Handbook of Research on Grid Technologies and Utility Computing:
Concepts for Managing Large–Scale Applications

Emmanuel Udoh
Indiana University–Purdue University, USA

Frank Zhigang Wang
Cranfield University, UK

INFORMATION SCIENCE REFERENCE

Hershey · New York

Director of Editorial Content:	Kristin Klinger
Senior Managing Editor:	Jamie Snavely
Managing Editor:	Jeff Ash
Assistant Managing Editor:	Carole Coulson
Typesetter:	Jeff Ash
Cover Design:	Lisa Tosheff
Printed at:	Yurchak Printing Inc.

Published in the United States of America by
Information Science Reference (an imprint of IGI Global)
701 E. Chocolate Avenue
Hershey PA 17033
Tel: 717-533-8845
Fax: 717-533-8661
E-mail: cust@igi-global.com
Web site: http://www.igi-global.com/reference

and in the United Kingdom by
Information Science Reference (an imprint of IGI Global)
3 Henrietta Street
Covent Garden
London WC2E 8LU
Tel: 44 20 7240 0856
Fax: 44 20 7379 0609
Web site: http://www.eurospanbookstore.com

Library of Congress Cataloging-in-Publication Data

Handbook of research on grid technologies and utility computing : concepts for managing large-scale applications / Emmanuel Udoh and Frank Zhigang Wang, editors.
      p. cm.

Includes bibliographical references and index.
Summary: "This book provides a compendium of terms, definitions, and explanations of concepts, issues, and trends in grid technology"-- Provided by publisher.

ISBN 978-1-60566-184-1 (hardcover) -- ISBN 978-1-60566-185-8 (ebook) 1. Computational grids (Computer systems)--Handbooks, manuals, etc. I. Udoh, Emmanuel, 1960- II. Wang, Frank Zhigang, 1965-

  QA76.9.C58H353 2009
  004'.36--dc22

                    2009007145

British Cataloguing in Publication Data
A Cataloguing in Publication record for this book is available from the British Library.

All work contributed to this book is new, previously-unpublished material. The views expressed in this book are those of the authors, but not necessarily of the publisher.

Editorial Advisory Board

List of Contributors

Table of Contents

Section I
Introduction

Chapter I

Emmanuel Udoh, Indiana University–Purdue University, USA
Frank Zhigang Wang, Cranfield University, UK
Vineet R. Khare, Cranfield University, UK

Section II
Grid Scheduling and Optimization

Chapter II

Eric Aubanel, University of New Brunswick, Faculty of Computer Science, Canada

Chapter III

Enis Afgan, University of Alabama at Birmingham, USA
Purushotham Bangalore, University of Alabama at Birmingham, USA

Section III
Grid Security

Section IV
Grid Architecture, Services, and Economy

Section V
Grid Applications and Future Tools

Detailed Table of Contents

Section I
Introduction

The introductory section provides an overview of grid computing and discusses issues like grid evolution, potential users, trends and advances in grid infrastructure, web and grid services, international collaborations and emerging standards. It introduces the framework in which to understand the fundamental concepts of grid computing as contrasted from distributed computing and peer-to-peer computing as well as the current challenges.

Chapter I

  Emmanuel Udoh, Indiana University–Purdue University, USA
  Frank Zhigang Wang, Cranfield University, UK
  Vineet R. Khare, Cranfield University, UK

This chapter presents a historical record of the advent of Grid with a recourse to some basic definitions commonly accepted by most researchers. It discusses the current and potential users of Grid computing and the expected changes in the user base as it gains popularity. The role of the Internet infrastructure in shaping the grid evolution received detailed treatment. Furthermore, the chapter contrasts grid computing with distributed and peer-to-peer computing and highlighted the salient features. Finally, the chapter discusses the recent advances in Web and Grid service technologies, including international projects, emerging standards and organizations, and the current challenges faced by Grid researchers.

Section II
Grid Scheduling and Optimization

Grid Scheduling and Optimization deals with an important research topic in grid computing. In scheduling, one or more user jobs can be processed without knowing where the resources are or the owner of the resources. The efficiency and quality of service of job's execution must be guaranteed as resource management is determined by many and different organizational administrative policies. Several chapters presented in this section mirror the intensity of research on this topic. Chapters such as "Resource-Aware Load Balancing of Parallel Applications" review the wide range of solutions proposed for parallel applications and the need for performance comparisons, while the chapter "Data-Aware Distributed Batch Scheduling" addresses challenges and trends in data-aware scheduler with a focus on Stork case study. The section ends with two chapters on quality of service in grid computing.

Chapter II

Eric Aubanel, University of New Brunswick, Faculty of Computer Science, Canada

The problem of load balancing parallel applications is particularly challenging on computational grids, since the characteristics of both the application and the platform must be taken into account. This chapter reviews the wide range of solutions that have been proposed. It considers tightly coupled parallel applications that can be described by an undirected graph representing concurrent execution of tasks and communication of tasks, executing on computational grids with static and dynamic network and processor performance. While a rich set of solution techniques have been proposed, there has not been of yet any performance comparisons between them. Such comparisons will require parallel benchmarks and computational grid emulators and simulators.

Chapter III

Enis Afgan, University of Alabama at Birmingham, USA
Purushotham Bangalore, University of Alabama at Birmingham, USA

Grid computing has emerged as the next generation computing platform. Because of the resource heterogeneity that exists in the grid environment, user jobs experience variable performance. Grid job scheduling, or selection of appropriate mappings between resources and the application, with the goal of leveraging available capacity and imposed requirements is thus at the heart of successful grid utilization. Grid job scheduling can be viewed as a function of resource heterogeneity, resource and application availability, and application options. This chapter presents work that incorporates all of these factors to provision and present individual users with alternative job options in terms of cost and time tradeoffs. Inherently, this leads to more effective scheduling policies. To support these aims, a framework is introduced with a novel scheduling methodology that introduces new user-scheduler interaction levels and a new layer of scheduling that includes application parameter selection and parameter value optimization.

Chapter IV

Kuo-Chan Huang, National Taichung University, Taiwan
Po-Chi Shih, National Tsing Hua University, Taiwan
Yeh-Ching Chung, National Tsing Hua University, Taiwan

Most current grid environments are established through collaboration among a group of participating sites which volunteer to provide free computing resources. Therefore, feasible load sharing policies that benefit all sites are an important incentive for attracting computing sites to join and stay in a grid environment. Moreover, a grid environment is usually heterogeneous in nature at least for different computing speeds at different participating sites. This chapter explores the feasibility and effectiveness of load sharing activities in a heterogeneous computational grid. Several issues are discussed including site selection policies as well as feasible load sharing mechanisms. Promising policies are evaluated in a series of simulations based on workloads derived from real traces. The results show that grid computing is capable of significantly improving the overall system performance in terms of average turnaround time for user jobs.

Chapter V

Tevfik Kosar, Louisiana State University, USA

As the data requirements of scientific distributed applications increase, the access to remote data becomes the main performance bottleneck for these applications. Traditional distributed computing systems closely couple data placement and computation, and consider data placement as a side effect of computation. Data placement is either embedded in the computation and causes the computation to delay, or performed as simple scripts which do not have the privileges of a job. The insufficiency of the traditional systems and existing CPU-oriented schedulers in dealing with the complex data handling problem has yielded a new emerging era: the data-aware schedulers. This chapter discusses the challenges in this area as well as future trends, with a focus on Stork case study.

Chapter VI

Gianni Pucciani, CERN, European Organization for Nuclear Research, Switzerland
Flavia Donno, CERN, European Organization for Nuclear Research, Switzerland
Andrea Domenici, University of Pisa, Italy
Heinz Stockinger, Swiss Institute of Bioinformatics, Switzerland

Data replication is a well-known technique used in distributed systems in order to improve fault tolerance and make data access faster. Several copies of a dataset are created and placed at different nodes, so that users can access the replica closest to them, and at the same time the data access load is distributed among the replicas. In today's Grid middleware solutions, data management services allow users to replicate datasets (i.e., flat files or databases) among storage elements within a Grid, but replicas are often considered read-only because of the absence of mechanisms able to propagate updates and enforce replica consistency. This entry analyzes the replica consistency problem and provides hints for the development of a Replica Consistency Service, highlighting the main issues and pros and cons of several approaches.

Chapter VII

Ming Wu, Illinois Institute of Technology, USA
Xian-He Sun, Illinois Institute of Technology, USA

Rapid advancement of communication technology has changed the landscape of computing. New models of computing, such as business-on-demand, Web services, peer-to-peer networks, and Grid computing have emerged to harness distributed computing and network resources to provide powerful services. The non-deterministic characteristic of the resource availability in these new computing platforms raises an outstanding challenge: how to support Quality of Service (QoS) to meet a user's demand? This chapter conducts a thorough study of QoS of distributed computing, especially on Grid computing where the requirement of distributed sharing and coordination goes to the extreme. The research starts at QoS policies, and then focuses on technical issues of the enforcement of the policies and performance optimization under each policy. This chapter provides a classification of QoS metrics and policies, a systematic understanding of QoS, and a framework for QoS of Grid computing.

Chapter VIII

Zhihui Du, Tsinghua University, China
Zhili Cheng, Tsinghua University, China
Xiaoying Wang, Tsinghua University, China
Chuang Lin, Tsinghua University, China

This chapter first summarizes popular terms of QoS related concepts and technologies in grid computing, including SLA, End-to-End QoS Provision and Virtualization. Then a three layered general grid QoS provision model based on MetaServices is proposed. Operating mechanisms are discussed in detail, and the model can maintain grid QoS by defining QoS requirements in different levels and solve the QoS problems hierarchically. A prototype named PMGrid is designed and implemented based on the QoS provision model. PMGrid is a grid system for astronomy data processing. The results show that the PMGrid can maintain the QoS requirements of astronomy data processing.

Section III
Grid Security

Grid Security, which deals with authentication and authorization for use of grid resources, is a critical component for extending the grid technology beyond the academic realm. Due to the heterogeneity of the grid environments such as the different operating systems, policy decisions, software and hardware, security issues are a major source of concern for use and adoption of the grid virtualization solutions in the enterprise. It is therefore necessary to develop solutions to address these issues. The chapter "Trust and Privacy in Grid Resource Auctions," offers a look at the privacy preserving and verifiable auction protocols for secured electronic auctions and the implications of adopting them on grid architecture.

Chapter IX

Kris Bubendorfer, Victoria University of Wellington, New Zealand
Ben Palmer, Victoria University of Wellington, New Zealand
Ian Welch, Victoria University of Wellington, New Zealand

A Grid resource broker is the arbiter for access to a Grid's computational resources and therefore its performance and functionality has a wide-ranging influence on the utilization and performance of the Grid. Ideally, we want to avoid relying on a single 'trusted' resource broker because it may not be trustworthy. For example, a broker holding a resource auction could examine and reveal bid information to others, or defraud participants by subverting the auction results. The use of privacy preserving and verifiable auction protocols offers guarantees beyond those possible in real world auctions, making the electronic auctions as secure, or more secure, than their physical counterparts. This chapter provides the background to understand privacy preserving and verifiable auction schemes and discuss the implications of adopting them on Grid architecture. It then evaluates a range of potential secure auction schemes and identifies those that are most suitable to be adopted within for use in the Grid.

Section IV
Grid Architecture, Services, and Economy

Grid Architecture, Services and Economy, looks at a host of research directions in architecture, service and grid economy. The grid architecture defines the basic and interacting components for managing cross-organizational resource sharing. It focuses on the interoperability among the resource providers and users as well as the protocols at each layer of the architectural model. Currently, there are efforts to merge the grid architecture with service-oriented architectures (SOAs), autonomic computing and other open standards platforms. This will aid the construction of dynamic applications that leverage virtualized resources, as users of applications are now only concerned with the operational description of the service. Furthermore, concepts defined in grid economy help effective management of resources and application scheduling as cooperative and competitive trading of resources such as CPU cycles, storage, and network bandwidth leverage various grid resource allocation.

Chapter X

Sandro Fiore, University of Salento & CMCC, Italy
Alessandro Negro, CMCC, Italy
Salvatore Vadacca, CMCC, Italy
Massimo Cafaro, University of Salento & CMCC, Italy
Giovanni Aloisio, University of Salento & CMCC, Italy
Roberto Barbera, Università di Catania and Istituto Nazionale di Fisica Nucleare (INFN), Italy
Emidio Giorgio, INFN Sez. di Catania, Italy

Grid computing is an emerging and enabling technology allowing organizations to easily share, integrate and manage resources in a distributed environment. Computational Grid allows running millions of jobs in parallel, but the huge amount of generated data has caused another interesting problem: the management (classification, storage, discovery etc.) of distributed data, i.e., a Data Grid specific issue. In the last decade, many efforts concerning the management of data (grid-storage services, metadata services, grid-database access and integration services etc.) identify data management as a real challenge for the next generation petascale grid environments. This work provides an architectural overview of the GRelC DAS, a grid database access service developed in the context of the GRelC Project and currently used for production/tutorial activities both in gLite and Globus based grid environments.

    Man Wang, Tsinghua University, China
    Zhihui Du, Tsinghua University, China
    Zhili Cheng, Tsinghua University, China

Resource Management System (RMS), which manages the Grid resources and matches the applications' requests to the proper resources, is one of the most important and complex parts in Grid systems. In fact, because of the complexity of Gird environment, one resource management approach alone cannot satisfy different applications' requirement. Therefore, a novel Adaptive Resource Management (ARM) mechanism is provided here. This mechanism is based on multidimensional Grid QoS, which dynamically organizes Grid resources into Task Resources for feasible distribution. Moreover, this management mechanism can select appropriate management approach according to different applications' requirements, which is well adapted to dynamic Grid environment.

    Vineet R. Khare, Cranfield University, UK
    Frank Zhigang Wang, Cranfield University, UK

The need for a dynamic and scalable expansion of the grid infrastructure and resources and other scalability issues in terms of execution efficiency and fault tolerance present centralized management techniques with numerous difficulties. This chapter presents the case for biologically inspired grid resource management techniques that are decentralized and self organized in nature. To achieve the desired de-centralized resource management, these techniques model the self-organization observed in many natural complex adaptive systems. Using a few representative techniques, the authors review the literature on Bio-inspired Grid Resource Management. Based on this review the authors conclude that many such techniques have been successfully applied to resource discovery, service placement, scheduling and load balancing.

    Yuhui Deng, Cranfield University, UK
    Frank Zhigang Wang, Cranfield University, UK
    Na Helian, Metropolitan University, UK

Storage Grid is a new model for deploying and managing the heterogeneous, dynamic, large-scale, and geographically distributed storage resources. This chapter discusses the challenges and solutions involved in building a Service Oriented Storage (SOS) Grid. By wrapping the diverse storage resources into atomic Grid services and federating multiple atomic Grid services into composite services, the SOS Grid can tackle the heterogeneity and interoperability. Peer-to-peer philosophy and techniques are employed in the SOS Grid to eliminate the system bottleneck and single point of failure of the traditional centralized or hierarchical Grid architecture, while providing dynamicity and scalability. Because Grid service is not designed for critical and real-time applications, the SOS Grid adopts Grid service to glue the distributed and heterogeneous storage resources, while using binary code to transfer data. The proposed methods strike a good balance among the heterogeneity, interoperability, scalability and performance of the SOS Grid.

Chapter XIV

Dominic Cherry, Technicolor Network Services, UK
Maozhen Li, Brunel University, UK
Man Qi, Canterbury Christ Church University, UK

This chapter presents MediaGrid, a distributed storage system for archiving broadcast media contents. MediaGrid utilizes storage resources donated by computing nodes running in a distributed computing environment. A genetic algorithm for resource selection is built in MediaGrid with the aim to optimize the utilization of resources available for archiving media files with various sizes. Evaluation results show the effectiveness of MediaGrid in archiving broadcast media contents, and the performance of the genetic algorithm in resource utilization optimization.

Chapter XV

Maozhen Li, Brunel University, UK
Man Qi, Canterbury Christ Church University, UK
Bin Yu, Level E Limited, UK

The computational grid is rapidly evolving into a service-oriented computing infrastructure that facilitates resource sharing and large-scale problem solving over the Internet. Service discovery becomes an issue of vital importance in utilizing grid facilities. This chapter presents ROSSE, a Rough sets based search engine for grid service discovery. Building on Rough sets theory, ROSSE is novel in its capability to deal with uncertainty of properties when matching services. Services with WSDL interfaces or OWL-S interfaces can be registered with ROSSE and then be discovered.

Chapter XVI

Irfan Habib, University of the West of England, UK
Ashiq Anjum, University of the West of England, UK
Richard McClatchey, University of the West of England, UK

Due to some barriers to adoption we have not seen a proliferation of Grid Computing technologies throughout e-Science or other domains. This chapter outlines many issues that are a consequence to the existing Grid Middleware based approaches. The authors believe a Grid Operating system, or an operating system with built in Grid computing capability might be able to address the drawbacks of the existing infrastructure, leading to a fault tolerant, flexible and easy to use stack for rapid deployment of Grids. This chapter presents the motivation and issues which lead us to a Grid operating System and outline its design, implementation and evaluation details.

Chapter XVII

    Kurt Vanmechelen, University of Antwerp, Belgium
    Jan Broeckhove, University of Antwerp, Belgium
    Wim Depoorter, University of Antwerp, Belgium
    Khalid Abdelkader, University of Antwerp, Belgium

As grid computing technology moves further up the adoption curve, the issues of dealing with conflicting user requirements formulated by different users become more prevalent. In addition, the need to negotiate static sharing agreements between the different stakeholders in a grid system is time-consuming and offers limited incentive for resource owners to step into the grid's infrastructure in a provider role. Resource management approaches that are currently adopted in grids are not able to deal with these issues in a flexible, value-maximizing way because of their system-centric approach. This contribution presents a clear motivation for the use of economic forms of scheduling in grid computing environments to address these shortcomings. The authors also provide an introductory overview of the different forms of market mechanisms that have been adopted by researchers in the field. In addition, the authors present simulation results concerning the use of Vickrey auctions and commodity markets as market mechanisms for dynamic pricing in grid resource markets.

Chapter XVIII

    Rosario M. Piro, INFN and University of Torino, Italy

Large, geographically distributed and heterogeneous computing infrastructures, such as the Grid, often span multiple organizations and administrative domains. In such infrastructures, resource usage accounting, i.e. keeping track of the resources consumed by single users or entire organizations, is a non-trivial but very important task. This chapter introduces some general aspects and discusses the fundamental requirements that need to be fulfilled in order to guarantee an accurate resource usage accounting. Typical accounting procedures and current practices are described along with other related issues such as the normalization of resource usage information, the standardization of accounting interfaces, billing and charging, resource pricing, market-oriented resource allocation and economic scheduling.

Section V
Grid Applications and Future Tools

Grid Applications and Future Tools offers a way to solve challenging problems such as earthquake, climate/weather, financial and protein simulations. Grid technology can also be applied as a utility for commercial and noncommercial user. This last section of the handbook showcases the flurry of activities in applying the grid technology to various domains such as nuclear physics, biomedicine, image processing, e-science, simulation, business, global terrorism and national platforms.

Chapter XIX

Frans Arickx, University of Antwerp, Belgium
Jan Broeckhove, University of Antwerp, Belgium
Peter Hellinckx, University of Antwerp, Belgium
David Dewolfs, University of Antwerp, Belgium
Kurt Vanmechelen, University of Antwerp, Belgium

Quantum structure or scattering calculations often belong to a class of computational problems involving the aggregation of a set of matrices representing a linear problem to be solved. The authors discuss a number of approaches based on cluster and grid computing, and discuss the implementations and the respective merits and shortcomings. The authors consider MPI-based cluster computing in a self-scheduling paradigm, CoBRA (a cpu-harvesting desktop grid) in a farmer-worker paradigm, and a batch-computing paradigm on BEGrid (the Belgian research grid facility). It is observed that for all paradigms an efficient implementation is possible, yielding results within a comparable time frame.

Chapter XX

Gabriel Aparicio, Universidad Politécnica de Valencia, Spain
Fernando Blanco, CIEMAT, Spain
Ignacio Blanquer, Universidad Politécnica de Valencia, Spain
César Bonavides, UNAM Campus Morelos, Mexico
Juan Luis Chaves, Universidad de los Andes, Venezuela
Miguel Embid, CIEMAT, Spain
Álvaro Hernández, Universidad de los Andes, Venezuala
Vicente Hernández, Universidad Politécnica de Valencia, Spain
Raúl Isea, Fundacion IDEA, Venezuela
Juan Ignacio Lagares, CIEMAT, Spain
Daniel L. Aldama, CUBAENERGIA, Cuba
Rafael Mayo, CIEMAT, Spain
Esther Montes, CIEMAT, Spain
Henry Ricardo Mora, CUBAENERGIA, Cuba

In the last years an increasing demand for Grid Infrastructures has resulted in several international collaborations. This is the case of the EELA Project, which has brought together collaborating groups of Latin America and Europe. One year ago, the authors presented this e-infrastructure used, among others, by the biomedical groups for the studies of oncological analysis, neglected diseases, sequence alignments and computational phylogenetics. After this period, the achieved advances and the scientific results are summarized in this chapter.

Efficient approaches to computationally intensive image processing tasks are currently highly sought after. In this chapter, the authors show how a blackboard paradigm, originally developed for collaborative problem solving, can be used as an efficient and effective vehicle for distributed computation. Through the design of dedicated intelligent agents, typical image processing algorithms can be applied in parallel on multiple loosely coupled machines leading to a significant overall speedup as is verified in a series of experiments.

The BaBar experiment uses data since 1999 in examining the violation of charge and parity (CP) symmetry in the field of high energy physics. This event simulation experiment is a compute intensive task due to the complexity of the Monte-Carlo simulation implemented on the GEANT engine. Data needed as input for the simulation (stored in the ROOT format), are classified into two categories: conditions data for describing the detector status when data are recorded, and background triggers data for noise signal necessary to obtain a realistic simulation. In this chapter, the grid approach is applied to the BaBar production framework using the INFN-GRID network.

A framework is proposed that creates, uses, and communicates information, whose organizational dynamics allows performing a distributed cooperative enterprise in public environments, even over open source systems. The approach assumes the web services as the enacting paradigm possibly over a grid, to formalize interactions as cooperative services on various computational nodes of a network. The illustrated case study shows that some portions, both of processes and of data or knowledge, can be shared in a collaborative environment, which is also more generally true for any kind of either complex or resource demanding (or both) interaction that will benefit any of the approaches.

    Roberto Barbera, Università di Catania and Istituto Nazionale di Fisica Nucleare
    (INFN), Italy
    Valeria Ardizzone, Istituto Nazionale di Fisica Nucleare (INFN), Italy
    Leandro Ciuffo, Istituto Nazionale di Fisica Nucleare (INFN), Italy

The Grid INFN virtual Laboratory for Dissemination Activities (GILDA) is a fully working Grid test-bed devoted to training and dissemination activities. Open to anyone who wants to have its first hand experience with grid systems, GILDA has been adopted as the official training tool by several Grid projects around the world. All services, tools and materials produced in the past tutorials can be freely used by anyone who wants to learn and teach grid technology. Additionally, through a set of applications ported on its Grid Infrastructure, developers can identify components and learn by examples how to "gridify" their applications. This work presents the main features of such training-Infrastructure.

    Dirk Gorissen, Gent University–IBBT, Belgium
    Tom Dhaene, Gent University–IBBT, Belgium
    Piet Demeester, Gent University–IBBT, Belgium
    Jan Broeckhove, University of Antwerp, Belgium

The simulation and optimization of complex systems is a very time consuming and computationally intensive task. Therefore, global surrogate modeling methods are often used for the efficient exploration of the design space, as they reduce the number of simulations needed. However, constructing such surrogate models (or metamodels) is often done in a straightforward, sequential fashion. In contrast, this chapter presents a framework that can leverage the use of compute clusters and grids in order to decrease the model generation time by efficiently running simulations in parallel. The authors describe the integration between surrogate modeling and grid computing on three levels: resource level, scheduling level and service level. This approach is illustrated with a simple example from aerodynamics.

    Patrik Skogster, Rovaniemi University of Applied Sciences, Finland

Grid computing is becoming as essential part of different business analysis. In traditional business computing infrastructures data transfer occurs to and from computing resources at the network edges. On the other hand, most business activities are bound to space and location. The aim of this chapter is to describe the business use of geographic data (business intelligence) and Geographic Information System (GIS) grids. As conclusion business intelligence helps to improve productivity by giving users information they need when they need it most at the point of decision. Organizations that effectively use geographic information elements analyzing their risk portfolio and compliance activities can reduce costs and increase the clarity of their operations. Grid computing is an answer to the needs of efficient GIS aided analysis. When geographic data, grid computing and business information are combined, they create new possibilities to enhance and broaden the standpoints of already existing data within organizations.

Chapter XXVII

The emerging grid technology provides a secured platform for multidisciplinary experts in the security intelligence profession to collaborate and fight global terrorism. This chapter developed grid architecture and implementation strategy on how to connect the dots between security agents such as the CIA, FBI, police, custom officers and transport industry to share data and information on terrorists and their movements. The major grid components that featured in the architecture are the grid security portal, data grid, computational grid, semantic grid and collaboratory. The challenges of implementing this architecture are conflicting laws, cooperation among governments, and information on terrorist's network and interoperability problem.

This chapter focuses on the efforts to design and develop a standard pure Java API to access the metadata service of the EGEE Grid middleware, and provide at the same time a powerful object oriented framework to allow engineers and programmers to embed metadata features inside their own application, using a standard approach based on design patterns. A specific web interface is built on top of this framework that permits users and administrators to manage the metadata catalog, from any platform and everywhere, according to their own X.509-based credentials.

Efforts in Grid Computing, both in academia and industry, continue to grow rapidly worldwide for research, scientific and commercial purposes. Building a commanding position in Grid computing is crucial for India. The major Indian National Grid Computing initiative is GARUDA. Other major efforts include the BIOGRID and VISHWA. Several Indian IT companies too are investing a lot into the research and development of grid computing technology. Though grid computing is presently at a fairly nascent stage, it is seen as a cutting edge technology. This chapter presents the state-of-the-art of grid computing technology and the India's efforts in developing this emerging technology.

Chapter XXX

Hai Jin, Huazhong University of Science and Technology, China
Li Qi, Huazhong University of Science and Technology, China
Jie Dai, Huazhong University of Science and Technology, China
Yaqin Luo, Huazhong University of Science and Technology, China

A grid system is usually composed of thousands of nodes which are broadly distributed in different virtual organizations. Owing to geographical boundaries among these organizations, the system administrators suffer a great pressure to coordinate when grid system experiences a maintaining period. Furthermore, the runtime dynamicity of service state aggravates the complexity of tasks. Consequently, building an efficient and reliable maintaining model becomes an urgent challenge to ensure the correctness and consistency of grid nodes. In our experiment with ChinaGrid, a Dynamic Maintenance mechanism has been adopted in the fundamental grid middleware called ChinaGrid Support Platform. By resolving the above problems with system infrastructure, service dependency and service consistency, the availability of the system can be improved even the scope of maintenance extends to wider region.

Foreword

It is a great pleasure for me to write the foreword for this book. The quality of the presentations and the scope of recent topics provide the reader with an up-to-the-moment resource in the area of grid computing.

Grid technology enables the combination of geographically dispersed resources such as computer cycles, storage space, software and scientific devices into one large scale virtual environment that can be shared by multiple users.

In a similar fashion to an on-demand electric power utility, grid computing can eliminate underutilized computing capacity and leverage existing investments and best practices in an organization. It is therefore essential to keep educators, students, researchers and professionals abreast of changes in the ever-evolving grid concepts, protocols, applications, methods and tools [http://users.ipfw.edu/udohe/gridintro.htm].

The *Handbook of Research on Grid Technologies and Utility Computing: Concepts for Managing Large-Scale Applications* presents a variety of recent advances in grid technology. Contributions include articles on current trends and tools in grid computing, the impact of the grid on directions for future research and recent developments in grid technology and applications.

Section I of this book presents a comprehensive overview of the history of grid computing, accepted terminology and recent advances in web and grid service technology along with a discussion on emerging standards and the challenges faced by grid researchers.

In Section II, a collection of articles address some of the inherent problems in grid computing such as a performance comparison of load balancing techniques, grid scheduling to leverage available grid capacity and load sharing policies. Data management issues are a significant bottleneck over a distributed collection of heterogeneous and several papers in this section discuss various techniques for data handling along with current case studies and future trends.

The widespread acceptance of grid technology outside of the scientific community has been hindered by a perceived lack of security. Section III of this book presents an article which discusses current electronic privacy preserving schemes and their suitability for implementation in the Grid.

In Section IV the focus is on grid architecture, grid services and the economics of grid computing. Discussions cover the architecture of a grid database access service, an Adaptive Resource Management (ARM) mechanism, biologically inspired grid resource management techniques and storage systems for the Grid.

The final section of this book presents a collection of articles on grid applications in such areas as nuclear physics, biomedical studies, image processing, e-science, modeling, business and global terrorism. A significant growth in the number of international collaborations in a wide collection of application areas has been spawned by advances in grid infrastructure. This book presents a sampling of such collaborations and, as such, provides readers with an exciting glimpse into what grid computing can provide to research partnerships on a global scale.

Ruth E. Shaw

Professor and Dean, Faculty of Science, Applied Science & Engineering
University of New Brunswick, Saint John

Ruth. E. Shaw *is a professor of computer science and currently the dean of faculty of science, applied Science and engineering, University of New Brunswick, Saint John, Canada. Dr. Shaw has worked at UNB Saint John since 1980. She joined the faculty full-time in 1994; her recent research is in developing efficient algorithms for parallel processing. She has published over 50 papers in refereed journals and conference proceedings.*

Preface

Grid computing is an emerging computational field with a great impact in compute-intensive endeavors. As an offshoot of distributed computing, the grid can be harnessed to solve a single scientific or technical problem at the same time by deploying jointly computational resources such as computers, networks, data archives and instruments. It is cost-effective as organizations can share or pool together computing resources among geographically dispersed groups in a virtual environment.

Historically, the term grid computing stemmed from Ian Foster's and Carl Kesselman's seminal work in the nineties that liken the grid to electric power grid. The term has since been popularized by such academic works as SETI@home (that exploited cycle-scavenging networks or networked PCs) and other applications to grand challenge problems. Grid computing is becoming popular in the enterprise world after its origin in the academic and research communities, where it was successfully used to share resources, store data in petascale, and ultimately lower IT costs. There are several reasons for the embrace of the enterprise grids. In the nineties, the IT world was confronted with the high cost of maintaining smaller, cheaper and dedicated servers such as UNIX and Windows. There was the problem of application silos that lead to underutilized hardware resources; huge and ungainly systems that are costly to maintain and transform; and patchy and disintegrated information that cannot be fully exploited by the enterprise as a whole. Various surveys put the average utilization of servers in a typical enterprise to often much less than 20 percent. But with the increasingly available cheaper, faster and affordable hardware such as server blades, and operating systems like the open source Linux, the IT world embraced grid computing to save money on hardware and software.

The grid has since grown with the demand for more computational resources for problems in engineering, biology, military, climate or weather research. Complex simulations cause long runtimes or overtax modern computer systems and pooling computational resources together have proven to minimize runtimes. Such simulations can be efficiently executed in parallel or distributed across many nodes or processors in a grid environment. Even ad hoc or pro-active grids have emerged that are suitable for short-term collaborations or small-scale computations.

The growing importance of grid computing has been accompanied by numerous researchers around the world focusing on accumulating knowledge in this discipline. Therefore, to keep educators, students, researchers and professionals abreast of changes in the ever-evolving grid concepts, protocols, applications, methods and tools, I decided to launch a handbook project where researchers from all over the world would assist me in providing some necessary coverage on topical issues in the discipline.

The *Handbook of Research on Grid Technologies and Utility Computing: Concepts for Managing Large-Scale Applications* provides a comprehensive coverage of terms, concepts, processes, acronyms, important issues and trends in grid technology. With contributions from diverse experts, the handbook shares new ideas and best approaches among researchers, scholars and industry practitioners. The handbook is organized in five distinct sections, covering wide-ranging topics such as: (1) Introduction (2)

Grid Scheduling and Optimization (3) Grid Security (4) Grid Architecture, Services and Economy (5) Grid Applications and Future Tools. These sections are summarized as follows:

Section I, *Introduction,* provides an overview of grid computing and discusses issues like grid evolution, potential users, trends and advances in grid infrastructure, web and grid services, international collaborations and emerging standards. The chapter *"Overview of Grid Computing"* by Emmanuel Udoh, Frank Zhigang Wang and Vineet R. Khare, presents an excellent framework in which to understand the fundamental concepts of grid computing as contrasted from distributed computing and peer-to-peer computing as well as the current challenges.

Section II, *Grid Scheduling and Optimization,* deals with an important research topic in grid computing. In scheduling, one or more user jobs can be processed without knowing where the resources are or the owner of the resources. The efficiency and quality of service of job's execution must be guaranteed as resource management is determined by many and different organizational administrative policies. Several chapters are presented in this section mirroring the intensity of research on this topic. Eric Aubanel in *"Resource-Aware Load Balancing of Parallel Applications"* reviews the wide range of solutions proposed for parallel applications and the need for performance comparisons, while Tevfik Kosar in *"Data-Aware Distributed Batch Scheduling"* addresses challenges and trends in data-aware scheduler with a focus on Stork case study. Chapters such as *"Assisting Efficient Job Planning and Scheduling in the Grid"* by Enis Afgan and Purushotham Bangalore discuss work that offers individual users alternative job options in terms of cost and time tradeoffs in which a new layer of scheduling includes application parameter selection and parameter value optimization, while the chapter *"Effective Resource Allocation and Job Scheduling Mechanisms for Load Sharing in a Computational Grid"* by Kuo-Chan Huang, Po-Chi Shih and Yeh-Ching Chung, evaluates site selection policies and feasible load sharing mechanisms in a series of simulations. The section ends with two chapters on quality of service in grid computing from Ming Wu and Xian-He Sun as well as researchers Zhihui Du, Zhili Cheng, Xiaoying Wang and Chuang Lin.

Section III, *Grid Security*, which deals with authentication and authorization for use of grid resources, is a critical component for extending the grid technology beyond the academic realm. Due to the heterogeneity of the grid environments such as the different operating systems, policy decisions, software and hardware, security issues are a major source of concern for use and adoption of the grid virtualization solutions in the enterprise. It is therefore necessary to develop solutions to address these issues. The chapter from researchers Kris Bubendorfer, Ben Palmer and Ian Welch, *"Trust and Privacy in Grid Resource Auctions,"* offers a look at the privacy preserving and verifiable auction protocols for secured electronic auctions and the implications of adopting them on grid architecture.

Section IV, *Grid Architecture, Services, and Economy*, looks at a host of research directions in architecture, service and grid economy. The grid architecture defines the basic and interacting components for managing cross-organizational resource sharing. It focuses on the interoperability among the resource providers and users as well as the protocols at each layer of the architectural model. Currently, there are efforts to merge the grid architecture with service-oriented architectures (SOAs), autonomic computing and other open standards platforms. This will aid the construction of dynamic applications that leverage virtualized resources, as users of applications are now only concerned with the operational description of the service. For instance, the Web services architecture (WSA) enables and defines SOA, where services interact by exchanging XML (Extensible Markup Language) messages. Furthermore, concepts defined in grid economy help effective management of resources and application scheduling as cooperative and competitive trading of resources such as CPU cycles, storage, and network bandwidth leverage various grid resource allocation.

There are a couple of chapters in this section. Researcher Sandro Fiore and colleagues described a grid database access service in *"An Architectural Overview of the GRelC Data Access Service,"* while

Man Wang, Zhihui Du and Zhili Cheng discuss a mechanism based on multidimensional grid QoS in *"Adaptive Resource Management in Grid Environment."* In chapters *"Bio-Inspired Grid Resource Management"* and *"Service Oriented Storage System Grid"* Vineet R. Khare, Frank Zhigang Wang, Yuhui Deng and Na Helian address biologically inspired grid resource management techniques that are decentralized and self organized in nature as well as challenges involved in building a service oriented storage (SOS) grid. Rosario M. Piro in *"Resource Usage Accounting in Grid Computing"* and Kurt Vanmechelen, Jan Broeckhove, Wim Depoorter, and Khalid Abdelkader, in *"Pricing Computational Resources in Grid Economies"* focus on new approaches in grid economy. Maozhen Li and Man Qi, in *"Service Discovery with Rough Sets"* present ROSSE, a rough sets based search engine for grid service discovery. In *"On the Pervasive Adoption of Grid Technologies: A Grid Operating System"* by Irfan Habib, Ashiq Anjum and Richard McClatchey, the researchers emphasize the need to simplify the learning curve of grid technology (thus promote easy adoption) by integrating the grid system in an operating system environment.

Section V, *Grid Applications and Future Tools*, offers a way to solve challenging problems such as earthquake, climate/weather, financial and protein simulations. Grid technology can also be applied as a utility for commercial and noncommercial user. This last section of the handbook showcases the flurry of activities in applying the grid technology to various domains such as nuclear physics, biomedicine, image processing, e-science, simulation, business, global terrorism and national platforms.

In chapters *"Grid-Based Nuclear Physics Applications"* by Arickx Frans and *"Simulated Events Production on the Grid for the BaBar Experiment"* by Daniele Andreotti, Armando Fella and Eleonora Luppi, the researchers discuss MPI-based cluster computing in a self-scheduling paradigm and a batch computing paradigm as well as the grid approach to the BaBar production framework using the INFN-GRID network respectively. Gerald Schaefer and Roger Tait present how a blackboard paradigm can be used as an efficient and effective vehicle for distributed computation in *"Distributed Image Processing on a Blackboard System."* In the chapter *"Developing Biomedical Applications in the Framework of EELA,"* Gabriel Aparicio and colleagues apply grid to studies of oncological analysis, neglected diseases, sequence alignments and computational phylogenetics. Diego Liberati proposes a framework that creates, uses and communicates information over a distributed cooperative enterprise in public environments or open source systems, in *"A Framework for Semantic Grid in E-Science."*

In this final section, there are other chapters that capture the research trends in the grid realm. Roberto Barbera, Valeria Ardizzone and Leandro Ciuffo described a fully working grid test-bed devoted to training and dissemination activities in *"INFN virtual Laboratory for Dissemination Activities (GILDA)."* In the chapter *"Grid Enabled Surrogate Modeling"* Dirk Gorissen, Tom Dhaene, Piet Demeester and Jan Broeckhove present a framework that can leverage the use of compute clusters and grids in order to decrease the model generation time by efficiently running simulations in parallel. Patrik Skogster describes in *"GIS Grids and the Business Use of GIS Data"* the business use of geographic data (business intelligence) and geographic information system (GIS) grids. To further demonstrate the applicability of the grid concept to global security, Gokop Goteng, Ashutosh Tiwari and Rajkumar Roy in *"Grid Computing: Combating Global Terrorism with the WWW"* develop grid architecture and implementation strategy on how to connect the dots between security agents such as the CIA, FBI, police, custom officers and transport industry to share data and information on terrorists and their movements. Finally, Jyotsna Sharma in *"Grid Computing: The Technology and The Indian Initiatives"* and researchers Hai Jin, Li Qi, Jie Dai and Yaqin Luo in *"Dynamic Maintenance in ChinaGrid Support Platform"* describe the major efforts in grid platforms initiated in India and China respectively.

In conclusion, the capability of the web to link information over the Internet has popularized computer science to the public. But it is the grid that will enable the public to exploit data storage and computer power over the Internet analogous to the electric power utility (a ubiquitous commodity). In this vein, the handbook is a contribution to the growth of grid technology as a new IT infrastructure that allows modular hardware and software to be deployed collectively to solve a problem or rejoined on demand to meet changing needs of the user.

Emmanuel Udoh
Indiana University–Purdue University, USA

Frank Zhigang Wang
Cranfield University, UK

Acknowledgment

The editor would like to acknowledge several individuals for their contributions in the preparation of this handbook. Deep appreciation and gratitude is due to professor Frank Zhigang Wang, director of Centre for Grid Computing, Cranfield University, UK, for the cooperative assistance in acquiring the materials for the publication. Professor David Erbach, chair of computer science department at the Indiana – Purdue University, Fort Wayne, USA for the generous allocation of hardware and software resources and other sundry support.

Most of the authors of chapters included in this handbook also served as referees for chapters written by other authors. Thanks go to all those who provided constructive and comprehensive reviews. However, some of the reviewers must be mentioned as their reviews set the benchmark. Reviewers who provided the most comprehensive, critical and constructive comments include: Ruth Shaw (University of New Brunswick), Eric Aubanel (University of New Brunswick), Daniel Katz (Louisiana State University), Maozhen Li (Brunel University) and Yuhui Deng (Cranfield University).

Special credit should also go to the editorial and production team at IGI Global, whose contributions throughout the whole process from inception of the initial idea to final publication have been invaluable. Kristin M. Klinger approved the project and pushed for a coordinated completion of the work. Kristin Roth provided the initial editorial assistance, while Heather Probst, Julia Mosemann and Beth Ardner at the final stage prodded via e-mail for keeping the project on schedule. Their ideas and enthusiasm motivated me to successfully complete the project.

Special credit should also go to Ruth Shaw, who wrote the foreword and read a semi-final draft of the manuscript as well as provided helpful suggestions for enhancing its content. And last but not least, my wife, Agatha, and children for unfailing support and encouragement during the months it took to give birth to this book.

In all, I wish to thank the authors for their insights and excellent contributions to this handbook and the almighty God for the successful completion of the project even at trying time.

Emmanuel Udoh, Indiana University–Purdue University, USA
January 2009

Section I
Introduction

Chapter I
Overview of Grid Computing

Emmanuel Udoh
Indiana University–Purdue University, USA

Frank Zhigang Wang
Cranfield University, UK

Vineet R. Khare
Cranfield University, UK

ABSTRACT

This chapter presents a historical record of the advent of Grid with a recourse to some basic definitions commonly accepted by most researchers. It discusses the current and potential users of Grid computing and the expected changes in the user base as it gains popularity. The role of the Internet infrastructure in shaping the grid evolution received detailed treatment. Furthermore, the chapter contrasts grid computing with distributed and peer-to-peer computing and highlighted the salient features. Finally, the chapter discusses the recent advances in Web and Grid service technologies, including international projects, emerging standards and organizations, and the current challenges faced by Grid researchers.

INTRODUCTION

The computational grid emerged in 1990s from the works of Ian Foster and Carl Kesselman (Foster and Kesselman, 1999, 2003). The word "grid" is analogous to the electric power grid, which provides pervasive access to electrical power. Residential homes source power from the power plant through the distribution grid, which sometimes covers a region, a nation and even a continent. Similarly, computational grid is predicted to provide pervasive access to advanced computational resources to people across national boundaries. According to Foster and Kesselman (1999), the grid is a new class of infrastructure built on the Internet and the World Wide Web.

Using the Internet as a bedrock, the grid offers networked computer systems access not just to information but also to computing power. Sometimes, the grid is dubbed as Internet II (next-generation Internet). However, the grid differs from the Internet, as it is much more than a means of communication between computers. Today's Internet and web technologies address basic communication requirements, but not the computational tasks. The grid's mission is to provide the infrastructure and tools that make large-scale and secure resource sharing possible and straightforward. In this regard, the grid subsumes the traditional Internet. Nevertheless, the grid is not an alternative to "the Internet": it is rather a set of additional protocols and services that are built on Internet protocols and services to support the creation and use of computation- and data-enriched environments.

Scientists in many different fields today require world-wide collaborations, i.e. multi-domain access to distributed resources. But even as computer power, data storage, and communication continue to improve exponentially, computational resources are failing to keep up with what scientists demand. The advent of grid technologies could change the way that many institutions practice science. Grids provide access to large data processing power and huge data storage capabilities. Furthermore, as the grid grows its usefulness increases with availability of more resources. Scientists hope that with the help of the grid, vast computing resources around the world can be harnessed and shared to tackle some of the biggest challenges in medicine, physics, astronomy and engineering.

In this chapter, we present some definitions of grid computing accepted by most researchers. An examination of the historical record of the advent of grid and the current and potential users of grid computing was undertaken. We discuss how the basic Internet infrastructure has shaped the evolution of grid. The grid was also contrasted with the Internet and distributed computing. Finally, we discuss recent advances in web and grid service technologies, including international projects, emerging standards and organizations, and the current challenges faced by grid researchers.

BACKGROUND

Electrical Power Grid

Most of us have a pervasive access to electrical power. It is a little bit like the air we breathe: we don't really think about it until it is missing. Power is just "there," meeting our every need, constantly. It is only during a power failure like the 2003 North American Blackout, when we walk into a dark room and instinctively hit the useless light switch that we realize how important power is in our daily life. We use it for heating, cooling, cooking, refrigeration, light, sound, computation, and entertainment. Without it, life can get somewhat cumbersome. Electrical power is brought from the power plant to our houses through an amazing system called the power distribution grid, which sometimes covers a region, a nation and even a continent. For power to be useful in a home or business, transformers step transmission voltages (in the tens or hundreds of thousands of volts range) down to voltages of typically 100-250 volts. Through this regional, national or even continental distribution grid, finally we are down to the wire that brings power to our house. No matter if we live in a suburban or rural area, availability of electricity is the same. It is so public, in fact, that we don't even notice its existence anymore. Our brain ignores all of the power lines because we have seen them so often.

GRID AND GRID COMPUTING

The word "grid" is analogous to the electric power grid. According to Foster and Kesselman (1999), the grid is a new class of infrastructure built on the Internet and the World Wide Web. As shown in Figure 3, using the Internet as a bedrock, the grid offers all networked computers access not just to information but also to computing power.

Imagine being able to plug your computer into the wall and tapping into as much processing power as you need. Essentially, a customer gets computing power and storage capacity, not from his/her computer, but over the Internet on demand. According to Hermida (2001), "You pay for what you use, pretty much the way you do with electric power". This is the global vision of grid computing. A global computational grid will connect multiple regional and national computational grids to create a universal source of computing power. Such a huge computer network all over the world is known as the Great Global Grid (GGG).

Grid and Internet

Sometimes, the grid is being dubbed Internet II (next-generation Internet). However, the grid differs from the Internet as it is much more than a means of communication between computers. Contrarily, today's Internet and web technologies

address basic communication requirements, but not the computational tasks. The grid's mission is to provide the infrastructure and tools that make large-scale, secure resource sharing possible and straightforward. The grid provides huge data processing power. The grid will not only be what Internet I was supposed to be, it would also be better than its predecessor. In this regard, the grid enhances the traditional Internet. Nevertheless, the grid is not an alternative to "the Internet": it is rather a set of additional protocols and services that build on Internet protocols and services to support the creation and use of computation- and data-enriched environments. Any resource that is "on the grid" is also, by definition, "on the net" (Foster and Kesselman, 1999).

Grid and Distributed Computing

Grid Computing can be considered as a general form of distributed computing. The complexity of the grid, however, provides some distinguishing features (Stockinger, 2007). Number of organizations involved in a grid computing system can

Figure 1. The computational grid offers the ability of "grid computing" to plug into a network of computer systems and have access not just to information but also to computing power. The word "grid" is chosen by analogy with the electric power grid.

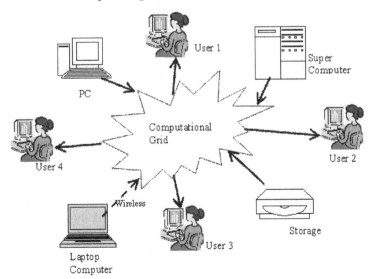

potentially be much higher than a distributed computing system. Distributed computing systems, generally, have 2-way requirements for communications and security, whereas these change to N-way requirements in case of grid computing. Finally, the requirements for heterogeneous resource utilization are much stricter in case of grid computing.

MAIN FOCUS

Grid Users

Scientists in many different fields today require world-wide collaborations, i.e. multi-domain access to distributed resources. Even as computer power, data storage, and communication continue to improve exponentially, computational resources are failing to keep up with what scientists demand of them. The advent of grid technologies could change the way that many institutions practice science. Grids provide access to large data processing power and huge data storage capabilities. Furthermore, as the grid grows its usefulness increases with more availability of resources.

Scientists hope that with the help of the grid, vast computing resources around the world can be harnessed and shared to tackle some of the biggest challenges in medicine, physics, astronomy and engineering. Large communities of possible GRID users are in:

- High Energy Physics
- Environmental studies: Earthquakes forecast, geologic and climate changes
- Biology, Genetics,
- Earth Observation
- Astrophysics,
- New composite materials research
- Astronautics

All institutions currently maintain their own computing facilities but, until now, these have largely existed as islands of computation that rarely work together. At times the computational resources are in use, whereas at others they are relatively dormant. Every day, billions of dollars worth of computing power is applied to displaying nifty screen savers. The grid uses that idle computing power to solve computationally intensive problems. In finance, research, engineering, product testing, and operations, a wide range of computationally intensive problems can be solved quickly by distributing tasks to idle desktop computers. The main motivation behind grid computing is to make this task easy.

The GGG Era

The Great Global Grid (GGG) era is on its way. Using the Internet as a bedrock, the grid is intended to succeed the WWW. It would dramatically change human capabilities and society with enormous benefits and implications. Everybody is likely to be impacted by the grid in a similar way that we are by the Internet.

Consider this scenario – a customer plans to attend an international conference to be held in San Francisco next month. Today, what he/she needs to do first is to book an air ticket by visiting a flight tickets website that syndicates many airline companies; then he/she needs to visit another website for hotel bookings that syndicates hotel content from several hotel companies to book a hotel room; finally, he/she may have to visit a car rental website that aggregates content from a broad range of rental car suppliers to hire a car for stay in San Francisco. In an ideal GGG era, a customer just needs to issue a command to the grid "get a cheap flight to San Francisco on such and such date, find a five star hotel there for 3 nights and a rental car as well." Everything will be sorted out during a single visit! Such a scenario is likely to happen because the grid is expected to be highly intelligent (compared with the Internet) attributing to its enormous computing power. The grid (for travel in this instance)

Figure 2. Evolutionary history of information technology

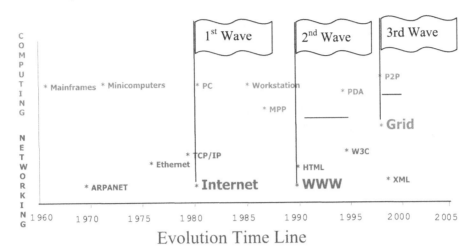

The second wave originated in Europe and made big waves throughout the world in the 1980s. In 1980, Tim Berners-Lee in CERN (Central European Radiation Network) wrote a notebook program, "Enquire-Within-Upon-Everything", which allowed links to be made between arbitrary nodes. Each node had a title, a type, and a list of bi-directional typed links. "ENQUIRE" ran on Norsk Data machines under SINTRAN-III. This is the origin of the WWW, which electronically links the Internet users' web pages (Internet & WWW history 2003).

will offer users choice, convenience, guaranteed quality by integrating a rich blend of direct travel-related services (accommodation, dining, transport, recreation and entertainment) and other ancillary services (insurance, software, content, finance, weather, news, maps etc.).

The advent of the grid urges the third wave (Figure 2) in Information Technology (IT) after the Internet and World Wide Web (WWW). The Internet is considered the first wave IT revolution. The second wave is associated with the browser and the World Wide Web, which allowed information sharing across the Internet. The third wave, the grid, allows users to collaborate and share, not just information, but resources and services, such as high-performance computing facilities, large data archives, remote sensing instruments and digital libraries (Ross-Flanigan, 2003).

The first wave, also referred to as "Internet," began in USA in the late 1960s. The global Internet's progenitor was the ARPAnet project, which was sponsored by the US Department of Defense in 1968. The Advanced Research Projects Agency (ARPA)'s program plan for the ARPAnet was entitled as "Resource Sharing Computer Networks" (Internet & WWW history 2003). The Internet physically links geographically distributed computers.

Due to the rapid expansion of the Internet, the WWW is seen as no longer serving the current needs of scientists. The advent of the grid (Figure 3) promises to make it possible for scientific collaborations to share resources on an unprecedented scale, and for geographically distributed groups to work together in ways that were previously impossible. The Great Global Grid (GGG) is expected to be the third IT wave. A big push for the development of the grid has come from CERN, the place where the WWW was invented.

The Great Global Grid will provide a wealth of opportunities for entrepreneurs, consumers, and investors. It will come in the form of universal broadband access, unlimited network server availability, global virtual malls, real-time enterprise

Figure 3. Computing food chain

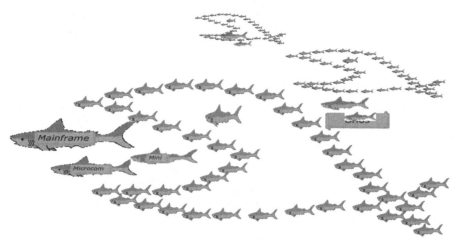

Computing Food Chain: Grids swallowing others...

computing. It's the firstborn offspring of the Internet; only it will be sleeker, smarter, more agile and more compliant than its predecessor. Potentially, it could eclipse the unprecedented economic expansion from 1992 to 1999 (Malone 2001). Forbes predicts that if history holds true the grid will be a USD 20 trillion industry (nearly twice the current Gross Domestic Product) by the year 2020. Even if it is only one-tenth that size, it will still constitute an economic revolution (Malone 2001). Within this wave, it is the widespread use of "Web Services" (defined as loosely coupled components that communicate via XML interfaces), combined with a "grid computing model" (in which every user and his access device is both a client and a server and is both a provider and consumer of *information*) will cause a revolutionary upheaval in the way various industries are structured and businesses are conducted (Pollock and Benjamin 2002). The third wave of IT revolution is heading our way.

GRID STANDARDS ORGANIZATIONS

Software and grid services developers working in various organizations across the world seek to conform to conventions and standards widely adopted by the grid community. These standards are provided by various organizations. The Global Grid Forum (GGF, www.ggf.org) is the primary standards setting body for the grid. The GGF works with many organizations throughout industry that influence grid standards and policies, including those for security and virtual organizations. The GGF is a community-driven set of working groups that are developing standards and best practices for wide-area distributed computing. It was formed in 1998 from the merger of the Grid Forum in North America, the Asia-Pacific Grid community, and the European Grid Forum (eGrid).

Other bodies include the Organization for the Advancement of Structured Information Standards (OASIS), the World Wide Web Consortium (W3C), the Distributed Management Task Force (DMTF), and various groups within Internet2 (Baker et al 2005).

- OASIS, a not-for-profit international organization formed in 1993, promotes industry standards for e-business and produces web services standards that focus primarily on higher-level functionality such as security, authentication, registries, business process execution, and reliable messaging.

- The W3C (www.w3.org), an international organization initiated in 1994 by Tim Berners-Lee to promote common and interoperable protocols, has partnered with the GGF in the Web services standards area.
- The DMTF (www.dmtf.org) is an industry-based organization founded in 1992 to develop management standards and integration technologies for enterprise and Internet environments. It formed an alliance with the GGF in 2003 for the purpose of building a unified approach to the provisioning, sharing, and management of grid resources and technologies.
- Internet2 (www.internet2.edu) is a consortium of groups from academia, industry, and government formed in 1996 to develop and deploy advanced network applications and technologies. Internet2 working groups related to grid standards include the Higher Education PKI Technical Activities Group, the Peer-to-Peer Working Group, and the Shibboleth project.

GRID STANDARDS

Efforts are underway in the GGF and OASIS to document "best practices," implementation guidelines, and standards for grid technologies. The most important grid standards include:

Open Grid Services Architecture

The most important grid standard to emerge is the Open Grid Services Architecture (OGSA), which aims to define a common, standard, and open architecture for grid-based applications (Foster et al. 2002). It represents an evolution towards a grid system architecture based on web services concepts and technologies (http://www.globus.org/ogsa/). A web service is a software system (often

Web APIs accessible over a network) designed to support interoperable machine-to-machine interaction over a network. These software systems can be executed on a remote system hosting the requested services.

Web Services Resource Framework

Web Services Resource Framework or WSRF (http://www.globus.org/wsrf/) is a set of web service specifications being developed by the OASIS organization. These specifications describe how to implement OGSA capabilities using Web services.

MAJOR INTERNATIONAL GRID PROJECTS

There are many national and international grid projects across the world. Here we only mention a few major projects due to space limitations.

e-Science (UK)

The UK e-Science program started in April 2001 as an ambitious GBP 120M effort to change the dynamic of the way science is undertaken by exploiting the emerging grid infrastructures to enable global collaborations in many key areas including engineering, astrophysics, medical research, healthcare, chemistry and environment (Taylor 2002). Many regional e-Science centers within nine UK universities and over 60 UK companies are involved in the core technology program. In addition, there is large international involvement as well.

TeraGrid (U.S.)

The TeraGrid project (http://www.teragrid.org/) is funded by the National Science Foundation (http://www.nsf.gov/) and includes nine partners within the U.S. Using high-performance network connections, the TeraGrid integrates high-performance computers, data resources and tools, and high-end experimental facilities around the U.S. Currently, TeraGrid resources include more than 250 teraflops of computing capability and more than 30 petabytes of online and archival data storage, with rapid access and retrieval over high-performance networks.

NAREGI (Japan)

National Research Grid Initiative or NAREGI (http://www.naregi.org/HPCAsia2004-ws.html) is a collaborative project among industry, academia and government, initiated by the Ministry of Education, Sports, Culture, Science and Technology (MEXT). It is expected to have a 100+ teraflops of computing capability by 2007.

EGEE (Europe)

The Enabling Grids for E-sciencE or the EGEE project (http://www.eu-egee.org/) is funded by the European Commission and brings together scientists and engineers from more than 90 institutions in 32 countries world-wide. The EGEE Grid consists of over 30,000 CPU in addition to about 5 petabytes of storage, and maintains 30,000 concurrent jobs on average.

CNGrid (China)

The China National Grid Project or the CNGrid Project (http://www.cngrid.org/en_index.htm) is supported by the "High Performance Computer and its Kernel Software " project, which is a key project in the National High-Tech R&D Program. CNGrid is equipped with independently developed grid oriented high performance computers (Lenovo DeepComp 6800, Dawning 4000A) and constitutes an open grid environment with 8 nodes including Hong Kong. Independently developed

grid software are used to sustain the grid environment and the development of application grid. The total computing capacity is 17 TFlops.

DEISA (Europe)

The Distributed European Infrastructure for Supercomputing Applications or DEISA supercomputing Grid (http://www.deisa.org/grid/) is a European research infrastructure resulting from the integration of national High Performance Computing (HPC) infrastructures. This integration of national resources – using modern grid technologies – is expected to contribute to a significant enhancement of HPC capability and capacity in Europe. The DEISA infrastructure's aggregated computing power will be close to 190 Teraflops in 2007

FUTURE TRENDS

Grid technology is evolving and certain trends are discernible. Generally, grid is becoming popular and acceptable in the industry. This trend will continue as the technology matures and becomes more profitable. There is also the growing resolution of the issue of multiple grids versus a single global grid and where to apply them. Other challenges such as grid economics, the problems of resource allocation and the security of un-trusted parties running grid applications are being addressed to sustain the general acceptance of grid as the next IT wave. Furthermore, the grid community is still short of established standards for dynamic and autonomic resource provisioning, which hampers vendor interoperability. With focused efforts, there will be improvements in grid standards that will be incorporated in emerging grid products. In all, the emerging service-oriented architecture and semantic grid will greatly impact grid growth in the near future.

CONCLUSION

The advent of the grid promises to make it possible for scientific collaborations to share resources on an unprecedented scale, by enabling coordinated problem solving in dynamic and multi-institutional setups. At present there are dozens of major grid projects in scientific and technical computing/research. Industrial interest is also growing rapidly due to the wealth of opportunities for entrepreneurs, consumers, and investors alike. Currently, we are observing a transition phase from pure academic research to industrial applications. This will aid the growth and will help achieve the goal of pervasive access to computing by making it available to users from non-scientific community. However, there are many pressing challenges that remain. These include – standardization of grid architectures and protocols, more decentralized resource management techniques, establishing and extending grid community and pursuing the research to address next-generation systems.

REFERENCES

Baker, M., Apon, A., Ferner, C., & Brown, J. (2005). Emerging grid standards. *Computer, 38*(4), 43-50.

Foster, I., & Kesselman, C. (1999). The grid: Blueprint for a new computing infrastructure. San Francisco: Morgan Kaufmann Publishers, Inc.

Foster, I., & Kesselman, C. (2003). The grid: The first 50 years, lovelace lecture at British computer society (BCS). Lovelace Medal Presentation, London, UK.

Foster, I., Kesselman, C., Nick, J. M., & Tuecke, S. (2002). The physiology of the grid: An open grid services architecture for distributed systems integration. Retrieved June 30, 2007, from http://www.globus.org/alliance/publications/papers/ogsa.pdf

Hermida, A. (2001). Computing power on tap. BBC News online. Retrieved June 30, 2007, from http://news.bbc.co.uk/2/hi/science/nature/1470225.stm

Internet & World Wide Web History (2003). Retrieved June 30, 2007, from www.elsop.com/wrc/h_web.htm

Malone, M., S. (2001). Internet II: Rebooting America, Forbes online. Retrieved June 30, 2007, from http://members.forbes.com/asap/2001/0910/044.html

Pollock, A., and Benjamin, L. (2002). Why Web Services and Grid Computing will Turn the Travel Industry on Its Head – and Why that's a Good Thing!. White Paper, DestiCorp.

Ross-Flanigan, N. (2003). MGRID to lead to third wave of computing, The University record online, University of Michigan. Retrieved June 30, 2007, from http://www.umich.edu/~urecord/0203/May05_03/08.shtml

Stockinger H. (2007). Defining the Grid: A Snapshot on the Current View, *Journal of Supercomputing*, Springer Verlag. Retrieved June 30, 2007, from http://www.springerlink.com/content/906476116167673m/

Taylor, J. (2002). Plenary keynote, GGF 5. Retrieved June 30, 2007, from www.gridforum.org/Meetings/ggf5/plenary/Mon/

KEY TERMS AND DEFINITIONS

Distributed Computing: In distributed computing, parts of a program run simultaneously on two or more computers that are communicating with each other over a network.

Grid Computing: It involves resource sharing and coordinated problem solving in dynamic and multi-institutional virtual organizations.

OGSA: Open Grid Services Architecture or OGSA is a grid standard that aims to define a common, standard, and open architecture for grid-based applications.

Virtual Organization: It can consist of multiple independent organizations linked through a computer network. These independent organizations share skills and resources to achieve their goals.

Virtualization: It is an interface often provided with grid services to hide the complexity of the underlying resources.

Web Service: A web service is a software system (often Web APIs accessible over a network) designed to support interoperable machine-to-machine interaction over a network.

WSRF: Web Services Resource Framework or WSRF is a set of Web Service specifications being developed by the OASIS organization. These specifications describe how to implement OGSA capabilities using Web services.

Section II
Grid Scheduling and Optimization

Chapter II
Resource–Aware Load Balancing of Parallel Applications

Eric Aubanel
University of New Brunswick, Faculty of Computer Science, Canada

ABSTRACT

The problem of load balancing parallel applications is particularly challenging on computational grids, since the characteristics of both the application and the platform must be taken into account. This chapter reviews the wide range of solutions that have been proposed. It considers tightly coupled parallel applications that can be described by an undirected graph representing concurrent execution of tasks and communication of tasks, executing on computational grids with static and dynamic network and processor performance. While a rich set of solution techniques have been proposed, there has not been of yet any performance comparisons between them. Such comparisons will require parallel benchmarks and computational grid emulators and simulators.

INTRODUCTION

Distributed high performance computing (HPC) applications have formed an important class of grid applications from the early days of the I-Way (DeFanti et al., 1996; Foster and Kesselman, 1999) to the TeraGrid (http://www.teragrid.org) of today. The main reason is that the aggregation of multiple parallel computers permits problem solutions that require more resources than are available in a single system. Many of these applications, such as partial differential equation (PDE) solvers, can be described by an undirected graph representing concurrent execution of tasks and communication between tasks, as in Foster's PCAM design methodology (Foster, 1995). Parallel execution requires partitioning of the application's graph in such a way that communication between the resulting subgraphs is minimized and the load is roughly balanced. These subgraphs must be mapped to the processors of a parallel computer. In many cases partitioning is only required once before execution of the application begins. However, in situations where the computational requirement of tasks varies with time, as in adaptive mesh refinement methods, the graph may need to be repartitioned to re-balance the computational load of processors (Schloegel, Karypis and Kumar, 2003; Teresco, Devine, and Flaherty, 2005). Here we use the term "load balancing" to refer to both static partitioning and dynamic repartitioning. This load balancing problem becomes particularly challenging when a homogeneous parallel computer is replaced by a heterogeneous computational grid.

Load balancing using graph partitioning is a well-established research area that has resulted in a number of popular software tools used by computational scientists (Schloegel, Karypis and Kumar, 2003). Several approaches have been proposed for this NP-hard problem. Many employ a multilevel approach (Schloegel, Karypis and Kumar, 2003), which collapses (coarsens) the graph recursively, partitions the smallest graph, and refines the partition as the graph is un-coarsened. One critique of classical graph partitioners is that minimizing the number of edges cut by a partition misrepresents the actual communication volume (Hendrickson, 1998), but in many cases this metric still provides a reasonable estimate of the total communication volume of the parallel application. In reality, however, it is the time (due to computation and communication) spent by the slowest processor that determines the execution time of a parallel application. This becomes particularly important when the computational platform is heterogeneous in processor and network performance, in which case the number of edges cut by a partition is a poor measure of parallel overhead. We call resource-aware load balancing the partitioning and mapping of an application's graph to a heterogeneous computational platform, either before execution begins or periodically during execution.

Recent work has begun to address the problem of resource-aware load balancing. This includes DRUM, JOSTLE, MinEX, PaGrid, PART, and SCOTCH, among others. Our goal is to review and contrast these recent efforts and discuss the many avenues for future work. A comprehensive review of this area has not been published to date (Li and Lan, 2004; Devine et al., 2005).

BACKGROUND

Since heterogeneous computing is a broad research area and there are many definitions of computational grids, we define the characteristics of the applications and platforms that we are considering.

Applications

We consider tightly-coupled parallel applications that can be described by an undirected graph representing concurrent execution of tasks and communication between tasks. The most important class concerns the numerical solution of PDEs (Schloegel, Karypis and Kumar, 2003), but such applications also include molecular dynamics problems (Koenig and Kalé, 2007) and cellular automata (Cappuccio et al., 2001). Parallel execution requires partitioning of the application's graph in such a way that communication between the resulting subgraphs is minimized and the load is roughly balanced. These applications are typically iterative, with alternating communication and computation phases (Botadra et al., 2007). Although partial overlap is possible, the entire communication overhead cannot be overlapped with computation because of the dependency between subsequent iterations. Scheduling of operations on dense matrices on heterogeneous systems has been studied (Dongarra and Lastovetsky, 2006), but is not considered here. We are also not concerned here with scheduling of independent tasks or scheduling of workflows represented by directed graphs, but with scheduling of the components of a single parallel program, defined as the use of multiple resources executing concurrently to solve a single problem.

Platforms

High capacity grid platforms are dedicated to high performance computing (HPC) applications and generally consist of an aggregation of multiple HPC clusters (e.g. the TeraGrid) and are space-shared, that is processors only execute a single user's process(es) at a time. The clusters may be located in one organization, or they may be more spread out geographically, which can pose additional problems of high latencies. *High throughput* grid platforms aim to take advantage of spare compute cycles on processing nodes that may be dedicated to multiple users at the same time and hence are time-shared. This latter class can consist of local or global networks of computers, and can be either within one organization (Chien, 2003) or be simply a collection of individual computers on the Internet (Anderson, 2004). While high throughput grids are mainly useful for scheduling independent tasks they can also be used for parallel applications, and therefore both types of grids will be considered here. For more on classification of computational grids, see Dongarra and Lastovetsky (2006) and Stockinger (2007).

Grid computing platforms can be heterogeneous in many ways, whether due to varying processor and network link performance, available memory, or system software, to name a few (Dongarra and Lastovetsky, 2006). Here we consider only processor and network heterogeneities, since they alone significantly complicate the load balancing problem. Such heterogeneities can be static or dynamic, and the load balancing strategies differ significantly for both cases. Processor heterogeneity can be static due to the presence of processors of varying potential performance, and can be dynamic for time-shared platforms.

Network heterogeneity can be static due to the presence of slow and fast links, and can be dynamic due to the varying performance over time of wide-area networks. It should be noted that the load balancing algorithms discussed here are not only applicable to grids, but are also valid for single clusters that have static or dynamic heterogeneities.

MAIN FOCUS

Since the load balancing problem is NP-hard, exact solutions are only possible for graphs too small to be useful (see, e.g., Attiya and Hamam, 2004, and references therein), since a typical application graph will have well over one thousand vertices. Load balancing algorithms fall into two classes: static and dynamic. Resource-aware algorithms also consider static and dynamic processor and network characteristics.

Static Load Balancing

The simplest type of heterogeneity to deal with is due to fixed differences between processors. Varying processor performance can be accommodated by weighting the size of subgraphs of a partition, which can be easily incorporated into homogeneous partitioners, such as METIS (Karypis and Kumar, 1998). Accommodating static network heterogeneity is more challenging, and a number of approaches have been taken. These can be classified into two classes: partitioning and mapping, and hierarchical partitioning.

A number of partitioners, including SCOTCH, JOSTLE, and PaGrid, partition and map the application graph onto a weighted platform graph. To our knowledge, SCOTCH (Pellegrini and Roman, 1996) was the first partitioner of this type. Mapping of graphs to certain types of platform graphs (e.g. hypercube) has been well studied (Grama et al., 2003), but here we are considering mapping of arbitrary application graphs to arbitrary platform graphs. SCOTCH employs recursive bisection of both the mesh and platform graphs. At each step the two graphs are bipartitioned, while maintaining a balanced load of vertices, and a subset of vertices is mapped onto a subset of processors when the size of the subset of processors is equal to one. JOSTLE (Walshaw & Cross, 2001) is a multilevel graph partitioner that uses a variant of the Kernighan-Lin algorithm and a cost function based on total communication cost (as does SCOTCH). While JOSTLE produces partitions that are balanced in terms of vertices of the application graph, it does not take into account the communication cost of each processor when load balancing. This can produce imbalanced partitions, with processors connected by slow links having higher execution times than the rest (Wanschoor and Aubanel, 2004). The initial version of PaGrid (Huang, Aubanel and Bhavsar, 2003, 2006) used a multilevel graph partitioning approach, with refinement based on minimization of total communication cost, as in JOSTLE, augmented by a load balancing stage based on estimated execution time in the final uncoarsening phase. The next version (Wanschoor and Aubanel, 2004) improved PaGrid by using the estimated execution time cost function at all levels of refinement. PaGrid was further improved by incorporating latency into the estimated execution time (Aubanel and Wu, 2007). Adams and Price (2004) proposed a Boltzmann machine neural network for the partitioning and mapping problem, in which multiple simulated annealings are performed. Their approach lends itself to parallelization, but may still be costly for large problems. Recent work by Moulitsas and Karypis (2006) has investigated adapting the METIS algorithm to first balance the load of processors, followed by an additional stage that modifies this partition to minimize the communication volume. They also discuss briefly the possibility of using a similar approach to PaGrid, where the estimated execution times of processors is balanced and the maximum time is minimized.

The hierarchical partitioning approach has been taken by projects such as DRUM, Charm++, PART, and by the work of Otero et al. (2005). The first two are dynamic load balancers and will be discussed in the next section. PART (Chen and Taylor, 2002) uses simulated annealing, with a cost function based on estimated execution time. It first partitions the mesh into c subgraphs, where c is the number of clusters, then partitions each subgraph for the processors in each cluster, and finally performs a global retrofit. This computationally intensive algorithm requires a parallel implementation. Otero et al. (2005) use METIS to partition the graph into c subgraphs, and then partition each subgraph into two classes: subgraphs containing only boundary nodes communicating with other clusters and those containing only communications local to the cluster. This allows slow remote communications to be overlapped with computation.

While many problems involve dynamic applications and/or dynamic platforms, and hence require dynamic load balancing, static load balancing is still important, since initial assignment of tasks is crucial to the performance of dynamic load balancing. As well, many algorithmic techniques developed for static partitioners can also be applied to dynamic ones.

Dynamic Load Balancing

These algorithms have traditionally been designed to handle parallel applications where during execution either the mesh is adaptively refined (AMR) or the computational load varies over time. They begin with a static partitioning of the initial graph, then periodically monitor the load of processors, followed by reassignment of vertices to balance the load as required. This reassignment can be accomplished either by graph repartitioning or by diffusion algorithms (Schloegel, Karypis and Kumar, 2003; Teresco, Devine and Flaherty, 2005). These algorithms must not only balance the load and minimized inter-processor communication in the parallel application, but also must minimize the cost of reassigning vertices, which can be significant.

Dynamic load balancing algorithms can easily be extended to deal with dynamic processor heterogeneity. Minyard and Kallinderis (2000) applied an octree-based method for the initial partition and repartitions of a computational fluid dynamics application. They used runtime measurements to determine the need for load balancing due either to mesh adaptation or to changes in the runtime environment. Rao (2006) modified an explicit finite element solver to periodically check the load of processors and then used a simple load balancing algorithm. He indicated that a more scalable solution could use diffusion algorithms to minimize redistribution cost. Dobber, Koole and van der Mei (2004) performed experiments on dynamic load balancing of a red/black SOR algorithm on the Planetlab computational grid (http://www.planet-lab.org), using exponential smoothing to predict processor performance.

Network heterogeneity can be taken care of directly, in a manner similar to the graph partitioning and mapping algorithms discussed above, or indirectly, by performing hierarchical partitioning. In the case of load balancers that employ diffusion algorithms, care should be taken to include the varying performance of network links when evaluating redistribution cost (Rao, 2006; Rotaru and Nageli, 2004). The GrACE adaptive runtime system supports AMR applications on dynamic heterogeneous systems (Sinha and Parashar, 2002). Load balancing is done using a capacity metric determined for every processor, from the system state monitored using the Network Weather Service tool (http://nws. cs.ucsb.edu). MinEX (Das, Harvey and Biswas, 2002) is a multilevel dynamic partitioner that minimizes the estimated execution time of the application. It refines partitions by moving vertices from overloaded to underloaded processors in order to minimize the variance in processor execution times. Petcu, Vizman and Paprzycki

(2006) used a heuristic partitioning algorithm called Largest Task First with Minimum Finish Time and Available Communication Cost for load balancing of a multi-block CFD application in a heterogeneous computing environment. Here grid blocks are scheduled to processors, taking into account dynamically varying performance of the platform.

Hierarchical approaches are commonly used in this area. The Dynamic Resource Utilization Model (DRUM) is used in Zoltan, a parallel computing toolkit, to collect information about the processors and network of the computing platform (Devine et al., 2005; Teresco, Devine and Flaherty, 2005). DRUM uses a weighted sum of processor and communication cost for each node in a tree structure that represents the network topology. Different partitioning algorithms can be applied at different levels of the tree, for example fast geometric algorithms can be used to partition within a shared memory compute node where communication costs are negligible. Lan, Taylor and Li (2006) used a hierarchical algorithm to balance the load between and within clusters for adaptive cosmological simulations. This deals to some extent with the hierarchical networks of computational grids without treating communication cost directly. Koenig and Kalé (2007) incorporated resource-aware load balancing into the Charm++ parallel programming language and runtime system. They used METIS to first partition into one subgraph per cluster, and then partition within each cluster. This means partitions must be recomputed from scratch at each load balancing step ("scratch-map" repartitioning; see Schloegel, Karypis and Kumar, 2003), which can have significant overhead, but the problem size they tested was quite small (3000 nodes).

Platform Modeling

The load balancing algorithms described here employ a wide range of metrics to represent platform performance. Processor performance alone can be modeled using either benchmarks or monitoring of the application. More interestingly, different approaches have been taken to represent the total communication and computation cost and the network topology. For the former, terms representing communication and computation costs are either simply summed (MinEX, PART), or the terms are weighted in acknowledgment of the varying importance of the two terms for different applications (DRUM, PaGrid). It is not clear whether it is better to represent the network topology directly, or indirectly via a hierarchical approach. The former approach does have the advantage that it can deal with a more kinds of heterogeneous platforms. Finally, consideration of the importance of the number (sensitive to latency) and size of messages (sensitive to bandwidth) may be important (Aubanel and Wu, 2007).

Summary

This review has revealed a wide range of solutions to the resource-aware load balancing problem, which are summarized in Table 1. What is evidently missing is a performance comparison between them, which it not possible at present, since they address applications with different characteristics. In order to compare them two things are needed: benchmark applications and simulators/emulators of grid computing systems.

Table 1. Classification of resource-aware load balancing algorithms

Static	Partition and Map
	Recursive bipartition: SCOTCH (Pellegrini & Roman, 1996)
	Multilevel refinement:
	METIS (Karypis & Kumar, 1998)
	JOSTLE (Walshaw & Cross, 2001)
	PaGrid (Huang, Aubanel & Bhavsar, 2003, 2006; Wanschoor & Aubanel, 2004; Aubanel & Wu, 2007)
	Neural network: Adams & Price (2004)
	Adaptation of METIS: Moulitsas & Karypis (2006)
	Hierarchical
	Simulated annealing: PART (Chen & Taylor, 2002)
	Using METIS: Otero et al. (2005)
Dynamic	**Processor Heterogeneity**
	Octree, CFD: Minyard & Kallinderis (2000)
	Explicit FEM: Rao (2006)
	Red-black SOR: Dobber, Koole, & van der Mei (2004)
	Network Heterogeneity
	AMR: GrACE (Sinha & Parashar, 2002)
	Multilevel refinement: MinEX (Das, Harvey, & Biswas, 2002)
	Multi-block CFD: Petcu, Vizman, & Paprzycki (2006)
	Hierarchical
	Tree-based model: DRUM (Devine et al., 2005; Teresco, Devine, & Flaherty, 2005)
	Adaptive Cosmological: Lan, Taylor, & Li (2006)
	Scratch-map using METIS: Charm++ (Koenig & Kalé, 2007)

A consistent set of parallel benchmarks (of the type described in the Background section) is required in order to perform a fair comparison (Ghazinour et al., 2008). However these benchmarks should not just be run on whatever heterogeneous system is at hand. For reproducible and comparable results they should be run on a standard set of simulated or emulated heterogeneous platforms. We know of no published benchmarks, other than Ghazinour et al. (2008). However, some work has been done on simulation (Liu and Chien, 2006) and on emulation (Koenig and Kalé, 2007; Canon and Jeannot, 2006).

FUTURE TRENDS

An important question that has not been addressed by the work surveyed here is whether it is better to select a subset of the processors of a computational grid at runtime instead of using them all. Moldable scheduling has been proposed to address this question for scheduling of homogeneous parallel applications (Cirne and Berman, 2003). This needs to be extended to heterogeneous platforms.

In dynamic load balancing there is a tradeoff between the benefit and cost of potentially complex redistribution strategies. This will likely be explored further, with future tools perhaps making available a choice of multiple strategies.

One important issue that has not been addressed here is fault tolerance. This is particularly important for high throughput platforms where member nodes may join and leave the grid frequently, but also for large high capacity grids, whose large size means that node failures are likely during the execution of an application. Solutions to this problem should recognize that MPI is the dominant programming paradigm in the HPC community and is likely to remain so for a while. Therefore solutions that require minimum alteration of existing code should be explored. Already, much work has been done on making MPI fault-tolerant, for example in OpenMPI (http://ww.open-mpi.org).

Finally, much of the above work relies on the local nature of inter-task communication. Many new types of simulations use graphs with highly irregular connectivity, posing a challenge to graph partitioners. Techniques such as hypergraph partitioning are being explored to deal with such graphs (Devine et al., 2005).

CONCLUSION

A rich set of solution techniques have been proposed for the problem of resource-aware load balancing of parallel applications, considering the static and dynamic heterogeneities of computational grids. In practice, the best approach will depend on the characteristics of the application and of the platform. These techniques need to be incorporated into software platforms (as in the case of Zoltan), and performance comparison of different approaches is necessary to characterize the balance between model sophistication, overhead, and solution quality.

REFERENCES

Adams, J. R., & Price, C. C. (2004). Boltzmann algorithms to partition and map software for computational grids. In *Proceedings of the 18th International Parallel and Distributed Processing Symposium, High Performance Grid Computing Workshop.*

Anderson, D. P. (2004). BOINC: A system for public-resource computing and storage. *Fifth IEEE/ACM International Workshop on Grid Computing.*

Attiya, G., & Hamam, Y. (2004). Two phase algorithm for load balancing in heterogeneous distributed systems. *12th Euromicro Conference on Parallel, Distributed and Network-Based Processing* (pp. 434-439).

Aubanel, E., & Wu, X. (2007). Incorporating latency in heterogeneous graph partitioning. In *Proceedings of the 21st Intl. Parallel and Distributed Processing Symposium, Workshop on Parallel and Distributed Scientific and Engineering Computing (PDSEC).*

Botadra, H., Cheng, Q., Prasad, S.K., Aubanel, E., & V. Bhavsar, V. (2007). iC2mpi: A platform for parallel execution of graph-structured iterative computations. In *Proceedings of the 21st Intl. Parallel and Distributed Processing Symposium, Workshop on Parallel and Distributed Scientific and Engineering Computing (PDSEC).* March 2007, Long Beach California.

Canon, L., & Jeannot, E. (2006). Wrekavoc: A tool for emulating heterogeneity. In *Proceedings of the 20th Intl. Parallel and Distributed Processing Symposium, Heterogeneous Computing Workshop (HCW).*

Cappuccio, R., Cattaneo, G., Erbacci, G., & Jocher, U. (April 2001). A parallel implementation of a cellular automata based model for coffee percolation. *Parallel Computing, 27*(33), 685-717.

Chen, J., & Taylor, V. E. (2002). Mesh partitioning for efficient use of distributed systems. *IEEE Transactions on Parallel and Distributed Systems, 13*(1), 67-79.

Chien, A. A. (2003). Architecture of a commercial enterprise desktop grid: The entropia system. In F. Berman, G.C. Fox, & A.J.G. Hey, *Grid computing: Making the Global Infrastructure a Reality.* John Wiley & Sons, Ltd.

Cirne, W., & Berman, F. (2003). When the herd is smart: Aggregate behavior in the selection of job request. *IEEE Transactions on Parallel and Distributed Systems, 14*(2), 181-192.

Das, S. K., Harvey, D. J., & Biswas, R. (2002). MinEX: A latency-tolerant dynamic partitioner for grid computing applications. *Future Generation Computer Systems, 18*(4), 477-489.

DeFanti, T. A., Foster, I., Papka, M. E., Stevens, R., & Kuhfuss, T. (1996). Overview of the I-way: Wide-area visual supercomputing. *International Journal of High Performance Computing Applications, 10*(2-3), 123-131.

Devine, K. D., Boman, E. G., Heaphy, R. T., Hendrickson, B. A., Teresco, J. D., Faik, J., et al. (2005). New challenges in dynamic load balancing. *Applied Numerical Mathematics, 52*(2-3), 133-152.

Dobber, M., Koole, G., & van der Mei, R. (2005). Dynamic load balancing experiments in a grid. *International Symposium on Cluster Computing and the Grid (CCGrid)* (pp. 1063-1070), Vol. 2.

Dongarra, J., & Lastovetsky, A. (2006). An overview of heterogeneous high performance and grid computing. In B. Di Martino, J. Dongarra, A. Hoisie, L. Yang & H. Zima (Eds.), *Engineering the grid: Status and perspectives.* American Scientific Publishers.

Foster, I. (1995). *Designing and building parallel programs.* Addison Wesley.

Foster, I., & Kesselman, C. (1999). *The grid: Blueprint for a new computing infrastructure.* San Francisco, CA: Morgan Kaufmann Publishers, Inc.

Ghazinour, K., Shaw, R.E., Aubanel, E., & Garey, L.E. (2008) A linear solver for benchmarking partitioners. In *Proceedings of the 22nd Intl. Parallel and Distributed Processing Symposium, Workshop on Parallel and Distributed Scientific and Engineering Computing (PDSEC).*

Grama, A., Karypis, G., Kumar, V., & Gupta, A. (2003). *Introduction to parallel computing* (2nd ed.). Addison-Wesley.

Hendrickson, B. (1998). Graph partitioning and parallel solvers: Has the emperor no clothes? *Workshop on Parallel Algorithms for Irregularly Structured Problems* (LNCS 1457, 218-225).

Huang, S., Aubanel, E. E., & C., V. (2006). PaGrid: A mesh partitioner for computational grids. *Journal of Grid Computing, 4*(1), 71-88.

Huang, S., Aubanel, E., & Bhavsar, V. C. (2003). Mesh partitioners for computational grids: A comparison. *International Conference on Computational Science and its Applications* (LNCS 2267-2269, 60-68).

Karypis, G., & Kumar, V. (1998). Multilevel k-way partitioning scheme for irregular graphs. *Journal of Parallel and Distributed Computing, 48*(1), 96-129.

Koenig, G. A., & Kalé, L. V. (2007). *Optimizing distributed application performance using dynamic grid topology-aware load balancing.* Paper presented at the 21st. International Parallel and Distributed Processing Symposium.

Lan, Z., Taylor, V. E., & Li, Y. (2006). DistDLB: Improving cosmology SAMR simulations on distributed computing systems through hierarchical load balancing. *Journal of Parallel and Distributed Computing, 66*(5), 716-731.

Li, Y. W., & Lan, Z. L. (2004). A survey of load balancing in grid computing. *First International Symposium on Computational and Information Science* (LNCS 3314, 280-285).

Liu, X., & Chien, A. A. (2006). Realistic large-scale online network simulation. *International Journal of High Performance Computing Applications, 20*(3), 383-399.

Minyard, T., & Kallinderis, Y. (2000). Parallel load balancing for dynamic execution environments. *Computer Methods in Applied Mechanics and Engineering, 189*(4), 1295-1309.

Moulitsas, I., & Karypis, G. (2006). *Architecture aware partitioning algorithms.* (Tech Rep. No. 06-001). University of Minnesota.

Otero, B., Cela, J. M., Badia, R. M., & Labarta, J. (2005). Data distribution strategies for domain decomposition applications in grid environments. *6th International Conference on Algorithms and Architectures for Parallel Processing, ICA3PP.* (LNCS 3719, 214-224).

Pellegrini, F., & Roman, J. (1996). SCOTCH: A software package for static mapping by dual recursive bipartitioning of process and architecture graphs. In *Proceedings of the International Conference and Exhibition on High-Performance Computing and Networking: HPCN Europe 1996* (pp. 493-498).

Petcu, D., Vizman, D., & Paprzycki, M. (2006). Heuristic load balancing for CFD Codes executed in heterogeneous computing environments. *Scalable Computing: Practice and Experience* (SCPe), *7*(2), 15-24.

Rao, A.R.M. (2006). Explicit nonlinear dynamic finite element analysis on homogeneous/heterogeneous parallel computing environment. *Advances in Engineering Software, 37*(11), 701-720.

Rotaru, T., & Nägeli, H. (2004). Dynamic load balancing by diffusion in heterogeneous systems. *Journal of Parallel and Distributed Computing, 64*(4), 481-497.

Schloegel, K., Karypis, G., & Kumar, V. (2003). Graph partitioning for high-performance scientific simulations. In J. Dongarra, et al. (Eds.), *The sourcebook of parallel computing.* Morgan Kaufmann.

Sinha, S., & Parashar, M. (2002). Adaptive system sensitive partitioning of AMR applications on heterogeneous clusters. *Cluster Computing, 5*(4), 343-352.

Stockinger, H. (2007). Defining the grid: A snapshot on the current view. *The Journal of Supercomputing, 42*(1), 3-17.

Teresco, J., Devine, K., & Flaherty, J. (2005). Partitioning and dynamic load balancing for the numerical solution of partial differential equations. In *Numerical solution of partial differen-*

tial equations on parallel computers. Springer Verlag.

Walshaw, C., & Cross, M. (2001). Multilevel mesh partitioning for heterogeneous communication networks. *Future Generation Computer Systems, 17*(5), 601-623.

Wanschoor, R., & Aubanel, E. (2004). Partitioning and mapping of mesh-based applications onto computational grids. *Fifth IEEE/ACM International Workshop on Grid Computing* (pp. 156-162).

KEY TERMS AND DEFINITIONS

Dynamic Load Balancing: Assignment of tasks to a computational platform, with the objective of balancing the work assigned to processors. When the tasks are interdependent an additional objective is to minimize communication between processors. The load balance is monitored during execution of the application, and the assignment is modified if required, while trying to minimize the communication cost of migrating tasks.

Heterogeneous Computing: Design and implementation of algorithms for computing platforms with heterogeneous characteristics, such as processor and network performance.

High Capacity Computational Grid: A grid platform dedicated to high performance computing (HPC) applications and generally consisting of an aggregation of multiple HPC clusters. These grids are space-shared, that is processors only execute a single user's process(es) at a time. The clusters may be located in one organization, or they

may be more spread out geographically, which can pose additional problems of high latencies.

High Throughput Computational Grid: A grid platform that aims to take advantage of spare compute cycles on processing nodes. These nodes may be dedicated to multiple users at the same time and hence are time-shared. These grids can consist of local or global networks of computers, and can be either within one organization or be simply a collection of individual computers on the Internet.

Graph Partitioning: In the context of parallel computing, the partitioning of a graph (representing concurrent execution of tasks and communication between tasks) into disjoint subgraphs, where the communication between subgraphs is minimized and the load is roughly balanced.

Resource-Aware Load Balancing: Assignment of tasks to a computational platform, taking into account its heterogeneous characteristics, with the objective of balancing the work assigned to processors. The tasks may be independent, or may have interdependencies described in a graph or digraph. In the latter case an additional objective is to minimize communication between processors. The assignment may be static, that is decided before tasks execute, or dynamic, that is tasks are assigned as conditions change.

Static Load Balancing: Assignment of tasks to a computational platform, before execution takes place, with the objective of balancing the work assigned to processors. When the tasks are interdependent an additional objective is to minimize communication between processors. This assignment is then fixed for the duration of the computation.

Chapter III
Assisting Efficient Job Planning and Scheduling in the Grid

Enis Afgan
University of Alabama at Birmingham, USA

Purushotham Bangalore
University of Alabama at Birmingham, USA

ABSTRACT

Grid computing has emerged as the next generation computing platform. Because of the resource heterogeneity that exists in the grid environment, user jobs experience variable performance. Grid job scheduling, or selection of appropriate mappings between resources and the application, with the goal of leveraging available capacity and imposed requirements is thus at the heart of successful grid utilization. Grid job scheduling can be viewed as a function of resource heterogeneity, resource and application availability, and application options. This chapter presents work that incorporates all of these factors to provision and present individual users with alternative job options in terms of cost and time tradeoffs. Inherently, this leads to more effective scheduling policies. To support these aims, a framework is introduced with a novel scheduling methodology that introduces new user-scheduler interaction levels and a new layer of scheduling that includes application parameter selection and parameter value optimization.

INTRODUCTION

Over the past few years, grid computing (Foster and Kesselman, 1999) has gained popularity as the emerging architecture for next-generation high performance distributed computing. Goal of providing ubiquitous access to distributed, High Performance Computing (HPC) resources that are shared between multiple organizations through "virtualization" and "aggregation", is only as efficient as its overall perception by the end users though. In order to realize this goal, grid middleware provides a standard set of services for authentication, authorization, resource allocation and management, job submission and monitoring, as well as data transfer and management (Berman et al., 2003), thus providing necessary abstractions from individual resources. Because grid provides access to heterogeneous pool of resources, grid job scheduling, or selection of appropriate mappings between resources and application, is at the heart of grid success. However, this scheduling process is perplexed with complexities due to resource availability, application and resource dependencies (Berman, 1998), as well as user goals and requirements. In order for grid to gain wide spread appeal and make efficient use of available resources, grid scheduling needs to be raised to the level where it can accommodate for such aspirations. User experience has to be tailored to support the individual user and provide them with the options they need and desire.

Access to grid resources is typically handled through a job submission interface (*e.g.,* a web-based portal (Gannon et al., 2003), command line interface) where the user is requested to supply job options and parameters. Options requested depend on the scheduling engine employed behind the submission interface and can range from as few as application name and job input files to as many as an individual application supports (*e.g.,* requirements for number of processors employed, amount of memory needed, speed of data transfer). If the latter grid job submission interface is perceived from a perspective of a typical user, such as an applied scientist, all the available resources and choices might appear equivalent and inherent differences would not be recognized, while the selection of which resource to run the job on might be random or based on previous experiences. In addition, once a routine has been established, even though the resource availability, input data, algorithms, or even the applications change, the user may always use the same resource and/or options. The resulting observation is that grid experience does not meet user's expectations while leading to underutilized and inefficient use of resources (in terms of both, cost and time).

Grid job scheduling can be viewed as a function of resource heterogeneity, resource and application availability, *and* application options. In this paper, a grid scheduling framework is presented that advances grid job scheduling to include all of above stated parameters. Through incorporation of these factors, the goal of this work is to provision and present users with concrete and detailed options regarding their jobs, as well as provide more effective and efficient scheduling policies. To support these aims, the framework introduces a novel scheduling methodology that introduces new user-scheduler interaction levels and a new layer of scheduling that includes application parameter selection and parameter value optimization. To accommodate for the overall framework goals, individual components within the proposed framework will allow *specification of application requirements*, enabling initial application registration on the grid, an *application profiling system* developed and customized for data analysis tools, *data analysis* tools geared toward job parameter optimization, and resource-job *cost normalization* environment enabling comparisons between resource cost provider formats. These tools act as support mechanisms for the framework as a whole to assist users with planning and scheduling their job execution on the grid.

Aim of this work is to realize cost-to-application-runtime tradeoffs from user's perspective. This is accomplished by providing job scheduling alternatives, thus providing support for situation-oriented user requirements and considerations. The act of resource selection and scheduling is the central point in all aspects of the grid and, as the grid evolves, will be a key to account management and cost tracking. Providing users with easily understood and applicable, yet targeted job alternatives is thus a key requirement for the grid to see wide overall acceptance.

BACKGROUND

As stated earlier, application execution time is dependent on many factors (Xia et al., 2004). Executing an application in a grid environment exponentially increases influence, dependency, and complexities of such factors. While the user is constrained by resource availability, selection of many other factors influencing job execution time can be controlled. Several key factors can often be found to have significant influence on application execution time and cost, showing importance of proper resource selection and job parameterization. We define *job parameterization* as an understanding and selection of job parameters (*i.e.,* user controllable and application dependent options that can be changed when submitting a job, such as number of processors employed, algorithm used, and data distribution) that are algorithm, input data, and resource dependent. These dependencies can be categorized into three major areas: hardware influence, algorithm influence, and job parameters influence. Full analysis and job execution influence details on mentioned areas can be found in (Afgan and Bangalore, 2007).

Based on stated facts, it can be concluded that scheduling of jobs in heterogeneous grid environment poses a significant challenge. In more traditional HPC environments, where a user had access to a handful of resources, the user could have experimented and adjusted their job parameters to obtain necessary, tuned, and reusable job parameters. In grid environments though, due to the highly dynamic state of resources and applications, jobs need to be automatically adapted to the changing grid environment by automatically handling parameterization, node failure, dynamic resource availability and cost. Involved complexity results in inability of users to perform this task manually and thus automated methods are required. This is the job of schedulers. Today, two main types of schedulers exist, namely local

resource management (LRM) systems and distributed resource management (DRM) systems. The main characteristic of LRMs (*e.g.,* LSF, PBS, SGE, Condor) is that they reside directly on a resource and have full information and control of the underlying system. This enables tight control over the resource and allows the scheduler to deliver desired level of Quality of Service (QoS) to the users. At the same time, DRMs are characterized as being higher level LRMs. DRMs do not have direct control over underlying resources but rather rely on aggregated information from multiple LRMs and enable scheduling of jobs on multiple resources from a unified interface. Because in distributed and grid environments DRMs do not have the direct control of the resources, the scheduling becomes more difficult to implement due to failures, missing and/or stale information, lesser control, and similar scenarios of having to operate at a more abstract level. Nonetheless, various grid job schedulers (*i.e.,* DRMs) are available today (*e.g.,* Abramson et al., 2002; Bose et al., 2004; Huedo at al., 2004) that successfully alleviate some of the job submission and scheduling efforts. If individual schedulers are categorized though, they can fairly well be classified by the following scenario:

1. User supplies a job request
2. Scheduler checks resource availability and
    - Submits the job *as is* (some projects (*e.g.* Buyya et al., 2000; 2005) optimize around user supplied request) or
    - *Queues* the job until necessary resources become available

The framework proposed in this paper builds on top of such approaches and introduces two new components in grid scheduling, namely *provisioning of job alternatives and options to the user* and *job parameterization*, as discussed in the next section.

MAIN FOCUS

Grid adoption can be seen as a result of tendency to obtain capabilities such as increased performance, increased resource availability, improved resource utilization, or decreased cost. Any of these capabilities are inherently provided through automation of job submission and job management processes. Although current grid schedulers accomplish much of required effort, there are still many required components of the job submission process that are not automated by the schedulers, primarily because schedulers are not aware of user preferences and requirements. As the grid advances into a wide spread use in the commercial sector, high requirements will be imposed on automation and insight into various aspects of user presence on the grid (*e.g.,* cost analysis, performance tradeoffs, and resource usage). As a step in the direction of reducing this gap, this paper describes a framework supporting advancements in the following areas:

- *Focus on the individual user* by providing them with concrete job options presenting a range of cost vs. time tradeoffs and allowing them to make the final decision, thus supporting higher level of QoS
- *Optimize job parameters* for the application during job scheduling

Focus on individual user is realized through two-way user-scheduler interaction. Typical user-scheduler interaction involves user submission of job requirements upon which scheduler acts. Supporting two-way communication allows a scheduler to devise a set of options (as discussed below) for a user job and presentation of those to the user in easily understood terms (*e.g.,* cost vs. time tradeoff). A user can then select the most appropriate option, as it corresponds to their current situation. The second advancement, acting as one of support tools for deriving job options, involves job parameterization. In Background

Section above, variability of job runtimes were related not only to resources but also to selection of underlying algorithms and selection of various application and job options. Including job parameterization into the job scheduling introduces a new layer of grid scheduling where not only are the resources carefully selected, but also the job options are customized for selected resource. Proper parameterization can transition a poorly behaving resource into a highly competitive one (Afgan & Bangalore, 2007). From a resource owner perspective, the result can be seen as transparent optimization of resource capabilities realizing additional scheduling options, better resource utilization, and longer resource lifetime. From an end user perspective, this can be beneficial in reducing job cost as well as improving overall job performance.

Through support of stated advancements, user will become savvy of various alternatives currently available to them and will be able to make targeted decisions relating job execution time and associated cost. Rather than being presented with a myriad of options, not knowing what to select, and if and how those options interrelate, they will be provided with a carefully selected set of application invocation alternatives and matching tradeoffs. Based on their needs, preferences, and abilities they can make the appropriate selection from this small subset of all possible alternatives.

Accomplishment of stated goals is realized through a framework that includes understanding of application performance variability across heterogeneous environment, determination of required information to perform necessary comparisons, mechanisms for information capturing and analysis, and support for user-job value dependency. The framework components are depicted in Figure 1 and their functionality and interactions can be summarized as follows:

- *AppDB* (Application Performance Database), similar to Prophesy project (Taylor et al., 2000), but working at an application

Figure 1. Vertically integrated view of framework components

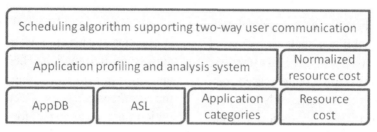

level, is a dedicated system aimed at capturing historical application runtime data. Information captured includes a wide range of application, job, and resource specific information that can provide insight into execution relationship between application and resource, relationship between selected job parameters and execution time, relationship between values of those parameters and execution time, application scalability, application efficiency, as well as accounting information. This information is later used by the scheduler component to enable mapping of job parameters and options to currently available resources through a guided fashion and thus enable job submission optimization.

- *ASL* (Application Specification Language) (Afgan and Bangalore, 2007a) stores persistent, application specific data into a document that can be reviewed, built upon, and used through a standard set of interfaces. Complementary to Job Submission Description Language (JSDL) (Anjomshoaa et al., 2005) that allows capturing of job specific requirements and Resource Description Language (RDL) (Anjomshoaa et al., 2005) capable of capturing individual resource information, ASL is capable of capturing application specific information. ASL is developed with a goal of assisting application developers by allowing them to describe purpose of the application, its requirements, and special constraints. This information can

subsequently be used to extract application performance information and dependencies on resources and job parameters.

- *Application categories* is another information repository module that, based on defined application categories (Afgan, Bangalore & Gray), provides a scheduler with insight into general application behavior and thus guides scheduling procedures. This idea is based on the observation that applications of similar type exhibit similar behavior and can thus be scheduled in similar ways (Tsouloupas and Dikaiakos, 2003). This module provides both, a safeguard in case needed application information is not available though AppDB or ASL as well as a set of guidelines to follow during scheduling.

- *Resource cost* establishes the requirement of this system that operates under Posted Price Model (Buyya et al., 2000).

- *Application profiling and analysis (APA) system* is the process of applying analysis and optimization techniques to perform data analysis over the *Application Information Services (AIS)* data (composed of AppDB, ASL, and Application Categories) and currently available resources to obtain application specific and user oriented set of scheduling calculations. The APA system is the key aspect of this framework where job options are explored through combination of lookup and optimization methods with the goal of creating a set of job-to-resource mappings. These mappings are based and optimized on currently available information about an application and resources. Further details on optimization of resource utilization and job parameters can be found in (Afgan and Bangalore, 2007b, 2008).

- *Normalized Resource Cost* is a module that normalizes job requirements and resource cost across many resource providers and job options. It includes normalization ranging from variable pricing modes (*e.g.,* flat rate of $1/CPUhr vs. millions of instructions) to variable parameterization options (*e.g.,* use of 10 CPUs at Site 1 executing for 1 hour vs. 6 CPUs at Site 2 executing for 1 hour as well or combination of using multiple sites simultaneously for partial job submissions when scheduling parameter sweep applications).

- *Scheduling algorithm* coordinates all the above components including resource monitoring, data analysis, job parameterization and management, and resource cost normalization to be presented to the user in terms of tradeoffs and options. While the application profiling and analysis system derives possible combinations of job-to-resource assignments, the scheduling algorithm selects and presents a subset of those. The selection of

the subset can be guided by user profiles to either select options a user would be more interested in (*e.g.,* more cost effective or more time sensitive alternatives) or to fully automate the process based on the user profile by selecting most likely option. Because of the described difficulties of working at the level of a DRM, available information may not be current for an extended period. There is no automated way to avoid this constraint, but rather the airline industry model is adopted, where the user has a limited time to make a selection after the options are presented to them. Alternatively, if advance reservation models are supported, user selection could be guaranteed by the system.

As just stated, AppDB, ASL, and Application Categories together compose an *Application Information Services (AIS)*. APS, in its entirety, is complete and can be somewhat redundant with respect to the application-specific data. Because information available in the grid is dynamic and transient, this approach was necessary to provide and, in turn, maximize available information to the APA system. This enables targeted and specific manipulation and optimization of collected data. Throughout the APA system, and grid in general,

Figure 2. Sample screenshot of job execution options allowing a user to observe job tradeoffs

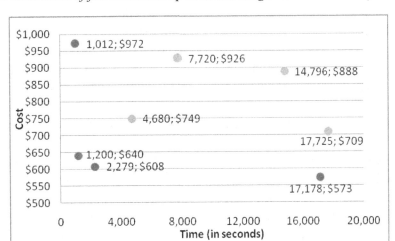

users are constrained by resource availability. Thus, any job scheduling, and associated application and resource usage optimization, can only operate under those constraints. As such, the goal of APA and AIS is to provision and provide a set of alternative options available to a user under the constraints of resource availability complemented by application-specific information.

A sample of what a user may experience during job submission process is shown in Figure 2 where various possibilities for submitting job runtimes and associated job cost are depicted. Each of the shown options is mapped to currently available resources that are also appropriately parameterized, automatically on user's behalf. Provisioning the user with such options does not only greatly simplify job submission process but more importantly, introduces the user to the possible and viable options, which they may not have even been aware of. In addition, singly dominated options can be color-ranked to provide automated prioritization of job tradeoffs (by using Pareto-set selection). Examples of such tradeoffs include extremes such minimum time and minimum cost, but also mid-range benefits where optimality of time vs. cost is presented to the user (similar to (Yu at al., 2007). Another application where such scheduling techniques are employed is the recent version of Dynamic BLAST (Afgan and Bangalore, 2008; Afgan et al., 2006).

FUTURE TRENDS

Grid computing is stepping out of research labs alone and making its entrance into widespread, general use (Amazon, 2008; Fox and Pierce, 2007; Sun, 2008). Once in the commercial sector, certain and strict rules will have to imposed on resource usage relating to resource utilization and associated job cost. Methods for historical usage tracing and accountability will have to exist. All these requirements will be justified by the economics of the overall system. This system will thus have to

provision options for its use and not impose many defaults by implicit automation. Work described in this paper is a step in that direction because it offers options for the user as are pertinent to the given user. Future advancements of this work, as well as other upcoming technologies (*e.g.*, Jia et al., 2007), will have to advance reliability of predictions presented to the user. More stringent methods of resource selection and performance prediction need to be established and brought to production levels. Earlier efforts, concretely involving job runtime prediction in heterogeneous environment (Downey, 1997; Gibbons, 1997; Smith et al., 1998), have resulted in variable performance. With the advent of mentioned economic requirements and guidelines relating to resource sharing and usage, such methods will have me modified and improved to yield accountable results.

CONCLUSION

Grid job scheduling has been an active area of research over the past several years due to the complexities involved and dependencies between applications and resources. This article grid scheduling framework supports a novel approach to grid job scheduling where new interaction methods between user and scheduler are introduced and are supported by a new layer of application parameter scheduling. The introduced two-way user-scheduler interaction provides new options for the scheduler and user supporting ideas of job options and tradeoffs. Such interaction levels raise awareness of grid capabilities and grid usability for individual users. Cost tradeoffs can be more concisely and appropriately observed by users leading to higher QoS. In addition, by incorporating application and job parameterization on top of scheduling that considers only resource availability, resource utilization is increased and it provides additional job customization opportunities. The overall research aim is to hide accidental complexities involved with job scheduling and provide estimates of job runtime to individual users. This goal supports individual user more closely, thus yielding higher user utility and better grid acceptance.

REFERENCES

Abramson, D., Buyya, R., & Giddy, J. (2002). A computational economy for grid computing and its implementation in the Nimrod-G resource broker. *Future Generation Computer Systems, 18*(8).

Afgan, E., & Bangalore, P. (2007a). Application specification language (ASL) – A language for describing applications in grid computing. *The 4th International Conference on Grid Services Engineering and Management - GSEM 2007,* Leipzig, Germany (LNCS, pp. 24-38).

Afgan, E., & Bangalore, P. (2007b). Performance characterization of BLAST for the grid. In *Proceedings of the IEEE 7th International Symposium on Bioinformatics & Bioengineering (IEEE BIBE 2007)* (pp. 1394-1398). Boston, MA: IEEE.

Afgan, E., & Bangalore, P. (2008). Experiences with developing and deploying dynamic BLAST. In *Proceedings of the 15th ACM Mardi Gras conference, Workshop on Grid-Enabling Applications* (pp. 38). Baton Rouge, LA: ACM.

Afgan, E., Sathyanarayana, P., & Bangalore, P. (2006). Dynamic task distribution in the grid for BLAST. *Granular computing 2006* (pp. 554-557). Atlanta, GA: IEEE.

Amazon. (2008). *Amazon elastic compute cloud* (Amazon EC2). Retrieved February 18, 2008, from http://www.amazon.com/gp/browse.html?node=201590011

Anjomshoaa, A., Brisard, F., Drescher, M., Fellows, D., Ly, A., McGough, S., et al. (2005). *Job submission description language (JSDL) specification, Version 1.0* (Tech. Rep. No. GFD-R.056). Global Grid Forum (GGF).

Berman, F. (1998). High-performance schedulers. In I. Foster & C. Kesselman (Eds.), *The grid: blueprint for a new computing infrastructure* (pp. 279-309). San Francisco, CA: Morgan Kaufmann Publishers, Inc.

Berman, F., Hey, A., & Fox, G. (Eds.). (2003). *Grid computing: Making the global infrastructure a reality.* New York: John Wiley & Sons.

Bose, A., Wickman, B., & Wood, C. (2004). *MARS: A metascheduler for distributed resources in campus grids* (pp. 110-118).

Buyya, R., Abramson, D., & Giddy, J. (2000). *An economy driven resource management architecture for global computational power grids.* Paper presented at the 2000 International Conference on Parallel and Distributed Processing Techniques and Applications (PDPTA 2000), Las Vegas, NV.

Buyya, R., Murshed, M., Abramson, D., & Venugopa, S. (2005). Scheduling parameter sweep applications on global Grids: A deadline and budget constrained cost-time optimization algorithm. *Software - Practice & Experience, 35*(5), 491-512.

Downey, A. (1997). Predicting queue times on space-sharing parallel computers. In *Proceedings of the International Parallel Processing Symposium (IPPS ,97)* (pp. 209-218). Geneva, Switzerland.

Foster, I., & Kesselman, C. (Eds.). (1999). *The grid: Blueprint for a new computing infrastructure* (1st ed.). Morgan Kaufmann Publishers.

Fox, G., & Pierce, M. (2007). *Grids challenged by a Web 2.0 and multicore sandwich.* Paper presented at Cluster Computing and the Grid (CCGrid), Rio de Janeiro, Brazil: IEEE.

Gannon, D., Fox, G., Pierce, M., Plale, B., Laszewski, G. v., Severance, C., et al. (2003). *Grid Portals: A scientist's access point for grid services.* Global Grid Forum (GGF).

Gibbons, R. (1997). *A historical application profiler for use by parallel schedulers.* (LNCS 1291, 58-77).

Huedo, E., Montero, R. S., & Llorente, I. M. (2004). A framework for adaptive execution on grids. *Journal of Software - Practice and Experience, 34,* 631-651.

Jia, Y., Michael, K., & Rajkumar, B. (2007). Multi-objective planning for workflow execution on grids. *Grid Computing 2007* (pp. 10-17). Austin, TX.

Smith, W., Foster, I., & Taylor, V. (1998). Predicting application run times using historical information. In *Proceedings of the Workshop on Job Scheduling Strategies for Parallel Processing* (pp. 122-142). Springer-Verlag.

Sun. (2008). *Sun Grid.* Retrieved February 18th, 2008, from http://www.sun.com/service/sungrid

Taylor, V., Wu, X., Geisler, J., Li, X., Lan, Z., Stevens, R., et al. (2000). Prophesy: An infrastructure for analyzing and modeling the performance of parallel and distributed applications. *High Performance Distributed Computing (HPDC) 2000* (pp. 302-303). Pittsburgh, PA.

Tsouloupas, G., & Dikaiakos, M. (2003). GridBench: A tool for benchmarking grids. In *Proceedings of 4th International Workshop on Grid Computing (Grid2003)* (pp. 60-67). Phoenix, AZ: IEEE.

Xia, H., Dail, H., Casanova, H., & Chien, A. A. (2004). The MicroGrid: Using online simulation to predict application performance in diverse grid network environments. In *Proceedings of the Second International Workshop on Challenges of Large Applications in Distributed Environments (CLADE)* (pp. 52- 61). Honolulu, HI.

Yu, J., Kirley, M., & Buyya, R. (2007). Multi-objective planning for workflow execution on Grids. *Grid 2007* (pp. 10-17). Austin, TX: IEEE/ACM.

KEY TERMS AND DEFINITIONS

Aggregation: It is collection of dispersed resources into a readily available pool of resource that can be simultaneously be used to complete a task

Grid Computing: It is a form of distributed computing where, through networking and middleware, possibly geographically distributed and heterogeneous resources are aggregated and virtualized into a seamless resource pool available to its users.

Grid Application: An application that is capable of executing in a grid environment with a goal of taking advantage offered by grid environment, such as heterogeneous and dynamic resource availability.

Grid Job Scheduling: It is the process of goal-driven resource selection in grid computing for a given application at a given moment in time that is constrained by resource availability and application options.

Job Parameterization: Refers to targeted selection of application options and values for those options, each of which can alter job execution variables (*e.g.,* execution time, cost).

Scheduling Optimization: It refers to grid job scheduling with a mathematically targeted goal of obtaining an optimal solution under current constraints, such as an optimum in combined execution time and cost).

Virtualization: Refers to abstraction of low level details otherwise associated with resource access in grid computing to simplify cross computer communication.

Chapter IV
Effective Resource Allocation and Job Scheduling Mechanisms for Load Sharing in a Computational Grid

Kuo-Chan Huang
National Taichung University, Taiwan

Po-Chi Shih
National Tsing Hua University, Taiwan

Yeh-Ching Chung
National Tsing Hua University, Taiwan

ABSTRACT

Most current grid environments are established through collaboration among a group of participating sites which volunteer to provide free computing resources. Therefore, feasible load sharing policies that benefit all sites are an important incentive for attracting computing sites to join and stay in a grid environment. Moreover, a grid environment is usually heterogeneous in nature at least for different computing speeds at different participating sites. This chapter explores the feasibility and effectiveness of load sharing activities in a heterogeneous computational grid. Several issues are discussed including site selection policies as well as feasible load sharing mechanisms. Promising policies are evaluated in a series of simulations based on workloads derived from real traces. The results show that grid computing is capable of significantly improving the overall system performance in terms of average turnaround time for user jobs.

INTRODUCTION

Grid computing (Foster and Kesselman, 1999) has recently become a promising trend in high performance computing. Many universities, research institutes, and commercial companies have been devoted to the development of related technologies and applications (Globus Alliance, 2007; Open Grid Forum, 2007; Platform, 2007; IBM Grid Computing, 2007; and Sun Grid Engine, 2007). Among various grid architectures and applications is the **computational grid** which aims to integrate computing resources located at different places and managed by different authorities to achieve **load sharing** and better resource utilization.

This article explores computing scenarios related to *high throughput computing* and *on-demand computing* discussed in (Berman et al., 2003), which are concerned with improving overall system performance on a **computational grid** through appropriate **workload** management approaches. A **computational grid** has to provide strong incentive for participating sites to join and stay in it. Participating sites are concerned with the performance improvement brought by the **computational grid** for the jobs of their own local user communities. Feasible and effective **load sharing** is key to fulfilling such a concern.

BACKGROUND

Without grid computing users can only run jobs on their local site. The owners or administrators of different sites are interested in the potential benefit of participating in a **computational grid** and whether such participation will result in better service for their local users by improving the job turnaround time. Therefore, it is important to ensure that grid computing can bring performance improvement and that the improvement is achieved in the sense that all participating sites benefit from the collaboration. In the other words, no participating sites' average turnaround time of their local jobs would increase after joining the **computational grid**.

Heterogeneity is another important issue in a **computational grid**. Many previous work (Bucur and Epema, 2003; Ernemann et al., 2002; Zhang et al., 2006) have shown significant performance improvement for multi-site **homogeneous** grid environments. However, in the real world a grid usually consists of heterogeneous sites that differ in configuration and computing speed. **Heterogeneity** puts a challenge on designing effective **load sharing** methods. Methods developed for **homogeneous** grids have to be improved or even redesigned to make them effective in a heterogeneous environment. This article addresses the potential benefit of sharing jobs among different sites in a speed-heterogeneous **computational grid** environment. Related issues are discussed, including **job scheduling** for feasible **load sharing** and **site selection** for processor allocation.

Job scheduling for parallel computers has been a subject of research for a long time. As for grid computing, previous work discussed several strategies for a grid scheduler. One approach is the modification of traditional list scheduling strategies for usage on a grid (Hamscher et al., 2000; Ernemann et al,. 2002). Some economic based methods are also being discussed (Buyya et al., 2002; 2003; Zhu et al., 2005; Ernemann et al., 2002). In this article we explore non-economic scheduling and allocation policies for a speed-heterogeneous grid environment.

England and Weissman in (England and Weissman, 2004) analyzed the costs and benefits of **load sharing** of **parallel jobs** in the **computational grid**. Experiments were performed for both **homogeneous** and heterogeneous grids. However, in their work simulations of a heterogeneous grid only captured the differences in the numbers of processing nodes and **workload** characteristics. The computing speeds of nodes on different sites are assumed to be identical. In this article we deal with **load sharing** issues regarding heterogeneous grids in which nodes on different sites may have different computing speeds.

For **load sharing** there are several methods for selecting which site to allocate a job. Earlier simulation studies in the literature (Huang and Chang, 2006; Hamscher et al., 2000) showed the best results for a selection policy called *best-fit*. In this policy a particular site is chosen on which a job will leave the least number of free processors if it is allocated to that site. However, these simulation studies are performed based on a **computational grid** model in which nodes on different sites all run at the same speed. In this article we explore possible **site selection** policies for a heterogeneous **computational grid**. In such a heterogeneous environment nodes on different sites may run at different speeds.

MAIN FOCUS

To facilitate **load sharing** by allowing efficient dynamic job migration without the need for recompilation, in the following simulation studies, all computing nodes in the **computational grid** are assumed to be binary compatible. This is not uncommon since many grid platforms are established by connecting together binary-compatible PC clusters located at different places. The grid is heterogeneous in the sense that nodes on different sites may differ in computing speed and different sites may have different numbers of nodes. All nodes on each site run at the same speed. The **computational grid** integrates these sites and shares their incoming jobs. For the sake of simplicity, we assume a global grid scheduler which handles all **job scheduling** and **resource allocation** activities. The local schedulers are only responsible for starting the jobs after their allocation by the global scheduler. Theoretically, a single central scheduler could be a critical limitation concerning efficiency and reliability. However, practical distributed implementations are possible, in which site-autonomy is still

maintained but the resulting schedule would be the same as created by a central scheduler (Ernemann et al., 2004).

Our simulation studies were based on publicly downloadable **workload** traces (Parallel Workloads Archive, 2007). We used the SDSC's SP2 **workload** logs as the input **workload** in the simulations. The **workload** log on SDSC's SP2 contains 73496 records collected on a 128-node IBM SP2 machine at San Diego Supercomputer Center (SDSC) from May 1998 to April 2000. After excluding some problematic records based on the *completed* field in the log, the simulations in this article use 56490 job records as the input **workload**. In the SDSC's SP2 system the jobs in this log are put into five different queues and all these queues share the same 128 processors on the system. In the following simulations this **workload** log will be used to model the **workload** on a **computational grid** consisting of five different sites whose **workloads** correspond to the jobs submitted to the five queues respectively. The numbers of processors on these five sites are 8, 128, 128, 128, 50, respectively. The number of processors on each site is determined according to the maximum number of required processors of the jobs belonging to the corresponding queue for that site.

To model the speed difference among participating sites we define a speed vector, speed=(sp1,sp2,sp3,sp4,sp5), to describe the relative computing speeds of all the five sites in the grid, in which the value 1 represents the computing speed resulting in the job execution time in the original **workload** log. In addition to the baseline **workload** on SDSC's SP2, we generate additional **workloads** for further simulation study by increasing the average job execution time of the baseline **workload**. More specifically, we generate different **workloads** by multiplying each job's execution time by a load factor. For a fixed inter-arrival time, increasing job execution time typically increases utilization. We defined a load vector of positive real numbers, load=(ld1,ld2,ld3,ld4,ld5), where ld1 to ld5 are the corresponding load factors for site1 to site5, used to produce new job execution time by multiplying them to the original job execution time in the baseline **workload**. The values of load factors on for different sites might be different. Therefore, through appropriate manipulation of the load factors, we can arrange different utilization levels for different sites.

In the following simulation studies, different sites in the **computational grid** are viewed as different processor pools and each job must be allocated to exactly one site. No jobs can simultaneously use processors on multiple sites. Two kinds of policies are important regarding **load sharing** in a **computational grid**: *job scheduling* and *site selection*. **Job scheduling** determines the sequence of starting execution for the jobs waiting in the queue. On the other hand, **site selection** policies choose an appropriate site among a set of candidate sites for allocating a job according to some specified criteria.

Previous research work shows that the *best-fit* **site selection** policy (Huang and Chang, 2006; Hamscher et al. 2000) can bring significant performance improvement to a **homogeneous computational grid** under both FCFS (First-Come-First-Serve) and the SJF (Smallest-Job-First) policies. We use the average turnaround time of all jobs as the comparison criterion in all simulations. The SJF policy was shown to outperform other non-FCFS policies, including *conservative backfilling, first-available, largest-first*, in (Huang and Chang, 2006). Here, the word "smallest" means requiring the least number of processors. In the *best-fit* policy a particular site is chosen for a job on which the job will leave the least number of free processors if it is allocated to that site.

However, in the real world a **computational grid** is usually heterogeneous, at least, in the aspect of computing speeds at different sites. Figure 1 shows that the *best-fit* **site selection** policy without considering the speed difference

among participating sites may result in even worse performance than the original non-grid architecture.

In a heterogeneous grid environment an intuitively promising approach is the *fastest one* policy, which chooses the site with the fastest computing speed among all the sites with enough free processors for a specific job. However, simulation results showed that the *fastest-one* policy did not always outperform the *best-fit* policy in all cases. In the following, we propose an *adaptive* policy, which tries to dynamically make the better choice between the *best-fit* and the *fastest-one* policies at each **site selection** activity. The decision is made based on a calculation of which policy can further accommodate more jobs for immediate execution after the current job's allocation, through a simulated processor allocation process. The *adaptive* policy works as shown in Box 1.

Figure 2 shows that the *adaptive* policy has potential for outperforming the *best-fit* and the *fastest-one* policies in some cases. We also performed a series of 120 simulations representing all kinds of relative speed sequences for the 5 sites for permutations of speed=(1, 3, 5, 7, 9), in the **computational grid**. In the 120 simulations, among the three policies the *adaptive* policy is the most stable one. It is never the last one and always quite close to the best one in performance for all the 120 cases, while the other two policies would lead to poor performance in some cases, being distant from the best and the second policies. Therefore, while it is not clear whether the *best-fit* or the *fastest-one* policy could achieve better performance under current grid configuration and **workload**, it may be good to play it safe by adopting the proposed *adaptive* policy.

In most current grid systems, participating sites provide their resources for free with the expectation that they can benefit from **load sharing**. Therefore, it is important to ensure that **load sharing** is performed in a feasible manner. Feasibility could be a good incentive for

Figure 1. Load sharing performance in a heterogeneous grid using best-fit policy

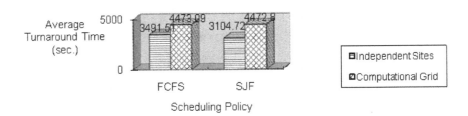

speed=(0.6, 0.7, 2.4, 9.5, 4.3) load=(1,1,1,1,1)

Box 1.

```
//When allocating a job, run this algorithm to select an appropriate site for it;

Let np(n) be an array of the number of currently available processors at each site
     work(n) be a temporary working space
     TempQueue be a temporary job queue

BestFitCount = 0;
FastestOneCount = 0;

Copy the content of waiting queue to TempQueue;
Copy the content of np to work;
While (TempQueue is not empty)
   {
     Pick up the first job in TempQueue;
     Try to find a site for this job according to the best-fit policy;
     If (site i is found for allocation)
        {
np(i) = np(i) – the job's required amount of processors;
BestFitCount++;
        }
     Else //no site can accommodate this job
        Break;
   }
Copy the content of waiting queue to TempQueue;
Copy the content of np to work;
While (TempQueue is not empty)
   {
     Pick up the first job in TempQueue;
     Try to find a site for this job according to the fastest-one policy;
     If (site i is found for allocation)
        {
np(i) = np(i) – the job's required amount of processors;
FastestOneCount++;
        }
     Else //no site can accommodate this job
        Break;
   }
If (BestFitCount > FastestOneCount)
     Adopt the best-fit policy to allocate this job;
Else
     Adopt the fastest-one policy to allocate this job;
```

Figure 2. Performance of the adaptive policy

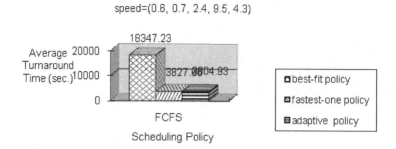

Figure 3. Detailed process of the feasible load sharing policy

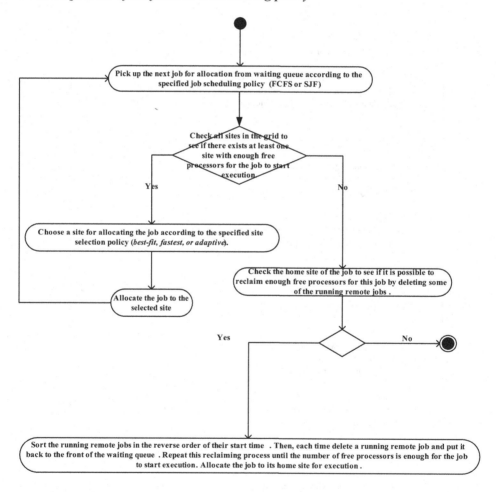

attracting computing sites to join a **load sharing computational grid**. In this article, we define the feasibility of **load sharing** to be such a property which ensures the average job turnaround time of each participating site is improved without exception. In the following we describe a feasible **load sharing** policy which works as follows. When the grid scheduler chooses the next job

Table 1. Average turnaround times (sec.) for speed=(1,3,4,4,8) and load=(5,4,5,4,1)

	Entire grid	Site 1	Site 2	Site 3	Site 4	Site 5
Independent sites	9260	14216	10964	10199	6448	57
Ordinary load sharing	4135	191	4758	4799	3881	559
Feasible load sharing	4152	193	4750	4798	3939	57

Table 2. Average turnaround times (sec.) for speed=(5,4,3,2,1,) and load=(3,3,3,3,3)

	Entire grid	Site 1	Site 2	Site 3	Site 4	Site 5
Independent sites	7839	582	5650	7168	11083	1387
Ordinary load sharing	4091	184	5253	4278	4285	338
Feasible load sharing	4149	184	5226	4348	4369	338

from the waiting queue and finds that there exists no single site with enough free processors for this job's immediate execution, instead of simply keeping the job waiting in the queue the grid scheduler inspects the status of the job's home site to see if it is possible to make enough free processors by reclaiming a necessary amount of occupied processors from some of the running remote jobs. If so, it deletes a necessary amount of these running remote jobs to collect enough free processors and re-submits the deleted remote jobs directly to the front of the waiting queue to be re-scheduled to other sites for execution. This feasible **load sharing** policy tries to achieve feasibility by giving local jobs a higher priority than remote jobs at the cost of the re-scheduled remote jobs' turnaround times being increased. Figure 3 describes the detailed process when the grid scheduler tries to schedule the jobs according to the feasible **load sharing** policy.

Tables 1 and 2 evaluate the effects of the feasible **load sharing** policy in heterogeneous **computational grids** with different speed and load configurations. The SJF scheduling policy and the *fastest-one* **site selection** policy are used in the simulations. The results first show that not all configurations would lead to unfeasible grid computing where some sites get degraded performance after joining the grid. The configuration

in Table 1 led to unfeasible grid computing when adopting ordinary **load sharing** policy, while the configuration in Table 2 did not. The feasible load sharing policy could incur resource reclaiming overheads which might lead to larger average job turnaround time at some sites as shown in Tables 1 and 2. However, comparing the performances of the ordinary and feasible **load sharing** policies in Tables 1 and 2 indicates that the resource reclaiming overheads are small. Moreover, as shown in Table 1, the feasible **load sharing** policy has great potential to avoid unfeasible grid computing which the ordinary **load sharing** policy might lead to. With the ordinary **load sharing** policy the performance at site 5 was degraded after joining the grid. On the other hand, the feasible **load sharing** policy is shown to be able to achieve a somewhat more feasible **load sharing** result in the sense that no sites' performances were sacrificed.

FUTURE TRENDS

In the **load sharing** policies described in the previous sections, different sites in the **computational grid** are viewed as independent processor pools. Each job can only be allocated to exactly one of these sites. However, one drawback of this multi-pool processor allocation is the very likely internal fragmentation (Ernemann et al., 2002) where no pools individually can provide enough resources for a certain job but the job could get enough resources to run if it can simultaneously use more than one pool's resources. Allowing multi-site parallel execution is a promising solution. However, multi-site parallel execution in a heterogeneous **computational grid** requires further study and development of **site selection** policies.

In a grid environment where multi-site parallel execution cannot be easily supported, adaptive processor allocation for moldable jobs (Feitelson et al., 1997) is another possible approach to improving system utilization and shortening waiting times for user jobs at the cost of increased job execution time. The combined effects of increased execution time and reduced waiting time for adaptive processor allocation need further study. Workflow computing is another trend where the submitted jobs are not simple serial or parallel programs. Instead, the jobs consist of a set of serial or parallel programs with specified execution or data dependencies among them. Workflow computing in a **computational grid** presents new challenges for **job scheduling** and processor allocation.

CONCLUSION

Most current grid environments are established through collaboration among a group of participating sites which volunteer to provide free computing resources. Each participating site usually has its own local user community and computing jobs to take care of. Therefore, feasible **load sharing** policies that benefit all sites are an important incentive for attracting computing sites to join and stay in a grid environment. Moreover, a grid environment is usually heterogeneous in nature at least for different computing speeds at different participating sites. This **heterogeneity**

presents a challenge for effectively arranging **load sharing** activities in a **computational grid**. This article explored the feasibility and effectiveness of **load sharing** activities in a heterogeneous **computational grid**. Several issues are discussed including **site selection** policies as well as feasible **load sharing** mechanisms. Promising policies are evaluated in a series of simulations. The quality of scheduling and allocation policies largely depends on the actual grid configuration and **workload**. The improvements presented in this article were achieved using example configurations and **workloads** derived from real traces. The outcome may vary in other configurations and **workloads**. However, the results show that grid computing is capable of significantly improving the overall system performance in terms of average turnaround time for user jobs.

REFERENCES

Berman, F., Fox, G. & Hey, T. (2003). The grid: past, present, future. In F. Berman, G.C. Fox, & A.J.G. Hey (Eds.), *Grid computing* (pp. 51-63). New York: Wiley.

Bucur, A. I. D., & Epema, D. H. J. (2003) The performance of processor co-allocation in multi-cluster systems. In *Proceedings of the Third IEEE International Symposium on Cluster Computing and the Grid (CCGrid'03)* (pp. 302).

Buyya, R., Giddy, J., & Abramson, D. (2000). An evaluation of economy-based resource trading and scheduling on computational power grids for parameter sweep applications. In *Proceedings of the Second Workshop on Active Middleware Services (AMS2000), In conjunction with the Ninth IEEE International Symposium on High Performance Distributed Computing (HPDC 2000)*, Pittsburgh, USA.

Buyya, R., Abramson, D., Giddy, J., & Stockinger, H. (2002). Economic models for resource management and scheduling in grid computing.

The Journal of Concurrency and Computation: Practice and Experience (CCPE), Special Issue on Grid Computing Environments.

England, D., & Weissman, J. B. (2004). Costs and benefits of load sharing in computational grid. *10th Workshop on Job Scheduling Strategies for Parallel Processing* (LNCS 3277).

Ernemann, C., Hamscher, V., Yahyapour, R., & Streit, A. (2002). Enhanced algorithms for multi-site scheduling. In *Proceedings of 3rd International Workshop on Grid Computing, in conjunction with Supercomputing 2002* (pp. 219-231). Baltimore, MD, USA.

Ernemann, C., Hamscher, V., Schwiegelshohn, U., Streit, A., & Yahyapour, R. (2002). On advantages of grid computing for parallel job scheduling. In *Proceedings of 2nd IEEE International Symposium on Cluster Computing and the Grid (CC-GRID 2002)* (pp. 39-46). Berlin, Germany.

Ernemann, C., Hamscher, V., Streit, A., & Yahyapour, R. (2002). On effects of machine configurations on parallel job scheduling in computational grids. In *Proceedings of International Conference on Architecture of Computing Systems, ARCS 2002* (pp. 169-179).

Ernemann, C., Hamscher, V., & Yahyapour, R. (2002). Economic Scheduling in Grid Computing. *8th International Workshop on Job Scheduling Strategies for Parallel Processing.* (LNCS 2537, pp. 128-152).

Ernemann, C., Hamscher, V., & Yahyapour, R. (2004). Benefits of global grid computing for job scheduling. In *Proceedings of the Fifth IEEE/ACM International Workshop on Grid Computing (GRID'04)* (pp. 374-379).

Feitelson, D., Rudolph, L., Schwiegelshohn, U., & Sevcik, K. C. (1997). Theory and practice in parallel job scheduling (LNCS 1291, pp. 1-34).

Foster, I. & Kesselman, C. (1997). Globus: A metacomputing infrastructure toolkit. *The International Journal of Supercomputer Applications and High Performance Computing, 11*(2), 115-128.

Foster, I., & Kesselman, C. (1999). *The grid: Blueprint for a new computing infrastructure.* Morgan Kaufmann Publishers, Inc.

Globus Alliance. (2007). Retrieved August 10, 2007, from http://www.globus.org/

Hamscher, V., Schwiegelshohn, U., Streit, A., & Yahyapour, R. (2000). Evaluation of job-scheduling strategies for grid computing. In *Proceedings of the 7th International Conference on High Performance Computing, HiPC-2000* (pp. 191-202). Bangalore, India.

Huang, K. C., & Chang, H. Y. (2006). An integrated processor allocation and job scheduling approach to workload management on computing grid. In *Proceedings of the 2006 International Conference on Parallel and Distributed Processing Techniques and Applications (PDPTA'06)* (pp. 703-709). Las Vegas, USA.

IBM Grid Computing. (2007). Retrieved August 10, 2007, from http://www-106.ibm.com/developerworks/grid/

Open Grid Forum. (2007). Retrieved August 10, 2007, from http://www.ogf.org

Parallel Workloads Archive. (2007). Retrieved August 10, 2007, from http://www.cs.huji.ac.il/labs/parallel/workload/

Platform. (2007). Retrieved August 10, 2007, from http://www.platform.com/

Sun Grid Engine. (2007). Retrieved August 10, 2007, from http://wwws.sun.com/software/gridware/sge.html

Zhang, W., Cheng, A. M. K., Hu, M. (2006, April). Multisite co-allocation algorithms for computational grid. In *Proceedings of the 20th International Parallel and Distributed Processing Symposium* (pp. 8).

Zhu, Y., Han, J., Liu, Y., Ni, L. M., Hu, C., & Hua, J. (2005). TruGrid: A self-sustaining trustworthy grid. *Proceedings of the First International Workshop on Mobility in Peer-to-Peer Systems (MPPS) (ICDCSW'05)* (pp. 815-821).

KEY TERMS AND DEFINITIONS

Computing Grid: A kind of grid computing platform that focuses on integrating computing resources at different places for solving computing-intensive problems or applications.

Feasible Sharing: A computational grid is feasible if it can bring performance improvement and the improvement is achieved in the sense that all participating sites benefit from the collaboration. That means no participating sites' average turnaround time for their jobs get worse after joining the computational grid.

Grid Computing: An IT infrastructure that can dynamically integrate various resources together for use based on specific need. Those resources may be located on different places and managed by different organizations or authorities, connected through public or private networks.

Job Scheduling: It determines the sequence of starting execution for the submitted jobs waiting in the queue.

Load Sharing: Jobs submitted at a local site and waiting in a queue can be migrated to remote sites for immediate execution or reduced waiting time.

Processor Allocation: It is concerned with the assignment of the required number of processors for a specific job.

Site Selection: It chooses an appropriate site among a set of candidate sites in a computational grid for allocating a job according to some specified criteria.

Chapter V
Data–Aware Distributed Batch Scheduling

Tevfik Kosar
Louisiana State University, USA

ABSTRACT

As the data requirements of scientific distributed applications increase, the access to remote data becomes the main performance bottleneck for these applications. Traditional distributed computing systems closely couple data placement and computation, and consider data placement as a side effect of computation. Data placement is either embedded in the computation and causes the computation to delay, or performed as simple scripts which do not have the privileges of a job. The insufficiency of the traditional systems and existing CPU-oriented schedulers in dealing with the complex data handling problem has yielded a new emerging era: the data-aware schedulers. In this chapter, we discuss the challenges in this area as well as future trends, with a focus on Stork case study.

INTRODUCTION

Modern scientific applications and experiments become increasingly data intensive. Large experiments, such as high-energy physics simulations, genome mapping, and climate modeling generate data volumes reaching hundreds of terabytes (Hey, 2003). Similarly, data collected from remote sensors and satellites are also producing extremely large amounts of data for scientists (Tummala and Kosar, 2007; Ceyhan & Kosar, 2007). In order to process these data, scientists are turning towards distributed resources owned by the collaborating parties to provide them the computing power and storage capacity needed to push their research forward. But the use of distributed resources imposes new challenges (Kosar, 2006). Even simply sharing and disseminating subsets of the data to the scientists' home institutions is difficult. The systems managing these resources must provide robust scheduling and allocation of storage resources, as well as the efficient management of data movement.

One key benefit of distributed resources is that it allows institutions and organizations to gain access to resources needed for large-scale applications that they would not otherwise have. But in order to facilitate the sharing of compute, storage, and network resources between collaborating parties, middleware is needed for planning, scheduling, and management of the tasks as well as the resources. The majority of existing research has been on the management of compute tasks and resources, as they are widely considered to be the most expensive. As scientific applications become more data intensive, however, the management of storage resources and data movement between the storage and compute resources is becoming the main bottleneck. Many jobs executing in distributed environments are failed or are inhibited by overloaded storage servers. These failures prevent scientists from making progress in their research.

According to the 'Strategic Plan for the US Climate Change Science Program (CCSP)', one of the main objectives of the future research programs should be *"Enhancing the data management infrastructure"*, since *"The users should be able to focus their attention on the information content of the data, rather than how to discover, access, and use it."* (CCSP, 2003). This statement by CCSP summarizes the goal of many cyberinfrastructure efforts initiated by DOE, NSF and other federal agencies, as well the research direction of several leading academic institutions.

NSF's 'Cyberinfrastructure Vision for 21st Century' states that *"The national data framework must provide for reliable preservation, access,*

analysis, interoperability, and data movement" (NSF, 2006). The same report also says: *"NSF will ensure that its efforts take advantage of innovation in large data management and distribution activities sponsored by other agencies and international efforts as well."* According to the NSF report on 'Research Challenges in Distributed Computing Systems', *"Data storage is a fundamental challenge for large-scale distributed systems, and advances in storage research promise to enable a range of new high-impact applications and capabilities"* (NSF, 2005).

It would not be too bold to claim that **the research and development in the computation-oriented distributed computing has reached its maturity, and now there is an obvious shift of focus towards data–oriented distributed computing.** This is mainly due to the fact that existing solutions work very well for computationally-intense applications, but inadequately address applications which access, create, and move large amounts of data over wide-area networks.

Accessing and transferring widely distributed data can be extremely inefficient and can introduce unreliability. For instance, an application may suffer from insufficient storage space when staging-in the input data, generating the output, and staging-out the generated data to a remote storage. This can lead to trashing of the storage server and subsequent timeout due to too many concurrent read data transfers—ultimately causing server crashes due to an overload of write data transfers. Other third party data transfers may stall indefinitely due to loss of acknowledgment. And even if transfer is performed efficiently, faulty hardware involved in staging and hosting can cause data corruption. Furthermore, remote access will suffer from unforeseeable contingencies such as performance degradation due to unplanned data transfers, and intermittent network outages.

Traditional distributed computing systems closely couple data handling and computation. They consider data resources as second class entities, and access to data as a side effect of computation. Data placement (i.e. access, retrieval, and/or movement of data) is either embedded in the computation and causes the computation to delay, or performed as simple scripts which do not have the privileges of a job. The insufficiency of the traditional systems and existing CPU-oriented schedulers in dealing with the complex data handling problem has yielded a new emerging era: the data-aware schedulers. One of the first examples of such schedulers is the Stork data placement scheduler, developed by Kosar and Livny (2004).

The DOE – Office of Science report on 'Data Management Challenges' defines data movement and efficient access to data as two key foundations of scientific data management technology (DOE, 2004). The DOE report says: *"In the same way that the load register instruction is the most basic operation provided by a CPU, so is the placement of data on a storage device… It is therefore essential that at all levels data placement tasks be treated in the same way computing tasks are treated."* and refers to the work by Kosar and Livny (2004). The same report also states that *"Although many mechanisms exist for data transfer, research and development is still required to create schedulers and planners for storage space allocation and the transfer of data."*

In the remaining sections of this article, we give some background information on the evolution of data-aware distributed computing; give details of the first batch scheduler specializing in data management: Stork; and conclude with future trends in this area.

BACKGROUND

In the old days, the CPU was responsible for carrying out all data transfers between I/O devices and the main memory at the computer hardware level. The overhead of initiating, monitoring and actually moving all data between the device and the main memory was too high to permit efficient

utilization of CPU. To alleviate this problem, additional hardware was provided in each device controller to permit data to be directly transferred between the device and main memory, which led to the concepts of DMA (Direct Memory Access) and I/O processors (channels). All of the I/O related tasks are delegated to the specialized I/O processors, which were responsible for managing several I/O devices at the same time and supervising the data transfers between each of these devices and main memory (Bic and Shaw, 1974).

On the operating systems level, initially the users had to write all of the code necessary to access complicated I/O devices. Later, low level I/O coding needed to implement basic functions was consolidated to an I/O Control System (IOCS). This greatly simplified users' jobs and sped up the coding process (Deitel, 1990). Afterwards, an I/O scheduler was developed on top of IOCS that was responsible for execution of the policy algorithms to allocate channel (I/O processor), control unit and device access patterns in order to serve I/O requests from jobs efficiently (Madnick and Donovan, 1974).

When we consider scheduling of I/O requests at the distributed systems level, we do not see the same recognition given them. They are not considered as tasks that need to be scheduled and monitored independently. I/O and computation is closely coupled at this level, and I/O is simply regarded as a side effect of computation. In many cases, I/O is handled manually or using simple scripts which require baby-sitting throughout the process. There are even cases where the data is dumped to tapes and sent to the destination via postal services (Feng, 2003).

Kosar and Livny (2004) introduced the concept that "data placement" activities in a distributed computing environment must be first class citizens just like the computational jobs. In that work, they have presented a framework in which data placement activities are considered as full-edged jobs which can be queued, scheduled, monitored, and even check-pointed. They have introduced the first batch scheduler specialized in data placement and data movement: Stork. This scheduler implements techniques specific to queuing, scheduling, and optimization of data placement jobs, and provides a level of abstraction between the user applications and the underlying data transfer and storage resources.

Later, Bent et al. (2004) introduced a new distributed file system, the Batch-Aware Distributed File System (BADFS), and a modified data-driven batch scheduling system (Bent, 2005). Their goal was to achieve data-driven batch scheduling by exporting explicit control of storage decisions from the distributed file system to the batch scheduler. Using some simple data-driven scheduling techniques, they have demonstrated that the new data-driven system can achieve orders of magnitude throughput improvements both over current distributed file systems such as AFS as well as over traditional CPU-centric batch scheduling techniques which are using remote I/O.

Kosar et al (2005) has designed and implemented a complete *data placement subsystem* for distributed computing systems, similar to the I/O subsystem in operating systems. This subsystem includes the specialized scheduler for data placement (Stork), a higher level planner aware of data placement jobs, a knowledgebase which can extract useful information from history logs, failure detection and classification mechanism, and some runtime optimization tools. This data placement subsystem provides complete reliability, a level of abstraction between errors and users/applications, ability to achieve load balancing on the storage servers, and to control the traffic on network links.

Kosar has been recently leading an NSF funded project called PetaShare (2007), which is a distributed data archival, analysis and visualization cyberinfrastructure for data-intensive collaborative research. PetaShare responds to the urgent need of scientists who work with large-scale data generation, sharing and collaboration requirements. PetaShare aims to enable domain scientists to

focus on their primary research problem, assured that the underlying infrastructure will manage the low-level data handling issues. The key technologies that are being developed in this project include data-aware storage systems, data-aware schedulers, and cross-domain metadata scheme which take the responsibility of managing data resources and scheduling data tasks from the user and perform these tasks transparently. An initial prototype of PetaShare is being deployed at five Louisiana campuses. It will leverage 40 Gigabit per second Louisiana Optical Network Initiative (LONI) infrastructure to make the interconnections, fully exploiting high bandwidth low latency optical network technologies.

We believe that these were only the initial steps taken towards a new paradigm in data-intensive computing: the data-aware batch schedulers. This trend will continue since the batch schedulers are bound to take the data into consideration when making scheduling decisions in order to handle the data-intensive tasks correctly and efficiently.

DATA-AWARE SCHEDULER: STORK

In this section, we will present the key features of the first batch scheduler specialized in data placement and data movement: Stork. Stork is especially designed to understand the semantics and characteristics of data placement tasks, which can include: data transfer, storage allocation and de-allocation, data removal, metadata registration and un-registration, and replica location.

Stork uses the ClassAd (Raman et al., 1998) job description language to represent the data placement jobs. The ClassAd language provides a very flexible and extensible data model that can be used to represent arbitrary services and constraints. This flexibility allows Stork to specify job level policies as well as global ones. Global policies apply to all jobs scheduled by the same Stork server. Users can override them by specifying job level policies in job description ClassAds.

Stork can control the number of concurrent requests coming to any storage system it has access to, and makes sure that neither that storage system nor the network link to that storage system get overloaded. It can also perform space allocation and de-allocations to make sure that the required storage space is available on the corresponding storage system. The space allocations are supported by Stork as long as the corresponding storage systems have support for it. The ideal case would be the destination storage system support space allocations, as in the case of NeST (2007), and before submitting a data transfer job, a space allocation job is submitted in the workflow. This way, it is assured that the destination storage system will have sufficient available space for this transfer.

Unfortunately, not all storage systems support space allocations. For such systems, the data placement scheduler needs to make the best effort in order not to over-commit the storage space. This is performed by keeping track of the size of the data transferred to, and removed from each storage system which does not support space allocation. When ordering the transfer requests to that particular storage system, the remaining amount of available space, to the best of the scheduler's knowledge, is taken into consideration. This method does not assure availability of storage space during the transfer of a file, since there can be external effects, such as users which access the same storage system via other interfaces without using the data placement scheduler. In this case, the data placement scheduler at least assures that it does not over-commit the available storage space, and it will manage the space efficiently if there are no external effects.

In some cases, two different jobs request the transfer of the same file to the same destination. Obviously, all of these request except one are redundant and wasting computational and network resources. The data placement scheduler catches such requests in its queue, performs only one of them, but returns success (or failure depending on the return code) to all of such requests. We want to highlight that the redundant jobs are not canceled or simply removed from the queue. They still get honored and the return value of the actual transfer is returned to them. But, no redundant transfers are performed. In some other cases, different requests are made to transfer different parts of the same file to the same destination. These type of requests are merged into one request, and only one transfer command is issued. But again, all of the requests get honored and the appropriate return value is returned to all of them.

Stork can interact with higher level planners and workflow managers. This allows the users to schedule both CPU resources and storage resources together. Kosar and Livny (2004) have introduced a new workflow language capturing the data placement jobs in the workflow as well. The enhancements made to the workflow manager (i.e. DAGMan) allows it to differentiate between computational jobs and data placement jobs. The workflow manager can then submit computational jobs to a computational job scheduler, such as Condor or Condor-G, and the data placement jobs to Stork.

Stork also acts like an I/O control system (IOCS) between the user applications and the underlying protocols and data storage servers. It provides complete modularity and extendibility. The users can add support for their favorite storage system, data transport protocol, or middleware very easily. This is a very crucial feature in a system designed to work in a heterogeneous distributed environment. The users or applications may not expect all storage systems to support the same interfaces to talk to each other. And we cannot expect all applications to talk to all the different storage systems, protocols, and middleware. There needs to be a negotiating system between them which can interact with those systems easily and even translate different protocols to each other. Stork has been developed to be capable of this. The modularity of Stork allows users to insert a plug-in to support any storage system, protocol, or middleware easily.

We want to give a case study of how Stork can improve the performance of data transfers by using the information it extracts from the data placement job submit files. This example is auto-tuning of protocol-specific network parameters for data transfers.

Sophisticated protocols developed for wide area data transfers like GridFTP allow tuning depending on the environment to achieve the best performance. While tuning by itself is difficult, it is further complicated by the changing environment. The parameters which are optimal at the time of job submission may no longer be optimal at the time of execution. The best time to tune the parameters is just before execution of the data placement jobs. Determining the environment characteristics and performing tuning for each job may impose a significant overhead. Ideally, we need an infrastructure that detects environmental changes and performs appropriate tuning and uses the tuned parameters for subsequent data placement jobs. A monitoring and tuning infrastructure such as the one presented by Kola et al. (2005) can provide the necessary information to the scheduler to tune up protocol-specific network parameters for data placement jobs.

The Stork scheduler can use the information provided by the monitoring and tuning infrastructure to set optimal I/O block size, TCP buffer size and the number of TCP streams for the data transfer from a given node X to a given node Y. Statistics for each link involved in the transfers are collected regularly and written into a file, creating a library of network links, protocols and auto-tuning parameters. An example of this library entry is shown below:

```
[
  link = "slic04.sdsc.edu - quest2.
ncsa.uiuc.edu";
  protocol = "gsiftp";
  bs = 1024KB; //block size
  tcp_bs = 1024KB; //TCP buffer
size
  p = 4; //parallelism
]
```

Before performing every transfer, Stork checks its auto-tuning library to see if there are any entries for the particular hosts involved in this transfer. If there is an entry for the link to be used in this transfer, Stork uses these optimized parameters for the transfer. Stork can also be configured to collect performance data before every transfer, but this is not recommended due to the overhead it will bring to the system.

In an experiment to test this feature, we submitted 500 data transfer requests to a traditional batch scheduler and to the Stork server. Each request was to transfer a 1.1GB image file (total 550 GB) using GridFTP. We used third-party globus-url-copy transfers without any tuning and without changing any of the default parameters.

The average data transfer rate that the traditional scheduler could get was only 0.5 MB/s. After a while, Stork started gradually tuning the network parameters. Every 15 minutes, Stork obtained the tuned-up values for I/O block size, TCP buffer size and the number of parallel TCP streams from the monitoring and tuning infrastructure. Then it applied these values to the subsequent transfers. Figure 1 shows the increase in the performance after Stork tunes up the network parameters. We got a speedup of close to 20 times compared to transfers with a traditional scheduler.

CONCLUSION AND FUTURE TRENDS

The insufficiency of the traditional distributed computing systems and existing cpu-oriented batch schedulers in dealing with the complex data handling problem has yielded a new emerging era: the data-aware batch schedulers. One of the first examples of such schedulers is the Stork data placement scheduler. In this article, we have discussed the limitations of the traditional schedulers in handling the challenging data scheduling problem of large scale distributed applications; gave our vision for the new paradigm in data

Figure 1. Protocol-specific network parameter tuning by Stork

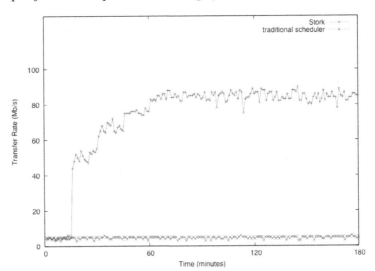

intensive scheduling; and elaborated on our case study: the Stork data placement scheduler.

We believe that Stork and its successors are only the initial steps taken towards a new paradigm in data intensive computing: the data-aware batch schedulers. This trend will continue since the batch schedulers are bound to take the data dependencies and data movement into consideration when making scheduling decisions in order to handle the data-intensive tasks correctly and efficiently.

REFERENCES

Bent, J., Thain, D., Arpaci-Dusseau, A., & Arpaci-Dusseau, R. (2004, March). Explicit control in a batch-aware distributed file system. In *Proceedings of the First USENIX/ACM Conference on Networked Systems Design and Implementation*.

Bent, J. (2005). *Data-driven batch scheduling*. Ph.D. Dissertation, University of Wisconsin-Madison.

Bic, L., & Shaw, A. C. (1974). The organization of computer systems. In *The logical design of operating systems*. Prentice Hall.

CMS (2007). The Compact Muon Solenoid Project (CMS). Retrieved from, http://cmsinfo.cern.ch/.

CCSP (2003). Strategic plan for the US climate change science program. *CCSP Report*.

Ceyhan, E. & Kosar, T. (2007). Large scale data management in sensor networking applications. To appear in *Secure Cyberspace Workshop*. Shreveport, LA.

Deitel, H. M. (1990). I/O Control System. In *An introduction to operating systems*, Addison-Wesley Longman Publishing Co., Inc.

DOE (2004, March-May). The data management challenge. *Report from the DOE Office of Science Data-Management Workshops*.

Feng, W. (2003). High performance transport protocols. *Los Alamos National Laboratory*.

Kola, G., Kosar, T., & Livny, M. (2005). Runtime adaptation of grid data-placement jobs. *Scalable Computing: Practice and Experience, 6*(3), 33-43

Kosar, T., & Livny, M. (2004, March). Stork: Making data placement a first class citizen in the

Grid. In *Proceedings of 24th IEEE International Conference on Distributed Computing Systems (ICDCS 2004)*, Tokyo, Japan.

Kosar, T., Son, S., Kola, G., & Livny, M. (2005). Data placement in widely distributed environments. In L. Grandinetti (Ed.), *Grid Computing: The New Frontier of High Performance Computing* (pp. 14). Elsevier Press.

Kosar, T. (2006, June). A new paradigm in data intensive computing: Stork and the data-aware schedulers. In *Proceedings of Challenges of Large Applications in Distributed Environments (CLADE 2006) Workshop*. Paris, France.

Hey, T. & Trefethen, A. (2003). The data deluge: An e-Science perspective. In *Grid computing - Making the global infrastructure a reality* (pp. 809-824). Wiley and Sons.

Madnick, S. E., & Donovan, J. J. (1974). I/O Scheduler. In *Operating Systems*. McGraw-Hill, Inc.

NeST (2007). *Network Storage Technology*. http://www.cs.wisc.edu/condor/nest

NSF (2005). Research challenges in distributed computer systems. *NSF WorkshopReport*.

NSF (2006, January). NSF's Cyberinfrastructure Vision for 21st Century Discovery. *NSF Cyberinfrastructure Council Report*.

PetaShare (2007). Retrieved from, http://www.petashare.org

Raman, R., Livny, M., & Solomon, M. (1998, July). Matchmaking: Distributed resource management for high throughput computing. In *Proceedings of the Seventh IEEE International Symposium on High Performance Distributed Computing (HPDC7)*. Chicago, Illinois.

Tummala, S. & Kosar, T. (2007). Data management challenges in coastal applications. To appear in *Journal of Coastal Research*.

KEY TERMS AND DEFINITIONS

Batch Scheduling: Scheduling and execution of a series of jobs in the background "batch" mode, without any human interaction.

Condor: It is a batch scheduling system for computational tasks. It provides a job queuing mechanism and resource monitoring capabilities. It allows the users to specify scheduling policies and enforce priorities.

Condor-G: It is an extension of Condor, which allows users to submit their jobs to inter-domain resources by using the Globus Toolkit functionality. In this way, user jobs can get scheduled and run not only on Condor resources but also on PBS, LSF, LoadLeveler, and other grid resources.

DAGMan: It manages dependencies between tasks in a Directed Acyclic Graph (DAG), whrere tasks are represented as nodes and the dependencies between tasks are represented as directed arcs between the respective nodes.

Data Placement: It encompasses all data movement related activities such as transfer, staging, replication, space allocation and de-allocation, registering and unregistering metadata, locating and retrieving data.

Distributed Computing: It is a type of parallel computing where different parts of the same application can run on more than one geographically distributed computers.

Stork: It is a specialized scheduler for data placement activities in heterogeneous environments. Stork can queue, schedule, monitor, and manage data placement jobs and ensure that the jobs complete.

Chapter VI
Consistency of Replicated Datasets in Grid Computing

Gianni Pucciani
CERN, European Organization for Nuclear Research, Switzerland

Flavia Donno
CERN, European Organization for Nuclear Research, Switzerland

Andrea Domenici
University of Pisa, Italy

Heinz Stockinger
Swiss Institute of Bioinformatics, Switzerland

ABSTRACT

Data replication is a well-known technique used in distributed systems in order to improve fault tolerance and make data access faster. Several copies of a dataset are created and placed at different nodes, so that users can access the replica closest to them, and at the same time the data access load is distributed among the replicas. In today's Grid middleware solutions, data management services allow users to replicate datasets (i.e., flat files or databases) among storage elements within a Grid, but replicas are often considered read-only because of the absence of mechanisms able to propagate updates and enforce replica consistency. In this entry we analyze the replica consistency problem and provide hints for the development of a Replica Consistency Service, highlighting the main issues and pros and cons of several approaches.

INTRODUCTION

Replica consistency is the property exhibited by a set of data items, such as files or databases located at different nodes of a Grid, that contain the same information; when these data items are modifiable, all of them should be updated (or *synchronized*) so that consistency is maintained. Replica consistency is a very well studied research topic and has its roots in distributed systems as well as in distributed database management systems, where it is sometimes referred to as *external consistency* (Cellary et al., 1988). Replica consistency is obviously related to data replication, a technique that is used pervasively in Grids to achieve fast data access, high availability, increased fault tolerance, and better load balancing. Data replication involves databases, files, and possibly other units of information, such as objects or records, and relies on the functions provided by "plain" file systems, storage systems, database management systems, and middleware services. Currently, existing Grids offer scarce support, if any, for data consistency. Often, data is considered to be read-only, i.e. data is consistent by definition since no updates are allowed on existing data items.

The rest of this entry presents an introduction to the problem in the Background section, where the key concepts are introduced. Furthermore, the data management capabilities provided by middleware services currently used in some of the largest Grids are reviewed, pointing out their approach to replica management and support for replica synchronization. The core analysis of the problem is presented in the Main Focus section, where the main issues in the development of a Replica Consistency Service for Data Grids are discussed.

BACKGROUND

Data Replication

Data replication is a technique that is most commonly used in distributed database management systems and is tightly coupled with the transaction system. For example, a relational database management system can have identical copies at three geographically different sites, each holding a full copy of the data. End users can place their SQL queries to any of the replicas: distributed transactions are then used to make sure that data does not get corrupted by multiple writers.

Simply put, data consistency makes sure that different data copies are synchronized, i.e., have the same values.

In Grid computing, data replication is done at different levels of granularity than in traditional, distributed relational database management systems. In particular, Grids often replicate entire files rather than database objects. Furthermore, data synchronization and therefore consistency has to be managed by "external" services which often do not provide a unique interface for reading and writing data based on traditional database transactions. In the rest of this article we concentrate on the specific issues of Data Grids. However, before we go into the details of replica consistency in Grids, let us first review typical data replication components and services that are commonly used in Grid computing.

A Data Grid typically offers a *Replica Management Service* (RMS), a middleware component that creates replicas of files (rather than relational databases) on request by applications or possibly in a transparent way in order to optimize data access. This service uses a *Replica Catalogue* (RC) to keep track of the replicas. The RMS may also rely on a *Replica Optimization Service* (ROS) to select dynamically the best[1] replicas to be accessed by a given application.

Such file replication tools must then implement policies concerning the following major issues:

- *When and where to create or remove replicas*? A replication service should perform dynamic replication (Ranganathan, 2001), that is the automatic creation and removal of replicas based on different system parameters and/or user needs.
- *Data location and cataloguing.* Replicas can be created and removed in the course of time: they are created somewhere when needed and they must be deleted when they are no longer used. How does a user or application, or the RMS itself know where a replica is, at a certain point in time? To this

end, *replica catalogues* (Chervenak et al., 2002) are normally used.

- *Replica synchronization*. When a replica must be updated, how are the other replicas synchronized with the new content? How is *replica consistency* enforced throughout the system? This is the topic of this entry.

Users of a RMS need not be aware of the existence of replicas. Normally, they refer to a file by a *logical name* that identifies the information carried by the file, independently of the physical location of its replicas. Applications relying on the RMS pass the logical name to the service that retrieves from the RC the *physical names* specifying the actual locations of the replicas.

Replicas are created using RMS client tools, such as the Globus Data Replication Service (Chervenak et al., 2005) or LCG Data Management tools (Peris et al., 2004) (which most of the times rely on lower level services like GridFTP), and kept on *Storage Elements* (SE) of different types. A storage element is a complex system that may support a hierarchy of storage systems, such as fast disk caches, long term and high capacity disks, and tapes. Different types of storage elements exist, providing support for different access protocols. Efforts in promoting the usage of a standard interface for heterogeneous SEs are present (Shoshani, 2003). A storage element may replicate data internally to optimize file access, but this kind of replication is independent of the RMS and will not be discussed further.

Replica management services usually replicate files and possibly file collections, but they offer no support for the replication of data stored in relational or object-oriented databases. Database replication relies on the proprietary mechanisms provided by the database management systems. For example, in the project WLCG, Worldwide LHC Computing Grid (WLCG, 2007), Oracle Streams is used for unidirectional replication of Oracle Databases. Replication of databases is especially important for the availability and

reliability of the Grid middleware services since most of them use databases to keep track of service specific metadata that is frequently updated.

Database replication has different and usually more complex requirements with respect to file replication. Databases can be large, they must be accessed through their management systems, and they cannot just be copied as a whole, but need to be installed with a rather complex procedure. Furthermore, different sites may want to keep copies of the same data in database systems provided by different vendors: this is called *heterogeneous replication*. In the remainder of this article we will discuss the requirements and features for both file and database replication and their synchronization.

Key Concepts

Depending on the application (counting also middleware services as applications), data to be replicated may be stored in a file or a file collection, a database or a database table, or an object stored in a file or in a database. We will use the term *dataset* to cover these possibilities.

Datasets may be *structured* or *unstructured*. A dataset is structured if a user/application accesses it by means of record-oriented operations. A relational database is a typical example of a structured dataset that is accessed through SQL commands. Unstructured datasets are those whose internal structure is either unknown or ignored for the purposes of replication, and are accessed by users/applications by means of file management operations, local or remote file I/O protocols. Unstructured datasets will also be referred to as *flat files*.

We distinguish between the logical *contents* of a dataset, i.e., the information it carries, and its physical instances, called *replicas*. A *logical dataset* (or *dataset* for short) may then be defined as an abstract entity composed of its contents and its *logical name*. To each logical dataset is associated a set of replicas, each identified by a *physical name*. Replicas can be stored at a particular location (on a file system, database or mass storage system) and accessed by the users/applications with some sort of access protocol.

A replica contains a physical representation of the dataset contents and as observed before, different representations are possible for a given dataset. A *semantic function* maps a representation to the contents: for flat files the semantic function is the identity function, while for structured datasets it is the mechanism that extracts information from the replica (in a database, it is simply the query-processing interpreter).

Replica Synchronization Protocols

A *replica synchronization protocol* is performed by any system (such as a distributed database manager or a Grid middleware service for file replication) whose purpose is to maintain a set of replicas consistent. Several such protocols have been proposed, each aimed at satisfying different sets of requirements that arise in different environments. For example, in Grid environments it is often not possible to keep all replicas up-to-date, and at any given time one or more replicas might be outdated. Depending on the application, certain more relaxed consistency requirements and states can be defined (Düllmann, 2002; Gray, 1997; Breitbart, 1997). For instance, certain applications can deal with datasets that are outdated for several minutes, sometimes even hours. If this feature is known *a priori*, adequate consistency models can be chosen.

In particular, we can distinguish between two main approaches:

- **Synchronous, or eager synchronization**. In this approach, all replicas for a given logical dataset are updated within the same transaction, with a protocol that usually is a variation of the basic *two-phase commit protocol* (Özsu et al., 1999). This has the consequence that no single replica can be accessed during the update process but after the transaction all replicas have the same physical state and they are consistent. Although high data consistency is a desirable feature, this approach has important limitations for distributed systems and in particular for Data Grids: replicas need to be locked which can result in long "downtimes" of replicas due to update contention. When no timeout or quorum systems are used, disconnected sites can block an update operation indefinitely.

- **Asynchronous (or lazy) synchronization**. The second approach tries to overcome the problem of distributed locks by updating only a subset of replicas during an update transaction and propagating the update to the other replicas at a later time. Certainly, some of the replicas will be outdated for a certain period, which is the price for speeding up the write access and increasing data availability.

In order to further characterize replica consistency mechanisms, we introduce more definitions. When using lazy synchronization a simple and reliable solution is where a replica is designated as *master* or *primary replica*. In single-master systems, the unique master replica is the only one that can be modified by users, while the other replicas (*slave* or *secondary replicas)* are updated by the replica synchronization protocol. Secondary replicas are useful to speed up read operations. In case of failures at the master site that compromise the use of the master replicas, an *election algorithm* (Garcia-Molina, 1982) can be used among secondary replicas to elect a new master replica.

Multi-master solutions can expose the system to *update conflicts*. Conflict resolution is a highly application specific problem. With low write access rates or when the semantics of the application allows the resolution of a conflict without affecting the normal behavior and performance of the system, multi-master solutions can be implemented – increasing data availability and speeding up both read and write operations.

Depending on how the update of a replica is performed, we can further classify synchronization protocols distinguishing between push versus pull based and log versus content transfer systems (Saito et al., 2005).

Existing Support for Replica Consistency

Today, most of the commercial database management systems provide replication features with mechanisms enforcing consistency; Oracle Streams, IBM DB Replication and Microsoft SQL Server are some of the best known ones. However, in this case the replication is homogeneous in that it regards databases of the same vendor, with a few exceptions[2].

As regards Grid environments, no consistency service has been yet developed in important middleware solutions such as the Globus Toolkit and the LHC Computing Grid. Both these solutions do provide file replication features, but the automatic management of replica consistency is not supported. A prototype Grid service for maintaining consistency of replicated files *and* databases can be found in (Domenici et al., 2006).

The SDSC Storage Resource Broker (SRB, 2007) instead provides a rather complete set of replication and consistency management features including synchronous and asynchronous approaches.

Other studies in replica consistency management can be found in (Yu et al., 2002) and (Susarla et al., 2005) but their application in a production Grid environment has not yet been considered.

MAIN FOCUS

The need for replica consistency mechanisms in Grid environments has been pointed out early in (Stockinger, 2001), (Düllmann et al., 2002) and (Casey et al., 2003), but few solutions have been proposed so far.

This is partly due to the fact that many applications that are driving the development of Grid middleware[3] expect to use modifiable datasets in the future, but currently use mostly read-only data. As a consequence, requirements for replica consistency are still unclear. More precise requirements will be defined when users begin to try new models of computation and data access.

Issues in Designing a Replica Consistency Service

The design of a Replica Consistency Service (RCS) as part of a Grid middleware is faced with many difficult issues that derive from specific properties of a Grid environment.

In general, being replica consistency a highly application-specific problem, designing one consistency management mechanism for different applications requires finding trade-offs on many different design choices. In the next paragraphs we review some of the most important issues that need to be dealt with, providing hints for the design of a Replica Consistency Service (Pucciani, 2008).

Scalability. First of all, any Grid infrastructure involves the management of many sites, hence, in case of flat files[4] it is likely that there is the need to deal with several thousands of replicas, some of which could not be continuously available. Thus, update propagation algorithms must be properly designed to provide good performance also with large numbers of replicas. Keeping the design simple can be the key to success; whenever possible, single master solutions are the recommended way to provide fast read access and high data availability.

Security. Security issues must be considered in the development of a RCS. Communication with the service should be secure; this means that the service should deal with authentication, authorization, privacy, and integrity issues. The Grid Security Infrastructure (GSI) provided by the Globus Toolkit is widely adopted as an integrated solution to security problems, and it is based on the public key infrastructure. The GSI can be easily integrated in a Grid service.

Replica location. Replica location services and replica catalogues are used in Grid middleware to store the association between a logical dataset and all its replicas. Among the most used implementations we cite the Globus Replica Location Service (RLS) (Chervenak et al., 2002) and the LCG File Catalogue (LFC). The RCS has two options: interfacing with this catalogue or implementing its own replica catalogue. Both options have advantages and disadvantages. Using an external replica catalogue would avoid duplicating information and complicating the system. On the other hand, the integration with an external service should be carefully planned and would require such catalogues to be modified. For example, not all the logical datasets registered in a replica catalogue need the consistency management, like read-only datasets. For datasets that do require consistency management, some new attributes (e.g. master/slaves, fresh/stale, version number) should be added to each replica's metadata.

Efficient file transfer. An efficient file transfer tool should be used for update propagation. File transfer services for Grid computing are normally built on top of the GridFTP protocol. The RCS should use either GridFTP or higher level services to efficiently propagate updates to possibly thousand of replicas. Most of the Storage Elements support the GridFTP protocol, making it a good choice to solve the file transfer issue in the RCS. Note that GridFTP is optimized for transferring rather big amounts of data with relatively big file sizes. This is partially due to the fact that TCP/IP works more efficiently with larger than with smaller file sizes due to the TCP window size tuning and a "slow start up" with smaller window sizes. Performance tests have shown that transfers of smaller data items (up

to about 5 MB) can be achieved more efficiently using alternative approaches such as SOAP with attachment (Sciolla, 2007).

SE heterogeneity. A Grid connects many different resources. Storage Elements, where datasets are stored, can have different implementations and different access protocols. Although a standard interface could be available in the next few years (Shoshani, 2003), a RCS should interface with different SEs.

Lock management functionalities should be provided by the SE since, in certain scenarios, the access to a replica may need to be blocked to avoid concurrent accesses.

Disconnected nodes. The RCS should be able to complete the synchronization of replicated datasets even when some of them are not available. Quorum mechanisms could be used to ensure that an update propagation process can execute when at least a given number of replicas are available, and it should be possible to select this number depending on the application requirements. Synchronization of unavailable replicas should be retried as soon as they become available.

Metadata consistency. The RCS should provide synchronization capabilities both for application and middleware services. Many middleware services in fact use replication for fault tolerance and reliability. One example can be found in the Globus RLS, where catalogues are replicated but consistency management is not supported. This leads us to consider, as already stated in this article, the consistency of both files and databases, that is the subject of the next paragraph.

Database consistency. A Replica Consistency Service to be used in a Grid middleware should be able to manage the consistency of both applications' data and middleware services' data.

Many Grid services in fact use persistent data stores, usually relational databases, to save critical information. In order to provide fault tolerance and increase the performance of these services, such data are often replicated over several sites, and hence a consistency mechanism is needed to enforce consistency among these replicas.

Practical examples of replicated services that use relational database are the Globus Replica Location Service and the LCG File Catalogue. Such services usually can be implemented using backend databases from different vendors. Oracle databases are a common choice for larger sites. In other cases, open source databases (often MySQL and PostgreSQL) are good alternatives. Thus, cross-vendor replication also needs to be supported by a Replica Consistency Service. Cross-vendor or heterogeneous database synchronization requires that the RCS is built using pluggable modules to interface with many different software packages.

Differences in the SQL dialects used by database vendors must be taken into account, both by limiting the use of non-standard SQL, and by providing some translation capabilities.

Unidirectional Oracle to MySQL synchronization has been tested in the CONStanza project (Domenici et al., 2006). Another open source software that provides heterogeneous replication through a Java based data extraction, transformation and loading tool is Enhydra Octopus (Octopus, 2007). A third example for a Grid database replication system is presented in (Chen, 2007). The problem of concurrency control in distributed heterogeneous databases in a Grid environment is studied in (Taniar, 2007).

Although they present different characteristics, file synchronization and database synchronization have common features that should be exploited to provide a general and flexible Replica Consistency Service.

FUTURE TRENDS

In general, the Grid software developers deal more with the efficient replication and replica selection of read-only datasets than with update synchronization and consistency. One of the reasons for that is that there are not many use cases of the latter kind in "classical" Grid applications. On the other hand, database research has shown that update replication comes at some cost in terms of data availability, so that only certain applications can fully profit from replicated data with update features. Just as replica consistency has become an essential property in distributed databases and certain file systems, the same will occur in Grid infrastructures.

Further, considering that Grid computing is a rapidly emerging domain, it is likely that new applications, outside the scientific field, will arise in the next few years, providing more requirements for the implementation of a Replica Consistency Service.

CONCLUSION

We have presented the problem of replica consistency in Grid environments and discussed possible solutions to be considered when implementing such a system. Nowadays many Grid applications deal with read-only replicas; for this reason Grid middleware frameworks do not provide any support for replica synchronization. Another reason is that replica synchronization is a highly application specific domain, and providing a universal solution suitable for multiple dataset types and access patterns is very difficult. In this entry we analyzed the main issues in developing a Replica Consistency Service (RCS) in a Grid environment, suggesting practical approaches. Some of these approaches have been implemented and tested in a prototype service described in (Domenici et al., 2006) that allows for the synchronization of both files and heterogeneous database replicas. We expect that future Grid applications will have more stringent requirements for replica consistency; this will help to better characterize the design of the RCS and will also speed up the implementation of reliable solutions.

REFERENCES

Baud, J.P, Casey, J., Lemaitre, S., Nicholson, C., Smith, D., & Stewart, G. (2005). *LCG Data Management: from EDG to EGEE.* GLAS-PPE/2005-06.

Breitbart Y., & Korth, H. F. (1997). Replication and consistency: Being lazy helps sometimes. In *Procedings of the 16th ACM SIGACT-SIGMOD-SIGART Symposium on Principles of Database Systems.*

Casey, J. et al. (2003). Next-generation EU DataGrid data management services. In *Proceedings of the Conference for Computing in High Energy and Nuclear Physics (CHEP 2003)*, La Jolla, California.

Cellary, W., Gelenbe, E., & Morzy, T. (1988). *Concurrency control in distributed database systems.* Amsterdam: North-Holland.

Chen, Y., Berry D., & Dantressangle P., (2007). Transaction-based grid database replication. In *Proceedings of the UK e-Science All Hands Meeting.*

Chervenak, A., Deelman, E., Foster, I., Guy, L., Hoschek, W., Iamnitchi, A., et al. (2002). Giggle: A framework for constructing scalable replica location services. In *Proceedings of the Int'l. ACM/IEEE Supercomputing Conference (SC 2002).* IEEE Computer Society Press.

Chervenak, A., Schuler, R., Kesselman, C., Koranda, S., Moe, B., & Wide (2005). Area data replication for scientific collaboration. In *Proceedings of 6th IEEE/ACM Int'l Workshop on GridComputing (Grid2005).*

Domenici, A., Donno, F., Pucciani, G., & Stockinger, H. (2006). Relaxed data consistency with CONStanza. *Sixth IEEE International Symposium on Cluster Computing and the Grid (CCGrid06).* Singapore: IEEE Computer Society.

Domenici, A., Donno, F., Pucciani, G., Stockinger, H., & Stockinger, K. (2003). Replica consistency in a data grid. In *Proceedings of the IX International Workshop on Advanced Computing and Analysis Techniques in Physics Research*, Tsukuba, Japan.

Düllmann, D., Hoschek, W., Jean-Martinez, J., Samar, A., Stockinger, H., & Stockinger, K. (2002). Models for replica synchronisation and consistency in a data grid. In *Proceedings of 10th IEEE Symposium on High Performance and Distributed Computing (HPDC-10).* IEEE Computer Society Press.

Garcia-Molina, H. (1982). Elections in a distributed computing system. *IEEE Transaction on Computers, 32.*

Gray, J., Helland, P., O'Neil, P., & Shasha. D. (1997). The dangers of replication and a solution. In *Proceedings of the 1996 ACM SIGMOD International Conference on Management of Data* (pp. 173-182).

LCG-3D (2007). *Distributed deployment of databases for LCG.* Retrieved from https://twiki.cern.ch/twiki/bin/view/PSSGroup/LCG3DWiki

Octopus (2007). *Enhydra octopus, JDBC data transformation.* Retrieved from http://www.enhydra.org/tech/octopus/

Özsu, M.T., & Valduriez, P. (1999). *Principles of distributed database systems.* Prentice Hall.

Peris, A.D., Lorenzo, P.M, Donno, F., Sciabà, A., Campana, S., & Santinelli, R. (2004). *LCG-2 User Guide, v2.1.*

Pucciani, G. (2008). *The replica consistency problem in data grids.* Ph.D. Thesis, Information Engineering, University of Pisa, Italy.

Ranganathan, K., & Foster, I. (2001). Identifying dynamic replication strategies for a high performance data grid. In *Proceedings of the International Grid Computing Workshop*, Denver, CO.

RLS (2007). Data management: Key concepts of RLS. Retrieved from http://www.globus.org/toolkit/docs/4.0/data/key/rls.html

Saito, Y., & Shapiro, M. (2005). *Optimistic replication.* ACM Computing Surveys.

Sciolla, C. (2007). *Implementazione e valutazione di un sistema di trasferimento file basato su SOAP in ambiente GRID.* Master's Thesis at the University of Pisa.

Shoshani, A. (2003). Storage resource managers: Essential components for the grid. In J. Nabrzyski, J.M. Schopf, & J. Weglarz (Eds.), *Grid resource management: State of the art and future trends.* Kluwer Academic Publishers.

SRB (2007). The SDSC storage resource broker. Retrieved from, http://www.sdsc.edu/srb/index.php/Main_Page

Stockinger, H. (2001). *Database replication in world-wide distributed data grids.* Ph.D. Thesis, Institute of Computer Science and Business Informatics, University of Vienna, Austria.

Susarla, S., & Carter, J. (2005). Flexible consistency for wide area peer replication. In *Proceedings of the 25th International Conference on Distributed Computing Systems.*

Taniar D., G. S. (2007). Concurrency control issues in grid databases. *Future Generation Computer Systems 23*(1).

WLCG (2007). *Worldwide LHC computing grid.* Retrieved from http://lcg.web.cern.ch/LCG/

Yu, H., & Vahdat, A. (2002). Design and evaluation of a Conit-based continuous consistency model for replicated services. *ACM Transactions on Computer Systems (TOCS).*

KEY TERMS AND DEFINITIONS

Data Replication: Having and managing more copies of datasets. These copies are typically synchronized.

Replica Catalogue: Used to locate replicas (physical locations) which are mapped to logical file names.

Logical File Name: A name used to identify a set of replicated files.

Physical File Name: The name of a replicated file which defines its location.

Replica Management System: A Grid service that takes care of replicating datasets and keeping track of locations in a Replica Catalogue.

Replica Consistency: The property exhibited by a set of replicas that contain the same information.

Replica Synchronization: The task of updating replicas in order to enforce their consistency.

Strict Synchronization: Updating all the replicas of the same dataset in a single transaction to make sure that replicas are never outdated.

Lazy Synchronization: Allowing for certain delays in the update process, i.e. replicas can be outdated for a certain time.

Heterogeneous Database Synchronization: Used to enforce consistency among replicated databases of different vendors.

ENDNOTES

[1] The "best" replica in this case is chosen considering access speed and supported protocols.

[2] Oracle Streams can use Oracle Heterogeneous Connectivity technology to replicate data from an Oracle system to a non-Oracle (Informix, MS SQL Server and Sybase) system. IBM DB2 can share and replicate data with an Informix database.

3   It is the case, for example, in the WLCG middleware, where High Energy Physics experiments mainly use the Grid to perform analysis on read-only files.

4   In case of replicated databases the number of replicas can range from a few units to a few tens of replicas.

Chapter VII
Quality of Service of
Grid Computing

Ming Wu
Illinois Institute of Technology, USA

Xian-He Sun
Illinois Institute of Technology, USA

ABSTRACT

Rapid advancement of communication technology has changed the landscape of computing. New models of computing, such as business-on-demand, Web services, peer-to-peer networks, and Grid computing have emerged to harness distributed computing and network resources to provide powerful services. The non-deterministic characteristic of the resource availability in these new computing platforms raises an outstanding challenge: how to support Quality of Service (QoS) to meet a user's demand? In this chapter, we conduct a thorough study of QoS of distributed computing, especially on Grid computing where the requirement of distributed sharing and coordination goes to the extreme. We start at QoS policies, and then focus on technical issues of the enforcement of the policies and performance optimization under each policy. This chapter provides a classification of QoS metrics and policies, a systematic understanding of QoS, and a framework for QoS of Grid computing.

INTRODUCTION

With the advance of network technology, many new distributed computing models are being constructed to harness geographically distributed computing and communication resources, such as business-on-demand, Web services, peer-to-peer networks, and Grid computing. Typical examples of these systems include WebSphere, Gnutella, Skype, Seti@home, Condor, PPLive (a P2P television network), and Globus (Wu, 2006). The system size of these systems scales from hundreds of nodes to tens of thousands of nodes, and even more. In these systems, resources are shared and collaborated to provide services/functionalities such as online shopping, online telephony and television, teleimmersion, online control of scientific instrumentation, and resource pooling. Much effort is being made in the standardization of protocols and interface for service orchestration and resource collaboration in these environments (Foster and Kesselman, 2004). With the maturity of these systems, when more and more users to use them as day-to-day computing infrastructure, Quality of Service (QoS) of these newly-emerged computing platforms is becoming more and more important.

QoS study was focused on QoS control and delivery in a dedicated environment where resources are controlled and managed in a centralized mechanism. In a shared network environment like a Grid, where resources are shared among different applications and managed within different organizations and domains, there are several new issues related to QoS support that do not arise in a single computer system. The first issue is the variation of resource availability, the accessibility of a system resource to an application. This variation may be due to resource contention, dynamic system configuration, software or hardware failures, and other factors beyond the control of a user. The uncertainty of resource availability presents a big challenge on guaranteed application quality delivery. The second issue is parallel processing. The total workload of a large scale application is often partitioned into smaller pieces, called subtasks. These subtasks are then allocated to resources in a distributed system to be processed concurrently. The challenge of parallel processing in a shared network environment lies on that the computing resources may be heterogeneous and have individual availability patterns. The third issue is non-centralized control. In a general Grid environment, the computing resources are autonomous. Local schedulers schedule local jobs and the Grid scheduler does not have the control of the local jobs.

Because of these difficulties, a suitable and broadly applicable QoS solution has been elusive. This is especially true for Grid computing, where the requirement of distributed sharing and coordination goes to the extreme. QoS is a known technical hurdle preventing a broader adoption of Grid computing for which there has been no well-conducted QoS study to balance the need of Grid tasks and local jobs. Some efforts have been made to address the issues of sharing. Distributed systems, such as Condor, NetSolve, Nimrod, and Globus (Foster and Kesselman, 2004), support Grid computing and facilitate resource sharing and collaboration. These systems adopt different QoS policies, usually implicitly, and try to provide a satisfactory QoS under their adopted policies. These policies often support QoS for one side and sacrifice that of the other – they perform well for certain applications but do not provide a satisfactory solution for general Grid computing.

Without a better understanding of the impact of resource reservation on QoS an appropriate decision cannot be made. Recently, a prototype of QoS system, Grid Harvest Service (GHS) has been developed at Scalable Software System lab in Illinois Institute of Technology (Wu and Sun, 2006). GHS is based on a fundamental understanding of QoS of Grid computing in two stages: policymaking and optimization mechanisms. Policymaking decides the QoS policy of resource sharing among Grid tasks and local jobs. Optimization mechanisms obtain an optimum QoS under each QoS policy. They are integrated solutions of advanced performance modeling, resources management, and scheduling algorithms. These QoS optimization mechanisms provide a comprehensive investigation of the impact of system characteristics, such as resource sharing, non-centralized control, heterogeneity, and dynamics; and application characteristics, such as parallel processing, computation or communication, hard guarantee or soft guarantee, on the application QoS delivery in Grid computing (Wu et al, 2006).

This chapter is organized as follows. We first introduce the concept and classification of quality of service. We then discuss the challenges in QoS delivery in Grid Computing and identify the limitations in some current efforts. Next, we summarize a list of existing QoS policies and propose some new QoS policies. QoS models are then given to estimate the application performance under different resource sharing policies. Based on QoS models, we study various task scheduling strategies and resource management mechanisms to improve application quality. Some initial experimental results are also presented to verify these optimization mechanisms. Finally, we present a system overview of Grid Harvest Service system.

BACKGROUND

Quality of Service involves customer satisfaction, quality measurement and management, and quality improvement. Quality may mean different things for different applications, users, and domains. Thus, quality of service can be defined from different aspects. Some of definitions found online are given as follows:

- Quality of service is the idea that transmission rates, error rates, and other characteristics can be measured, improved, and, to some extent, guaranteed in advance.
- Quality of service is a general term that incorporates bandwidth, latency, and jitter to describe a network's ability to customize the treatment of specific classes of data.
- Quality of service is a measurable set of parameters that define the level of service that a service provider can be held accountable for.
- Quality of service is the ability to define a level of performance in a data communications system.

These definitions describe some details of quality of service, such as rates, parameters, performance, provider et al. A more general definition is given by Chalmers and Sloman (1999), "QoS defines nonfunctional characteristics of a system, affecting the perceived quality of the results. In multimedia this might include picture quality, or speed of response, as opposed to the fact that a picture was produced or a response to stimuli occurred." (p. 4).

In a distributed environment, there might be a large number of similar or equivalent resources provided by different parties. To select appropriate resources for running their applications, therefore, users can not only consider functional characteristics of the applications. QoS requirements such as execution time (deadline) and expenditure limit (budget) should also be considered. Depending on application's requirement, different users might be interested in different QoS metrics. For example, in middleware systems, people are interested in reliability and performance, availability. In data networks, the QoS study generally focuses on domain-specific dimensions such as bandwidth, latency, jitter, and loss. Based on the previous work in (Yu and Buyya, 2005), we list five dimensions of QoS Metrics as follows.

Performance. Performance is the most widely used QoS metric. It includes time, bandwidth and latency, transaction/service rate, et al.

Cost. Task cost represents the cost associated with the execution of applications. Cost is an important factor, since organizations need to operate according to their financial plan.

Security. Security refers to confidentiality of the execution of applications and trustworthiness of resources. Security QoS metrics include confidentiality, integrity, non-repudiation of sending, and authentication/

Reliability. In general, reliability is the ability of a system to perform and maintain its functions in routine circumstances, as well as hostile or unexpected circumstances.

Fidelity. Fidelity refers to the measurement related to the quality of the output of applications. Fidelity reflects how well a product is being produced and how well a service is being rendered. An example of quantitative fidelity of online video play is picture detail, picture color accuracy, video rate, video smoothness, audio quality and video/audio synchronization.

After identifying the application QoS requirements, we need to develop effective mechanisms to meet the end-users' QoS need. This task is often done by developing a QoS architecture. Depending on the application specific QoS interests and the resource management policies in the system, many QoS architectures have been designed and developed (Chalmers and Sloman, 1999). These QoS architectures are usually composed of three major subsystems: QoS specification, QoS provision, and QoS management.

QoS Specification. QoS specification allows users describe their applications' QoS requirements and management policies. This information will be used to select appropriate QoS provision and management mechanisms. QoS specification includes QoS metric specification, Level of service, and QoS management policy.

QoS Provision Mechanisms. QoS provision mechanisms determine how to allocate resources to applications to support user-supplied QoS specification. It is static resource management and used in the establishment of resource commitment. QoS provision mechanisms include QoS mapping, Admission control, and Resource reservation protocol.

QoS Management Mechanisms. Different from QoS provision mechanisms where static resource management is performed, QoS management mechanisms provide dynamic resource management to monitor and maintain application QoS at runtime and to adapt the system change if possible. The goal of QoS management is to ensure that the contracted QoS is sustained. QoS management mechanisms include QoS monitoring, QoS maintenance and QoS adaptation.

The generalized QoS architecture provides us a good picture of QoS support in a distributed system. However, it does not support QoS delivery in emerging distributed systems such as Skype, Seti@home, Condor, and Globus where resources are shared among local jobs and Grid tasks. The current QoS mechanisms focus on QoS support in a central control system, where resources are managed in a single administration domain or resources in different organization can be managed by the same resource management policy. Moreover, current QoS architectures provide an isolated QoS support. Resources are reserved and managed to guarantee QoS only for the application to be deployed. What the impact of this resource reservation and management on QoS of other applications, such as local jobs, is unknown.

MAIN FOCUS

A good QoS solution requires a comprehensive investigation of the complex interaction between system characteristics, such as resource sharing, non-centralized control, heterogeneity, and dynamics; and application characteristics, such as parallel processing, computation or communication, hard guarantee or soft guarantee. To provide a uniformed QoS solution for general Grid computing, we propose to develop a software solution through increasing the fundamental understanding of QoS of Grid computing. We specifically study the relation between the QoS of Grid tasks and the QoS of local jobs and investigate the influence of resource reservation on local jobs. We divide the fundamental understanding of QoS into two stages: policymaking and optimization mechanisms. Policymaking decides the QoS policy of resource sharing among Grid tasks and local jobs. Optimization mechanisms obtain an optimum QoS under each QoS policy. Optimization mechanisms in turn consist of advanced performance modeling, resources management, and scheduling algorithms. The interference of Grid tasks and local jobs are considered in modeling. Task schedulers choose the best set of resources to optimize the application QoS based on the information provided by performance modeling. Resource management collects application and resource information, enforces the QoS policy, and carries out the scheduling decisions. This top-down study not only leads to a better understanding of QoS between the Grid tasks and local jobs, it also gives a constructive solution

QoS Policymaking and Optimization Mechanisms

Grid computing requires the coordination of distributed network resources to solve non-trivial applications. The distributed resources may belong to different virtual organizations, shared by Grid tasks and local jobs, and are often autonomic controlled. A Grid management system has no control over the usage pattern of the shared resources. The uncertainty of resources makes QoS of Grid computing hard to achieve. In recent years, some efforts have been made to address the issues of sharing. But most existing QoS support is built under certain tacit assumptions. They often support QoS of one side in the cost of sacrifice another. For instance, seti@home gives the priority to local jobs. The Grid task executes only when no local jobs are running. There is no QoS for Grid tasks. Resource reservation has been proposed for Grid computing (Foster, 2004). Resource reservation reduces system utilization and may disturb the normal operation of local jobs. The question, then, is how much resources need to be reserved for how long and on which resources. Currently the decision is made based on the demand of the Grid task or let the local scheduler to make the decision. To lead a better understanding of QoS, we first need to understand the QoS policies.

In Grid environments the quality of service has to be supported on shared resources. Recognizing that the sharing has two sides, Grid tasks and local

jobs, and the QoS concerns of the two sides are quite different, we specifically study the relationship between the QoS of Grid tasks and the QoS of local jobs and intend to develop a system solution to meet the need of both sides simultaneously, or at least balance the requirements. In practice, there are three resource sharing policies widely used in the Grid computing community.

- **The best-effort policy.** In best-effort policy, local jobs have higher priority than a Grid task. A Grid task is allowed to execute only when there is no local jobs running. During the execution of the Grid task, if any local jobs arrive, the Grid task is either suspended or terminated. In Grid computing, we are more interested in the first scenario because Grid tasks are usually stateful large-scale scientific applications. In practice, the keyboard and mouse activities are usually monitored to detect the local job running status. The best-effort policy is adopted in the Seti@home project to utilize the idle computation cycles of hundreds of thousands of machines to detect intelligent life outside Earth. A more general platform to support best-effort policy is Condor, which can be configured to run Grid tasks on desktop machines only when they are idle. This policy is best for independent, non-time constraint Grid tasks.

- **The real-time policy.** In real-time policy, Grid tasks have a higher priority over local jobs. According to the Grid task QoS requirement, a certain computing resources (CPU, Memory, I/O, network) are reserved for the dedicated use of the Grid task. This reservation is fixed during the execution of the Grid task. The real-time policy is adopted in the GASA project. It is often used for resource allocation in supercomputer centers, in which a number of nodes in a cluster system or in a group of cluster are reserved for running of a scientific application. This policy is best for test the potential of Grid computing and within a virtual organization where a priority can be defined globally.

- **The competing policy.** In the competing policy, a Grid task competes for resources with local jobs. The good part of the competing policy is that every one is equal; no one has to sacrifice for another. The bad part, on the other hand, is there is no guaranteed QoS for any one. This policy is usually applied in public domains, such as campus computing environments. For example, AppLeS (Berman et al, 2003) project support this policy so that workstations in their systems are harvested to increase the computing throughput.

Besides the three existing QoS policy, we identify two new resource sharing policies which has the potential to be applied in a general distributed environment to enrich the different relationship between local jobs and Grid tasks in terms of their qualities.

- **The constrained policy.** In the constrained policy, the QoS of Grid tasks or local jobs has to be maintained at certain level. Meeting the QoS is first priority of the constrained policy. For instance, if the constrained is to maintain the local job QoS at certain level, then resources only can be reserved to Grid tasks when the reservation does not reduce the local job QoS below the QoS level. In the meantime, Grid scheduler should reserve as mush as resources possible for its gains as long as the constraint condition is not violated. This provides a compromised resource sharing policy where a certain part of resource is dedicated to a Grid task under the condition that local job QoS is affected within a limitation.
- **The balanced policy.** In the balanced policy, both the quality of Grid tasks and

the quality of local jobs are considered and measured with some given criteria. The balanced policy can be viewed as a further extension of the constrained policy. Instead of enforcing QoS constraint on either side of applications, the balanced policy weighs the priorities of both sides' QoS requirements. When there is no enough resources to support QoS, the both sides will suffer together with predefined proportion.

The policy list is incomplete and is only an initial point. The balanced policy, for instance, may lead to different policies based on different tradeoffs and concerns; different policies may need to be combined and adopted at different time to support the QoS of a given application. The competing policy may have different QoS goals: optimizing the Grid task performance, minimizing the slowdown of local jobs, or some weighted combinations. In addition, the Grid tasks, or local jobs, themselves may have different QoS needs and should be treated separately.

After a QoS policy is chosen, the next question is how to achieve an optimum quality under the given policy. Quality is often measured in terms of performance. Improving quality then becomes an optimization problem. For example, for the best-effort service, we should partition and schedule the Grid task in such a way to optimize its execution time; for the real-time service we should schedule the Grid task appropriately to minimize the QoS degradation of local jobs. A more complex task is to optimize the performance of both Grid tasks and local jobs under a balanced QoS policy. The optimization mechanisms in turn rely on advanced performance modeling, resource management, and scheduling algorithms. Figure 1 presents the relationship of QoS policies, optimization goals, and optimization mechanisms in Grid computing.

QoS Modeling in Grid Computing

QoS modeling estimates the impact of resource availability on application quality. In a shared network environment, there are many factors incurring the variation of resource availability, such as resource contention between local jobs and a Grid task, resource failure of hardware and software, dynamic system configuration. In this chapter, we focus on studying the effect of the resource contention on application quality in terms of performance (the term of QoS modeling and performance modeling are used exchangeable in this context). Depending on resource sharing policies, different performance models are needed to identify the impact of resource sharing on application quality. We discuss best-effort performance model and real-time performance model in this chapter. They are used to estimate the application completion time under computation resource sharing. The impact of communication resource sharing on application performance can be found at (Wu, 2006). Notice that the appliance of these QoS models is not limited to resource contention. They can be extended to study the effect of resource failure on application performance.

We assume a Grid environment is composed of heterogeneous resources $\{m_1, m_2, ..., m_n\}$. Each machine in the system has its own computing capacity, τ_i, and memory availability, a_i. Three additional parameters, λ_i, ρ_i, and σ_i are introduced to describe usage pattern of a shared resource. Based on the observation of shared machine usage pattern, we assume that the local job processing follows M/G/1 queuing system. We describe the characteristics of a resource in a distributed system with τ_i, λ_i, ρ_i, and σ_i.

- τ_i: the computing capacity of the machine m_i.
- λ_i: the arrival rate of local jobs on machine m_i.
- ρ_i: the resource utilization on machine m_i.
- σ_i: the standard deviation of service time of local jobs on machine m_i.

Computation modeling for best-effort service. We have introduced a performance modeling for best-effort service. The model predicts QoS, in terms of completion time, of a Grid task (Gong et al, 2002) – allowing a set of appropriate network resources to be chosen for optimal execution time. It is derived from a combination of rigorous stochastic analysis and intensive simulation and designed for large-scale applications. The model considers the heterogeneous machine utilization and computing capacity, heterogeneous job arrival rate as well as heterogeneous service distributions. The effects of machine utilization, computing power, and local job service and task

Figure 1. QoS policy and optimization mechanisms

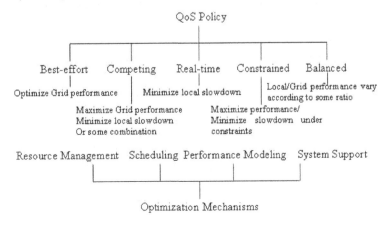

allocation on the completion time of Grid task are individually identified.

In the best-effort service, the Grid task is given a lower priority than the local job so that the Grid task is less intrusive. We suppose the execution of the Grid task is interrupted by local jobs S times. Each busy period for local jobs running is Y_i ($1 \leq i \leq S$). The completion time of the sub-task on machine m_k can be expressed as:

$$T_k = w_k / \tau_k + Y_{k1} + Y_{k2} + ... + Y_{kS_k} \qquad (1)$$

$Y_{ki} (1 \leq i \leq S_k)$ is the computing time consumed by sequential jobs and S_k is the number of interruption due to local job arrivals on machine k. By defining

$$U(S_k) = \begin{cases} 0, & if \quad S_k = 0 \\ Y_{k1} + Y_{k2} + ... + Y_{kS_k}, & if \quad S_k > 0 \end{cases}$$

$$\qquad (2)$$

we can obtain the distribution of T_k as shown in eq. (3) in Box 1.

If the distribution of $\Pr(U(S_k) \leq u \mid S_k > 0)$ can be identified, we can calculate the distribution of sub-task completion time. Using the well-known result in queuing theory, we can get the mean and variance of sub-task completion time:

$$E(T_k) = \frac{1}{1 - \rho_k} \frac{w_k}{\tau_k}, \qquad (4)$$

$$V(T_k)) = \frac{\rho_k}{(1 - \rho_k)^3} \frac{(\theta_k^2 + 1)}{\mu_k} \frac{w_k}{\tau_k}. \qquad (5)$$

The mean and variance of $U(S_k)$ given $S_k > 0$ are thus calculated as:

$$E(U(S_k) \mid S_k > 0) = \frac{1}{1 - e^{-\lambda_k w_k}} \frac{1}{1 - \rho_k} \frac{w_k}{\tau_k},$$

$$\qquad (6)$$

$$V(U(S_k) \mid S_k > 0) =$$

$$\frac{1}{1 - e^{-\lambda_k w_k}} \frac{\rho_k}{(1 - \rho_k)^3} \frac{(\theta_k^2 + 1)}{\mu_k} \frac{w_k}{\tau_k} \qquad (7)$$

where $\rho_k = \lambda_k / \mu_k$ is the machine utilization and $\theta_k = \sigma_k \mu_k$ is the coefficient of variation of service. Compared to the execution time of a Grid task, $T = \frac{w}{\tau}$, on a dedicated machine with the same computing capacity τ and workload w, the speed of the machine seen by the Grid task is slowed down by a factor of $(1-\rho)$.

The completion time of a Grid task is the maximum of each sub-task completion time. After the distribution of the completion time of sub-task w_k is identified, the cumulative distribution function of the remote parallel task completion time can be calculated as shown in eq. (8) in Box 2, where $\kappa_{max} = Max\{w_k / \tau_k\}$. κ_{max} denotes the maximum of the minimum execution time on each machine m_k ($1 \leq k \leq n$).

Simulation results indicate that Gamma, Lognormal or Weibull are among the best-fit distributions to describe the $\Pr(U(S_k) \leq u \mid S_k > 0)$. When the machine utilization is less than 15%, the Gamma distribution is the best. The Weibull distribution favors $\Pr(U(S_k) \leq u \mid S_k > 0)$ when machine utilization is medium. If the utilization is higher than 50%, the Lognormal distribution may be the best choice. In general, the Gamma distribution is appropriate for the calculation of $\Pr(U(S_k) \leq u \mid S_k > 0)$.

Box 1.

$$\Pr(T_k \leq t) = \begin{cases} e^{-\lambda_k w_k / \tau_k} + (1 - e^{-\lambda_k w_k / \tau_k}) \Pr(U(S_k) \leq t - w_k / \tau_k \mid S_k > 0 & if \quad t \geq w_k / \tau_k \\ 0, & otherwise \end{cases} \qquad (3)$$

Box 2.

$$\Pr(T \le t) = \begin{cases} \prod_{k=1}^{n} [e^{-\lambda_k w_k / \tau_k} + (1 - e^{-\lambda_k w_k / \tau_k}) \Pr(U(S_k) \le t - w_k / \tau_k \mid S_k > 0)] & if \quad t \ge \kappa_{\max} \\ 0, & otherwise \end{cases} \tag{8}$$

Experimental Results. To verify the accuracy and feasibility of QoS models, we have conducted experimental testing on different cluster systems at the Argonne and Oak Ridge national laboratories, as well as in IIT. The most widely used platforms are the Sunwulf cluster and the DOT Grid Testbed. Sunwulf is a heterogeneous 84-node Sun ComputeFarm at IIT. The DOT connects clusters at ANL, NCSA, NU, UC, UIC, and IIT via the advanced "I-Wire" network. Each cluster is composed of one sever and multiple computing nodes. Local jobs on each resource in these test platforms are simulated with different job arrival rates and service rates, which follows the observation of over one million real-life processes generated from different academic workloads in Berkeley, as well as the machine usage pattern observation by researchers at Wisconsin-Madison, Maryland, Carnegie Mellon, et al (Harchol-Balter, 2002).

To evaluate the prediction accuracy of our performance model, we define the prediction error as $\left| \frac{Prediction_{period} - Measurement}{Measurement} \right|$. We have tested the Cactus application on the DOT Grid Testbed. Cactus, a numerical simulation of a 3D scalar field produced by two orbiting astrophysical sources, is used as our test application. In the test, we use the parallel version of Cactus application. It decomposes the 3D scalar field into sub-fields and each sub-field along with a small overlap region is mapped onto a different processor in the cluster. In the experiments, we use one server and one node from the IIT cluster, three nodes from the ANL cluster, and three nodes from the UC cluster. Two factors influence the accuracy of this kind actual testing, workload determination and system software interference. As a user we only

can estimate the workload of Cactus based on its iteration number and input values – which is error prone. Also the underlying DOT management system may take CPUs away from time to time. Nevertheless, our experiment results show the model working well even with these two factors. The expectation and variance of the prediction error get smaller with increase in application's work demand. When the parallel task execution time reaches 16 hours, the predication error (both mean and variance) is less than 6%.

Computation modeling for real-time service. In real-time service, certain resources are reserved for Grid tasks so their QoS can be guaranteed. This reservation may degrade the QoS of local jobs. In queuing systems, a commonly used QoS measure is the mean waiting time, which is defined as the average waiting time of local jobs. To determine whether a reservation is accepted or not, local users are naturally concerned about how much the average waiting time is affected. Let W_a denote the mean waiting time of local jobs after reservation and W_b denote the mean waiting time of local jobs before reservation. We introduce a new metric, relative slowdown (S_R) to measure the impact of resource reservation on the QoS of local jobs.

Definition The *relative* slowdown of local jobs on a resource for a given reservation is the ratio of the average waiting time with reservation and the average waiting time without reservation.

We name the new performance metric as the relative slowdown because W_a / W_b has a similar format as the performance metric in the queuing system, slowdown, which is defined as the ratio of the waiting time and the job's workload. In this study, we focus on the reservation of CPU resource. We use κ to represent the reserved part of CPU resource. We call it the reservation ratio.

Two queuing disciplines are widely used in a general computer system for choosing which job in the queue is to be serviced next. They are first-come-first-serve (FCFS) and round-robin (RR). In a FCFS queue, jobs are served in the order of their arrival times. After one is finished, the next one will be served. In a RR queue, each job in the queue is served in a quantum of time and all jobs are served in turn. We have shown in an M/G/1 FCFS queuing system, the mean waiting time after reservation and the relative slowdown, are

$$W_a = \frac{1}{1-\kappa}\phi(\lambda, \rho, \sigma, 1-\kappa)\lambda^{-1},$$

$$S_R = \frac{1}{(1-\kappa)}\left(\frac{\phi(\lambda, \rho, \sigma, 1-\kappa)}{\phi(\lambda, \rho, \sigma, 1)}\right), \quad (9)$$

respectively, where

$$\phi(\lambda, \rho, \sigma, c) = \rho + \frac{\rho^2 + \lambda^2\sigma^2}{2(c-\rho)}.$$

$\rho = \lambda/\mu$ is machine utilization and σ is the service time standard deviation.

In an M/G/1 RR queuing system, the mean waiting time after reservation and the relative slowdown, are

$$W_a = \frac{\rho}{\lambda(1-\kappa-\rho)},$$

$$S_R = \frac{1-\rho}{(1-\kappa-\rho)}. \quad (10)$$

Please note that $1 - \rho > \kappa > 0$ holds in the above equation.

We have introduced the S_R metric to describe the impact of resource reservation on local job completion time. What is the effect of reserva-

tion on the Grid task execution time is another interesting problem. Let ϖ denote the workload of the Grid task, T denote the completion time of the Grid task and τ denote the resource computing capacity of a resource where the Grid task executes. Since the reserved CPU resource is dedicated to the execution of the Grid task, the task completion time can be expressed as

$$T = \frac{\varpi}{\kappa\tau}$$

On the other hand, if a Grid task has a requirement of the completion time, T, we can calculate the correspondent reservation ratio:

$$\kappa = \frac{\varpi}{T\tau}.$$

Experimental Results. A simulator of an M/G/1 queuing system was built to test the model for real-time service. The simulator is composed of a local job generator, a waiting queue, a scheduler, and a server. Both FCFS and RR queuing disciplines are supported in the simulator. The proposed model was tested with the bounded Pareto job lifetime distribution (Harchol-Balter, 2002). We measured the mean and variation of percentage prediction error with different reservation periods from 2000 seconds to 10000 seconds when the reservation ratio is 0.2 and the utilization is 0.15. The predicted value is the calculated relative slowdown given by formula (9) and (10) derived from the proposed model and the measured value is the QoS degradation of local jobs collected from simulation results. We observe that both mean and deviation are very small. The maximum prediction error observed in simulation is 1.15%. The mean and deviation of the prediction error tends to be smaller with the increase of the reservation period. These simulation results demonstrate that the computation model for real-time service can accurately capture the effect of reservation on the QoS degradation of local jobs.

Task Scheduling and Allocation

Task scheduling is an essential part of a QoS system. It selects appropriate resources in a shared environment to satisfy the user's QoS requirement. Based on a local resource's QoS policy, the task scheduling component in a QoS system chooses an appropriate QoS model to estimate the application performance on each resource or combination of resources (for parallel processing). In this way, the resource or a set of resource where the application desired QoS can be satisfied is identified. The task scheduling component then allocates the application to these resources.

Most task scheduling systems, including LSF, PBS Pro, Sun Grid Engine/CODINE, and Maui Scheduler (El-Ghazawi et al, 2004), are designed for dedicated and stable computing environments. The Condor system provides a matchmaking mechanism for distributed computing to allocate resources with a publish/request framework. It is aimed to match the software and hardware needs of the application, and not design to solve QoS tradeoff issues. In the PEGASUS and CHIMERA workflow management systems (Deelman et al, 2003; Foster et al, 2002) and in the AppLeS scheduling system (Berman et al, 2003), scheduling decisions are made based on the deterministic estimation of resource availability provided by NWS. These systems assume that Grid applications and local jobs compete for resources. From the QoS point of view, these systems intend to optimize the QoS of Grid tasks under the competing QoS policy. GASA (Grid Advance Reservation API), a subsystem of Globus project, provides mechanism for resource reservation so that applications can receive a certain level of service. The Legion system also supports resource reservation. In these systems, a scheduling decision is made only based on the QoS requirement of the Grid application. From the QoS point of view, these systems adopt the real-time service policy without considering the impact of reservation on the QoS of local jobs. These existing works are useful and provide

isolated solutions. An in-depth study of QoS is needed to integrate and extend existing results for a general QoS solution of Grid computing.

Besides the application QoS requirement, there are many other factors affecting the design of effective scheduling algorithms, such as affordable scheduling cost, application types (parallel program or meta-task), and QoS policies. Different emphasis on these factors leads to various scheduling algorithms. However, whatever factors are considered, task scheduling of a distributed application, in general, includes several basic steps: resource selection, task partition, and QoS evaluation. Resource selection is to choose a subset of the available resources. Task partition can be either partitioning or grouping. Partitioning divides a parallel program into subtasks and then assigns each subtask to a resource in this subset. Grouping clusters subtasks in a meta-task and then assigns each set of subtasks to a resource. QoS evaluation is to estimate the application quality for a given task partition plan. The basic process of task scheduling is given as follows.

- **Step 1.** Select a resource set from a list of available resources;
- **Step 2.** Partition a Grid task into a set of subtasks and allocate each subtask in the resource set based on resource availability prediction;
- **Step 3.** Estimate the application quality under this partition plan using a QoS model;
- **Step 4.** Go back to Step 1, until all possible machine sets have been examined. Choose the resource set where the task allocation plan gives the best-estimated application quality.

The strategy used in each step depends on the application specific information and the system specific information. In step 1, based on the size of available resources and affordable scheduling cost, different resource selection mechanisms can be chosen. If the number of available resources is small, an exhaustively resource selection method is usually applied to find an optimal solution. If we have a large number of available resources, a heuristic algorithm should be applied for a near-optimal solution. In step 2, if we only consider the effect of CPU resource availability on application quality, we can apply a CPU-only task partition strategy. If we also need to consider memory resource availability, we will utilize a memory-conscious task partition methodology.

In step 3, a QoS model is selected to estimate application quality based on the application QoS requirement. If the Grid task requires a real-time service, reservation-based QoS models are used. Otherwise, the best-effort or competing QoS model is utilized. According to local resource QoS policies, we can choose different reservation-based models. When the resource owner supports the constrained policy, the constrained model is applied. When the resource owner supports the real-time policy, the real-time model is used. The balanced model is used when the resource owner prefer a balanced QoS level between local jobs and the Grid task. We name their corresponding scheduling as constrained task scheduling, real-time task scheduling, and balanced task scheduling respectively. In real-time task scheduling, our goal is to minimize the reservation failure probability in meeting the performance (deadline) requirement of a Grid task. In constrained task scheduling, our goal is to optimize the QoS of a Grid task while maintaining the QoS of local jobs at a certain level. Experimental results have shown these QoS oriented scheduling algorithms work well in a Grid environment (Wu, 2006).

Software System Support of QoS

Different QoS models, task scheduling algorithms, and resource management mechanisms are needed for each resource sharing policy and application QoS requirement. To apply these optimization mechanisms, a QoS system should be developed to provide system support of QoS delivery in shared environments. While QoS support in Grid computing is very challenging and our study of QoS of shared environments is still in its initial phase, we have developed a prototype of QoS system, Grid Harvest Service (Wu and Sun, 2006; Sun and Wu, 2007). GHS consists of five subsystems: resource management, QoS measurement, QoS modeling, performance prediction, and task scheduling. In the resource management subsystem, GHS supports three general resource sharing policies: reservation-based, competing, and best-effort. Notice that the reservation-based policy can be further divided into real-time policy, constrained policy, and balanced policy. In the measurement subsystem, GHS provides QoS monitoring for both local jobs and Grid tasks. Utilizing the built QoS models for each shared policy, the performance prediction subsystem can estimate the application performance and predict the resource availability. They are performed by the application-level prediction component and the system-level prediction component respectively. In the task scheduling subsystem, GHS has task partition, task scheduling, task rescheduling, and task execution components. Based on applications QoS requirement and QoS estimation, the task scheduling selects an appropriate machine set. The generated scheduling plan is performed by the task execution component. Figure 4 depicts the design structure of GHS.

GHS can be deployed based on some existing pioneering work and software. In the resource management, current software systems already support three resource sharing policies: real-time, competing, and best-effort. For example, Condor and Seti@home support best-effort QoS policy. They can detect resource availability by monitoring local users' activities on mouse and keyboard. In Globus and VAS, DSRT and classic cluster resource management system such as PBS are used to provide time-sharing/space-sharing resource reservation. Notice that, with the support of our proposed reservation-based QoS models, these resource management tools can be further extended to support the constrained policy and the balanced policy. In AppLeS project, the default process scheduling in OS on local resources is used to support the competing policy. In the PEGASUS and CHIMERA workflow management systems and in the AppLeS and GHS scheduling system, current scheduling system can be extended by introducing the QoS-oriented task scheduling algorithms discussed in this section.

The design of GHS is component-oriented. It could be easily integrated into other Grid services and vice visa. The relation between the major components of the GHS system (shaded areas) and other Grid services is depicted in Figure 3. The Task Manager, which is responsible for task management, is located in the Application layer. It sends a request to the Scheduling component in the Collective layer for resource allocation. The Scheduling component contacts the Index service provided by WS Monitoring and Discovery System to locate potential available resources. The Prediction component can also serve other Grid Service, such as the Grid-enabled Programming System (GEPS), Problem Solving Environment (PSE), in a Grid runtime system. The Prediction component accesses the performance database

to estimate the task completion time. The Performance Communication Manager (PCM) component is used to collect performance data, which could be exchanged through the GridFTP services based on the communication infrastructure provided by the GSI service in the Connectivity layer. In the Fabric layer, the Performance Data Manager (PDM) component on each resource is responsible for measuring system and application information by using various sensors.

FUTURE TRENDS

During recent years, Grid architectures are gradually emerging into service-oriented architectures (SOAs). Providing the high-level quality of service needed for users is becoming a basic requirement of a Grid system (Foster, 2006). Grid systems are not only used to solve complex scientific computation problem, but also needed for support of complex web services. The current efforts on QoS support are mainly focused on application performance. An interesting problem arises, whether these QoS optimization mechanism can be applied in service-oriented computing? In a

Figure 2. System design of grid harvest service

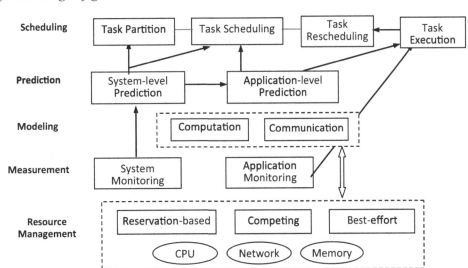

service-oriented computing environment, the performance may not be the only QoS metric. Users may be interested in other QoS characteristics, such as security, cost, and reliability. How to balance these QoS requirements is also a challenging problem. These issues require us to further increase the fundamental understanding of quality of service of Grid computing. This may include identifying new QoS policies; in-depth understanding of existing policies; automatic policy deployment for choosing an appropriate policy under a given scenario; dynamic policy adjustment where different policies may be adopted at different time for the best fit. Based on these work, a more advanced QoS system can be built to automatic choose an appropriate policy, and automatic adjust QoS parameters at runtime to optimize the quality of services.

CONCLUSION

Quality of service of Grid computing is a challenging but timely important problem. While intensive research has been conducted in QoS in recent years, most existing results are ad hoc and there is no taxonomy or a systematic understanding of the QoS under resource sharing. In this chapter, we present a thorough research to increase the fundamental understanding of QoS of Grid computing and promote system software to support QoS of Grid computing automatically. Our QoS is focused on the resource sharing of the Grid tasks and local jobs. We first introduce a QoS taxonomy based on QoS policies. The corresponding optimization issues of each QoS policies are identified next. Performance modeling and task scheduling algorithms are then presented to illustrate the solutions of selected optimization issues. Experimental results have shown

Figure 3. Integrating GHS into grid computing

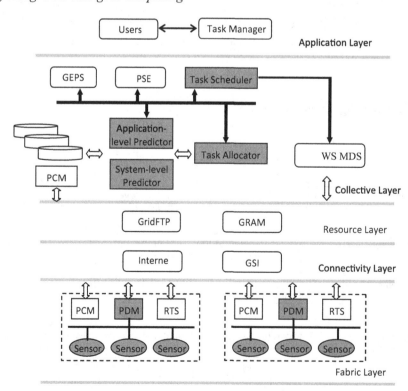

the feasibility and functionality of the proposed solutions. The QoS taxonomy and its associated optimization mechanisms form a framework whereas an automatic system support of QoS of Grid computing can be developed upon.

REFERENCES

Berman F., Wolski R., Casanova H., & Cirne W. (2003). Adaptive computing on the grid using AppLeS. *IEEE Transactions on Parallel and Distributed Systems, 14*(4) 369-382.

Chalmers, D., & Sloman M. (1999). A survey of quality of service in mobile computing environments. *IEEE Communications Surveys and Tutorials, 2*(2), 2-10.

Deelman E., Blythe J., Gil Y., & Kesselman C. (2003). Mapping abstract complex workflows onto grid environments. *Journal of Grid Computing, 1*(1) 25-39.

El-Ghazawi T., Gaj, K., & Alexandridis N. (2004). A performance study of job management systems. *Concurrency and Computation: Practice and Experience, 16*(13) 1229-1246.

Foster I., (2006). Globus toolkit Version 4: Software for service-oriented systems. *IFIP International Conference on Network and Parallel Computing* (LNCS 3779, 2-13).

Foster I. & Kesselman C. (2004). The Grid2: Blueprint for a new computing infrastructure. Morgan-Kaufman.

Foster I., Roy A., & Sander V. (2000). A quality of service architecture that combines resource reservation and application adaptation. In *Proceedings of the 8th International Workshop on Quality of Service (pp.* 181-188), Pittsburgh, PA.

Foster I., Voeckler J., Wilde M. & Zhao Y. (2002). *Chimera: A virtual data system for representing, querying, and automating data derivation.* Paper presented at Scientific and Statistical Database Management.

Gong L., Sun X.H. & Waston E. F. (2002). Performance modeling and prediction of non-dedicated network computing. *IEEE Trans. on Computers, 51*(9), 1041-1055.

Gupta A., Lin B. & Dinda P. (2004). Measuring and understanding user comfort with resource borrowing. In *Proceedings of the 13th IEEE International Symposium on High Performance Distributed Computing*, Honolulu, Hawaii.

Harchol-Balter, M. (2002). Task assignment with unknown duration. *J. ACM, 49*(2) 260-288.

Nurmi D., Brevik J., & Wolski R. (2003). *Modeling machine availability in enterprise and wide-area distributed computing environments* (UCSB Computer Science Tech. Rep.CS2003-28), 2003.

Sun X.-H., & Wu M. (2003). Grid harvest service: A system for long-term, application-level task scheduling. In *Proceedings of 2003 IEEE International Parallel and Distributed Processing Symposium*, Nice, France.

Sun X.-H., & Wu M. (2007). Quality of service of grid computing: Resource sharing. In *Proceedings of the 6th International Conference on Grid and Cooperative Computing* (pp. 395-402).

Wolski, R., Spring N. T., & Hayes J. (1999). The network weather service: A distributed resource performance forecasting service for metacomputing. *Journal of Future Generation Computing Systems, 15*(5-6) 757-768.

Wu M., Sun X.-H., & Chen Y. (2006). QoS oriented resource reservation in shared environments. In *Proceedings of the 6th IEEE International Symposium on Cluster Computing and the Grid* (pp. 601-608).

Wu M., & Sun X.-H. (2006). Grid harvest service: A performance system of grid computing. *Journal of Parallel and Distributed Computing, 66*(10), 1322-1337.

Wu, M. (2006). *System support of quality of service in shared network environments*. Dissertation, Department of Computer Science, Illinois Institute of Technology.

Yu, J., & Buyya, R. (2005). Taxonomy of Workflow management systems for grid computing. *Journal of Grid Computing, 3*(3-4), 171-200.

KEY TERMS AND DEFINITIONS

Quality of Service (QoS): QoS defines non-functional characteristics of a system, affecting the perceived quality of the results.

QoS Architecture: The structure or structures of a software system, which comprise QoS specification component, QoS provision component and QoS management mechanisms.

QoS Metric: A set of parameters to describe and measure the application QoS characteristics such as performance, cost, reliability, security and fidelity.

QoS Modeling: The process of building performance models to identify the impact of system parameters and application parameters on application QoS.

Resource Management: The management and control of applications running on resources to enforce specific QoS policies, and carry out the scheduling decisions.

Resource Reservation: A resource allocation where the system reserves physical resources of host machines or network resources for an application or a class of services. It includes CPU reservation, memory reservation, disk reservation and network reservation.

Task Scheduling: The process of task scheduling partitions a Grid application into sub-tasks and assigns each sub-task to a selected set of resources based on the pre-developed QoS models to support or optimize user required application QoS.

Chapter VIII
QoS in Grid Computing

Zhihui Du
Tsinghua University, China

Zhili Cheng
Tsinghua University, China

Xiaoying Wang
Tsinghua University, China

Chuang Lin
Tsinghua University, China

ABSTRACT

This chapter first summarizes popular terms of QoS related concepts and technologies in grid computing, including **SLA**, **End-to-End QoS Provision** *and* **Virtualization**. *Then a three layered general* **grid QoS** *provision model based on* **MetaServices** *is proposed. Operating mechanisms are discussed in detail, and the model can maintain* **grid QoS** *by defining QoS requirements in different levels and solve the QoS problems hierarchically. A prototype named* **PMGrid** *is designed and implemented based on the QoS provision model.* **PMGrid** *is a grid system for astronomy data processing. The results show that the* **PMGrid** *can maintain the QoS requirements of astronomy data processing.*

INTRODUCTION

Grid computing has been developing rapidly in recent years. Various Grid applications have involved the QoS (Quality of Service) provision problems. Since the Grid system is in essence a widely distributed and dynamically interactive system, QoS provision solutions for the Grid system are difficult and also very important.

Researches on Grid QoS started in the early 2000's. There have been many research hotspots during these years in the Grid QoS provision area, such as, resource reservation, QoS-based scheduling, Service Level Agreement, End-to-End QoS Provision, data transmission with QoS provision, and Virtualization technologies and so on.. In this paper, we will try to clarify the basic concept of Grid QoS, establish a simple and unified Grid QoS provision model, and introduce some important Grid QoS technologies.

Grid QoS can be defined as a set of parameters on the collective behavior of one or more services in the Grid environment to prioritize different requirements. In fact, Grid QoS indicates the non-functional requirements for services provided by the Grid infrastructure. It provides criteria which can be used to measure the behavior and operations of a Grid system. Reliability, scalability and cost are typical examples of QoS requirements.

QoS requirements can be either descriptive (subjective) or accurate (objective). One QoS requirement can be the cumulative effect of multiple aspects of the behavior and operations in Grid services. Since the high-level users often use descriptive and comprehensive requirements, the Grid infrastructure should be capable of analyzing and parsing these requirements into some low-level and accurate requirements. Vice versa, the Grid infrastructure should also be able to integrate some low-level requirements into high-level and descriptive requirements.

From another point of view, Grid QoS requirements can be elastic or inelastic. Elastic QoS requirements can take advantage of an arbitrary amount of services available in current Grid environment. On the contrary, inelastic QoS requirements often require the Grid services to reach a certain level in order to function - any more than required will be redundant and any less will cause the services non-functioning. These two different kinds of QoS requirements usually need different supporting or scheduling mechanisms.

In fact, Grid QoS provision is a must only when there is insufficient resource capacity and thus various services are competing in the Grid environment. Namely, the QoS provision is not necessary when there is enough capacity. Although the Grid infrastructure is designed in concept to provide powerful computing ability and massive storage, as the Grid users' requirements increase with the fast deployment of Grid computing, Grid QoS provision becomes a very essential feature of the Grid infrastructure.

BACKGROUND

Before the descriptions of the Grid QoS provision model later in the part of "main focus", technology hotspots of Grid QoS provision are discussed as the background in this section, including: Grid QoS negotiation protocols designed based on SLA, such as SNAP; End-to-End QoS Provision, concept borrowed from networks (Sander et al 2001); and Virtualization technologies which have been introduced into the area of Grid computing recently.

Agreement Protocols

In order to maintain a QoS-guaranteed communication path between services, the Service Level Agreement (SLA) is employed into Grid environment.

An SLA is a formal negotiation agreement between two parties. It is a contract that exists between customers and service providers. It records the QoS requirement of services, priorities, responsibilities, guarantee etc. (Wikipedia – Service Level Agreement).

In Grid computing, SLAs are instantiated via the Service negotiation and Acquisition Protocol (SNAP), which provides contract lifetime management (Czajkowski et al., 2002). SNAP proposes three different types of SLAs: Task service level agreements (TSLA), Resource service level agreements (RSLA), and Binding service level agreements (BSLA). It also defines an internal bundling model. Based on the standard form of SNAP, various Grid services keep consulting and interacting. For more detailed information of SNAP, please refer to the relevant descriptions in (Czajkowski et al 2002).

End-to-End QoS Provision

In 1996, Campbell et al discussed an End-to-End QoS Provision framework (Campbell et al 1996). They tried to establish a QoS provision layered system from the top down. They stated five basic principles of the End-to-End QoS Provision, based on which, the End-to-End QoS Provision framework can be divided into two areas: the QoS specification and the QoS implementation mechanism.

The QoS specification is a kind of unified description between a QoS object and a QoS-guaranteed system. The so-called "QoS object" is the principal part of QoS management. For example, in traditional network studies, the packet is a typical kind of QoS objects. Similarly, we treat the jobs submitted to the Grid systems as QoS objects in the context of Grid environment.

The QoS implementation mechanism is a concrete implementation of QoS norms, which can be further classified into three categories: QoS provision mechanisms; QoS control mechanisms and QoS management mechanisms.

Virtualization Technology

Virtualization technology is a hot topic nowadays in the area of architectures in computer science. Researches on Grid QoS have also paid attention to this revolutionary technology. This subsection discusses the benefit brought from Virtualization techniques to Grid QoS provision.

The Virtualization is defined as a technique for hiding the physical characteristics of computing resources from the way in which other systems, applications, or end users interact with those resources. This includes making a single physical resource (such as a server, an operating system, an application, or a storage device) appear to function as multiple logical resources; and making multiple physical resources (such as storage devices or servers) appear as a single logical resource (Enterprise Management Associates quote).

In the early 1970s, Madnick and Donovan had analyzed the system security and isolation in virtual machines in (Madnick and Donovan, 1973). In 2003 and 2004, many researchers tried to run Grid applications on virtual machines and tried to figure out the problems resulted by this action. In (Figueiredo et al., 2003), a case for Grid computing on virtual machine was studied. In (Sundararaj and Dinda, 2004), the virtual network used in virtual-machine-based Grid computing was discussed. These researches have clarified the possible difficulties for Grid applications running on virtual machines. Later, a concept called Virtual Workspace was introduced into Grid computing (Keahey et al., 2005; Keahey et al., 2005).

The advantages of leveraging Virtualization techniques in Grid computing are summarized as follows: resource isolation, consolidation, security, customization, and encapsulation. (Figueiredo et al., 2003; Rosenblum et al., 2005)

MAIN FOCUS

A General Grid QoS Provision Model

Based on the research of MetaServices (Du et al., 2004), a general Grid QoS provision model is described and specific Grid QoS technologies can be adopted by this model.

The concept of MetaService is abstracted to identify the essential management functions which should be provided in an OGSA-based Grid environment, and this concept divides the Grid services into two categories: MetaServices (management services) and resource services. MetaServices are used to manage other Grid resource services. Meanwhile, they have the same syntax as resource services.

Traditional networks tried to make the core of the network as simple as possible, which requires complex end devices and thus makes it difficult to guarantee QoS during the message transmission through network. In Grid computing, the infrastructure should be complex and powerful, and hence the end users' devices can be designed as simple as possible.

Figure 1 shows a general Grid QoS provision Model. Three roles are contained in the model, including consumer services or applications, MetaServices and resource services, as depicted in Figure 1. The top-down QoS provision procedure driven by the requirements involves following steps:

1. Consumer services/applications provide QoS requirements of different tasks/jobs, and MetaServices transform/divide the requirements into different parts which can be satisfied by the resource services.
2. MetaServices negotiate with both consumer services and resource services to sign contracts which are acceptable and feasible for both sides.
3. After that, the MetaServices assign the tasks/ jobs to contracted resource services to get services with the expected QoS capability.

The bottom-up procedure driven by other services/resources involves following steps:

1. Resource services provide QoS capabilities of different tasks/jobs to MetaServices.
2. MetaServices transform/merge the capabilities into different requirements which can be satisfied by the consumer services/ applications.
3. Then the similar negotiation and execution procedure will be done.

Different kinds of MetaServices, QoS transforming technologies, QoS mapping, resource reservation and QoS-based scheduling methods, will be involved in the two procedures. In this model, the roles of customer services and resource services are relative, which means that the resource services can also provide QoS requirements to the resource services in lower levels to implement their QoS capabilities.

QoS Technologies in the Model

In Figure 1, each level has a specific QoS technology. Hereafter, we will discuss them in this model in detail.

Figure 1. The general grid QoS provision model

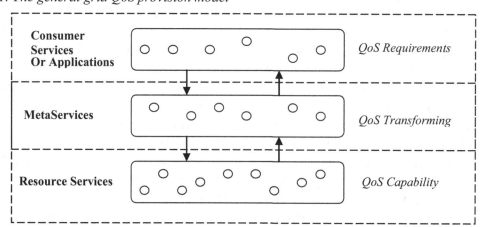

1. **QoS requirement:** It means how to describe the requirements of consumer services/applications, such as performance requirements and cost requirements. Compared with QoS requirements of the traditional network, these requirements are application level requirements. Thus, the resource services should make the lower levels QoS, such as QoS of the IP level and the physical level etc., transparent to MetaServices and customer services. In order to keep the mutual communication, the description standards of QoS requirements should be established. The acceptable QoS requirements can be described from different aspects, such as accessibility, administrability, availability, dependability, reusability, and scalability.

2. **QoS transforming:** It means a set of technologies in practical scenarios, including QoS negotiation, resource reservation, QoS mapping, and QoS-based scheduling.

   a. **QoS negotiation:** Including negotiation mechanisms among consumers, brokers and resource providers. The QoS negotiation mechanism is very important in making a contract and providing surveillance of executing the contract. Service Level Agreement (SLA) is a technology imported into the Grid computing area from the networking research area, in order to support the QoS negotiation in Grid computing. There are negotiation protocols used in Grid computing such as Service Negotiation Agreement Protocol (SNAP) (Czajkowski et al., 2002).

   b. **Resource reservation:** Resource reservation is an effective way to maintain the requirement of some high-level or real-time application. The concept originally comes from the traditional telecommunication area.

   c. **QoS mapping:** In the hierarchical structure of Grid systems, the QoS requirement is mapped from level to level. Different levels concentrate on different aspects, and thus a mapping method is needed to map the functions of different levels.

   d. **QoS-based scheduling:** Different resource providers can provide different services. Scheduling algorithms can select an optimized way to schedule tasks or distribute data onto different resources according to the requirements of users or orchestrator. Weighted Round Robin and Weighted Fair Queuing are typical QoS-based scheduling algorithms.

3. **QoS capabilities:** To supply the basic capabilities of services and devices to meet the QoS requirements.

Hotspots Integration

As discussed in the part of "Background" previously, the research hotspots can be integrated into the Grid QoS provision model as hotspots integration.

Agreement protocols technology can be easily integrated into the QoS provision model proposed in section 2. It is a very basic technology used in QoS negotiation.

The end-to-end principle originated from network and its emphasis is to keep the network as simple as possible. It is opposite from our view of the Grid infrastructure – complex in the core but simple in end devices. However, we can't ignore that the technologies in End-to-End QoS Provision will certainly bring a better QoS to Grid environment. In the Grid QoS provision model proposed in the last section, End-to-End QoS Provision technologies can be used on the MetaService level.

The Virtualization technology is becoming more mature and practical. The objective of facilitating resource sharing and collaboration matches the concepts of Grid computing. Maybe in the near future, these two technologies will cooperate with each other and finally merge together, providing a powerful and new computation environment.

In the Grid QoS provision model, virtual machines can be integrated as the enabling technology of Grid infrastructure to support resource isolation, customization, and adjusting. Virtual machines can be the basis of the Grid QoS provision model at the resource service level which provides the basic QoS capacity.

Prototype

Previously, we have proposed a prototype system called PMGrid (Wang et al 2007), which is a grid system designed based on MetaService, and it is implemented to perform astronomy data processing. Figure 2 shows the architecture of PMGrid in the context of the general grid QoS provision model proposed in this paper.

Astronomy data processing requires high quality of services. Hence, in PMGrid, we developed MetaService negotiable through SLA, and a specific Error Processing Service is designed in order to report the runtime errors for users to find.

In order to maintain the End-to-End QoS Provision, the communication schemes between levels are designed based on XML, which assures that the QoS requirements can be transformed to appropriate parameters in different levels.

At the resource services level, Virtualization mechanisms can take effect. Since different services in astronomy data processing requires different resource. For example, the Online Data Reception service needs little computing capability, but it should not be disturbed by other services at any time; and the Full Analysis service requires a great amount of CPU cycles. In this case, the benefits of Virtualization mechanisms can be leveraged, including consolidation and customization to give the services a suitable environment in capability, and resource isolation and security to maintain an undisturbed environment for the services.

Figure 3 shows the representations of astronomy data before and after processed in the prototype system PMGrid.

FUTURE TRENDS

At last, we will talk about the future research trends of Grid QoS. As far as we could see, the future of QoS researches will focus on the following topics:

Figure 2. The architecture of PMGrid

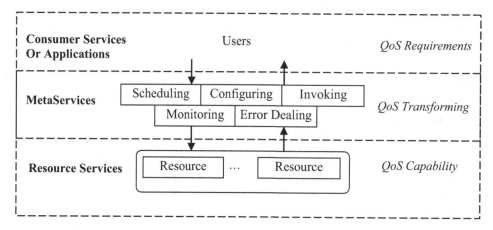

Figure 3. An example of astronomy data processing in PMGrid

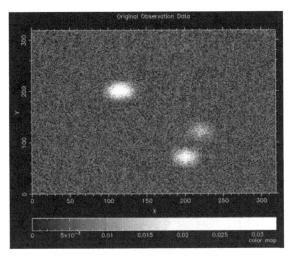

(a) representations of data before processing

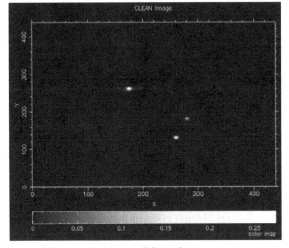

(b) representations of data after processing

- **Agreement Protocols:** In order to maintain the on-demand services in Grid computing, SLA will still be a very hot area to explore (Burchard et al., 2005), e.g. how to setup an Auditing and Accounting framework in practical scenarios by SLA.
- **Virtualization:** Although some progress has been made (Keahey et al., 2006), the current condition of Virtualization technologies used in Grid computing is still too limited. Maybe in the near future, with the development of Virtualization techniques, a mature framework will be established, and real Grid applications can run under virtualized platforms with QoS guarantees.
- **Scheduling algorithms:** Scheduling algorithms will always be important under the present architecture of Grid computing (Li et al., 2007; He et al., 2004). Fortunately, scheduling algorithms can be found in many other research areas besides Grid QoS.
- **Surveillance and monitoring:** In such a global infrastructure as grid, how to monitor and control the Grid behaviors is a very

important problem (Kim and Kang, 2006). At the same time, how to use the surveillance data to get useful information to optimize the Grid infrastructure is an even more important task. Some modern techniques like data mining may be very useful and can be employed in the processing and analysis of massive monitoring data.

CONCLUSION

This paper proposes the definition of Grid QoS, describes a Grid QoS provision model and summaries the hotspots of QoS research areas in Grid computing. These contents have three advantages:

1. Help people to understand the scope of Grid QoS and get a general idea of what Grid QoS is.
2. Review the hotspots of QoS researches in Grid computing and help people to learn the trends and know what to do in further researches on Grid QoS.

3. Propose a general Grid QoS provision model.

REFERENCES

Burchard, L.O., Linnert, B., Heine, F., Hovestadt, M., Kao, O., & Keller, A. (2005). A quality-of-service architecture for future grid computing applications. In *Proceedings of 19th IEEE International Parallel and Distributed Processing Symposium*, Berlin, Germany.

Campbell, A., Aurrecoechea C., & Hauw, L. (1996). A review of QoS architectures. In *Proceedings of 4th International Workshop on Quality of Service (IWQoS)*.

Cardellini, V., Colajanni, M., & Yu, P.S. (2000). Geographic load balancing for scalable distributed Web systems. In *Proceedings of 8th International Symposium on Modeling, Analysis and Simulation of Computer and Telecommunication Systems*, IEEE Computer Society, San Francisco, CA, USA (pp. 20-27).

Czajkowski, K., Foster, I., Kesselman, C., Sander, V., & Tuecke, S. (2002). SNAP: A protocol for negotiating service level agreements and coordinating resource management in distributed systems. (LNCS 2537, 153-183).

Du, Z.H., Lau, F.C.M., Wang, C.L., Lam, W.K., He C., Wang X.G., Chen Y. & Li S.L. (2004). Design of an OGSA-based MetaService architecture. In *Proceedings of Grid and Cooperative Computing—GCC2004* (LNCS 3251, 167-174).

Enterprise Management Associates. *A quote from this Information Technology analyst firm.*

Figueiredo, R., Dinda, P., & Fortes, J.A.B. (2003). A case for Grid computing on virtual machines. In *Proceedings of 23rd International Conference on Distributed Computing Systems* (pp. 550-559).

Hafid, A., & Bochmann, G. (1998). Quality of service adaptation in distributed multimedia applications. *ACM Springer-Verlag Multimedia Systems Journal, 6*(5), 299-315.

He, L., Jarvis, S.A., Spooner, D.P., Chen, X., & Nudd, G.R. (2004). Dynamic scheduling of parallel jobs with QoS demands in multi-clusters and grids. In *Proceedings of 5th IEEE/ACM International Workshop on Grid Computing*, Coventry, UK (pp. 402-409).

Keahey, K., Chase J. & Foster, I (2006). Virtual playgrounds: managing virtual resources in the grid. In *Proceedings of 20th IEEE International Parallel and Distributed Processing Symposium*, IL, USA.

Keahey, K., Foster I., Freeman T., & Zhang X. (2005). Virtual Workspaces: Achieving quality of service and quality of life in the Grid. *Scientific Programming*. IOS Press.

Keahey, K., Foster I., Freeman T., Zhang X., & Galron D. (2005). Virtual Workspaces in the Grid. (LNCS 3648, 421-431).

Kim, D.H. & Kang K.W. (2006). Design and implementation of integrated information system for monitoring resources in Grid computing. In *Proceedings of 10th International Conference on Computer Supported Cooperative Work in Design*, Korea (pp. 1-6).

Li, Y.H., Zhao, D.P., & Li J. (2007). Scheduling algorithm based on integrated utility of multiple QoS attributes on service Grid. In *Proceedings of 6th International Conference on Grid and Cooperative Computing*, Dalian, China (pp. 288-295).

Madnick, S. E., & Donovan J. J. (1973). Application and analysis of the virtual machine approach to information system security and isolation. In *Proceedings of ACM SIGARCH-SYSOPS Workshop on Virtual Computer Systems*, Boston, MA. (pp. 210-224).

Rosenblum, M., & Garfinkel, T. (2005). Virtual machine monitors: current technology and future trends. *Computer 38*(5), 39-47.

Sander, V., Adamson W., Foster I., & Roy A. (2001). *End-to-end provision of policy information for network QoS*. In *Proceedings of the Tenth IEEE Symposium on High Performance Distributed Computing (HPDC-10)*. IEEE Press.

Sundararaj, A., & Dinda, P. (2004). Towards virtual networks for virtual machine grid computing. In *Proceedings of 3rd USENIX Conference on Virtual Machine Technology*.

Wang, M., Du, Z.H., Cheng, Z.L., & Zhu, S.H. (2007). A pipeline virtual service pre-scheduling pattern and its application in astronomy data processing. *Simulation, 83*(1), 123-132.

Wikipedia – Service Level Agreement. Retrieved from, http://en.wikipedia.org/wiki/Service_Level_Agreement

KEY TERMS AND DEFINITIONS

Grid QoS: A set of quality requirements on the collective behavior of one or more services in Grid environment to prioritize different requirements.

Grid Middleware: Software designed to standardize and to ensure that the implementation of Grid application complied with Grid unified norms.

MetaService: Services abstracted to identify the essential management functions which should be provided in an OGSA based Grid environment.

Resource Reservation Protocol (RSVP): A network layer protocol designed to reserve resources across a network for integrated services over Internet.

Service Level Agreement: An agreement describes the user requirements for QoS by XML-based description language. It is defined in a unified service interface in order to achieve QoS service management, consultation and agreement.

Virtual Machine: A number of discrete identical execution environments on a single computer, each of which runs an operating system (OS). This can allow applications written for one OS to be executed on a machine which runs a different OS, or provide execution "sandboxes" which provide a greater level of isolation between processes than is achieved when running multiple processes on the same instance of an OS.

Virtual Workspace: A framework, which allows a Grid client to define an environment in terms of requirements (such as resource requirements or software configuration), manage it, and deploy the environment in the Grid environment (Keahey and Galron et al., 2005).

Section III
Grid Security

Chapter IX
Trust and Privacy in Grid Resource Auctions

Kris Bubendorfer
Victoria University of Wellington, New Zealand

Ben Palmer
Victoria University of Wellington, New Zealand

Ian Welch
Victoria University of Wellington, New Zealand

ABSTRACT

A Grid resource broker is the arbiter for access to a Grid's computational resources and therefore its performance and functionality has a wide-ranging influence on the utilization and performance of the Grid. Ideally, we want to avoid relying on a single 'trusted' resource broker because it may not be trustworthy. For example, a broker holding a resource auction could examine and reveal bid information to others, or defraud participants by subverting the auction results. The use of privacy preserving and verifiable auction protocols offers guarantees beyond those possible in real world auctions, making the electronic auctions as secure, or more secure, than their physical counterparts. In this chapter, we provide the background to understand privacy preserving and verifiable auction schemes and discuss the implications of adopting them on Grid architecture. We then evaluate a range of potential secure auction schemes and identify those that are most suitable to be adopted within for use in the Grid.

INTRODUCTION

One of the vital components of any Grid computing infrastructure is the resource broker. A Grid resource broker is the arbiter for access to a Grid's computational resources and therefore its performance and functionality has a wide-ranging influence on the utilization and performance of the Grid. Market based mechanisms, such as auctions, have often (Buyya, Abramson, Giddy, and Stockinger, 2002; Bubendorfer, Komisarczuk, Chard, and Desai, 2005; Chien, M., and W., 2005) been promoted as a solution for scalable resource economies because they are naturally decentralized, efficient and produce optimal allocations. Another advantage of such market-based mechanisms is that they are a natural fit with the principles of Utility computing (Eerola et al., 2003; Komisarczuk, Bubendorfer, and Chard, 2004) and efforts towards Grid commercialization (Dimitrakos et al., 2003; Graupner, Kotov, Andrzejak, and Trinks, 2003).

Ideally, we want to avoid relying on a single 'trusted' resource broker because it may not be trustworthy. For example, a broker holding a resource auction could examine the bids and reveal this information to others, or defraud participants by subverting the auction results. However, we can protect bid values by using a privacy preserving auction scheme. Fraud can be prevented by adding a verification protocol to the auction. The use of privacy preserving and verifiable auction protocols offers guarantees beyond those possible in real world auctions, making the electronic auctions as secure, or more secure, than their physical counterparts. The use of privacy preserving and verifiable auction protocols enables the construction of open and user centric Grid architectures. Indeed, it is possible to imagine such market oriented technologies underpinning peer based user-centric Grid communities, in which users can contribute and consume computing power on demand, purchase services and collectively provide the computing infrastructure.

In this chapter, we provide the background to understand privacy preserving and verifiable auction schemes and discuss the implications of adopting them on Grid architecture. We then evaluate a range of potential secure auction schemes and identify those that are most suitable to be adopted within for use in the Grid.

BACKGROUND

Auctions are favored as an efficient solution to the challenge of distributed resource allocation in both economic (Buyya et al., 2002; Bubendorfer et al., 2005; Chien et al., 2005) and can also be successfully applied in noneconomic (Malone, Fikes, Grant, and Howard, 1988) resource allocation systems. There are four main types of auction protocol; the English, Dutch, Sealed-Bid, and what has since become known as the Vickrey auction protocol. The English auction is the conventional open outcry, ascending price, multiple bid protocol. The Dutch auction is an open outcry, descending price, single bid protocol. The Sealed-Bid, or tender, is a sealed single bid, best price (1st price) protocol in which all bids are opened simultaneously. The Vickrey auction is similar to the Sealed-Bid auction, except that the winning bidder pays the amount of the second bid (2nd price). The second price bid mechanism results in a dominant strategy of truthful bidding in private value auctions, that is, bidding your true value will always give the best return regardless of other bidders strategies. It is worth noting that the revenue equivalence theorem states that all of the four main auction protocols return the same revenue in private value auctions (Vickrey, 1961), hence the selection of an auction protocol usually depends on implementation pragmatics such as messaging requirements.

When it comes to computational auctions however, it may not be possible to achieve QoS goals with a single representative good as the basis for resource allocations. Execution resources form an indivisible set, related and conditional upon the availability of each other. Game theorists term this as the combinatorial allocation problem (CAP) (Rothkopf, Pekec and Harstad, 1995), in which a set of components have a synergistic value that exceeds the sum of the individual parts. Because of preferential combinations and possible substitutions, bidders have preferences not just for particular items, but for collections of items. The Generalized Vickrey Auction (GVA) (MacKie-Mason and Varian, 1994) extends the 2nd price Vickrey auction protocol to address the CAP.

Figure 1 illustrates a combinatorial auction in which Alice is the auctioneer, Jane wants apples only if she can also have oranges, Bob wants all of the goods but does not need all of them and Sam needs all of the goods together. The highest revenue of $4 is generated by allocating the apples and oranges to Jane, the bananas to Bob and nothing to Sam. For a combinatorial 2nd price auction the price paid by the winner, is their bid less a discount equal to their contribution to the revenue from the auction. This discount is simply calculated by removing the winner from the auction and re-computing the result, the difference in revenues is the '2nd price' discount. The difference between the two values is the winner's discount. Solving a single GVA auction is *NP*-hard (Rothkopf, Pekec and Harstad, 1995), and for this reason there are a number of optimized variations (Nisan and Ronen, 2000; Parkes, 2001), and approximations (Lehmann, Oallaghan and Shoham, 2002) that reduce the computation time.

MAIN FOCUS

All auction protocols have known problems when deployed into an electronic market. An exhaustive analysis of these protocol considerations is detailed in (Sandholm, 1996), however, it is worth detailing a few examples. Both the English and Vickrey auctions suffer from self-enforced bidder collusion. All auctions reveal some information, for example, the Dutch auction reveals the winner and their bid, the English auction will reveal the valuations of all bidders (except the winner, who has not yet reached their maximum valuation), and the Vickrey auction will reveal the winner and the price of the second bid but not the bidder of the second price or the price bid by the winner. A compromised or corrupt auctioneer may reveal all the bid values in the case of both sealed bid auctions; and in the Vickrey auction, may misrepresent the amount the winner must pay. In addition, the values of past bids can be collected and either used in future auctions, or passed on to colluding bidders – *"Even if current information can be safeguarded, records of past behavior can be extremely valuable, since historical data can be used to estimate willingness to pay."'* (Varian, 1995).

Figure 1. A combinatorial auction

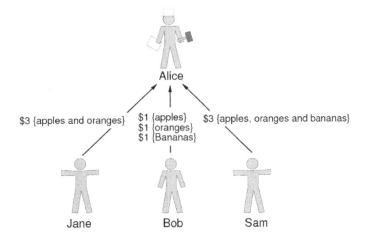

Trust and Auctioneers in the Grid Economy

If a Grid economy relies on a 'trusted' auctioneer, we have to satisfy to all users as to who owns, controls or audits the auctioneer, where it is placed, and how the auction data is secured. However, a 'trusted' auctioneer does not mean that the auctioneer is trustworthy. Suppose Alice is running a sealed bid auction for her own (and others delegated) resources. The auction is exposed as a webservice, with the auction's interface described using a machine-processable XML format allowing machine-to-machine interaction (Booth et. al., 2003). The auction webservice is hosted by Sam. Users Bob and Jane *trust* Alice and use their own programs to submit bids to her auction as shown in Figure 2.

There are many potential problems with this auction. Sam or Alice can examine the bids and potentially reveal this information to others - many bidders would prefer their bids to remain private. Alice could also refuse to count certain bids in the auction, while Sam could filter bids preventing Alice from including them in the auction. Alice could easily defraud the organizations that have delegated resources to her. Alice could: choose a winner regardless of the bid values to *favor* certain users, choose the winner correctly but report a reduced price and pocket the difference

herself, or award the most profitable bids to her own resources. A large amount of trust is placed in Alice with no way of determining if she has correctly executed the auction, in effect Alice is acting as a black box allocator.

We can prevent Alice or Sam from learning and potentially revealing private information by hiding the bid values in such a way that *still permits Alice to correctly compute the outcome of the auction*. This type of auction is privacy preserving, where the bid values are hidden by encryption or obfuscation. Figure 3 shows Alice holding a privacy preserving sealed bid auction.

In such a privacy-preserving auction, Alice cannot manipulate or misrepresent the bid values (to take a cut). Alice also cannot preferentially favor her resources as the actual values are hidden until the winner and the resource allocation is determined, at which time, only the winning bid value(s) are revealed. However, while a privacy-preserving auction offers significantly better guarantees, we still do not know if all of the bids were counted, and we also do not know if the auction protocol was computed correctly.

The trustworthiness of a privacy-preserving auction can be further enhanced with the addition of a verification scheme. A verifiable privacy-preserving auction is shown in Figure 4. A verification scheme allows bidders and other third parties to verify offline that the auction was

Figure 2. A resource auction

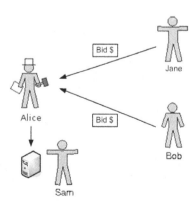

Figure 3. A privacy preserving resource auction

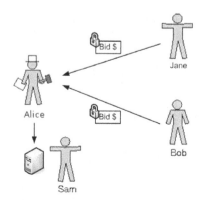

Figure 4. A verifiable privacy preserving resource auction

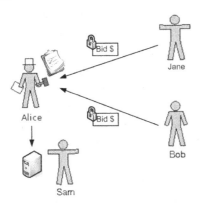

executed correctly and that all bids were considered in the result.

The verification gives bidders confidence that their bids have been counted and that the auction result has been computed correctly. A nice property is that the owners of any resources delegated to Alice can also verify the auction to make sure they are getting the correct amount of money from Alice. The combination of verification and privacy preservation eliminates the need to trust Alice.

Techniques for Implementing Privacy Preserving and Verifiable Auctions

A number of techniques are used to implement privacy preserving auction protocols and verification schemes. The cryptographic techniques most often used to implement privacy-preserving auctions are summarized below:

- **Homomorphic encryption:** Is used to encrypt the bid values while still allowing operations to be performed on them (Yokoo and Suzuki, 2002; Brandt, 2006).
- **Polynomial secret sharing:** Is used to spread the bid values over several auctioneers (Kikuchi, 2002) while still allowing bid comparisons. The values of bids are hidden in the degree of a polynomial.

- **Garbled circuit**: Uses a circuit composed of virtual Boolean gates to conduct the auction (Cachin, 1999; Naor, Pinkas and Sumner, 1999). This circuit is created and garbled by an auction issuer and sent to an auctioneer to execute. The garbling of the circuit prevents the auctioneer from discovering any bid values while still allowing the circuit to compute the auction result.

Verification for use with auction protocols has been most often implemented using one of the following techniques:

- **Zero knowledge proofs:** To prove the auction was correctly executed while revealing no other information (Brandt, 2006).
- **Range proofs:** Have also been used to prove that an encrypted value is the largest in a set of encrypted values (Lipmaa, Asokan and Niemi, 2002).
- **Cut and choose verification:** Is used in the garbled circuits protocol (Naor et al., 1999) where x copies of a garbled circuit are constructed for the auction and x-1 randomly chosen copies are opened before the auction to check they have been correctly constructed.

Architectural Implications for the Grid

When Grids cross organizational boundaries to become ad-hoc collections of resources with multiple owners, we strike the problem of establishing how we can trust other organizations and their software during resource allocation. This is especially true in on-demand Grids and Market Oriented Grid or Utility computing, where such allocation decisions can have very real financial implications. Privacy preserving auction protocols prevent an auctioneer from identifying bidders and acting to advantage, or to disadvantage certain bidders. These auctions also prevent the auctioneer from stealing and distributing commercially sensitive bid information. Verifiable auction protocols allow independent verification of an auctioneer's actions and therefore provide cryptographic guarantees that the outcome of the auction includes all bids and that the outcome of the auction was computed correctly. Combining both privacy preserving and verifiable auction protocols removes the need to trust an auctioneer – be they actually trustworthy or not. In effect the auctions become transparent and auditable, rather than operating as black boxes in which we have to place our trust in the outcomes, yet have no means to determine if our trust was well placed.

As there is no longer any need to trust an auctioneer that acts as a resource broker or scheduler, we can build new Grid architectures. Removing the need to establish trust enables Grid allocation architectures that are user-centric, peer oriented, open and dynamic. From this flexibility we should also see improvements in reliability, availability and accessibility. Resource auctions can be executed safely using *any* computing resources contributed by *any* provider, and as such, as the size of the Grid increases, additional untrustworthy computing resources can be deployed or redeployed dynamically to meet any subsequent growth in the number of resource auctions. Verifiable auctions remove the need to treat either a trusted auctioneer or privacy preserving protocol as a black box, and provide an audit trail by which incorrect allocations and pricing can be detected. Using this approach, virtual organization can safely auction delegated resources without having to trust any of the individual members of the virtual organization. If a member of a virtual organization, was found to be committing fraud or simply incorrectly programmed, then detection of this behavior would allow the virtual organization to suspend or perhaps redeploy the resources contributed by that member. The results from the verification process could also be used to feed into reputation service.

AUCTION TAXONOMY

We have constructed a feature centric taxonomy of secure sealed bid auction schemes and note those that also include verification. The taxonomy provides a framework in which to compare the features of secure auction protocols, and serves to identify those which are suitable to be deployed within a Grid economy. We consider the following attributes of secure auction protocols:

- **Price Flexibility:** Permits sufficient range and combinations of prices to be generated by the bidders. Some schemes restrict this in different ways i.e., by defining a finite range and granularity of bid values to reduce encryption costs.
- **Verifiability:** Allows the result of an auction to be checked
  - **Group:** Only allows parties that were taking part in the auction to verify the auction process.
  - **Public:** Allows any third party to verify the auction process regardless of whether they were taking part in the auction.
- **Type Flexibility:** The scheme supports multiple types of auction:
  - **Single:** Supports more than one winner determination scheme, e.g. 1st price, 2nd price, and $(M + 1)^{st}$ price for multiples of the single good.
  - **Combinatorial:** Supports auctions where combinations of goods can be bid for.
- **Bid Privacy:** To provide privacy in auctions, the bids are encrypted. The information to decrypt these bids is distributed in two main ways:
  - **Trust Model:** Bids are encrypted. The information to decrypt these bids is then distributed amongst some number of parties:

> ➤ **Threshold** trust is shared among a set of n hosts. Unless a certain number (a quorum) of this set of hosts are corrupt, the privacy of the scheme is preserved.
>   - **t,n:** The (t,n) if less than t auctioneers of the n are subverted and colluding, then the auction is secure.
>   - **n,n:** The (n,n) unless all n of the auctioneers are subverted and colluding, the auction is secure.
> ➤ **Two Party** trust is distributed between two separate parties who must not collude to ensure that the auction is secure.

∘ **Level:** when bid privacy is provided, it can provide different levels of privacy. These levels of privacy are grouped as follows:

> ➤ **0:** Only the winning bidder and the price they paid are revealed.
> ➤ **1:** In addition to the information leakage of level 0, one other piece of information is revealed. For example, apart from the information revealed by level 0, the fourth highest bid could also be revealed.
> ➤ **m:** (only applicable to combinatorial auctions): in addition to the information revealed at level 0, all maximum bids for any combination of goods is revealed.
> ➤ **s:** In addition to the information leakage of level 0, it is also possible to recover bid statistics. For example, the maximum bid, the average bid, and the standard deviation of bids.
> ➤ ***:** All of the bid values are available to the auctioneer after the auction.

- **Bid Anonymity:** If the bidder is kept anonymous, then the value of their bid cannot be associated with them.

Table 1 identifies which attributes and features are implemented by the surveyed privacy preserving and/or verifiable auction schemes.

Mechanism Evaluation for the Grid Context

We have three main requirements from our discussion of architectural implications for the Grid: (1) we should be able to avoid having to trust a single auctioneer; (2) we should be able to verify that the auction was conducted correctly; and, (3) we should be able to provide strong bid privacy.

We want a scheme that avoids trusting a single auctioneer because this represents a single point of failure. Ideally, the auctions should be capable of being run by a dynamic set of auctioneers who cooperate. This provides reliability, availability and accessibility. In terms of our taxonomy, only bid privacy schemes using threshold trust meet this requirement. All the schemes except for Garbled Circuits (Juels and Szydlo, 2003; Naor et al., 1999) and 2-Server (Cachin, 1999) meet this requirement. The (t,n) schemes providing the guarantees as long as a certain proportion of the hosts are not compromised and (n,n) schemes providing the guarantees as long as all of the hosts are compromised.

Even though a distributed scheme is less likely to be compromised, no scheme is perfect so it is still necessary to be able to verify that the auction has been conducted correctly. We may not want to verify each auction; we may only want to audit a proportion to give us confidence. However, we do not want to do this at the expense of bid privacy because we do not want to give advantage to any parties by revealing bid valuations. Schemes that provide these guarantees are: Franklin and Reiter (Franklin and Reiter, 1995), Bidder Resolved (Brandt, 2006), Five Models (Peng et al., 2003),

Table 1. Taxonomy of privacy preserving auction protocols

Auction Scheme	Flexible Bidding	Verifiability: Grp	Verifiability: Pub	Type Flex.: Single	Type Flex.: Comb.	Trust Model – Threshold: t,n	Threshold: n,n	Trust Model: 2pty	Bid Privacy – Level: 0	1	m	s	*	Bidder Anon.
Franklin &Reiter (Franklin & Reiter, 1995)	•	•		•		•							•	•
Garbled Circuits (Juels & Szydlo, 2003; Naor et al., 1999; Palmer, Bubendorfer, & Welch, 2007b)	•	•			•			•	•					
Bidder Resolved (Brandt, 2006)			•	•			•		•					
Five Models (Peng, Boyd, Dawson, & Viswanathan, 2003)	•		•	•		•			•					
SGVA (K. Bubendorfer et al., 2005; Yokoo & Suzuki, 2002)	•		•	•	•	•						•		•
Poly. (Kikuchi, 2002)	•	•		•		•			•					
PolyGVA (Kris Bubendorfer & Thomson, 2006; Suzuki & Yokoo, 2002)	•				•	•					•			
2 Server (Cachin, 1999)	•	•		•				•		•				
Comb. Bid Res. (Nzouonta, 2003)					•	•			•					
HKT (Harkavy, Tygar, & Kikuchi, 1998)				•		•			•					
Extended HKT (Peng, Boyd, Dawson, & Viswanathan, 2002)	•		•	•		•			•					•
Verifiable Scheme (Parkes, Rabin, Shieber, & Thorpe, 2006)			•	•			• (n=1)						•	
Receipt Free (Chen, Lee, & Kim, 2003)			•	•				•	•					
No Threshold (Lipmaa et al., 2002)		•		•				•				•		
Non Interact. (Baudron & Stern, 2001)	•			•			• (n=1)		•					
GW Micali (Peng, Boyd, & Dawson, 2005)			•	•			•		•					
Yet Another (Ham, Kim, & Imai, 2003)	•		•	•		•			•					•
Extended vSGVA (Palmer, Bubendorfer, & Welch, 2007a)			•	•		•			•					

Polynomial (Kikuchi, 2002), Extended HKT (Peng et al., 2002), Verifiable scheme (Parkes et al., 2006), GW Micali (Peng et al., 2005), Yet Another (Ham et al., 2003) and vSGVA (Palmer et al., 2007a).

Grid users will not use any of these schemes if they believe that their privacy is compromised because bid valuations released to the wrong parties can allow them to subvert future auctions. Therefore, strong privacy guarantees are required such as only revealing the winning bidder and the price they paid at the end of the auction while keeping all other bid information secret. Of the schemes meeting our first two criteria, this rules out Franklin and Reiter, Five Models and Verifiable Scheme.

Although the six remaining schemes meet our requirements, the majority only allow auctions for single types of goods. In reality, many Grid resource allocation decisions require determination of allocations of combinations of goods (CAP). At present, the only scheme meeting our requirements and supporting combinatorial auctions is vSGVA. This is an extension of the SGVA (Yokoo and Suzuki, 2002) scheme through the addition of verification.

FUTURE TRENDS

As the Grid matures, a vision of a truly global Grid computing infrastructure (Assunção, Buyya, and Venugopal, in press) has started to emerge as a basis for on demand or utility computing. In this global grid computational resources are acquired on demand and provided with an agreed quality of service. This view of the Grid can be further extended from the current institutional model, to one where participation is open to all, and resources may be used or potentially provided by the general public, institutions or companies. The technologies discussed in this chapter, by minimising the need for prearranged trust through a combination of distribution of

trust and verification, will enable the emergence of new marketplaces for trading application services, computation, bandwidth and storage within such a global Grid. Looking even further ahead, it is possible to imagine such market oriented technologies underpinning peer based user-centric Grid communities, in which users can contribute and consume computing power on demand, purchase services and collectively provide the computing infrastructure. This could provide resources to support ubiquitous computing scenarios such as those envisioned by the MIT Project Oxygen (Rudolph, 2001).

However much work remains to be done. Additional research needs to be done in providing frameworks and infrastructures to support the development of market oriented Grid Software. More specifically, research needs to be carried out to improve the performance of the auction schemes outlined in this chapter. A number of the verification techniques in this chapter could also be applied to general computation, for example (Min et al., 2005), these could be applied to webservices to verify that they have executed correctly for their given input.

CONCLUSION

On demand (or utility computing) is one of the motivators of the Grid economy, although the same basic economic techniques can be usefully applied for resource allocation in other Grids such as, clusters, scientific Grids and sensor Grids. Underpinning the Grid economy are resource markets and the means of interacting with them. Ultimately a Grid economy represents a paradigm shift within the Grid community, where resources are traded, negotiated, allocated, provisioned, and monitored based on users quality of service requirements. The Grid economy will underpin the evolution of the Grid from a collection of computational islands into a global computational environment capable of delivering different levels of service, risk and cost, depending on the preferences of the user. When the resources being allocated are spread across varied administrative domains and ownership, the allocations of the resource allocator (in our case auctioneer) must provide confidence in the outcome. Essentially economic interactions must provide privacy and trustworthiness before the Grid economy will be widely adopted, especially in a competitive economic environment. Verifiable privacy preserving auctions satisfy these requirements, permitting any Grid or Utility computing provider to hold a resource auction for its (and others') resources without needing to be trusted or even trustworthy.

REFERENCES

Assunção, M. D. d., Buyya, R., & Venugopal, S. (in press). InterGrid: a case for internetworking islands of Grids. *Concurrency and computation: practice and experience*.

Baudron, O., & Stern, J. (2001). *Non-interactive private auctions*. Paper presented at the 5th International Financial Cryptography Conference, Grand Cayman, BWI, 19-22.

Booth, D., Haas, H., McCabe, F., Newcomer, E., Champion, M., Ferris, C., & Orchard, D. (2003). *Web services architecture, W3C working draft 8 August 2003*. Retrieved December 4th, 2007, from http://www.w3.org/TR/2003/WD-ws-arch-20030808/.

Brandt, F. (2006). How to obtain full privacy in auctions. *International Journal of Information Security, 5*(4), 201-261.

Bubendorfer, K., Komisarczuk, P., Chard, K., & Desai, A. (2005). *Fine grained resource reservation and management in grid economics*. Paper presented at the International Conference on Grid Computing and Applications.

Bubendorfer, K., & Thomson, W. (2006). *Resource management using untrusted auctioneers in a*

Grid economy. Paper presented at the Second IEEE International Conference on e-Science and Grid Computing.

Buyya, R., Abramson, D., Giddy, J., & Stockinger, H. (2002). Economic models for resource management and scheduling in Grid computing environments. *Concurrency and Computation: Practice and experience, 14*(13-15), 1507-1542.

Cachin, C. (1999). *efficient private bidding and auctions with an oblivious third party*. Paper presented at the ACM Conference on Computer and Communications Security.

Chen, X., Lee, B., & Kim, K. (2003). Receipt-free electronic auction schemes using homomorphic encryption. Paper presented at the 6th International Conference on Information Security and Cryptology (pp. 259-273).

Chien, C. H., M., & W. (2005). *Market-oriented multiple resource management and scheduling in Grid computing*. Paper presented at the Advanced Information Networking and Applications (AINA'05).

Dimitrakos, T., Mac Randal, D., Yuan, F., Gaeta, M., Laria, G., Ritrovato, P., et al. (2003). *An emerging architecture enabling grid based application service provision*. Paper presented at the Seventh IEEE International Conference on Enterprise Distributed Object Computing Conference.

Eerola, P., Konya, B., Smirnova, O., Ekelof, T., Ellert, M., Hansen, J. R., et al. (2003). Building a production grid in Scandanavia. *Internet Computing, IEEE, 7*(4), 27-35.

Franklin, M., & Reiter, M. (1995). *The design and implementation of a secure auction service*. Paper presented at the Proc. IEEE Symp. on Security and Privacy.

Graupner, S., Kotov, V., Andrzejak, A., & Trinks, H. (2003). Service-centric globally distributed computing. *IEEE Internet Computing, 7*(4), 36-43.

Ham, W., Kim, K., & Imai, H. (2003). *Yet another strong sealed-bid auctions.* Paper presented at the Symposium on Cryptography and Information Security (SCIS).

Harkavy, M., Tygar, J. D., & Kikuchi, H. (1998). *Electronic auctions with private bids.* Paper presented at the 3rd USENIX Workshop on Electronic Commerce.

Juels, A., & Szydlo, M. (2003). *A two-server, sealed-bid auction protocol.* Paper presented at the Proc. 6th Financial Cryptography Conference (FC 2002).

Kikuchi, H. (2002). *(M+1)st-price auction protocol.* Paper presented at the 5th International Financial Cryptography Conference.

Komisarczuk, P., Bubendorfer, K., & Chard, K. (2004). *Enabling virtual organisations in mobile networks.* Paper presented at the Fifth IEE International Conference on 3G Mobile Communication Technologies.

Lehmann, D., Oallaghan, L. I., & Shoham, Y. (2002). Truth revelation in approximately efficient combinatorial auctions. *Journal of the ACM (JACM), 49*(5), 577-602.

Lipmaa, H., Asokan, N., & Niemi, V. (2002). *Secure Vickrey auctions without threshold trust.* Paper presented at the 6th International Financial Cryptography Conference.

MacKie-Mason, J. K., & Varian, H. R. (1994). *Generalized Vickery auctions* (Working Paper). University of Michigan.

Malone, T. W., Fikes, R. E., Grant, K. R., & Howard, M. T. (1988). Enterprise: A market-like task scheduler for distributed computing environments. In *The Ecology of Computation* (pp. 177-205). North-Holland: Elsevier Science Publishers.

Min, Y., Shao-yin, H., Zhi, W., Zunping, C., dilin, M., & Chuanshan, G. (2005). *PICC: a secure mobile agent framework based on garbled circuit.* Paper presented at the 19th International Conference on Advanced Information Networking and Applications.

Naor, M., Pinkas, B., & Sumner, R. (1999). *Privacy preserving auctions and mechanism design.* Paper presented at the 1st ACM Conference on Electronic Commerce.

Nisan, N., & Ronen, A. (2000). *Computationally feasible VCG mechanisms.* Paper presented at the 2nd ACM conference on Electronic commerce.

Nzouonta, J. (2003). *An algorithm for clearing combinatorial markets* (Technical Report No. CS-2003-23). Florida Institute of Technology.

Palmer, B., Welch, I., & Bubendorfer, K. (2007a). *Adding verification to a privacy preserving combinatorial auction* (No. CS-TR-07-3). School of Mathematics, Statistics and Computer Science at Victoria University of Wellington.

Palmer, B., Bubendorfer, K., & Welch, I. (2007b). *Combinatorial auctions using Garbled circuits* (No. CS-TR-07-2). School of Mathematics, Statistics and Computer Science at Victoria University of Wellington.

Parkes, D. C. (2001). *An iterative generalized Vickery auction: Strategy-proofness without complete relevation.* Paper presented at the AAAI Spring Symposium on Game Theoretic and Decision Theoretic Agents.

Parkes, D. C., Rabin, M. O., Shieber, S. M., & Thorpe, C. A. (2006). *Practical secrecy-preserving, verifiably correct and trustworthy auctions.* Paper presented at the 8th International Conference on Electronic Commerce.

Peng, K., Boyd, C., & Dawson, E. (2005). *A multiplicative homomorphic sealed-bid auction based on goldwasser-micali encryption.* Paper presented at the 8th International Conference on Information Security.

Peng, K., Boyd, C., Dawson, E., & Viswanathan, K. (2002). *Robust, privacy protecting and publicly verifiable sealed-bid auction.* Paper presented at the 2nd International Conference on Information, Communications and Signal Processing.

Peng, K., Boyd, C., Dawson, E., & Viswanathan, K. (2003). *Five Sealed-bid auction models.* Paper presented at the Australasian Information Security Workshop Conference on ACSW Frontiers.

Rothkopf, M. H., Pekec, A., & Harstad, R. M. (1995). *Computationally manageable combinatorial auctions.* New Jersey, USA: DIMACS, Center for Discrete Mathematics and Theoretical Computer Science, Rutgers.

Rudolph, L. (2001). *Project oxygen: Pervasive, human-centric computing - An initial experience.* Paper presented at the 13th International Conference on Advanced Information Systems Engineering.

Sandholm, T. W. (1996). *Limitations of the Vickery auction in computational multiagent systems.* Paper presented at the Second International Conference on Multi-Agent Systems.

Suzuki, K., & Yokoo, M. (2002). *Secure combinatorial auctions by dynamic programming with polynomial secret sharing.* Paper presented at the 6th International Financial Cryptography Conference.

Varian, H. R. (1995). *Economic mechanism design for computerized agents.* Paper presented at the Usenix Workshop on Electronic Commerce.

Vickrey, W. (1961). Counterspeculation, auctions and competitive sealed tenders. *The Journal of Finance, 16*(1), 8-37.

Yokoo, M., & Suzuki, K. (2002). *Secure multiagent dynamic programming based on homomorphic encryption and its application to combinatorial auctions.* Paper presented at the First International Joint Conference on Autonomous Agents and Multiagent Systems.

KEY TERMS AND DEFINITIONS

Auction: The sale of some item or items where an auctioneer is selling to a set of bidders who place bids. An auction employs dynamic pricing dependant on the values of the bids.

Combinatorial Allocation Problem: How to efficiently allocate the items in a combinatorial auction to the bidders in an optimal way.

Combinatorial Auction: An auction where there is more than one heterogeneous item for sale. Bidders can place bids on combinations of specific items.

Encryption: To alter data using a secret code so that it is unidentifiable to unauthorized parties. Authorized parties can use a code to decrypt the data to it's original form.

Grid Economy: The grid economy is a market in which computing resources and services are bought and sold on demand.

Grid Resource Broker: A grid resource broker is a grid application scheduler that is responsible for resource discovery, selection, scheduling, and deployment of computations over resources.

Privacy Preserving: Maintaining the confidential nature of some item. An auction can be said to be privacy preserving if any confidential data sent to the auctioneer that does not need to be revealed to complete the auction remains confidential.

Trust: Reliance placed on a party for some purpose such as correctly computing an auction result, or not revealing private information.

Trustworthy: Deserving of trust, often due to past actions or reputation.

Verification: To check that some process has been correctly completed. Verification of an auction involves at the minimum checking that the auction protocol has been correctly executed, and that all bids have been counted.

Section IV
Grid Architecture, Services, and Economy

Chapter X
An Architectural Overview of the GRelC Data Access Service

Sandro Fiore
University of Salento & CMCC, Italy

Giovanni Aloisio
University of Salento & CMCC, Italy

Alessandro Negro
CMCC, Italy

Roberto Barbera
Università di Catania and Istituto Nazionale di Fisica Nucleare (INFN), Italy

Salvatore Vadacca
CMCC, Italy

Emidio Giorgio
INFN Sez. di Catania, Italy

Massimo Cafaro
University of Salento & CMCC, Italy

ABSTRACT

Grid computing is an emerging and enabling technology allowing organizations to easily share, integrate and manage resources in a distributed environment. Computational Grid allows running millions of jobs in parallel, but the huge amount of generated data has caused another interesting problem: the management (classification, storage, discovery etc.) of distributed data, i.e., a Data Grid specific issue. In the last decade, many efforts concerning the management of data (grid-storage services, metadata services, grid-database access and integration services, etc.) identify data management as a real challenge for the next generation petascale grid environments. This work provides an architectural overview of the GRelC DAS, a grid database access service developed in the context of the GRelC Project and currently used for production/tutorial activities both in gLite and Globus based grid environments.

INTRODUCTION

Grid computing (Berman, 2003) is an emerging and enabling technology allowing organizations to easily share, integrate and manage resources in a distributed environment. As an advanced form of distributed computing, grids link together servers, data sources, sensors and applications into a single system by means of a specific glue named *grid middleware*. All of these components can be very heterogeneous (different operating systems, multiple hardware platforms and architectures) and geographically dispersed.

Starting from the first distributed testbeds (I-WAY, GUSTO, etc.) a lot of efforts have been devoted to the improvement of grid services to support enhanced job submission, efficient file transfer, distributed resources monitoring and so on. However, the early attempts of grids were mainly related to the aggregation of computational power trying to address large scale computational problems. These efforts demonstrated the potential of a Computational Grid to run millions of jobs in parallel, but the huge amount of generated data has caused another interesting problem: the management (classification, storage, discovery etc.) of distributed data, i.e., a Data Grid specific issue.

In the last decade many efforts concerning the management of data (grid-storage services, metadata services, grid-database access and integration services etc.) identify data management as a real challenge for the next generation petascale grid environments. Raw data management, that relates to storage services, file transfer protocols, reliable file transfer services, storage resource managers etc. are obviously very important, but may be useless without something enabling (i) the discovery of a file within a distributed collection, (ii) metadata search and browsing, (iii) the classification of a set of output results, etc. These features make feasible the management of such a high scale production activity.

Both system (to support grid services) and application-level (for researchers and scientists) metadata often rely on relational and XML databases that can obviously be distributed and heterogeneous. Grid Services for database access and integration (Watson, 2003) are now capturing the interest of the grid community since they play a strategic role and provide added value to a grid production environment.

The biggest European Production Grid (EGEE) aims at providing researchers in academia and in-

dustry with access to major computing resources. The EGEE infrastructure, composed of standard PCs interconnected through high performance links on the Internet, is a suitable infrastructure for handling a large number of computational tasks. Research and development activities related to EGEE have generally focused on cpu-bound applications where data is stored in files.

Nowadays, in the EGEE project, a special attention has been paid to grid database access because there is an urgent need to interconnect pre-existing and independently operating databases. This requirement, addressed by the GRelC middleware, is common to many e-Science applications willing to use the EGEE grid environment; in particular, among the others, to the bioinformatics and astrophysics communities.

BACKGROUND

This Section introduces the Grid Database Access Service concept, describing the main existing approaches (front-end and embedded) and then dealing with two case studies: GRelC and OGSA-DAI. We will also highlight the main differences between the two research projects from several points of view: programming language, client support, security, data access and integration services, etc. Finally, we will briefly discuss the convergence issues related to the novel OGF DAIS specifications.

Grid Database Access Service: General Description

A Grid Database Access Service enables the virtualization of both relational and non- relational (i.e., XML-DBs) database systems within a Grid environment. It must provide secure, transparent, robust and efficient access to heterogeneous and distributed databases exposing standard interfaces to enable interoperability with other grid components and/or services.

Several research projects exploit the *service-in-the-middle* or *front-end* approach to provide such kind of functionalities, that is, they focus on the development of a transparent, secure and robust grid interface to existing DBMSs.

The rationale behind the *front-end* approach is strongly related to the development of a new data grid service:

- Providing a unified grid interface to data sources (both relational and XML);
- Loosely coupling with back-end data sources (no change to existing databases, i.e., both data and schema, is required);
- Concealing the DBMS heterogeneity at different levels;
- Hiding the physical database location;
- Providing a Web Service interface to address interoperability;
- Supporting grid security protocols such as GSI (Grid Security Infrastructure) (Tuecke, 2001) and Virtual Organization oriented role-based management.

On the contrary, vendor-specific products (i.e. Oracle 10g, 2005 and Oracle 11g, 2007) (Goyal and Lawande, 2006) basically exploit an embedded approach that is very different from the front-end one because it:

- Is basically tightly coupled with the vendor data management solution;
- Focuses on the development/enhancement of a particular DBMS;
- Provides a grid-enabled solution based on market needs/requirements and enterprise environments (intra-grid).

This work provides an architectural overview of the GRelC DAS, a grid database access service (exploiting the front-end approach) developed in the context of the GRelC Project and currently used for production/tutorial activities both in gLite and Globus based grid environments.

Grid Database Access Services: GRelC and OGSA-DAI

Since 2001, the need to access and integrate databases and to develop grid-enabled databases technologies has been identified as a challenging scientific activity. Research projects such as GRelC since 2001, (Aloisio, 2005) and OGSA-DAI since 2002, (Antonioletti, 2005; Karasavvas, 2005) have been providing solutions in this field addressing this important subject for the scientific community.

In this subsection, we discuss and highlight the main differences between the two research projects trying to take into account key issues such as: programming language, client support, security, data access and integration services, etc.

The Open Grid Services Architecture Data Access and Integration (OGSA-DAI) is a project (conceived by the UK Database Task Force) concerning the development of middleware to support access and integration of data from separate data sources via the grid. Moreover, it is also connected with international standardization activities related to Grid Data Management (Open Grid Forum DAIS-WG and the Globus Alliance).

The main differences between the two middleware (which both exploit a full service oriented approach), are listed below.

- *The programming language.* Java (OGSA-DAI) against C (GRelC) for grid services. Java Swing (OGSA-DAI) against Qt (GRelC) for graphical interfaces and JSP/Servlet (GRelC) for the GRelC Portal.
- *Client* and *administration support.* Currently, OGSA-DAI does not provide a CLI (Command Line Interface), whereas a complete *CLI* as well as a *data grid portal* solution is offered by GRelC to end-users and administrators.
- *Security (authorization).* The GRelC DAS provides both local and global (even combined) authorization by exploiting data

access policies on the GRelC DAS side (for local authorization) and VOMS (Virtual Organization Membership Service) (Alfieri 2003) attributes and roles (for global authorization) on the VOMS server side. OGSA-DAI VOMS support is now an ongoing activity of the OMII-Europe project; concerning local authorization the schema adopted by OGSA-DAI does not exploit data access policies defined at the grid service level, because it entirely relies on the back-end framework. However, the two services provide full GSI support.

- *Data access and integration services.* OGSA-DAI provides a distributed query processor for data integration (no constraints about database schemas). The GRelC project offers a grid enabled P2P solution (which is out of the scope of this work), providing data integration among different grid databases (an inherent constraint is that the grid-databases must have the same schema).

- *Key issue.* An extensible framework for OGSA-DAI leveraging the activity concept (unit of functionality) and allowing users to plug-in their own. An efficient data grid service (from a performance point of view) for GRelC, able to outperform direct database connection.

Finally, since the two teams are working on WS-DAI-compliant releases (OGF family of specifications for data access and integration), novel *interoperability schemas* and advanced data integration scenarios could be soon defined, deployed and tested. This convergence issue is fundamental for the development of higher and loosely coupled (with the underlying grid database management layer) data grid services.

MAIN FOCUS

In this section we introduce the GRelC Data Access Service, starting from a general description of the grid service, highlighting its main features and requirements and then discussing in detail architectural aspects (both in the large and in the small). Deployment on existing grids both for production and tutorial purposes is also discussed.

GRELC DAS Introduction and General Description

The GRelC DAS is a general purpose data grid service for database access, query and management. It was conceived within the context of the Grid Relational Catalog (GRelC) Project at the University of Salento, Italy. This service acts as a standard front-end for database access on the grid. It provides both basic and advanced primitives to transparently access, query, manage and interact with different data sources, concealing the back-end heterogeneity, Globus GSI and VOMS, security details, connection and other low level issues. It currently (i) exploits the Web-Services paradigm (WS-I based), (ii) it is compatible with Globus and gLite grid middleware/environments and (iii) it provides grid-enabled query mechanisms leveraging compression, chunking, prefetching and streaming to enhance performance on a wide area network/grid environment. Moreover, it supports both global (by means of VOMS) and local (on the GRelC DAS side) authorization levels, increasing flexibility, manageability and scalability in role and policy management.

The main goal of this data grid service is to efficiently, securely and transparently manage *databases on the grid*, across virtual organizations, with regard to modern grid standards and specifications (OGSA and WSRF compliant) as well as existing middleware such as Globus, gLite, etc.

GRELC DAS Architecture in the Large

The GRelC DAS architecture has been designed in order to satisfy the following requirements: transparency, efficiency, robustness, interoperability, extensibility and scalability. In the following we describe the GRelC DAS architecture, motivating specific choices that have been made in order to fulfill and completely address all of the cited service requirements.

The GRelC DAS Architecture in the large (see Fig. 1) is made up of the following components: (i) data sources, (ii) GRelC Data Access Service, (iii) Metadata Catalogue, (iv) Client applications and (v) GRelC Portal.

Let us now delve into details in order to fully understand the proposed grid database service solution.

- *Data sources:* represent the databases hosted by the end-users; legacy systems or new databases that need to be accessed in grid can be configured as grid-db (virtualized data sources) by means of a Grid DAS. Obviously, data sources can be very heterogeneous, in

nature, from different point of views: data model, data format, query language, etc. It is worth noting here that the GRelC DAS is able to manage several grid-databases at the same time. Moreover, the process regarding the *porting of an existing DB in grid* is not invasive and it is entirely automated from an end-user point of view. Data is left on the back-end system and just metadata information is imported within the GRelC DAS Metadata Catalogue. Since several DBMS must be supported, an extensible standard database access interface interacting with different back-ends, has been designed and developed (satisfying and addressing the transparency requirement with regard to heterogeneous data sources and uniform data access).

- *GRelC DAS:* in our architecture it represents the grid service providing efficient and secure access to data sources. It allows both user-centric and VO-centric database management in grid. Within the depicted architecture, the GRelC DAS acts as a standard interface to relational and non-relational (XML) data sources. In order to

Figure 1. GRelC DAS architecture in the large

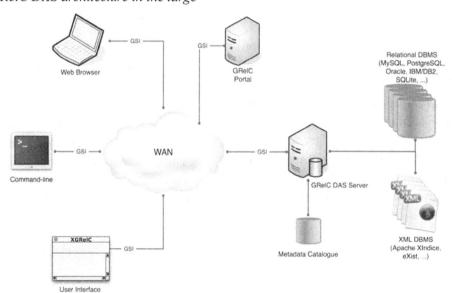

satisfy the interoperability requirement, the GRelC DAS leverages a Web Services oriented approach (WS-I). Moreover, new OGF specifications are also under development in order to provide a WS-DAI compliant interface. Efficiency is fully addressed by means of different query mechanisms and data delivery able to provide high level of performances. An intensive stress test demonstrated the robustness of the provided data grid service. Additional details about performance tests can be found in (Fiore, 2007).

- *Metadata Catalogue*: it is a system database (relational) for the GRelC DAS. It runs on top of Postgresql and stores information about users, VOs, data access control policies, grid-databases (DBMS type, port, login etc.), and so on. To further improve performances, the Metadata Catalogue can be managed through an embedded DBMS (i.e. SQLite). This way service robustness and reliability as well as performances are increased owing to the fact that the Metadata Catalogue does not rely on external DBMS servers.

- *Client Applications*: several software solutions are currently available client side for the *end-users* to access and interact with the GRelC DAS. Some examples are the Command Line and the XGRelC Graphical User Interface based on the Qt libraries. Moreover, developers can take advantage of a wide SDK for their applications. Support is currently provided for the Java, C and C++ programming languages.

- *GRelC Portal*: it represents an ubiquitous and seamless access interface to the GRelC DAS which does not require additional software installation and configuration. It entirely replaces the CLI, providing a high level interface, requiring just a browser for all of the data access and management activities. It allows managing users/ACL/ VOs and submitting queries via web as well

as checking GRelC DAS activity (through logging facility), etc. Access and location transparency as well as pervasiveness are intrinsically well solved and addressed by the adopted web approach and technologies. The portal is able to provide user-friendly access to GRelC DAS functionalities simplifying the interaction between the users and the data grid environment. It is worth noting here that, concerning grid database access, integration and management, no other grid software (at the time the paper is being written) is able to *fully* address via web, grid database issues, as in the case of the GRelC Portal. Moreover, contextual online-help and rich tutorial web pages are also available.

The GRelC data management solution is therefore not just a Grid DAS, but a complete data management environment trying to satisfy data-oriented user's requirements and needs.

GRELC DAS Architecture in the Small

Starting from the GRelC DAS architecture in the large, we now delve into details to provide a strong analysis and description (GRelC DAS architecture in the small) about internal components and modules. As shown in Fig. 2, the GRelC DAS is a very complex service composed of several modules. The most important ones are: GRelC DAS Front-end, User Management, Host Management, VO Management, Grid-DB Management, Data Access, Standard Data Access Interface Relational (SDAIR) and Standard Data Access Interface XML (SDAIX).

In the following we discuss them in detail describing technological, internal and security issues.

- The *GRelC DAS Front-end* (a WS-I based interface) listens for incoming client requests.

Figure 2. GRelC DAS architecture in the small

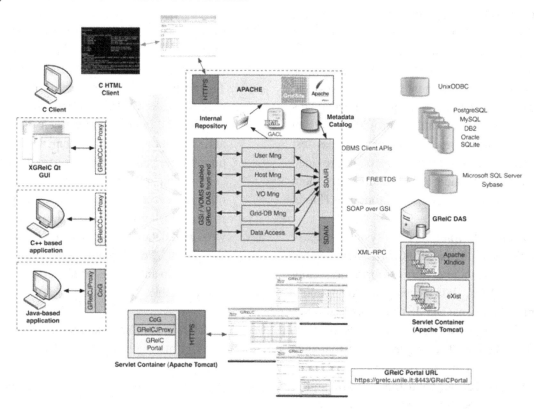

Moreover, (i) it provides a pre-threaded support to enhance performances (w.r.t. server response time, server throughput and scalability), (ii) it relies on the GSI protocol for security (mutual authentication and authorization processes based on X509v3 certificates and access control lists), and (iii) it supplies VOMS-based role management to enhance flexibility and scalability in a multi-VO grid environment (Fiore, 2007). Finally, it is responsible to setup the user's environment (i.e., the user's privileges mask);

- The *User Management* module provides support to add, delete and manage grid-users on the GRelC DAS side. Three main classes of users can be defined: end-user, grid-db-admin and super-user. Management of grid-user privileges is under the responsibility of this module;

- The *Host management* component provides a set of methods to manage both the list of machines on which physical databases are running and the DMS (Data Management System, e.g. RDBMS, XMLDB-Engine) instances deployed on those machines. A DMS is characterized by several parameters such as login, password, port, hostname etc. that must be provided to link the GRelC DAS to the data resources;

- The *VO-Management* module provides functionalities related to Virtual Organization and Grid-Database authorization. For instance, to enable a registered VO on a particular Grid-DB it is fundamental to define the (VO,Grid-DB) association. This means that (to preserve local policies against global ones) VO_1 users with VOMS-based privileges on Grid-DB$_1$ are not able to access Grid-DB$_1$ unless the (VO$_1$,Grid-DB$_1$)

association is locally defined on the GRelC DAS side by exploiting this module;

- The *Grid-DB Management* component provides several functionalities connected with the management (create, drop, update and register) of Grid-Database/Logical Data Space. By our definition, a Grid-Database *is a collection of one or more databases logically interrelated (distributed over a grid environment) which can also be heterogeneous and contain replicas, accessible through a Grid-DataBase Management System front-end. It represents an extension and a virtualization of the Database concept in a grid environment"*. *Create, drop* and *update* apply only to the Logical Data Space (defined as *"the virtualized space where a Grid-Database can be managed by the Grid-DBMS"*) whereas the register operation applies to the Grid-Database because it represents the mapping between the Logical Data Space and the physical data source (it also implies that all of the metadata belonging to the data source schema are automatically imported into the GRelC DAS Metadata Catalogue). This functionality allows porting one-shot in grid a legacy database without knowing anything about its data contents and schema;

- The *Data Access* component provides functionalities connected with the access to the data source. The most important one is the Query Management that supplies users with several kinds of grid-enabled queries exploiting compression, chunking, pre-fetching and streaming to address efficiency and extreme performances in grid environments. Additional details, comparisons and tests related to the performances of the queries provided by the GRelC DAS can be found in (Fiore, 2007);

- The *Standard Data Access Interface Relational (SDAIR)* provides transparent and uniform access to relational databases

through a plug-in architecture based on dynamic libraries. Currently, available plug-ins are related to the following DMBSs: PostgreSQL, MySQL, SQLite, Unix ODBC, IBM/DB2, Oracle, Microsoft SQL Server (via FreeTDS). This library is equally used both for application-level and system-level databases. The provided APIs allow performing on the relational back-end system the following actions: bind and unbind to a database, query submission, transaction management, concurrency management as well as access to metadata schema information (tables, attributes, constraints, data types, etc.);

- The *Standard Data Access Interface XML (SDAIX)* provides transparent and uniform access to XML databases through the same type of plug-in based architecture. Available plug-ins are related to eXist and XIndice (via XML-RPC) and libxml2-based documents. In this case the available APIs allow carrying out on the XML data sources query submission, document update, insert, delete, etc.

It is worth noting here that *logging* activities are performed within all of the described modules/ libraries in order to keep track of all of the operations carried out server-side by the users. Grid-DB administrators can set the logging level (debug, production, test, verbose) and client commands to remotely check various logs are also available for administration. All of the described modules are written in C for performance reasons and user support concerning the SDK is currently available for C, C++ and Java developers.

Deployment on Existing Grids

Nowadays the GRelC DAS is deployed on several grids:

- The Grid INFN virtual Laboratory for Dissemination Activities (GILDA) t-infrastructure for training activities. Launched in 2004 by the EGEE partner INFN, GILDA (Andronico, Barbera et al., 2005) is a fully operational Grid testbed devoted to dissemination activities; it provides both users and system administrators with a practical hands-on approach to gLite based Grid systems. Within the EGEE context, GILDA acts as a crucial component of the project's t-Infrastructure (training infrastructure) programme, helping to pass on knowledge and experience, as well as computing resources, to the scientific community and Industry. A training version of the GRelC DAS is already available for tutorial activities on the Grid CT Wiki;

- The Euro-Mediterranean Centre for Climate Change for ES-Metadata management, searching and browsing. Indeed, climate modelling applications require the management of huge amounts of data (on the order of petabytes) (i) heterogeneous with regard to the format (ii) that must be arranged in optimized hierarchical storage systems and (iii) need to be efficiently classified to simplify data discovery exploiting metadata searching;

- LIBI National project for bioinformatics database access and management. The Italian FIRB LIBI ("International Laboratory for Bioinformatics") project, funded by the Italian Ministry for the University and Research, proposes the setting up of an advanced Bioinformatics and Computational Biology Laboratory focusing on the central activities of basic and applied research in modern Biology and Biotechnologies.

FUTURE TRENDS

Data and Computational Grids cope with different issues, which span management of remote resources, job submission, job monitoring, file transfer, database/storage access, etc. Historically there was a different interest from scientists, researchers, end-users and commercial vendors on these two faces of the same medal. While at the beginning more efforts and interest were mainly devoted to Computational Grids, in the last years Data Grids have been deserving the required attention being a crucial point for academic and industrial partners. Since 2002, at first GGF (Paton, 2002; Raman, 2002) and EGA, and now OGF addressed standardization on grid data management topics releasing a set of specifications concerning Data Format Description Language, Grid File System, Grid Storage Management, GridFTP, etc. Interesting activities about Database Access and Integration recently (Antonioletti, 2006) produced the WS-DAI (Web Service Data Access and Integration) family of specifications (WS-DAI, WS-DAIR and WS-DAIX) which defines a set of web service interfaces to relational or XML data resources.

The keyword highlighted by this standardization activity is *interoperability*, which can be achieved by different grid middleware providing reference implementations of these specifications.

This way, high level data grid services such as data integration services or grid dataflow engines could:

- Exploit an underlying Grid DAS without knowing its internal details;
- Work simultaneously with different Grid DAS (without making any changes to the software);
- Be developed by third-party research teams without tightly coupling the software;
- Really provide data interoperability scenarios in grid contexts.

The GRelC Team is currently testing and certifying a WS-DAI compliant production release of the GRelC DAS (converging towards this standard), since interoperability is one of the main requirements addressed by the GRelC Project.

CONCLUSION

Data Grid middleware provides a set of services to access, share, manage and integrate massive amounts of data distributed across heterogeneous and geographically dispersed grid resources. We presented an architectural overview of the GRelC DAS (a data grid service developed within the context of the GRelC project) describing its internal modules and libraries, highlighting its main features and back-end support for relational and XML data sources. Moreover, information about the current deployment on different Grid Environments was also reported to provide some examples related to the current end-user communities, the dissemination efforts, the integration with gLite based releases and so on. In the future, the GRelC DAS will move towards the emerging WS-DAI family of specifications to address interoperability.

REFERENCES

Alfieri, R., Cecchini, R., Fiaschini, V., Dell'Agnello, L., Frohner, A., Gianoli, A., etl al. (2003). VOMS, an Authorization System for Virtual Organizations. In *Proceedings of the 1st European Across Grids Conference* (pp. 33-40).

Aloisio, G., Cafaro, M., Fiore, S., & Mirto, M. (2005). The grid relational catalog project. In L. Grandinetti (Ed.), *Advances in parallel computing, "Grid computing: The new frontiers of high performance computing"* (pp. 129-155). Elsevier.

Andronico, G., Ardizzone, V., Barbera, R., Catania, R., Carrieri, A., Falzone, A., et al. (2005). In *TRIDENTCOM 2005. GILDA: The Grid INFN Virtual Laboratory for Dissemination Activities.* (pp. 304-305).

Antonioletti, M., Krause, A., Paton, N. W., Eisenberg, A., Laws, S., Malaika, S., et al. (2006). The WS-DAI family of specifications for web service data access and integration. *ACM SIGMOD Record, 35*(1), 48-55.

Antonioletti, M., Atkinson, M. P., Baxter, R., Borley, A., Chue Hong, N. P., Collins, B., et al. (2005). The design and implementation of grid database services in OGSA-DAI. *Concurrency and Computation: Practice and Experience, 17*(2-4), 357-376.

Berman, F., Fox, G., & Hey, T. (2003). The grid: Past, present, future. In F. Berman, G.C. Fox, & A.J.G. Hey (Eds.), *Grid computing* (pp. 51-63). New York: Wiley.

Fiore, S., Negro, A., Vadacca, S., Cafaro, M., Mirto, M., & Aloisio G. (2007). Advanced Grid database management with the GRelC data access service. In *Proceedings of the 5th International Symposium on Parallel and Distributed Processing and Applications (ISPA07)* (LNCS 4742, 683-694).

Fiore, S., Cafaro, M., Negro, A., Vadacca, S., Aloisio, G., Barbera, R., et al. (2007). GRelC DAS: A Grid-DB access service for gLite based production Grids. In *IEEE Proceedings of the Fourth International Workshop on Emerging Technologies for Next-generation GRID (ETNGRID 2007).* (pp. 261-266).

Goyal, B., & Lawande, S. (2006). Enterprise grid computing with Oracle. New York: McGraw-Hill.

Karasavvas, K., Antonioletti, M., Atkinson, M. P., Chue Hong, N. P., Sugden, T., Hume, A. C., et al. (2005). Introduction to OGSA-DAI Services (LNCS 3458 1-12).

Paton, N. W., Atkinson, M. P., Dialani, V., Pearson, D., Storey, T., & Watson, P. (2002). *Database access and integration service on the Grid.* Global Grid Forum OGSA-DAIS WG.

Tuecke S. (2001). Grid security infrastructure (GSI) roadmap. Retrieved from, http://www.

gridforum.org/security/ggf1_-200103/drafts/ draft-ggf-gsi-roadmap-02.pdf

Raman, V., Narang, I., Crone, C., Haas, L., Malaika, S., Mukai, T., et al. 2002). *Data access and management services on Grid.* Global Grid Forum 5.

Watson, P. (2003). Databases and the Grid. In F. Berman, G.C. Fox, & A.J.G. Hey (Eds.), *Grid computing* (pp. 363-384). New York: Wiley.

KEY TERMS AND DEFINITIONS

Combined Authorization: The authorization process performed on the Grid DAS side exploiting both Global and Local Authorizations to provide the maximum level of scalability, flexibility and manageability.

Global Authorization: The authorization process performed on the Grid DAS side exploiting Community Authorization extensions (VO-based) present into the user's credentials (e.g., proxy).

Grid-DBMS: A distributed system which automatically, transparently and dynamically manage Data Resources, according to the Grid state, in order to maintain a desired performance level. It must offer an efficient, robust, intelligent, transparent, uniform access to Grid-Databases by means of a Grid Data Access Service (Grid-DAS) interface.

Grid Data Access Service: The Grid-DBMS virtualized access interface to Grid-Databases.

Grid-Database: A collection of one or more databases logically interrelated (distributed over a grid environment) which can also be heterogeneous and contain replica, accessible through a Grid-DBMS front end. It represents an extension and a virtualization of the Database concept in a grid environment.

Local Authorization: The authorization process performed on the Grid DAS side exploiting local policies/roles stored on the Grid-DAS Metadata Catalogue and managed by the Grid DAS administrator.

Logical Data Space: The virtualized space where a Grid-Database is managed by the Grid-DBMS.

Chapter XI
Adaptive Resource Management in Grid Environment

Man Wang
Tsinghua University, China

Zhihui Du
Tsinghua University, China

Zhili Cheng
Tsinghua University, China

ABSTRACT

Resource Management System (RMS), which manages the Grid resources and matches the applications' requests to the proper resources, is one of the most important and complex parts in Grid systems. In fact, because of the complexity of Grid environment, one resource management approach alone can not satisfy different applications' requirement. Therefore, a novel Adaptive Resource Management (ARM) mechanism is provided here. This mechanism is based on multidimensional Grid QoS, which dynamically organizes Grid resources into Task Resources for feasible distribution. Moreover, this management mechanism can select appropriate management approach according to different applications' requirements, which is well adapted to dynamic Grid environment.

INTRODUCTION

All the facilities, which can be shared and utilized in Grid environment, can be viewed as Grid resources, such as machines, services, and networks. The most predominant quality of Grid is the seamless resources sharing and cooperation in large distributed areas. Central to the Grid system is the **Resource Management System (RMS)**, which manages the Grid resources and matches the applications' requests to the proper resources.

At this point, the most common purposes of **Resource Management System** in such a complex environment can be separated into two categories: system-centric policy and user-centric policy. The former attempts to optimize system-wide measurement of performance, while the latter concentrates on delivering maximum utility to the users of the system based on their QoS requirements (Buyya, et al, 2005).

Generally, the functions of RMS include resource storage, resource organization/ discovering, **resource matching**/allocating, and resource monitoring/recovery. According to Ding (2002), most RMSs have a common service process as follows. When an application makes requests, the RMS adds them into the request queue and then schedules them to different RM (Resource Management) servers for mapping. After that, the RM servers discover the proper resources and establish the relationship between the requests and the resources. Finally, the discovered resources are available to the application.

The literature records a great deal of research on RMS since the onset of Grid research. In Grid computing architecture, the Grid resource management component (Foster and Kesselman, 2004; Krauter, 2002) is a fundamental **middleware**. Being widely adopted by the industry to build a Grid, the **Globus Toolkit** provides a set of components for Grid control, management, and execution. The Globus Resource Management and Allocation (GRAM) component is a classic resource management example and the Monitoring and Discovery Service (MDS) component facilitates the selection of Grid resources. Some other systems, such as DI-Gruber (Dumitrescu, 2005), utilize Globus components.

Although much contributing work has been done in this field, an efficient RMS in Grid environment is still a challenging and important problem due to the following reasons:

1. Resources in Grid environment are geographically distributed, and in most cases they belong to different autonomously administered domains, which use resource management approaches and control models.
2. Resources in Grid environment are heterogeneous. One level resource management can not control all of them well.
3. Resources in Grid are dynamic. For example, the resources' joining and leaving are dynamic, and the current resources performance is changing.

As a result, in the last few years, along with the development of application requests, the **adaptive resource management** has become popular. Duran-Limon (2004) points out two aspects— openness and ease of use, which are essential to achieving adaptive resource management in middleware. However, some contributing work (Dai, 2008; Kyong, 2006) have been done in this field.

BACKGROUND

Currently, there are different research interests and technologies in RMS as follows :

Resource Description

From Ian Foster (2004) point of view, the primary goal of Grid resource management is to establish a common proposal, through which the resource provider agrees to provide the ability for resource consumers to execute some tasks. For resource consumers, they should provide their requests based on resources' characters. As a result, there should be some rules for resource description. The widely used languages for resource description in Grid environment are RSL (Resource Specification Language) in **Globus Toolkit** and ClassAds in Condor. In industry, as the basic modeling technology used for abstracting and managing resources in the Grid, CIM (Common Information Model) will hold the definitions of the resources managed in the Grid.

Resource Orgnization and Discovery

For efficient utilization, it is necessary to organize the physical resources into some logical level, and the conception of virtual organization (VO) is established. A **virtual organization** (VO) is a set of individuals and/or institutions defined by certain sharing rules form, such as direct access to computers, software, data, services, and other resources, as required by a range of collaborative problem-solving and resource-brokering strategies emerging in industry, science, and engineering. This sharing is, necessarily, highly controlled, with resource providers and consumers defining clearly and carefully just what is shared, who is allowed to share, and the conditions under which sharing occurs (Foster, 2001).

In Grid environment, when requests come from Grid entities, the Grid Information Service (GIS), a Grid **middleware** component which maintains information about all resources in a VO, is responsible for launching resource discovery and lookup. There are several solutions in different Grid projects such as Globus and Legion to implement such information services. MDS-2 (Monitoring and Discovery Service) (Czajkowski, 2001) is one solution provided by **Globus Toolkit.** In the work of Keung(2003), the performance of MDS-2 is valued, and a better understanding of the performance of the GRIS (Grid Resource Information Service) and subsequently the GIIS (Grid Index Information Service) leads to a more standard way of formalizing the performance of a Grid Information Service.

Resource Mangement Model

Unlike conventional resource management model, which takes a system-centric approach, new economic models based on microeconomic and macroeconomic principles for resource management have been proposed (Huhns & Stephens, 2000). According to Buyya (2005), these models, such as commodity market models, posted price models, and bargaining models, can "place the power in the hands of both resource owners and users—they can make their own decisions to maximize the utility gained and profit".

Generally, most existing Grid RMS typically addresses these requests through a two-tiered approach, such as Digruber (Dumitrescu, 2005). But in large scale system, large message traffic between resource managers may occur. Moreover, it is not easy to define and implement hierarchical management and operational policies. As a result, some literatures (El-Darieb& Krishnamurthy, 2006) provide a more scalable and robust Grid resource management model.

Quality of Service

The Grid **QoS** research took place around the beginning of this century. Along with the development of Grid resource management, Grid QoS plays a more and more significant role. OGSA (open Grid services architecture) (Foster, 2002), OGSI (open Grid services infrastructure) (Tuecke, 2003) and WS-resource framework (WSRF) (Czajkowski, 2004) require all services should provide the seamless QoS. Many problems in Grid resource management can be concluded to the research of QoS. QoS management covers a range of different activities, from resource selection and allocation to resource release. Regardless of the context, a QoS management system should address the following needs (Al-Ali, 2003):

- Specifying QoS requirements.
- Mapping QoS requirements to resource capabilities.
- Negotiating QoS with resource owners, where a requirement cannot be exactly met.

- Establishing SLA (Service Level Agreement) with clients.
- Reserving and allocating resources.
- Monitoring parameters associated with a QoS session.
- Adapting to varying resource quality characteristics.
- Terminating QoS sessions.

Foster (1999) proposed the Globus Architecture for Reservation and Allocation (GARA) to enable programmers and users to specify and manage end-to-end QoS for Grid-based applications. It also provides a uniform mechanism for making QoS reservations for different types of Grid resources like processors, networks and storage devices. In Khanli and Analoui (2006), a novel solution to guarantee the Quality of Service in Grid computing environment by using Active Database is presented. It accommodates some actions to be down automatically by inserting, deleting or updating transactions. As a result the best matching is obtained by using the most up to date information.

MAIN FOCUS

In fact, because of the dynamic character and complexity of Gird environment, one resource management approach alone can not satisfy different applications requirement. Therefore, a novel **Adaptive Resource Management** (ARM) mechanism is provided here. Based on different applications' requirements, the mechanism selects the management approaches in different levels.

Figure 1 shows the ARM mechanism. In this mechanism, the resources in grid are organized into three different levels: Grid resources, **Computing Unit** (CU) and Task Resource.

A CU (Computing Unit) is a group of resources which have close physical relationship with each other. Furthermore, usually a CU can be regarded as the smallest unit which can perform certain functions required by an application. For example, a computer with services deployed on it can be viewed as a CU because it can execute an application or part of it. A CU is a physical/positional conception rather than a logical conception. The CUs in the distributed systems are heterogeneous, and for different CUs the hardware environments, processing abilities are different.

Task Resource is also a group of resources. Different from Computing Unit, it combines the CUs from a logical level. A Task Resource is mainly responsible for an application/tasks execution.

Based on the general requests of an application, multidimensional Grid QoS is described. For simplicity, we separated an application's requests into 3-dimentions, and the relevant **multidimensional Grid QoS** includes:

1. **Time.** The time T includes two categories, one is the application's response time RT and the other is the application's execution time ET. If RT does not meet the application's requests, RT_QoS=0. If RT meets the application's requests, the smaller the RT is, the bigger the RT_QoS is. ET_QoS has the similar definition.

2. **Cost.** The Cost C here is the total cost of resources when an application is completed successfully. If the C does not meet the application's requests, C_QoS=0. On the contrary, the value of C_QoS increases along with the decrease of the value of C.

3. **Satisfaction.** The Satisfaction S means the user's satisfaction with the final results without considering the time and cost. The accuracy of the results is one example. S_QoS is in direct ratio to S.

Then, the total **multidimensional Grid QoS** MGQ is calculated as formula 1:

Figure 1. Adaptive resource management mechanism

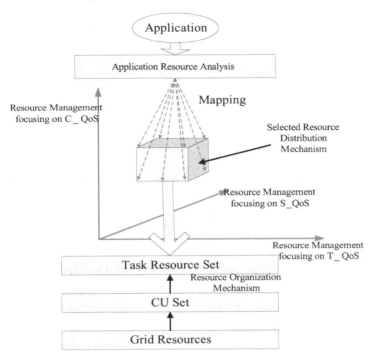

$$MGQ = p_1 \times (RT\_QoS + ET\_QoS) + p_2 \times C\_QoS + p_3 \times S\_QoS \qquad (1)$$

where, $p_1 + p_2 + p_3 = 1$ and $p_1, p_2, p_3 >= 0$.

Adaptive Resource Management is focused on applications, and its key idea is that, according to the application's different QoS requests, different management approaches are utilized. In this paper, the ARM mechanism can be viewed as a 3-dimensional space, and each dimension is related to one QoS request defined in this paper. In fact, each application's requests are always in a range rather than a point. As a result, based on an application's requests range, a "Cube" can be found in the ARM space. After that, the relevant approach, held by different RM server, can be used to do the resource management work.

Generally, the serving process of ARM mechanism includes four steps:

- **Step 1:** Analyze the applications' requests, and transfer them into three dimensions QoS.

- **Step 2:** According to the QoS, map the requests into the management mechanism space, select the proper approach "Cube" and then allocate the requests into the relevant RM server.

- **Step 3:** In the RM server based on the selected "Cube", guided by the selected approach, find the candidate Task Resources, organized by Resource Organization Mechanism for the application.

- **Step 4:** Guided by the selected approach, select the optimal Task Resource for the application by Resource Distribution Mechanism, and also save several Task Resources for backup.

The details are explained as follows:

1. Analyze the applications' requirements, and transfer them into three dimensions QoS. The ARM mechanism proposed in this paper is focused on the application level, i.e,

113

resource management is based on different applications' different requests. So, the first step is to transfer applications' requests into the form accepted by ARM. Based on the QoS, the Application Resource Analysis part separates the requests into Time, Cost, and Satisfaction three dimensions, and sets the coefficient p_1, p_2, p_3 according to users' requests. For example, in telescope data processing, due to the large amount of data waiting to be processed, the Time request has highest priority, and the p_1 can be set bigger than p_2 and p_3. After this step, the application's QoS requests can be defined in a certain range, which is the precondition of selecting the resource distribution mechanism.

2. The relationship among Cubes, ARM space, the management approaches and RM servers.

    The ARM space can be viewed as a whole Cube and the space can also be separated as several Cubes. How to separate the ARM space into different Cubes depends on the applications in the Grid system. No matter how "big" a Cube is, only one management approach is provided for it. Moreover, it is easy to separate a huge Cube into several smaller ones and implement them with new approaches, just according to the applications.

    An example is provided here. Under the military background, Information Grid plays an important role. There are several kinds of applications, such as making strategies, executing commands and supporting logistics. Each dimension of QoS can be separated into low, middle and high three parts. Then, based on this QoS request, the ARM space can be separated into 27 Cubes. Accordingly for the application that requires high RT_QoS, ET_QoS, C_QoS, S_Qos can use the method, including resource preemption, resource reservation, and more

accurate scheduling algorithm, to ensure the QoS requirement. On the contrary, for the application that requires low RT_QoS, ET_QoS, C_QoS, S_Qos, some simple methods like random resource selection could be applied to assign the resources.

The RM servers implement the concrete approaches. In the former RMS, RM servers are mostly homogeneous. Here, in ARM mechanism, the relationship between RM servers and management approaches are many-to-one. That is, one RM server implements one management approach, while a same approach can be adopted by more than one RM servers.

3. Task Resources organization mechanism.

    In the ARM mechanism, the resources are organized in three levels, as Figure 2 shows. The Task Resources are configured dynamically according to different applications' requests.

In Grid environment, many resources can offer the same effect and different groups of resources can all satisfy an application's requests. A Task Resource is such a set of resources that can meet all requests of an application. Obviously, more than one Task Resources can support the execution of an application. Therefore, a particular purpose of ARM is to provide applications a group of Task Resources, one of which will be chosen and the rest serve as backups. The Resources Organization mechanism is responsible for organizing the distributed CUs into Task Resources. There are two tables maintained in ARM for organization. The first is CU table. This table is used to record the Grid Resources based on different CUs. Because CU is a physical conception, this table is not changed too much. The other table is for concrete applications. Once an application comes, the Resource Organization mechanism adds a row for it, and based on the selected approach, combines several available CUs to cover all required resources to form diversity Task Resources. The

Figure 2. Resource organization level

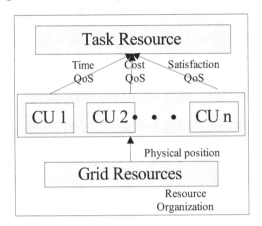

relevant items in the table will be deleted right after the application completion.

Compared with other RMS, the AMR presented in this paper has the following characters.

1. The mechanism organizes the grid resources in a three-level way, which makes the matching process application-specific.
2. The mechanism offers an open and easy way for users to find more appropriate management approach for their applications. Most current ARM systems provide the ability, such as variable parameters. However, the mechanism proposed here provides many approaches for different applications, which is more "adaptive".
3. Grid QoS is an important research field. This mechanism introduces 3-dimentional QoS to classify the application, which can satisfy the QoS quickly.

FUTURE TRENDS

Although there are many literatures working on this area, there is still plenty of challenging work to do. As far as we could see, the future of Grid resource management will focus on three topics:

- How can resource management preserve the autonomy of organizations hosting the resources?
- How can resource management mechanisms be more scalable?
- How can resource management deal with dynamic situation, such as recourses' joining or leaving dynamically?

CONCLUSION

This paper proposes the definition of resource management in Grid environment, reviews hotspots in this area, and presents Adaptive Resource Management (ARM) mechanism. This mechanism is based on multidimensional Grid QoS, which dynamically organizes Grid resources into Task Resources for feasible distribution. This management mechanism can select appropriate management approach according to different applications' requirements, which is well adapted to dynamic Grid environment.

REFERENCES

Al-Ali, J., Hafid, A., Rana, F., & Walker, W. (2003). QoS adaptation in service oriented grids. In *Proceedings of the 1st International Workshop on Middleware for Grid Computing (MGC 2003)*, Brazil. Retrieved from, http://mgc2003.lncc.br/cam_ready/MGC289_final.pdf

Buyya, R., Abramson, D., & Venugopal, S.(2005). The grid economy. *In Proceedings of the IEEE, 93*(3), 698 – 714.

Czajkowski, K., Ferguson, DF., Foster, I., Frey, J., Graham, S., Seduknin, I., et al. (2004). *The WS-resource framework* (Version 1.0). Retrieved from, http://www-106.ibm.com/developerworks/library/ws-resource/ws-wsrf.pdf

Czajkowski, K., Fitzgerald, S., Foster, I., & Kesselman, C. (2001). Grid information services for distributed resource sharing. *In Proceedings of the 10th IEEE Int. Symposium on High-performance distributed computing (HPDC-10)* (pp. 181-194), San Francisco, CA.

Dai, Y.S., Xie, M., & Poh, K.L. (2008). Availability modeling and cost optimization for the Grid resource management system. *Systems, Man and Cybernetics, Part A, IEEE Transactions, 38*(1), 170-179.

Ding, Q., Chen, G. L., & Gu, J. (2002). A unified resource mapping strategy in computational Grid environments. *J. Softw., 13*(7), 1303-1308.

Dumitrescu, C., Raicu, I., & Foster, I. (2005). DI-GRUBER: A distributed approach for grid resource brokering. In *Proceedings of the International Conference on High Performance Computing, Networking and Storage.*

Duran-Limon, H.A., Blair, G.S., & Coulson, G. (2004). Adaptive resource management in middleware: A survey. *Distributed Systems Online, 5*(7).

El-Darieb, M., & Krishnamurthy, D. (2006). A scalable wide-area Grid resource management framework. *International Conference on Networking and Services (ICNS'06)* (pp. 76).

Foster, I., & Kesselman, C. (1999). A distributed resource management architecture that supports advance reservation and co-allocation. In *Proceedings Of The International Workshop on Quality of Service* (pp. 27-36).

Foster, I., Kesselman, C., & Tuecke, S. (2001). The anatomy of the Grid: enabling scalable virtual organizations. *Int. J. Supercomput. Appl., 15*(3), 200-222

Foster, I., Kesselman, C., Nick, JM., & Tuecke, S.(2002). *The physiology of the Grid: An open Grid services architecture for distributed systems integration.* Retrieved from, http: //www.gridforum. org/ogsi-wg/drafts/ogsa_draft2.9_2002-06-22. pdf

Foster, I., & Kesselman, C. (2004). *The Grid 2: Blueprint for a new computing infrastructure.* San Fransisco: Morgan Kaufmann Publishers.

Huhns, M. & Stephens, L. (2000). Mutiagent systems and societies of agents. In G. Weiss (Ed.) *Multiagent systems.* Cambridge, MA: The MIT Press.

Keung, H.N.L.C., Dyson, J.R.D., Jarvis, S.A., & Nudd, G.R.(2003). Performance evaluation of a Grid resource monitoring and discovery service. *Software, IEEE Proceedings, 150*(4), 243-251.

Khanli, L.M., & Analoui, M. (2006). Grid-JQA a new architecture for QoS-guaranteed Grid computing system. In *Proceedings of the 14th Euromicro International Conference on Parallel, Distributed, and Network-Based Processing (PDP'06)* (pp. 268-271).

Krauter, K., Buyya, R., & Maheswaran, M. (2002). A taxonomy and survey of Grid resource management systems for distributed computing. *International Journal of Software: Practice and Experience, 32*(2), 135-164.

Kyong, H. K., Buyya, R., & Kim, J.(2006). Imprecise computation Grid application model for flexible market-based resource allocation. *Cluster Computing and the Grid, 2006. CCGRID 06. Sixth IEEE International Symposium on Volume 1, 5.*

The Globus Toolkit (n.d.). Retrieved from, http:// www.globus.org/toolkit/

Tuecke, S., Czajkowski, K., Foster, I., Frey, J., Graham, S., Kesselman, C., et al. (2003). Open grid services infrastructure (OGSI) Version 1.0. Retreived from, http://forge.gridforum.org/projects/ ggf-editor/document/draft-ogsi-service-1/en/1

KEY TERMS AND DEFINITIONS

Computing Unit: A group of grid resources having close physical relationship with each other and can be used as a basic unit for executing a task.

GARA: Globus Architecture for Reservation and Allocation, which enables programmers and users to specify and manage end-to-end QoS for Grid-based applications. It also provides a uniform mechanism for making QoS reservations for different types of Grid resources, such as processors, networks and storage devices.

Grid Resource: All abilities which can be shared and used in Grid environment.

GRAM: Globus Resource Management and Allocation, a component that allows remote user jobs to request another system's resources and supports status monitoring of remote jobs.

QoS in Grid Resource Management: A set of measurements and differentiations on the collective behavior of services in grid resource management.

Resource Management: The way of providing grid resources to users by satisfying both requests of users and providers.

Task Resource: A group of CUs which cover all the resources required by a certain application.

Chapter XII
Bio–Inspired Grid Resource Management

Vineet R. Khare
Cranfield University, UK

Frank Zhigang Wang
Cranfield University, UK

ABSTRACT

The need for a dynamic and scalable expansion of the grid infrastructure and resources and other scalability issues in terms of execution efficiency and fault tolerance present centralized management techniques with numerous difficulties. In this chapter we present the case for biologically inspired grid resource management techniques that are decentralized and self organized in nature. To achieve the desired de-centralized resource management, these techniques model the self-organization observed in many natural complex adaptive systems. Using a few representative techniques, we review the literature on Bio-inspired Grid Resource Management. Based on this review we conclude that many such techniques have been successfully applied to resource discovery, service placement, scheduling and load balancing.

INTRODUCTION

In computational grids resources vary in complexity and type. They may include computers, storage space, sensors, software applications, and data. A Grid is a collection of heterogeneous resources and can be characterized by its large scale and dynamic nature. In most existing grid systems, management of these resources is centralized. Due to the heterogeneous and dynamic nature of grid resources, fluctuating resource demands, and the presence of different control policies in different domains the centralized management has its limitations. Further, the need for a dynamic and scalable expansion of the grid infrastructure and resources and other scalability issues in terms of execution efficiency and fault tolerance present these centralized management techniques with numerous difficulties. These limitations have been identified by many researchers (Iamnitchi and Foster, 2001; Lamehamedi, 2005; Pavani and Waldman, 2006; Wolski et al., 2003) in the past.

Resource discovery, for instance, is significantly difficult for traditional centralized services because resources are owned by various administrative organizations and are shared under local policies that define which resources are to be shared when (e.g. dependent on local computing load) and with whom (Iamnitchi and Foster, 2001). Lamehamedi (2005) notes that, in most cases, system administrators are responsible for installing software, granting and controlling access to resources. It is argued that such configurations are not suitable for dynamic and scalable expansion of the grid infrastructure and resources. Addition of new nodes is dependant on the intervention of system administrators. Similarly, a node cannot leave without system pre-configuration. Enabling dynamic node addition and deletion while providing efficient access to resources on the data grid presents considerable challenges to system designers. Centralized grid resources allocation and scheduling is also proving to be a performance bottleneck. It is argued (Wolski et al., 2003) that it is not a scalable solution either in terms of execution efficiency (the resource broker or scheduler can become a bottleneck) or fault tolerance (the allocation mechanism is a single point of failure).

These traditional and centralized resource management mechanisms work well within single grid clusters but are not suitable for multiple Grids (Ching et al., 2002). Provision of services across such platforms requires a distributed resource management mechanism with capabilities beyond traditional centralized management. A self-organized approach to resource management

can provide the infrastructure for a reliable and a consistent Grid.

BACKGROUND

The universe is full of systems that are complex and constantly adapting to their environment. Examples of these systems include human economies, the ecosystem and the weather system. These, so called complex adaptive systems (CAS), are characterised by the absence of a centralised control, dynamism and large scales. The components (or agents) of these complex adaptive systems interact with each other according to some simple local rules. These simple interactions, however, result in self-organisation and complex behaviors.

The Grid As A Complex Adaptive System

A grid computing system can also be seen as a CAS. It is by nature a complex combination of hardware, software and network components. Geographically distributed nature of resources that make up the grid infrastructure, along with their heterogeneity and different control policies in different domains, make the availability of these resources dynamic and conditional upon local constraints. The consumers of the resources are the users who have specific requirements which are expressed in terms of CPU speed, storage capacity, network bandwidth, etc. To achieve the desired de-centralized resource management the self-organization observed in many natural CAS systems can be modeled in the context of grid computing.

Emergent Behavior in Nature

Foraging in ant and bee colonies, predator and obstacle avoidance in fish schools, bird flocks and animal herds are examples of *emergent behavior* observed in nature. The behavior of individual creatures based on simple rules gives rise to a richer, more complex collective behavior. These emergent behaviors, observed in nature, have been modeled in the past to explore collective (or distributed) problem solving without centralized control or the provision of a global model. These models are collectively called Swarm Intelligence (SI) models and are characterized by their decentralized and self-organizing nature. Like their natural counterparts, these are made of simple agents that interact with each other and with their environment based on some simple local rules to produce complex global behaviors. Examples of these models include ant colony optimization (Dorigo and Stutzle, 2004), particle swarm optimization (Kennedy and Eberhart, 1995) and flocking simulations (Reynolds, 1987).

MAIN FOCUS

Ant Colony Optimization

In this chapter we shall be focusing on the Ant Colony Optimization (ACO), which has received a great deal of attention in the context of grid resource management recently. The ACO meta-heuristic was first described by Dorigo (1992) as a technique to solve the traveling salesman problem, and was inspired by the ability of real ant colonies to efficiently organize the foraging behavior of the colony using chemical pheromone trails as a means of communication between the ants. ACO algorithms have since been widely employed on many other combinatorial optimization problems including routing, frequency assignment and scheduling problems (Dorigo and Stutzle, 2004).

Making use of evaporating pheromone trails, an ACO algorithm can adapt to transient conditions like network congestion, node failure, link failure etc. The use of the distributed agents (ants) working in parallel and independent of each other obviates the need to maintain global state across

all nodes, which might not available due to the scale and dynamism of the task. This distributed and self-organizing nature of ACO algorithms makes them particularly suited for grid resource management. Many researchers have identified this match and have used ACO for grid resource management. In the following we present some examples of distributed and self-organized resource management (DSRM) techniques from the literature.

ARMS: An Agent-Based Resource Management System

ARMS (Cao et al., 2002) utilizes an agent-based methodology for distributed resource management. Although it does not use an ACO algorithm, we present it here for two reasons – (1) it is a distributed resource management mechanism and (2) it is used as a framework for another application, presented later, that uses ACO for load balancing (Cao, 2004). It consists of a hierarchy of identical agents with same functionality. Each agent is viewed as a representative of a grid-resource at a meta-level of resource management and contributes to both – service advertisement and service discovery. The service information corresponding to each grid resource can be advertised within the agent hierarchy and agents can cooperate with each other to discover available resource. This is achieved by maintaining various Agent Capability Tables (ACTs) that contain service information of other agents. Separate ACTs can be used to record service information of local resources and similar information received from lower agents and higher agent in the hierarchy. These ACTs are kept coherent either by *Data-pull* or *Data-push* methods. In *Data-pull,* each agent asks other agents for their service information either periodically or upon a request arrival. In *Data-push,* each agent provides other agents with its service information either periodically or when it is changed. Upon arrival of a service request an agent queries its ACT, first looking for the requested service in local resources, followed by lower agents and finally the higher agent. If the service is not found, the agent either forwards the request to the higher agent or terminates the request. ARMS represent a self-organizing and distributed RMS, however, due to its fixed structure, it is not expected to be fault tolerant against node or link failures.

Self-Organizing Load Balancing

This work (Cao, 2004) incorporates an additional self-organizing mechanism for automatic grid load balancing in the ARMS system discussed earlier. It uses ants to distribute jobs evenly among available resources. The load balancing system is implemented at two layers. Job schedulers for clusters are used for local grid management and these local schedulers are integrated with ARMS agents for management at the higher level. The iterative ant algorithm used for load balancing can be described as follows. Each ant wanders from one ARMS agent to another for m steps, keeping track of the most overloaded agent found so far. This is followed by another m steps, where it finds the most under-loaded agent. In the following step the ant suggests the most overloaded and most under-loaded agents to balance their jobs.

A Hybrid Ant Algorithm for Scheduling Independent Jobs

Ritchie and Levine (2004) present an ACO algorithm that, when combined with local and tabu search, can find efficient schedules of independent computational jobs in a heterogeneous computing environment. Here it is assumed that global information about the jobs and resources is available and the expected running time of each individual job on each processor is used for the purpose of scheduling jobs on processors. A pheromone table is maintained, which is used by ants to share information about good processors for particular jobs. This table has a single (real-valued) entry for each job-processor pair in the

problem. In each iteration, the global best ant or the iteration best ant updates the pheromone trail. In addition to the pheromone values, ants also use a heuristic based on problem specific information to build their solution. Another similar approach towards task scheduling using ACO is described in (Fidanova and Durchova, 2006). Both of these require complete information about the environment in terms of expected execution time for all task and resource pairs. Hence these are centralized and are not expected to scale well. For these reasons and the space restrictions the details of their implementation are omitted here. Instead, in the following, we describe another technique, in detail, which does not need to maintain global state across all nodes.

Algorithms for Self-Organization and Adaptive Service Placement

An algorithm based on Ant Colony Optimization for adaptive resource allocation in dynamic grid environments is proposed by Andrzejak and colleagues (Andrzejak et al., 2002). It provides a suitable and adaptive placement of services or applications on resources, which prevents overloading server environments and the communication infrastructure, keeps resource utilization and response times in balance, and achieves higher availability and fault-tolerance.

A set of ants is used to discover resources required for every application or service. A *service manager* for each service s is created which controls the set of ants. Each ant contains information about resource requirements for s and other cooperating services in a list. It also contains the current communication requirements among the services in the list. Each ant discovers a partial solution to the allocation problem. This partial solution contains a sub-set of services (S) and servers (V). A metric, called the partial objective function (POF), is used to compare these partial solutions. POF is derived from a weighted sum of two quantities; the sum of traffic costs between the services (in S) on a pair of servers (in V) weighted by the distance of the servers and the variance of the processing capacity usage among the servers (in V). This objective function does not only prevent overloading server environments, but also helps in placing services in such a way that the communication demand among them is kept under check. Each ant travels from one server to another choosing the servers along the path based on a probability computed locally. On each server (v), the ant evaluates the score of the server in respect to each service (s) from its list. For each pair (s,v), this placement score expresses how well this server is suitable to host the service. This score is the POF value calculated for the (partial) assignment of the services to the servers already done by the ant, together with the mapping of s to v. For this calculation, S is chosen as the current service and the set of all services already assigned, and V is chosen as the current server and all servers that the ant has already visited.

The ant assigns the service s from its list, with the highest score, to the server v. It also updates a pheromone table stored on the current server. This table contains *pheromone scores* for certain pairs (service, server). Those are essentially weighted sums of placement scores of the ants that evaluated this particular (service, server)- pair. Neighboring servers periodically exchange these tables and provide the mechanism to disseminate local information across the system. The pheromone table is used to help an ant to decide which server to visit next. The ant moves to the server v, which is not too distant and the corresponding (s,v) pair value is highest among all unassigned services. If no such pair is found in the table, ant chooses a set of servers with most recently updated pheromone scores and with the highest pheromone scores. One server is chosen randomly from this set as the next server. This approach helps in identifying servers with free resources.

After assigning all the services in its list to servers, each ant reports back to the service man-

ager and terminates. After comparing the partial solutions obtained by all the ants the service manager decides if the current assignment (if any) is worse than the best ant solution by a certain threshold. This decision may result in a possible rearrangement of service placements.

AntHill Framework

The AntHill framework (Babaoğlu et al., 2003) introduces a new approach for designing peer-to-peer (P2P) systems. The approach includes a multi-agent system and evolutionary programming. The framework has three different entities: ants, nests and services. In the context of a grid computing system a nest is any machine, which is running AntHill and is capable of performing computations and hosting resources. Each nest can join and leave the network, giving the AntHill framework the desired dynamic property. Each nest provides local applications with a set of services using autonomous agents (ants). Services have a distributed nature and can range from a distributed indexing service for a file sharing application (Babaoğlu et al., 2003) to a load balancing service (Montresor et al., 2002). These ants can travel around the nest network, interacting with various nests and cooperating with other ants, to solve the task at hand. The core of an ant is the algorithm it uses and should be adapted according to the service.

Messor (Montresor et al., 2002) is an example of such an algorithm and is used for load balancing. It is inspired from the object collection activity observed in several species of natural ants. These natural ants group objects in their environment (e.g., dead corpses) into piles to clean up their nests. It has been shown that this behavior can be simulated with artificial ants and without using a leader or a central control (Resnick, 1997). Each artificial ant wanders randomly in the environment. When it encounters an object, it collects it, if it is not carrying anything at the moment. Otherwise, it drops the object that it is carrying next to the encountered object. Despite the simplicity of the rules followed by individual ants, the group as a whole manages to group objects into clusters. Messor uses a variation of this algorithm. Each ant not carrying an object wanders about randomly until it finds an object and picks it up. Each ant carrying an object only drops it when it has finished wandering about for a while without encountering other objects. In this instance, the ant colony tries to disperse the objects uniformly over the environment. This algorithm forms the basis for distributed load balancing in Messor. Advantages of this approach stem from it decentralized architecture. Each nest is capable of producing new jobs and introducing them to the network. It is suitable for heterogeneous and dynamic environments. Further, it also scores well in terms of scalability. One disadvantage of Messor is that it cannot organize computations based on the memory, storage, and computing requirements of jobs, so in some cases it might be less efficient.

FUTURE TRENDS

As the Grid popularity grows, areas such as aerospace, automotive, financial markets, government and life sciences are becoming more and more Grid savvy. For a discussion on adoption of grid solutions in industry please refer to Linesch (2007). Beyond its academic and research roots as Grid expands in commercial organizations, there is a potential for grid resource trading among these organizations. Trading of resources among these organizations enables them to utilize their resources more effectively. Idle resources can be used as a source of revenue or traded for other resources needed at a later stage. Again, self-organization is likely to be the key to the working of a system that can enable trading of such grid resources. Grid resource trading (Briquet and de Marneffe, 2006) is one area that is expected to benefit most from the application of such distrib-

uted and self-organizing resource management (DSRM) schemes.

Standardization of these techniques, like any other in the grid domain, is also expected to feature prominently. Having demonstrated the promise of DSRM techniques, researchers and developers must now look at ways to facilitate their integration into a grid system. The Distributed Resource Management Application API (DRMAA), described in the Open Grid Forum's Grid Final Document number 22 (Brobst et al., 2007), provides a generalized API to distributed resource management systems (DRMSs). Conforming to DRMAA, would not only gain a wider acceptance for these DRMSs, but also will benefit the application builders.

CONCLUSION

Heterogeneous and dynamic nature of grid resources, their multiple ownership and requirements for their dynamic and scalable expansion call for distributed and self-organized resource management (DSRM) techniques. Various techniques inspired from nature have been used in the past to achieve this decentralized resource management. In particular, Ant Colony Optimization has received a great deal of attention in this regard, lately. Natural ants can be viewed as powerful problem-solvers with sophisticated collective intelligence. Composed of simple interacting agents, this intelligence lies in the networks of interactions among individuals and between individuals and the environment.

This collective intelligence is modeled in ACO algorithms and can be utilized to achieve the desired distributed and self-organized grid resource management system. In this chapter we have presented some such techniques from literature. These include, resource discovery, service placement, scheduling and load balancing techniques – all based on ACO algorithm or its variant. These techniques emphasize the importance of decentralized resource management and give us an indication of the role bio-inspired algorithms can play in their implementation.

The research in this area, however, lacks in two key aspects. Firstly, there is a need for comparative studies, which contrast DSRM techniques against the traditional ones. Such studies are a must for a wider adoption of DSRM techniques in the Grid community. Secondly, there is also a need for real-world implementations of such bio-inspired DSRM techniques. Simulation studies have demonstrated their potential. The next phase must demonstrate their applicability on a realistic Grid platform, using real-world tests.

REFERENCES

Andrzejak, A., Graupner, S., Kotov, V., & Trinks, H. (2002). *Algorithms for self-organization and adaptive service placement in dynamic distributed systems* (Tech. Rep. No. HPL-2002-259). Palo Alto: HP Laboratories.

Babaoğlu, Ö., Meling, H., & Montresor, A. (2003). Anthill: A framework for the development of agent-based peer-to-peer systems. In *Proceedings of the 22nd International Conference on Distributed Computing Systems* (ICDCS'02), Vienna, Austria.

Briquet, C., & de Marneffe, P. (2006). Grid resource negotiation: Survey with a machine learning perspective. In T. Fahringer (Ed.), *Proceedings of the 24th IASTED international Conference on Parallel and Distributed Computing and Networks* (pp. 17-22). ACTA Press, Anaheim, CA.

Brobst, R., Chan, W., Ferstl, F., Gardiner, J., Robarts, J. P., Haas, A., et al. (2007). *Distributed resource management application API specification 1.0*. OGF Grid final documents. Retrieved October 29, 2007, from http://www.ogf.org/documents/GFD.22.pdf.

Cao, J. (2004). Self-organizing agents for Grid load balancing. In *Proceedings of the Fifth IEEE/ACM international Workshop on Grid Computing* (pp. 388-395). GRID. IEEE Computer Society, Washington, DC.

Cao, J., Jarvis, S. A., Saini, S., Kerbyson, D. J., & Nudd, G. R. (2002). ARMS: An agent-based resource management system for grid computing. *Scientific Programming, 10*(2), 135-148.

Ching, A. L. M., Sacks, L., & McKee, P. (2002). Super resource-management for Grid computing. *In Proceedings of the London Communications Symposium (LCS 2002)*, London.

Dorigo, M. (1992). *Optimization, learning and natural algorithms*. PhD thesis, DEI, Polytecnico di Milano, Milan, Italy. (in Italian).

Dorigo, M., & Stutzle, T. (2004) *Ant colony optimization*. The MIT Press.

Fidanova, S., & Durchova, M. K. (2006). Ant algorithm for Grid scheduling problem. In *Proceedings of the 5th International Conference on Large-Scale Scientific Computing* (pp. 405-412).

Iamnitchi, A., & Foster, I. T. (2001). On fully decentralized resource discovery in Grid environments. In C. A. Lee (Ed.), *Proceedings of the Second international Workshop on Grid Computing*. London: Springer-Verlag (LNCS 2242, pp. 51-62).

Kennedy, J., & Eberhart, R. C. (1995). Particle swarm optimization. In *Proceedings of IEEE International Conference on Neural Networks* (pp. 1942-1948).

Lamehamedi, H., Szymanksi, B. K., & Conte, B. (2005). *Distributed data management services for dynamic data Grids* (Tech. Rep. No. 05-16). Computer Science, Rensselaer Polytechnic Institute.

Linesch, M. (2007). *Grid - Distributed computing at scale, An overview of Grid and the Open Grid Forum*. OGF Grid final documents. Retrieved

October 29, 2007, from http://www.ogf.org/documents/GFD.112.pdf

Montresor, A., Meling, H., & Babaoğlu, Ö. (2002). Messor: Load-balancing through a swarm of autonomous agents. In *Proceedings of the 1st International Workshop on Agents and Peer-to-Peer Computing* (pp. 125-137). Springer Berlin / Heidelberg.

Pavani, G. S., & Waldman, H. (2006). Grid resource management by means of ant colony optimization. In *Proceeding of the third International Workshop on Networks for Grid Applications* (GridNets 2006), San Jose, CA, USA.

Resnick, M. (1997). *Turtles, termites, and traffic jams - explorations in massively parallel microworlds*. Cambridge, MA: MIT Press.

Reynolds, C. W. (1987). Flocks, herds, and schools: A Distributed behavioral model. *Computer Graphics*, *21*(4), 25-34.

Ritchie, G., & Levine, J. (2004). A hybrid ant algorithm for scheduling independent jobs in heterogeneous computing environments. In *Proceedings of the 23rd Workshop of the UK Planning and Scheduling Special Interest Group*.

Wolskĩ, R., Brevik, J., Plank, J., & Bryan, T. (2003). Grid resource allocation and control using computational economies. In F. Berman, A. Hey, & G. Fox (Eds.), *Grid computing - Making the global infrastructure a reality* (pp. 747-771). New York: J. Wiley.

KEY TERMS AND DEFINITIONS

Agent-Based Systems: These are composed of multiple independent / autonomous agents which are collectively capable of achieving goals difficult for an individual agent or a monolithic system.

Ant Colony Optimization: Ant Colony Optimization or ACO is a Swarm Intelligence technique inspired by the ability of real ant colonies to efficiently organize the foraging behavior of the colony using chemical pheromone trails as a means of communication between the ants.

Complex Adaptive Systems: They are *complex* in that they are diverse and made up of multiple interconnected elements and *adaptive* in that they have the capacity to change and learn from experience.

Emergent Behavior: Emergence refers to the way complex systems and patterns arise out of a multiplicity of relatively simple interactions.

Grid Resource Management: Efficient and effective deployment of Grid resources when they are needed.

Heuristic Methods: These methods, found through discovery and observation, are known to produce incorrect or inexact results at times but likely to produce correct or sufficiently exact results when applied in commonly occurring conditions.

Self-organization: It is a process in which the internal organization of a system, normally an open system, increases in complexity without being guided or managed by an outside source. Self-organizing systems typically exhibit emergent behavior.

Swarm Intelligence: Emergent behavior, observed in numerous natural entities, is modeled to explore collective (or distributed) problem solving without centralized control or the provision of a global model. These models are collectively called Swarm Intelligence models and are characterized by their decentralized and self-organizing nature.

Chapter XIII
Service Oriented Storage System Grid

Yuhui Deng
Cranfield University, UK

Frank Zhigang Wang
Cranfield University, UK

Na Helian
Metropolitan University, UK

ABSTRACT

Storage Grid is a new model for deploying and managing the heterogeneous, dynamic, large-scale, and geographically distributed storage resources. This chapter discusses the challenges and solutions involved in building a Service Oriented Storage (SOS) Grid. By wrapping the diverse storage resources into atomic Grid services and federating multiple atomic Grid services into composite services, the SOS Grid can tackle the heterogeneity and interoperability. Peer-to-peer philosophy and techniques are employed in the SOS Grid to eliminate the system bottleneck and single point of failure of the traditional centralized or hierarchical Grid architecture, while providing dynamicity and scalability. Because Grid service is not designed for critical and real-time applications, the SOS Grid adopts Grid service to glue the distributed and heterogeneous storage resources, while using binary code to transfer data. The proposed methods strike a good balance among the heterogeneity, interoperability, scalability and performance of the SOS Grid.

INTRODUCTION

According to a new report from IDC (IDC white paper, 2007), 161 exabytes of digital information were created and copied in 2006. The growth will continue to increase exponentially. The amount of information in 2010 will surge more than six fold to 988 exabytes which amounts to a compound annual growth rate of 57%. About 70% of the digital information will be generated by individuals over the next three years. The data will be stored in a large number of data centers which are distributed across the Internet. The data centers may have completely heterogeneous operating systems, computer architectures, and IT infrastructures.

The explosive growth of data has been identified as the key driver to escalate storage requirements. There are two major technologies which impact the evolution of storage systems. The first one is parallel processing such as redundant arrays of inexpensive disks (RAID) (Gibson, et al, 1988). The second one is the influence of network technology on storage system architecture. Network based storage systems such as network attached storage (NAS) and storage area network (SAN) (Gibson and Meter, 2000; Morris and Truskowski, 2003) offer a robust and easy method to control and access large amounts of storage resources. However, the ever increasing amounts of data generated worldwide incur a significant impact on the storage systems we have today (Min, et al, 2005). It requires more sophisticated techniques and more flexible and reliable storage systems to store and manage the data (e.g. providing petabytes and even exabyte storage capacity, and aggregate bandwidth over 100 GB/s). Undoubtedly, NAS and SAN cannot meet the requirements. It is a big challenge to design an autonomous, dynamic, large-scale and scalable storage system which consolidates distributed and heterogeneous storage resources to satisfy both the bandwidth and storage capacity requirements.

A Grid is a flexible, secure, coordinated resource sharing among dynamic collections of individuals, institutions, and resources (Foster, et al, 2001). The objective is to virtualize resources including computers, networks, instruments and so on and allow users and applications to access the resources in a transparent manner. A Grid environment may consist of hundreds or even thousands of geographically distributed and heterogeneous resources to match the requirements imposed by all kinds of Grid applications. Grid computing has emerged as an important new field, distinguished from conventional distributed computing by its focus on large scale resource sharing and high performance orientation. Table 1 illustrates the characteristics of Grid and data storage.

Drawing inspiration from the Grid computing community, a storage Grid system is supposed to be able to satisfy the ever-increasing data storage requirements. The main goal of the storage Grid is to shield the heterogeneity of geographically distributed and diverse storage systems involved in the data storage and provide storage resources on demand for every authorized Grid user. Based on the existing Internet infrastructure, the storage Grid is a virtual organization which combines geographically distributed and heterogeneous storage systems into a logical community with only minimal administrative requirements.

BACKGROUND

In recent years, several research projects have investigated techniques in designing storage systems in a Grid environment. Storage Resource Broker (SRB) (Storage resource broker, 2007) supports

Table 1. Characteristics comparison of Grid and data storage

Grid Characteristics	Data Storage Characteristics
Large scale or global distribution	Worldwide
Dynamic coordination	Ever-increasing
Collaborative virtual organizations	Require Interoperability
User transparent	Involve large quantity of heterogeneous storage resources
Secured communication	High security, privacy, and reliability

shared collections that can be distributed across multiple organizations and heterogeneous storage systems. SRB offers some Grid functionality including a Virtual Organization (VO) structure for data and information, handling multiplicity of platforms, resource and data types, and seamless authorization and authentication to data and information stored in distributed sites. Distributed Parallel Storage System (DPSS) (Distributed parallel storage system, 2007) provides high speed parallel access to remote data and the DPSS servers are transparent to applications. It is currently being integrated into Globus and SRB. DataCutter (2007) is a middleware infrastructure that enables processing of large scale scientific datasets stored in archival storage systems in a Grid environment.

The above work has made important strides in designing storage systems in a Grid environment. However, the systems discussed use incompatible protocols and standards for accessing data. Each of these systems is designed to satisfy specific requirements and applications.

Building a distributed Grid consolidated by many heterogeneous resources demands that we extract and standardize some common patterns. A Grid Service is becoming a basic application pattern for a Grid because the service provides a standard means of interoperating between different applications running on a variety of platforms. A Grid Service enables heterogeneous environments to be integrated and reconciled to accomplish complex tasks, which significantly increase the versatility of a Grid. Recently, there have been some research efforts to wrap resources into a Grid Service to perform specific tasks. Smith et al (2004) designed a service oriented ad hoc Grid as a spontaneous fusion of cooperating heterogeneous computing nodes into a logical community without a preconfigured fixed infrastructure. Peng et al (2005) proposed a High Performance Computing (HPC) cluster service architecture for Grid computing and utility computing. With the architecture, Grid users are able to deploy a HPC cluster based on the requirements of their Grid jobs.

In order to construct a scalable, large-scale, geographically distributed, and heterogeneous storage Grid, Deng and Wang (2007) proposed and designed a storage Grid enabled by Grid Service based on an existing Grid environment (GT4). Figure 1 shows the system architecture.

The basic ideas are to wrap heterogeneous storage resources into Grid Services and take advantage of the existing Grid environment to discover and locate the resources.

MAIN FOCUS

The objective of storage management is to maximize the overall resource utilization of the storage systems by intelligently allocating the available storage resources among the applications above it, thus guaranteeing on-demand storage requirements. Due to the increasing storage requirements, the manageability of the dynamic and heterogeneous storage resources has become a dominant criterion in evaluating storage solutions, as the cost of storage management often outweighs the cost of the storage devices themselves by a factor of three to eight (Patterson, 2002).

Figure 1. Architecture of the service oriented storage system grid

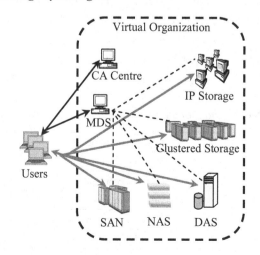

At the Center for Grid Computing, Cranfield University, the Service Oriented Storage (SOS) Grid has been proposed and designed to address the management of large-scale and heterogeneous storage systems. Experiences from the SOS project illustrate that building a large-scale storage Grid has to deal with the following challenges: heterogeneity, interoperability, scalability, and performance perspective.

Heterogeneity

Since the first disk drive was introduced by IBM in 1956, storage technology has experienced considerable development. Large numbers of storage devices, storage protocols, transport mechanisms, physical connections, topology, and associated software techniques (e.g., disk drives, magnetic tapes, Enhanced Integrated Drive Electronics (EIDE), Small Computer System Interface (SCSI), Fiber Channel (FC), Internet Small Computer System Interface (ISCSI), Direct Attached Storage (DAS), Network Attached Storage (NAS), and Storage Area Network (SAN), etc) have been devised (Patterson, et al,1998; Gibson and Meter, 2000).

The ever increasing amount of data (IDC white paper, 2007) will be stored in a large number of data centers which are geographically distributed on the Internet. The data centers may employ completely different storage devices, storage protocols, storage system architectures, operating systems, etc. How to tackle the heterogeneity of a large-scale storage system, while still providing high resource utilization, is a big challenge. Most of the current research has been focused on large-scale, high bandwidth and scalability, with a few isolated studies on limited heterogeneity. The reader is referred to (Deng and Wang, 2007) for a comprehensive discussion of heterogeneous storage systems.

All Web Services use Extensible Markup Language (XML) at their core because of the portability and ease of machine processing it offers.

A Web Service provides interfaces described by a machine-processable Web Services Description Language (WSDL) document, and other systems can interact with the service using Simple Object Access Protocol (SOAP) messages. But Web Services are stateless and transient, because the Web Service cannot keep state from one invocation to another, and does not have the concept of service creation and destruction to manage its lifecycle. Web Services Resource Framework (WSRF) is a family of six Web Services specifications that build on SOAP, WSDL, and WS-Addressing to define the WS-Resource approach for modelling and managing state in a Web Service context.

A Grid Service is a stateful Web Service with an associated lifetime which provides a set of interfaces through which Grid users may interact. The latest Open Grid Service Architecture (OGSA) defines a set of platform independent protocols and standards for creating, naming, and discovering persistent and transient Grid Service instances. For example, the client program can be programmed in C++ under Windows, while the Grid Service is programmed in Java under Linux. A Grid Service provides the virtualization of available resources at the system independent level, and allows transparent access to heterogeneous systems. The hardware, operating system, and underlying implementation of a service are all shielded from the caller of a Grid Service. Even the service instance of a deployed Grid Service is system independent, since it is specified to be handled by a service factory called a gatekeeper. By wrapping the heterogeneous storage resources into Grid Services, the SOS Grid leverages the heterogeneity successfully.

Interoperability

Interoperability between heterogeneous storage systems guarantees seamless storage consolidation by using standard interfaces. It is crucial for a storage system which involves large amounts of heterogeneous storage resources. Interoperability normally exhibits one or all of the following capabilities: 1) data/knowledge exchange; 2) coordinated behaviour; and 3) cooperative problem solving (Wong, 2005). To achieve a seamless interoperability of a storage Grid, the requests invoked by users should be able to cross the boundary of one storage resource and enter another storage resource. For example, if the storage resource of one location cannot meet a data requirement, it should be able to negotiate and borrow some storage resources from another location, and unite the different storage resources to satisfy the data requirement. A proper load balancing also requires the support of interoperability to relay the messages among multiple different institutions or domains, thus adjusting the workload among multiple distributed resources dynamically. However, the geographically distributed storage resources involved in a large-scale storage Grid normally reside in different institutions or different administrative domains. The institutions or administrative domains could employ completely different system architectures, protocols, and interfaces.

Athanasopoulos et al. (2006) discussed the dimensions of interoperability and developed a generic service model that can leverage the interoperability among Web, Grid and P2P services. In contrast to their method, the interoperability of SOS is achieved by employing a Grid Service. A Web Service is designed to support interoperable machine-to-machine interaction over a network. A Grid Service inherits the features naturally since it is a stateful Web Service with an associated lifetime. A Grid Service combines the Web Service and WSRF to provide a service based Grid environment that enables heterogeneous environments to be integrated and reconciled to accomplish complex tasks. By using a Grid Service, it is easy to construct a heterogeneous and Internet-scale storage system which guarantees interoperability. Because the Grid Service uses HTTP to transmit messages (such as the service request and response), this is a major advantage to build geographically distributed applications which cross Internet-scale and organizational boundaries, because most of the proxies and firewalls will not disturb HTTP traffic.

Scalability

The scalability of a storage system refers to the ability to provide satisfied capabilities including storage capacity, performance and fault tolerance when the system is increased in size in order to meet the data requirements. Watson (2005) divided the scalability of a storage system into many dimensions including data throughput, storage capacity, robustness, name service, clients, data distribution, security, management, etc. He discussed the architectural approach and the implementation choice in each dimension.

In Service Oriented Computing (SOC), developers and users can solve complex problems by combining basic services as a composition service and ordering them to best suit their problem requirements. Service composition can significantly accelerate rapid application development, service reuse, and complex service consummation (Milanovic and Malek, 2004; Srivastava and Koehler, 2003). Drawing experiences from the SOC, the SOS project regards a single storage service as one atomic service. Multiple atomic services can be automatically combined together as a composite service in terms of requirements. A composite service normally consists of an abstract workflow and a number of atomic services. The work flow depends on the requirements of users. For example, a user may submit a storage request with 500GB storage capacity and 500KB sustaining bandwidth. There could be a number of service candidates which can meet the requirements. To satisfy the data requirement and maximize the resource utilization of the candidate services, the Grid scheduler should be able to choose the storage resources from different storage services in terms of the resource utilization, geographical location, and etc. How to select a suitable atomic service in terms of the workflow is an important issue. We will address the issue by discussing the Grid scheduler in the future trend section.

The SOS Grid is based on GT4 which consists of a Monitoring and Discovery System (MDS), a Certificate Authentication (CA) centre and Grid service providers (see Figure 1). All Grid services are registered in the MDS. MDS is a key component which provides basic mechanisms for resource discovery and monitoring in a typical Grid environment. The interaction between the Grid services and Grid users is mediated through the MDS. There is typically one MDS per VO, but in a large VO, several MDSs are normally organized in a hierarchy. Traditional approaches maintain a centralized MDS or a set of hierarchically organized MDSs to index resource information in Grid. However, two reasons limit the efficiency of the traditional approach. The first, the centralized approach and the root node of the hierarchical method have the inherent drawback of a single point of failure. The second, the approaches cannot scale well to a large-scale and geographically distributed system across the Internet. To solve this problem, the SOS Grid organizes the MDSs in a peer-to-peer manner which guarantees the scalability and dynamicity (Deng, et al, 2008). Figure 2 depicts the resource discovery of the SOS Grid.

The major steps of resource discovery are labelled with the sequence number as defined in the following descriptions. (1) A request initiated by a Grid user is submitted to MDS2. (2) Once the request is received, the MDS2 searches the VO Two. (3) If satisfied Grid services (storage resources) are found in the domain, the MDS2 will notify the corresponding service provider which has the required resources to communicate with the user directly (e.g. call GridFTP to transfer data). (4) Otherwise, the MDS2 forwards the request to its neighbours MDS1 and MDS3. (5) The MDS1 and MDS3 will simultaneously repeat the operations as MDS2 did in step (2) and step (3) to achieve inter-VO parallelism.

Figure 2. Resource discovery of the SOS grid

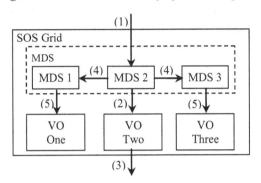

According to the above discussion, the storage oriented Grid Service can be considered as a basic building block of an infinite storage pool which provides a good scalability through its inherent parallelism, and facilitates simple incremental resource expansion (to add storage resources, one just adds storage services). According to the model of pay as you grow, Grid users can stack simple modular storage service piece by piece as demand grows instead of buying monolithic storage systems.

Performance Perspective

The SOS Grid employs Grid Service to glue the heterogeneous storage systems which are distributed across Internet together to execute complex Grid applications. The core of Grid Service is XML which offers portability and ease of machine processing, because both the WSDL and SOAP are based on XML. Due to the involved XML, requests and replies become much larger and parsing the XML messages on both the sender and the receiver side incurs additional overhead. Tian et al. (2004) discovered that sending 589 bytes of content involves additional 3363 bytes by using Web Service. Mani and Nagarajan (2002) reported that XML's way of representing data takes more than 400% overhead compared with a binary representation.

In order to investigate the overhead involved in the XML processing, we measured the registration time when a service provider registers a storage service in the local container with three different computers. The registration mainly involves small SOAP messages processing. The three computers are an Intel 550MHz machine with 128MB memory (Computer1), an Intel 1.6 GHz machine with 256MB memory (Computer2), and a Centrino duo 1.66 GHz machine with 1GB memory (Computer3). Table 2 illustrates the registration overhead of the three different computers.

The use of XML introduces a fixed amount of overhead on each request of Grid Service. The less data being moved, the higher this overhead is relative to the data transfer portion of the request. According to Table2, the overhead of Grid Service may lead to low performance and inefficient utilization of the storage resources in the storage Grid. It is obviously not a good idea for a service oriented storage Grid to transfer all data in XML especially for the critical real-time applications. The SOS Grid wraps heterogeneous storage resources into Grid Service and deploys the service in a Grid environment, therefore, we can take advantage of the Grid Service to discover and locate the heterogeneous storage resources which are transparent to the Grid users. However, the data transfer still uses binary code (typically GridFTP in a Grid environment) rather than XML to maintain the performance. The approach strikes a good balance between the transparency and efficiency of Grid Service.

FUTURE TRENDS

A large-scale and distributed storage Grid may have to support hundreds of thousands different applications. Different applications could have different performance requirements. However, all data accesses of applications are eventually transformed to I/O requests, and storage systems typically treat the I/O requests equally. For example, an I/O intensive application can incur noticeable performance degradation of other applications which share the same storage resource. Therefore, the Quality of Service (QoS) of the storage service will be an important issue.

A composite storage service can offer linear scalability of performance and storage capacity by combining multiple atomic services which are distributed. However how to select the suitable atomic services is a challenge for the Grid scheduler. Grid scheduler is in charge of scheduling jobs or applications where resources are distributed over a large-scale or multiple administrative domains. To increase the efficiency of resource utilization, an intelligent Grid scheduling mechanism may be able to match a specific requirement with suitable storage resources automatically by negotiating between the resource providers and the resource consumers. However, the scheduler in a Grid environment normally does not have full control of resources, information about the resources in grid is often unreliable, the behaviours of applications running on the Grid are usually difficult to predict. All these reasons make Grid scheduling far more difficult to realize. More research efforts should be invested in solving this challenge (Deng and Wang, 2007).

An intelligent dynamic data replication mechanism which automatically places the data replicas where they are needed is crucial to performance of an Internet-scale storage Grid. First, it improves the aggregate bandwidth by providing simultane-

Table 2. Registration overhead of three different computers

	Computer1	Computer2	Computer3
Overall	11195 ms	8636 ms	1182 ms
XML processing	11129 ms	8596 ms	1162 ms
Percentage	99.4%	99.5%	98.3%

ous data access to multiple data copies. Second, it reduces the latency between the data provider and data consumer by copying the data near the data consumer, because the latency is incurred not only by the protocol stack of Grid Service, but also by the distance of the communication. Therefore, it is possible to support data intensive or critical applications by introducing a dynamic data replication mechanism. The SOS Grid can also mitigate the performance requirements of a network by storing the correlated data closely to enhance the data locality, thus reinforcing the loosely coupled Grid Service.

CONCLUSION

The manageability of large-scale and heterogeneous storage resources has long been a challenge in the storage community. The ever increasing storage demands force us to rethink storage system architecture and data organization with more focus on heterogeneity, interoperability and scalability. Drawing inspiration from Grid computing community, the SOS Grid attempts to investigate and tackle the problems. By wrapping the diverse storage resources into atomic Grid Services and federating multiple atomic Grid Services into composite services, the SOS Grid makes an important stride in solving the heterogeneity, interoperability and scalability. Because Grid Service is not designed for the critical real-time applications (e.g. data storage), the SOS Grid employs Grid Service to glue the geographically distributed and heterogeneous storage resources, while still using binary code to transfer data. The method strikes a good balance among the performance, heterogeneity, interoperability and scalability.

REFERENCES

Athanasopoulos, G., Tsalgatidou, A., & Pantazo-glou, M. (2006). Interoperability among hetero-geneous Services. In *Proceedings of the IEEE International Conference on Services Computing* (pp.174-181).

Distributed parallel storage system project (2007). Retrieved from, http://wwwdidc.lbl.gov/DPSS/.

DataCutter (2007). Retrieved October 7, 2007, from http://www.cs.umd.edu/projects/hpsl/ResearchAreas/DataCutter.htm

Deng, Y., & Wang, F. (2007). A heterogeneous storage grid enabled by grid service. *ACM SIGOPS Operating Systems Review, 41*(1), 7-13.

Deng, Y., & Wang, F. (2007). Opportunities and challenges of storage grid enabled by grid service. *ACM SIGOPS Operating Systems Review, 41*(4), 79-82.

Deng, Y., Wang, F., Helian, N., Wu, S., & Liao, C. (2007). Dynamic and scalable storage management architecture for Grid oriented storage device. *Parallel Computing, 34*(1).

Foster, I., Kesselman, C., & Tuecke, S. (2001). The anatomy of the Grid: Enabling scalable virtual organizations. *International Journal of High Performance Computing Applications, 15*(3), 200-222.

Gibson, G., & Meter, R. V. (2000). Network attached storage architecture. *Communications of the ACM, 43*(1), 37-45.

Gibson, G., Stodolsky, D., Chang, F., Courtright II, W., Demetriou, C., Ginting, E., et al. (1995). The Scotch parallel storage system. In *Proceedings of 40th IEEE Computer Society International Conference* (pp. 403-410).

IDC white paper. (2007). The expanding digital universe: A forecast of worldwide information growth through 2010. Retrieved October 7, 2007, from http://www.emc.com/about/destination/digital_universe/

Mani, A., & Nagarajan, A. (2002). Understanding quality of service for Web services. Retrieved

October 7, 2007, from http://www-106.ibm.com/developerworks/library/ws-quality.html.

Milanovic, N., & Malek, M. (2004). Current solutions for web service composition. *IEEE Internet Computing, 8*(6), 51-59.

Min, W. H., Wilson, W. Y., Ngi, Y. H., Wang, D., Li, Z., Hong, L. K., et al. (2005). Dynamic storage resource management framework for the Grid. In *Proceedings of the 22nd IEEE / 13th NASA Goddard Conf. on Mass Storage Systems and Technologies*, (pp. 286-293).

Morris, R.J.T., & Truskowski, B. J.(2003).The evolution of storage systems. *IBM System Journal, 42*(2), 205-217.

Patterson, D. A. (2002, January). Availability and maintainability >> Performance: New Focus for a new century. *Key Note Lecture at FAST '02*.

Peng, L., Ng, L. K., & See, S. (2005). YellowRiver: A flexible high performance cluster computing service for Grid. In *Proceedings of the 8th International Conference on High Performance Computing in Asia-Pacific Region (HPCASIA'05)* (pp. 553-558).

Srivastava, B., & Koehler, J. (2003). Web service composition—Current solutions and open problems. IN *Proceedings of the ICAPS 2003 Workshop on Planning for Web Services* (pp. 28-35).

Smith, M., Friese, T., & Freisleben, B. (2004). Towards a service-oriented Ad Hoc grid. In *Proceedings of the 3rd International Symposium on Parallel and Distributed Computing/Third International Workshop on Algorithms, Models and Tools for Parallel Computing on Heterogeneous Networks (ISPDC/HeteroPar'04)* (pp. 201-208).

Storage resource broker (2007). Retrieved October 7, 2007, from http://www.sdsc.edu/srb/index.php/Main_Page

Tian, M., Voigt, T., Naumowicz, T., Ritter, H., & Schiller, J. (2004). Performance considerations for mobile web services. *Computer Communications, 27*(11), 1097-1105.

Wong, A. K. Y., Ray, P., Parameswaran, N., & Strassner, J. (2005). Ontology mapping for the interoperability problem in network management. *IEEE Journal on Selected Areas in Communications, 23*(10), 2058-2068.

KEY TERMS AND DEFINITIONS

Grid Scheduler: Grid scheduler is in charge of scheduling jobs or applications where resources are distributed across a large scale or multiple administrative domains.

Grid Service: A grid service is a stateful web service with an associated lifetime which provides a set of interfaces through which grid users may interact.

Storage Grid: Storage grid is a virtual organization which federates the geographically distributed and heterogeneous storage systems into a logical community with only minimal administrative requirements, while providing scalability and interoperability.

Storage Interoperability: Storage interoperability provides seamless resource consolidation and cooperation among a large number of heterogeneous storage resources by using standard interfaces.

Storage Management: Storage management indicates a virtualization method which is employed to maximize the overall resource utilization of the storage systems by intelligently allocating the available storage resources among the applications above it, thus guaranteeing on-demand storage requirements.

Storage Scalability: Storage scalability is the ability to provide satisfied capabilities including storage capacity, performance and fault tolerance when a storage system is increased in size in order to meet the data requirements.

Storage Service Composition: Storage service composition indicates combining available atomic storage services as composition service to meet the data requirements of complex applications.

Web Service: Web service is defined by W3C as a software system designed to support interoperable machine to machine interaction over a network. A web service provides interfaces described by a machine-processable WSDL document, and other systems can interact with the service using SOAP messages.

Chapter XIV
A Distributed Storage System for Archiving Broadcast Media Content

Dominic Cherry
Technicolor Network Services, UK

Maozhen Li
Brunel University, UK

Man Qi
Canterbury Christ Church University, UK

ABSTRACT

This chapter presents MediaGrid, a distributed storage system for archiving broadcast media contents. MediaGrid utilizes storage resources donated by computing nodes running in a distributed computing environment. A genetic algorithm for resource selection is built in MediaGrid with the aim to optimize the utilization of resources available for archiving media files with various sizes. Evaluation results show the effectiveness of MediaGrid in archiving broadcast media contents, and the performance of the genetic algorithm in resource utilization optimization

INTRODUCTION

It was the mid 1950s when the Ampex Corporation's Quadraplex professional video tape recording system was first widely available. Since then, production, storage and playout of television programs has been centered on magnetic tape technologies. Recently, the advancement of disc based, server technologies has had an impact on the broadcast industry. There is now an increasing trend towards the 'tape-less' production environment (Watkinson , 1990).

It is now possible to shoot an entire programme's material directly to disc and edit it using software tools, such as Avid or Apple's Final-Cut Pro. A completed programme can be delivered to a transmission playout centre using an optical fibre channel network. Here, the content is reviewed and verified from a video server before playing-out as a video stream, at the scheduled time, to the transmitter. Recent consumer gadgets like Personal Video Recorder systems allow a viewer to record or time-shift their favourite shows. At no point in this example has the programme content ever touched a piece of magnetic tape.

Server based transmission has been widely used in broadcast infrastructure. In the multi-platform, multi-channel environment, transmission playout from the server is preferred whenever possible. Two of the many advantages are, being able to preview any part of the content close to transmission without having to worry about whether there is enough time to spool the tape back to the start of the programme. Also, it is possible to view the end of the file (on an alternative server output), whilst the beginning is being transmitted. This level of media access is not possible with tape.

Transmission playout servers are specialist items of broadcast equipment which translate content between a file stored on a disc array and a real-time MPEG video stream. When the programme's scheduled air-time occurs, the server plays back the file, under control of an automation system, and outputs an MPEG video stream. Because they are highly specified, these are costly machines with a current price ranging from £40k-£70k each, depending on capacity. Their storage capacity therefore comes at a premium. There is an upper limit on both the number of files each server can hold and the total storage capacity. Due to the cost of these machines, their capability is not a suitable option for longer term storage and archive.

The past few years have witnessed a rapid development of grid computing (Foster and Kesselman, 1998; Li and Baker, 2005; Berman et al., 2003), a computing paradigm to facilitate utilization of resources on the Internet. This article presents MediaGrid, a light-weighed storage system for archiving broadcast media content utilizing resources dispersed in a distributed environment. We applied the concept of grid computing aiming to provide a novel solution to the problem of not having enough storage space to hold the ever-increasing mass of media content. As such, it performs a single function of the material management systems within a broadcast infrastructure.

It is worth noting that MediaGrid is related to GridCast (Harmer et al., 2003). The scope of the GridCast project is much broader, aiming to provide all the basic functions required within a broadcast material or content management system. The extent of this scope includes content sharing, browsing and trafficking, as well as assisting in broadcast scheduling. The GridCast project implements these functions as Web services using open standards and the Globus Toolkit (Sotomayor and Childers, 2005). MediaGrid can be plugged into GridCast as an archive service exploiting desktop PC storage at each site, so could be part of the content storage and retrieval process.

BACKGROUND

Figure 1 shows how and where server based technology is being used within a broadcast infrastructure. This diagram is based on the design model of an existing transmission playout centre.

The pale green blocks represent the areas where the transmission infrastructure is still predominantly broadcast specific, single purpose, proprietary equipment. In the presentation chain, this is equipment such as the video mixer, DVE (Digital Video Effects) processors, and data bridges or inserters. DVEs provide 'real-time' vision processing such as keying and manipulating video layers, providing effects like picture squeezes, captions and picture-in-picture overlays. Data bridges add data, such as teletext subtitling

Figure 1. An overview of a broadcast playout infrastructure

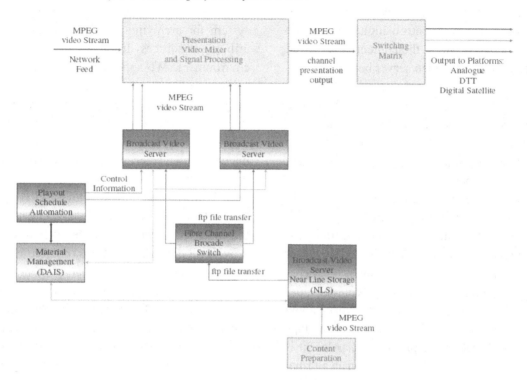

information, or wide-screen-signal coding to the video signal. This data is broadcast with the pictures and decoded at the receiver.

The switching matrix, often called a video router, creates cross-point between video-bandwidth input and output busses. These are used to switch the processed signal onwards to its destination. In the case of this diagram describing a playout centre, the outputs feed the delivery platforms. The main television delivery platforms are: Analogue Terrestrial Transmission (ATT), Digital Terrestrial Transmission (DTT) using the DVB-T standard in the UK, and Digital Satellite Transmission (DSAT). In the UK, digital cable delivery is usually a re-broadcast relay of DSAT.

Content preparation areas often include broadcast video tape machines, linear editing, and broadcast signal monitoring equipment. The remaining blocks in the diagram represent the functions which are provided by equipment traditionally purposed in Information Technology roles, albeit evolved to a higher specification.

Servers, databases and computer remote control (automation), have been adapted and enhanced by manufacturers. These become available for deployment into a broadcast infrastructure.

A multi-channel broadcast automation system may consist of several processors which each carry out a specific function. One may be used to send remote control instructions in real-time, others may offer a user interface to an operator. Another may run DAIS services (Database Access and Integration Service) which provide material management functions.

Primarily, material management keeps track on whether or not broadcast material exists, or if it is missing i.e. not available for its scheduled transmission slot. If it does exist, the database keeps records as to which servers hold a copy and instigates a file copy process to move material into the scheduled playout server prior to the scheduled air-time. In the model being described, the files are moved across a fibre-channel network.

In addition to the basic function of keeping track of if and where media content files are held, it also provides a mechanism to release the material as 'cleared for transmission'. This is used to prevent un-cleared or 'work in progress' files being inadvertently broadcast. Once the material is transmitted, house-keeping routines periodically purge the file from the servers, thus preventing them from becoming full.

A significant quantity of programme material is delivered to the transmission playout centre on tape. Getting the content onto the video servers and preparing the files requires skilled effort from a technical operator. If a programme is scheduled for a repeat transmission, the investment of time and effort in preparing the file is lost where the file is deleted due to lack of storage capacity. Unnecessary duplication of effort is wasteful and counter-productive, but is the unfortunate outcome if the scheduled repeat is to occur. As much as 40% of a channel's output may be processed more than once because of storage capacity limitations when repeats are scheduled.

MAIN FOCUS

Figure 2 shows how MediaGrid can be used in a broadcast playout infrastructure for media content management. MediaGrid provides a low-cost solution to meet the need for increasing archive storage capacity for broadcast media.

On a basic level MediaGrid can be described as one system which discovers and harvests distributed unused storage resources on desktop PCs connected by a network, and exploits this capacity for the purpose of archiving. It uses simple messages passed between components to coordinate FTP file transfers. The system's state is preserved by the server components keeping records in tables within a database. Figure 3 shows the MediaGrid user interface. In the fol-

Figure 2. The architecture of MediaGrid

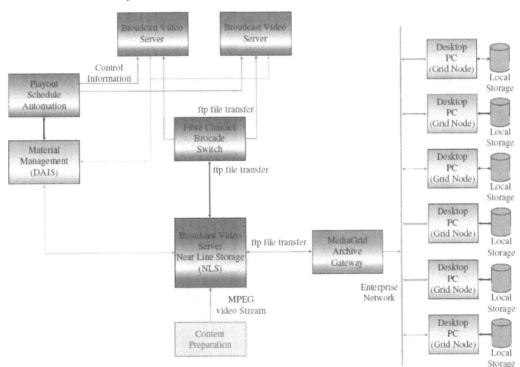

lowing sections, we briefly describe the major components of MediaGrid.

Resource Discovery

Resource discovery is a key requirement and is achieved through client nodes advertising their spare storage capacity to the server. When a file is successfully archived onto a client node, a copy of the database record is kept on the client machine. In the event that a client node disappears from the network (the user shuts down the machine, for example), all the records relating to that client are deleted from the database. If it subsequently returns, the Resource Manager detects that it has discovered a previously lost node and uses the client's copy of the records to restore the server's database. The previously lost archived file(s) now becomes available again.

When the client node is started, the total free capacity on the local disc is detected. This detection required interaction with the underlying operating system. From the total free space detected, an amount is subtracted for use by the

local machine's user. The remaining capacity may be donated to MediaGrid. A check is carried out to see how many archived files the client holds. A storage capacity advertisement message *StoreAd* is then sent to the server's Resource Manager.

On receipt of a *StoreAd* message, the Resource Manager checks to see if the discovered resource is one which is already known. If it is, its record is updated. If not, a check is made on the number of files held by the client. This information is contained in the *StoreAd* message. If the client holds no files, then it is assumed to be a newly discovered resource, and a new record made in the resource table.

If the client does hold files, but there is no resource record, then this must be the rediscovery of a previously lost node. In this event, a message is passed back to the client asking for a copy of the archive table records. These records contain the detail as to the archived files currently stored on the client. The reply is used to re-populate the information in the archive table. As this is now a known resource, a new resource record is also written. When a resource record is written,

Figure 3. The user interface of MediaGrid

a timestamp for when this occurs is included in the record.

Detecting a Lost Client

It is possible that a client PC may not be reached on the network (if the user has powered it down, for example). It is the Resource Manager's task to detect that the client is no longer contactable. This is achieved through a system of polling messages.

Periodically, a message is sent from the server (Resource Manager) to the client requesting an updated *StoreAd* message. The frequency with which this occurs is configurable in the Resource Manager's .ini file. The client would normally respond, resulting in an updated record being written in the resource table. Having sent requests to all the known clients, the Resource Manager waits. The waiting time is linked to the configurable frequency with which the request messages are sent.

After waiting, the Resource Manager calculates a cut-off point as being some time in the past, based on a multiple of the configurable polling frequency. It then searches the resource table for records which are older than the calculated cut-off point. Any records which are found to be out of date will relate to previously discovered resources that have not replied to a number of poll messages. They are therefore considered lost.

The record relating to each lost client is deleted from the resource table. A message is sent to the Archive Manager module, where the records of files stored on the lost client are also deleted.

Storing a File in the Archive

Once a client is selected for archiving files, a message is then sent to the Archive Manager requesting the transfer. On receiving the message, the Archive Manager 'locks' the resource. This is a flag in the resource table that prevents that particular client being chosen again as a resource, whilst the transfer takes place.

Next, a job number is generated. The job number is derived from the precise instant of time that the job was created. This enables the Archive Manager to allocate easily a unique number. The job number and job record is intended to be part of a mechanism for use by the Transfer Manager to make the transfer process resilient. A message is sent to the Transfer Manager, signaling a job record has been created.

On receipt of this message, the Transfer Manager queries the job record and sends a message to the client PC. The message contains the filename of the required file, and given that the file already exists in the server's pending folder, the client simply becomes an FTP client and transfers the file to its local disc. On completion, the FTP reply code is checked for a successful transfer. A message is passed back to the Transfer Manager and passed-on to the Archive Manager. A record of the stored file is made in the archive table, and a copy of that record sent back to the client for local storage.

Having completed the transfer process, the 'lock' flag is removed, the job record deleted, and the file deleted from the server's pending folder.

Retrieving a File from the Archive

Once a file is selected for retrieval, a message is passed to the Archive Manager. The archive table is queried to find which client is holding the file. As before, the client's resource record is locked, a job number generated and a job record written. The Transfer Manager module is then informed, via a message from the Archive Manager. The request is passed-on to the client.

On receipt of the retrieval request, the client becomes an FTP client, and deposits the file in the server's returned folder. The FTP reply code is tested for a successful transfer and a message sent back to the Transfer Manager notifying the completion of the request.

The success message is passed back to the Archive Manager and the archive record for that file is deleted. The process completes when the 'lock' flag is removed, the job record deleted, and a message passed back to the client. This message triggers the locally stored copy of the record, and the archived file itself, to be deleted.

Resource Utilization Optimization

Resources in MediaGrid are mainly storage spaces denoted by computing nodes and files to be archived. One challenging issue is how to maximally utilise storage resources available in MediaGrid for file archiving. To this purpose, a genetic algorithm is designed for optimizing resource utilization.

To be able to successfully implement a genetic algorithm, the problem of matching pending files to storage resources must first be coded into chromosomes. Each chromosome is made up of a number of genes, each gene representing one part of a complete solution. Therefore, each chromosome represents one of the many possible solutions to the problem of selecting a storage resource for each and every file in the pending list.

The genetic algorithm is implemented in such a way that the position of each gene in the chromosome is used to represent a file in the pending list. For example, the third gene in the chromosome represents the third file in the pending list. The integer value given to each gene represents the storage resource that would be used to store it. Each chromosome is, therefore, a sequence of numbers whose length matches the length of the list of pending files, and whose values indicate various resource selections.

A population of chromosomes is taken and tested for fitness. For each generation cycle, the fittest solutions are kept and the weakest discarded. Those discarded are replaced by new chromosomes which are crossbred from the fittest of the previous generation. The fitness function is defined in the following way.

Let

- p_i be the ith computing node, $1 \leq i \leq n$.
- $C(p_i)$ be the storage capacity denoted by node p_i.
- $U(p_i)$ be the utilised capacity on node p_i.

Then, the fitness function f can be defined using the following formula:

$$f = \min \sum_{i=1}^{n} (C(p_i) - U(p_i))$$

EXPERIMENTAL RESULTS

The scenario used in testing had a server and six client machines connected by an Ethernet network. The client machines advertised their spare capacity which was used to store a batch of eleven files.

The test scenario requires the genetic algorithm to find a solution to allocate one of the six storage resources to each of the eleven files, whilst minimizing fragmentation. The harvested capacity from each machine is considered as a collection of 8MB chunks, plus some remainder (fragmented) capacity which is considered wasted. Therefore, the problem to be solved is not simply allocating a storage client with enough capacity to hold the file, but also grouping the files most efficiently such that the remaining capacity is multiples of 8MB chunks.

Each of the six client machines has a hard-disc capacity of 6GB. Together they donated a pool of 17.5GB, which was available to the server to store the eleven GXF (general exchange format) files. The files, when archived to the client machines, utilised approximately 4% of the donated capacity.

The eleven files chosen were broadcast quality GXF files taken from a video server. The GXF files were a variety of commercial spot clips of 10, 20 and 30 seconds duration. These files were those that would be broadcasted from a video server during a commercial break, between programme parts. The eleven files, when played back to back, have a total running duration of three and a half minutes and represent the contents of an entire commercial break.

We compared the implemented genetic algorithm with the following three resource allocation schemes.

- **Random.** The Random scheme queries the resource table for all clients whose capacity is greater than the file to be submitted. From the returned resources, a client is chosen at random. This scheme might be used to prevent the same client node being repeatedly chosen.

- **Largest.** The Largest scheme queries the resource table for all clients whose capacity is greater than the file to be submitted. From the returned resources, the client with the largest storage capacity is chosen. This method might be used to preserve the maximum disc capacity for the client users as, using this method, clients with less spare capacity would be chosen last.

- **Smart.** The Smart scheme also queries the resource table for all clients whose capacity is greater than the file to be submitted. From the returned resources, the client with the least storage capacity is chosen. This method might be used to preserve the largest single chunk available to the archive. The client with the largest capacity is only ever selected if there is no other choice.

Figure 4 presents the results of this group of tests showing the change (difference) in fragmented (waste) capacity across the system using the four resource allocation schemes. It is evident that the genetic algorithm reduces the fragmented capacity, whilst the other schemes made little change or increased it. It is worth noting the Smart scheme is worse than Random in resource utilization. The reason is that the capacity donated by the clients does not inherently form neat multiples of 8MB chunks. Before the files were submitted there is a level of pre-existing fragmentation, or waste.

In evaluating the performance of the resource allocation schemes, it is necessary to consider the resulting change, or difference, in fragmentation.

Figure 4. Effectiveness of the four schemes in reducing storage fragments

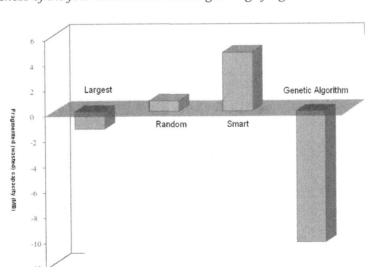

The Smart scheme selects the client which has donated the smallest capacity which is greater than the size of the file. In the test scenario, the donated capacities were all significantly larger than the files to be stored. For the Smart scheme, this resulted in selection of the same client, i.e. that which had donated the least capacity.

Following the submission of files for storage, the amount of fragmentation impacts the total number of available 8 MB chunks. This can be seen from Figure 5. The reduction in fragmented capacity through the use of the genetic algorithm has resulted in a gain of 1 or 2 additional chunks over the other selection methods.

FUTURE TRENDS

In optimizing the genetic algorithm, the results showed that the parameters giving the best overall result did not converge at the same rate as others during early generations. In these generations, a smaller population showed greater improvement in fitness. Future work could look at further optimizing the performance of the genetic algorithm. This would focus on using a dynamic population size in an attempt to get the algorithm to converge to a near optimal solution after fewer generations (Greene 2001; Maheswaran et al., 1999; Zomaya and Teh, 2001). In addition, the predictable and

group genetic algorithm (Li et al., 2006) could also benefit from resource utilization in MediaGrid.

With the development of Web services technologies (Curbera et al., 2002), the computing grid is evolving as a service-oriented computing infrastructure (Atkinson et al., 2005). Open Grid Services Architecture (OGSA)(Foster et al., 2002), promoted by the Open Grid Forum (OGF, http://www.ogf.org) as a standard service-oriented architecture (SOA) for grid applications, has facilitated the evolution. It is expected that Web Services Resource Framework (WSRF) (Czajkowski et al., 2004) will be acting as an enabling technology to drive this evolution further. The promise of SOA is the enabling of loose coupling, robustness, scalability, extensibility, and interoperability for large-scale grid systems (Papazoglou et al., 2005). We intend to extend MediaGrid with SOA technologies for enhanced scalability and robustness.

CONCLUSION

Grid computing is still evolving with new technologies and standards being designed and implemented. It is envisioned that more and more grid applications will be available to benefit users by utilizing resources on the Internet. MediaGrid set out with the intention of proving a concept. This

Figure 5. Effectiveness of the four schemes in utilizing resources

concept was to use several desktop PC's hard discs collectively as a means of distributed file storage. The purpose behind the concept was to expose a possible solution to meet the increasing demand for midterm, archive file storage for broadcast media. This problem is evident in transmission playout centres where the number of channels or delivery platforms is increasing.

REFERENCES

Atkinson, M., Roure, D., Dunlop, A., Fox, G., Henderson, P., Hey, A. J. G., Paton, N. W., Newhouse, S., Parastatidis, S., Trefethen, A. E., Watson, P., & Webber, J. (2005). Web service grids: an evolutionary approach. Concurrency - Practice and Experience, 17(2-4), 377-389.

Berman, F., Fox, G. and Hey, T. (2003). The grid: Past, present, future. In F. Berman, G.C. Fox, & A.J.G. Fox (Eds.), *Grid computing* (pp. 51-63). New York: Wiley.

Curbera, F., Duftler, M., Khalaf, R., Nagy, W., Mukhi, N., & Weerawarana, S. (2002). Unraveling the Web services: An introduction to SOAP, WSDL, and UDDI. *IEEE Internet Computing, 6*(2), 86-93.

Czajkowski, K., Ferguson, D. F., Foster, I., Frey, J., Graham, S., Sedukhin, I., et al. (2004). The WS-Resource framework. Retrieved March 5, 2004, from http://www.globus.org/wsrf/specs/ws-wsrf.pdf. (last access: June 2007)

Foster, I., & Kesselman, C. (1998). *The Grid, blueprint for a new computing infrastructure.* San Francisco: Morgan Kaufmann Publishers Inc..

Foster, I., Kesselman, C., Nick, J. M., & Tuecke, S. (2002). Grid services for distributed system integration. *IEEE Computer, 35*(6), 37-46.

Greene, W. A. (2001). Dynamic load-balancing via a genetic algorithm. In R. Bilof, & L. Palagi (Eds.), *13ᵗʰ IEEE International Conference on Tools with Artificial Intelligence*, (pp. 121-129), Dallas: IEEE Computer Society.

Harmer, T. J., Donachy, P., Perrott, R.H., Chambers, C., Craig, S., Mallon, B., et al. (2003). In C. Simon (Ed.), *UK e-Science all hands meeting 2003*, Nottingham. Retrieved June 2007, from http://www.nesc.ac.uk/events/ahm2003/AHMCD/

Li, M., & Baker, M. (2005). *The Grid: Core technologies.* England: Wiley.

Li, M., Yu, B., & Qi, M. (2006). PGGA: A predictable and grouped genetic algorithm for job scheduling. *Future Generation Computer Systems, 22*(5), 588-599.

Maheswaran, M., Ali, S., Siegel, H. J., Hensgen, D., & Freund, R. F. (1999). Dynamic mapping of a class of independent tasks onto heterogeneous computing systems. *Journal of Parallel and Distributed Computing, 59*(2), 107-131.

Papazoglou, M.P., Traverso, P., Dustdar, S., Leymann, F., & Krämer, B.J. (2005). Service-oriented computing: a research roadmap. In F. Curbera, B. J. Krämer, M. P. Papazoglou (Eds.), *Service Oriented Computing (SOC)*. Germany: Schloss Dagstuhl.

Sotomayor, B., & Childers, L. (2005). *Globus toolkit 4: Programming java services.* Morgan Kaufmann.

Watkinson, J. (1990). *The art of digital video.* Focal Press.

Zomaya, A.Y., & Teh, Y.H. (2001). Observations on using genetic algorithms for dynamic load-balancing. *IEEE Transactions on Parallel and Distributed Systems, 12*(9), 899-911.

KEY TERMS AND DEFINITIONS

Globus: A major middleware technology for developing grid applications.

Grid Computing: A distributed computing paradigm that facilitates resource utilization and large scale problem solving on the Internet.

Open Grid Services Architecture (OGSA): Promoted by Open Grid Forum and enabled by Web services technologies, OGSA is a standard architecture for next generation service oriented grids.

Job Scheduling: A process to map computing jobs to resources.

Service Oriented Architecture (SOA): An architecture to facilitate loose coupling of software components.

Web Services: An XML based standard middleware technology for developing interoperable service-oriented distributed systems.

Web Services Resource Framework (WSRF): A set of specifications that models stateful resources with Web services.

Chapter XV
Service Discovery with Rough Sets

Maozhen Li
Brunel University, UK

Man Qi
Canterbury Christ Church University, UK

Bin Yu
Level E Limited, UK

ABSTRACT

The computational grid is rapidly evolving into a service-oriented computing infrastructure that facilitates resource sharing and large-scale problem solving over the Internet. Service discovery becomes an issue of vital importance in utilizing grid facilities. This chapter presents ROSSE, a Rough sets based search engine for grid service discovery. Building on Rough sets theory, ROSSE is novel in its capability to deal with uncertainty of properties when matching services. Services with WSDL interfaces or OWL-S interfaces can be registered with ROSSE and then be discovered.

INTRODUCTION

The past few years have witnessed the rapid development of grid computing, a computing paradigm that can be employed to utilise various resources on the Internet. The evolution of grid computing can be divided into the following stages:

- **Parallel computing** is targeted at high performance computing using parallel computers of which each has multiple processors. A parallel library such as MPI (Message Passing Interface, http://www-unix.mcs. anl.gov/mpi/) or PVM (Parallel Virtual Machine, http://www.csm.ornl.gov/pvm/)

can be used to make multiple processors of a supercomputer work together to achieve high performance. Parallel computing environment focuses on high performance and utilize dedicated resources.

- **Cluster computing** is a computing paradigm that couples inexpensive personal computers in a LAN to utilise resources. Most cluster computing environments employ a master-slave mode with one master node and multiple working nodes. Compared with parallel computing environments, a cluster is cheap to deploy, and the capacity of resources can increase dynamically. Unlike parallel computing environments, resources in a cluster environment can be non-dedicated, and can be effectively shared. Software technologies such as Condor (http://www.cs.wisc.edu/condor/), PBS (Portable Batch System, http://www.openpbs.org/), LSF (Load Sharing Facility, http://www.platform.com/Products/Platform.LSF.Family/), Sun Grid Engine (http://www.sun.com/software/gridware/) can be used to build a cluster computing environment.

- **Meta-computing** is a computing paradigm that can be used to build a large scale computing environment on top of cluster computing environments and parallel computing environments. A meta-computing environment is characterised by coupling heterogeneous resources which may spread across organizational boundaries. Globus (http://www.globus.org) and Legion (http://legion.virginia.edu/) are two representative middleware technologies for developing meta-computing systems.

- **Grid computing** aims to provide a uniform interface for people to utilise various virtualised resources on the Internet for computing on demand. Grid computing is a kind of meta-computing but focuses on large scale computing environments. A number of grid middleware technologies are available including Globus, EGEE (Enabling e-Science in Europe, http://www.eu-egee.org/) gLite (http://glite.web.cern.ch/glite/), CNGrid (China National Grid) VEGA GOS (http://www.cngrid.org/en_index.htm), Open Middleware Infrastructure Institute UK (OMII-UK, http://www.omii.ac.uk/), NorduGrid Advanced Resource Connector (http://www.nordugrid.org/middleware/), XtreemOS (http://www.xtreemos.eu/), ChinaGrid Support Platform (http://www.chinagrid.edu.cn/cgsp).

Standards are needed to make grid systems interoperable. Building on Web services technologies (Curbera et al., 2002), the global grid forum (now is open grid forum, http://www.ogf.org) promotes Open Grid Services Architecture (OGSA) (Foster et al., 2002) as a standard service-oriented architecture (SOA) for the next generation of grid systems. In the context of OGSA, it is envisioned that various physical resources such as processors/CPUs, disk storage, network links, instrumentation and visualisation devices as well as applications and software libraries would be exposed as services. Discovering services of interest from a large grid environment becomes an issue of vital importance in utilizing grid facilities. This article introduces ROSSE (Li et al., 2006; Yu et al., 2006), a Rough sets (Pawlak, 1982) based search engine for service discovery in the grid infrastructure.

BACKGROUND

Grid services are implemented as software components, the interfaces of which are used to describe their functional and non-functional properties (attributes). Publishing (advertising) services in a grid environment means that service-associated properties are registered with a service registry. Service discovery involves a process of matching service properties of a user query with that of a service advertisement.

In a large-scale grid system, service publishers and requestors may use their pre-defined properties to describe services. Therefore, uncertainty of service properties exists when matching services. For a property used in one service advertisement, it may not be used by another service advertisement within the same service category. As can be seen from Table 1, property P_1 used by service S_1 for its advertisement does not appear in the advertisement of service S_2. Similarly, property P_3 used by service S_2 for its advertisement does not appear in the advertisement of service S_1. When both services S_1 and S_2 are matched with a service query using properties P_1, P_2, and P_3, property P_3 becomes an uncertain property in matching service S_1, and property P_1 becomes an uncertain property in matching service S_2. Consequently, both services S_1 and S_2 cannot be discovered because of uncertainty of properties even though the two services may be of interest to the user.

It is worth noting that properties used in a service advertisement may have dependencies, e.g. property P_3 may be dependent on property P_2 in describing service S_1. Similarly, property P_1 may be dependent on property P_2 as well in describing service S_2. Both services S_1 and S_2 can be discovered if the dependent properties P_1 and P_3 (which are uncertain properties in terms of the user query) are dynamically discerned in the matching process. To achieve high accuracy, service discovery must be able to deal with uncertain properties when matching services. To the best of our knowledge, no work to date has been reported to address this challenge.

Table 1. Two service advertisements with uncertain service properties

services	property	property	property
S_1	P_1	P_2	
S_2		P_2	P_3

As the computing grid is evolving towards a service-oriented computing infrastructure, service discovery has been a research focus in the grid community. Grid information services such as Globus MDS (Schopf et al., 2006) and R-GMA (Cooke et al., 2004) facilitate discovery of resources and services in a grid environment. However, they are restricted to keyword-based queries. UDDI (http://www.uddi.org) is an industry initiative for discovery of Web services. UDDI has been utilised by the grid community for discovery of grid services (Banerjee et al., 2005; Sinclair et al., 2005; Miles et al., 2003). Similar to Globus MDS, UDDI only supports keyword matching when searching for services. Various UDDI extensions have been proposed (ShaikhAli et al. 2003; Powles & Krishnaswamy, 2005; Miles et al., 2003) to enhance service discovery. Among them, UDDI-M (Miles et al., 2003) is flexible in attaching metadata defined in RDF triples to various entities associated with a service. Building on UDDI, the Grimoires service registry (Fang et al., 2005) supports multiple service description models and it takes into account robustness, efficiency and security issues.

Semantic Web (Lee et al., 2001) technologies can be used to further enhance service discovery. Services can be annotated with metadata whose relationships are typically defined with a service domain ontology. One key technology to facilitate service discovery with semantic annotations is OWL-S (Martin et al., 2004), an OWL (McGuinness and Harmelen, 2004) based ontology for encoding properties of Web services. OWL-S ontology defines a service profile for encoding a service description, a service model for specifying the behavior of a service, and a service grounding for invoking the service. Typically, a service discovery process involves a matching between the profile of a service advertisement and the profile of a service request using domain ontologies described in OWL. The service profile not only describes the functional properties of a service such as its inputs, outputs, pre-conditions, and effects (IOPEs), but also non-functional features such as name, category, and QoS related aspects of a service. Srinivasan et al. (2004) enhance UDDI for service discovery by embedding OWL-S in a UDDI registry. Paolucci et al. (2002) present a matchmaking algorithm for discovery of services with OWL-S interfaces. Building on this algorithm, a number of extensions are available. For example, Jaeger et al. (2005) introduce "contravariance" in matching inputs and outputs between service advertisements and service requests using OWL-S, Li et al. (2004) introduce a "intersection" relationship between a service advertisement and a service request, Majithia et al. (2004) introduce reputation metrics in matching services.

Besides OWL-S, another prominent effort for semantic annotations of services is Web Service Modeling Ontology (WSMO) (Roman et al., 2005), which is built on four key concepts – ontologies, standard Web services with WSDL interfaces, goals, and mediators. WSMO stresses the role of a mediator in order to support interoperation between Web services. A mechanism is also proposed for discovery of WSMO services (Keller et al, 2004).

Although the aforementioned approaches and algorithms are available to facilitate discovery of grid services, they require that properties used in a service advertisement should be explicitly expressed in a service query. As a result, these efforts cannot deal with uncertainty of properties when matching services. They potentially produce a low accuracy in service discovery. ROSSE builds on Rough sets to dynamically identify and reduce dependent properties which could be uncertain properties when matching services. In this way, ROSSE can achieve high accuracy in service discovery.

MAIN FOCUS

We have implemented ROSSE for service discovery. ROSSE has a graphical user interface for service registration as shown in Figure 1.

ROSSE has two registries for service registration, a UDDI registry and an OWL registry. The UDDI registry is used to register services with WSDL interfaces, and the OWL-S registry is used to register services with OWL-S interfaces. The UUID of a WSDL service registered with the UDDI registry is used to uniquely identify semantic annotation records of the registered service. In this way, WSDL services registered with ROSSE can be matched with semantic inferences instead of using keywords only. jUDDI (http://ws.apache.org/juddi) and mySQL (http://www.mysql.com) are used to build the UDDI registry and UDDI4J (http://uddi4j.sourceforge.net/) is used to query the registry. OWL-S API (http://www.mindswap.org/2004/owl-s/api) is used to parse OWL-S documents to register services with OWL-S interfaces with the OWL-S registry in ROSSE.

Service Publication

Services with WSDL or OWL-S interfaces can also be directly registered with ROSSE. Figure 2 shows a page to register a *vehicle* service that has a WSDL Interface, and Figure 3 shows the four steps used to semantically annotate the *vehicle* service. Figure 4 shows the registration of a zip code finding service with an OWL-S interface in ROSSE.

Figure 1. ROSSE user interface

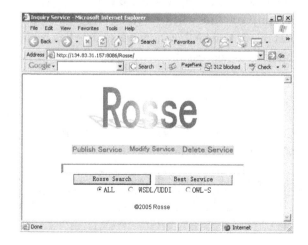

Figure 2. Registering a service that has a WSDL interface

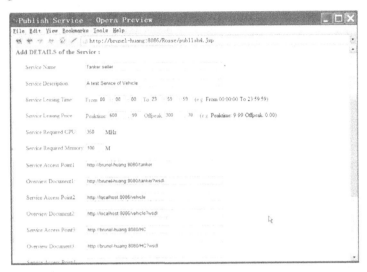

Figure 3. Annotating a vehicle service with semantic information

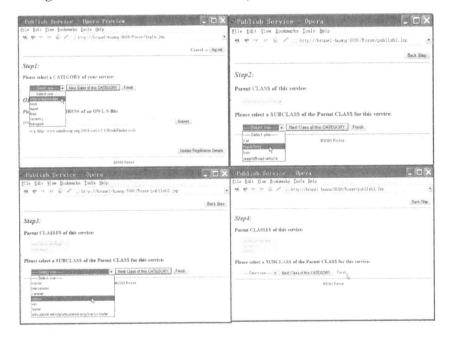

Properties Reduction with Rough Sets

Rough sets theory can be considered as a mathematical technique to deal with uncertainty in knowledge discovery. A fundamental principle of a Rough sets based learning system is to discover redundancies and dependencies between the given features of a problem to be classified. Rough sets theory approaches a given concept using lower and upper approximations.

Figure 4. Registering OWL-S services with ROSSE

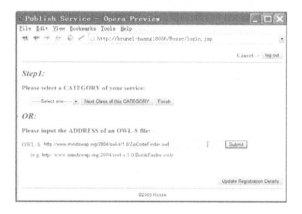

Let

- Ω be a domain ontology.
- U be a set of N advertised services whose properties are defined in Ω, $U = \{s_1, s_2, ..., s_N\}$, $N \geq 1$.
- P be a set of K properties that describe the N advertised services of the set U, $P = \{p_1, p_2, ..., p_K\}$, $K \geq 1$.
- P_A be a set of M properties that are relevant to the properties used in a service query Q in terms of Ω, $P_A = \{p_{A1}, p_{A2}, ..., p_{AM}\}$, $P_A \subseteq P$, $M \geq 1$.
- X be a set of advertised services that are relevant to the service query Q in terms of Ω, $X \subseteq U$.
- $\underline{X}$ be a lower approximation of the set X.
- $\overline{X}$ be an upper approximation of the set X.
- $[x]_{P_A}$ be a set of advertised services that are exclusively defined by the properties of the set P_A, x $\in U$.

According to Rough sets theory, we have

$$\underline{X} = \{x \in U : [x]_{P_A} \subseteq X\}$$

$$\overline{X} = \{x \in U : [x]_{P_A} \cap X \neq \varnothing\}$$

For a service property $p \in P_A$, we have

- $\forall x \in \underline{X}$, x definitely has property p.
- $\forall x \in \overline{X}$, x possibly has property p.
- $\forall x \in U - \overline{X}$, x absolutely does not have property p.

For a service query, there could be a large number of matched services. Based on the size of the set $\underline{X}$, user can dynamically determine the size of the set $\overline{X}$ which may maximise user satisfaction in service discovery.

Properties used in service advertisements may have some relationships with the properties used in a service query in terms of the definition of a domain ontology. For those properties that are marked with a *non-match* in a service advertisement, they will be considered as irrelevant properties when matching a service query. These irrelevant properties will not be considered in the process of service matchmaking.

Properties used by a service advertisement may have dependencies. A reduct is a set of properties (which are decisive properties) that are sufficient enough to discern advertised services relevant to a service query. Dependent properties are indecisive properties that can be reduced in discerning services.

All possible combinations of indecisive properties will be checked with an aim to compute a maximum set of indecisive properties. Some uncertain properties in service advertisements may be indecisive properties when matching a service query. As a result, these uncertain properties will not be considered in the process of matching services. In other words, some uncertain properties of a service advertisement will not affect the matching degree of the advertised service. Accordingly, the accuracy in matching services can be further improved.

Service Discovery

ROSSE can discover services with WSDL interfaces or OWL-S interfaces. It can also discover the best service from a number of service advertisements. ROSSE calculates a matching degree for each service advertisement related to a service request. Matching degrees are used to rank discovered services.

FUTURE TRENDS

It has been shown that finding a minimal reduct in Rough sets is a NP-hard problem when the number of attributes gets large (Skowron & Rauszer, 1992). Heuristic methods need to be investigated to speed up the process in service property reduction.

The number of services registered with ROSSE could be tremendous. Scalability is one the issues that need to be tackled. UDDI Version 3 (http://uddi.org/pubs/uddi_v3.htm) provides larger support for multiple registries, but the specification does not specify how these registries should be structured for enhanced scalability in service registration. Distributed Hash Table (DHT) based Peer-to-Peer (P2P) systems such as Chord (Stoica et al. 2003) and Pastry (Rowstron and Druschel, 2001) have shown their efficiency and scalability in content lookup. Scalability in ROSSE can be improved with DHT structured P2P systems.

Advertised services may be further described in terms of their non-functional properties related to quality-of-service (QoS) such as reliability and cost. One challenge is how to model such QoS data so that functionally matched services can be evaluated in terms of their QoS properties.

CONCLUSION

The grid is still evolving towards a service oriented computing infrastructure. It is envisioned that the grid will be acting as an operating system hosting a huge number of services utilising physical resources on the Internet. It is well known that Web search engines such as Google and Yahoo have played a critical role in the widespread uptake of the World Wide Web for information discovery. It is expected that service search engines like ROSSE would promote a wider uptake of the grid infrastructure in the near future.

REFERENCES

Banerjee, S., Basu, S., Garg, S., Garg, S., Lee, S.J., Mullan P., et al. (2005). Scalable Grid service discovery based on UDDI. In P. Henderson (Ed.), *Proceedings of the 3rd Int. Workshop on Middleware for Grid Computing* (pp. 1-6). Grenoble, France: ACM Press.

Cooke, A.W. et al. (2004). The relational Grid monitoring architecture: Mediating information about the grid. *Journal of Grid Computing, 2*(4), 323-339.

Curbera, F., Duftler, M., Khalaf, R., Nagy, W., Mukhi, N., & Weerawarana, S. (2002). Unraveling the web services: an introduction to SOAP, WSDL, and UDDI. *IEEE Internet Computing, 6*(2), 86-93.

Fang, W., Wong, S. C., Tan, V., Miles, S., & Moreau, L. (2005). Performance analysis of a semantics enabled service registry. In C. Simon (Ed.), *UK e-Science All Hands Meeting*, Nottingham.

Foster, I., Kesselman, C., Nick, J. M., & Tuecke, S. (2002). Grid services for distributed system integration. *IEEE Computer, 35*(6), 37-46.

Jaeger, M. C., Goldmann, G.R., Mühl, G., Liebetruth, C., & Geihs, K. (2005). Ranked matching for service descriptions using OWL-S. In *Proceedings of Communication in Distributed Systems (KiVS)*, Kaiserslautern, Germany.

Keller, U., Lara, R., Polleres, A., Toma, I., Kifer, M., & Fensel, D. (2004). *WSMO discovery*. Working Draft D5.1v0.1. Retrieved June 2007, from http://www.wsmo.org/2004/d5/d5.1/v0.1/20041112/ (last access: June 2007)

Lee, T.B., Hendler, J., & Lassila, O. (2001). The semantic Web. *Scientific American, 284*(4), 34-43.

Li, L., & Horrocks, I. (2004). A software framework for matchmaking based on semantic Web technology. *Int. J. of Electronic Commerce*, 8(4), 39-60.

Li, M., Yu, B., Huang, C., Song, Y. & Rana, O. (2006). Service Matchmaking with Rough Sets, Proceedings of the 6th IEEE International Symposium on Cluster Computing and the Grid (CCGRID'06) (pp. 123 – 130), Singapore.

Majithia, S., Ali, A.S., Rana, O., & Walker, D. (2004). Reputation-based semantic service discovery. In *Proc. of Int. Workshops on Enabling Technologies: Infrastructures for Collaborative Enterprises (WETICE)* (pp. 297-302). Modena, Italy: IEEE Computer Society.

Martin, D. L., et al. (2004). Bringing semantics to Web services: The OWL-S approach. In J. Cardoso & A.P. Sheth (Eds.), *Proceedings of the 1st Int. Workshop on Semantic Web Services and Web Process Composition (SWSWPC)* (pp. 26-42). San Diego: IEEE Computer Society.

Miles, S., Papay, J., Dialani, V., Luck, M., Decker, K., Payne, T., & Moreau, L. (2003). Personalised Grid service discovery. *IEEE Proceedings Software: Special Issue on Performance Engineering, 150*(4), 252-256.

McGuinness, D. L., & Harmelen, F. (2004). *OWL Web ontology language overview*. W3C Recommendation. Retrieved June 2007, from http://www.w3.org/TR/owl-features (last access: June 2007)

Paolucci, M., Kawamura, T., Payne, T., & Sycara, K. (2002). Semantic matching of Web service capabilities. In I. Horrocks & J. Hendler (Eds.), *Proceedings of the 1st International Semantic Web Conference (ISWC)* (pp. 333-347). Berlin: Springer-Verlag.

Pawlak, Z. (1982). Rough sets. *Int. J. of Computer and Information Science, 11*(5), 341-356.

Powles, A., & Krishnaswamy, S. (2005). Extending UDDI with recommendations: an association analysis approach. In S. Bevinakoppa, L.F. Pires, & S. Hammoudi (Eds.), *Proceedings of Web Services and Model-Driven Enterprise Information Services (WSMDEIS)* (pp. 45-54). Miami: INSTICC Press.

Roman, D., Keller, U., Lausen, H., Bruijn, J., Lara, R., Stollberg, M., et al. (2005). Web service modeling ontology. *Applied Ontology*, 1(1), 77-106.

Rowstron A., & Druschel, P. (2001). Pastry: Scalable, distributed object location and routing for large-scale peer-to-peer systems. In R. Guerraoui (Ed.), *Proceedings of Middleware 2001* (pp. 329-350). Heidelberg: Springer-Verlag.

Schopf, J. M., Pearlman, L., Miller, N., Kesselman, C., Foster, I., D'Arcy, M., et al. (2006). Monitoring the Grid with the Globus Toolkit MDS4. *Journal of Physics: Conference Series, 46*, 521–525.

ShaikhAli, A., Rana, O., Al-Ali, R., & Walker, D. (2003). UDDIe: An extended registry for Web service. *Proceedings of 2003 Symposium on Applications and the Internet Workshops (SAINT)* (pp. 85-89). Orlando: IEEE Computer Society.

Sinclair, B., Goscinski, A., & Dew, R. (2005). Enhancing UDDI for Grid service discovery by using dynamic parameters. In O. Gervasi, et al. (Eds.), *Proceedings of the Int. Conference on Computational Science and its Applications (ICCSA)* (pp.49-59). Singapore: Springer.

Skowron, A., & Rauszer, C. (1992). The discernibility matrices and functions in information systems. In R. Slowinski (Ed.), *Decision support by experience - Application of the rough sets theory* (pp. 331-362). Kluwer Academic Publishers.

Srinivasan, N., Paolucci, M., & Sycara, K.P. (2004). An efficient algorithm for OWL-S based semantic search in UDDI. In J. Cardoso & A.P.

Sheth (Eds.), *Proceedings of the 1st Int. Workshop on Semantic Web Services and Web Process Composition (SWSWPC)* (pp. 96-110). San Diego: IEEE Computer Society.

Stoica, I., Morris, R., Liben-Nowell, D., Karger, D., Kaashoek, M., Dabek, F., & Balakrishnan, H. (2003). Chord: A scalable peer-to-peer lookup protocol for Internet applications. *IEEE/ACM Transactions on Networks, 11*(1), 17-32.

Yu, B., Guo, W., Li, M., Song, Y., Hobson, P. & Qi, M. (2006). *Proceedings of Semantics, Knowledge and Grid, 2006 (SKG '06)* (pp. 80). Gulin, China: IEEE Computer Society.

KEY TERMS AND DEFINITIONS

MDS (Monitoring and Discovery Service): MDS is a grid information service provided by Globus.

Message Passing Interface (MPI): A specification for peer-to-peer communications in a parallel environment.

Open Grid Services Architecture (OGSA): Promoted by Open Grid Forum and enabled by Web services technologies, OGSA is a standard architecture for next generation service oriented grids.

OWL (Web Ontology Language): OWL is a W3C recommended language for describing domain ontologies.

OWL-S (OWL Web Service Ontology): OWL-S is an OWL-based Web service ontology providing a core set of markup language constructs for describing the properties and capabilities of Web services in unambiguous, computer-interpretable form.

Parallel Virtual Machine (PVM): PVM is a software system for developing parallel applica-

tions. Using PVM, a heterogeneous collection of UNIX and/or Windows systems can work as a single virtual machine.

RDF (Resource Description Framework): A metadata model for describing resources on the Internet.

R-GMA (Relational Grid Monitoring Architecture): R-GMA is an implementation of the GMA promoted by Open Grid Forum as a monitoring and information management service for distributed resources.

Semantic Web: An initiative to augment unstructured Web content as structured information and to improve the efficiency of Web information discovery and machine-readability.

Service Oriented Architecture (SOA): An architecture to facilitate loose coupling of software components.

UDDI (Universal Description, Discovery, and Integration): UDDI is an industry standard for Web services registration and discovery.

Web Service Modeling Ontology (WSMO): WSMO was developed by Digital Enterprise Research Institute (DERI), a leading European research institute in the field of Semantic Web and Semantic Web services (SWS) technology. It is a set of ontology specifications that provide a conceptual framework and a formal language for semantically describing all relevant aspects of Web services in order to facilitate the automation of discovering, combining and invoking electronic services over the Web. WSMO was submitted to the W3C for consideration in 2005.

Web Services Resource Framework (WSRF): A set of specifications that models stateful resources with Web services.

Web Services: An XML based standard middleware technology for developing interoperable service-oriented distributed systems.

Chapter XVI
On the Pervasive Adoption of Grid Technologies:
A Grid Operating System

Irfan Habib
University of the West of England, UK

Ashiq Anjum
University of the West of England, UK

Richard McClatchey
University of the West of England, UK

ABSTRACT

Due to some barriers to adoption we have not seen a proliferation of Grid Computing technologies throughout e-Science or other domains. This chapter outlines many issues that are a consequence of the existing Grid Middleware based approaches. The authors believe a Grid Operating system, or an operating system with built in Grid computing capability might be able to address the drawbacks of the existing infrastructure, leading to a fault tolerant, flexible and easy to use stack for rapid deployment of Grids. In this chapter, we present the motivation and issues which lead us to a Grid operating System and outline its design, implementation and evaluation details.

INTRODUCTION

Despite having made substantial advances during the last decade, ***grid computing*** is still neither pervasive nor widely deployed. Gartner predicted that by 2006 grid computing would mature sufficiently to leave the science laboratories and enter the business world (Gartner Group, 2003). But so far there have been only a few success stories, since only a subset of business applications are supported by existing grid infrastructures. To date the computing research community and particularly eScience projects have been the biggest beneficiaries of grid computing whereas other communities, such as user-centric fields like medical sciences, cannot easily implement existing grid architectures to support their applications. In Mattmann (2007), various requirements have been outlined which existing grid middleware do not support, thus increasing the cost of the adoption of grids for medical science. It is a similar story for enterprise computing where existing grid middleware is not scalable or lacks fault tolerance. Moreover they are mostly platform dependent and are insufficiently flexible to support enterprise applications. These issues in grid adoption can be traced to technical hurdles which arise as a consequence of the current approaches to grid computing. We are of the opinion that these hurdles originate from the current middleware approach to grid computing, as detailed below.

The *middleware* approach to grid computing was developed in science laboratories in which computing clusters distributed across the world are linked together in order to create grids to solve mainly compute and data intensive scientific problems. The role of grid middleware in this paradigm was to 'glue' the clusters together to achieve interoperability. Notable grid middleware included Globus (Foster and Kesselman, 1997), gLite (Laure, 2004) and UNICORE (Erwin and Snelling, 2001). This approach has however created some obstacles to grid adoption in other fields, since the cluster-oriented grids of today are not very suitable for user-centric computation, due in part to their complex operation and maintenance requirements. The main barriers (Ali, 2006) to the adoption of grid computing that result from the strong focus of current grid computing research on eScience are: the support for only limited application types (which mostly comprise highly parallel and batch applications), potentially inflexible network topologies, the steep learning curve required for configuring and maintaining a grid

with grid middleware, the lack of fault tolerance in the infrastructure and an inflexibility of virtual organization (VO) management software to create more fine grained VOs, as required by some applications. All of these limitations make grid computing in its present incarnation unsuitable for the common user with little computing expertise and make grid computing expensive for existing users to maintain.

As an example, one domain which is generally common-user centric is the biomedical field. In ***biomedical informatics*** there has been an exponential growth of data that has been generated and which needs to be assimilated and used by individual clinicians. As a result biomedical research has witnessed tremendous growth in terms of the adoption of technologies to facilitate research. To enable knowledge discovery and foster enhanced collaboration, medical sciences have increasingly turned towards grid computing (Freund, 2006). Another area which has already adopted grid computing is that of High Energy Physics (HEP) research. These two computing environments are radically different. HEP grids mostly involve non-interactive compute intensive batch applications that are fully supported in the existing grid infrastructures. Data privacy concerns are non-existent and there is minimal interaction of the user with the grid middleware. In contrast, in biomedicine data governance is required via national regulations, most applications are interactive and data-intensive, and the interaction of the researchers with the grid middleware is more extensive. Such kinds of applications are not easily supported with existing grid middleware. Moreover current grid middleware is designed for homogenous computing systems; one example, the EGEE glite middleware, is designed specifically for Scientific Linux for CERN only. Furthermore although there has been a push for platform independence via the WSRF/OGSA (Foster, 2005) standards, the emerging grid standard Globus is still Linux dependent. This is highly unsuitable for many domains like enterprise computing where the co-existence of multi-platform computers is necessary.

These differences in computing environments highlight the need for a generic grid computing system that is not specific to a community of users, as is the case nowadays. A so-called "*Grid Operating System*" is an important step towards such a pervasive grid computing system. In this paper we propose an approach which aims at bridging the gap between user-centric computing and eScience-centric grid computing, via a Grid Operating System built on a virtualized infrastructure. In Figure 1, we outline our objective of the integration of grid middleware functionality together with an execution environment provided by a modern cluster middleware into the machine operating system, in order to make a single unified system: the Grid Operating System (GridOS). This paper proceeds in the following manner: firstly in section 2 we will compare and contrast related work, discussing the research issues related to the system. In section 3, we detail the characteristics of a GridOS (PhantomOS), which will remove the barriers to the adoption of grid computing. Section 4 outlines how PhantomOS is aligned with emerging grid research and the paper closes with conclusions and future work plans.

BACKGROUND

There are many ways that a GridOS can be envisaged. In Ali (2006), the authors defined it to be "an operating system which transparently enables a user to peruse discovered distributed resources, to share resources in a decentralized fashion, to seamlessly launch and to migrate tasks on global resources giving the user an impression that one is using the local resources and to enable the control and monitoring of executed processes on a global scale through local means". According to this definition few systems qualify as grid operating systems, the closest ones being distributed operating systems. Recently new projects have emerged in this domain, including Vigne (Rilling, 2006) and XtreemOS (Johnson, 2007). The Vigne System (Rilling, 2006) is a grid operating system which aims to relieve users and programmers from the burden of dealing with the highly distributed and volatile resources of computational grids. Vigne focuses on three issues: i) grid level single system images to provide abstractions for users and programmers to hide the physical distribution of grid resources; ii) self-healing services to tolerate failure and reconfigurations in the grid and iii) self-organization to relieve administrators from manually configuring and maintaining VigneOS's services. Vigne plugs onto the Kerrighed Cluster system (Morin, 2004) which supports cluster middleware level issues. However Kerrighed has some limitations which would limit wide scale deployment. Kerrighed does not tolerate node failure; clusters cannot be bigger than 32 nodes and provide no symmetric multiprocessing and no 64-bit architecture support in its current version.

Figure 1. From Grid Middleware based approach to a Grid-OS approach

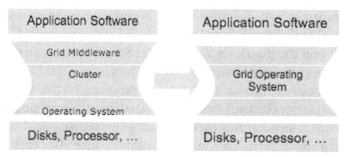

XtreemOS (Johnson et al., 2007) aims at the design and implementation of an open source GridOS with native support for VOs, capable of running on a wide range of underlying platforms, from clusters to mobiles. XtreemOS is focusing primarily on: extending the Linux kernel to support virtual organization creation and administration (XtreemOS-F); utilizing the core functionality provided by XtreemOS-F in order to provide general VO related services, and finally XtreemOS-FS, a file system to be built from scratch for supporting the replication of data across multiple sites for fault tolerance, by adapting an object-oriented approach to file systems.

The system outlined in this paper, PhantomOS, is geared towards providing an end-to-end stack for grid computing built on an open source platform. It focuses on scalable discovery services, fault tolerant virtual organizations and integrated virtualization at its core to provide security and a heterogeneous grid platform; many components are detailed in subsequent sections.

AN INTEGRATED APPROACH TO GRID COMPUTING

Our vision of PhantomOS targets the problems with the existing infrastructures, leading to a convergence of common user and business oriented computing with eScience-centric grid computing. The system is designed from the ground up to be grid computing enabled with platform virtualization being a central part of PhantomOS. The discovery service follows a hybrid client-server and peer-to-peer (P2P) model. Services detect each other with minimal configuration and form sub-grids, and an aggregation of sub-grids form a grid. The topology we have adopted enables the creation both of cluster-oriented grids, where individual clusters represent the virtualized combined resources of disparate machines, and *adhoc* grids to enable groups of users to form virtual organizations in order to share their resources.

Current grid application development environments present the user with non-transparent grids, increasing the complexity of creating grid applications. PhantomOS however enables users to natively deploy grid applications through virtual machines, without considering issues such as platform compatibility, software dependencies or domain specific issues. Security is another area rich with challenges in the current infrastructure. Grid middleware depends on a trust-based authentication scheme, and site level security is in the hands of the site administrators themselves. With virtualization site administrators have more fine grained control over their resources. Foreign computations run in virtual machines and cannot compromise host machines. On the other hand virtual machines will encapsulate user data and computations, securing it from external modification/access. In this paper we will restrict our discussion of PhantomOS to address problems of the existing grids by utilizing a virtualized infrastructure for supporting common user and business centric grid computing. This paper thus addresses two essential PhantomOS components:

- Deployment of a virtualized infrastructure for enabling flexible grids
- A two-tier super-peer based mechanism to allow the discovery of PhantomOS nodes

Further components including the data management, the self organization of the discovery service and virtualized networking and application development will be discussed in future publications.

Figure 2 presents the architectural layout of the system highlighting the relationship between the components covered in this paper. The two tier super-peer discovery service forms the back bone of PhantomOS. It caters for the discovery and integration of resources which grid users share. Details of the approach are discussed in section 3.3. The *Virtualized Infrastructure* (VI)

Figure 2. PhantomOS layered architecture

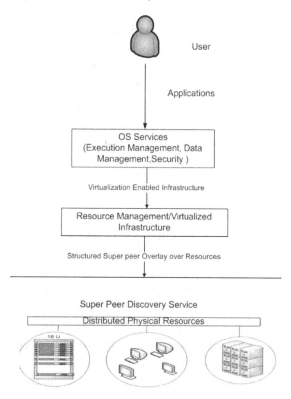

is a crucial component of the operating system. Its main purpose is to abstract heterogeneous computing resources and present them as a black box to users. Grid applications do not have to worry about fault tolerance, security, platform specific dependencies as well as platform heterogeneity issues. The users can design applications and, with the help of the VI, create bespoke clusters which suit their application's requirements. Additionally the VI is largely responsible for ensuring user application fault tolerance and security. Critical research issues in this domain are intra-hypervisor VM translation. There are a number of popular virtualization hypervisors, but not all are compatible, and in such an infrastructure compatibility must be ensured. Additionally the processes of snapshotting and VM migration are expensive and count as pure overhead. To deploy such an infrastructure over wide area networks, the costs in performing these operations must be reduced. The highest level grid services layer

is largely analogous to existing grid services in that it handles authentication/authorization as well as scheduling and resource brokering and data management.

Using a Virtualized Infrastructure to Tackle Issues of Existing Grids

The concept of *virtual organisations* (VOs) has been central to the idea of grid computing since its inception. Members of a VO are grid nodes that share common goals and policies. In the traditional grid computing paradigm users interact through portals which launch and deploy applications on VOs. The existing setup severely restricts the way VOs operate: they are not scalable (Novak, 2005), do not support dynamic membership and existing grids tend to be inflexible. Cluster administrators must ensure that they have installed up-to-date packages and often VOs have an homogenous software setup, which limits the kind of computations which can be carried out on grids. When scheduling grid applications many grid resource brokers do not consider the network as a resource and, as a consequence, network intensive applications suffer. Moreover, existing administrators cannot share their resources in a fine grained manner.

Virtualization has advanced in the last decade, and can be integrated into a grid infrastructure. PhantomOS aims to use platform virtualization and associated technologies to setup a virtualized infrastructure for grids which, as we will demonstrate, can tackle many issues of the existing infrastructure.

There exist several different types of grids commonly defined as Service Grids, Data Grids and Compute Grids. Our proposed virtual infrastructure can tackle problems in all three major types of grids. Service Grids deploy standardized web services to expose functionality to the grid; grid applications mainly use these services in a platform independent manner. Because Service Grids are based on a client-server paradigm, availability is a major issue in these grids and grid applications may crash if a single service is not available. Often entire portions of the grid can become unavailable if some central component like a Grid Scheduler or Resource Broker crashes. One of the major uses of virtualization has been to rejuvenate software services in the event of failure. Deploying these services not in actual machines but in virtual machines, means that they can be decoupled from the physical resources. Hence if the physical resource is failing, the service virtual machine can be pre-emptively migrated away. In the case where the resource goes offline, a recent virtual machine snapshot of the service can be deployed on a new resource, minimizing disruption to the infrastructure. Load balancing can be achieved with migrations or virtual machine replication.

Data Grids are grids which share massive amounts of data; often grid applications in these are either query or data transformation applications. In many domains data is governed by regulations which complicate the scheduling and resource brokering in this environment. By using virtual machine wrapped processes, the process could migrate to data sources, execute data locally and transmit the result back to the user. Finally, Compute Grids are highly platform dependant. Computation designed, for example, on a single platform using Linux, can only be executed on Linux. Hence in any heterogeneous grids many resources might go unused. Thus when wrapping processes in virtual machines more resources than otherwise possible in traditional grids may be practical.

Another crucial component of the PhantomOS virtualized infrastructure is the use of virtual networking. Virtual networking is an extension of classical platform virtualization that creates a virtual overlay network over an existing network. With virtual networking disparate parts of a single workflow can communicate with each other across administrative boundaries in a secure, isolated manner. This creates a virtual cluster which spans multiple VOs. Application specific VOs are a possibility. For example the user may submit a Grid application which requires certain hardware, such as a specific FPU unit in the processor. A virtual grid node of those specific types of computers can be created and the user's application can then be deployed on that virtual cluster. Applications with more fine grained resource demands can be deployed over such a grid. Virtual networking is a technology which can enable PhantomOS to setup flexible grids, where the same grid can be shared by users having different interests. Additionally self reorganization based on application characteristics becomes a possibility. If the system recognizes that the virtual machines are excessively using network resources, the virtual machines can be migrated to more high speed grid nodes thus ensuring efficient application execution.

Platform Virtualization Hypervisor Evaluation

To explore the viability of a virtualized infrastructure-based grid using existing state-of-the-art *virtualization hypervisors*, we carried out extensive evaluations on both software-based hypervisors as well as emerging hardware assisted virtualization hypervisors. These benchmarks serve two purposes: to evaluate the overheads introduced by the state-of-the-art virtualization hypervisors and to determine if the overheads are sufficiently large to render the deployment of a virtualization infrastructure based grid infeasible. We selected the leading open source hypervisor Xen (Barham, 2003) and tested it in both para-virtualization (PVM) and in hardware assisted modes (HVM). We also evaluated KVM (http://kvm.qumranet. com), the hardware assisted hypervisor recently added to the Linux kernel. Evaluation criteria were chosen to study the following parameters: CPU and I/O efficiency, memory management efficiency as well as network performance. All hypervisors were benchmarked against the native platforms Linux kernel 2.6.18 SMP and the non SMP version. Xen PVM/HVM and KVM were benchmarked in an environment where each VM instance had:

1.   2.66 GHz Quad 64 bit Intel Xeon Processor, with first generation VT extensions
2.   1GB RAM and 2 GB Swap for each Virtual Machine
3.   Scientific Linux for CERN 4.5

Benchmarks were carried out by running eScience applications as well as micro benchmarks. One virtual machine was created for each test. Each application was selected to benchmark different areas. One of these, Geant4[1], is a toolkit for the simulation of the passage of particles through matter. It is a compute intensive application, and hence it is suitable for testing compute efficiency in eScience applications. ROOT[2] is a scientific data analysis framework; the stress benchmark, one of its applications, was selected due to its high disk I/O affinity and was used as a platform for benchmarking the I/O performance of various hypervisors. The standard ROOT stress benchmark was used to yield two sets of parameters: ROOTMARKS and Real time. ROOTMARKS is proportional to the CPU efficiency, and Real time, which illustrates the combined CPU as well as I/O performance.

For network performance an Iperf (http://dast.nlanr.net/projects/Iperf/) application was selected. Through the transfer of 1 GB of data, the bandwidth in the VM was determined. Bonnie[3], a popular Unix file system benchmark was used as a micro benchmark to test file I/O performance. Disk performance was determined by reading and writing 1 GB of data to the disk. The MMU benchmark was custom coded to generate non-swapping page faults and to efficiently determine how the OS instance managed non-swapping page faults.

All charts are normalized with respect to native system performance. The normalized performance of ROOTMARKS, network and disk I/O was calculated by:

Normalized Performance (Percentage) = (VM Performance/Native Performance) * 100

In terms of ROOT Real time, Geant4 and MMU benchmarks, as lower result was better, normalized, performance was calculated by:

Normalized Performance (Percentage)=(1/(VM Performance/Native Performance)) * 100

Results

CPU Benchmarks

Geant4 results are illustrated in Figure3a. As can be seen from the graph, Xen PVM and Xen HVM both have over 95% of native performance whereas KVM achieved only 85% of native performance. KVM recently added to the Linux kernel, is still in the experimental stages, hence we believe that Xen PVM and Xen HVM, being mature VMMs are reflective of their respective types of virtualization. The same results are reflected in Figure 3b, which illustrates the normalized ROOTMARKS performance. Xen uses various innovations to achieve high system performance, at the cost of modifying guest operating systems. Hardware assisted hypervisors also achieve close to native performance, with the advantage that they do not need modified guest operating systems, hence they support proprietary operating systems.

I/O Benchmarks

In Figure 3c we can see the normalized performance on the basis of the "real-time" from the ROOT stress benchmark (which includes both the CPU and the I/O time that the application spent in accessing the data). Figure 3d shows the results of the Bonnie benchmark results. At Stress event 1000, we can see abnormal performance for both

Figure 3. CPU and I/O benchmarks

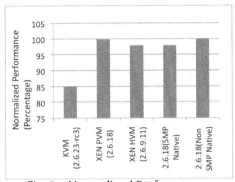

Fig. 3a: Normalized Performance on Geant4 Benchmark

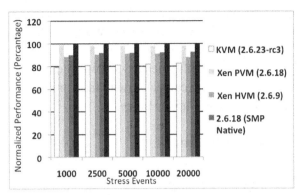

Fig. 3b: Normalized Performance for ROOTMARKS (Root Stress Benchmark)

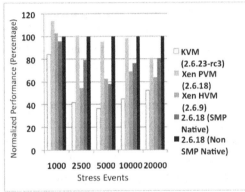

Fig. 3c: Normalized Performance on Real time (ROOT)

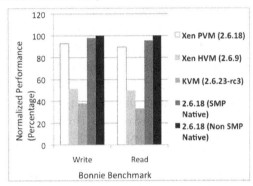

Fig. 3d: Normalized performance on Read and Write of 1 GB data

Xen PVM and HVM; the same trend is not observed at higher numbers of stress events, and we consider the higher range as a more accurate representation of the I/O efficiency of the hypervisors. Once again para-virtualization is best in terms of performance, whereas hardware-assisted virtualization technologies fare rather poorly; in KVM's case it is just over 40% of native performance. Existing hardware-assisted virtualization platforms compensate little for virtualizing memory and I/O access since both Xen HVM and KVM deploy the Qemu (Bartholomew, 2006) based I/O emulation. Qemu is a popular operating system emulator; both Xen HVM and KVM build on it. Many grid applications are highly I/O intensive hence poor I/O performance of hardware assisted hypervisors could discourage adoption.

MMU Benchmarks

The MMU benchmark was custom coded, and was made to generate page faults, which in turn was used to test the memory management of different kernels/hypervisors. The result is shown in figure 4a. According to (Barham, 2003), Xen does not handle page faults as quickly as system calls, and this lag is shown in our results. Again para-virtualization achieves the best performance, with Xen achieving close to 80% and Lguest at 50%. Memory access is important for scientific applications since many are multi-threaded and deal with large amounts of data in memory. An optimized memory access process can drastically reduce the execution overheads and improve application performance. Hardware-assisted virtualization engines manage to achieve only 40% of native performance. Software emulated MMU in hardware virtualized systems is expensive. Both KVM and Xen HVM use Qemu Software based MMU, and in each the memory access and address mappings are recalculated with cache tables being used to speed up the process.

Network Benchmarks

For network performance measurement, an application of Iperf was used for benchmarking. As can be observed from the results in figure 4b, there was a considerable gap between software based and hardware-assisted virtual hypervisors. Xen's Network I/O virtualization technique has been described in the literature (Apparao, 2006); Xen extends the concept of I/O rings to Network I/O. Hardware-assisted virtualization again relies on software to handle network I/O. Both Xen HVM and KVM use Qemu's Network I/O emulation.

Developing a Scalable Resource Discovery System

Various approaches have been used for ***resource discovery*** and are widely described in the research literature (Krauter, 2002). In most of the existing grid middleware, resource discovery is handled

in a centralized and/or hierarchical manner. For example, gLite 3.0 and Globus Toolkit 2.0 use MDS-2 which is built around the centralized index service GIIS. GT 4.0 uses an improved form of MDS 4.0[4] with minor changes to the underlying architecture. UNICORE too is built around a client-server approach. Most grid discovery services have cluster level granularity, and depend on the cluster middleware for low level discovery. Existing grids are not designed for nodes which have dynamic membership, however in various fields such grids are required. Also existing discovery services being based on client-server approaches are not scalable, therefore to provide for more scalability and due to the dynamic nature of resources a new kind of discovery system is required. Existing grid middleware is also not designed for fault tolerance.

Scalability is an essential requirement for any widely distributed system. There are numerous challenges in designing a scalable resource discovery service for such a widely distributed system. Adopting a pure P2P approach can radically reduce the Quality of Service (QoS) due to increased response times and a larger search space for resource discovery. Another challenge for developing a resource discovery scheme for a fine grained grid is to tackle the volatile nature of machines, both in terms of availability and rapid changes in

Figure 4. MMU and network benchmarks

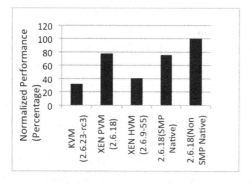

Fig. 4a: Normalized Performance for CPU cycles spent on Page fault handling

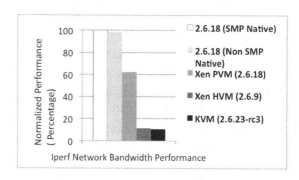

Fig. 4b: Normalized Performance on transferring 1 GB data

processing loads. Existing discovery services do not cater for such dynamic environments since the resources they have to support are dedicated. Information dissemination or other schemes will no longer give the true resource status and will also produce high network traffic. We believe that PhantomOS could serve as a means for the convergence of both grid and P2P environments. It could provide the necessary infrastructure for P2P environments to be introduced into a greater number of domains and move beyond simple data sharing. It would also enable grid environments to adopt the scalability of P2P environments. The convergence of both technologies will, as a result, lead to a more ubiquitous deployment of distributed applications.

Our Proposed Scheme and Architecture

Our proposed discovery scheme for PhantomOS is an enhancement over the approach of Mastroianni et al. (Mastroianni, 2005). The enhancements target certain issues, primarily dealing with the adaptability of our algorithm to hybrid grids and limiting the overhead of communication between the nodes in a single instance of resource discovery and usage. Certain enhancements deal with limiting the potential for all–to-all communication which plague existing peer-to-peer networks.

We introduce a two-tier based so-called *super-peer architecture*. The lower tier is a machine level granularity sub-grid, which consists of machines that have good network connectivity between them. Each sub-grid is represented by a super-peer, which is the most available machine within the vicinity of the sub-grid. At the upper tier the granularity is in terms of sub-grids, and these are grouped into regions depending on the geographical proximity of the super-peers. The regions are represented by a region peer, as shown in Figure 5. A virtual organization (VO) in this system can be at any level: it can consist of individual machines or can be an aggregation of entire sub-grids or of entire regions. Interactive applications will be handled at a machine-level

Figure 5. A two-tier Super-peer architecture

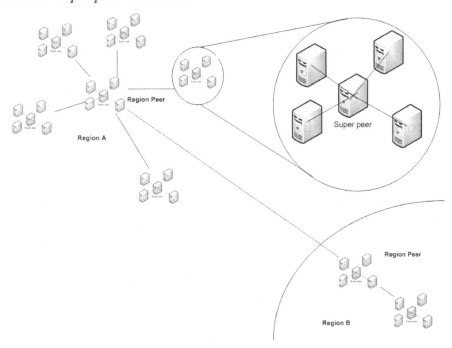

VO, whereas large-scale grid applications will require aggregations of entire sub grids.

The concept of a two-tier super-peer based system was developed for four reasons:

- To improve the network usage, by allowing a resource request to propagate to peers in close proximity, thus limiting overall network traffic, and improving response latency.
- To improve the quality of results, by propagating the request only when a suitable resource has been found, while limiting the network traffic as much as possible;
- To provide a scalable and efficient framework for PhantomOS. By dynamically grouping nodes into sub-grids, and clustering sub-grids into regions, the QoS is ensured for individual nodes, and the overall network efficiency is enhanced by limiting the flow of resource requests and
- To enable the creation of different kinds of grids, as required in different domains, from simple cluster oriented grids of today to the *adhoc* grids relevant to science and business.

Resource discovery mechanism in the context of a Compute Grid is explained separately in terms of tiers in the following sub-sections of this paper.

Resource Discovery at the Intra-Sub GridLevel

The sub-grid in our proposed scheme is analogous to a cluster of computers, and is the lower tier in the system. Resource discovery and brokering is carried out internally in the sub-grid in a semi-centralized fashion. The central server in the sub-grid is the super-peer, corresponding to the most available machine in the cluster, and has the responsibility of managing requests and providing a registration interface to new nodes. Upon joining

a sub-grid members register their presence with the super-peer. When a node of a sub-grid needs a resource, it sends a request query to its super peer which returns the list of resources matching the user's query constraints, if matching resources are available. If the super-peer cannot satisfy the request, it then forwards the query request to the region peer. Once the requesting machine has a list of the machines within the sub-grid it contacts each in a P2P fashion and the resource broker determines the suitability of the discovered nodes to execute the user application, leading to eventual migration of the job.

Resource Discovery at Intra and Inter-Region Level

If a resource request cannot be satisfied from within the sub-grid, the region peer comes into play. The region peer has a notion of the cumulative power of a sub-grid, and, based on this it takes a decision on which sub-grids have the required resources to compute the job. The cumulative power of a sub-grid is determined by aggregating individual resource descriptions and calculating a theoretical peak. When such sub-grids are found, the job request is forwarded to them and then the resource brokering and scheduling process takes place within the new sub-grid. If the region cannot satisfy the resource requirements it then contacts other regions in a P2P manner.

Resource Discovery for Resource Intensive Applications

Resource intensive applications are those applications which require more processing than any single machine can provide. The previous two subsections assume that the resources were being requested for a task which can be handled by a single machine. However for more complex workflows the two-tier super-peer model supports these applications as well. Given that the application designers can accurately declare the resources they require, with the help of the virtualized infrastructure the required resources can be aggregated into virtual sub-grids and the workflow can be deployed on it. Details of this approach will be outlined in future publications.

EMERGING GRID TRENDS

Recently, the convergence of both virtualization and grid computing with service-oriented architectures has been termed *"Cloud computing"* (Weiss, 2007). PhantomOS can be viewed as a scalable platform for a layered Cloud computing architecture. Through P2P discovery services and native support for virtualization, heterogeneous resources can be integrated into the grid fabric for dynamic and on-the-fly resources and services. Virtualization is becoming a key platform for resource and service isolation and can help large scale organizations and data centres to achieve fault tolerance and availability. The PhantomOS based virtualized infrastructure can thus be instrumental in infrastructure consolidation and to provide an homogeneous view of the global resources across multiple administrative domains which should lead to more efficient resource usage. This is a feature lacking in current generation Cloud computing initiatives (for example Amazon Elastic Compute Cloud[5] and VMware VI[6])

The transparent provision and management of services across different administrative domains, platforms and geographies is the most recent trend being increasingly adopted by research and industrial communities[7]. The dynamic provision of services coupled with the virtualization-based architecture of PhantomOS matches these latest trends in achieving resource and service migration, consolidation and isolation. The latest trend is to empower the core kernel to extend capabilities beyond the basic operating systems features and to enable virtualization and other related features as a kernel module. PhantomOS has the flexibility to exploit these features; we intend to achieve the local and global task, service and resource mappings by gridifying the Linux kernel using the capabilities made possible through virtualization.

CONCLUSION

Despite having made huge progress during the last decade, grid computing is not as pervasive as has been promised over recent years. This shortfall in use can be traced to obstacles coming from the strong focus on middleware in grid computing research and on a hitherto particular community of largely scientific and engineering users. This has led to some limitations in existing grid infrastructures in terms of interactive application support, resource discovery in highly dynamic environments and scalable topologies for grids with loosely coupled dynamic clusters. In addition, the infrastructure required in managing grids and the steep learning curve associated with maintaining contemporary grid middleware discourages potential users from adopting the grid. PhantomOS aims at the development of a pervasive general purpose grid computing platform for both common and existing grid users by converging user-centric computing with eScience-centric grid computing. The main contribution of this paper is to outline the underpinning technologies that enable us to achieve our aims. This paper has established mechanisms to tackle some of the problems of the existing infrastructure by deploying a virtualized infrastructure based grid. Moreover, a two-tier super-peer model based discovery topology aimed at converging centralized grid computing with the decentralized P2P architecture, leading to a potentially high QoS, scalable, self-organizing and fault tolerant grid was also described.

Future work includes the development of a prototype system which incorporates the components detailed in this paper, as well as a global meta-scheduling component. Interoperability with existing Grid middleware at the discovery and scheduling level is another direction of work. Evaluations on the integrated system and real world usage scenarios will be detailed in future publications.

REFERENCES

Ali, A., et al. (2006). *From Grid middleware to a Grid operating system*. Paper presented at the 5th International Conference on Grid and Cooperative Computing, Oct 21-24, 2006, Changhsa, China.

'Apparao, P., Makineni, S., & Newell, D. (2006). *Characterization of network processing overheads in Xen*. Paper presented at the First International Workshop on Virtualization Technology in Distributed Computing, 17 Nov 2006, Tampa, USA.

Barham, P., et al. (2003). Xen and the art of virtualization. In *Proceedings of the Nineteenth ACM Symposium on Operating Systems Principles*, October 19-22, 2003, Bolton Landing, USA.

Bartholomew, D. (2006). QEMU: A multihost, multitarget emulator. *Linux J.*

Erwin, D., & Snelling, D. (2001). UNICORE: A Grid computing environment. (LNCS 2150, pp. 825-834). Springer.

Foster, I., et al. (2005). *The open Grid services architecture, Version 1.0*. Informational document, global Grid forum (GGF).

Foster, I., & Kesselman, C. (1997). Globus: A metacomputing infrastructure toolkit. *Intl J. Supercomputer Applications, 11*(2),115-128.

Freund, J., et al. (2006). Health-e-Child: An integrated biomedical platform for Grid-based paediatrics. In *Studies in health technology & informatics* (pp. 259-270). IOS Press.

Gartner Group (2003, November). *Gartner predicts: Future of IT, symposium/ITxpo*. Cannes.

Johnson, I., Lakhani, A., Matthews, B., Yang, E., & Morin, C. (2007). XtreemOS: towards a Grid operating system with virtual organisation support. *UK eScience All Hands Meeting*, September 2007.

Krauter, K., Buyya, R., & Maheswaran, M. (2002). A taxonomy and survey of Grid resource management systems for distributed computing. *Software: Practice and experience (SPE), 32*(2), 135-164.

Laure. E. (2004). Middleware for the next generation grid infrastructure. In *Proceedings of the Computing in High Energy Physics Conference* (pp. 8-26).

Mastroianni, C., Talia, D., & Verta, O. (2005). A super-peer model for building resource discovery services in Grids: Design and simulation analysis. *European Grid Conference 2005*. (LNCS 3470, pp. 132-143).

Mattmann, C., et al. (2007). A reference framework for requirements and architecture in biomedical Grid systems. *IEEE International Conference on Information Reuse and Integration, 2007* (pp. 418-422). Las Vegas, NV.

Mocnik, J., et al. (2005).A discovery service for very large, dynamic Grids. *Sixth IEEE/ACM International Workshop on Grid Computing*.

Morin, C., et al. (2004). Kerrighed: A single system image cluster operating system for high performance computing. *International Conference on Parallel and Distributed Computing, Parallel Processing, 2790/2004* (pp. 1291-1294).

Rilling, L. (2006, August). Vigne: Towards a self-healing Grid operating system. *International Conference on Parallel and Distributed Computing, Dresden, Germany*.

Weiss, A. (2007). Computing in the clouds. *Networker, 11*(4), 16-25.

KEY TERMS AND DEFINITIONS

Discovery Service: A service in Grid computing which is responsible for the discovery of distributed resources.

Grid Computing: A model of distributed computing based on the dynamic sharing of resources between participants, organisations and companies with the aim of combining these resources and carrying out intensive computing applications or the processing of vast amounts of data.

Hypervisor: The software which enables virtualization in a system. Mostly denotes software which enables platform virtualization.

Peer to Peer: A computing model in distributed systems where constituent nodes interact with each other without centralized mechanisms.

Platform Virtualization: A virtualization model which creates a logical abstraction of a hardware platform. This logical abstraction is typically denoted as a "virtual machine", which is capable of simulating the capabilities of the concerned platform.

Super Peer: A model in peer to peer systems, where a node in the system represents a collection of independent peers which interact with the larger system through a centralized node. This peer is termed as the super peer.

Virtualization: A term that broadly refers to the abstraction of resources. Resources may include applications, platforms and systems.

ENDNOTES

[1]   http://www.geant4.org
[2]   http://root.cern.ch
[3]   http://www.textuality.com/bonnie/
[4]   http://www.globus.org/mds/
[5]   http://aws.amazon.com/ec2
[6]   http://www.vmware.com/products/vi/
[7]   http://www.reservoir-fp7.eu

Chapter XVII
Pricing Computational Resources in Grid Economies

Kurt Vanmechelen
University of Antwerp, Belgium

Jan Broeckhove
University of Antwerp, Belgium

Wim Depoorter
University of Antwerp, Belgium

Khalid Abdelkader
University of Antwerp, Belgium

ABSTRACT

As grid computing technology moves further up the adoption curve, the issues of dealing with conflicting user requirements formulated by different users become more prevalent. In addition, the need to negotiate static sharing agreements between the different stakeholders in a grid system is time-consuming and offers limited incentive for resource owners to step into the grid's infrastructure in a provider role. Resource management approaches that are currently adopted in grids are not able to deal with these issues in a flexible, value-maximizing way because of their system-centric approach. In this contribution, we will present a clear motivation for the use of economic forms of scheduling in grid computing environments to address these shortcomings. We also provide an introductory overview of the different forms of market mechanisms that have been adopted by researchers in the field. In addition, we present simulation results concerning the use of Vickrey auctions and commodity markets as market mechanisms for dynamic pricing in grid resource markets.

INTRODUCTION

Grid technology has reached a maturity level in which computational resources are being virtual-ized, shared and used on a global scale. Large scale deployments of the technology in production level academic environments are being driven by projects such as EGEE in Europe and TeraGrid in the

United States. These projects now make hundreds of teraflops in compute capacity and petabytes of storage capacity available to researchers in more than 40 countries. One of the crucial components of *grid middleware*, the software which enables the operation of a grid infrastructure, is the resource management system. This subsystem is responsible for mapping a user's request for service to resources available in the grid. Often this involves a two staged process in which a grid service, called the *resource broker*, first determines a set of suitable local resource managers based on the request's quality of service requirements. In the second stage, the local resource managers are contacted to fulfill the request by engaging the local resources they control (e.g. the set of CPUs in the cluster).

Currently, the resource management and scheduling approaches found in production level grid middleware have a strong focus on the efficient scheduling of jobs from a system-oriented point of view. This means that the broker schedules jobs in a way that maximizes the overall utilization of the infrastructure or that obtains the highest possible level of overall system throughput. These approaches to scheduling do not take into account the actual value grid users associate with their computations. As a result, the broker may be performing optimally from a system-oriented point of view, but suboptimally from a user-oriented point of view. The potential for value loss as a result of these suboptimal scheduling decisions increases with the load on the grid infrastructure and the heterogeneity of the valuations among users. As shown by Chun (2005), user valuations for allocations of motes on a sensor net testbed can vary by four orders of magnitude[1].

In addition, current resource management systems assume the existence of static bilateral sharing agreements between the different parties that contribute to the shared grid infrastructure. These agreements are often hard to negotiate, and result in limited flexibility and openness with respect to the integration of new parties in the

global grid infrastructure. As a result, several grid 'islands' or 'silos' emerge and the full potential of the infrastructure is not realized. This is partly due to the specific funding contracts under which grid resources are procured and brought into operation. Indeed, a currently debated topic is how to build grid infrastructures that are *sustainable* over the long term, i.e. that are self-supporting and do not require funding from a source that imposes the vision of global sharing of resources for their operation.

We believe that the introduction of an electronic market place for trading grid usage rights provides a promising approach to deal with the issues of openness, sustainability, and value maximization. Such a market place is open to all parties that wish to participate in the system as a provider or consumer. The incentives for (well-behaved) participation in such a market stem from a common value model and accounting system that charges or rewards the different parties involved, for their requested or delivered service.

Firstly, this differs from the negotiation model that is currently in place in which users need to lobby for access rights which are subsequently enforced by long term, static policies. A market-based approach allows for greater flexibility in terms of accepting new parties in the infrastructure and in terms of determining usage rights for users, resulting in a more open and agile grid infrastructure. This is especially important for the potential grid user base that is formed by small research institutions or SMEs. Their relative cost for maintaining and procuring computing infrastructure is high due to limited economics of scale and their often strongly fluctuating requirements. As a consequence, these users are not able to engage in *bartering* during negotiations of sharing agreements as they do not own a significant amount of computing infrastructure. On the other hand, this user base has the greatest potential for benefiting from the added value a grid infrastructure can provide. The possibility to pay for usage rights enables them to tap into this added value.

Secondly, the possibility of charging a cost for sharing resources provides an incentive for resource owners to take on a provider role in the grid. In this way, a well-organized market is an important step towards sustainable grid infrastructures that exhibit organic growth when demand exceeds supply due to economic incentives.

Thirdly, the market's operation and resulting prices fulfill the role of a communication bus over which the market participants transmit their valuation information. Depending on the *market mechanism* that is employed, this information can be used to prioritize conflicting servicing requirements in times of congestion in order to maximize the value of the grid infrastructure, as perceived by its users. The promise of value maximization also requires mechanisms to encourage parties to report their valuations truthfully. This implies that users are endowed with limited budgets to back their valuations and that the market mechanism has the property of *incentive compatibility* (Fudenberg, 1991) or leads to a *Bayes-Nash equilibrium* (Harsanyi, 1968).

One of the most important design considerations in the development of an electronic market place is the choice of the market mechanism that establishes dynamic prices for grid resources, based on current (and possibly future) demand and supply levels. This contribution will consider the use of *commodity markets* and *Vickrey auctions* (Vickrey, 1961) for pricing CPU resources and give an overview of existing approaches to pricing in grid economies. We show that it is possible to obtain fairly stable price levels in a distributed Vickrey auction organization, obtaining results that are close to the commodity market organization.

BACKGROUND

The idea of using economic principles in resource management is certainly not new. One of the first publications suggesting a market-based approach

is Sutherland (1968). In order to allocate time slots on a PDP-1 microcomputer he made users mark their desired time frame, together with a bid level, on a continuous roll of transparent paper. Every user was endowed with a limited budget of tokens that reverted to the user's account once they were used.

Important early prototypes of economic resource managers are Spawn (Waldspurger, 1992) and Popcorn (Regev, 1998). The Spawn system was the first to support concurrent applications using hierarchical funding structures to dynamically increase or decrease the parallelization degree of a distributed application. It used sealed-bid second-price auctions to form a spot market in which free time slices on CPU resources were traded. In the Popcorn system, goods called JOP (Java operations per second) were traded in a resource market using three alternative market mechanisms; Vickrey auctions, a simple double auction and a clearinghouse double auction. Price dynamics, social efficiency and price stability were analyzed and showed promising results for an environment with non-strategic buyers and sellers.

More recently, HP Labs developed an economic resource manager (Feldman, 2005) for grids using a proportional sharing mechanism in which a user obtains an allocation share on a resource that corresponds to the relative weight of its bid to all the other active bids on the resource. A *best-response algorithm* computes the optimal division of credits among the different resources, given the current price levels and the consumer's budgetary limits. AuYoung (2004) presents an economic resource manager which uses *combinatorial auctions* (Cramton, 2006) for allocating time slots on different motes in a sensor net testbed at Intel. A similar but richer approach (in terms of bid expressiveness), is adopted by Schnizler (2007) for grids. From a usage model point of view it is clear that adopting combinatorial auctions, in which a participant can submit a single bid for a combination of goods, is one of the most attractive organizations. It enables consumers to accurately define their valuations for specific collections of grid resources that are required by their applications. As such, it allows for expressing valuations that are conditional on the co-allocation of a set of resources. This eliminates the *exposure problem* (Bykowsky, 1995) users face when they need to participate in multiple auctions for acquiring the constituent parts of an allocation bundle. However, this approach suffers from high computational complexity which can mostly be attributed to the NP-completeness of determining the optimal set of winners in such an auction (Lehmann, 2006). In addition, the lower bounds on the communicative complexity of the value elicitation process in combinatorial auctions also inhibit their applicability for large scale economies, certainly in the case of general bidder valuations and when aiming for exact efficiency (Segal, 2006).

Aside from the applications within the grid domain (Abramson, 2002; Gomoluch, 2003; Wolski, 2006; Vanmechelen, 2006), (consult (Buyya, 2005) for an overview), economic models for resource sharing have also been applied to agent systems (Bredin, 2003; Dash, 2003), telecommunication networks (Haque, 2005), databases (Stonebraker, 1996) and data mining (Joita, 2007).

The work by Shneidman (2005) reinforces the promise of applying economically inspired forms of resource management. It also identifies the reasons for the limited penetration of these ideas in contemporary production level resource management systems, and the associated research challenges.

MAIN FOCUS

We now turn to our simulation study that compares two different dynamic pricing approaches for trading CPU resources in grid economies. Due to space considerations we cannot fully outline the details of the simulated provider and consumer agents and will focus on the two market mechanisms and their resulting outcomes. In short, consumers interact with the market to obtain resources for their independent and CPU-bound jobs. In doing so, they use a *valuation factor* which expresses their personal preference for resources, given the resource's performance characteristics. As a budget management policy, consumers spread out their expenditures evenly over a time period (the *allowance period*). Within their budgetary limits, consumers attempt to allocate as many resources as possible. In this contribution, providers are considered to be price takers and will therefore not impose reservation prices or throttle their supply to the market in order to obtain higher revenues. For a more detailed discussion we refer to (Vanmechelen, 2007).

Dynamic Pricing

In the following, we assume that our market mechanisms will set prices for one time unit of usage of a CPU resource, and that this price level is to be paid by the consumer as a fixed rate for the entire duration of the user's job.

The mechanism used for determining prices in both Vickrey auction and commodity market organizations is fundamentally different. In the commodity market, market-wide prices for different CPU categories are dynamically set in every pricing step by an optimizer, called the *Walrasian Auctioneer*. The categories introduced in the market reflect the performance class a traded CPU belongs to. The optimizer adjusts the price in order to bring the market to equilibrium by iteratively polling all market participants for their current supply and demand levels for each CPU category. This information is used to define an *excess demand* surface, i.e. the difference between current demand and supply as a function of the price vector over all CPU categories. An example of such an excess demand surface for a commodity market with two substitutable CPU categories is shown in Figure 1. Note that we use the Euclidean norm of the excess demand vector in the figure. The price formation process boils down to a minimization of the N-dimensional excess demand function through alterations of the market price vector. The global zero search algorithm that we adopt is a combination of the algorithm presented in (Stuer, 2007), which is an adaptation of Smale's algorithm (Smale, 1976), and a pattern search algorithm (Lewis, 2002) of which we use the implementation provided by Matlab's "Genetic Algorithm and Direct Search Toolbox".

The information gathering process for the demand and supply levels can be organized in a hierarchical, tree-based manner as depicted in Figure 2 in order to improve scalability. However, the actual price adjustment process needs to be performed by a centralized service. Multiple such pricing services could coexist in a deployed grid architecture, each forming market prices within its local region. This however, can no longer guarantee equilibrium market prices across all regions. In this sense, there is a trade-off between economic efficiency and scalability of the commodity market model in the setting of global grids.

In the auction market, each provider hosts a number of single-unit Vickrey auctions, one for each CPU that is available at that point in time. Consumers submit their sealed bids to the auctioneers of the CPUs they are interested in. The Vickrey auction allocates the CPU to the consumer with the highest bid, at the transaction price of the second highest bid (or zero if there is only one bidder). The fact that the consumer's transaction price does not depend on its own bid forms the basis for the incentive compatibility of the Vickrey auction. This means that a consumer has no incentive to place a bid which differs from its true value for the CPU, because no strategic advantage can be gained from this act.

Simulation

We resort to a simulated market environment for analyzing the commodity and auction market organizations. For this we use GES (Grid Economics Simulator), a Java-based discrete-time simulator that we developed to support research into different market organizations for economic Grid resource management. The simulator supports both non-economic and economic forms of resource management and allows for efficient comparative analysis of different resource management systems. We currently have built-in support for commodity markets, different forms of auctions (English, Dutch, Vickrey, combinatorial and double auctions), futures markets (Vanmechelen,

Figure 1. Excess demand surface for a commodity market with two CPU categories

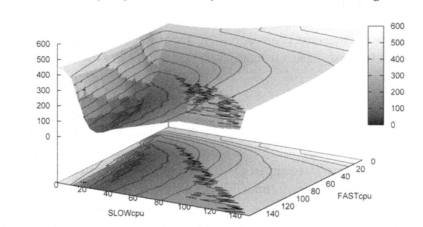

Figure 2. Tree-based excess demand propagation

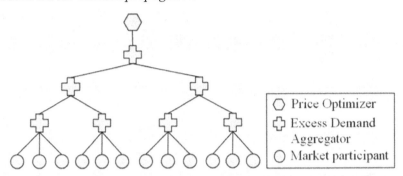

2008), fixed pricing as in (Buyya, 2002), and implementations of other market mechanisms such as the proportional sharing approach found in Tycoon (Feldman, 2005). Non-economic resource management is supported through FIFO, round robin, and priority schedulers. The simulator is equipped with a user interface for supporting efficient analysis and configuration of market scenarios. A persistency framework allows for storing both scenario configurations and configurations of the UI layout. A screen shot of the UI is shown in Figure 3.

The parameters for the simulated scenario are given in Table 1. For parameters that are specified with a range, we draw values from a uniform random distribution. Three groups of consumers with different budget levels are created by multiplying a consumer's base allowance with the respective allowance factor of its group. The valuation factors influence the additional value a consumer attributes to CPUs in the two highest performance categories.

In every simulated time step, pricing takes place through the commodity market mechanism, or as a result of bidding interactions in the auction market.

As shown in Figure 4, the average prices paid by the consumers are similar when the workload

Table 1. Simulation parameters

Parameter	Value
Number of consumers	100
Number of providers	50
Number of fast CPUs per provider	{1, 2, ... , 7}
Number of medium CPUs per provider	{3, 4, ... , 11}
Number of slow CPUs per provider	{9, 10, ... , 17}
Performance ratio of fast vs slow CPU	3.0
Performance ratio of medium vs slow CPU	2.0
Valuation factors	[1.0,1.5]
Job running time in time steps	{4, 5, ... , 8}
Number of jobs per consumer	{150, 151, ... , 500}
Base allowance	1,000,000 * [1.0,1.5]
Allowance factors consumer groups 1, 2, 3	{1.0, 2.0, 3.0}
Allowance period in time steps	800

Figure 3. Screenshot of the GES user interface

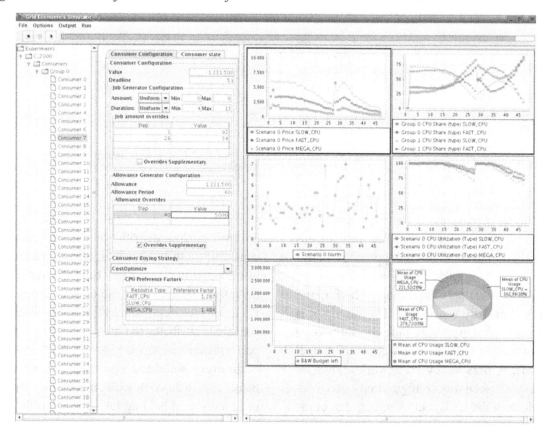

is kept constant during the simulation. The auction market shows a higher fluctuation in the price levels over the course of the simulation with a relative standard deviation (Snedecor, 1967), of 5.86% versus 1.62% for the commodity market. The deviation for the auction market prices does not include the instable price levels of the first 10 steps, if these are included, the deviation reaches 9.62%. Whereas the commodity market immediately brings the market to equilibrium through global optimization, the participants in the auctions still have to learn their optimal target parallelization degree, i.e. the amount of resources to bid on, through local interactions. This results in the extensive adjustments of the average CPU price paid at the beginning of the simulation.

Figure 5 shows the resulting prices for a scenario in which the initial workload is injected into the system every 45 simulation steps. Both market mechanisms dynamically adjust the price level to reflect the relation between demand and supply. This differs from the results presented in (Wolski, 2003) that show erratic pricing behavior for the auction market. A possible explanation for this is the complementarity of the goods traded in that study (CPU resources and storage). Further research is required however to provide a definite explanation for this behavior. We note that the two price peaks for the slow CPU category in the commodity market scenario are caused by the fact that no slow CPU resources are available for trade at those time instances. The equilibrium optimizer therefore generates a high price level for these resources in order to eradicate all demand in the market.

We note that in case of a dynamic market environment in which consumers and providers

Figure 4. Prices for the commodity market (left) and Vickrey auction market (right) under constant load

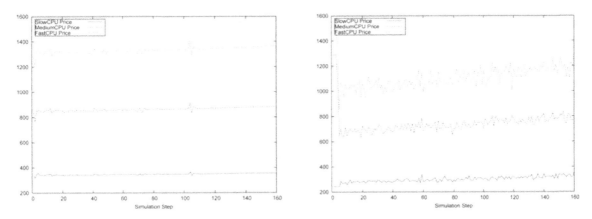

Figure 5. Prices under varying load for the commodity market (left) and Vickrey auction market (right)

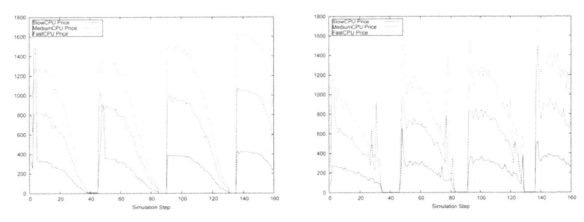

randomly leave and join the network, the sound properties of the commodity market also hold Abdelkader (2008).

Figure 6 compares the budget shares of three consumer groups in the market with their allocated shares of the infrastructure. In a fair market operation, these shares should correspond. We see that this is the case for the commodity market, in the Vickrey auction market correspondence is not achieved in the first simulation steps but gradually improves as the simulation progresses. This is a consequence of the incorrect estimations of the target parallelization degree by the consumer agents in the first steps of the simulation. Agents

with low budgets underestimate the market price which allows the wealthy agents to win all resource auctions, resulting in a 100% share of the infrastructure.

In terms of scalability, the commodity market induces significantly higher computational and communicative costs as a result of the N-dimensional price optimization process. The difference increases with the number of distinct commodities in the market. This limits the specificity by which users can express their valuations for grid resources. For details we refer to (Vanmechelen, 2007).

Figure 6. Budget and infrastructural shares as a cumulative average for the commodity market (left) and Vickrey auction market (right) under constant load

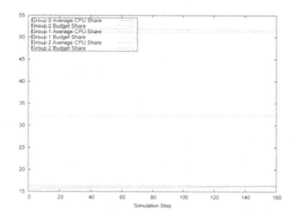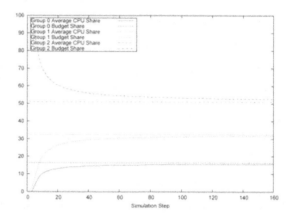

FUTURE TRENDS

Research into economic forms of grid resource management is gaining interest both in academia as in the industry, as evidenced by recent research activities partnered by HP (Lai, 2004), LogicaCMG (Altmann, 2007) and Sun Microsystems (Neumann, 2007). Within the context of the sixth framework programme of the EU IST, a number of projects have been accepted with a specific focus on this domain. SORMA (Neumann, 2007) focuses on the development and analysis of market mechanisms suitable for grid resource management. The GridEcon (Altmann, 2007) project concentrates on the new opportunities that an open grid service market can bring in terms of service orientation and realization of business value. The AssessGrid (Voss, 2007) project targets the issues of risk management that participants face when performing negotiations in a grid market place.

A number of important future trends and research opportunities include the development of bidding tools to support the user in its bidding process, field testing of market mechanisms and integration of these mechanisms through standardized interfaces in existing grid middleware, the integration of data dependencies and network characteristics in economic resource managers

with dynamic pricing, and the development of market mechanisms that allow more complex QoS constraints to be expressed. An example of this is the inclusion of complex workflows and workload dependencies. This requires a move from *spot markets* such as the ones presented in this contribution, to *futures markets*. We see a convergence here between research into next generation resource management systems that support advanced quality of service constraints through e.g. reservations, and economic resource management systems that rely on this evolution to accurately implement negotiated resource sharing contracts. Lastly, we observe that aside from the bottom-up approach which extends resource management systems to more advanced economic aware systems, there is a simultaneous stream of research that already assumes the existence of such systems and investigates the new business opportunities this technology will create (Stanoevska-Slabena, 2007).

CONCLUSION

The introduction of economic principles into grid resource management is a promising approach for building grid systems that are open, sustainable and that maximize perceived value for grid users.

A key aspect in the realization of this vision is the development of market mechanisms for pricing and trading grid resources. We have presented simulation results of two popular mechanisms for pricing computational grid resources in the form of Vickrey auction and commodity market models. Although the commodity market results in a more stable environment, this comes at a computational and communicative cost. In addition, this organization has limited support for fine-grained valuations because of the high communication costs when defining a large number of resource categories, and its centralized nature. The Vickrey auction organization leads to similar but less stable outcomes and supports fine-grained valuations at significantly lower communicative requirements.

REFERENCES

Abdelkader, K., Broeckhove J., & Vanmechelen, K. (2008). Commodity resource pricing in dynamic computational grids. In *Proceedings of the ACS/IEEE International Conference on Computer Systems and Applications (AICCSA '2008)*, IEEE Computer Society.

Abramson, D., Buyya, R., & Giddy, J. (2002). A computational economy for Grid computing and its implementation in the Nimrod-G resource broker. *Future Generation Computer Systems*, *18*(8), 1061-1074.

Altmann, J., Courcoubetis, C., Darlington, J., & Cohen, J., (2007). GridEcon – The economic-enhanced next-generation Internet. In J. Altmann, & D.J. Veit (Eds.), In *Proceedings of the 4th International Workshop on Grid Economics and Business Models*, Lecture Notes in Computer Science (LNCS 4685, pp. 188-193). Heidelberg: Springer-Verlag.

AuYoung, A., Chun, B.N., Snoeren, A.C., & Vahdat, A. (2004). Resource allocation in federated distributed computing infrastructures. In *Proceedings of the 1st Workshop on Operating System and Architectural Support for the On-demand IT Infrastructure*

Bredin, J., Maheswaran, R.T., Imer, C., Basar, T., Kotz, D., & Rus, D. (2003). Computational markets to regulate mobile-agent systems. *Autonomous Agents and Multi Agent Systems*, *6*(3), 235-263.

Buyya, R., Abramson, D., & Venugopal, S. (2005). The Grid economy. *Proceedings of the IEEE*, *93*(3), 698-714.

Buyya, R. (2002). *Economic-based distributed resource management and scheduling for grid computing.* Doctoral dissertation, Monash University, Australia.

Bykowsky, M., Cull, R., & Ledyard, J.O. (1995). Mutually destructive bidding: The FCC auction design problem. *Journal of Regulatory Economics*, *17*(3), 205-228.

Chun, B. N., Buonadonna, P., AuYoung, A., Chaki, N., Parkes, D.C., Shneidman, J., Snoeren, A.C., & Vahdat, A. (2005). Mirage: A microeconomic resource allocation system for sensornet testbeds. In *Proceedings of the Second IEEE Workshop on Embedded Networked Sensors* (pp. 19-28). Los Alamitos, CA: IEEE Society Press.

Cramton, P., Shoham, Y., & Steinberg, R. (Eds.). (2006). *Combinatorial auctions.* Cambridge, MA: MIT Press.

Dash, R.K., Parkes, D.C., & Jennings, N.R. (2003). Computational mechanism design: A call to arms. *IEEE Intelligent Systems*, *18*(6), 40-47.

Feldman, M., Lai, K., & Zhang, L. (2005). A price-anticipating resource allocation mechanism for distributed shared clusters. In *Proceedings of the 6th ACM conference on Electronic commerce* (pp. 127–136). New York: ACM Press.

Fudenberg, D., & Tirole, J. (1991). *Game theory.* Cambridge, MA: MIT Press.

Gomoluch, J., & Schroeder, M. (2003). Market-based resource allocation for Grid computing: A model and simulation. In *Proceedings of the 1st International Workshop on Middleware for Grid Computing* (pp. 211–218). Rio de Janeiro: PUC-Rio

Haque, N., Jennings, N. R. and Moreau, L. (2005). Resource allocation in communication networks using market-based agents. *International Journal of Knowledge Based Systems, 18*(4-5), 163-170.

Harsanyi, J. (1967). Games with incomplete information played by Bayesian players, I - III. *Management Science, 14*, 159-182, 320-334, 486-502.

Joita, L., Rana, O., Freitag, F., Chao, I., Chacin, P., Navarro, L., & Ardaiz, O. (2007). A catallactic market for data mining services. *Future Generation Computer Systems*, 23(1), 146-153.

Lai, K., Rasmusson, L., Adar, E., Sorkin, S., Zhang, L., & Huberman, B.A. (2004). *Tycoon: an implementation of a distributed market-based resource allocation system* (Tech. Rep. arXiv:cs. DC/0412038). Palo Alto, CA: HP Labs.

Lehmann, D., Müller, R., & Sandholm, T. (2006). The winner determination problem. In P. Cramton, Y. Shoham, R. Steinberg, R. (Eds.), *Combinatorial auctions* (pp. 297–317). Cambridge, MA: MIT Press.

Lewis, R., & Torczon, V. (2002). A globally convergent augmented Lagrangian pattern search algorithm for optimization with general constraints and simple bounds. *SIAM Journal on Optimization, 12*(4), 1075-1089.

Neumann, D., Stoesser, J., Anandasivam, A., & Borissov, N., (2007). SORMA – Building an open Grid market for Grid resource allocation. In J. Altmann, D.J. Veit (Eds.), *Proceedings of the 4th International Workshop on Grid Economics and Business Models* (LNCS 4685, pp. 194-200). Heidelberg: Springer-Verlag.

Regev, O., & Nisan, N. (1998). The POPCORN market – an online market for computational resources. In *Proceedings of the 1st International Conference on Information and Computation Economies* (pp. 148-157). New York: ACM Press.

Segal, I. (2006). The communication requirements of combinatorial allocation problems. In P. Cramton, Y. Shoham, & R. Steinberg, R. (Eds.), *Combinatorial Auctions* (pp. 265–294). Cambridge, MA: MIT Press.

Shneidman, J., Ng, C., Parkes, D.C., AuYoung, A., Snoeren, A.C., Vahdat, A., & Chun, B. (2005). Why markets could (but don't currently) solve resource allocation problems in systems. In *Proceedings of the 10th conference on Hot Topics in Operating Systems*. Berkeley: USENIX Association

Schnizler, B. (2007). *Resource allocation in the Grid: A market engineering approach*. Doctoral dissertation, Universitätsverlag Karlsruhe, Karlsruhe.

Smale, S. (1976). A convergent process of price adjustment and global Newton methods. *Journal of Mathematical Economics, 3*(2), 107-120.

Snedecor, G., Cochran, W.G. (1967). *Statistical methods* (pp. 62-64). Ames, IA: The Iowa State University Press.

Stanoevska-Slabena, K., Talamanca, C.F., Thanos, G.A., & Zsigri, C. (2007) Development of a generic value chain for the grid industry. In J. Altmann, & D.J. Veit (Eds.), *Proceedings of the 4th International Workshop on Grid Economics and Business Models* (LNCS 4685, pp. 44-57). Heidelberg: Springer-Verlag.

Stonebraker, M., Aoki, P.M., Litwin, W., Pfeffer, A., Sah, A., & Sidell, J. (1996). Mariposa: A wide-area distributed database system. *The International Journal on Very Large Databases, 5*(1), 48-63.

Stuer, G., Vanmechelen, K., & Broeckhove, J. (2007). A commodity market algorithm for pricing substitutable Grid resources. *Future Generation Computer Systems, 23*(5), 688-701.

Sutherland, I.E. (1968). A futures market in computer time. *Communications of the ACM, 11*(6), 449-451.

Vanmechelen, K., Stuer, G., & Broeckhove, J. (2006). Pricing substitutable Grid resources using commodity market models. In H.Y. Lee, & S. Miller (Eds.), *Proceedings of the 3rd International Workshop on Grid Economics and Business Models* (pp. 103-112). Singapore: World Scientific.

Vanmechelen, K., & Broeckhove, J., (2007). A comparative analysis of single-unit Vickrey auctions and commodity markets for realizing Grid economies with dynamic pricing. In J. Altmann, D.J. Veit (Eds.), *Proceedings of the 4th International Workshop on Grid Economics and Business Models* (LNCS 4685, pp. 98-111). Heidelberg: Springer-Verlag.

Vanmechelen, K., Depoorter, W., & Broeckhove, J., (2008). Economic Grid resource management for CPU bound applications with hard deadlines. In *Proceedings of the 8th IEEE International Symposium on Cluster Computing and the Grid (CCGrid 2008)*. Lyon (France), IEEE Computer Society.

Vickrey, W. (1961). Counterspeculation, auctions, and competitive sealed tenders. *Journal of Finance, 16*(1), 8-37.

Voss, K., Djemame, K., Gourlay, I., & Padgett, J., (2007). AssessGrid, economic issues underlying risk awareness in Grids. In J. Altmann, D.J. Veit (Eds.), *Proceedings of the 4th International Workshop on Grid Economics and Business Models* (LNCS 4685, pp. 170-175). Heidelberg: Springer-Verlag.

Waldspurger, C.A., Hogg, T., Huberman, B.A., Kephart, J.O., & Stornetta, W.S. (1992). Spawn: A distributed computational economy. *IEEE Transactions on Software Engineering, 18*(2), 103-117.

Wolski, R., Brevik, J., Plank, J.S., & Bryan, T. (2003). Grid resource allocation and control using computational economies. In F. Berman, G.C. Fox, & A.J.G. Hey (Eds.), *Grid Computing: Making the Global Infrastructure a Reality* (pp. 747-772). Chicester: Wiley and Sons.

KEY TERMS AND DEFINITIONS

Bayes-Nash Equilibrium: When a system is in a Bayes-Nash equilibrium, the best strategy for each participant is to be truthful, provided that all other participants are truthful as well.

Best-Response Algorithm: An algorithm that determines the strategy that produces the best possible immediate outcome for a bidder, taking other bidder's strategies as given.

Commodity Market: A market in which products are traded that have no qualitative difference.

Exposure Problem: The problem that occurs when bidders have to win several objects in a (set of) auction(s) but are exposed to the risk of not winning all of them as competition on some of these objects turns out to be tougher than expected.

Futures Market: A market in which goods are sold that are to be delivered at a certain point in the future, at a specified price.

Incentive Compatibility: A mechanism is incentive compatible if it is best for all participants to be truthful in their actions. This means that there is no strategic advantage to be gained by being dishonest.

Spot Market: A market in which goods are sold and delivered immediately.

Vickrey Auction: A second-price sealed-bid auction that has been proven to be incentive compatible. Bidders are not allowed to see each other's bids. The highest bidder wins the auction and pays a transaction price which corresponds to the bid of the second highest bidder.

Walrasian Auctioneer: A hypothetical entity that facilitates market adjustment in disequilibrium by announcing prices and collecting information about supply and demand at those prices without any disequilibrium transactions actually taking place.

Chapter XVIII
Resource Usage Accounting in Grid Computing

Rosario M. Piro
INFN and University of Torino, Italy

ABSTRACT

Large, geographically distributed and heterogeneous computing infrastructures, such as the Grid, often span multiple organizations and administrative domains. In such infrastructures, resource usage accounting, i.e. keeping track of the resources consumed by single users or entire organizations, is a non-trivial but very important task. This chapter introduces some general aspects and discusses the fundamental requirements that need to be fulfilled in order to guarantee an accurate resource usage accounting. Typical accounting procedures and current practices are described along with other related issues such as the normalization of resource usage information, the standardization of accounting interfaces, billing and charging, resource pricing, market-oriented resource allocation and economic scheduling.

INTRODUCTION

In the last years, Grid Computing has proven to be one of the most promising approaches to satisfying the ever growing computational power requirements by research and industry. Many globally distributed large-scale production Grids that span multiple organizations and administrative domains have been deployed. Such collaborative Grid Computing environments require not only mechanisms for a balanced access of many thousands of simultaneous users, but also specific middleware components that can keep track of the resources consumed by the single Grid users, as well as by entire organizations, in order to guarantee a fair sharing of available resources, allow for a balanced cost allocation among the participating organizations, and evaluate whether Grid service providers fulfill the established service level agreements (SLAs). But the need for an accurate accounting of resource usage will be even more pressing in future commercial Grid environments. Hence, resource usage accounting can be considered one of the key middleware tasks in Grid Computing.

However, accounting in a large, geographically distributed and heterogeneous computing infrastructure, such as the Grid, is not a trivial task. This article introduces some general aspects of Grid accounting and discusses some of the most important features an accounting system should have. Furthermore, economic aspects of Grid Computing (billing and charging, but also market-based resource allocation and economic scheduling) that rely on accurate accounting information are briefly described. Finally, some shortcomings of current Grid accounting practices and possible future developments are highlighted.

BACKGROUND

Accounting is often considered as an important basic service of the Grid's authentication, authorization and accounting (AAA) infrastructure. The resource usage information collected by a Grid accounting system could be used for diverse purposes. Apart from the analysis of usage statistics and summaries for single users or entire organizations, accounting information may, for example, be exploited by an automated policy management system to ensure Grid-wide quota enforcement (Ciaschini et al., 2006).

In a commercial context, resource usage information is essential to allow for billing and charging for the services rendered to remote users. But even in multi-organizational non-commercial environments, such as collaborative Grid infrastructures used by research and academia, in which single users are usually not charged for their resource

consumption, accounting information may be important for funding and cost allocation between the involved parties. Moreover, such usage data can help in predicting future demand for specific services and hence in improving the Grid infrastructure for the benefit of its users.

The need for a proper usage accounting exists also in traditional multi-user systems. But the dynamic nature, the global distribution, the high degree of heterogeneity (e.g. different Local Resource Management Systems on computational resources) and the division into different administrative domains of Grid infrastructures pose additional challenges in terms of decentralization, scalability and flexibility to Grid accounting systems (Thigpen et al., 2002). In turn, they can benefit from the Grid's authentication and authorization mechanisms to establish the identity and credentials of the Grid users that request the accounted services (Thigpen et al., 2002).

Requirements for Grid Accounting

In many cases, detailed information for single service requests is required (especially in a commercial or economic context), such as CPU time, run time, memory usage and start and end time in case of the execution of a "job" on a remote Computing Element (CE). Other use cases, however, involve the aggregation of accounting information in order to determine, for example, the total resources requested by a single user at a specific site or over the entire Grid, or the resources consumed for a specific project. To satisfy these different use cases, a Grid accounting system should be able to report usage data from fine (for single service requests/job submissions) to coarse (arbitrary aggregations) granularity.

An essential requirement is the ability to unequivocally assign usage records to the requesting Grid user and the corresponding home organization (e.g. in case of research institutes or companies on whose behalf the user is requesting a service). In practice, however, such an assignment is not trivial (computational resources, for example, are often managed by local batch systems, most of which record only local information for single jobs and are not aware that a job has entered their queues through a Grid middleware component/ gatekeeper) and not in all cases possible due to the complexity and wide range of different site configurations. On the LHC Computing Grid (see http://lcg.web.cern.ch/LCG/), for example, a considerable amount of "out-of-band" work is being performed through non-Grid interfaces to the computing resources.

Due to the potentially unlimited number of service instances and their users on Grid infrastructures, one of the major concerns for all Grid middleware components is the need for scalability without a significant loss of performance. This requirement can best be met through decentralization of management (including accounting). A distributed network of accounting servers, as for example provided by DGAS (Piro at al., 2003; http://www.to.infn.it/grid/accounting/), SGAS (Sandholm et al., 2004), GridBank (Barmouta and Buyya, 2003) and RUDA (Chen et al., 2005), does not rely on a less scalable centralized accounting repository, as it is used for example by APEL (Byrom et al., 2005). The distribution of accounting data over multiple databases, however, has the disadvantage that, for specific use cases, Grid-wide usage statistics may be more difficult to obtain. Some distributed systems, such as DGAS and RUDA, try to overcome this drawback by allowing the deployment of a hierarchical infrastructure of higher level accounting servers that can collect and aggregate usage information from multiple primary (or lower level) servers.

The importance of accounting information, especially in a commercial or economic context, demands strict security mechanisms for data transport through secure and authenticated communication channels, in order to guarantee integrity and reliability of the usage records. The need for integrity and completeness of accounting information demands also a high degree of robustness and fault-tolerance of the information gathering and storage process. Decentralized accounting procedures, apart from being more scalable (see above), may aid in avoiding single points-of-failure.

Since accounting systems often need to handle private information (e.g. usage statistics associated to specific user certificate subjects), the confidentiality of such information should be ensured by the adoption of strict access control mechanisms. That is, Grid users should be able to access only information regarding their own service requests/ jobs, while administrators or managers may have access to the accounting information regarding the group of users and/or services they are responsible for. Aggregated usage statistics that cannot be attributed to a single person can often be made public. In any case, when deciding upon such access rights, the applicable legislation for data privacy has to be considered.

Accounting Procedures

Typical accounting procedures in Grid environments can be described by means of the simple, layered model shown in Fig. 1. As can be seen, an accounting system, for being functional, requires more than just accounting servers that store usage records and associate them to service instances and the users that requested them. Resource usage has to be metered and the resulting records have to be collected from the service instances. This is usually accomplished by dedicated accounting sensors installed on the service hosts. For the purpose of usage data analysis an interface to the accounting system must be provided, such that the accounting data (for single requests or statistics) can be communicated to authorized clients. In a commercial context, an accounting system may also provide procedures for account balancing or billing and charging (described below), but such procedures may also be decoupled from the accounting system (as shown in the figure) or may be omitted in collaborative environments.

Figure 1. Simplified model of the accounting procedure

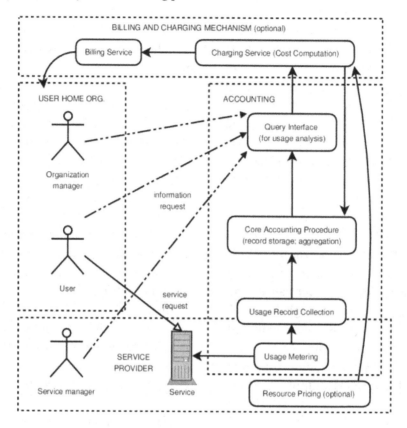

Some accounting systems, like DGAS, provide additional components for resource pricing, but these as well are not strictly necessary for the accounting task itself.

Accounting sensors for usage metering may come in different flavors, since they have to be capable of extracting the required usage information from heterogeneous service instance implementations (e.g. from widely differing Local Resource Management Systems, or batch systems, used for computational resources). The integration of local usage information (e.g. CPU time, run time, memory usage, execution start time) with Grid-related information (e.g. Distinguished Name of the user's certificate subject, Grid job ID) is not always straightforward (as mentioned above), but important in a Grid context.

Depending on the exact purposes for which usage information is gathered, the accounting procedures can foresee a *periodic* (i.e. in defined time intervals, for example once a day), *immediate* (i.e. upon service/job completion) or *real-time* (i.e. incrementally while furnishing a service) accounting of provisioned services. Most systems implement either periodic accounting (e.g. APEL) or immediate accounting (e.g. DGAS), since real-time accounting is difficult to realize and in many cases not required.

In practice, accounting procedures and requirements may differ from those described above, since different Grid environments may have different needs. For example, in Peer-to-Peer Grids (Foster and Iamnitchi, 2003), where participants can often freely join the system without stringent needs for authentication accounting solutions cannot rely on a trust relationship among parties, i.e. usage records obtained from remote resource providers cannot simply be trusted. Nonetheless, accounting for resource usage is important, because free-riding is a common behavior in peer-to-peer systems (Santos et al., 2005). A possible solution is an autonomous accounting scheme that is not based on the exchange of usage information and instead relies on the observed relative performance among peers (Santos et al., 2005). In such a case, however, many usage parameters, that cannot be directly observed by the consumer (such as CPU time and memory consumption), can at the most be estimated. Also for Campus Grids some of the requirements can be less stringent. Due to the limited scale, for example, centralized accounting solutions are in most cases sufficient.

Current Accounting Practices

Although the accounting tools used by the major Grid projects differ widely, their accounting practices usually reflect the simplified model depicted in Fig.1. Gratia, the accounting tool of the Open Science Grid (OSG; http://www.opensciencegrid. org), for example, implements periodic metering and inserts records into distributed accounting servers from where they are fetched for storage in a central repository. Both detailed job-level and summary accounting information is available through Web portals and Web Services interfaces.

On the TeraGrid (http://www.teragrid.org) resource consumption is metered by local, site-specific accounting systems. Local usage information is then converted into a shared format and forwarded to a central database (Beckman, 2005).

Most sites of the EGEE/LCG (Enabling Grids for E-sciencE; http://www.eu-egee.org) infrastructure use APEL to periodically meter resource usage and forward accounting records to a central database located at the Grid Operations Center (GOC). Usage statistics (but no detailed job information) are available through a Web portal. A notable exception is INFN-Grid (http://grid.infn. it) that constitutes the Italian EGEE/LCG sites and

uses DGAS for immediate usage metering and accounting on a distributed network of accounting servers. Usage information is available in the form of usage statistics as well as for single jobs. Accounting records are periodically converted to the format used by APEL to be forwarded to the GOC database.

Other Grid infrastructures/projects have adopted comparable solutions, such as SGAS, used by NorduGrid (http://www.nordugrid.org), or the Resource Usage Service of the UK National Grid Service (NGS; http://www.grid-support.ac.uk).

MAIN FOCUS

The following discussion briefly addresses some interesting and controversial issues related to resource usage accounting in Grid Computing. A more detailed discussion, however, is out of scope of this article.

Accounting and/vs. Monitoring

Although, as depicted in Fig. 2, there is some overlap between the accounting of resource usage and the monitoring of services and service requests, the final purpose of these two important middleware tasks is substantially different.

The monitoring activity can roughly be classified in infrastructure monitoring and application monitoring (Aiftimiei et al., 2007).

Application monitoring (we might more generally speak of service provision monitoring) aims at observing the status of the execution of service requests (e.g. status of a job execution or a file upload) and may also involve the determination of some usage information (hence the overlap with accounting, see Fig. 2). This allows users to keep track of their single service requests, but also to identify reasons for job failures (see for example Müller-Pfefferkorn et al., 2006).

Many existing monitoring tools, however, focus on infrastructure monitoring (Müller-

Figure 2. Accounting and/vs. monitoring

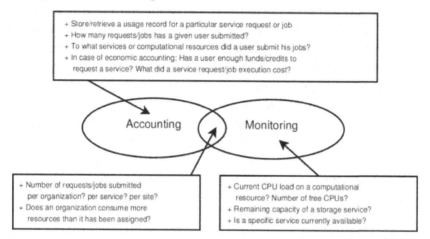

Pfefferkorn et al., 2006), providing information on services and sites, such as service status (up and running), CPU load, number of available CPUs, queue length, remaining storage space, number of queued requests, available bandwidth, etc. Such status information is usually unimportant for an accounting system, that, as described above, is concerned with accurately and reliably measuring and reporting resource consumption. Also, monitoring systems mostly gather information that is not directly associated with a particular person (with the exception of application monitoring) and consequently requires less stringent mechanisms for security and privacy.

Normalization of Usage Information

One of the most underestimated difficulties regarding Grid accounting is the normalization of accounting data originating from heterogeneous resources and service implementations. A part of the measured resource usage of an application (e.g. CPU time), for example, can depend significantly on the processor performance (and other characteristics) of the executing resource. How can usage records from heterogeneous resources be compared in a meaningful way? For this purpose additional information on resource characteristics, such as processing power, is required. However,

benchmarking Grid resources is still a research issue. In general, an accounting system needs to record the raw resource consumption plus additional characteristics regarding the service provider that allow for normalization, instead of storing already normalized usage values. This is necessary to guarantee that usage data remains valid in case normalization procedures should change.

Billing, Charging and Resource Pricing

As already mentioned, neither the pricing of nor billing and charging for services rendered are strictly required for Grid accounting, intended as the tracking of resource usage by Grid users (see for example Schnellmann and Redard, 2006). Especially in a commercial computing environment, however, mechanisms for cost computation and payment may be fundamental and are closely related to the accounting task, because they rely on accurate and reliable tracking of resource consumption. Due to this close relationship the meaning of the terms accounting, charging and billing are often not sufficiently delimited with respect to Grid Computing and easily become erroneously mingled (see Terms and Definitions).

Resource pricing (see Fig. 1) is the dynamic or manual assignment of a price to an offered resource or service. Charging is the assignment of a cost to a resource consumption. The two procedures may be integrated, but as depicted in Fig. 1, they can also be separated if pricing is intended per resource unit and cost computation takes information about both the price and the amount of consumed computational energy (Piro et al., 2003) as input. As also described by Morariu et al. (2006), charging is logically located on top of metering and accounting, but does not include billing, that is the delivery of charging information to the user and the processing of the payment (often by a trusted third party). These differences are, however, of a conceptual nature and implementations of accounting and/or charging and billing systems may unite the different concepts into a single framework. In any case, charging and service cost information should be fed back into the accounting system, as indicated in Fig. 1. Note that charging and billing may be of interest also in a non-commercial, collaborative context for a fair cost allocation to the participating organizations. In such a case it may be better to speak of "account balancing" rather than charging and billing.

Generally, the purpose of a Grid accounting system should not be to define (and hence limit) the economic interactions between users and resource owners, but to provide the necessary information to enable them.

Market-Oriented Resource Allocation and Economic Scheduling

The two major objectives associated with multi-user resource allocation in Grids are fairness among users and their applications and the balance between the overall throughput of the system and Quality of Service (QoS) for the single applications, thus seeking high utilization, but not at the expense of QoS and vice versa. This is particularly difficult when resource demand exceeds resource supply and when producers (resource owners) and consumers (resource users) have different goals, objectives, and strategies. Economic approaches to the problem of resource allocation ("computational economies") are widely believed to offer natural and decentralized self-regulating mechanisms that help in balancing demand and supply (see for example Buyya et al., 2005; Ernemann et al., 2002; Eymann et al., 2005; Shneidman et al., 2005; Thigpen et al., 2002; Wolski et al., 2001 and Wolski et al., 2003). However, it has to be noted that not all market-oriented approaches to resource allocation are scalable. Auction-based market models, for example, are difficult to realize in a decentralized manner. The same is true for approaches based on the computation of Grid-wide equilibrium prices that balance demand and supply.

Eymann et al. (2005) distinguish two types of interrelated markets: service markets, that regard the trading of application services, and resource markets, that regard the trading of computational and data resources. The commodities, i.e. tradable resource types, include (but are not limited to) computing power, memory usage, storage space, network bandwidth, and access to particular software libraries and data repositories, but also "value-added" higher level services (composed of other services).

The adoption of a computational economy model can not only help in balancing demand and supply, given an appropriate resource pricing scheme to attract or deter users according to the current service workload. It can also aid in efficiently assigning the incoming service requests to different service providers on the Grid (workload balancing by means of economic scheduling; see for example Piro et al., 2004 and Piro et al., 2006).

Although markets can provide appropriate mechanisms for resource allocation and workload balancing, their wide adoption on existing Grid infrastructures must overcome key challenges regarding not only conceptual and technical aspects (Cheliotis et al., 2005; Shneidman et al., 2005), but also the understanding, supporting, and using of the mechanisms (Shneidman et al., 2005).

FUTURE TRENDS

Current implementations of Grid accounting systems focus mainly on tracking the usage of processing power in terms of CPU time, run time, memory usage and other parameters describing the resource consumption of user applications/jobs. Grid infrastructures, however, may provide other services, such as storage space, databases, data mining services and value-added (composed) services. Network bandwidth and software licenses may be regarded as tradable resources as well. Although some resource type-specific research – for example on storage accounting (for tracking file size, upload, deletion, access, etc.) – is under way, for future Service-Oriented Architectures (SOAs), an accounting framework for generic services will be necessary.

The need for more generality will most likely have an impact on the Grid community's standardization efforts that aim at interoperability between different Grid implementations thus allowing for even larger collaborations. Two working groups of the Open Grid Forum (OGF; http://www.ogf.org) in particular are concerned with emerging standards related to Grid accounting.

The Usage Record (UR) Working Group defined an XML-based data format for the exchange of usage information. The current specification of the OGF UR (Mach et al., 2006), however, is very batch job specific and is therefore not suitable for the accounting of storage and other services.

The Resource Usage Service (RUS) Working Group is defining a Web Services-based interface to accounting systems for a standardized upload and retrieval of resource usage information in the form of OGF UR documents (Ainsworth et al., 2006). Such an interface may enable different implementations of accounting services to communicate with each other and is therefore

important for the interoperability of different Grid infrastructures (Piro et al., 2007).

An issue that will have to be addressed by the two working groups is the aggregation of usage information. The OGF UR specification, and consequently also the RUS interface, regard only "atomic" usage records (i.e. for single application runs/jobs). Therefore, only custom interfaces can currently be utilized to obtain aggregated/summarized usage statistics from the different Grid accounting systems.

CONCLUSION

Accounting is one of the most important tasks of Grid middleware, especially in large-scale infrastructures of both commercial and collaborative nature, where a tracking of resource usage is essential for charging/billing and fairness of resource sharing, respectively. An accurate resource usage accounting is fundamental for implementing user charging systems and market-oriented resource allocation mechanisms. In this article, we have briefly described the purpose and requirements of Grid accounting and a simplified, layered model of accounting procedures has been discussed. The research on issues regarding Grid accounting is still ongoing and hopefully the development of strategies for accounting generic services and the ongoing standardization, and thus improvement of interoperability, will help in overcoming current shortcomings of Grid accounting systems.

REFERENCES

Aiftimiei, C., Andreozzi, S., Cuscela, G., Donvito, G., Dudhalkar, V., Fantinel, S. et al. (2007). Recent evolutions of GridICE: A monitoring tool for Grid systems. In *Proceedings of the 2007 Workshop on Grid Monitoring* (pp. 1-8), Monterey, California, USA.

Ainsworth, J., Newhouse, S., & MacLaren, J. (2006). *Resource usage service (RUS) based on WS-I Basic Profile 1.0* (draft-ggf-wsi-rus-17). Global/Open Grid Forum. Retrieved August 30, 2007, from http://forge.ogf.org/sf/go/doc7965?nav=1

Barmouta, A., & Buyya, R. (2003, April). Grid-Bank: A Grid accounting service architecture (GASA) for distributed systems sharing and integration. In *Proceedings of the 17th Annual International Parallel and Distributed Processing Symposium* (pp. 245-252), Nice, France.

Beckman, P.H. (2005). Building the TeraGrid. *Philosophical transactions of the royal society A*, 363, 1715-1728.

Buyya, R., Abramson, D., & Venugopal, S. (2005). The Grid economy. In *Proceedings of the IEEE*, 93(3), 698-714.

Byrom, R., Cordenonsi, R., Cornwall, L., Craig, M., Djaoui, A., Duncan, A. et al. (2005). *APEL: an implementation of Grid accounting using R-GMA*. Paper presented at the UK e-Science All Hands Conference, Nottingham, UK.

Cheliotis, G., Kenyon, C., & Buyya, R. (2005). 10 Lessons from Finance for Commercial Sharing of IT Resources. In R. Subramanian, & B.D. Goodman (Eds.), *Peer to peer computing: The evolution of a disruptive technology* (pp. 244-264). Hershey, PA: Idea Group Publishing.

Chen, M.L., Geist, A., Bernholdt, D.E., Chanchio, K., & Million, D.L. (2005). The design and prototype of RUDA, a distributed Grid accounting System (LNCS 3482, pp. 29-38).

Ciaschini, V., Ferraro, A., Ghiselli, A., Rubini, G., Guarise, A., Patania, G. et al., (2006). *An integrated framework for VO-oriented authorization, policy-based management and accounting*. Paper presented at the Conference on Computing in High Energy and Nuclear Physics (CHEP'06), T.I.F.R. Mumbai, India.

Ernemann, C., Hamscher, V., & Yahyapour, R. (2002). Economic scheduling in Grid computing (LNCS 2537, pp. 128-152).

Eymann, T., Reinicke, M., Streitberger, W., Rana, O., Joita, L., Neumann, D., et al. (2005). Catallaxy-based Grid markets. *Multiagent and Grid Systems*, 1(4), 297-307.

Foster, I., & Iamnitchi, A. (2003). On death, taxes, and the convergence of peer-to-peer and Grid computing (LNCS 2735, pp. 118-128).

Mach, R., Lepro-Metz, R., Jackson, S., & McGinnis, L. (2006) *Usage Record -- Format Recommendation* (Version 1, GDF.98). Open Grid forum. Retrieved August 30, 2007, from http://www.ogf.org/documents/GFD.98.pdf

Morariu, C., Waldburger, M., & Stille, B. (2006). *An accounting and charging architecture for mobile Grids* (Tech. Rep. No. 2006.06). Zurich, Switzerland: University of Zurich, Department of Informatics (IFI).

Müller-Pfefferkorn, R., Neumann, R., Borovac, S., Hammad, A., Harenberg, T., Husken, M., et al. (2006). Monitoring of jobs and their execution for the LHC computing Grid. In *Proceedings of the Cracow Grid Workshop (CGW 06)*, Cracow, Poland.

Piro, R.M., Guarise, A., & Werbrouck, A. (2003). An economy-based accounting infrastructure for the DataGrid. In *Proceedings of the 4th International Workshop on Grid Computing* (pp. 202-204), Phoenix, AZ.

Piro, R.M., Guarise, A., & Werbrouck, A. (2004). Simulation of price-sensitive resource brokering and the hybrid pricing model with DGAS-Sim. In *Proceedings of the 13th International Workshops on Enabling Technologies: Infrastructures for Collaborative Enterprises (WETICE 2004)*, Modena, Italy.

Piro, R.M., Guarise, A., & Werbrouck, A. (2006). Price-sensitive resource brokering with the hybrid pricing model and widely overlapping price domains. *Concurrency and Computation: Practice and Experience, 18*(8), 837-850.

Piro, R.M., Pace, M., Ghiselli, A., Guarise, A., Luppi, E., Patania, G., et al. (2007). Tracing resource usage over heterogeneous Grid platforms: A Prototype RUS interface for DGAS. In *Proceedings of the 3rd IEEE International Conference on e-Science and Grid Computing 2007 (eScience2007)*, Bangalore, India.

Sandholm, T., Gardfjäll, P., Elmroth, E., Johnsson, L., & Mulmo, O. (2004). An OGSA-based accounting system for allocation enforcement across HPC centers. In *Proceedings of the 2nd International Conference on Service Oriented Computing*, New York, USA.

Santos, R., Brasileiro, F., Andrade, A., Andrade N., & Cirne, W. (2005). Accurate autonomous accounting in peer-to-peer Grids. In *ACM International Conference Proceeding Series, 117*, 1-6. *3rd International Workshop on Middleware for Grid Computing (MGC'05)*, Grenoble, France.

Schnellmann, P., & Redard, A. (2006). *Accounting for the authentication and authorization infrastructure (AAI) - Pilot Study* (Technical Report, version 1.0). Zurich, Switzerland: SWITCH - The Swiss Education & Research Network.

Shneidman, J., Ng, C., Parkes, D.C., AuYoung, A., Snoeren, A.C., Vahdat, A., & Chun, B. (2005). Why markets could (but don't currently) solve resource allocation problems in systems. In *Proceedings of the 10th Conference on Hot Topics in Operating Systems (HotOS X)*, Santa Fe, NM, USA.

Thigpen, W., Hacker, T.J., McGinnis, L.F., & Athey, B.D. (2002). Distributed accounting on the Grid. In *Proceedings of the 6th Joint Conference on Information Sciences* (pp. 1147-1150), Durham, North Carolina, USA.

Wolski, R., Plank, J.S., Brevik, J., & Bryan, T. (2001). Analyzing market-based resource allocation strategies for the computational Grid. *International Journal of High Performance Computing Applications, 15*(3), 258-281.

Woslki, R., Brevik, J., Plank, J.S., & Bryan, T. (2003). Grid resource allocation and control using computational economies. In F. Berman, G. Fox, & A. Hey (Eds.), *Grid computing: making the global infrastructure a reality* (pp. 747-772). John Wiley & Sons.

KEY TERMS AND DEFINITIONS

Accounting: *Accounting*, in the context of a computational infrastructure, is usually not defined as in finance, since it does not necessarily (but may) involve payment statements. It, instead, is defined as the gathering (including *Metering*), processing (e.g., aggregation) and reporting of resource usage information. Note that *Accounting* itself does not include *Billing* and *Charging*. The term "Economic Accounting" may be used in an economic context in which price or cost information is included in the *Usage Records*.

Billing: *Billing*, in a Grid context, can be defined as the collection and processing of *Charging* information and the delivery of a payment request to the user or its home organization (adapted from Morariu et al., 2006 and Schnellmann and Redard, 2006). Payments can also regard virtual credits rather than true money.

Charging: The assignment of a cost to a resource or service consumption. This cost may be determined from the prices per unit (see *Resource Pricing*) and the actual amount of consumed resources, or *Computational Energy*, that is determined by *Accounting* and stored in a *Usage Record*.

Computational Economy: An artificial economy, set up under a certain set of constraints in order to make it obey a certain set of economic principles, in which consumers are represented by users and their applications (or the Resource Brokers, or metaschedulers, on their behalf) and suppliers by the various Grid resource providers and their services (adapted from Woslki et al., 2003). Note that the term *"computational economy"* refers also to the utilization of computers to solve complex financial problems. In this article, however, it is intended exclusively to refer to artificial economies. In the context of Grid Computing, the term "Grid Economy" (Buyya et al., 2005) can be considered equivalent.

Computational Energy: The *Computational Energy* consumed by a service request is "the product of a performance factor or power p (e.g. a benchmark of CPU speed) and the amount of usage u (e.g. the CPU time), which ideally should be independent of the resource's characteristics." (Piro et al., 2003).

Metering: The measuring of a service request's resource consumption on the service host (or intermediate systems; e.g. routers in case of network resources) and the generation of the corresponding *Usage Record* to be fed into the *Accounting* system.

Resource Pricing: The dynamic or manual assignment, by the resource owner, of a price to an offered resource or service. If prices are determined per unit of *Computational Energy*, price information has to be fed into the *Charging* mechanism to compute the overall cost of a service request.

Resource Usage Service: The *Resource Usage Service* (RUS) is Web Services-based interface to *Accounting* systems, that is being defined by the RUS Working Group of the Open Grid Forum (OGF). The RUS interface (Ainsworth et al., 2006) allows for a standardized upload and retrieval of resource usage information in the form of OGF *Usage Record* documents.

Usage Record: Generally, each accounting record, that in some form describes the resources consumed by a service request, can be called a *Usage Record* (as we do in this article). However, the *Usage Record* (UR) is also a specific, syntactically well-defined XML document (Mach et al., 2006) for job usage information, that is defined by the UR Working Group of the Open Grid Forum (OGF).

Section V
Grid Applications and Future Tools

Chapter XIX
Grid–Based Nuclear Physics Applications

Frans Arickx
University of Antwerp, Belgium

Jan Broeckhove
University of Antwerp, Belgium

Peter Hellinckx
University of Antwerp, Belgium

David Dewolfs
University of Antwerp, Belgium

Kurt Vanmechelen
University of Antwerp, Belgium

ABSTRACT

Quantum structure or scattering calculations often belong to a class of computational problems involving the aggregation of a set of matrices representing a linear problem to be solved. We discuss a number of approaches based on cluster and grid computing, and discuss the implementations and the respective merits and shortcomings. We consider MPI-based cluster computing in a self-scheduling paradigm, CoBRA (a cpu-harvesting desktop grid) in a farmer-worker paradigm, and a batch-computing paradigm on BEGrid (the Belgian research grid facility). It is observed that for all paradigms an efficient implementation is possible, yielding results within a comparable time frame.

INTRODUCTION

Many computational problems belong to a class involving the aggregation of a set of matrices, representing a linear problem to be solved, and which represents a sizeable or major portion of the total computational load.

Microscopic quantum nuclear physics calculations are usually computationally intensive because of a multitude of degrees of freedom. The main aim in such calculations is to obtain a solution for bound or scattering states of the so-called Schrödinger equation. Exact solutions are impossible to obtain except for simplified model problems. A popular technique approximates the solution as an expansion in a complete basis. Such a basis is usually characterized by a multidimensional parameter space. This leads to extensive, but often highly parallelizable calculations of the class mentioned above.

In this paper we consider as an example of the matrix aggregation class of problems, and as a representative for many theoretical nuclear calculations, a description of light nuclei in a microscopic three-cluster model. As is often the case, we start from existing legacy code originally written in Fortran 90. This code is easily parallelizable into a large set of individual subcalculations. We then distribute the calculations on both a cluster (Beowulf) and a Grid (BEgrid) configuration. To solve the distribution of tasks we use 2 distinct approaches on the Beowulf (Gropp et al., 2003) system: task submission using the CoBRA middleware, and a self-scheduling approach based on MPI. On the BEgrid we take a scripting approach to properly submit the individual tasks.

We discuss the timing characteristics of the implementations, and discuss merits and shortcomings. Because of the differences in platforms and middleware, direct comparisons are difficult, but we then compare qualitatively. It is shown that for each of the distribution approaches an efficient implementation is possible within a comparable time frame.

BACKGROUND

Before focusing on the actual distribution, more insight into the actual problem and the possible distribution mechanisms is essential. This section discusses the actual nuclear physics problem and gives a brief introduction to each of the used distribution mechanisms (CoBRA, BeGrid and MPI)

The Nuclear Physics Problem

To obtain physical properties of quantum systems, such as atoms, nuclei or molecules, one needs to solve the Schrödinger equation. In order to solve it, proper boundary conditions must be chosen. The solutions, the so-called wave-functions, then allow for the calculation of physical quantities. The equation and its boundary conditions are usually too complex to be solved exactly for many-body systems (e.g. a nucleus), and approximations have to be introduced. One approach is to expand the wave-function on a discrete, infinite-dimensional, set of basis states. Substitution of this approximation in the equation and boundary conditions leads to a much simpler matrix equation in the expansion coefficients to be solved. The matrix formulation can be further simplified by choosing expansion bases with specified properties. The Modified J-Matrix model (Broeckhove et al., 2004) is such an approach, and has been applied to three-cluster nuclear systems (Vasilevsky et al., 2001). We consider it here to obtain scattering results for a three-particle configuration of a triton and two neutrons of ^5H.

The calculations essentially consist of two steps: (1) a CPU intensive calculation of the matrix elements in the matrix equation, and (2) the solution of the matrix equation. As step 2 can be obtained sequentially on a single node, we will only consider the distribution of step 1. The expansion basis for the solution of a three-cluster problem is enumerated by a set of indices. These are the hypermoment K, describing the three cluster geometry; relative angular momenta l_1 and l_2 between the three clusters coupled to the total angular momentum L, a constant of motion; the oscillator index n. The number of $(l_1 l_2)$ combinations depends on both K and L. The essential matrix to be determined is the energy matrix, denoted by

$$\left\langle K_i, (l_1, l_2)_i L, n_i \middle| \hat{H} \middle| K_j, (l_1, l_2)_j L, n_j \right\rangle = \tag{1}$$

$$\left\langle K_i, l_i, n_i \middle| \hat{H} \middle| K_j, l_j, n_j \right\rangle$$

where $\hat{H}$ is the Hamiltonian, or energy, operator, and i and j distinguish basis states; the right hand side in (1) simplifies the notation. The theory to obtain (1) (Vasilevsky et al. 2001) is well beyond the scope of this paper, but it can be broken down to

$$\left\langle\!\left\langle K_i, l_i \middle| \hat{H} \middle| K_j, l_j \right\rangle\!\right\rangle = \sum\sum\sum R(K_i, l_i, l_r, t)$$

$$\left\langle K_i, l_r \middle| \hat{H} \middle| K_j l_s \right\rangle\!\right\rangle_t R(K_j, l_s, l_j, t) \tag{2}$$

where $\langle\langle\rangle\rangle$ stands for a matrix over all n_i, n_j indices. The R factors (Raynal-Revai) are discussed in (Vasilevsky et al., 2001), and the range of index t depends on the nucleus (^5H) and its cluster decomposition ($t + n + n$). The granularity of the problem is clear from (2), and reduces the problem calculating all independent $\langle\langle K_i l_r | \hat{H} | K_j l_s \rangle\rangle$ matrices for fixed K_i, K_j and all allowed combinations l_r, l_s, t, followed by a summation to obtain (2).

The task graph for computing (2) is therefore relatively simple as all matrices can be calculated independently and in random order before being aggregated in (2). It therefore closely resembles a "bag of tasks" model.

In this paper we focus on an example calculation for $L = 0$ and $K = 0,2,4, \ldots, 16$, a range of $l_1 = l_2 = 0,1,\ldots,K/2$ values, and 45 t values (Broeckhove et al., 2007). All of the computational (legacy) code components are implemented in Fortran90. Individual tasks, each calculating a $\langle\langle K_i l_r | \hat{H} | K_j l_s \rangle\rangle$

matrix, are file based, meaning that they get their input from a series of files and write their results into one. All input files except one, a configuration file which contains the particular indices for the current computation, have a constant content for all tasks. The full ^5H results have been published in (Broeckhove et al., 2007).

Introduction to CoBRA

CoBRA is an acronym for Computational Basic Reprogrammable Adaptive grid, and is a Light-Weight robust grid middleware system with reconfigurable features.

CoBRA was introduced (Hellinckx et al., 2007) to fulfill the needs of different kinds of users ranging from developers to consumers. As this paper describes the distribution of a quantum physics problem we will focus on de the consumer point of view.

The CoBRA grid (see Figure 1 for an overview) is built up from three main components: the Broker, the Scheduler and the Workers. Only the First component is visible to the consumer. The consumer has three responsibilities (Hellinckx et al., 2007).

1. **Implement the taskmaster:** The consumer has to implement the three abstract methods of the abstract taskmaster class:
    - **GetData:** This method defines which data is transferred to the broker before execution.
    - **Run:** This method defines the execution process: Job Creation, Job Submission, Result data processing … (upper text frame in Figure 1)
    - **PutData:** This method transfers the taskmaster's resulting data to the consumer.
2. **Implement the job:** The consumer has to implement the three abstract methods of the abstract job class:

Figure 1. Distribution mechanism of the CoBRA grid

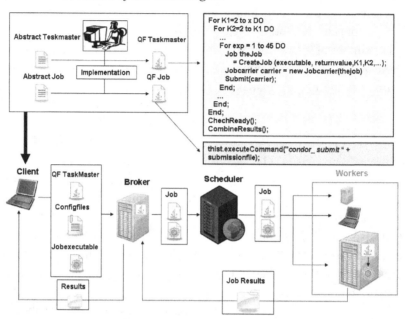

- **GetData:** This method defines which data is transferred from an external machine (in most cases the broker) onto the worker before execution.
- **Execute:** This method defines the actual implementation of a job ranging from plain java code to the execution of a compiled executable (lower text frame in Figure 1).
- **PutData:** This method transfers the job's resulting data to an external machine (in most cases the broker).

3. **Submit the Taskmaster to a CoBRA broker:** When the taskmaster and the job are implemented, the only remaining task of a consumer is to submit the taskmaster to a broker.

Introduction to BEgrid

The BEgrid (BEgrid, 2007) project involves an infrastructural collaboration between several universities and research institutes in Belgium, and is an example of a Heavy-Weight grid. It currently includes sites from the universities of

Antwerp, Ghent, Leuven and Brussels as well as other research institutions such as the Flanders Marine Institute. BEgrid is part of the North European ROC region of the EGEE project (see EGEE reference). Each site operates a cluster integrated in BEgrid, which totals to some 400 CPU's at the time of writing.

The LCG 2.7 middleware (see LCG reference), built on top of the well-known Globus Toolkit (see Globus reference), is used to operate this infrastructure. Most sites are transitioning to gLite (see gLite reference), a new generation middleware for the EGEE project. The middleware comprises a number of modules that cooperate to provide workload, data and information management services. A resource broker matches job requirements, which are expressed in JDL (Job Description Language), to the available computing elements (CEs) and subsequently forwards jobs to CEs. The CE virtualizes compute resources such as PBS, LSF or Condor farms, providing uniform access to heterogeneous compute back-ends. A user has the ability to state complex infrastructural and operational job requirements using a standardized information schema called GLUE.

The broker also supports user-defined ranking of resources based on soft QoS metrics such as the average queued time for a job at a resource.

All interactions with the Grid infrastructure take place from a user interface node which supports APIs, command line, and graphical interfaces to BEgrid.

Introduction to MPI

MPI stands for "Message Passing Interface". Briefly: MPI is a standard library specification for message-passing based parallel software (Dongara et al., 1996).

MPI can be characterized as follows:

- It is a specification - there is no "standard implementation".
- It is a standard - all implementations should be compile and link-level compatible.
- It is a library - no adaptations to the compiler or other steps in the build process are needed to use it except inclusion of the library itself.
- It exclusively addresses the "pure" message-passing programming model - even for those hardware platforms that use shared memory at the core (Gropp et al., 1997).

MPI was designed in the period 1992-1994 by the MPI-forum, an organization open to all specialists in the field, gathering more than 40 organizations in its fold: these consisted of parallel computer vendors, as well as portable software library writers and parallel application specialists.

MAIN FOCUS

Distributed program development often relies on the wrapping/refactoring of existing legacy codes. IBM has produced some interesting documents with guidelines concerning grid enablement of applications, as referred in Jacob et al. 2003, Kra 2004 and Machado 2004.

The first step in distributing the nuclear physics problem is shifting the original F90 code from a sequential to a task-based approach. In this process we were able to identify three separate computational steps in the calculation process: initial data retrieval/dissemination and task generation (done in a master process), task calculation (done in multiple parallel calculator processes to obtain the matrices $<<K_{l'}l_{r}|\hat{H}|K_{l'}l_{s}>>_{t}$ in (2)) and matrix generation and recombination (done in parallel recombinator processes to obtain the matrices $<<K_{l'}l_{i}|\hat{H}|K_{l'}l_{j}>>$), producing one matrix per $K_{l'}K_{j}$ combination to be calculated. Both calculators and recombinators take in new work as soon as they become available. The following three sections will reflect this strategy onto the different distribution mechanism and discuss the results.

CoBRA

CoBRA is by construction bag of task oriented, and is thus a good middleware candidate for the class of problems treated here.

The CoBRA implementation of the nuclear physics code calculates the matrices $<<K_{l'}l_{r}|\hat{H}|K_{l'}l_{s}>>_{t}$ appearing in the right hand side of (2), and recombines these results to obtain the final matrices $<<K_{l'}l_{i}|\hat{H}|K_{l'}l_{j}>>$. Implementing the distribution of the nuclear physics legacy code onto the CoBRA grid is straightforward.

First the *TaskMaster* class is extended. It creates and submits a job for each of the $<<K_{l'}l_{r}|\hat{H}|K_{l'}l_{s}>>_{t}$ matrices. The *GetData* method transfers the necessary input files to the broker machine. The *Run* method implements the task creation. For every task (the calculation of a single matrix) the appropriate input file is generated and an instance of the task class is created and submitted (code in the upper text frame in Figure 1). Finally In a final step the recombination is done on the broker machine. The implementation of the *PutData* method puts the resulting data on the submission machine.

Secondly the task class is extended. The implementation of the *GetData* method transfers the files, which are not available on the worker, from the broker to this worker. The *Execute* implementation runs the FORTRAN executable (code in the lower text frame in Figure 1). The implementation of the *PutData* method transfers the resulting data to the broker machine.

Table 1 compares a run with certain fixed parameters on a local machine with a run on the Co-BRA grid (1 Scheduler, 1 Broker, 20 Workers). The first row contains the values of the input parameter K. The second row lists the speedup results of the tests performed on the CoBRA infrastructure, and the third row lists the speedup normalized to a single node (NSpeedup). The speedup as a function of K is also shown in Figure 2.

The distribution implemented consists of a lot of tasks. The amount of tasks increases from 135 tasks for $K = 0$ to 18315 tasks for $K = 16$ and the average task length increases from 9 ms for $K = 0$ to 54 sec for $K = 16$. The large amount of small tasks for small K implies that the distribution overhead largely exceeds the execution time for the tasks. For $K \geq 6$ the mean task length is sufficiently large (above the black line in Figure 2) to achieve a speedup with respect to a single machine. For $K = 16$, the speedup is seen to almost reach its theoretical peak value equal to the number of workers involved (20).

BEgrid

The LCG middleware supports a batch oriented computing model, which nicely fits our problem as jobs are trivially parallel. One of the merits of distributing the computation on BEgrid is the efficiency of the implementation process itself: only 230 lines of bash scripting code were needed to capture all job distribution and execution logic. Though the highly parallel and independent nature of the distributed subtasks is certainly of influence, this is also directly related to the fact that core grid services for workload, data and information management as well as core security provisions, are delivered 'out-of-the-box'.

An aspect that has affected our job distribution scheme and has introduced some unavoidable complexity in the implementation, is the fact that long delays have been observed when submitting jobs and receiving their results. The computation time for individual indices of the problem also varies widely from a few seconds to a few hours. Therefore, it was deemed necessary to pack several core calculations in a single job. To determine the packing size, we monitored the number of queued jobs over all CE queues during the computation and adjusted workload size accordingly. The idea is that as long as all CE queues are sufficiently loaded to keep the compute resources busy, the submission delay will not affect the total wall-clock time of the computation.

It should be clear that the LCG middleware has no direct support to automatically handle the task graph, so that a scripting solution to implement this had to be used.

For the BEgrid tests, we reserved a part of the grid for performance testing and used 24 3.2 GHz Pentium 4 nodes at Antwerp and 8 dual-Opteron/244 nodes (1.8 GHz) at Leuven. This amounts to 33 normalized 3.2 CPUs which is the maximum reachable speedup factor on this setup.

Table 1. Speedup and of the nuclear physics calculation on the CoBRA grid. NSpeedup is the Speedup normalized to a single CPU.

K	0	2	4	6	8	10	12	14	16
Speedup	0.05	0.14	0.54	1.98	6.17	13.72	15.95	18.30	19.26
NSpeedup	0.003	0.007	0.099	1.98	0.309	0.686	0.798	0.915	0.963

Figure 2. Speedup of the nuclear physics calculation on the CoBRA grid as a function of K

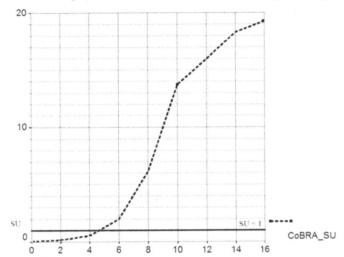

Both sites use a 1 Gigabit Ethernet interconnection. The user interface and resource broker were both located at Antwerp.

Table 2 shows the attained speedup factors, as well as the speedup normalized to a single node (= NSpeedup) for different values of K. Low speedup figures for $K < 10$ are caused by the fact that most of the tasks with low K have a very small execution time and that job submission delays are in the order of seconds, while result fetching delays are in the order of minutes. This makes it difficult to achieve optimal resource utilization in the beginning and at the end of the computation. The delays were not found to be caused by data transmission overhead but rather by the workload management system itself. From $K = 10$ onwards, the picture changes, as the mean execution time for these jobs rises significantly.

Comparing the timing results in Table 2 with those of the CoBRA calculation in Table 1 reveals from the normalized speedup that the overhead due to the LCG middleware is much larger. This is due to the fact that CoBRA runs on a "private" cluster without the need for specific security

Table 2. Sequential and distributed runtimes on BEgrid. NSpeedup is the Speedup normalized to a single CPU.

K	Sequential Execution	Distributed Execution	Speedup	NSpeedup
0	1s	7m57s	0.00	0.000
2	3s	9m00s	0.01	0.000
4	35s	16m27s	0.04	0.001
6	5m19s	16m59s	0.32	0.010
8	30m44s	18m54s	1.63	0.049
10	2h55m43s	18m42s	9.40	0.285
12	12h37m12s	49m36s	15.27	0.463
14	49h39m20s	2h01m05s	24.61	0.746
16	173h37m26s	6h07m31	28.30	0.858

aspects, whereas LCG is designed to distribute tasks over clusters with different administrative requirements.

MPI

In order to distribute the Nuclear calculation in a self-scheduled fashion, MPI provides us with the following primitives: Send()-Recv() calls, allowing for point-to-point communication between individual parallel processes and a collective Bcast() call, for broadcasting information from a single root process to all other parallel processes using only one call (Gropp et al., 1999).

As a proof-of-concept implementation in pure F90 turned out to be successful, a second step was decided upon in which part of the code base was ported over to C++ in order to make use of its object-oriented facilities and extendibility. This port would include most of the communication and parallel logic while most of the computational core (the "legacy code") was to be retained in F90.

For practical deployment of the software, we decided to use the MPI implementation called MPICH-2 (Gropp et al., 1996), mostly because: it is free (w.r.t. price and source code), it is widely supported on many platforms and for all the computer languages covered by the MPI standard (Fortran, C and C++), and lastly, it is one of the most feature-rich MPI implementations currently available on the market.

The results of this approach have been very satisfying. MPI allowed us to do the refactoring through gradual, incremental steps, instead of forcing us into a straight re-write. This enabled us to retain a major part of the original code base.

True to its aim, the MPICH-2 implementation allowed for combining multiple programming languages (with MPI calls being used in each) on multiple platforms.

Using MPI even allows us to choose any implementation which suits us best, enabling us to switch from MPICH-2 (mostly geared to classical cluster environments) to e.g. MPICH-G2 (Karonis

et al., 2003) (geared towards grid environments) without a change to the code base.

Finally, the major advantage of this approach is that the whole system is basically self-scheduling, with each slave (calculator or recombinator) getting itself new work once it is free to do so, without any planning overhead whatsoever. The whole task graph is thus being handled by the MPI master node.

We do not present explicit timings for these calculations, but refer to Broeckhove et al., 2007, where production results are presented for a more involved calculation (much larger matrices) than was performed for the CoBRA and BEgrid. Also, contrary to the CoBRA and BEgrid implementations, the recombination (or aggregation) of matrices was integrated in the self-scheduling approach, which makes direct comparison difficult. An evaluation of the results is however that up to $K=6$ an important overhead is present due to very short matrix calculation times leading to burst network transfers of relatively large result messages; from $K=10$ on, the speedup is steeply increasing up to almost maximal usage of all nodes, and very comparable to the CoBRA speedup results. This close behavior is somehow to be expected as both implementations ran on a comparable and "private" cluster.

FUTURE TRENDS

Distributed programming is becoming a standard to the modal software developers. This results into a rapid evolution towards different distribution paradigms each of them focussing on different kind of users. The differences in this chapter are clear: MPI focuses on skilled developers interested in high speed computing on local clusters (small roundtrip time); The BeGrid is used by skilled developers to perform high throughput calculations using resources all over the world; The CoBRA grid is straightforward to use even for less skilled programmers. It focuses on straightforward distribution on local area networks.

As high performance is essential in this particular Nuclear physics calculations MPI will be used in future implementations. Due to its straightforward way of programming the CoBRA paradigm will be used in future proof of concepts implementations.

CONCLUSION

Many microscopic nuclear physics calculations use a complete basis to mimic the true solution of the Schrödinger equation. This leads to a matrix equation of high dimension. The computation of such matrices is often highly parallelizable.

It was shown that both Light-Weight as well as Heavy-Weight Grid infrastructures allow for efficient execution.

Several implementations have been considered, using the original code base for the calculation of matrix elements (the so called legacy code) without modification or refactoring. We considered self-scheduling (MPI), master-slave (CoBRA) and submission scripting (BEgrid) solutions. All were successful and led to an efficient use of the involved compute power when the individual task lengths were sufficiently high, which in the current model calculation occurs at a high value of the parameter K.

We conclude that a broad spectrum of Grid infrastructures can be put to efficient use for an important class of microscopic nuclear physics calculations.

REFERENCES

BEgrid (2007). *The Belgian Grid for research*. Deployed through the Belgian federal and state government initiatives. Retrieved from, http://www.begrid.be

Broeckhove, J., Arickx, F., Vanroose, W., & Vasilevsky V. (2004). The modified J-Matrix method for short-range potentials. *Journal of Physics A: Mathematical and General, 37*, 1-13

Broeckhove, J., Arickx, F., Hellinckx, P., Vasilevsky, V. S., & Nesterov, A. V. (2007). The ⁵H resonance structure studied with a three-cluster J-matrix model. *Journal of Physics G: Nuclear and Particle Physics, 34*, 1955-1970

Dongara, J.J. & Walker, D. (1996). MPI: A standard message passing interface. *Supercomputer, 12*(1), 56-68

EGEE (n.d.). *Enabling Grids for E-science*. Project funded by the European Commission. Retrieved from, http://www.eu-egee.org.

gLite. *Middleware development initiative as part of the EGEE project*. Retrieved from, http://glite.web.cern.ch/glite/default.asp.

Globus Toolkit (n.d.). Retrieved from, http://www.globus.org/toolkit.

Fagg, G.E., Gabriel, E., Bosilca, G., Angskun, T., Chen, Z., Pjesivac-Grbovic, J., London, K. & Dongara, J. (2004). Extending the MPI specification for process fault-tolerance on high-performance computing systems. In *Proceedings of the International Supercomputer conference (ICS)*.

Gropp, W. & Lusk, E. (1997). A high-performance MPI implementation on a shared-memory vector supercomputer. *Parallel Computing, 22*(11), 1513-1526

Gropp, W., Lusk, E., & Skjellum, A. (1999). *Using MPI-Portable parallel programming with the message passing interface* (2nd ed.).

Gropp, W., Lusk, E., Doss, N., & Skjellum, A. (1996). A high-performance, portable implementation of the MPI message passing interface standard. *Parallel Computing, 22*(6), 789-828

Gropp, W., Lusk, E., & Sterling, T. (2003). *Beowulf cluster computing with Linux*. Cambridge, MA: The MIT Press.

Hellinckx, P., Arickx, F., Broeckhove, J., & Stuer G. (2007). The CoBRA Grid: A highly configurable lightweight Grid system. *International Journal of Web and Grid Services, 3*(3), 267-286

Jacob, B., Ferreira, L., Bieberstein, N., Gilzean, C., Girard, J., Strachowski, S., et al. (2003). Enabling applications for Grid computing with Globus. *IBM RedBooks SG24-6936-00* (pp. 43-69).

Karonis, N., Toonen, B. & Foster, I. (2003). MPICH-G2: A grid-enabled implementation of the message passing interface. *Journal of Parallel and Distributed Computing (JPDC), 63*(5), 551-563.

Kra, D. (2004, April). Six strategies for grid application enablement: Part 1. *IBM DeveloperWorks series* (pp. 1-8).

LCG (n.d.). *Worldwide Large Hadron Collider Computing Grid.* Project of the European Organization for Nuclear Research (CERN).

Machado, M. (2004, June). Enable existing applications for Grid. *IBM developerWorks series* (pp. 1-11).

Vasilevsky, V. S., Nesterov, A. V., Arickx, F., & Broeckhove, J. (2001). The algebraic model for scattering in three-s-cluster systems: Theoretical background. *Physical Review, C63 034606* (pp. 1-16).

KEY TERMS AND DEFINITIONS

BEgrid: Infrastructural Grid collaboration between several universities and research institutes in Belgium. BEgrid is part of the North European ROC region of the EGEE project.

Beowulf: Beowulf Clusters are scalable performance clusters based on commodity hardware, on a private system network, with open source software (Linux) infrastructure.

EGEE: EGEE stands for "Enabling Grids for E-sciencE". THe project is funded by the European Commission and aims to build on recent advances in grid technology and develop a service grid infrastructure which is available to scientists 24 hours-a-day. It currently consists of some 41,000 CPU's and some 5 PetaByte storage space, and typically runs about 100,000 jobs concurrently.

Globus: The **Globus Alliance** is a community of organizations and individuals developing fundamental technologies behind the "Grid," which lets people share computing power, databases, instruments, and other on-line tools securely across corporate, institutional, and geographic boundaries without sacrificing local autonomy. The **Globus Toolkit** is an open source software toolkit used for building Grid systems and applications. It is being developed by the Globus Alliance and many others all over the world. A growing number of projects and companies are using the Globus Toolkit to unlock the potential of grids for their cause.

MPI: MPI stands for "Message Passing Interface", and is a standard library specification for Message Oriented Middleware without modifications to compiler or system. It was designed for parallel and high performance computing

MPICH2: MPICH2 is an implementation of the Message-Passing Interface (MPI). The goals of MPICH2 are to provide an MPI implementation for important platforms, including clusters, SMPs, and massively parallel processors.

MPICH-G2: MPICH-G2 is a *grid-enabled* implementation of the MPI v1.1 standard. Using services from the Globus Toolkit® (e.g., job startup, security), MPICH-G2 allows to couple multiple machines, potentially of different architectures, to run MPI applications. MPICH-G2 automatically converts data in messages sent between machines of different architectures and supports multiprotocol communication by automatically selecting TCP for intermachine messaging and (where available) vendor-supplied MPI for intramachine messaging

LCG: LCG stands for "Large Hadron Collider Computing Grid", and its mission is to build and maintain data storage and analysis infrastructure for the entire high energy physics community that will use CERN's large hadron collider. It contributed significantly to the development of computing grids, particularly in Europe.

Chapter XX
Developing Biomedical Applications in the Framework of EELA

Gabriel Aparicio
Universidad Politécnica de Valencia, Spain

Fernando Blanco
CIEMAT, Spain

Ignacio Blanquer
Universidad Politécnica de Valencia, Spain

César Bonavides
UNAM Campus Morelos, Mexico

Juan Luis Chaves
Universidad de los Andes, Venezuela

Miguel Embid
CIEMAT, Spain

Álvaro Hernández
Universidad de los Andes, Venezuela

Vicente Hernández
Universidad Politécnica de Valencia, Spain

Raúl Isea
Fundacion IDEA, Venezuela

Juan Ignacio Lagares
CIEMAT, Spain

Daniel L. Aldama
CUBAENERGIA, Cuba

Rafael Mayo
CIEMAT, Spain

Esther Montes
CIEMAT, Spain

Henry Ricardo Mora
CUBAENERGIA, Cuba

ABSTRACT

In the last years an increasing demand for Grid Infrastructures has resulted in several international collaborations. This is the case of the EELA Project, which has brought together collaborating groups of Latin America and Europe. One year ago we presented this e-infrastructure used, among others, by the biomedical groups for the studies of oncological analysis, neglected diseases, sequence alignments and computational phylogenetics. After this period, the achieved advances and the scientific results are summarized in this chapter.

INTRODUCTION

EELA (E-Infrastructure shared between Europe and Latin America, see http://www.eu-eela.org) is a Project funded by the European Commission that began in January 2006. Its objective is building a digital bridge between the existing e-Infrastructure initiatives in Europe and those that were emerging in Latin America, through the creation of a collaborative network that shares an interoperable Grid infrastructure to support the development and test of advanced applications.

One of the areas of work is the identification and support of Grid enhanced applications. This scientific research covers several fields, but due to the high social impact in the Latin American society, one of the pillars of the Project is Biomedicine and, consequently, the applications that can be run on the Grid.

Some of them, falling in three typical categories of bioinformatics applications, computational biochemical processes and biomedical models, were selected and started to be deployed on the infrastructure for both production and dissemination purposes.

This document describes these biomedical applications running in the Project and the advances and scientific results that have been achieved, among others, in the field of cancer diseases, the drug discovery in Malaria, the determination of sequences in parasite diseases and in the HIV origin.

BACKGROUND

The realization of a common interoperable Grid testbed from existing resources in Latin America and Europe, distributed over 15 resource centers, was the first problem to overcome. For this purpose, the testbed was built upon the network infrastructure provided by GÉANT in Europe and RedCLARA in Latin America and interfacing with European and Latin American National Research and Education Networks (NREN).

The Pilot Testbed is organized in three layers: at the highest level, the EELA Operations Centre (old Grid Operations Centre) coordinates the interaction between the subordinate CORE Services Centers (CSC) and the Resource Centers (RCs) which provide computing power and data storage. At the base level we have the Additional Service Providers (ASPs) which provide support for services needed by proper operation of the Pilot Testbed but not directly related to the middleware utilized, such as Certification Authority management and Virtual Organization Management Services (VOMS) and File Catalogues.

EELA has integrated more than 1,500 computing cores and 60 TB of data storage available to the project users and has been accepted as member of The Americas Grid Policy Management Authority (TAGPMA), as well as new national Latin American Certification Authorities have been accredited too. EELA has two distinct VOs (EELA and EDTEAM) and accepts two particular High Energy Physics VOs (Alice and LHCb), accounting for 4 VO setups. EELA provides network services through standard modeling processes thus ensuring the required quality of service.

As EELA has adopted the gLite Middleware (see http://glite.web.cern.ch/glite/), EELA has tight interactions with EGEE (see http://www.eu-egee.org/) and with the Joint Research Program GEANT2. The compatibility between different middleware is another concern of the Project and is one of the future research lines of EELA, to be carried out in collaboration with the peer-to-peer OurGrid Project (see http://www.ourgrid.org/). In addition, several Globus components, such as the GridWay Metascheduler (Huedo et al., 2005) have been adopted in order to run the applications and their inner dependencies in a successful way.

Various disciplines in the realm of biomedicine have experienced drastic progresses on development of models, tools and procedures which make use of the extensive computer cycles and data storages. The White Paper on HealthGrid (see, http://whitepaper.healthgrid.org) identifies five key areas: Genomics; Proteomics; Medical Imaging; Human Body Simulation; and Epidemiology. These issues apply to the whole society and, in particular, to the Latin American countries.

More powerful tools improved by the Grid technology will foster physicians and biologists to improve their scientific position. For example, in the case of new drugs, this is even more relevant, since the main targets for Latin America countries are different from Europe, because many of them suffer from neglected diseases (such as malaria or dengue) which are not considered by the main pharmaceutical companies due to their low economic profit.

The target for the biomedical part of the Project is to deploy Grid applications for the biomedical Latin American community to improve their research excellence and to foster the use of Grids in this community.

Grid biomedical applications typically fall into four categories:

- Bioinformatics applications, where we can find genomic, genetic or proteomic analysis which expands the use of biological tools;
- Development for computational biology, which is the improvement of new application components in Java, C++, Python and so on,, applied to molecular biology and chemical interaction studies;
- Bio-model simulation, used to simulate structural, flow or electrical bio-model; and,
- Medical imaging, ideal for image post-processing and sharing.

Because of the interest in the Latin American society, the Project partners selected applications in the first three areas. BLAST and Phylogeny as bioinformatics applications, WISDOM as computational biochemical processes and GATE for the biomedical simulation. A more detailed explanation of the applications can be found in (Cardenas et al. 2006). Besides, it is important

to mention that two applications from the portfolio of mature EGEE (see http://www.eu.egee.org) biomedical applications have been selected: GATE and WISDOM. All these applications already respond to users' needs and have proven their interest on EGEE. This source of mature applications was selected to ensure that already working applications could be deployed at the very start of the EELA project. Moreover, the deployment on EELA also implies a very important knowledge transfer. In addition to this, the rest of the tools are a novel approach to the Grid which completes the scope from other different Biomedical Projects such as SHARE (see http://www.share-project.org/) of BioinfoGRID (see http://www.share-project.org/).

MAIN FOCUS: THE APPLICATIONS

GATE

The C++ platform based on the Monte Carlo GEANT4 software (Agostinelli, 2003) GATE (GEANT4 Application for Tomographic Emission) (Jan, 2004) models nuclear medicine applications, such as Positron Emission Tomography (PET), Single Photon Emission Computed Tomography (SPECT) or radiotherapy dosimetry within the OpenGATE collaboration (see, http://opengate-collaboration.healthgrid.org).

Radiation therapy requires a previous computing of the intensity and location of the radioactive sources for the specific location and size of the tumour. Nowadays, simplified analytical methods are currently used to provide quick sub-optimal solutions, but iterative methods, such as Monte Carlo, provide much more accurate results, specially when the information about the tissues of the patients are considered.

However, the main problem of iterative methods is their high computational cost. This can be tackled by using a Grid infrastructure by means of splitting of the particles in different computing resources and the random seeds to avoid dependent sequences. In this way, speed-up goes above 20 and the computing problem is reduced to less than 15 minutes as can be seen in Figure 1 by using an Intel Xeon CPU 3.06 GHz.

As a result, the objective of GATE is to use the Grid environment to reduce the computing time of Monte Carlo simulations providing a higher accuracy in a reasonable period of time

WISDOM

The Wide in Silico Docking of Malaria (WISDOM) application (Jacq, 2006) consists in the deployment of a high throughput virtual screening platform in the perspective of in-silico drug discovery for Malaria diseases. Every year 350-500 million cases of malaria occur worldwide and at least 1.5 million people die, most of them young children in sub-Saharan Africa. The development of new drugs in-silico is faster and much cheaper than the experimental docking, which is restricted to the most successful ligands obtained after the simulation process. WISDOM consists in a set of scripts, procedures and applications for dividing ligand databases and target experiments on a coordinated community of users who execute the docking process on the grid.

BiG: BLAST in Grids

The study of the functionality of the different genes and regions is one of the most important efforts on the analysis of the genome. If the queries and the alignments are well designed both functional and evolutionary information can be inferred from sequence alignments since they provide a powerful way to compare novel sequences with previously characterized genes.

The Basic Local Alignment Search Tool (BLAST) (Altschul, 1997) finds regions of local similarity between sequences. The program compares nucleotide or protein sequences to databases and calculates the statistical significance of matches. This process of finding similar sequences is very computationally-intensive since the searching alignment of a single sequence is not a costly task, but normally, thousands of sequences are searched at the same time.

The biocomputing community usually relies on either local installations or public servers, such as the NCBI (see http://www.ncbi.nlm.nih. gov) or the gPS@ (see http://gpsa.ibcp.fr), but the limitations on the number of simultaneous queries make this environment inefficient for large tests. Moreover, since the databases are periodically updated, it will be convenient to do the same with the results of previous studies.

Figure 1. Comparison of GATE use

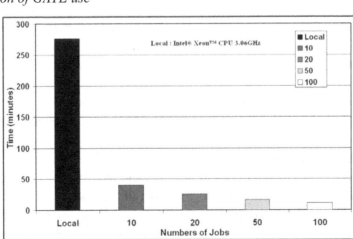

BLAST has been the first application success-fully ported to the Grid by EELA, producing BiG in this way. For doing this, different approaches (Aparicio et al. 2006) can be found because of the number of fragments to be analyzed and the periodical updating of the information will be increased. EELA has adopted the availability of an independent Grid-enabled version (Aparicio, 2007) integrated on the Bioinformatics Portal of the Universidad de los Andes (see http://www.cecalc.ula.ve/blast) providing registered users with results in a shorter time.

Basically the users access the service (based on MPIBLAST, Darling, 2003) with an easy interface with high compatibility through this web portal and, after that, to the EELA Grid with a Gate-to-Grid, i. e., an EELA Grid node which provides a WSRF-Based web interface by means of JAVA programs. Thus, multiple database queries can be done by parallel process, so this data partition in a Grid approach gives scalability with huge quantities of data. Since BiG divides sequences into blocks, a block is assigned to an EELA Grid job and, then, with a single block, as many output files as databases used are generated.

The security is provided by means of a My-Proxy server which generates manually and temporally certificates that will be retrieved by the UI when required. This will also allow the existence of long-living jobs by using proxy re-newal. Besides, some improvements in the return of a selected number of hits and not all of them if it is required in this way and a new system monitoring method have been achieved in the post-processing stage

Bayesian Estimation of Phylogeny: MrBayes

A phylogeny is a reconstruction of the evolutionary history of a group of organisms used throughout the life sciences, as it offers a structure around which to organize the knowledge and data accumulated by researchers. Computational phyloge-netics has been a rich area for algorithm design over the last 15 years.

The inference of phylogenies with computational methods is widely used in medical and biological research and has many important applications, such as gene function prediction, drug discovery and conservation biology (see the work of Lesheng in http://www.nus.edu.sg/comcen/svu/publications/hpc_nus/sep_2005/ParallelMrBayes.pdf).

The most commonly used methods to infer phylogenies include cladistics, phenetics, maxi-mum likelihood, and Markov Chain Monte Carlo (MCMC) based Bayesian inference. These last two depend upon a mathematical model describing the evolution of characters observed in the included species, and are usually used for molecular phy-logeny where the characters are aligned nucleotide or amino acid sequences.

Due to the nature of Bayesian inference, the simulation can be prone to entrapment in local optima (Altekar, 2004). To overcome local op-tima and achieve better estimation, the MrBayes program (Ronquist, 2003) has to run millions of iterations (generations) which require a large amount of computation time. For multiple sessions with different models or parameters, it will take a very long time before the results can be analyzed and summarized.

The phylogenetic tools are widely demanded by the Latin America bioinformatics community. A Grid service for the parallelized version of Mr-Bayes application is planned to be developed by means of a simple interface that will be deployed on the bioinformatics portal of Universidad de los Andes (see http://portal-bio.ula.ve/) in a similar way to that done for BiG.

However, the parallelization model of any phylogenetic tool is different from the approach followed on BiG. Finer-grain parallelism is present and database splitting is not possible. More efficient approaches are being studied to enlarge the availability of resources for this problem, which typically is bounded by memory constraints. Besides, a control of the failures of the jobs submitted must be implemented in order to avoid the typical MPI drawbacks.

RESULTS AND FUTURE TRENDS

GATE

Nine Cuban centers will test, as users, the results of the simulation of radiotherapy treatments using realistic models that GATE provides in two main oncological problems:

- Thyroid Cancer (the diseases of thyroids are one of the 5 main causes of endocrinology treatments (Navarro, 2004); and
- Treatment of metastasis with P32 isotopes (Alert, 2004) by means of the brachytherapy improving the knowledge on the doses captured from the different tissues by accurate simulation.

The application has been used in many areas such as dosimetry, development of detectors, Positron Emission Tomography technology and so on (see for example the OpenGATE collaboration in http://opengatecollaboration.healthgrid.org/publications/), but up to now, no use in these two oncological problems has been performed.

The EELA consortium has provided the support for the installation and integration of a standalone Grid site in Cuba where the simplest jobs concerning Monte Carlo simulations can currently be run using the GILDA framework to access the system and to interact with the environment. For those cases where the computer load is greater, a previous preparation of the job will be done in Cuba and, after that, the necessary material will be brought physically to other EELA sites with a higher bandwidth in order to do the submission process. For this purpose, GATE has been installed in several EELA sites.

Because of all these reasons, the expected impact is very important, many cases are being studied and an important step beyond in the diagnosis of the aforementioned diseases will be reached. Some medical results are expected through 2007.

As a conclusion and added value, Grid will increase the performance to the application, but in this case, it will even be more important, since it is an enabling technology opening the doors to a new range of applications and possibilities. All the centers from Cuba are expected to bring to the EELA community around 90 cases per month.

WISDOM

The magnitude of WISDOM is really high. In its first coordinated Data Challenge on malaria, 46 million ligands were docked in 39 days using EGEE grid (information available from http://wisdom.healthgrid.org/index.php?id=142) in a process that would have taken 80 years in a state-of-the-art PC. The number of executed jobs on 1758 CPUs was 72751. Thus, 1.5 TB of results were produced.

The interest of the EELA partners centered in three actions:

- The study of new targets for new parasitology diseases;
- The selection of new targets for malaria; and,
- The contribution with resources for the WISDOM Data Challenge.

Thus, a well-established platform in this tool already exists, so EELA had to contribute to it with a new push, not only coming from supporting calculations by means of more computational resources. The WISDOM initiative has performed its second High-Throughput virtual Docking of million of chemical compounds available in the databases of ligands to several targets in the fall of 2006. In this WISDOM Data Challenge-II (see http://wisdom.healthgrid.org/index.php?id=139) the Universidad de Los Andes (ULA) has proposed two targets in Plasmodium vivax, which is of special interest in the Latin American society: the binding site is in the loop Asn117 until Tyr125; and, the loop SER117 until Tyr125.

These targets have been accepted by the consortium and the first of them has been already docked within the EELA as was agreed by the WISDOM DC-II decision-makers. This process has been coordinated by Universidad Politécnica de Valencia (UPV) and all the EELA sites have acted as donor of computational and storage resources, running effectively more than 40% of the jobs in the Latin American sites. The results will be presented in future works.

Each target requires executing 2422 jobs which take around 1 CPU day each. This large demand of resources is being tackled with the collaboration of resources from institutions of Brazil, Mexico, Venezuela, Spain and Italy. At the end of 2006, half of the experiment has been completed producing 53 GB of results due to 100% of the jobs have been run with a total effective running time of 228 CPU days.

Currently, the WISDOM Project is focused on a framework specially designed for the data analysis since 2TB of data were expected. To do so, a workflow based on DIANE (Distributed Analysis Environment, see http://cern.ch/diane) was designed in Phyton for the using of distributed information which is stored independently in a way that the researcher doesn't know its allocation. DIANE is a lightweight distributed framework for parallel scientific applications in master-worker model which takes care of all synchronization, communication and workflow by means of a communication between the nodes by the CORBA standard (Moscicki, 2004).

On the one hand, for the EELA infrastructure, WISDOM-DC II has been a crucial test; on the other hand, this high completion in the docked process has debugged some unexpected problems in the original files.

BiG

The use of BiG in a parallel way is a first conclusion because of the good scalability in Grid. Thus, to show the right use of a parallel version, the data are as follows. The alignment of 3000 sequences in a row in a CE of 30 nodes takes 9h 18m 50s (i.e., 11.18 s/seq), meanwhile the alignment of the same number of sequences, but in CEs of 20 nodes takes 8h 36m 51s (10.34 s/seq). The optimal ratio is found in 2 CEs of 15 nodes (see Figure 2 for details) and, beyond this point, there is no gain in the addition of new CEs.

Figure 2. Parallel approach for a BiG performance analysis

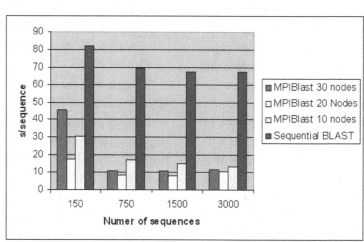

As was aforementioned, BiG has been the first own application ported to the Grid by the EELA consortium and, at the same time, has given to the bioinformatics community a new powerful tool to use BLAST with a high computational power. Other approaches to port BLAST to the Grid has been performed afterwards (see Trombetti et al., 2007).

Another important asset is shown in Figure 3, where the use of Grid technology is showed. There, we can see that the use of sequential BLAST for 3000 sequences takes 67.34 s/sequence and, the same sequences, but in a one 20 nodes cluster, takes 10.34 s/sequence and so on.

BiG has been used for searching similar sequences and inferring their function in parasite diseases such as the Leishmaniasis (mainly Mexican leishmania), Chagas (mainly Trypanosoma Cruzi) and Malaria (mainly Plasmodium vivax) producing in this way several scientific results of interest from the first moment. For example, work on the complete genome of the Plasmodium falciparum for the identification of dihydrofolate reductase (DHFR) antigenic proteins has already been done. At the same time, it means a technical innovation in the field and the first "own EELA application" running in the Grid.

In a year of life of BiG its use statistics are: 836 jobs executed; 263,4 CPU days consumed; and, 4.6 CPU hours per job (1.1 CPU hours of standard deviation).

The future plans for the BiG service will go through three main issues:

- Increasing the availability of resources through the integration of both parallel and sequential processing engines;
- Increasing the usage of the application giving support to outstanding experiments. An experiment identified consists on the multiple alignment of a metagenome sample involving the complete genomes of 20 bacteria. This will require processing several hundred thousands of sequences, and CPU years. A supporting environment is being developed to monitor, retrieve and combine the results from a large scale of operations; and,
- Increasing the awareness on the user community. Another real interest of BiG is that it is able to identify similarities in genetic sequences that can be used in a second phase as candidates for medical drugs. Thus, these candidates would be docked in the framework of WISDOM and, in a third and final step, a row of in vitro experiments with the best targets would be carried out.

Figure 3. Grid approach for a BiG performance analysis

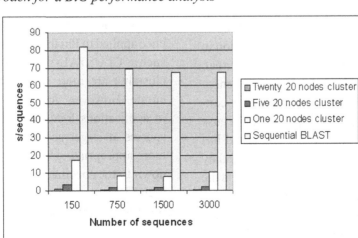

MrBayes

The first test performed in a parallel version of MrBayes were about a simply phylogeny to demonstrate that humans become from primates. It just showed that the use of Grid is of great advantage since the number of trees grows with the number of taxons (sequences) according to:

$$R_n = \prod_{i=3}^{n+1} (2i - 5) \qquad (1)$$

where the effect is even higher if trees with root (Rn) are used since i (taxons) runs to n+1 instead of n.

After that first test, the use of Directed Acyclic Graph (DAG) technique has also been checked. Thus, 121 sequences from the Papillomavirus as input under the same script have been used to reproduce the diversity of PV types; in this work, a successful comparison with (Villiers, 2004) was done.

Another work has been done with 13 sequences from gene fragment in Human Immunodeficiency Virus type 1 (HIV-1) population because of its well-known transmission history (Leitner, 1996). We analyzed a simulated data set using MrBayes software. A calculation of 10 million generations under the simulation model (NY98), sampling every 5000 generations, was performed.

Since we have as a reference the tree from Leitner (Leitner, 1996) for comparison, it is possible to determine the adequacy of a Grid environment in Phylogeny. In our case, we have selected the phylogeny which reproduces the transmission in the human inmunodeficiency virus type 1 (Leitner, 1997; Leitner, 1999). Since these last references show the "True phylogenetic" tree, we can conclude that the use of Grid is appropriate because our result obtained with the NY98 method has been the same that the one already published by Leitner in 1996 (see Figure 4). The service via the web portal was made available on June 2007. Up to now, the CPU consume has been of 965 CPU hours in 24 jobs. It is important to outline that

Figure 4. Molecular tree constructed using the NY98 model (tree obtained with Treeview)

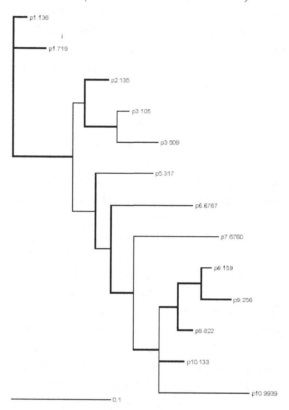

97% of this time has been invested in two main jobs, which are representative in resource consume according to the users' profile. In this task force, more than 2000 sequences equivalent to 4•107 iterations are going to be analyzed producing an estimation of consumption of 3 CPU years.

For future plans we can say that MrBayes is a well-known, effective tool for Bayesian inference applied to Phylogenetics. Other approaches, such as CLUSTAL-W (see http://www.ebi.ac.uk/clustalw) are more scalable, although less accurate. However, accuracy can be less critical in applications focused on the classification of species at larger scope. Bayesian methods are more appropriate when the level of details goes down to the specimen. Thus, a service based on CLUSTAL-W will be provided to complement the offer of services.

In this way, MrBayes has been ported to the Grid with several approaches (see for example https://mrbayes.dev.java.net/ where it has been done by means of utility computing), but the novelty of EELA is based on the scientific results and the way that they are also obtained in the Grid environment, this is, HIV and Papillomavirus.

New EELA Applications

The EELA project has currently four biomedical pilot applications running and the support of the portal developed at ULA, but is also looking for new ones. For this purpose, it is offering its support with initiatives like Grid Schools (see http://www.eu-eela.org/egris1/index.html & http://www.cecalc.ula.ve/EGRIS-2/) and the possibility of signing a Memorandum of Understanding for further collaboration.

As a result, other biomedical applications such as EMBOSS (see http://emboss.sourceforge.net/what/#Overview) will be ported to the Grid very soon creating in this way a new application called GrEMBOSS. With this free Open Source software analysis package specially developed for the needs of the molecular biology user community EELA will keep on working in the biomedical field as well as increasing their users. The versions that will be ported are the latest released, i.e., 4.0 and 4.1. Both binaries and databases will be stored in the Storage Elements and will be registered on the LFC by means of the GFAL library. The script for the submission of jobs from a UI automates all the necessary commands and deals with the databases and the EMBOSS tool in order to obtain the final results transparently for the user.

Currently, the SE of Instituto de Ciencias Nucleares (UNAM) has installed the GrEMBOSS files and test databases, but the huge databases from NCBI and EMBL are still to be mirrored. Once the distribution of binaries and databases to other EELA SEs are overcome, the scripts to access GrEMBOSS will be distributed and the integration of a web interface (wEMBOSS, see

http://www.wemboss.org) will be done as near goals.

In addition, new tools developed for the simulation of the effects of the radiation in the human body have joined recently the EELA Project. They are GAMOS and MIRaS, which will complete the scope of GATE since they are also based on GEANT4 and Monte Carlo simulations, but their application is not in the field of Nuclear Medicine.

GAMOS (Geant4-based Architecture for Medicine-Oriented Simulations) is a powerful plug-in based tool to ease the use of GEANT4 to non-computer experts and, at the same time, provide easily all the functionality of GEANT4 to more advanced users (Arce and Rato, 2006; Arce and Rato, 2007). The objective of GAMOS is to provide a software framework that serves the inexperienced user to simulate a project without having to code in C++ and with a minimal knowledge of GEANT4, and at the same time, let an advanced user add new functionality and easily integrate it with the rest of GAMOS functionality. The plug-in concept provides at the user to choose different simulation components (geometry, physics, user actions...) and to combine them in a simple way.

MIRaS is an integrated code useful to Medical Imaging, Radiotherapy treatment and Simulation and to ease the Medical Image analysis (Lagares, 2007). The main goals of MIRaS are to provide a single interface for the user, to manipulate and to analyze multiple types of images from some or different image techniques simultaneously. It also lets verification of previous plans of radiotherapy treatments, using free available Monte Carlo (MC) codes like BEAMnrc, GAMOS and others. The MC technique requires a high computational performance. For this issue a GRID environment is the right way to solve these kinds of problems.

Actually, the computation time, using full MC, is very slow (around hours in a PC cluster) (Lagares, 2006 and Leal, 2003). The main goal of MIRAS implies reducing the computer time in some minutes or seconds. This can be a very useful tool in the daily clinical context.

MIRaS is based on an open source code and it promises to be a useful tool for research centers and hospitals. From the point of view of some hospitals:

- It will be a way to obtain a tool to calculate a radiotherapy plans, on institutions were do not exist a Treatment Planning System (TPS) for Radiotherapy, but where they have an available few numbers of CPUs.
- It will be the tool to check the TPS (obtained with analytical commercial codes).
- To check and to solve the distributions dose for a high complexity, research and new techniques of radiotherapy.

This software could be of a great interest in hospitals in the Latin-America area or, in general, in countries with a minimum computer infrastructure.

All these applications have signed the MoU with EELA on March 2007 (GrEMBOSS) and June 2007 (the rest) and the first tests on the EELA infrastructure have already begun.

CONCLUSION

The EELA e-infrastructure is permitting various collaborative groups in Latin America to use more powerful computational resources than those available on their centers. This achieves that the lines of investigation stated in the document are feasible as the computational requirements for them are being met. As a result, thyroid cancer and the treatment of metastasis are being studied by means of the GATE application and two loops in the Plasmodium vivax have been docked for a further in vitro work.

BiG has been used for searching similar sequences and inferring their function in parasite

diseases such as the Leishmaniasis (mainly Mexican leishmania), Chagas (mainly Trypanosoma Cruzi) and Malaria (mainly Plasmodium vivax) producing in this way several scientific results of interest from the first moment. For example, work on the complete genome of the Plasmodium falciparum for the identification of dihydrofolate reductase (DHFR) antigenic proteins has already been done.

Phylogeny has been used in the Grid environment to reproduce the diversity of Papillomavirus types and to find the transmission history of HIV.

ACKNOWLEDGMENT

The authors would like to express their acknowledgement to the EELA Project (European Commission contract 026409) for providing the e-Infrastructure in which this work has been performed.

REFERENCES

Agostinelli, S. (2003). GEANT4—A simulation toolkit. *Nuclear Instruments and Methods in Physics Research A, 506*, 250-303.

Alert, J. & Jiménez J. (2004). Tendencias del tratamiento radiante en los tumores del sistema nervioso central. *Rev Cubana Med*, 43, 2-3.

Altekar, G., Dwarkadas S., Huelsenbeck J.P. & Ronquist F. (2004). Parallel metropolis coupled Markov chain Monte Carlo for Bayesian phylogenetic inference. *Bioinformatics*, *20*, 407-415.

Altschul, S.F. (1997). Gapped BLAST and PSI-BLAST: a new generation of protein database search programs. *Nucl. Acids Res, 25*, 3389-3402.

Aparicio, G. (2006). Blast2GO goes Grid: Developing a Grid-enabled prototype for functional genomics analysis. *Studies in Health Technology and Informatics, 120,* 194-204.

Aparicio, G., Blanquer I., Hernández V. & Segrelles D. (2007). BLAST in Grid (BiG): A Grid-enabled software architecture and implementation of parallel and sequential BLAST. In J. Casado, R. Mayo, & R. Muñoz (Eds.), *Proceedings of the Spanish Conference on e-Science Grid Computing* (pp. 11-22). Madrid: CIEMAT Press.

Arce, P., & Rato, P. (2006). GAMOS: A user-friendly and flexible framework for medical applications. *GEANT4 Collaboration Workshop and Users Conference,* LIP, Lisbon, Portugal.

Arce, P., & Rato, P. (2007). GAMOS status and plans. *12th GEANT4 Collaboration Workshop and Users Conference,* Hebden Bridge, United Kingdom.

Cárdenas, M. (2006). Biomedical Applications in EELA. *Studies in Health Technology and Informatics, 120,* 397-400

Darling, A., Carey, L. & Feng, W. (2003). The design, implementation, and evaluation of mpiBLAST. In Proceedings of the *4th International Conference on Linux Clusters: The HPC Revolution* (In conjunction with the ClusterWorld Conference & Exp San Jose).

De Villiers, E.M. (2004). Classification of papillomaviruses. *Virology, 324,* 17-27.

Huedo, E, Montero, R.S., & Llorente I.M. (2005). The GridWay framework for adaptive scheduling and execution on Grids. *Nova Science,* 6, 1-8.

Jacq, N. (2006). Demonstration of in silico docking at a large scale on Grid infrastructure. *Studies in Health Technology and Informatics, 120,* 155-157

Jan, S. (2004). GATE: A simulation toolkit for PET and SPECT. *Phys. Med. Biol., 49,* 4543-4561.

Lagares, J.I., Soler, J.D., Arce, P., Pereira, G., & Embid, M. (2007). The MIRaS (Medical Image Radiotherapy and Simulation) C++ Radiotherapy Simulation Module. *Xth EFOMP Congress,* Pisa, Italy.

Lagares, J.I., Arce, P., Soler, J.D., Pereira, G., & Embid, M. (2007). The MIRaS (Medical Image Radiotherapy and Simulation) project. *4th International Conference on Imaging Technologies in Biomedical Sciences, ITBS 2007.* Milos Conference Center G. Eliopoulos, Milos Island, Greece.

Lagares, J.I. (2006). Monte Carlo parallelized solution for patients under dynamic radiotherapy treatment. *Science and supercomputing in Europe* (pp. 520-524).

Leal, A., Sánchez-Doblado, F., Arráns, R., Roselló, J. V., Carrasco, E., & Lagares, J.I. (2003). Routine IMRT verification by means of an automatic MC simulation system. *Int. J. Rad. Oncol. Biol. Phys, 56*(1) 58-68.

Leitner, T. (1996). Accurate reconstruction of a known HIV-1 transmission history by phylogenetic tree analysis. *Proc. Natl. Acad. Sci. USA, 93* (pp. 10864-10869).

Leitner, T., Kumar, S., & Albert, J. (1997). Tempo and mode of nucleotide substitutions in gag and env gene fragments in Human Immunodeficiency Virus Type 1: Populations with a known transmission history. *Journal of Virology, 71,* 4761–4770.

Leitner, T., & Albert, J. (1999). The molecular clock of HIV-1 unveiled through analysis of a known transmission history. *Proc. Natl. Acad. Sci. USA, 96* (pp. 10752–10757).

Moscicki, J.T., Lee, H.C., Guatelli, S., Lin, S.C., & Pia, M.G. (2004). Biomedical Applications on the GRID: Efficient management of parallel jobs. In *NSS IEEE 2003, Rome.* Retrieved from,http://it-proj-diane.web.cern.ch/it-proj-diane/papers/DIANE-NSS2004.pdf

Navarro, D. (2004). Epidemiología de las enfermedades del tiroides en Cuba. *Rev Cubana Endocrinol, 15.*

Ronquist, F., & Huelsenbeck, J.P. (2003). MrBayes 3: Bayesian phylogenetic inference under mixed models. *Bioinformatics, 19*, 1572-1574.

Trombetti, G.A., Merelli, I., Orro, A., & Milanesi, L. (2007). BGBlast: A BLAST Grid implementation with database self-updating and adaptive replication. *Stud Health Technol Inform, 126*, 23-30.

KEY TERMS AND DEFINITIONS

Applications Grid: It shares and reuses application codes but uses software technologies like service oriented architectures that facilitate sharing business logic among multiple applications.

BiG: BLAST in Grids uses the Basic Local Alignment Search tool to find regions of local similarity between sequences by comparing nucleotide or protein sequences to databases and by calculating the statistical significance of matches.

EELA Infrastructure Grid: This grid pools, shares and reuses infrastructure resources such as hardware, software, storage and networks across multiple applications between Europe and Latin America

EMBOSS: Free Open Source software analysis package which covers several molecular biology tools.

GATE: C++ platform based on the Monte Carlo GEANT4 software, which models nuclear medicine applications, such as Positron Emission Tomography (PET), Single Photon Emission Computed Tomography (SPECT) or radiotherapy dosimetry

Grid Computing: A style of computing that dynamically pools IT resources together for use based on resource need. It allows organizations to provision and scale resources as needs arise, thereby preventing the underutilization of resources (computers, networks, data archives, instruments).

Phylogeny: A reconstruction of the evolutionary history of a group of organisms used throughout the life sciences

WISDOM: Wide in Silico Docking of Malaria is the proposition of new inhibitors by means of periodic Data-Challenges and further analysis

Chapter XXI
Distributed Image Processing on a Blackboard System

Gerald Schaefer
Loughborough University, UK

Roger Tait
University of Cambridge, UK

ABSTRACT

Efficient approaches to computationally intensive image processing tasks are currently highly sought after. In this chapter we show how a blackboard paradigm, originally developed for collaborative problem solving, can be used as an efficient and effective vehicle for distributed computation. Through the design of dedicated intelligent agents, typical image processing algorithms can be applied in parallel on multiple loosely coupled machines leading to a significant overall speedup as is verified in a series of experiments.

INTRODUCTION

Despite continuous increases in processor speeds, many image processing tasks remain computationally intensive. Partly this is due to researchers "keeping up" with the technology and developing more complex but better working algorithms, and partly because typical image sizes also continually grow due to improved technologies. It is therefore not uncommon that some algorithms take a relatively long time to run. While this is typically not a big obstacle for home users, a more feasible approach needs to be adopted in large scale image acquisition and processing environments or in real time or near-real time domains.

Conveniently, many image processing algorithms are inherently parallel and therefore well suited to a distributed implementation. An important consideration when parallelising such algorithms is the architecture of the host system

(Jamieson *et al.*, 1992). A tightly-coupled system comprises of one machine with multiple processors. In this case, data distribution is not necessary. In contrast, a loosely-coupled architecture, consisting of multiple computers in different locations will require distribution, communication, and accumulation mechanisms.

In this chapter we will only consider loosely-coupled systems as they are by far more common due to the high costs of tightly-coupled systems. We will show that by employing a distributed blackboard architecture consisting of several intelligent agents known as knowledge sources (KSs) it is possible to perform parallel image processing on a loosely-coupled system and achieve a significant performance gain when utilising a number of different machines.

BACKGROUND

In a tightly-coupled architecture all processors share the same main memory and work, concurrently, on the same data. Consequently, this type of system largely eliminates the need for explicit message passing between concurrent tasks. Multithreaded programming allows applications to branch into independent concurrent threads and is not restricted to shared-memory multiprocessor architectures. In general, multi-threaded applications are well suited to multi-processor architectures. This is because individual threads can run concurrently on different processors. As multi-threaded applications share the same address space, they cause considerably fewer overheads than the creation of an equivalent number of processes.

In a loosely-coupled architecture, parallel image processing tasks typically consist of four main steps: image distribution, local processing, data transfer during processing, and segment accumulation. Distribution is the process of dividing an image into segments each of which is assigned to a unique processor (Taniguchi *et al.*,

1997). Under a duplicate distribution scheme each processor is sent an exact copy of the original image. Alternatively, more complex schemes can be adopted where an image is divided into a variable sized matrix (Nicolescu and Jonker, 2000). After distribution, each processor applies local image processing to its allocated segment. When data allocated to other processors are required, they are transferred by inter-processor communication. Finally, after application of the parallel algorithm, segments are accumulated into a resulting image.

Inter-processor communication is required when data allocated to other processors are needed, and can be categorised into groups based on their pattern of data access (Seinstra, Koelma and Geusebroek, 2002). These patterns also represent a strategy for synchronisation between communicating processors. One-to-one access is common in tasks such as image brightening or colour correction, where an output pixel maps directly to a pixel in the input image. Alternatively, a one-to-many relationship exists in neighbourhood operators, such as edge detection filters, which calculate an output based on a function of the input pixel's immediate neighbourhood. Naturally, the handling and transmission of non-contiguous data differs from data stored as contiguous blocks. Data stored randomly in memory causes additional overheads due to its packing into a contiguous buffer before transmission (Hoare, 1985).

Multiagent systems offer the possibility of directly representing the individual components of a complex system (Murch and Johnson, 1998) and are inherently suitable for distributed implementation. The behaviour that is encapsulated within an agent gives it the ability to adapt, interact and evolve within the environment in which it exists. An agent makes decisions based upon memory, internal state and information received from other agents. If multiple agents are hosted on independent computers within the same network, communications coupled to a control module are used to achieve interaction and collaboration.

Multiple agents have been utilised in several parallel image processing environments, where decisions are made based on simple behaviour. In one such example intelligent agents are employed to detect homogeneous features in natural objects (Harrovet *et al.*, 1998). In (Lueckenhaus and Eckstein, 1997) a three-layered architecture for automatic parallelisation of image analysis tasks is presented. In the initial layer, image processing operators are selected for parallelisation. Then execution of the operator is carried out in parallel by multiple agents. Management of the overall system is provided by a third layer which represents an image operator database.

A BLACKBOARD ARCHITECTURE FOR PARALLEL IMAGE PROCESSING

In this chapter we present a parallel image processing approach based on a distributed blackboard architecture. Blackboard systems are based on the analogy of a group of experts working together to solve a common problem by writing their ideas onto a common blackboard (Engelmore and Morgan, 1998). Such architectures have emerged from their 1970s origins as a suitable host for multiagent implementations (Jufeng *et al.*, 2004). Traditional implementations are constructed from three distinct components including a blackboard, expert agent modules known as knowledge sources (KSs), and a control unit. The blackboard represents an area of shared memory where agents can store and retrieve information. Agents can be implemented in any programming style, e.g. as a rule base, neural networks, fuzzy logic, or procedural modules. Also known as the scheduler, the control unit monitors changes on the blackboard and is used to determine the focus of attention. The focus of attention can be described as the selection of an agent to be activated or selection of a solution to pursue.

DARBS (Distributed Algorithmic and Rule-based Blackboard System) is a distributed blackboard architecture based on a client/server model, in which the server functions as the blackboard and client modules as KSs (Nolle, Wong and Hopgood, 2001). The blackboard system that we present here is based on DARBS and comprises three different types of knowledge sources: a Distributor KS, Worker KSs, and a Manager KS (Tait, Schaefer and Hopgood, 2006).

The Distributor knowledge source splits an image into segments which are then placed on the blackboard. A segment list which is locally maintained by the Distributor KS is initialised in preparation for new data. Selection of an image is performed either automatically when in batch mode, or manually after an image viewer has been shown. System data defining various parameters is then added to the blackboard. This includes image processing operator parameters, the number of segments into which an image is divided, the size of border between segments, and the size of the original image. Next, using the number of segments and border size, the image is divided into segments. Resulting segments are then compressed, accumulated in the local segment list, and sent to the blackboard.

Worker knowledge sources take segments from the blackboard and perform local processing. The division of an image into segments means that the tasks performed by each Worker KS are identical. As a consequence, behaviours of all Worker KS are also identical. In order to achieve co-ordination of multiple identical Worker KSs, each Worker KS is assigned an index. Because Worker KSs act for the majority of their time upon data with corresponding indices, the indexing scheme is also used to assign image segments to Worker KSs. Thus, for instance Worker n KS fetches segment n from the blackboard.

Retrieval of some parameter information is the first task of the Worker n KS. Once retrieved, parameters associated with the image processing operator are extracted. The Worker n KS then waits to be triggered. When this happens, segment *n* is retrieved from the blackboard. The retrieved segment is then decompressed and processed using the assigned image processing operations. Once processed, segment *n* is compressed and returned to the blackboard and the Worker KS terminates.

The Manager knowledge source collects processed segments and constructs a resulting image, while co-ordinating Worker KS activities. The initial task performed by the Manager KS is clearance of a locally maintained segment list, in preparation for new data and fetching the necessary parameter information (the number of segments, border size, and original image size) from the blackboard. The waiting Worker KSs are then triggered to commence processing. The Manager KS now waits for the workers to terminate and retrieves the processed segments from the blackboard. Each retrieved segment is decompressed and added to the locally maintained processed segment list. Once all processed segments have been accumulated, a resulting image is constructed and can be viewed on screen or stored automatically.

EXPERIMENTS

In order to evaluate the efficiency of our framework, a number of algorithms were selected. The algorithms represent image processing operators that demonstrate a range of computational complexities. In order for extensive testing to be carried out, the algorithms chosen are easily scalable.

Convolution is a simple mathematical operation that multiplies two sets of numbers; in the field of image processing a kernel and an image. This property allows implementation of image processing operators, whose output is a combination of inputs values. Selected for testing purposes, mean filtering (Davies, 1990) is one such convolution-based operator whereby the intensity variation between a pixel and its neighbours is reduced which is why it is often employed for noise reduction. During filtering, pixel intensities in an input image are replaced with the statistical mean of the neighbourhood or kernel that surrounds them. A small kernel is usual for such implementations.

Due to this small kernel size and the resulting relatively low complexity of the algorithm it was expected that our distributed blackboard approach did not yield any improvements in terms of processing speed for mean filtering. Rather, a drop in performance was measured which can be attributed to the communication overheads associated with KS management.

Histogram equalisation represents a method that distributes pixel intensities uniformly throughout the intensity range of an image and is often used to enhance the contrast of images. In more complex conditions where a global histogram does not capture the regional statistics of an image, local histogram equalisation (Dale-Jones and Tjahjadi, 1993) has become a well established technique. For each pixel in the input image, a kernel representing neighbourhood pixels is constructed. The intensity of the central pixel is then set based on the equalised histogram of the constructed kernel. Crucially, the kernel is required to be of sufficient size in order to capture the regional statistics of the image.

In Figure 1 we show the experimental results obtained from performing local histogram equalisation on our distributed blackboard, as a plot of processing time against the number of knowledge sources employed. For comparison, the execution time of a non-distributed sequential single processor implementation is also shown. Although the processing time of a single Worker KS exceeds that of the sequential implementation, which is to be expected due to communication overheads, it can be seen that the average execution time reduces from approximately 2 minutes to 35 seconds when 8 Worker KSs are employed.

Figure 1. The sequential and distributed processing speeds of local histogram equalisation with increasing number of Worker KSs

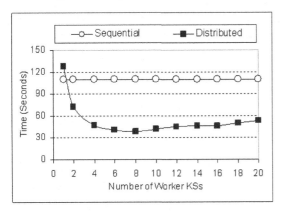

Figure 2. The sequential and distributed processing speeds of adaptive thresholding with increasing number of Worker KSs

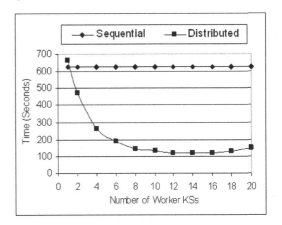

Thresholding is a process used to divide an image into foreground and background components. In conventional thresholding all pixels are compared with a global threshold level and set accordingly. In contrast, in adaptive thresholding (Umbaugh, 1998) the threshold level is dynamically changed over an entire image. Typically, adaptive thresholding is used on images which contain variable lighting conditions or shadows. This is because the algorithm assumes that smaller image regions contain more uniform illumination conditions than the image as a whole. For each pixel in the input image, a kernel representing neighbourhood pixels is constructed. Using the kernel, an optimum threshold level is then calculated by determining the between-class variance of its intensity histogram (Otsu, 1979). The employed kernel needs to be of sufficient size to cover foreground and background pixels as otherwise the between-class variance cannot be computed accurately.

Here, larger speedups were achieved. The results, given in Figure 2 highlight how processing time is drastically reduced from 11 minutes for a single Worker KS, to approximately 2 minutes when 14 KSs are employed.

FUTURE TRENDS

As we have demonstrated, distributed blackboard systems can be used for efficient parallel image processing. However, as has been seen, one problem is that after a certain number of agents there are no further speed increases to be gained. This is due to a saturation effect of the blackboard and stems from the fact that communication between the blackboard and the knowledge sources is hindering the task of parallelisation. More effective control of this will hence enable even further improvements.

In the general field of parallel image processing it will be interesting to see how systems and algorithms will be able to incorporate recent processors that contain 2 or more processing units. Of even more interest will be a true synthesis between loosely-coupled and tightly-coupled systems in one effective framework.

CONCLUSION

High image resolutions coupled with complex algorithms have increased the demand for high speed processing capabilities. In this chapter we have presented a distributed blackboard that is capable for efficient parallel image processing. Image segments are split, processed in a distributed way by intelligent agents and re-assembled. Experimental results, based on complex image processing tasks such as local histogram equalisation and adaptive thresholding, have confirmed the efficiency of our approach. These tests show that the time constraints associated with a variety of image processing tasks can be successfully alleviated.

REFERENCES

Dale-Jones, R., & Tjahjadi, T. (1993). A study and modification of the local histogram equalisation algorithm, *Pattern Recognition, 26*, 1373-1381.

Davies, E.R. (1990). *Machine vision: theory, algorithms, practicalities.* Academic Press, London.

Engelmore, R., & Morgan, T. (1998). *Blackboard systems.* New York: Addison-Wesley Publishers.

Harrovet, F., Ballet, P., Rodin, V., & Tisseau, J. (1998). ORIS: Multiagent approach for image processing. In *Proc. Parallel and Distributed Methods for Image Processing* (pp. 57-68).

Hoare, C.A.R. (1985). *Communicating sequential processes.* Prentice Hall, New York.

Jamieson, L.H., Delp, E.J., Wang, C., Li, J., & Weil, F.J. (1992). A software environment for parallel computer vision. *Computer, 25*, 73-77.

Jufeng, W., Hancheng, X., Xiang, L., & Jingping Y. (2004). Multiagent based distributed control system for an intelligent robot. In *Proc. IEEE International Conference on Services Computing*, 633-637.

Lueckenhaus, M., & Eckstein, W. (1997). Multiagent based system for parallel image processing. *Proc. Parallel and Distributed Methods for Image Processing* (pp. 21-30).

Murch, R., & Johnson, J. (1998). *Intelligent software agents.* New York: Prentice Hall.

Nicolescu, C., & Jonker, P. (2000). Parallel low-level image processing on a distributed memory system. In *Proc. 15th Workshop on Parallel and Distributed Processing* (pp. 226-233).

Nolle, L., Wong, K.C.P., & Hopgood, A.A. (2001). DARBS: A distributed blackboard system. *Research and Development in Intelligent Systems XVIII*, 161-170.

Otsu, N. (1979). A threshold selection method for gray level histograms. *IEEE Transactions on Systems, Man and Cybernetics*, 9, 62-66.

Seinstra, F.J., Koelma, D., Geusebroek, J.M. (2002). A software architecture for user transparent parallel image processing. *Parallel Computing, 28*, 967-993.

Tait, R.J., Schaefer, G., & Hopgood, A.A. (2006). iDARBS – A distributed blackboard system for image processing. In *Proc. 13th International Conference on Systems, Signals and Image Processing*, 431-434.

Taniguchi, R., Makiyama, Y., Tsuruta, N., Yonemoto, S., & Arita, D. (1997). Software platform for parallel image processing and computer vision. In *Proceedings of Parallel and Distributed Methods for Image Processing* (pp. 2-10).

Umbaugh, S. (1998) *Computer vision and image processing.* New York: Prentice Hall.

KEY TERMS AND DEFINITIONS

Blackboard Architecture: An artificial intelligence application based on and analogous to a group of experts seated in a room with a large blackboard working as a team to solve a common problem.

Distributed Agents: Software entities, designed to execute as independent threads and on distributed processors, capable of acting autonomously in order to achieve a pre-defined task.

Loosely-Coupled Hardware Architecture: Architecture that consists of multiple separate machines each with their own processor and memory.

Parallel Image Processing: A distributed execution of an image processing algorithm on multiple processors.

Tightly-Coupled Hardware Architecture: Architecture that consists of one machine with several processors that share the same memory.

Chapter XXII
Simulated Events Production on the Grid for the BaBar Experiment

Daniele Andreotti
Ferrara University, Italy

Armando Fella
CNAF Bologna Centre, Italy

Eleonora Luppi
Ferrara University, Italy

ABSTRACT

The BaBar experiment uses data since 1999 in examining the violation of charge and parity (CP) symmetry in the field of high energy physics. This event simulation experiment is a compute intensive task due to the complexity of the Monte-Carlo simulation implemented on the GEANT engine. Data needed as input for the simulation (stored in the ROOT format), are classified into two categories: conditions data for describing the detector status when data are recorded, and background triggers data for noise signal necessary to obtain a realistic simulation. In this chapter, the grid approach is applied to the BaBar production framework using the INFN-GRID network.

INTRODUCTION

In the early 1990s, the high energy physics community had to solve the problems of storing and processing the large quantities of data that are produced by experiments that span over several years. In fact, high energy physics experiments have very complex instrumentation, involving large collaborations from widely dispersed institutions and produce enormous amounts of data. Data would have been too much for one institution to handle so they needed to share resources using distributed computing. For these reasons, it is necessary to have efficient communication among the various institutions in the world and access to very large computing power. A computational grid comes in handy. A computational grid is a hardware and software infrastructure that provides dependable, consistent, pervasive, and inexpensive access to high-end computational capabilities (Foster and Kesselman, 1998).

The current dominant BaBar experiments are Belle (Belle, 2007) in Japan and CDF (CDF, 2007) at Fermilab in USA. Belle experiment started in 1998, while the CDF has been operational since 2001. Together with future experiments at CERN's Large Hadron Collider (LHC) (Bird et al., 2005), these experiments will produce roughly **15 Petabytes** of data each year. Other particle physics experiments are already producing huge quantities of data for analysis, which may need grid implementation. These experiments have to manage the migration from a traditional computing model to the evolving grid based model.

BACKGROUND

The BaBar experiment (Cowan, 2007), developed at SLAC (Stanford Linear Accelerator Center), Stanford University, studies the violation of charge and parity (CP) symmetry, a well known topic in the high energy physics field. The universe presents a composition where the difference between matter and anti-matter is subtle, and thus the experiment is geared towards understanding why matter prevails on anti-matter. High-energy electrons and positrons continuously collide every 250 million times per second to create rare B-meson and anti-B-meson. Such events are recorded for further analysis.

High speed electronics events require about 30kB of storage for each event. Some events are reconstructed from raw data and then separated ("skimmed") into approximately 200 data streams according to their physics properties. These data streams are made available as datasets for analysis and used by 600 researchers based at 75 institutes in 10 countries. The data streams result in increased storage requirements as each event is duplicated in different streams but each data stream can be analyzed more quickly. The BaBar experiment has accumulated to date about 525 fb-1 integrated luminosity.

Another important task, called Simulation Production (SP), is focused on the simulation of the experiment to reconstruct events produced through a simulation based on the Monte Carlo method that compares real data with the theoretical model. Accurate simulations, based on the Monte Carlo method, need fast reprocessing of data for distributing a large amount of simulated events for analysis purpose.

All information concerning the detector, like calibrations and efficiencies, represent its status during data acquisition and are called condition data. This information is mandatory for describing the real state of the system during the generation of simulated events. Along with condition data, other important information is represented by the background triggers component, the noise recorded when data are taken, that addresses the requirement for a realistic reconstruction of simulated events. At least three times as many simulated events are needed as data events. With the traditional production system, each simulated event takes 4 seconds on a modern processor and results in 20kB of storage.

In order to speed up data access for the huge amount of events produced, both types of data are stored following the ROOT (Brun and Rademakers, 1997) framework schema that allows one to represent data as objects, describing parameters like energy, speed and trajectory as attributes that can be easily accessed through specific methods, by the code in charge of analyzing them.

Data for the simulation process are usually aggregated into bunches of runs of 2000 events each (up to 6000) and allocated among all sites belonging to the collaboration in order to be generated in a distributed way. All results are then sent back to the main center at SLAC where are stored and deployed to BaBar members.

In the traditional model, each site belonging to the collaboration sets up specific computing resources and events are spread over local farms of dedicated CPUs centrally managed by local administrators. On each farm, a complete BaBar software release needs to be installed locally or made available to the batch nodes via network file system. A number of servers must be maintained locally: the location of the experimental and simulated data is provided by a MySQL database. The system requires a great deal of local customization with each dedicated farm maintained by a local production manager. Load balancing between independent farms has to be done manually. Monitoring of jobs during production is difficult and there is no way to automatically ensure that all resources are available before commencing a production run. Despite these drawbacks, the system has run with greater than 98% efficiency. (Smith, Blanc, Bozzi, Andreotti and Khan, 2006)

In this paper, we describe the implementation of a new model based on the grid paradigm in order to provide a production workflow where scalability is improved concerning the number of computing resources involved.

MAIN FOCUS

INFN-Grid Project

Italy's National Institute for Nuclear Physics started the INFN-Grid project (INFNGrid, 2002) and in 2002 implemented the first national grid. More than 30 farms located over the whole country are INFN grid sites, providing storage and computing facilities, and cooperating in developing a distributed computing model based on EGEE gLite middleware. Nowadays many others kind of applications are run on the INFN Grid. The main organizations involved in developing and

exploiting grid infrastructure are represented by the LHC experiments located at CERN.

The actual middleware implemented is based upon the official gLite 3.0.0 (Burke, et al., 2007) and is provided along with different profiles for setting up the components of the architecture as follows:

- **User Interface (UI):** Represents the official interface for the user to the grid environment. Through specific commands it is possible to submit a job previously defined to check its status during execution and to retrieve the result at job completion.
- **Resource Broker (RB):** This element is in charge of collecting user's jobs and spreading them over the grid using a routing algorithm capable of balancing the workload. A match between requirements of the job and resources provided is performed for each single site involved.
- **Computer Element (CE):** Represent the official gate of each site grid farm. CE accepts jobs provided by the RB and distributes them over the underlying processing farm. CE is the standard farm gatekeeper. It hides the heterogeneous LRMS (Local Resource Manager System) layer. In particular, the LRMS works as a job queue distributor and resource modeler. Similar examples are LFC, PBS, Condor and so on.
- **Worker Node (WN):** A single machine equipped with one or more CPUs in charge of executing jobs provided by CE.
- **Storage Element (SE):** Provides storage facilities for user's data.

Groups of users that share a common interest to achieve a specific target are classified into Virtual Organizations (VO) (Foster, Kesselman and Tuecke, 2001) , a logical schema that allows members of the same community to easily and securely access and share resources and information. In order to belong to a VO, each user needs a personal digital certificate for identity and authorization to resources in one's own group.

Job Definition

Grid jobs must be properly defined using a specific format before being submitted to the grid. Job Description Language (JDL) (Datamat, 2001) supplies the right syntax, a sequence of coupled attribute-value, to define a job's requirements along with all details needed for correct execution. For example, a simple "Hello world" job is shown in Box 1.

This job executes the command "echo Hello World" on a WN, writing its output to the file hello.out. After the job has ended both files hello.log and hello.err are automatically retrieved.

BABARGRID

BaBar software releases (Geddes, 1998), are made up groups of packages like binaries and libraries, that are periodically distributed. A production release is developed at SLAC and each external site can easily download and install it locally using specific tools. Releases contain all the software developed for the experiment, not just for simulation purpose, therefore the size is pretty huge (1.5 GB). This doesn't match with requirements of a large distributed environment like the Grid, since it's very hard to try to manage such quantity of data on several sites keeping everything in sync.

In order to bypass this limit, a custom application has been written to extract from a main release just the part of the software concerning the Monte Carlo simulation for events production, including all the components needed to create a small package (a tar archive of about 70 MByte) that can be easily installed everywhere in order to work independently from the main release.

The step just described is mandatory for making BaBar simulation software compatible with the Grid model. The package is then installed to those CE belonging to sites involved in the production task, using the standard grid job submission procedure, and exported to WNs through a shared area. The whole procedure is performed by a special user with specific rights.

Input data provided for the simulation process are stored using the ROOT format. The data should be largely distributed to be easily localized and accessed by WNs on the grid. The architecture of Xrootd (Hanushevsky, 2004) servers provides reliable file transfer, asynchronous data access and multithreading management of client's requests. All data are installed on dedicated machines along with server daemons and replicated on four sites belonging to the INFN-Grid: CNAF, Ferrara, Padova and Pisa. Locations involved in production without a local copy of the data can remotely access Xrootd servers through a specific protocol. All sites belonging to the production group are marked with a special tag in order to define a pool of computing farms where BaBar jobs can run safely.

The traditional model implemented in BaBar provides a set of Perl (Kirrily, 2002) scripts, called ProdTools (Smith, 2001), to manage the whole

Box 1.

```
Executable = "/bin/echo";                          # main command to
Arguments = "Hello World ";                        # parameters used by the executable
StdOutput = "hello.out";                           # output file
StdError = "hello.err";                            # error log file
OutputSandbox = {"hello.out","hello.err"};         # list of files to retrieve after job ending
```

production workflow that can be summarized by the following steps:

- **Build:** A range of assigned runs (jobs) is built locally. Each run is provided with all information needed to produce a specific sequence of events.
- **Submit:** Runs are sent as jobs to a batch system that takes care of executing them
- **Merge:** Results are merged into collection of data ready to be exported to SLAC
- **Export:** Merged collections are transferred to the main repository at SLAC

ProdTools concerning job forwarding are modified to comply with the grid submission system along with scripts assigned to build runs allocated so that a custom JDL file including the right information to run on the grid is generated.

Workflow

The user is in charge of managing production logs on the UI to build a range of runs and establish a connection with the main database at SLAC for collecting all data related to the type of events generated for each single job. The submission is performed through the standard grid tools to the RB dedicated to BaBar, which spreads jobs over the grid balancing the workload on the sites

involved. Jobs are queued by the selected CE until they are able to run on an available WN. The execution step runs the main application used in BaBar to generate simulated events while contacting the Xrootd server closest to the node where job is running. Output is registered into the grid catalogue (LFC) and then moved to a SE. LFC is a distributed file catalogue where files can be classified using a Logical File Name (LFN) that provides a set of facilities to make the data transfer more reliable. The procedure has been implemented taking into account different kind of error that could happen during this step. Results are then retrieved on the UI, where after a check is merged into collections and then transferred to SLAC (Brew, Wilson, Castelli, Adye, Luppi, and Andreotti, 2006). The whole workflow on the grid is managed by a custom application, installed on the UI, in charge of monitoring production and collecting results.

Monitor

A custom application has been developed to monitor job status on the grid, along with other information like workload on sites involved, historical data and production rate. In order to provide a full control on a job's life cycle, this tool has been installed on the UI to track both grid states, obtained via middleware calls, and

Figure 1. Sites distribution for BaBar SP

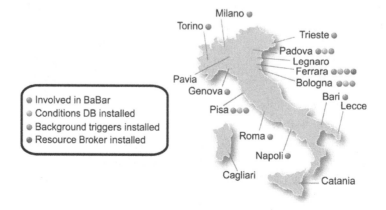

Figure 2. Production workflow

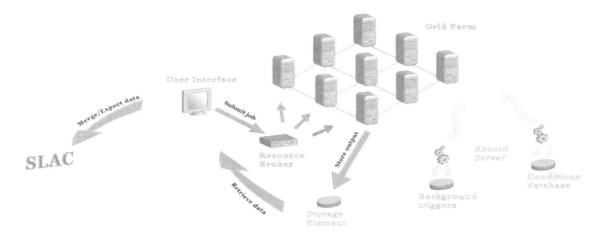

Figure 3. Web monitor

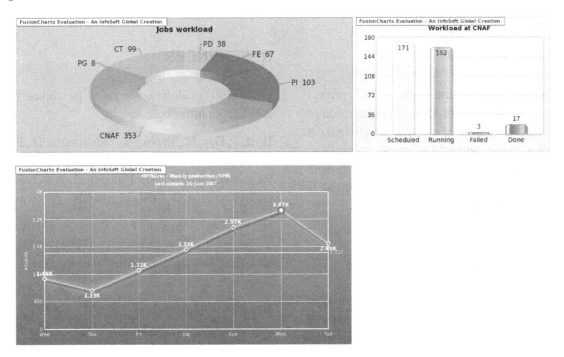

ProdTools states, like "build", "merged" and "transferred".

All information is displayed via a web front-end interface, while the backend is implemented using the Round Robin Databases (RRD) (Oetiker, 2005) toolkit. The interface provides statistical plots concerning the status of jobs from when they are built until they are retrieved, showing each intermediate step. The main application periodically checks jobs transitions, resubmits wrong runs and retrieves completed jobs on the UI.

Figure 4. Million of events produced per site worldwide

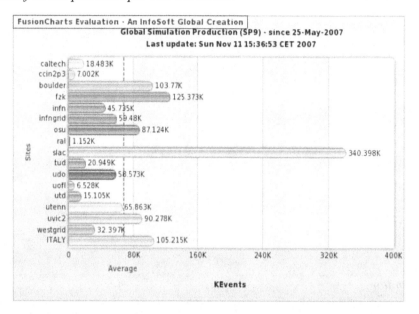

FUTURE TRENDS

The future plans for the BaBar GRID project include migration from LCG to gLite middleware and the merging of specific steps to make it comply with standard grid submission workflow. The knowledge gained working on this project represents a useful reference for further models that could be developed in the future.

CONCLUSION

The Italian production rate was about 60 million events in the last 3 months, reaching a peak of 14 million events per week and about 600 jobs running simultaneously on 8 INFN-GRID sites. Compared to last year, the INFN BaBar simulation production doubled. A low failure rate (2%), mostly due to the wrong site configuration, implied that the architecture implemented provided a stable and reliable platform for a distributed and intensive computing task like BaBar Simulation Production. (Fella, Andreotti, & Luppi, 2007)

REFERENCES

Belle (2007). *Belle home page*. Retrieved Feb. 2007, from http://belle.kek.jp/

Bird, I., Bos, K., Brook, N., Duellmann, D., Eck, C., Fisk, I., et al. (2005). *LHC Computing Grid*. Retrieved June 20, 2005, from http://lcg.web.cern.ch/LCG/tdr/LCG_TDR_v1_04.pdf

Brew, C.A.J., Wilson, F.F., Castelli, G., Adye, T., Luppi, E., & Andreotti, D. (2006). BABAR experience of large scale production on the Grid. *E-science*, 151.

Brun, R. & Rademakers, F. (1997). ROOT – An object orientated data analysis framework. *Nucl. Instr. and Methods*, A 389, 81.

Burke, S., Campana, S., Delgado Peris, A., Donno, F., Mendez Lorenzo, P., Santinelli, R., et al. (2007). *GLite 3 user guide*. Retrieved January 17, 2007, from https://edms.cern.ch/file/722398/1.1/gLite-3-UserGuide.pdf

CDF (2007). *The collider detector at Fermilab*. Retrieved Feb. 2007, from http://www-cdf.fnal.gov/

Cowan, R. (2007). *BaBar public Web home page.* Retrieved May 16, 2007, from http://www-public. slac.stanford.edu/babar/

Datamat. (2001). *Job Description Language how to.* Retrieved December 12, 2001, from http:// www.grid.org.tr/servisler/dokumanlar/DataGrid-JDL-HowTo.pdf

Fella, A., Andreotti, D., & Luppi E. (2007). *Events simulation production for the BaBar experiment using the grid approach content.* Paper presented at the Third EELA Conference, Catania, Italy.

Foster, I., & Kesselman, C. (1998). *The Grid: blueprint for a new computing infrastructure.* Morgan Kaufmann Publishers, Inc.

Foster, I., Kesselman C., & Tuecke S. (2001). *The anatomy of the Grid - Enabling scalable virtual organizations.* Retrieved 2001, from http://www. globus.org/alliance/publications/papers/anatomy. pdf

Geddes, N. I. (1998). *BaBar software release structure.* Retrieved November 18, 1998, from http://www.slac.stanford.edu/BFROOT/www/ Computing/Environment/NewUser/htmlbug/ node14.html

Hanushevsky, H. (2004). *The Next Generation Root File System.* Paper presented at CHEP04, Interlaken, Switzerland.

INFNGrid (2002). *The Italian Grid infrastructure.* Retrieved December 2002, from http://grid. infn.it/

Kirrily R. (2002). *A brief introduction.* Retrieved March 2002, from http://perldoc.perl.org/perlintro.pdf

Oetiker, T. (2005). *Write your own monitoring software with RRDtool.* Retrieved August 3, 2005, from http://oss.oetiker.ch/rrdtool/pub/oscon2005-slides.pdf

Smith, D. (2001). *ProdTools man pages.* Retrieved December 10, 2001, from http://www.slac.stan-ford.edu/BFROOT/www/Computing/Offline/ Production/prodtools.pdf

Smith, D. A., Blanc, F., Bozzi, C., Andreotti, D., & Khan, A. (2006). Babar Simulation Production – A millennium of work in under a year. *Nuclear Science, IEEE Transactions on 53*(3), 1299–1303.

KEY TERMS AND DEFINITIONS

BaBar Import/Export Tools: The main tasks the BaBar collaboration carries out at remote sites are the event reconstruction, the simulation production and the physics data analysis. Despite the fact that each duty needs to access a different data type and database metadata information, only one import/export software suite is shared between all the site managers.

BaBar Software: BaBar software is organized in terms of packages. A package is a self-contained piece of software intended to perform a well defined task. Some packages may not be usable on their own, requiring integration with others. A software release consists of a coherent set of packages together with the libraries and binaries created for various machine architectures.

Distributed Computing: The distributed computing paradigm envisages the execution of particular software on two or more computational systems. The software can be developed for a pure parallel computation (e.g. parallelism on data, on task, instruction level parallelism) or can be managed by a dependency structure as a pipeline or farm model. In the BaBar scenario the computational tasks are performed using data parallelism on a distributed computer farm (twenty farms in 5 countries) and on LCG/gLite based Grid in Italy and UK.

Grid Monitoring: The INFN-Grid` infrastructure includes several monitoring systems for different purposes and granularity. Monitor activity can focus on resources status and services availability at each site or across the grid as a whole and display useful data aggregated per site, service and VO.

LFC: LCG File Catalog. It is a high performance file catalogue that addresses availability and scalability issues storing both logical and physical file mappings.

Monte Carlo Method: A statistical approach ideal for those kind of problems that are too complicated to solve using analytical methods and that guarantees accurate results when applied several times to the problem domain. A classical example is the computation of the value of π generating couples of random numbers, (x,y). The ratio of the number of couples that satisfy the rule: $x^2+y^2<=1$ and the total number of couples generated is an approximation of $\pi/4$. The more random couples that are generated, the more accurate the approximation is.

ROOT: A set of frameworks on data analysis that can be easily extended to the Object Oriented approach implemented. Data are represented as objects that can be accessed to retrieve all information needed for further computation.

Chapter XXIII
A Framework for Semantic Grid in E-Science

Diego Liberati
Politecnico di Milano, Italy

ABSTRACT

A framework is proposed that creates, uses and communicates information, whose organizational dynamics allows performing a distributed cooperative enterprise in public environments, even over open source systems. The approach assumes the web services as the enacting paradigm possibly over a grid, to formalize interactions as cooperative services on various computational nodes of a network. The illustrated case study shows that some portions, both of processes and of data or knowledge, can be shared in a collaborative environment, which is also more generally true for any kind of either complex or resource demanding (or both) interaction that will benefit any of the approaches.

INTRODUCTION

One of the reasons for executing an experiment in a distributed way might be not just to share both data and computational power or to assign specific task to selected sites, but also to share developed software and even more importantly, competency. It would imply the need to consider not all the resources within a Grid as almost equivalent at the same logical level, but to partition them in classes of equivalence, and to share collaborative work on a specific sub-task only within the specialized sub-cluster. That may allow logically equivalent outputs, possibly with either different approaches and/or diverse performances. Autonomous agents (Amigoni et al., 2007) are believed to be of a great help in order to support optimal resource allocation dealing with such kind of constraints. In particular, the exemplifying field here used, in the framework of e-science, is the bioinformatics and systems biology growing arena, that may not require a unique big site for experiments like particle physics, but are amenable to a virtual collaboration among different sites. At the end-user level, addressing multidisciplinary distributed science, the proposed framework would thus also appear as a kind of Semantic Web (Bosin et al., 2006a) that enables transparent document sharing, metadata annotations and semantic integration (Hendler, 2003) over a Grid. Since both Grid Computing and Semantic Web deal with interoperability, it becomes apparent that, from the e-science perspective, they would both be necessary. Neither technology on its own alone can achieve the full e-science vision. This integration, called *Semantic Grid,* would serve as the infrastructure for this vision (De Roure, 2004). Thus, since ICT models, techniques and tools are rapidly gaining grounds, there is a true hope to move towards the realization of effective distributed and cooperative scientific laboratories.

BACKGROUND

Four main classes of methodological approaches to the experiments can be easily identified within the investigated field as follows:

- *Process Simulation and Visualization* of the already available information sources. This is a very widely studied class, pertaining also to computational biochemistry among other disciplines, on which we will deliberately not speculate within this paper, but focus instead on the following three classes, on which more results have been recently contributed. It is mentioned on the human-computer interaction issues discussed by Liberati (2008a).

- *Supervised or Unsupervised Classification* of observed events without inferring any correlation nor causality, such as in clustering (Garatti et al., 2007), and neural networks (Babiloni et al., 2000; Vercesi et al., 2000; Drago et al., 2002).

- *Machine Learning:* Rule Generation (Muselli and Liberati, 2002) and Bayesian Networks (Bosin et al., 2006b) are able to select and link salient features involved variables in order to understand relationships (Liberati, 2008b) and to extract knowledge on the reliability, and possibly causal relationships among related cofactors [Paoli et al. 2000] via tools like logical networks (Muselli and Liberati, 2000) and Cart-models.

- *Identification of the Process Dynamics,* through either ad hoc non linear models (Chignola et al., 2000), Piece-Wise Affine Identification (Ferrari-Trecate et al., 2003) of Hybrid dynamical-logical processes, or simplified linear (Baraldi et al., 2007) mass-action (De Nicolao et al., 2000; Sartorio et al., 2000; Sartorio et al., 2002) models (Liberati, 2008c) of the underlying Systems Biology (Sacco et al., 2007).

Such classes might have an impact on the design of the experiment and of its execution modality - in terms of execution resources. Beyond mediating possibly different repositories, they may require recursive approaches and hence intense computation either on a single specialized node or in a grid structure.

MAIN FOCUS

Sometimes, it is of interest to identify how an experiment can be mapped onto a service-oriented model over a grid. As a case study, we focus on an experiment (related to the identification of process dynamics as introduced in the previous section): the piecewise affine identification problem (Ferrari-Trecate et al., 2003). Piecewise affine identification associates temporal data points in the multivariable space in such a way to determine both a sequence of linear sub-models and their respective regions of operation. It does not even impose any continuity at each change in the derivative. It exploits a clustering algorithm, in which the three following steps are executed:

- *Step 1 – Local linear identification*: small sets of data points close to each other belong to the same sub-model. Thus, for each data point, a local set is tentatively built, collecting the selected point together with a given number of its neighbors. For each local data set, a linear model is identified through least squares procedure.
- *Step 2 – Clustering.* The algorithm clusters the parameter vectors of the identified models and thus the corresponding data points.
- *Step 3 – Piecewise affine identification.* Both the linear sub-models and their regions are estimated from the data in each subset. The coefficients are estimated via weighted least squares, taking into account the confidence measures. The shape of the polyhedral region characterizing the domain of each model may be obtained via Linear Support Vector Machines (Vapnik, 1998).

The *K-means* algorithm is employed, and can be (re)used several times. As an independent step, the clustering activity can be either assigned to a dedicated node, or distributed over the Grid, also depending on both its dimensionality and the complexity of the employed algorithm. Also the algorithm deputed to define the regions in which every linear model is valid may be one of the many general purpose available for such task (here a simple Support Vector Machine is chosen). As such, it can also be thought as a separate re-usable module, useful in many other problems. Moreover, the weighted least square module is another possible re-usable e-service, being already used twice within this kind of experiment, and being quite general purpose approach to many other kinds of scientific problems implying the need to identify a linear regression as a sub-problem.

On the other hand, K-means is also re-usable when simply clustering is just needed, possibly initialized by partitioning it orthogonal to the principal components (Garatti et al, 2007) in order to overcome the typical clustering drawbacks. A prototypical portal has thus been implemented as described in (Bosin et al., 2007a), constituting a sort of open source firmware (Bosin et al., 2007b), in order to set the framework (Bosin et al., 2008a) for such a cooperative environment (Bosin et al., 2008b), whose application to other virtual enterprises (Bosin et al., 2008c) is an inspiration for framework designed in this paper. The prototype allows for instance the researcher in one Milano site, besides linking other sites in term of computing resources and data repositories, to link another Milano site specialized in some peculiar kind of clustering, such as a Cagliari site specialized in Bayesian networks or a Genoa site specialized in Logical networks, but not yet involved within the grid. This does not necessarily imply that clustering is only performed in Milano, nor logical or Bayesian network in the specialized sites. On the contrary, only special allocations within each of such classes is reserved to the specific site when no other is competent enough, while other approaches to the same class are more shared and then dynamically allocated under the usual Grid protocol. Security issues can also be dealt with, even resorting to techniques in part similar to those applied to scientific workflow, namely identification of the suspect behaviors via selection of the salient features involved in such measures.

FUTURE TRENDS

It is rational to extend such framework beyond bioinformatics, either within or beyond e-science. In this sense, neuro-informatics (Liberati, 2008d) appears to be of similar complexity, switching from the biological cellular level to the systemic medical perspective. Like in bioinformatics, also in neuro-informatics it appears easier to reach a critical mass of diverse competencies by virtual cooperation than by physical concentration. Such concept, besides allowing every scientist within the network to cooperate with every other without the need of moving, does also help in overcoming digital divide. Thus less IT poor but competent potential contributors can be integrated in such grid project. besides, other applications, like geo-informatics are intrinsically substantially distributed not just people-wise, but even more with respect to physical data sources.

CONCLUSION

A framework is proposed that creates, uses and communicates information, whose organizational dynamics allows performing a distributed cooperative enterprise in public environments, even over open source systems. The approach assumes the web services as the enacting paradigm over a grid, to formalize interactions as cooperative services on various computational nodes of a network. A framework is thus proposed that defines the responsibility of e-nodes in offering services and the set of rules under which each service can be accessed by e-nodes through service invocation. By discussing a case study, the chapter deals with specific classes of interactions that can be mapped into a service-oriented model whose implementation will be carried out in a prototypical public environment. The illustrated experiment shows that some portions, both of processes and of data or knowledge, can be shared in a collaborative environment, possibly over a Grid. Finally, as aforementioned, any kind of complex or resource demanding (or both) interaction will benefit of the general purpose approaches espoused in this chapter and described more in detail in some of the referenced papers.

REFERENCES

Amigoni, F., Fugini, M.G., & Liberati, D. (2007) Design and execution of distributed experiments. In *Proceedings of the 9th International Conference on Enterprise Information Systems, (ICEIS'07)*, Madeira, June.

Babiloni, F., Carducci, F., Cerutti, S., Liberati, D., Rossini, P., Urbano, A., et al. (2000). *Comparison between human and ANN detection of laplacian-derived electroencephalographic activity related to unilateral voluntary movements. Comput Biomed Res, 33,* 59-74.

Baraldi, P., Manginelli, A.A., Maieron, M., Liberati, D., Porro, C.A. (2007). *An ARX model-based approach to trial by trial identification of fMRI-BOLD responsens. NeuroImage, 37,* 189-201.

Bosin, A., Dessì, N., Fugini, M.G., Liberati, D., & Pes, B. (2006a). Applying enterprise models to design cooperative scientific environments (LNCS 3812, pp. 281-292). Springer-Verlag.

Bosin, A., Dessì, N., Liberati, D., & Pes, B. (2006b). Learning Bayesian classifiers from gene-expression MicroArray data. *Lecture Notes in Artificial Intelligence, 3849,* 297-304.

Bosin, A., Dessì, N., Fugini, M.G., Liberati, D., & Pes, B. (2007a). *The future of portals in e-science.* In A. Tatnall (Ed.), *Encyclopedia of portal technology and applications* (pp. 413-418). Hershey, PA: IGI Global.

Bosin, A., Dessì, N., Fugini, M.G., Liberati, D., Pes, B. (2007b). ALBA architecture as a proposal for OSS collaborative science. In K. St.Amant & B. Still (Eds.), *Handbook of research on open source software* (pp. 68-78). Hershey, PA: IGI Global.

Bosin, A., Dessì, N., Fugini, M.G., Liberati, D., & Pes, B. (2008a). Setting the framework of collaboration for E-science. In N. Kock (Ed.), *Encyclopedia of E-Collaboration* (pp. 82-88). Hershey, PA: IGI Global.

Bosin, A., Dessì, N., Fugini, M.G., Liberati, D., & Pes, B. (2008b). ALBA cooperative environment for scientific experiments. In M. Freire & M. Pereira (Eds.), *Encyclopedia of Internet technologies and applications* (pp. 52-58). Hershey, PA: IGI Global.

Bosin, A., Dessì, N., Fugini, M.G., Liberati, D., & Pes, B. (2008c). Virtual enterprise environments for scientific experiments. In G. Putnik & M. Cunha (Eds.), Encyclopedia *of networked and virtual organizations*. Hershey, PA: IGI Global.

Chignola, R., Schenetti, A., Chiesa, E., Foroni, R., Sartoris, S., Brendolan, A., Tridente, G., Andrighetto, G., & Liberati, D. Forecasting the growth of multicell tumour spheroids: implications for the dynamic growth of solid tumours. *Cell Proliferat, 33*, 219-229.

DeNicolao, G., Liberati, D., & Sartorio, A. (2000). Stimulated secretion of pituitary hormones in normal humans: a novel direct assessment from blood concentrations. *Ann Biomed Eng, 28*, 1131-1145.

De Roure, D., & Hendler, J. (2004). E-Science: The grid and the semantic Web. *IEEE Intelligent Systems, 19*(1).

Drago, G.P., Setti, E., Licitra, L., & Liberati, D. (2002). Forecasting the performance status of head and neck cancer patient treatment by an interval arithmetic pruned perceptron. *IEEE T Bio-Med Eng, 49*(8), 782-787.

Ferrari, Trecate G., Muselli, M., Liberati, D., Morari, M. (2003). A clustering technique for the identification of piecewise affine systems. *Automatica, 39*, 205-217.

Garatti, S., Bittanti, S., Liberati, D., Maffezzoli, P. (2007). An unsupervised clustering approach for leukemia classification based on DNA micro-arrays data. *Intelligent Data Analysis, 11*(2), 175-188.

Hendler, J. (2003). Science and the semantic Web. *Science, 299*(5606).

Liberati, D. (2007). Identification through data mining. In J. Janczewski & A.M. Colarik (Eds.), *Cyber warfare and cyber terrorism* (pp. 374-380). Hershey, PA: IGI Global.

Liberati, D. (2008a). Attention facilitation via multimedia stimulation. In I.K. Ibrahim (Ed.), *Handbook of research on mobile multimedia*. Hershey, PA: IGI Global.

Liberati, D. (2008b). Multi-target classifiers for mining in bioinformatics. In M. Song & & Y.-F. Wu (Eds.), *Handbook of research on text and web mining technologies*. Hershey, PA: IGI Global.

Liberati, D. (2008c). System theory: From classical state space to variable selection and model identification. In L. Tomei (Ed), *Encyclopedia of information technology curriculum integration*. Hershey, PA: IGI Global.

Liberati, D. (2008d). Information technology in brain intensive therapy. In N. Wickramasinghe & E. Geisler (Eds.), *Encyclopedia of healthcare and information systems*. Hershey, PA: IGI Global.

Muselli, M., & Liberati, D. (2000). Training digital circuits with hamming clustering. *IEEE T Circuits I, 47*, 513-527.

Muselli, M., & Liberati, D. (2002). Binary rule generation via hamming clustering. *IEEE T Knowl Data En, 14*(6), 1258-1268.

Paoli, G., Muselli, M., Bellazzi, R., Corvò, R., Liberati, D., & Foppiano, F. (2000). Hamming Clustering techniques for the identification of prognostic indices in patients with advanced head and neck cancer treated with radiation therapy. *Med Biol Eng Comput, 38*, 483-486.

Sacco, E., Farina, M., Greco, C., Busti, S., De-Gioia, L., Fantinato, S., et al. (2007). Molecular and computational analysis of regulation of hSos1, the major activator of the proto-oncoprotein Ras. *Proc SysBioHealth*.

Sartorio, A., Pizzoccaro, A., Veldhuis, J., Liberati, D., DeNicolao, G., & Faglia (2000). Abnormal LH pulsatility in women with hyperprolactinaemic amnorrhoea normalizes after bromocriptine treatment: Deconvolution-based assessment. *Clin Endocrinol 52*(6), 703-712.

Sartorio, A., De Nicolao, G., & Liberati, D. (2002). An improved computational method to assess pituitary responsiveness to secretagogue stimuli. *Eur J Endocrinol, 147*(3), 323-332.

Vapnik, V. (1998). *Statistical learning theory.* New York: Wiley.

Vercesi, A., Sirtori, C., Vavassori, A., Setti, E., & Liberati, D. (2000). Estimating germinability of Plasmopara Viticola oospores by means of neural networks. *Med Biol Eng Comput, 38*, 109-112.

KEY TERMS AND DEFINITIONS

Bioinformatics: Application of computer science to huge biological problems.

e-Science: A virtual way to build a scientific community over an information and communication technology infrastructure.

Grid Computing: A style of computing that dynamically pools IT resources together in order to dynamically allocate resources depending on needs. It allows organizations to provision and scale resources as needs arise, thereby preventing their underutilization.

Neuroinformatics: The application of computer science to natural neuronal networks investigation.

Semantic Grid: A semantic web implemented over a Grid architecture.

Semantic Web: Information processing model in which computers can explicitly associate meanings or parse relationships between data without direct human intervention.

Service-Oriented Architecture: A kind of software design allowing a variety applications to interact regardless of specific technology like programming languages and operating systems.

Systems Biology: The application of the systems and control theory to complex Biological problems.

Virtualization: It allows sharing of the same resources by multiple users as needs arise as if they were co-located even if they are not.

Chapter XXIV
Grid INFN Virtual Laboratory for Dissemination Activities (GILDA)

Roberto Barbera
Università di Catania and Istituto Nazionale di Fisica Nucleare (INFN), Italy

Valeria Ardizzone
Istituto Nazionale di Fisica Nucleare (INFN), Italy

Leandro Ciuffo
Istituto Nazionale di Fisica Nucleare (INFN), Italy

ABSTRACT

The Grid INFN Virtual Laboratory for Dissemination Activities (GILDA) is a fully working Grid test-bed devoted to training and dissemination activities. Open to anyone who wants to have its first hand experience with grid systems, GILDA has been adopted as the official training tool by several Grid projects around the world. All services, tools and materials produced in the past tutorials can be freely used by anyone who wants to learn and teach grid technology. Additionally, through a set of applications ported on its Grid Infrastructure, developers can identify components and learn by examples how to "gridify" their applications. This work presents the main features of such training-Infrastructure.

INTRODUCTION

Launched in 2004 by the Italian National Institute for Nuclear Physics (INFN), GILDA (the Grid INFN virtual Laboratory for Dissemination Activities) is a fully working Grid test-bed devoted to dissemination activities. This infrastructure is open to anyone who wants to have a first hand experience with grid systems. Actually, GILDA can be an important tool for at least three main user categories:

- **Grid newcomers:** People willing to start learning how to use a grid infrastructure;
- **Grid application developers:** Through a set of applications ported on GILDA,

developers can identify components and learn by examples how to "gridify" their applications;

- **Tutors:** GILDA has been developed keeping training in mind. Thus, all services, tools and materials produced in the past tutorials can be freely used by anyone who wants to teach grid technology.

Indeed, GILDA has been adopted as the official training tool by several Grid projects, such as EGEE, EELA, EU-IndiaGRID, EUMEDGRID, EUChinaGRID, ICEAGE, and several others, becoming a "de facto" standard training-Infrastructure (hereafter t-infrastructure) in Europe and in several other parts of the world for a dissemination of Grid Computing.

The GILDA objectives can be summarized as follows:

- To raise awareness of Grid Computing benefits
- To provide customized formats for dissemination events, according to the skills of attendants
- To facilitate appropriate free on-line content and services for training purposes
- To encourage the use of a complete t-infrastructure by new communities

This article aims at presenting an overview of GILDA facilities as well as to invite the reader to try such t-infrastructure.

BACKGROUND

Computational and storage limitations are key issues for organizations that depend on computation-intensive applications. Such organizations are frequently affected by market pressures to reduce deployment time and maintenance costs. Hence, they may be looking for ways to improve the effectiveness of their infrastructure or their

business processes through transformation, or seeking opportunities for innovation that will benefit the business. Grid is not the answer by itself, but in many of these cases, it can certainly play an important role, allowing immediate productivity and benefits and giving more choice and control on how to purchase and leverage IT power for competitive advantage. The grid vision is to expand parallel and distributed computation, providing a virtualization of heterogeneous compute and data resources, supporting security policy based resource allocation and prioritization. The grid is ideal for any applications requiring excellent performance and scalability for their compute-intensive processes (e.g. Monte Carlo simulation, engineering CAD simulations, protein modeling, 3D rendering, archaeology investigation etc.).

In this context, the GILDA Project was born with the aim of offering a one-of-a-kind service for those interested in testing the grid, using gLite (2007) and the EGEE infrastructure with their own systems. GILDA offers either basic experiences through the "Try the Grid" walkthrough in minutes or intensive and in-depth training by helping users willing to develop applications to port them into a Grid environment.

DISSEMINATION INSTRUMENTS

The main objectives of GILDA activity are to encourage and help new and existing communities, to support them for improvement or migration of their applications to the Grid infrastructure, to accelerate the adoption of grid technologies, and to increase the satisfaction of those currently using the Grid service throw the communities' feedback. Training activities are a key component of the knowledge dissemination process, ensuring that all users fully understand the characteristics of the offered grid services and that they have enough expertise to properly use the available grid infrastructure. In order to accomplish the main objectives, several dissemination instruments are used. A brief description of the instruments is presented below.

GILDA Tutorials for Applications Developers

Porting an application into a Grid environment has never been an easy and straightforward task. In order to enable application developers to get used to the main Grid functionalities, an advanced tutorial has been created fully dedicated in teaching them in how to gridify their application. Such training events are the perfect scenario to put application experts in tight collaboration with Grid experts. Hence, the GILDA Team has acquired a good experience in transferring knowledge and know-how to new communities by helping them to integrate their application into several grid projects infrastructures.

GILDA Tutorials for Sysadmin

Tutorials for grid system administrators are organized by the GILDA team to meet the needs of computer centers interested in joining GILDA test-bed. Usually, for a novice user, installing and configuring a new Grid node is not an easy task. In that scenario, a step-by-step guide is described to help user during the troubleshooting stage.

Tutorials are divided into three parts: a theoretical part, a practical one and the hands-on section. In each presentation, the GILDA tutors use slides to show the main steps necessary to install and configure a grid element. Then, in the hands-on section all participants try to install a grid element by themselves, assisted by tutors. Training material is composed of multimedia slides, a Wiki website and a set of "Virtual Services", detailed below. The most important stage during the preparation of a tutorial is to set up the machines used for the grid node installation: to make it easy, a virtualization technique such as VMware® is adopted by all organized tutorials. In this way, all participants have their own Virtual Machines

on which they can work with minimum efforts required from the system administrators.

GILDA Wiki Website

The GILDA Wiki has been created mainly with the purpose of documenting and organizing the huge amount of training material produced so far. Its content is freely available on the Web for every interested user. Moreover, this site is not a simple on-line documentation repository, but an important collaborative tool used by the whole project team. Thus, all registered user can contribute feeding the site with useful training material. The Wiki site is an information source for three target audiences: users, site administrators and application developers. Regarding the users' content, the available material is subdivided into three different complexity levels (basic, medium and advanced), while the site administrators area consists of step-by-step procedures to install and configure grid services. Finally, the developers section presents the middleware functionalities that can be integrated into the source code.

GILDA Virtual Services

Through the use of the virtualization technique, it is possible to carry out all grid elements. This instrument has many benefits, such as increasing services' portability and reducing both the time to put a site in operation and the number of real machines required.

METHODOLOGY

By its nature, GILDA is one of the key enabler of the "virtuous cycle" to attract and support new communities. Its workflow is presented below:

1.   A novice user can get the feeling of what is Grid Computing and what applications can run on a grid infrastructure by simply using

the Grid Demonstrator which is available all the time. A screenshot of Grid Demonstrator is shown in Figure 1;

2. An interested user, participating in a tutorial event or an induction course, can go through all the mandatory procedure of the request of a personal digital certificate and subscription to a Virtual Organization and then use the grid tutor machine;

3. A community, interested in testing the grid, can join GILDA and try to port its applications on its test-bed, in a smaller scale, all problems of interfacing the grid services available before entering the huge e-Science infrastructure.

4. Various applications from different communities ported on GILDA can be incorporated into the Grid Demonstrator enriching the portfolio of examples that can be demonstrated to new people.

A site, wanting to set up a computing or a storage resource for a grid infrastructure can join GILDA and solve, at a smaller scale, all the problems of installation and proper configuration of the machines.

TECHNOLOGY DESCRIPTION

The GILDA test-bed consists of 20 sites on four continents (Europe, Africa, Latin America and Asia), using heterogeneous hardware to act as a "real world" grid environment. It is made up of all the components of a larger Grid project, including services, resources and monitoring systems tools. To allow use of the test-bed, it also features a Virtual Organization (VO) and a real Certification Authority (CA) that grants two-week certificates for the test use of the GILDA infrastructure. In addition, it runs the latest production (and stable) version of the LCG middleware (2006), being also compatible with gLite (2007), the EGEE's middleware solution. In order to ease the access to its t-infrastructure, GILDA also provides a grid portal called GENIUS (Barbera, 2003), where different usages are supplied, such as basic content for novice users and full featured ones for more in depth tutorials and demonstrations. At a more advanced level, GILDA offers a one-of-a-kind service for those interested in testing the Grid and gLite with their own software, offering a more intensive and in-depth introductions to the Grid. In a couple of weeks, a user can be trained in Grid usage, his/her software can be modified to run on the Grid environment and finally, a Genius

Figure 1. Screenshot of grid demonstrator

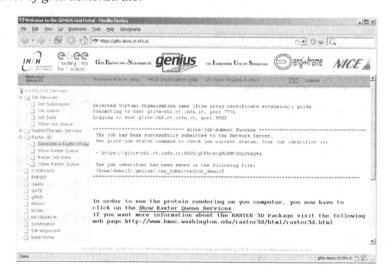

service can be created to increase the visibility of the work that has been done.

AVAILABLE APPLICATIONS

The grid environment will require many new skills both for scientists that need to learn how to work in new environments, and for application developers that have to learn how to write and optimize code for use in grids so as to better utilize grid resources. As consequence, disciplinary support is also essential to carry on grid knowledge management and grid education, both generic and towards specific application domains. In GILDA, a set of "case study" of integrated applications is created, so that scientist or code's developers can explore and compare different approaches for the integration process of their application on Grid Infrastructure. Currently GILDA applications portfolio covers a large range of different research domains. A short list of applications ported into GILDA test-bed is presented below.

GATE

Gate is a C++ platform based on the Monte Carlo Geant4 software (Cirrone, 2005). It has been designed to model nuclear medicine applications, such as PET (Positron Emission Tomography)

and SPECT (Single Photon Emission Computed Tomography) among the OpenGATE collaboration. Its functionalities combine ease of use with making the platform responsive to radiotherapy and brachytherapy treatment planning.

RASTER 3D

Raster3D is a set of tools for generating high quality raster images of proteins or other molecules. It uses an efficient software Z-buffer algorithm which is independent of any graphics hardware. Figure 2 illustrates the input interface and the generated output of this application.

Hadron Therapy

Hadron Therapy simulates the beam line and particles revelators used in the proton-therapy facility CATANA (Centro di AdroTerapia e Applicazioni Nucleari Avanzate), that is active even at INFN-LNS. Here 62 MeV (62 million of electron volts) proton beams, accelerated by a superconductive cyclotron, are employed for the treatment of some kind of ocular tumors.

gMOD

gMOD is a new application offering a video on demand service. A user can browse a catalog of

Figure 2. Raster R3 running on GILDA grid demonstrator

 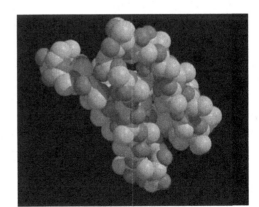

movie trailers and request one to be streamed in real time to his/her workstation using the power of the grid. Movies can also be chosen by querying an underlying metadata catalog using one or more attributes. The role feature of the Virtual Organization Membership Services (VOMS) is exploited to define normal users and catalog managers. gMOD represents a very interesting use case for the grid both in entertainment and distributed digital contents management.

EGEODE

Egeode (Expanding Geosciences On Demand) application is a seismic processing generic platform for research and education, based on Geocluster, an industrial application, used in production, that includes several standards tools for signal processing, simulation and inversion (model optimization).

GEMS

Gems (Grid-based European Molecular Simulator) project implements a simulation environment to perform the study of reaction dynamics of complex chemical systems.

Volcano Sonification

Current knowledge of volcanic eruptions does not yet allow scientists to predict future eruptions. This application represents an attempt to put the scientific community one step nearer to the eruption predictability by means of the sonification of volcano seismograms. Thus, the translation of the patterns of Mount Etna (Italy) and Mount Tungurahua's (Ecuador) volcanic behavior into sound waves has been carried out. Data sonification is currently used in several fields and for different purposes: science and engineering, education and training. It acts mainly as data analysis and interpretation tool.

FUTURE TRENDS

The t-infrastructure provided by GILDA will be continuously used by many EU funded projects, since several project proposals submitted to the 7th Framework Program Calls expressed their intention to use GILDA facilities as part of their training program.

In addition, the growing number of users has encouraged the GILDA team to announce the incorporation of some new features. These features are:

- The gLibrary service (Calanducci, 2006), an extensible, robust, secure and easy-to-use system to handle digital assets stored as files in a grid infrastructure. It offers an intuitive web interface to browse the available entries, since its powerful set of attribute filters, can find an asset in just a matter of seconds. gLibrary is a flexible system that can be used for different purposes. Its modular architecture enables different communities to easily adopt this tool to build their own digital libraries by defining types and categories according to their needs.
- Secure Storage Service, a service carried out by UNICO S.r.l. in close collaboration with INFN Catania in the context of the TriGrid VL Project . This service provides users with a set of tools for storing confidential data (e.g. medical or financial data) in a secure way and in an encrypted format on the grid storage elements. The data stored in this way is accessible and readable by authorized users only. Moreover, it solves the insider abuse problem preventing also the administrators of the storage elements from accessing the confidential data in a clear format.

The Grid Database Access Service (GRelC) aims to provide a set of advanced data grid service to transparently, efficiently and securely manage databases in a grid environment (Fiore, 2007). This framework, developed by University of Lecce – Italy and SPACI Consortium (The Italian Southern Partnership for Advanced Computational Infrastructures), is currently used to support bioinformatics experiments on distributed and huge data bank. The framework provides a uniform access interface to access and interact with heterogeneous DBMS such us PostgreSQL, MySQL, Oracle, DB2, SQLite, and so on.

CONCLUSION

GILDA represents a very valuable tool in the Italian INFN Grid Project as well as in several Grid projects around the world where GILDA is adopted. Indeed, its t-infrastructure has been used by more than 160 induction courses and demonstrations.

Through GILDA a broad range of users are able to get quick and easy access to a "real world" grid environment. Furthermore, GILDA facilities are open to any organizations or educational institutions who wants to adopt it in their Grid training programs.

In that sense, the main business benefits of adopting GILDA can be summarized as follows:

- It is free;
- No costs to leverage grid resources that are required to use it;
- It is the first place where a user gain experience on Grid Computing;
- It provides an affordable and pleasant experience in Grid training;
- It provides a good infrastructure where business applications can try "gridifying" operation exploiting GILDA team support.
- It improves local research activity quality by providing more power computation and storage resources;

- It equally promotes international cooperation and partnership.

REFERENCES

Barbera, R., Falzone A., & Rodolico A. (2003). *The GENIUS Grid Portal.* Paper presented at Conference for Computing in High Energy and Nuclear Physics (CHEP 2003), La Jolla, California, USA.

Barbera, R., Ardizzone, V., & Ciuffo, L. N. (2007). *Grid training and dissemination facilities: The GILDA experience.* Paper presented at IST-Africa Conference, Maputo, Mozambique.

Calanducci, T., Cherubino, C., Ciuffo, L.N., & Scardaci D. (2006*). gLibrary - Digital asset management system for the Grid.* Retrieved August 22, 2007, from https://glibrary.ct.infn.it/glibrary/

Cirrone, G.A.P., & Cuttone, G. (2005) Implementation of a new Monte Carlo-GEANT4 Simulation tool for the development of a proton therapy beam line and verification of the related dose distributions. *IEEE Transactions on Nuclear Science, 52*(1), 262-265.

EEGE (2007). *Enabling Grids for E-sciencE.* Retrieved August 21, 2007, from http://www.eu-egee.org/

EELA (2007). *E-Infrastructure shared between Europe and Latin America.* Retrieved August 21, 2007, from http://www.eu-eela.org/

EUChinaGRID initiative (2007). Retrieved August 21, 2007, from http://www.euchinagrid.org/

EUIndiaGrid (2007). *Joining European and Indian Grids for e-Science network community.* Retrieved August 21, 2007, http://www.euindi-agrid.org/

EUMEDGRID (2007). *Empowering eScience across the Mediterranean.* Retrieved August 21, 2007, from http://www.eumedgrid.org/

Fiore S., Cafaro M. & Aloisio G. (2007). *GRelC DAS: A Grid-DB Access Service for gLite Based Production Grids.* Paper presented at the Fourth International Workshop on Emerging Technologies for Next-generation GRID (ETNGRID 2007), Paris, France.

GENIUS Portal (2007). Retrieved August 21, 2007, from https://genius.ct.infn.it/

GILDA (2007) *Grid Infn Laboratory for dissemination activities.* Retrieved August 21, 2007, from https://gilda.ct.infn.it/

GILDA Grid Demonstrator (2007) Retrieved August 21, 2007, from https://glite-demo.ct.infn.it/

GILDA Wiki (2007). Retrieved August 21, 2007, from https://grid.ct.infn.it/twiki/bin/view/GILDA/WebHome

gLite (2007). *Lightweight middleware for Grid computing.* Retrieved August 21, 2007, from http://glite.web.cern.ch/glite/

ICEAGE (2007). *The international collaboration to extend and advance Grid education.* Retrieved August 21, 2007, from http://www.iceage-eu.org/

Kranzkmuller, D. (2006). White Paper. *e-Infrastructure Reflection Group, version 1.2* (pp. 67), from http://www.e-irg.org

LCG Middleware (2006). Retrieved August 21, 2007, from ttp://lcg.web.cern.ch/LCG/activities/middleware.html

KEY TERMS AND DEFINITIONS

Certification Authority: A trusted third party for signing certificates for network entities. Other network entities can check the signature to verify that a CA has authenticated the bearer of a certificate.

E-Infrastructure: Short term for Electronic Infrastructure, i.e., all ICT based resources (distributed networks, computers, storage devices, software etc.) and support operations which facilitate the collaboration among research communities by sharing resources, analysis tools and data.

EGEE: Enabling Grids for E-SciencE (EGEE) is an EU funded project to build a 24/7 Grid Production Service for scientific research. Already serving many scientific disciplines, it aims to provide academic and industrial researchers with access to major computing resources, independent of their locations. The EGEE project is led by CERN, the European Organization for Nuclear Research, and involves over 70 partner institutions across Europe, Asia and the United States.

Middleware: Software that sits between the operating system and application programs and provides a set of common services to them.

T-Infrastructure: Short for Training Infrastructure, i.e., specialized e-infrastructure devoted for educational purposes, including software, data and computer systems required to deliver courses and to support tutees and learners.

VO: Virtual Organization is a group of individuals or institutions who can use and share information and computational resources in a grid system.

gLite: A Grid middleware developed by the EGEE project

Chapter XXV
Grid Enabled
Surrogate Modeling

Dirk Gorissen
Gent University–IBBT, Belgium

Tom Dhaene
Gent University–IBBT, Belgium

Piet Demeester
Gent University–IBBT, Belgium

Jan Broeckhove
University of Antwerp, Belgium

ABSTRACT

The simulation and optimization of complex systems is a very time consuming and computationally intensive task. Therefore, global surrogate modeling methods are often used for the efficient exploration of the design space, as they reduce the number of simulations needed. However, constructing such surrogate models (or metamodels) is often done in a straightforward, sequential fashion. In contrast, we present a framework that can leverage the use of compute clusters and grids in order to decrease the model generation time by efficiently running simulations in parallel. We describe the integration between surrogate modeling and grid computing on three levels: resource level, scheduling level and service level. Our approach is illustrated with a simple example from aerodynamics.

INTRODUCTION

Computer based simulation has become an integral part of the engineering design process. Rather than building real world prototypes and performing experiments, application scientists can build a computational model and simulate the physical processes at a fraction of the original cost. However, despite the steady growth of computing power, the computational cost to perform these complex, high-fidelity simulations are still enormous. A simulation may take many minutes, hours, days or even weeks (Gu, 2001; Lin et al., 2005; Qian et al., 2006). This is especially evident for routine tasks such as optimization, sensitivity analysis and design space exploration as noted below:

"...it is reported that it takes Ford Motor Company about 36-160 hrs to run one crash simulation. For a two-variable optimization problem, assuming on average 50 iterations are needed by optimization and assuming each iteration needs one crash simulation, the total computation time would be 75 days to 11 months, which is unacceptable in practice" (Wang and Shan, 2007, p1).

Consequently, scientists have turned towards upfront approximation methods to reduce simulation times. The basic approach is to construct a simplified approximation of the computationally expensive simulator, which is then used in place of the original code to facilitate Multi-Objective Design Optimization (MDO), design space exploration, reliability analysis, and so on (Simpson, 2004). Since the approximation model acts as surrogate for the original code, it is referred to as a *surrogate model* or *metamodel*.

While the time needed for one evaluation of the original simulator is typically in the order of minutes or hours, the surrogate function, due to its compact mathematical notation, can be evaluated in the order of milliseconds. However, in order to construct an accurate surrogate one still requires evaluations of the original objective function, thus cost remains an issue. The focus of this paper is to discuss one technique to reduce this cost even further using distributed computing. By intelligently running simulations in parallel, the "wall-clock" execution time, in order to come to an acceptable surrogate model can be considerably reduced.

We present a framework that integrates the automated building of surrogate models with the distributed evaluation of the simulator. This integration occurs on multiple levels: resource level, scheduling level and the service level. Each of these will be detailed below.

BACKGROUND

Surrogate Modeling

Surrogate models play a significant role in many disciplines (hydrology, automotive industry, robotics, ...) where they help bridge the gap between simulation and understanding. The principal reason driving their use is that the simulator is too time consuming to run for a large number of simulations. A second reason is when simulating large scale systems, for example: a full-wave simulation of an electronic circuit board. Electro-magnetic modeling of the whole board in one run is almost intractable. Instead the board is modeled as a collection of small, compact, accurate surrogates that represent different functional components (capacitors, resistors, etc.) on the board.

There are a huge number of different surrogate model types available, with applications in domains ranging from medicine, ecology, economics to aerodynamics. Depending on the domain, popular model types include Radial Basis Function (RBF) models, Rational Functions, Artificial Neural Networks (ANN), Support Vector Machines (SVM), and Kriging models (Wang and Shan, 2007).

An important aspect of surrogate modeling is sample selection. Since data is computationally expensive to obtain, it is impossible to use traditional, one-shot, full factorial or space filling designs. Data points must be selected iteratively, there where the information gain will be the greatest (Kleijnen, 2005). A sampling function is needed that minimizes the number of sample points selected in each iteration, yet maximizes the information gain of each sampling step. This process is called adaptive sampling, but is also known as active learning, Optimal Experimental Design (OED), and sequential design.

Grid Computing

Almost two decades old, grid computing has become an established computing paradigm that integrates heterogeneous resources (computers, networks, data archives, instruments, etc.) in an interoperable virtual environment crossing both geographical and institutional boundaries (Berman, 2003). These resources are coordinated to provide transparent, dependable, pervasive and consistent computing support to a wide range of applications. These applications can perform either distributed computing, high throughput computing, on-demand computing, data-intensive computing, collaborative computing or multimedia computing.

A grid computing user interacts with the raw grid resources through a software layer, referred to as the middleware. The middleware is responsible for managing the grid resources (access control, job scheduling, resource registration and discovery, etc.), abstracting away the details and presenting the user with a consistent, virtual computer to work with. A large number of general purpose middleware have been developed, examples include: Globus, Unicore, Legion, JGrid and VgrADS.

SUrrogate MOdeling (SUMO) Toolbox

The SUMO Toolbox (Gorissen, 2006) is an adaptive tool that integrates different modeling approaches and implements a fully automated, global surrogate model construction algorithm. Given a simulation engine, the toolbox automatically generates a surrogate model within the predefined accuracy and time limits set by the user. However, at the same time keeping in mind that there is no such thing as a 'one-size-fits-all', different problems need to be modeled differently.

Therefore the toolbox was designed to be modular and extensible but not be too cumbersome to use or configure. Different plugins are supported: model types (neural networks, Kriging, splines, ...), model parameter optimization algorithms (BFGS, GA, PSO, ...), adaptive sample selection (density based, gradient based, ...), and sample evaluation (local, on a cluster or grid). The behavior of each component is configurable through a central XML configuration file and components can easily be added, removed or replaced by custom, problem-specific, implementations. This is illustrated in Figure 1.

The SUMO toolbox has been successfully applied to a very wide range of fields ranging from combustion modeling in metallurgy to structural mechanics modeling in the car industry. Its success primarily due to its flexibility, self tuning implementation, and its ease of integration into the larger computational science and engineering pipeline.

It is instructive to go through the control loop of the toolbox: First an initial set of samples is chosen according to some experimental design. Based on this initial set, one or more surrogate models are constructed and their parameters optimized according to an optimization algorithm (e.g., pat-

Figure 1. SUMO toolbox plugins

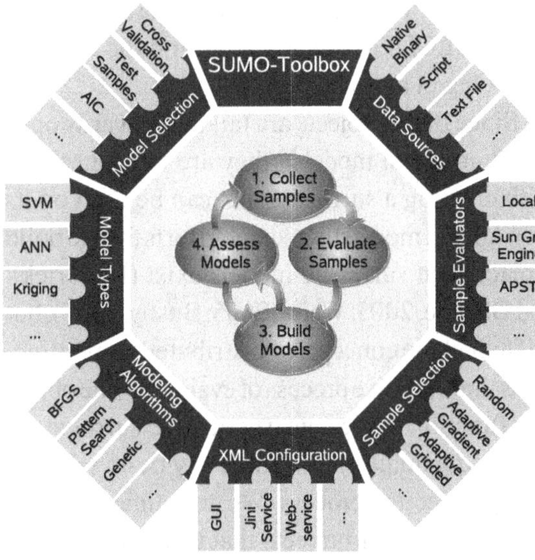

tern search). Models are assigned a score based on one or more measures (e.g., cross validation) and the model parameter optimization continues until no further improvement is possible. The models are then ranked according to their score and new samples are selected based on the top k models. The model parameter optimization resumes and the whole process repeats itself until one of the following three conditions is satisfied: (1) the maximum number of samples has been reached, (2) the maximum allowed time has been exceeded, or (3) the user required accuracy has been met.

MAIN FOCUS

Integrating Grid Computing and Surrogate Modeling

Research efforts that integrate surrogate modeling and design space exploration with grid computing can be divided into two categories: those catered towards design optimization and those geared towards the building of standalone global surrogate models.

The first category is by far the most populous: there are many grid-enabled optimization frameworks which can be applied to different problem domains. The most notable are Nimrod/O (Abramson, 2001), DAKOTA (Giunta and Eldred, 2000), GEODISE (Eres, 2005), and the work by Y. S. Ong et al (Ng, 2005).

Since these projects are tailored towards optimization (local models), they are not concerned with creating a surrogate that can be used on its own (global models). Research efforts that do build replacement surrogate models exist (Hendrickx and Dhaene, 2005; Weiss, 2005; Busby, 2007), but fail to include concepts of distributed computing. Thus the repetitive process of evaluating the objective function while constructing the surrogate is done sequentially, nor is there any tie-in with the sample selection process. We were unable to find evidence of other projects that tackle this.

Integration: Resource Level

When constructing a global surrogate model for an expensive simulation engine the largest computational bottleneck is performing the necessary simulations. An obvious step is to harness the power of the grid and run the simulations in parallel. By distributing the evaluation back-end of the toolbox, (the *Sample Evaluator*) the overall run time of the SUMO Toolbox can be significantly reduced.

A high level design diagram is shown in Figure 2.

The Sample Evaluator (SE) can be seen as a kind of Application Aware Scheduler (AAS) that forms the glue between the modeler and the middleware. It is responsible for translating modeler requests (i.e., evaluations of data points) into middleware specific jobs (e.g., <Task> tags in the case of APST, jdl files in the case of LCG), polling for results, and returning them to the modeler. The SE is implemented as a set of Java interfaces and base classes that are sub classed for each of the supported middlewares. This point is worth emphasizing. There are a large number of distributed middlewares available and their usage varies significantly between institutions. Therefore it is important not to restrict the integration to one particular middleware. The SE must be designed in such a way that different backends can be easily added and replaced (i.e., the SE acts as a meta-scheduler). At the same time the SE should hide as much of the complexity of the grid as possible. Besides a few configuration options, the user should not have to worry about the intricacies of each job authentication or submission system.

How this works in practice is illustrated in Figure 3. There is a separate delegate for each step in the sample evaluation process. The workflow is as follows: The modeler selects a number of data points that need to be simulated and sends them to the SE. The SE passes them on to the distributed backend (specified in the configuration file, in

Figure 2. High level components

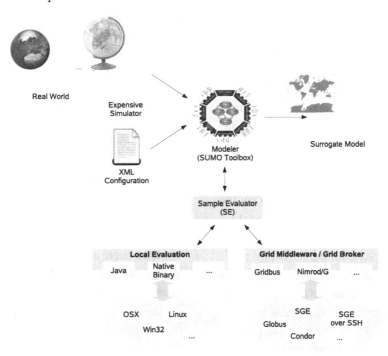

Figure 3. SGE sample evaluator backend

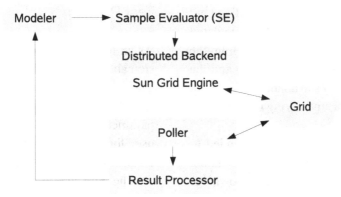

this case Sun Grid Engine (SGE)) that translates each data point into a middleware specific job request, stages the necessary input files, and submits it to the grid. A poller object is then instantiated which monitors the job state (finished, failed, running, waiting, ...). If a completed job is detected, the poller notifies a result processor object which takes care of retrieving the results and returning them back to the modeler. If a job failure is detected, the simulation is automatically re-submitted k times before regarding the job as permanently failed.

Thus, in sum, adding support for a new middleware (e.g., Condor) means providing a new {Distributed Backend, Poller, Result Processor} triplet.

Integration: Scheduling Level

Simply running simulations in parallel already gives a significant performance improvement. Performance can be improved even further if the intelligence of the SE is increased. It should be realized that not all data points are equally important, a partial ordering exists. For example, data points lying close to interesting features (e.g., extrema, domain boundaries), or far from other data points have a higher priority. These priorities are assigned by the sample selection algorithm and dynamically managed by the input queue which is a priority queue. Consequently, the priorities are reflected in the scheduling decisions made by the SE and distributed backend (simulations with higher priority are done first). The priority queue can have different management policies. For example, a policy can be to let the priority decrease with time unless interest in a sample point is renewed.

Additionally, the number of simulations to run (as requested by the modeler) is not fixed but changes dynamically. This number is calculated based on average time needed for modeling, the average duration of a single simulation, and the number of compute nodes available at that point in time. In this way the underlying resources are always used optimally.

Eventually this scheme will be extended to directly integrate the SE with the grid information system used (e.g., Ganglia). Combining knowledge on **real-time** system load, network traffic, ... with data point priorities would allow the SE to achieve an optimal *job-host* mapping (i.e., the data points with the highest priority should be scheduled on the fastest nodes).

Integration: Service Level

The previous two subsections exemplify the main reasons for traditionally turning to grid computing: computational power. However, the past few years Service Oriented Architectures (SOA) have become an increasingly popular (if not dominant) way to think about the grid. In this regard the grid is a heterogeneous collection of services, where each service provides access to a particular resource. Examples include services providing access to: a printer, a high performance numerical library, storage space, or CPU power. Users can connect to these services using standard technologies such as Jini or SOAP and use them as part of complicated workflows.

In this sense, "automated construction of surrogate models" is a prime example of a service that a scientist or engineer can use to delegate surrogate model construction to. The advantages are obvious: there are no setup or maintenance costs and interfacing is straightforward. Thus surrogate model construction can easily be integrated into the larger engineering design process, enhancing productivity.

Example Application

Test Problem

As an intuitive example to illustrate the discussion above we present the following application. The goal is to model the aerodynamic properties (lift, drag) of a winged box kite given 4 geometric parameters: h_1, h_2, w_1, w_2. This model can then be used for optimization, visualization, or as part of an educational kite design tool.

The kite and the different parameters are shown in Figure 4. We shall use this example to illustrate integration on the resource and scheduling level.

The example is interesting since it is easy to grasp and explain, but complex enough since the relationships between the variables are not immediately obvious. Additionally it is a good example, although it is somewhat academic, of what a surrogate model is used for. For example, an engineer may be interested in what parameter assignment gives the optimal lift/drag ratio. Instead of having to solve the full flow equations

Figure 4. Winged box kite

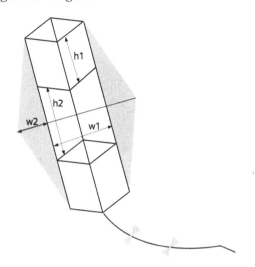

for each assignment a global surrogate model can be constructed that gives insight into the relationships between the different parameters (design space exploration) and help identify promising optima. The simulation code is freely available from NASA[1], written in Java, and was only slightly modified by the authors. The running time is quite short, about one minute, but long enough to be useful and illustrative.

Experimental Setup

The simulation code is distributed on a shared pool of 256 Sun Fire V20z nodes, running SUSE Linux and Matlab R2007a, administered by Sun Grid Engine (SGE) and accessible through a remote head node (meaning the toolbox has to tunnel job submissions through SSH). The resource pool is available through a number of submission queues and the toolbox dynamically switches to the queue with highest availability. The SUMO toolbox starts with an initial Latin hypercube sample distribution of 50 samples (in the 4D design space) and runs up to a maximum of 1000. The number of samples selected each iteration is selected dynamically and samples with higher priorities are scheduled first. For this example, a fully sequential approach would require 16-19 hours or computation time.

As a surrogate model type Kriging models are used. Initially developed within Geo-statistics, Kriging models (also referred to as Gaussian Process (GP) models) have become particularly popular in recent years due properties such as natural uncertainty estimation, interpolation, and fast training times. It is for these reasons that Kriging is used here, though other surrogate model types could have been used just as well.

The quality of a surrogate model is determined by k-fold cross validation (using a root mean square error function). To improve the modeling process the input parameters were scaled to [-1,1].

Results

Figure 5 shows the final Kriging surrogate for the lift (for discrete values of w_1, w_2). A full discussion of the model is out of scope for this paper. In sum we can say the model agrees with intuition: The most lift occurs when the area of the kite is the largest (high h_1, w_2) and the least lift where the area is smallest. Interestingly though, the lift also increases for high h_2, low h_1, and $w_2 = -1$. This could point to a potential inaccuracy of the model or a subtlety of the simulation code. More input from a domain export would be needed in order to fully understand the relationships.

The total simulation time for the experiment was only 1.2 hours with an average availability of 20 nodes. Compared with a purely sequential approach this results in a speedup factor of about 15[2]. The speedup is not the only quality metric. Recall that the SUMO Toolbox handles all interfacing with the grid automatically and transparently (even through ssh). Besides some initial configuration (user credentials, executable path, ...) no user intervention is required.

FUTURE TRENDS

The application of grid computing concepts and application aware scheduling to global surrogate

Figure 5. Final Kriging model for the lift (w_1, w_2 are plotted at 3 discrete intervals: -1, 0, 1)

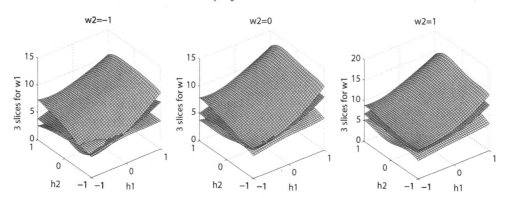

modeling is still an open field. Most of the work so far has been done on the lowest level of integration with already promising results (Gorissen, 2006). The problem here is interfacing with the different middleware in a flexible, extensible manner. Each middleware has its own characteristics and semantics which makes it difficult to support different middleware in a transparent way. Luckily, work on different meta-schedulers (e.g., GridWay, ProActive) and standardization efforts (CoG kit, DRMAA, ...) is underway to tackle this problem. The future should bring promising results in this respect.

Concerning the higher levels of integration, the authors know of no other related work. So much still remains to be done. It will be interesting to see how the problems of priority management integration with resource information will be tackled. In this respect there is a vast body of knowledge available from the scheduling communities in operating systems, distributed systems and grid-economics that surrogate model researches can leverage.

Finally, integration at the service level will play a very important role in bringing advanced surrogate model construction techniques closer to the scientists and engineers that need them. Easy, standardized (programmatic) access to a surrogate model construction service will greatly help engineers to faster explore, optimize and understand the design space of their problem without all the usual installation, configuration and interfacing costs.

CONCLUSION

Due to the computational complexity of current simulation codes, the use of *global* surrogate modeling techniques has become standard practice among scientists and engineers alike. However, these techniques are still very much applied in a one shot manner (collect data, do a regression, evaluate the model). More adaptive, integrated approaches have been described in literature (Farhang-Mehr and Azarm, 2005; Busby, 2007) but have found little or no use outside the labs that designed them. In addition, the authors found no evidence of the use of distributed computing in the global surrogate model construction process, thus expensive simulator evaluations are still being performed sequentially. Even if parallelization is used, integration with the sample selection and scheduling layer is lacking.

In this chapter we have made the case for the use of distributed computing while building global surrogate models. The use of grid computing allows one to run expensive simulations in parallel (resource level), optimally make use of available resources (scheduling level) and make surrogate modeling algorithms easily available to the engineers that need them (service level).

We have presented an adaptive framework based on the SUMO Toolbox that achieves this and can be downloaded from http://www.sumo.intec. ugent.be.

REFERENCES

Abramson, D., Lewis, A., Peachey, T., & Fletcher, C. (2001). An automatic design optimization tool and its application to computational fluid dynamics. In *Proceedings of the 2001 ACM/IEEE conference on supercomputing* (pp. 25–25).

Berman, F., Fox, G., & Hey, T. (2003). The Grid: past, present, future. In F. Berman, G. Fox, & T. Hey (Eds.), *Grid computing - making the global infrastructure a reality*. John Wiley & Sons.

Busby, D., Farmer, C. L., & Iske, A. (2007). Hierarchical nonlinear approximation for experimental design and statistical data fitting. *SIAM Journal on Scientific Computing, 29*(1), 49-69.

Eres, M. H., Pound, G. E., Jiao, Z., Wason, J. L., Xu, F., Keane, A. J., et al. (2005). Implementation and utilization of a grid-enabled problem solving environment in Matlab. *Future Generation Comp. System, 21*(6), 920-929.

Farhang-Mehr, A., & Azarm, S. (2005). Bayesian meta-modeling of engineering design simulations: a sequential approach with adaptation to irregularities in the response behavior. *International Journal for Numerical Methods in Engineering, 62*(15), 2104-2126.

Giunta, A., & Eldred, M. (2000). Implementation of a trust region model management strategy in the DAKOTA optimization toolkit. In *Proceedings of the 8th AIAA/USAF/NASA/ISSMO symposium on multidisciplinary analysis and optimization*. Long Beach, CA.

Gorissen, D., Hendrickx, W., Crombecq, K., & Dhaene, T. (2006). Integrating gridcomputing and metamodelling. In *Proceedings of 6th IEEE/ ACM international symposium on cluster computing and the grid (CCGrid 2006)* (p. 185-192). Singapore.

Gu, L. (2001). A comparison of polynomial based regression models in vehicle safety analysis. Paper DETC/DAC-21063, *Proceedings of DETC'01 ASME 2001 Design Engineering Technical Engineering Conferences and the Computers and Information in Engineering Conference*, Pittsburgh, PA, 9-12 September .

Hendrickx, W., & Dhaene, T. (2005). Multivariate modelling of complex simulation-based systems. *Proceedings of the IEEE NDS 2005 conference* (pp. 212-216).

Kleijnen, J. P., Sanchez, S. M., Lucas, T. W., & Cioppa, T. M. (2005). State-of-the-art review: A user's guide to the brave new world of designing simulation experiments. *INFORMS Journal on Computing, 17*(3), 263-289.

Lin, Y.-C., Fregly, B., Haftka, R., & Queipo, N. (2005). Surrogate-based contact modeling for efficient dynamic simulation with deformable anatomic joints. In *Proceedings of the tenth international symposium on computer simulation in biomechanics* (p. 23-24).

Ng, H.-K., Ong, Y.-S., Hung, T., & Lee, B.-S. (2005). Grid enabled optimization. In *Advances in Grid Computing - EGC 2005* (LNCS, 296-304).

Qian, Z., Seepersad, C. C., Joseph, V. R., Allen, J. K., & Wu, C. F. J. (2006). Building surrogate models based on detailed and approximate simulations. *Journal of Mechanical Design, 128*(4), 668-677.

Simpson, T. W., Booker, A. J., Ghosh, D., Giunta, A. A., Koch, P. N., & Yang, R.-J. (2004). Approximation methods in multidisciplinary analysis and optimization: A panel discussion. *Structural and Multidisciplinary Optimization, 27*(5), 302-313.

Wang, G. G., & Shan, S. (2007). Review of metamodeling techniques in support of engineering design optimization. *Journal of Mechanical Design*, *129*(4), 370-380.

Weiss, L., Amon, C., Finger, S., Miller, E., Romero, D. & Verdinelli, I. (2005). Bayesian computer-aided experimental design of heterogeneous scaffolds for tissue engineering. *Computer Aided Design*, *37*, 1127-1139.

KEY TERMS AND DEFINITIONS

Experimental Design: The theory of Design of Experiments (DOE) describes methods and algorithms for optimally selecting data points from an *n* dimensional parameter space. A simple example, say you have to select 1000 points from a 3-dimensional space (*n*=3). This can be done randomly, using a full factorial design (an equal number of points in every dimension, i.e., 10x10x10) or according to a Latin hypercube. These are 3 basic examples of an experimental design.

Meta-Scheduler: A meta-scheduler is a software layer that abstracts the details of different grid middlewares. In this way a client can support multiple submission systems while only having to deal with one protocol (that used by the abstraction layer). An example of a meta-scheduler is GridWay (www.gridway.org).

Middleware: The middleware is responsible for managing the grid resources (access control, job scheduling, resource registration and discovery, etc.), abstracting away the details and presenting the user with a consistent, virtual computer to work with. Examples of middlewares include: Globus, Unicore, Legion and Triana.

Sequential Design: For a high number of dimensions, *n > 3*, it quickly becomes impossible to use traditional space filling experimental

designs since the number of points needed grows exponentially. Instead data points must be chosen iteratively and intelligently, there where the information gain is the highest. This process is known as sequential design, adaptive sampling or active learning.

Service Oriented Architecture (SOA): SOA represents an architectural model in which functionality is decomposed into small, distinct units (services), which can be distributed over a network and can be combined together and reused to create applications.

Surrogate Model: This is a model that approximates a more complex, higher order model and used in place of the complex model (hence the term *surrogate*). The reason is usually that the complex model is too computationally expensive to use directly, hence the need for a faster approximation. It is also known as a *response surface model* or a *metamodel*.

Workflow: A workflow is a set of tasks (=nodes) that process data in a structured and systematic manner. In the case that each node is implemented as a service, a workflow describes how the services interact and exchange data in order to solve a higher level problem.

ENDNOTES

[1] http://www.grc.nasa.gov/WWW/K-12/InteractProgs/index.htm

[2] Using a middleware incurs an extra overhead (submission, staging, polling, ...) which explains a speedup < 20

Chapter XXVI
GIS Grids and the Business Use of GIS Data

Patrik Skogster
Rovaniemi University of Applied Sciences, Finland

ABSTRACT

Grid computing is becoming as essential part of different business analysis. In traditional business computing infrastructures data transfer occurs to and from computing resources at the network edges. In the other hand, most business activities are bound to space and location. The aim of this chapter is to describe the business use of geographic data (business intelligence) and Geographic Information System (GIS) grids. As conclusion business intelligence helps to improve productivity by giving users information they need when they need it most at the point of decision. Organizations that effectively use geographic information elements analyzing their risk portfolio and compliance activities can reduce costs and increase the clarity of their operations. Grid computing is an answer to the needs of efficient GIS aided analysis. When geographic data, grid computing and business information are combined, they create new possibilities to enhance and broaden the standpoints of already existing data within organizations.

INTRODUCTION

Modern businesses live in an information economy. For a long time it has been acknowledged that all business activities are time-bound and that time management is an important business activity (Lawson, 2001; Lee, 1999; Negroponte, 2000). Good management of time can lead to competitive advantage.

However, many data cannot be used efficiently because of the tremendous amount of information and the difficulty of the process and transfer through a network. So how to develop internet technology to solve these problems becomes a difficult problem (Shen et al. 2004). Fortunately, grid computing provides the method of solving this problem effectively. Grid computing is a resources sharing model that may solve the current network resources imbalance problem. (Shen et al., 2004).

Grid computing is becoming as essential part of different business analysis. It has been a popular tool in academia for many years but has recently become more popular in industries such as entertainment, finance, pharmaceutical, manufacturing, engineering and energy. Grid environment, the description, discovery, and monitoring of resources (e.g. hardware, software, data, instruments) is complex due to the diversity, large numbers, transient membership, dynamic behavior, and geographical distribution of the entities where a user might be interested. (Jie et al., 2007).

In traditional business computing infrastructures data transfer occurs to and from computing resources at the network edges. The data movement occurs between servers and databases within the data centre. The grid computing model is very different, as it distributes the processing load to the compute resources at the network edge

In the other hand, most business activities are bound to space. Business services are very often bound to the location of the customer – such as health care, primary education or barber shop, or the location of a specific resource, such as a travel attraction or production plant. It has been recognized that the management and production of **spatial information** is relevant (Breunig, 1996; Dennis and Carte, 1998; Keenan et al. 1999; Pick et al., 2000, Mineter et al., 2000). One trace of theory considering time and space leads to the concept of asset specificity central to the theory on transaction costs (Suomi, 1990; Williamson, 1985). Any asset can be specific because it is time or place bound. Asset specificity will cause transaction costs and is also harmful. Business service networks will be able to use specialized services by the application of grid computing to the service orientation of enterprise software. The data containing locational information, spatial data, can be utilized in various applications, e.g. map drawing, location planning in retailing and

modeling environmental phenomenon such as floods. The tools for these analyses are called Geographic Information Systems (**GIS**). **GIS** is a rapidly growing technological field that incorporates graphical features with tabular data in order to assess real-world problems.

MAIN FOCUS

The aim of this article is to describe the business use of GIS data and GIS grids. For the purposes of this article, grid computing is defined as dynamically matching jobs of certain computational requirements with available resources that meet those requirements. Furthermore, it is assumed that the computational resources are widely distributed across the enterprise; the resources are, in fact, composed of a large number of desktop (Foster et al., 2001).

BACKGROUND

Application of **spatial information** has longer traditions in public administration than in private business. Warfare, a privilege of public authority, is tightly bound to geographical data. Establishment and maintenance of different infrastructure, such as roads, electricity and telecommunication networks is mainly the task of public authority. In all of these, managing spatial data is crucial. In statistics production geographical data is often also in a key position and statistics production is usually a part of public administration. Postal services – as special case of logistics - are deeply involved with spatial data, and this area also used to be a part of public services, so as for example weather forecasting, a very spatial information intensive activity.

However, private business is taking up the topic very fast. There is nowadays the whole separate industry working with and producing spatial data. This industry can be called sector 1 industry as it comes to spatial and grid data. In addition there is a bigger, diverse industry needing spatial information in its activities. In a similar vein, this can be called sector 2 industry.

Spatial data can be collected through scanners, remote sensing devices, GPS receivers, government agencies, social organizations and commercial companies. As the consequence of development of data collecting devices and information networks, the updating of GIS data is getting more frequent. All these result in larger and larger volume of source data involved in GISs. In addition, since data sources are increasingly involved in **GIS**, data formats used in **GIS** are getting more various, which means a GIS is required to support multiple data formats. All these issues make it harder to store all datasets in a single site. Usually, these datasets belong to different custodians that are dispersed geographically and logically.

In the retail location planning area, for example, there is a large demand for modeling different phenomenon. A term describing the current trend in the integration of various business information and GIS is called business intelligence and GIS (**BI-GIS**). The major problem – when applying data to solutions – is the incompatibility of data. Data formats vary, data collecting standards differ, the quality of data keeps changing etc. However, also the lack of workstation performance has become a problem because of the growing size of information (databases) and the need for visualize the results. One solution for this problem is the grid computing.

It has been estimated that up to 80% of all data stored in corporate databases may have a spatial component (Franklin, 1992). Spatial data and geographical data should be differentiated, though. Spatial data is any data that tells about the special relationships between objects, more precisely information that describes the distribution of things upon the surface of the earth, information concerning the location, shape and relationships among geographic features (Walker,

1993; DeMers, 1997). This includes remotely sensed data as well as map data.

Geographical data is a subset of that and is connected to the geographical coordinates of the earth. It is data which record the shape and location of a feature as well as associated characteristics, which define and describe the feature. For example, areas of woodland can be located according to co-ordinate grid system references and its attribute data such as constituent tree type, seasonality or average height can also be recorded.

ESSENCE OF SPATIAL DATA

Spatial interpolation is widely used in geographical information systems to create continuous surfaces from discrete data points. The creation of such surfaces, however, can involve considerable computation, especially when large problems are addressed, because of the need to search for neighbors on which to base interpolation calculations. Computational Grids provide the computing resources to tackle spatial interpolation in a timely way. (Wang and Armstrong, 2003).

Spatial data should be three-dimensional to be exact. However, in many applications two dimensions are enough. Especially geographical data is often just in two dimensions. To bind these two terms, the term geospatial information has been used in this article.

A spatial data grid, as its name implies, will provide spatial data management and correlative services based on spatial data. The spatial data grid manages multi-scale and multi-precise spatial data, including a vector and a raster image. This spatial data can be stored in databases or files according to the requirement. A grid provides two kinds of services: basic services and incremental services. Basic services are services every grid nodes need to support e.g. data browsing, queries and economic attribute statistics.

Spatial data grid nodes provide basic services and incremental services. A spatial data grid node is the main part of spatial data management, is the provider of corresponding services. So its capacity, safety and robust, closely connect with the efficiency and stabilization of a system. The basic, principal parts of a grid node are data management **middleware** and **metadata** management **middleware**. Grid services will map to concrete physical resources by **middleware**.

Middleware will not limit the store mode of spatial data. Three types of systems, a **database system**, a **file system** or a **hybrid system** can be used. In this way, every grid node can choose patterns for a building repository according to actual situation, also can use stored spatial data productions furthest. But the precondition is that an abstract level providing standard, a coherent Application Programming Interface (**API**) should be built on store systems.

Many service and production activities are deep involved in three-dimensional spatial planning and operations, often in very small scale indeed, such as stevedoring, plumbing, surgery, warehousing, or computer chip planning.

The architecture of a grid GIS is actually the running structure of a grid GIS. It decides the stability and extensibility of the whole system. The architecture of grid computing defines many protocols and **API**s between grid nodes. It ensures various kinds of operations and applications of grid system to run successfully (Globus, 2008).

Therefore, geospatial information elements can be divided into e.g. following categories:

- Location (is data presented in common ways, such as coordinates, addresses?)
- Units and Scales (what is the sampling density?)
- Resolution (spatial or temporal?)
- Measurement standards and quality (which standards are used?)
- Reporting (**Metadata** and its quality).

SPATIAL DATA APPLICATION AREAS IN BUSINESS

A classical way of looking at business activities is that of Porter's value chain (Figure 1). It is used also in this article as a framework to discuss use of spatial data in grid computing within different business analysis solutions.

The value chain tells that all companies are involved in different networks, as do many other contemporary articles too (Borgatti and Foster, 2003; Shapiro and Varian, 1999; Weitzel, Wendt and v. Westarp, 2000). The networks are usually dynamic and do have some geographical attributes, but as special cases they could be static or just virtual ones with no permanent physical nodes.

Parallel processing is the use of multiple computer processors, in co-operation, to speed

Figure 1. The value chain by Michael Porter (Porter and Millar, 1985)

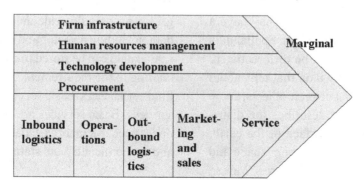

execution of one application. This is unfortunately still considered an esoteric research branch of geo-processing, with many academic and commercial software developers being unconvinced of the benefits or need for these methods, other than in the use of parallel database products for concurrent queries. Instead developers rely on the continuing advance of single processor performance to meet most evolving needs. Although this may explain the lack of commercial investment in parallel geographic information technology, it must be remembered that the history of computing is filled with technology-driven advances, and application developers tend to find reasons, sometimes justifiable ones, to use all available resources. (Mineter et al., 2000)

The company infrastructure is the most permanent part of a firm. That is why it is of crucial importance as it comes to spatial planning. Where to locate different business nodes for resource acquisition, production and customer contact are all key spatial questions. This can be called the Spatial Data Infrastructure (SDI).

Even human resources management can be bound to physical location. For example, the whole concept of science parks is fermented with the idea that high-tech business should grow in the proximity of universities. (Adams, 2006) In the whole globe scale, economic activity is fast moving to e.g. China, India and similar low-cost countries after cheap labor.

Technology development is usually not very tightly connected to space. However, some technologies are focusing on specific spatial characteristics: mining, off-shore activities, oil and gas industries, icebreaking technology, etc.

Procurement can or can not be connected with the grid computing. It is trendy to speak of global sourcing (Drtina, 1994; Gibson and McGuire, 1996; Halhead, 1995). However, sometimes space-bound grid computing is the only possibility. Tourism, for example, is often a very space-bound activity. Pioneers in procurement

planning have been firms such as oil companies or mining companies that have to track down natural resources around the globe. Interesting in their activity is also that in addition to mastering geographical data in three dimensions. They have to keep a close eye on time, for example in order to understand where oil could be stored in the ground. The same close connection between time and place can be seen e.g. in modern weather forecasting.

Grid operations are a very broad term within the spatial data analysis. In service industries, many services are bound to the place where the customer is, also to space. Planning for retail outlets is a good example of this, so as tourism discussed above. Many operations need space-bound resources, such as raw-materials. Again, knowledge work operations are usually not tightly place-bound.

Outbound logistics has the same characteristics as inbound logistics. The trend seems to be that companies want to be rather close to big customer masses than close to the raw-materials. For example, the paper industry has seen a tremendous change in this.

Marketing and sales are usually seen as global activities with no space-specific characteristics. All marketing activities, however, have to be limited to some geographical areas, and some, such as personal marketing, need actually very close spatial planning. A classic example is the traveling salesman problem: how to visit all the capitals of e.g. the United States or Europe with as little traveling as possible.

To end up with a somewhat simplifying framework, perhaps there are companies whose activities are place-bound and those whose activities are not. The three critical business areas containing place specificity and the need for powerful grid analysis are the inflow of factors of production (procurement), the actual production or operations activity, and the contact with the customer. This framework is presented in Figure 2.

Figure 2. Situations of place specificity

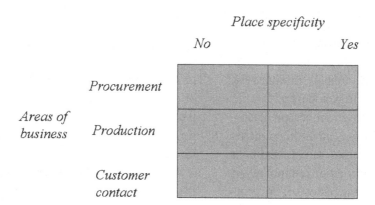

ESSENCE OF GIS

The key word to this technology is Geography - this usually means that the data (or at least some proportion of the data) is spatial, in other words, data that is in some way referenced to locations on the earth. Coupled with this data is usually data known as attribute data. Attribute data generally defined as additional information, which can then be tied to spatial data.

Data is the core of any **GIS**. There are two primary types of data that are used in GIS. A geodatabase is a database that is in some way referenced to locations on the earth. Geodatabases are grouped into two different types: vectors and rasters. Coupled with this data is usually data known as attribute data. Attribute data generally defined as additional information, which can then be tied to spatial data. Documentation of GIS datasets is known as **metadata**.

Grid GIS is the application of grid computing on GIS field. Shen et al. (2004) have presented its conception from various points. First, the target of grid computing is to share resources and data and every node to work together, which suits to the needs of GIS projects. A main characteristic of a grid is to share all kinds of resources under some specific regulars, including data, applications, computing capacity, and these regulars can ensure that all kinds of resources in the grid system work well together.

Second, grid computing must have many techniques to ensure resources sharing and cooperation so as to share all kinds of resources and make them cooperate well with one another. There must be many criteria to ensure the security and communication of every part of the whole system.

Hardware comprises the equipment needed to support the many activities of GIS ranging from data collection to data analysis. The central piece of equipment is the workstation, which runs the GIS software and is the attachment point for ancillary equipment. Data collection efforts can also require the use of a digitizer for conversion of hard copy data to digital data and a GPS data logger to collect data in the field. The use of handheld field technology is also becoming an important data collection tool in GIS. With the advent of web-enabled GIS, web servers have also become an important piece of equipment for GIS. An application about the use of grid computing and GIS is a web-service called Google Maps.

CASE GOOGLE MAPS

Google Maps (for a time named Google Local) is a free web mapping service application and technology provided by Google (Google, 2008). It powers many map-based services including the Google Maps website, Google Ride Finder and embedded maps on third-party websites via the Google Maps **API**. It offers street maps, a route planner, and an urban business locator to numerous countries around the world. At the same time as the release of the Google Maps **API**, Yahoo released their own Maps **API**. A related product is Google Earth, a standalone program for Microsoft Windows, Mac OS X and Linux which offers enhanced globe viewing features.

Google Maps features a map that users can pan (by dragging the mouse) and zoom (by using the mouse wheel). Users may enter an address, intersection or general area to quickly find it on the map. Users can also search for businesses and attractions (for example, theatres, restaurants and hotels) in or near a given place. Like many other map services, Google Maps can generate driving directions between any pair of locations in the United States and Canada and within certain other countries. It shows turn-by-turn instructions, an estimate for the trip time, and the distance between the two locations.

The "link to this page" link on each Google Maps map targets a URL which can be used to find the location on the map at a later time. The latitude and longitude can be used as input to NASA World Wind or TerraServer-USA, which in some cases have higher-resolution imagery.

Like many other Google web applications, Google Maps uses JavaScript extensively. As the user drags the map, the grid squares are downloaded from the server and inserted into the page. When a user searches for a business, the results are downloaded in the background to insertion into the side panel and map - the page is not reloaded. Locations are drawn dynamically by positioning a red pin on top of the map images.

As the Google Maps code is almost entirely JavaScript and XML, some end-users reverse-engineered the tool and produced client-side scripts and server-side hooks which allowed a user or website to introduce expanded or customized features into the Google Maps interface.

Using the core engine and the map/satellite images hosted by Google, such tools can introduce custom location icons, location coordinates and **metadata**, and even custom map image sources into the Google Maps interface. The script-insertion tool Greasemonkey provides a large number of client-side scripts to customize Google Maps data. Combined with photo sharing websites, a phenomenon called "memory maps" has emerged. Using copies of the satellite photos of their home towns or other favorite places, the users take advantage of image annotation features to provide personal histories and information regarding particular points of the area.

Google created the Google Maps **API** to facilitate developers integrating Google Maps into their web sites with their own data points. It is a free service, which currently does not contain ads, but Google states in their terms of use that they reserve the right to display ads in the future. When the Google Maps **API** first launched, it lacked the ability to geocode addresses, requiring you to manually add points in (latitude, longitude) format. This has since been rectified.

Google now allows its **API** users to perform geocoding. Geocoding is the process of assigning geographic identifiers (e.g., codes or geographic coordinates expressed as latitude-longitude) to map features and other data records, such as street addresses. Also media can be geocoded, for example where a picture was taken, IP addresses, and anything that has a geographic component. With geographic coordinates these features can be mapped and entered into Geographic Information Systems.

FUTURE TRENDS AND CHALLENGES

Using GIS applications is a common procedure for several business operators even already today. In the future the usage of different GIS solutions will increase both in traditional areas but also within new application fields because of the needs of more precise and accurate information for less time. Technology that exploits the multidimensional database paradigm provides unique capabilities to explore data in an intuitive and interactive way. The capability of linking or synchronizing several views of the same information in a context of interactive exploration of data brings new possibilities. This creates the need for efficient grid computing.

Nowadays there still are some challenges that GIS faces when it is combined with grid computing. There is no agreement on standards. The spatial data quality varies. There is a need for good **metadata** and standard formats. There is also a strong need for educating specialists that can combine GIS and grids.

CONCLUSION

Business intelligence helps to improve productivity by giving users information they need when they need it most at the point of decision. It helps to find new potential business areas and customers. One of the main market research applications of GIS is the ability to profile existing customers into classifications and then to use these categories to target potential new customers in areas of low market share (Birkin and Clarke 1998). On the other hand; risk management being embedded in its culture is essential to the success of the risk management process.

Among the most critical challenges is determining how much risk an entity is prepared for. Organizations that effectively use geographic information elements analyzing their risk portfolio and compliance activities can reduce costs and increase the clarity of their operations. Effective risk management requires, though, a risk assessment culture that supports a holistic approach to the identification and management of risk throughout

an organization. Risk management aided by GIS should therefore be part of an organization's strategy and planning processes and also an integral component of corporate governance. Importantly, an integrated risk management system develops the control environment, which provides reasonable assurance that the organization will achieve its objectives with an acceptable degree of residual risk. Grid computing is an answer to the needs of efficient GIS aided analysis.

When geographic data, grid computing and business information are combined, they create new possibilities to enhance and broaden the standpoints of already existing data within organizations. They provide longitudinal evaluations of changes in available data and information by holding constant one or more fixed query parameters. They support multi-perspective (i.e., multiple user class types) for organizational evaluations of geospatial data over common areas of interest. They also support pre-acquiring evaluations of expensive or difficult to acquire data. They are suitable for focused or tailored geospatial analyses. Business operators will have new problems to solve, though. One of them is the evaluation of the compatibility of GIS tools and intended geographic information data sources (Meeks and Dasgupta, 2004).

REFERENCES

Adams, S. B. (2006). Stanford and Silicon Valley: Lessons on becoming a high-tech region. *California Management Review, 48*(1), 29-51.

Birkin, M. & Clarke, G. (1998). GIS, geodemographics, and spatial modeling in the U.K. Financial Service Industry. *Journal of Housing Research, 9*(1), 87-111.

Borgatti, S., P., & Foster, P., C. (2003). The network paradigm in organizational research. *Journal of Management, 29*(6), 991-1031.

Breunig, M. (1996). *Integration of spatial information for geo-information systems.* Berlin, New York: Springer.

DeMers, M.N. (1997). *Fundamentals of geographic information systems.* New York: John Wiley & Sons.

Dennis, A. R., & Carte, T. A. (1998). Using geographical information systems for decision making: Extending cognitive fit theory to map-based presentations. *Information Systems Research, 9*(2), 194-203.

Drtina, R. E. (1994). The outsourcing decision. *Management Accounting, 75*(9), 56-62.

Foster, I., Kesselman, K., & Tuecke, S. (2001). The anatomy of the Grid: Enabling scalable virtual organizations. *International Journal of Supercomputer Applications, 2001*(3), 200-222.

Franklin, C. (1992). An introduction to geographic information systems: linking maps to databases, *Database 15*(2), 13-21.

Gibson, R., & McGuire, E. G. (1996). Quality control for global software development. *Journal of Global Information Management, 4*(4), 16-22.

Globus (2008). The Globus Project. Argonne National Laboratory USC Information Sciences Institute, Grid Architecture. Available from: http://www.globus.org

Google (2008). Available from http://maps.google.com

Halhead, R. (1995). Breaking down the barriers to free information exchange. *Logistics Information Management, 8*(1), 34-37.

Keenan, P. B., Grimshaw, D. J., Pick, J. B., & Ostyn, F. (1999). Panel: IS and GIS: mapping the way forward. In *Proceedings of the Seventh European Conference on Information Systems.* Copenhagen.

Lawson, M. B. (2001). In praise of slack: Time is of the essence. *The Academy of Management Executive, 15*(3), 125-136.

Lee, H. (1999). Time and information technology: Monochronicity, polychronicity and temporal symmetry. *European Journal of Information Systems, 8*(1), 16-26.

Meeks, W.L., & Dasgupta, S. (2004). Geospatial information utility: An estimation of the relevance of geospatial information to users. *Decision Support Systems, 38*(1), 47-63.

Mineter, M.J., Dowers, S., & Gittings, B.M. (2000). Towards a HPC Framework for integrated processing of geographical data: encapsulating the complexity of parallel algorithms. *Transactions in GIS, 4*(3), 245-261.

Negroponte, N. (2000, Jun 19). Will everything be digital? *Time, 155,* 86-87.

Pick, J. B., Hettrick, W. J., Viswanathan, N., & Ellsworth, E. (2000). Intra-censal geographical information systems: Application to binational border cities. *Proceedings of the Eighth European Conference on Information Systems.* Vienna.

Porter, M. E., & Millar, V. E. (1985). How information gives you competitive advantage. *Harvard Business Review, 64*(4), 149-160.

Shapiro, C., & Varian, H. R. (1999). *Information rules: a strategic guide to the network economy.* Boston: Harvard Business School Press.

Shen, Z., Dongping, M., & Qinghui, S. (2004). Architecture design of Grid GIS and its applications on image processing based on LAN. *Information Sciences, 166*(1-4), 1-17.

Suomi, R. (1990). Lowering transaction costs with information technology. *Nordisk Försäkringstidskrift, 70*(4), 264-285.

Walker, R. (ed.) (1993). *AGI Standards Committee GIS Dictionary.* Association for Geographic Information.

Wang, S. & Armstrong, M.P. 2003. A quadtree approach to domain decomposition for spatial interpolation in Grid computing environments. *Parallel Computing, 29*(10), 1481-1504.

Wei, J., Cai, W., Wang, L., & Procter, R. (2007). A secure information service for monitoring large scale grids. *Parallel Computing, 33*(7-8), 572-591.

Weitzel, T., Wendt, O., & v. Westarp, F. (2000). Reconsidering network effect theory. *Proceedings of the Eighth European Conference on Information Systems.* Vienna.

Williamson, O. E. (1985). *The economic institutions of capitalism. Firms, markets, relational constructing.* New York: The Free Press.

KEY TERMS AND DEFINITIONS

API: Originally Advanced Programming Interface but now more commonly known by its near synonym, Application Programming Interface, is any defined inter-program interface.

BI-GIS: GIS systems added with technologies, applications, and practices for the collection, integration, analysis, and presentation of business information and also sometimes to the information itself. BI systems provide historical, current, and predictive views of business operations, most often using data that has been gathered into a data warehouse or a data mart and occasionally working from operational data.

Databases (DBS): A system or software designed to manage a database, and run operations on the data requested by numerous clients. Typical examples of DBS use include accounting, human resources and customer support systems.

File System: A method for storing and organizing computer files and the data they contain to make it easy to find and access them.

GIS: A geographic information system (GIS), also known as a geographical information system or geospatial information system, is a system for capturing, storing, analyzing and managing data and associated attributes which are spatially referenced to the Earth. Grid Information Service (GIS) is a core component in the Grid software infrastructure.

Hybrid System: Dynamical systems with interacting continuous-time dynamics (modeled by differential equations) and discrete-event dynamics (modeled by automata).

Metadata: Metadata are data about data. An item of metadata may describe an individual datum, or content item, or a collection of data including multiple content items.

Middleware: Software that sits 'in the middle' between applications (e.g., a word processing program) working on different operating systems (Unix, Windows, z/OS, etc.). It is similar to the middle layer of a three-tier single system architecture, except it is stretched across multiple systems or applications. Examples include database systems, telecommunications software, transaction monitors and messaging-and-queuing software.

SDI: Spatial Data Infrastructure or SDI is a framework of spatial data, metadata, users and tools that are interactively connected in order to use spatial data in an efficient and flexible way.

Spatial Information: Information including locational elements.

Chapter XXVII
Grid Computing:
Combating Global Terrorism with the World Wide Grid

Gokop Goteng
Cranfield University, UK

Ashutosh Tiwari
Cranfield University, UK

Rajkumar Roy
Cranfield University, UK

ABSTRACT

The emerging grid technology provides a secured platform for multidisciplinary experts in the security intelligence profession to collaborate and fight global terrorism. This chapter developed grid architecture and implementation strategy on how to connect the dots between security agents such as the CIA, FBI, police, custom officers and transport industry to share data and information on terrorists and their movements. The major grid components that featured in the architecture are the grid security portal, data grid, computational grid, semantic grid and collaboratory. The challenges of implementing this architecture are conflicting laws, cooperation among governments, and information on terrorist's network and interoperability problem.

INTRODUCTION

Terrorism can be defined as the use of violence to cause harm, large-scale destruction and fear in order to force change in societal behaviour or to force a society to acquiesce to the goals of the terrorist(s) (Garrison, 2007). Another definition by Ruby (2002) is that terrorism is politically motivated violence perpetrated in a clandestine manner against non-combatants in order to create a fear state of mind in an audience different from the victims. From these definitions, the September

11th attack can be seen as a way of sending dangerous signals to the U.S. government to change its policies against some interest groups rather than the real victims of the attack.

Terrorism dates back as far as 2000 years ago. Some of the early terrorist attacks were carried by the Jewish resistant group known as Sicarii-Zealots (AD 66-72) whose targets are the Romans in Judea. Others are the reign of terror in France (1793-1794), the Anarchists in Europe (1871-1914), the Soviet Revolution (1917), the Irish Rebellion (1919-1921) and Terrorism in the Middle-East and Islamic Fundamentalism (1960s-date). However, the sophistication, targets, victims, perpetrators, causes and justifications offered by terrorists and their collaborators have changed significantly over the years.

Never in the history of the world had terrorism received attention as in the 21st Century. Terrorists have attacked cities like London, Madrid, Moscow, World Trade Centre, Pentagon and Mumbai. These attacks usually witnessed mass wanton destruction of lives and properties with devastating and lasting psychological, socio-political and economic consequences. Very recently, a major terrorist attack was exposed and stopped at Heathrow Airport in London on August 10, 2006 due to efficient, pervasive, secured, coordinated and timely distributed access to information by the intelligence personnel leading to the arrest of about 24 national and international suspects. Another two attempts were thwarted in London and Glasgow early this year again. It appears that timely distributed information about terrorists' activities is a great strategy in combating the menace of terrorism. This is where grid computing can play a great role with its pervasive, secured, dynamic and distributed data and information services. Grid computing connects islands of information sources and link different agents around the world to collaborate and respond immediately to disasters (Assuncao and Buyya, 2005). This form of collaboration is possible through efficient high volumes of data

processing using data clustering techniques for counter-terrorism (Rajasekaran et al., 2005).

BACKGROUND

September 11, 2001 could have passed like any day if only the United States intelligence agencies had been better equipped with pervasive and coordinated information technology systems. According to a U.S. Department of Defence report, ample relevant data was captured and stored in U.S. foreign intelligence databases but were not used because of inadequate coordinated distributed information technology (IT) that can enable sharing and analysis of information in the databases for prompt decision (Popp et al., 2004). The ultimate goal of using distributed IT for counter-terrorism is to empower users within the intelligence community (CIA, FBI, etc) with virtualised information so that they can anticipate and pre-empt terrorists' attacks through faster and agile analyses of collaborative multiple foreign agencies databases across the world (Popp et al., 2004). However, current IT infrastructures including high performance computing (HPC) do not have the scalability and robustness to handle biometric data workloads (Moretti et al., 2006). Moretti et al. (2006) observed that the emerging grid technology has the capability to handle data intensive biometric information of individuals collected from check points. Currently the U.S. has a terrorism watch list of approximately 350, 000 individuals (Moretti et al., 2006; The Washington Post, 2006). As the trend of terrorism increases, this list will also increase. This is where grid computing can play a role in handling the data and computational intensive nature of biometric data analysis of terrorists' watch list. Grid computing is a large-scale distributed technology which uses its secured, pervasive, independent, autonomic and dynamically coordinated features to provide sharing of resources (data, information, hardware, software, sensors, CCTV, etc) and collaboration among multidisciplinary virtual organisations (VO) (Foster and Kesselman, 1999). The use of grid computing to link professionals within virtual organisation such as transport industry and intelligence departments with databases to alert security and intelligence officers on terrorists' threats looks attractive to counter-terrorism organisations (Bebee and Thompson, 2004).

This chapter is divided into six sections. The first section introduces terrorism and brief historical background as well as some examples of recent terrorist attacks. It defines grid computing and why grid is a suitable information technology infrastructure to combat global terrorism. The second section discusses the implications of terrorists' attacks. The third section provides a grid framework and its components that can be used to tackle terrorism. The fourth section highlights the benefits of using grid computing to combat global terrorism. The fifth section highlights the challenges in implementing the framework. The sixth section gives a brief summary and conclusion.

Some Major Terrorists Attacks

Examples of some major terrorists' attacks are the bombings of Mubai (2006), Mogadishu (2006), London (2005), Madrid (2004), World Trade Centre and the Pentagon (2001). Others are Oklahoma (1995), Lockerbie (1988) and Nairobi (1988). The distributed nature of terrorists' networks around the world and the large-scale destruction of both human and material resources calls for the adoption of large-scale distributed technology that can securely identify high risks incidents and inform security agents such as custom, police and transport industry for prompt action. One way the U.S. Department of Defence is addressing the need for more effective counter-terrorism is by building improved modelling and simulation capabilities (Boris, 2002). Grid computing appears to suit this purpose with its secure, pervasive, autonomous and ubiquitous characteristics.

MAIN FOCUS

This section aims at identifying the important role grid computing and large-scale distributed technologies can play in combating terrorism.

The Place of Grid Computing in Combating Global Terrorism

During the Cold War era, innovation and technology was put to use in spying, detecting and outsmarting players. Each player knew what the other was up to by building and mounting sophisticated surveillance satellites and that put fear on each side which discourage them from actually using the weapons they possess. This is a case of the saying that he who wants peace tomorrow should prepare for war today. In the same manner, the approach tends to evolve with improvement in weaponry technology. For example, the stabilisation of explosives as dynamite in 1867 saw bombs replacing shorthand guns as weapon of choice by 19th century terrorists, aircraft hijacking declined with improvements in aircraft security and metal detectors in 1970s, the smuggling of liquid explosives in the form of hydrogen peroxide recently in London Heathrow airport on the 10th August 2006, there is now strict liquid detecting policy (Falkenrath, 2001). In summary, terrorists seize any loophole in security to perpetrate their acts. Putting tight security in place scares terrorists from perpetrating their intended acts, including suicide bombing. It is in this light that after studying the characteristics of grid computing and terrorists' networks around the world, a grid computing framework for counter-terrorism is proposed.

Grid Computing and Terrorism

Grid computing is defined as a 21st century distributed computing infrastructure which uses its secured, dependable, pervasive, dynamic, coordinated and reliable features to solve large-scale computational, data and information related problems. Terrorism is a global problem which enjoys the support of some network group of individuals and governments around the world and whose activities are large-scale destruction of lives and property. Grid computing is a large-scale network that solves large-scale problems and can connect the dots among intelligence offices, custom departments and transport systems to stop terrorists' attempts. This is possible because grids permit heterogeneous platforms (software and hardware) to communicate and share intelligence information (Davis et al., 2004). The components of grid computing and proposed framework to combat terrorism are discussed next.

It is important to mention here that technology such as grid computing is aimed at preventing the damages caused after terrorists' attacks. This is possible if traces or clues leading to attacks are captured and communicated promptly to counterterrorist security agents.

Primary Clues

Primary clues are traces that suggest and prompt suspicions that there is possible likelihood of imminent terrorist attack. These traces are information captured in CCTVs and databases. These pieces of information when matched with biometric information through pattern analysis may prompt suspicion on whether or not there should be terror alert. For example, the 07/07 London attack in 2005, CCTV captured the images of the terrorists at Luton train station. This was a vital primary clue that if it were properly mined, the 07/07 attack could have been thwarted. Capturing primary clues is vital in thwarting attacks. For example, police used CCTV image to prosecute Mohammed and his co-terrorists in the failed 10/08 London attempt. They (terrorists) were about to use hydrogen peroxide explosives to bomb 10 planes that were about to take off to the US. Fortunately enough, they were caught midway. Other clues could be suspicious substances

(liquids) or items in a bag. All these are primary clues that if properly captured using data grid can be mined to avoid attacks using autonomous and ubiquitous grid computing capabilities. Effective data mining of primary clues requires linking information systems directly to intelligence agencies using organisational infrastructures that can take timely and coordinated actions (Garrick et al., 2004).

Secondary Clues

Secondary clues are the destructions that occur after a successful terrorist attack. This is what grid technology aims to avoid. It should not reach this stage. Primary clues are the important features grid technology needs to capture to avoid the emergence of secondary clues. The following sections will discuss the components of grid computing that are needed to capture, store and mine primary clues.

Computational and Data Grids

Effective security goes beyond protecting physical structures which has always been the tradition, but should incorporate means of controlling the movement of terrorists. Data Grid can contain all the databases of collaborating foreign intelligence offices around the world. Distributed access to databases is guaranteed by Grid Access Secondary Storage (GASS) and Data Access and Integration (DAI) services. The Grid-Database Management System in Data grids has virtualised capabilities to hold information. Computational grid nodes using Grid Resource Allocation Manager (GRAM) have the capability to manage dynamic resource sharing among distributed intelligence offices securely. Middleware can overcome the interoperability among heterogeneous software, hardware and computational resources in the various geographical locations. With recent introduction of biometric data capture for all travellers around the world, Data grid will play a great role in mining these data and alerting security operatives on suspicions. Integrating collection of databases into a single data warehouse that can be used in dynamic federated grid environment supports counter-terrorism activities (Choucri et al., 2004).

Grid Problem Solving Environments (PSE)

PSE platform provides collaborative knowledge sharing and visualisation of results from the analysis of the databases, alerting foreign intelligence offices promptly on suspicions. The distributed nodes at intelligence offices offer collaboration within a secured Grid PSE safe from the terrorists and their collaborators. The goal of using PSE is to provide an environment for intelligence personnel to have easy access to all tools, resources and patterns related to terrorists' intentions around the world. Globalisation and migration have made borders of many technologically advanced countries entry points for terrorists. Information technology is being used for border surveillance to check illegal immigrants and terrorists enter-

ing some countries in Europe (Kowsloski, 2003). Figure 1 shows the arrangements of Grid tools for collaborative analysis that can potentially be mounted at airports, rail stations and borders to further help intelligence agents in fighting terrorism.

In Figure 1, Data Grid is central to other grid tools that need coordination for effective collaboration. This is because the major components of the arrangement such as computational grid, semantic grid, visualisation grid, pattern analysis tools, biometric matching tools and foreign language analysis tools need to have access to the stored data in data grid to perform any action. For example, biometric matching tools need to get access to the fingerprint, iris scan or facial scan of terrorists captured and stored within data grid to make comparisons with a person who is being suspected to be a terrorist.

Grid Information Service (GIS)

GIS in conjunction with metadata from databases is used for decision support on real time basis. GIS

Figure 1. Arrangement of distributed grid components to capture and mine data

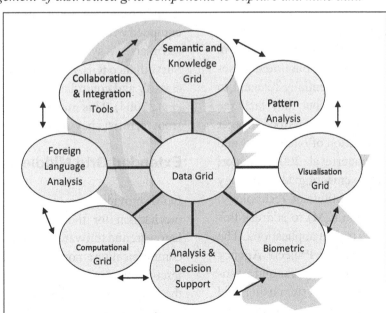

consists of Grid Resource Information Service (GRIS) which holds information on terrorist's identity, map of a city, biometric information, and so on. All GRIS are saved in GIIS (Grid Information Index Service). The Universal Description, Discovery and Integration (UDDI) service uses this information to autonomously discover, select, and send messages to Grid nodes (Pattnaik et al., 2003) alerting them on possible terrorists' activity. Predictive pattern analysis, categorisation, and clustering algorithms are useful analysis tools in Grids to track down terrorists networks.

Semantic Grid

Semantic Grid is a knowledge-based grid that gives meaning to representations of grid components (Roure et al., 2003). The Semantic Grid and ontology are used to capture and interpret patterns and foreign languages. Terrorists communicate to perpetrate their acts using various languages. The Semantic Grid can help transcript, translate, and summarise any language into English language. The Semantic Grid will match biometric information of terrorists with translated communication and connects to visualisation Grid and Geographical Positioning Service (GPS) for analysis. Pattern analysis identifies terrorists' activities using relationship extractions. It has been noted by the National Research Council in the US that there are private and public databases that contain information potentially relevant to counter-terrorism programs, but they lack the context definitions (metadata), access tools to other databases and the extraction of meaningful and timely information (Choucri et al., 2004). Choucri et al. (2004) developed a semantic grid technology at MIT (Massachusetts Institute of Technology) called Context Mediation (CM) to address this problem for counter terrorism applications. The Defence Advanced Research Projects Agency (DARPA) in collaboration with Hicks and Associates (H & A) are building a system using grid and web architecture that incorporates Semantic

Web to create novel data sharing and collaboration network to support counter terrorism capabilities (Babee and Thompson, 2004).

IMPLEMENTATION FRAMEWORK

Although grid computing is a new technology, it has the potential of being implemented at airports, rail stations and other strategic buildings and locations around the world. The components likely to attract this implementation are discussed below.

Grid Security Infrastructural (GSI) Portal

GSI in conjunction with web portal will provide a secured common authentication and authorisation logon feature through a single-sign proxy protocol (Novotny, 2003). The encryption facility of proxy certificate authorisation allows intelligence officers to have access to distributed databases across foreign intelligence offices around the world. Biometric (iris scan and finger print) authentication at grid entry points (portal) can also be used to generate unique identifiers for intelligence agents (Lambert and Leonardt, 2004). The grid is also equipped with systems that can detect abuse from intruders. A system called Grid-based Attack Surveillance (GBAS) is used to detect, monitor, classify and control attacks to grid systems (Wu et al., 2004). This makes grid technology secure from terrorists having access to the system.

Extended Grid Middleware (EGM)

EGM provides the brokering and negotiation mechanism for the distributed heterogeneous hardware and software platforms. This allows easy communication among intelligence officers of different countries. The guiding principle of EGM is the same as OGSA (Open Grid Services Architecture) such as coordinated resource sharing and problem solving in dynamic multi-institutional organisations (Babee and Thompson, 2004).

Counterterrorist Grid Collaboratories (CGC)

CGC is a specialised collection of distributed virtual resources specifically meant to feed all intelligence offices around the world with information on terrorists. CGC concept is adopted from the Index Service (IS) in Globus Toolkit. IS maintains information on all registered resources and services by obtaining resource properties from Aggregator Sources such as the Query Aggregator Source, Notification Aggregator Source and Execution Aggregator Source. The trigger mechanism in Globus enables Index Service information to be refreshed at specific intervals of time so that new happenings are recorded on the fly. In this manner, CGC allows sharing of sensitive databases and analysis results for pattern matching among specific virtual organisations charged with counterterrorist responsibility using IS collaboratories (Perrow, 2006).

Distributed Wireless Transport Grid Systems (DWTGS)

Transport systems such as air and rail are target points for terrorists. Key aircrafts and rails should have wireless Grids equipped with sensors biometric and digital forensic identification systems that send signals to all Grid nodes at Intelligence offices on suspicions. CCTV and surveillance equipment are mounted at all entrances and strategic places at airports and rail-stations and are connected directly to DWTGS for instant transmission to all CGCs.

Figure 2 is the implementation framework. The GRID with nodes node 1, node 2, …., node n can be used by collaborators to access physical entities as resources or services. Physical entities such as Geographical Positioning Service (GPS), CCTV, sensors, biometric databases of terrorists and visualisation equipment are published as resources on the grid. Dynamic coordination using tools for pattern analysis and predictive modelling to trace terrorist's networks on the fly will help in connecting the 'dots'. Information sharing among law enforcement agencies has been a key challenge

Figure 2. Implementation framework

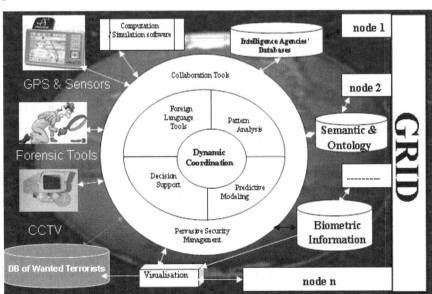

addressed by various governments. For example, FBI operates databases such as the Criminal Justice Information Services Division (CJIS), National Crime Information Centre (NCIC), Integrated Automated Fingerprint Identification System (IAIFIS) and National Instant Criminal Background Check System (NICBCS) to watch terrorists' movements (Ham and Atkinson, 2002). Ham and Atkinson (2004) observed that these systems are separate and lack real time coordination query system to track down terrorists. A grid system such as the one described in Figure 2 is capable of providing dynamic real time coordination for the different databases.

The implementation framework uses at its centre the dynamic coordination capability of grid computing to coordinate the real time interactions among pattern analysis tools, predictive modelling tools, decision support tools and foreign language interpretation tools. These tools also have access to various distributed databases that store biometric information and transactions carried out by terrorists. The framework also coordinates interactions by physical grid entities such as CCTV, GPS and sensors. Figure 1 is to be setup at airports, rail stations, intelligence offices and borders of countries to check terrorists' activities.

Visualisation Grid with Virtual Reality Network (VGVRN)

VGVRN is connected to DWTGS and CGC and produces real images and analyses results of patterns of terrorists' activities on real time basis. VGVRN will be located in all foreign intelligence offices around the world and real time discussion on the motion CCTV images monitoring real activities of terrorists.

Dynamic Ubiquitous and Autonomic Grid Computing (DUAGC)

The ultimate goal is that this system of tracking down terrorists happens without much interfer-

ence. DUAGC will allow the system to manage itself and send signals on its perceived environment and the analysis extracted from database patterns.

Figure 3 is a scenario of how grid computing components that are discussed above can be used to thwart attacks. This is how it works. The biometric information of terrorists is tracked, their networks tracked, their bank and arms transactions tracked and this is happening in a country that aids terrorism, then using pattern analysis tools may help security agents to arrive at decisions that there is the likelihood of terrorist attack. This will help to track down suspicious movements of terrorists (Goldstein, 2006). A grid system called Biometric Grid (BMG) is used to control access and verify individuals based on their physiological characteristics (Ming and Ma, 2007). BMG is a complete suite of grid system built on Globus Toolkit. It has web portal-based virtual organisation, large-scale biometric database and service-oriented collaboration tools that can be used for secure, fast and non-intrusive identification of people to check global terrorism by the homeland security agents (Ming and Ma, 2007). BMG suits well with the concept described in Figure 3.

BENEFITS AND FUTURE TRENDS

The benefits of this system are enormous. The obvious benefit is saving innocent lives and wanton destruction of properties through secure collaboration among countries and security agencies as they share security information on terrorists' networks (Kumagai, 2006). The threat to globalisation and international trade is another benefit of using grid computing for counterterrorism activities. It is estimated that the September 11th disaster alone resulted in a global economic lost of about $300 billion and about 200, 000 jobs were lost (GAO, 2002). Tourism and economic growth will be recorded in a world free of terrorists' threat.

Figure 3. Scenario of how to trace terrorists' networks through their activities

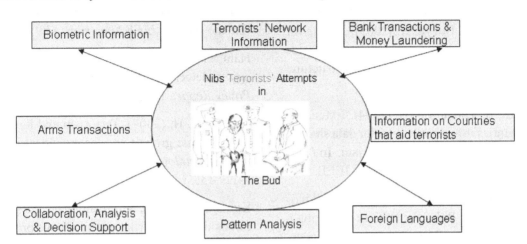

Future trend in counterterrorism research is aimed at implementing this framework. This is an analysis and review of grid computing technology to combat terrorism. More so, as great cities of the world such as New York, London, Mumbai, Paris and others become overpopulated, crime rate and terrorism may increase and the complexity to tackle this problem requires the use of future generation technologies such as grid computing, autonomic computing and ubiquitous computing (Sweet and Cass, 2007). Future research issues on combating terrorism with grid computing should include chemical and biological weapons detecting grid systems. Advanced information technology has a role to play in fighting chemical and biological terrorism but little success has been recorded in this area (Siegrist, 2000). Such advanced crisis management strategy is to incorporate the why, when, where, who and how prepared the intelligence departments are to deal with attacks (Paraskevas and Arendell, 2007).

CONCLUSION

Technology needs to play crucial role in the war on terror. Grid computing looks suitable for secure collaboration among countries and security agencies to fight terrorism. The primary clues gathered from CCTV footages and other databases can be mined for distribution to alert security agents promptly using data grid, computational grid and autonomous computing. This chapter proposed a framework for building such technology. Benefits of this technology are saving lives and properties, safe international trade and globalisation and global tourism. However, the war on global terrorism will continue for some time due to its negative implications. Apart from the psychological implication of causing fear and trauma, the adverse effect on global economy, tourism, transport industry, supply change management and globalisation calls for a technological solution that will address the trend (Koh, 2007). Some of the challenges in implementing this framework are getting the cooperation of governments and intelligence agencies to share their databases, the different legal laws in different countries on terrorism and the cost of building and maintaining the system. In conclusion, grid is a new but fast maturing technology that can be used to tackle the coordinated and dynamic nature of global terrorism.

REFERENCES

Assuncao, M., & Buyya, R. (2005). A case for the world wide Grid: Interlinking islands of Grids to create an evolvable global cyberinfrastructure. *Technical Report, 43(3)*.

Bebee, B., & Thompson, B. (2004). Extending rich semantics in an architecture for data sharing and collaboration for counter terrorism. In *IEEE Aerospace Conference Proceedings*. IEEE.

Boris, J. (2002). The threat of chemical and biological terrorism: Roles for HPC in preparing a response. In *Computing in science and engineering-HPC and national security*. IEEE

Choucri, N., Madnick, S. E., Moulton, A., Siegel, M. D., & Zhu, H. (2004). Information integration for counter terrorism activities: Requirements for context mediation. In *Proceedings of the 2004 IEEE Aerospace Conference*.

Davis, D. M., Baer, G. D., & Gottschalk, T. D. (2004). 21st Century simulation: exploiting high performance computing and data analysis. *Interservice/Industry Training, Simulation and Education Conference (I/ITSEC) 2004, 1517*, 1-14.

Falkenrath, R. A. (2001). Problem of preparedness: U.S. readiness for a domestic terrorist attack. *International Security, 25*(4), 147-186.

Foster, I., & Kesselman, C. (1999). *The Grid: Blueprint for a new computing infrastructure*. Morgan Kaufmann Publishers Inc.

GAO. (2002). Washington DC, USA: GAO; 2002 May 29.

Garrick, B.J., Hall, J.E., Kilger, M., McDonald, J.C., O'Toole, T., Probst, P.S., et al. (2004). Confronting the risks of terrorism: Making the right decisions. *Reliability Engineering and System Safety 86*(2), 129-176 .

Garrison, A. (2007). Terrorism: The nature of its history. *Criminal Justice Studies. 16*(1), 39-52.

Goldstein, H. (2006). Modelling terrorists: New simulators could help intelligence analysts think like the enemy. *IEEE Spectrum, 43*(9), 18-26.

Ham, S., & Atkinson, R. D. (2002). Using technology to detect and prevent terrorism. *Technical Policy Report*. Progressive Policy Institute, 102.

Koh, W. T. H. (2007). Terrorism and its impact on economic growth and technological innovation. *Technology forecasting & social change*, 74129-138. Elsevier.

Kumagai, J. (2006). Nine cautionary tales: If terrorists decide to strike again, are we prepared? Not really, as these scenarios of extremism make clear. *IEEE Spectrum, 43*(9), 28-37.

Lambert, H. D., & Leonhardt, C. F. (2004). Federated authentication to support information sharing: Shibboleth in a bio-surveilance information Grid. *International Congress Series*, 1268135-140.

Ming, A, & Ma, H. (2007). Proposal of an architecture for a biometric Grid. *LNCS, 44*(39),195-208.

Moretti, C., Faltemier, T. C., Thain, D., & Flynn, P. J. (2006). Challenges in executing data intensive biometric worloads on a desktop Grid. Tech Report (pp. 13).

Novotny, J. (2003). The Grid portal development kit. In F. Berman, G.C. Fox, & A.J.G. Hey (Eds.), *Grid computing: Making the global infrastructure a reality* (pp. 657-673). England: John Wiley & Sons Ltd.

Paraskevas, A., & Arendell, B. (2007). A strategic framework for terrorism prevention and mitigation in tourism destination. *Tourism management*. Elsevier.

Pattnaik, P., Ekanadham, K., & Jann, J. (2003). Autonomic computing and Grid. In F. Berman, G.C. Fox, & A.J.G. Hey (Eds.), *Grid computing: Making the global infrastructure a reality* (pp. 351-361). England: John Wiley & Sons Ltd.

Perrow, C. (2006). Shrink the targets: We can't defend everything, so we should take steps that protect against both terrorism and natural disasters. *IEEE Spectrum, 43*(9), 38-41.

Popp, R., Armour, T., Senator, T., & Numrych, K. (2004). Countering terrorism through information technology. *Communications of the ACM, 47*(3), 36-43.

Rajasekaran, S., Ammar, R., Demurjian, S., & Greenshields, I. (2004). Strategies to process voluminous data in support of counter-terrorism. *IEEEAC, 1253*(8).

Roure, D., Jennings, N. R., & Shadbolt, N. R. (2003). The semantic Grid: A future e-Science infrastructure. F. Berman, G.C. Fox, & A.J.G. Hey (Eds.), *Grid computing: Making the global infrastructure a reality* (pp. 437-470). England: John Wiley & Sons Ltd.

Ruby, C. L. (2002). The definition of terrorism. *Analyses of Social Issues and Public Policy, 2*(1), 9-14.

Siegrist, D. (2000). Advanced information technology to counter biological terrorism. *ACM SIGBIO, 20*(2), 2-7.

Sweet, W., & Cass, S. (2007). How to fight crime in real time: New York City's rapid data retrieval accelerates investigations. *IEEE Spectrum, 44*(6), 46-49.

The Washington Post (2006). 325,000 on terrorism list.

Wu, J., Cheng, D., & Zhao, W. (2004). Detecting Grid-abuse attacks by source-based monitoring. In *Proceedings of the 1st International Workshop on Security*.

Yuan, E., & Wenzel, G. (2002). Enabling total information awareness with Grid services. *IEEEAC, 6-2980*(1209).

KEY TERMS AND DEFINITIONS

Autonomic Computing: A grand challenge computing paradigm that enables computing systems and its interacting components to manage themselves or adapt to situations without the interference of a human systems administrator.

Biometric Information: Unique biological traits of human beings such as finger print and iris for unique identification of terrorists.

Collaboration: Sharing of security information about terrorists and their networks among countries and security agencies to fight terrorism.

Forensic Technology: A technology used for investigation and identification of facts surrounding a crime, sometimes using carbon related chemicals around the crime scene.

Grid Computing: Future generation distributed computational infrastructure that enables secure, dependable, scalable and dynamic collaboration among virtual organisations.

Portal: A uniform entry point for all grid users to access grid resources and services.

Resource Grid: Resources are data, information, software, hardware, sensors and instruments which are shared by grid users.

Semantic Grid: Knowledge-based grid computing which gives meaning to actions and components of resources based on the rules and language of the profession the resources are used for.

Service Standard: Grid functionalities such as reliable file transfer (RFT), resource management (GRAM), security of resources through authentication and authorisation (GSI) and other customised functionalities are called grid services.

Terrorism: The act of causing fear on the society by using force or violence to harm or destroy lives and properties by persons or group of persons for certain political or religious reasons so that authorities can succumb to some demands.

Ubiquitous Computing: A grand challenge computing paradigm that enables pervasive distribution of computational resources for effective collaboration.

World Wide Grid: Mechanism for linking islands of global grid resources for collaboration.

Chapter XXVIII
Accessing Grid Metadata through a Web Interface

Salvatore Scifo
Cometa Consortium, Italy

ABSTRACT

This chapter focuses on the efforts to design and develop a standard pure Java API to access the metadata service of the EGEE Grid middleware, and provide at the same time a powerful object oriented framework to allow engineers and programmers to embed metadata features inside their own application, using a standard approach based on design patterns. A specific Web interface is built on top of this framework that permits users and administrators to manage the metadata catalog, from any platform and everywhere, according to their own X.509-based credentials.

INTRODUCTION

AMGA service is the implementation of the metadata interface designed by the ARDA team for the official metadata service of the EGEE Grid middleware. It is a complete but simple interface to use. The service is flexible enough to support dynamic schemas in many application domains as well as hierarchical metadata structure definitions. The service presents a high degree of scalability to deal with large number of entries

(several millions) and the security aspect is fully compliant with the Grid Security. AMGA has been designed to hide network latency (based on TPC/IP communication protocol) as well as provide local replicas for off-line access. Its database independent replication supports grid environment heterogeneity and avoids the presence of single point of failure. As a grid service, developers provide only command line client and APIs (PHP, C/C++, Python and Java). In this paper, we describe both the basic API and a web interface to achieve access to the AMGA metadata sever from any platform. The AMGA Web Interface provides a powerful interface to access and manage GRID metadata according to X.509-based credentials. To be authenticated to the AMGA server, the user needs just a web browser and a valid X509 digital certificate released by one's Grid Virtual Organization Certification Authority. After a successful login, one can browse the hierarchy of collections and inspect schema/ permissions as well as the list of entries. One can create a new collection, define a metadata schema for it, edit entries, and finally perform queries against its attribute. The AMGA web interface follows the three-layer architecture of J2EE and adopts the framework as a data access layer.

BACKGROUND

This work is closely linked to the metadata service of the gLite, the middleware of the EGEE Grid European project. Within the gLite architecture, the data management system (DMS) is an essential part that enables users and applications to handle data and metadata without referring to the complex details of the computing environment. DMS provides APIs and Client tools to store, locate, access, retrieve and move files dispersed on the distributed virtual File System. From the functional point of view, gLite DMS offers two fundamental macro features: file management and metadata management. The first one (performed by the file catalogue service and the storage resource manager), involves the storing abilities (save file, copy file, read file, list file), placing abilities (replica file, transfer file) and security stuff (ACL for files, users roles). The second one (implemented by the metadata catalogue), offers database schema virtualization (metadata handling, intelligent search), file cataloguing and file searching. Fig.1 shows data management system modules and their interrelations.

The data storage is the subsystem that manages data manipulation so that users and/or applications can access and manage their own files. The data movement subsystem enables any other Grid services or any clients (users and/or applications) to move file from/to a site, (a site is the smallest, complete and auto consistent hardware/software resource organization within a Grid infrastructure). The data catalogue subsystem keeps track of file location in the distributed file system and store short information (as comment) about them. Finally, metadata catalogue service allows user to associate descriptive attributes (metadata schema) with files, publish these attributes online in order to make them available to end users and client applications. The history of evolution of gLite middleware does not contain relevant metadata experiences, we can find only two file catalogue services: LFC (LCG file catalogue) and FiReMan (file and replica manager). LFC is capable of storing a simple string comment for each file entry, while FiReMan allows associated information such as a couple of key and value. Since the use of FiReMan has been deprecated, the newest AMGA service handles cataloguing and indexing more efficiently. AMGA is a dedicated service that handles metadata for each file on the grid and it was designed to fulfill the needs of different groups of users like high energy physics which primarily demand high performance access, as well as biomedical sciences which require very strict authentication and fine grained access controls. In order to understand and meet the users' needs, AMGA was developed in close collaboration with the different user groups and a common metadata access interface was thus designed. Several applications are currently using AMGA to store their metadata. Some of them are: MDM (medical data manager), GANGA, Health-e-Child, WISDOM, Bio Med Portal, gLibrary, ADAT (Archivio Digitale Antico Testo) and GSAF (Grid Storage Access Framework).

For instance, the MDM application uses AMGA to save relational information on medical images stored on the grid, plus information on patients and doctors in several tables. User applications can retrieve images based on their metadata for further processing. Access restrictions are fundamentally important for the MDM application because the stored data is highly confidential and fine-grained access control is therefore necessary. GANGA (a physics analysis tool for the Atlas and LHCb experiments) uses AMGA to store the status of jobs running on the Grid in order to control their workflow. AMGA's simple relational database features are mainly used to ensure consistency when several GANGA clients of the same user are accessing the stored information remotely. The Health-e-Child project aims at developing an integrated healthcare platform for European pediatrics, providing seamless integration of traditional and emerging sources of biomedical information. The long-term goal of the project is to provide uninhibited access to universal biomedical knowledge repositories for personalized and preventive healthcare, large-scale information-based biomedical research and training, and informed policy making.

WISDOM (Wide In Silico Docking On Malaria) initiative aims to demonstrate the relevance and the impact of the grid approach to address drug discovery for neglected and emergent diseases. The grid infrastructure is used here to organise and accelerate disease research. The acronym WISDOM, comes from the first screening large scale experiment against malaria, and is now used as a generic name for the initiative. Bio Med Portal is a Grid application which gathers several medical use cases and emphasizes the benefit that a Grid service could provide to distant research groups of doctors, bioinformatics engineers, application developers, libraries and tools developers, middleware developers, grid service providers and infrastructure maintainers. The gLibrary application uses AMGA in a similar mode to MDM, but it provides several schemas to store information regarding images, texts, documents, movies or music. Another difference is that there is only a library manager to update the library while MDM updates are triggered by many image acquisition systems. ADAT is a prototype of Digital Archive for Cultural Heritage. It archives many ancient manuscripts using Grid as digital repositories. At server side, AMGA provides to ADAT all the

Figure 1. DMS architecture view

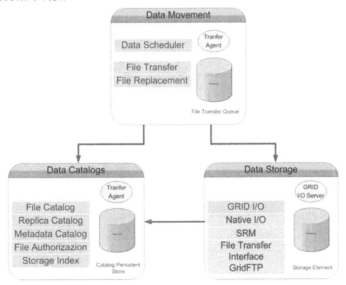

support for metadata cataloging management. At client side, users of ADAT are able to perform queries to find digitalized books. Finally, GSAF is an Object Oriented java framework designed to access and manage data and metadata by application. It embeds AMGA Java framework to offer a unified API that keeps track of all files spread over the whole Grid system and manage them easily, hiding the big fragmentation of the whole Grid data management services.

MAIN FOCUS

The first point we focused on is the availability of a standard pure Java API which offers the basic building blocks to allow generic clients to interact with the Grid metadata service. This API follows the standard client/server architecture based on TCP/IP protocol that ensures a very fast connection and data exchange. The second point was geared towards the realization of an object oriented framework that has a plug-in for general purpose applications for metadata on a Grid. Its design covers several object oriented design patterns that make the module generic enough and adaptable by any application. Finally, we devel-

oped a web interface (on top of the framework) to achieve access and manage the metadata catalog from any platform.

Web Application Overview

AMGA Web Interface is a J2EE (Java 2 Enterprise Edition) web application developed with pure Java technologies (Java Servlet, Java Server Pages, Custom Tag Library). As is shown in the Figure 2, the application design follows the standard multi-layer web application architecture consisting of a data presentation layer, a logic application layer and a data access layer. The data presentation layer consists of all web pages that allow users to access all features provided by the metadata catalog using only a common web browser. These pages publish dynamic contents managed by DHTML and Ajax (Asynchronous JavaScript And XML) libraries and any displayed information is coherent with the status of the information stored into the AMGA Server backend. The web pages work with both logic components to perform data manipulation and access components to retrieve and publish data. The logic application layer is made up of all the software modules that encapsulate the implementation of the provided

Figure 2. Layered architecture view

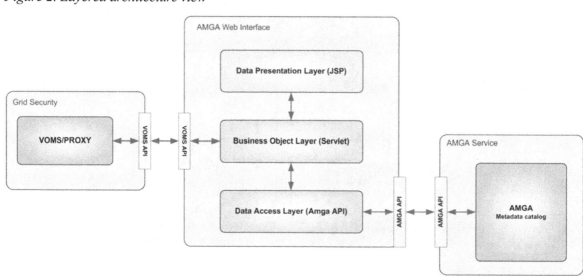

features (metadata handling and manipulation). It is the core of the application and it is designed to be a plug-in for general purpose applications that adopt metadata on Grid. Its design covers several object oriented design patterns (singleton, strategy, factory, template, iterator and composite methods) that make the module generic enough and adaptable by any application that needs to integrate Metadata usage.

The data access layer implements all software components that provide mechanisms to retrieve data from the AMGA server and publish them as dynamic contents on the web. This layer is built on top of the Java API.

Web Application Architecture

Figure 3 describes the software architecture of the application. Every AMGA logical entity (collection, entry, attribute, group, users and access rights) are mapped in to specific software modules according to a vertical design. This ensures a very clean and simple software architecture with a high degree of cohesion and decoupling.

The management web pages module implements the presentation layer, allowing user to provide its own proxy certificate to the application engine (through the homologous VOMS Manager) as well as covering all functional requirement regarding metadata manipulation. It collects all necessary web forms to submit information and tables for data presentation. The adoption of DHTML and Ajax (Asynchronous JavaScript And XML) makes the layout user friendly while techniques to separate presentation from logic (custom tags) make software maintenance easy. The managers - VOMS, collection, entry, attribute, group and user - belong to the logic layer. These components work as services invoked by the overlying web pages. VOMS manager interacts with the VOMS server in order to build a proxy certificate that allow a user to use metadata catalog. The group and user managers provide methods to manage groups and users and define the access control list for each collection. Collection manager implements all available operations on the set of entries.

The entry manager works with file entries and metadata instances, while the attribute manager manages the metadata schema.

Framework Software Design

AMGA service is accessible through the Java API in three different ways: low level usage, medium level usage and high level usage. Low level mode is complete and self consistent but close to the AMGA communication protocol (low level

Figure 3. System architecture view

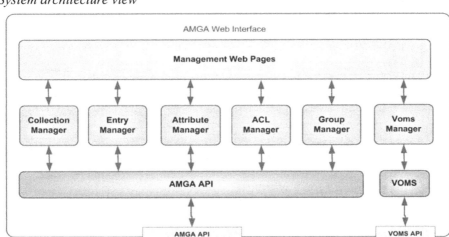

commands and syntax). Developer must know the right syntax of all commands and write a lot of code to send command and parse results. The medium level mode is built on top of the API and is more user friendly to the developers. It provides a complete data object model for all the involved logical entities (collection, entry, attribute, user, group and so on.), and a complete list of collection builders to execute query and searches as well a iterate or manipulate results. This API provides also a specific object that wraps the most used command while using the all aforementioned components as a basic client. Users must however still know the properties of the client object and

the correct behavior of its methods. No design patterns are provided and dependencies of syntax are still present. Finally, the high level mode wraps the basic API providing an object oriented framework. The framework hides all API complexity supplying several object oriented design patterns to improve code reuse and free hand to deal with the business logic by developers. The framework implements the object model of the service behavior by offering operations, execution context, collections, iterators and so on.

The core of the framework is designed to be a black box in order to be easily embedded into several applications independently of their

Figure 4. AMGA framework model

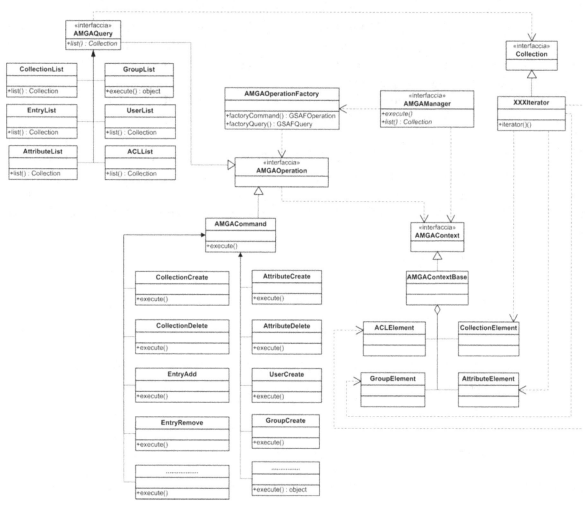

Figure 5. Collection management module of the web Interface

domains. Object-oriented analysis and design (OOAD) approach has been used in order to model the AMGA service as a group of interacting and collaborating objects. Each object represents some entity of interest in the system being modeled, and is characterized by its class, its state, and its behavior. Inside the framework, any instance of each data object composes the AMGA context base. This object is used as execution environment for each AMGA operation. The AMGA operation interface defines all functions allowed in the data set, and each function is bound inside a specific class identified by an operation code (command pattern). Both type of operation: command, which changes the state of the storage and query that performs only searches and returns the result set as a standard Java collection are supported as shown in the Fig. 4. Finally, the AMGA manager object is able to execute all algorithms embedded inside any AMGA operation. Developers may, in order to perform any wanted operation (functional object model), need to instantiate the context, quantify it with the right parameters (the data object model instances) according to the business rules of their application and pass it to the appropriate manager that execute it (template and strategy pattern combined together).

FUTURE TRENDS

This work embraces the new trend to Grid Systems and the European Community considers the Grid a suitable infrastructure for providing Digital Repositories and/or support for Digital Libraries. To maximize this trend, the Grid must evolve to a user friendly collection of services, opened to generic users rather than specialists such as researchers, technicians and professionals. This "humanization" process is line with the Web 2.0 directives, that allow service accessibility via http/https protocols from anywhere and shielded network and grid details. AMGA Web Interface is an attempt to interface and administrate the Grid Metadata Catalog. Furthermore, it is the first and the only existing interface for accessing metadata remotely (within the gLite middleware). Normally, users can interface Grid metadata catalog through some command line tool installed in dedicated machines called User Interface (UI). In order to do this, each user needs: a user account on a Grid UI; a net access to the Grid UI; VPN (Virtual Private Network) solution to access the Grid UI that resolve problems with firewalls and security details. Fig.5 shows a screen shot of the collection management module of the web interface.

Another important aspect of the system is the engine. All metadata functions are collected in a stand alone framework designed to be reusable in many different application domains. This model enables developers to design and develop grid applications easily and quickly, eliminating the big knowledge gap between classic developer and grid specialized developer. Finally, since any kind of applications belonging to the digital archive domain is metadata centric (metadata are the heart of any archiving and cataloguing process), it is evident how the current application enriches the flexibility of the Grid middleware by providing an administrative tool for catalog administrators, an authoring tool for catalog users and a powerful development tool for archive engineers.

CONCLUSION

The main idea of the present work is to provide a unified and standard mechanism to develop application (web or desktop, belonging to any domains), without requiring developers need to understand the syntax of the AMGA communication protocol or implementing their own object model any applications. In this way, any application that has a standard layered architecture can adopt this framework as a data access layer that can interact with the AMGA Service.

Currently, this project aims to become the official web oriented user interface for the Metadata Catalog of the EGEE middleware and several research groups use it to provide metadata on the Grid. The GILDA team (Grid INFN Laboratory for Dissemination Activities) adopts it for dissemination and training courses about metadata usage.

There are some noteworthy user groups of this resource. The Bio Med Portal project (sponsored by Bio-Lab, DIST University of Genoa), is geared towards a Bio Medical Informatics Framework that merges traditional clinical health records with the newest ones called Bio Medical Informatics records. This portal uses the Grid Data Services to store, organize and retrieve patient data as well as manipulate metadata. Another relevant adopter is the AIURI Project (carried out by COPPE – Federal University of Rio De Janeiro in collaboration with the EELA project). It aims at the construction of a high performance cooperative academic environment for education and research on computational intelligence. It has facilities for database access, visualization tools and appropriate user interfaces to perform data and text mining algorithms. Finally, the engine is also integrated within the GSAF framework in order to keep track of files spread over the distributed Storage System and retrieve them easily using descriptive metadata. The future thrust is to improve the query engine, provide a more powerful and complete query tool for complex and intelligent searches, as well as a JDBC-like for both on and off-line analysis. In all, the system provides facilities for metadata creation, a useful interface, a powerful authoring system and a simple plug-in for applications.

REFERENCES

Albrand, S., & Fulachier, J. (2004). ATLAS metadata interfaces (AMI) and ATLAS metadata catalogs. *Computing in high energy and nuclear physics (CHEP 2004),* Interlaken, Switzerland.

Baud, J.P., & Lemaitre, S. (2005). *The LHC File Catalogue (LFC),* HEPIX 2005, Karlsruhe, Germany.

Berman, F., Fox, G. and Hey, T. (2003). The Grid: Past, present, future. In *Grid computing.* New York: Wiley.

Calanducci, A. (2006). *gLibrary: A Multimedia contents management system on the Grid.* EGEE User Forum, CERN, Switzerland.

Deelman, E., Singh, G., Atkinson, M. P., Chervenak, A., Hong, N.P.C., Kesselman, C., et al.

(2004). *Grid-based metadata services.* Paper presented at the 16th International Conference on Scientific and Statistical Database Management (SSDBM'04), Santorini Island, Greece.

Doherty, T. (2006). *Development of gLite Web Service based security components for the ATLAS metadata interface,* EGEE User Forum, CERN, Switzerland.

Estrella, F., Kovacs, Z., LeGoff, J.M., & McClatchey, R. (2001). MetaData objects as the basis for system evolution (LNCS 2118, 390-399).

Foster, I. & Kesselman, C. (2001). A data Grid reference architecture. In *Proceedings of the ACM/IEEE SC2001 Conference.*

Foster, I., (2002). *The physiology of the Grid: An open Grid services architecture for distributed systems integration - globus project.*

Montagnat, J. (2006). Bridging clinical information systems and Grid middleware: A Medical Data Manager. In *Proc. HealthGrid 2006,* Valencia, Spain.

No, J., & Park, H. (2005). GEDAS: A data management system for data Grid environments. *Computational Science – ICCS 2005* (pp. 485-492).

Padala, P. & Shin, K. (2006). GVU: A view-oriented framework for data management in Grid environments. *High Performance Computing - HiPC 2006* (pp. 629-640).

Samaras, G., Karenos, K., & Christodoulou, E. (2004). A Grid service framework for metadata management in self-e-learning networks. *Grid Computing 2004* (pp. 260-269).

Santos, N., & Koblitz, B. (2005). Metadata services on the Grid. In *Proc. of Advanced Computing and Analysis Techniques (ACAT'05),* Zeuthen, Berlin.

Santos, N. & Koblitz, B. (2006). *Distributed metadata with the AMGA metadata catalog.* Paper presented at Workshop on Next-Generation Distributed Data Management. HPDC-15, Paris, France.

Torterolo, L., Corradi, L., Canesi, B., Fato, M., Barbera, R., Scifo, S., et al. (2007). A new paradigm to design, implement and deploy Grid oriented application: A biomedical use case. *Proceedings of the Symposium Open Grid,* Palermo, Italy.

Zhu, C. (2007). *Construction of a Webportal and user management framework for Grid.* Paper presented at the 21st International Symposium on High Performance Computing Systems and Applications (HPCS'07), Saskatoon, Saskatchewan, Canada.

KEY TERMS AND DEFINITIONS

API: An application programming interface is a set of declarations of the functions (or procedures) that an operating system, library or service provides to support requests made by computer programs. Language-dependent APIs are available only in a particular programming language. They utilize the syntax and elements of the programming language to make the API convenient to use in this particular context. Language-independent APIs are written in a way that means they can be called from several programming languages. This is a desired feature for a service-style API which is not bound to a particular process or system and is available as a remote procedure call.

Applications Grid: It shares and reuses application code but uses software technologies like service oriented architectures that facilitate sharing business logic among multiple applications.

Design Pattern: In software engineering, it is a general reusable solution to a commonly occurring problem in software design. A design pattern is not a finished design that can be transformed directly into code. It is a description or template for how to solve a problem that can be used in many different situations. Object-oriented design patterns typically show relationships and interactions between classes or objects, without specifying the final application classes or objects that are involved. Algorithms are not thought of as design patterns, since they solve computational problems rather than design problems. Not all software patterns are design patterns. Design patterns deal specifically with problems at the level of software design. Other kinds of patterns, such as architectural patterns, describe problems and solutions that have alternative scopes.

Framework: It is a basic conceptual structure used to solve or address complex issues. A software framework is a re-usable design for a software system (or subsystem). A software framework may include support programs, code libraries, a scripting language, or other software to help develop and glue together the different components of a software project. Various parts of the framework may be exposed through an API or be themselves API.

Grid Computing: A style of computing that dynamically pools IT resources together for use based on resource need. It allows organizations to provision and scale resources as needs arise, thereby preventing the underutilization of resources (computers, networks, data archives, instruments).

Information Grid: This grid shares information across multiple consumers and applications. It unlocks fragmented data from proprietary applications by treating information as a resource to be shared across the grid.

Infrastructure Grid: This grid pools, shares and reuses infrastructure resources such as hardware, software, storage and networks across multiple applications.

Metadata: (meta data, or sometimes meta-information) is "data about data", of any sort in any media. An item of metadata may describe an individual datum, or content item, or a collection of data including multiple content items. The word meta comes from the Greek, where it means 'after' or 'beyond'. In epistemology, the word means "about (its own category)"; thus metadata is "data about the data". Metadata is used to facilitate the understanding, characteristics, and management usage of data. The metadata required for effective data management varies with the type of data and context of use. In a library, where the data is the content of the titles stocked, metadata about a title would typically include a description of the content, the author, the publication date and the physical location.

Middleware: A computer software that connects software components or applications. The software consists of a set of enabling services that allow multiple processes running on one or more machines to interact across a network. This technology evolved to provide for interoperability in support of the move to coherent distributed architectures, which are used most often to support and simplify complex, distributed applications. It includes web servers, application servers, and similar tools that support application development and delivery. Middleware is especially integral to modern information technology based on XML, SOAP, Web services, and service-oriented architecture.

Object Model: A collection of objects or classes through which a program can examine and manipulate some specific parts of its world. In other words, the object-oriented interface to some service or system. Such an interface is said to be the *object model of* the represented service or system.

Provisioning: The allocation of resources to consumers on demand. A system determines specific need of the consumer and provides the resources as requested.

Virtualization: A form of abstraction that provides location- and technology-transparent access of resources to the consumer. It decouples the tight connections between providers and consumers of resources, thus allowing sharing of the same resources by multiple users as needs arise.

X.509: In cryptography, is an ITU-T standard for a public key infrastructure (PKI) and Privilege Management Infrastructure (PMI). X.509 specifies, amongst other things, standard formats for public key certificates, certificate revocation lists, attribute certificates, and a certification path validation algorithm.

Chapter XXIX
Grid Computing Initiatives in India

Jyotsna Sharma
Thapar University, India

ABSTRACT

Efforts in Grid Computing, both in academia and industry, continue to grow rapidly worldwide for research, scientific and commercial purposes. Building a commanding position in grid computing is crucial for India. The major Indian National Grid Computing initiative is GARUDA. Other major efforts include the BIOGRID and VISHWA. Several Indian IT companies too are investing a lot into the research and development of grid computing technology. Though grid computing is presently at a fairly nascent stage, it is seen as a cutting edge technology. This paper presents the state-of-the-art of grid computing technology and the India's efforts in developing this emerging technology.

INTRODUCTION

The term 'Grid' brings to mind an interconnected system of an electricity distribution network of power stations and high tension cables. The grid computing paradigm is similar to the electrical power grid because of similar properties like transparency, availability, pervasiveness and utility. Grid computing aims to extend this analogy by transparently integrating distributed computing resources, which may belong to different organizations, hiding their specificities and presenting a homogeneous interface to the users. Just as one may plug in a cell-phone charger into the wall socket and have no idea from where the electricity comes from, one may submit a job to a 'computational grid' without having any idea from where the computing power and resources are coming from. Grid computing is an approach to distributed computing that spans not only locations but also organizations, machine architectures and software boundaries to provide unlimited power, collaboration and information access to everyone connected to a grid (Foster, 2003). Just as an Internet user views a unified instance of content via the Web, a grid user essentially sees a single, large virtual computer (IBM, n.d.).

Though grid computing is presently at a fairly nascent stage, it is seen as a cutting edge technology. This paper aims to present the state-of-the-art of grid computing and attempts to survey India's efforts in developing this emerging technology. The major initiatives of Brazil, Russia and China are also included in order to provide a report on the grid computing efforts of the BRIC countries.

BACKGROUND

The term 'Grid Computing' is relatively new and means a lot of different things to a lot of different people (Jennifer, 2003). The grid concepts and technologies were first expressed by Foster and Kesselman in 1998. Built on the pervasive Internet standards, grid computing enables research-oriented organizations to solve problems that were infeasible to solve due to computing and data-integration constraints. Grids also reduce costs through automation and improved IT resource utilization. Grids help optimize the infrastructure to balance workloads and provide extra capacity for high-demand applications (Chawla, 2007). Grid computing can increase an organization's agility, enabling more efficient business processes and greater responsiveness to changing business and market demands.

Grid computing uses the resources of several computers connected by a network (usually the internet) to solve large-scale computation problems. These computers need not be the powerful supercomputers or mainframes. They could be the personal computers, running different operating systems on many hardware platforms. A study showed that more than 90% of the computer power remained free most of the time in case of normal desktops (Chopra, 2007). This idle time on several

thousands of computers throughout the world is used through the scheme of CPU scavenging to handle applications that would otherwise require the power of expensive supercomputers. In the SETI@home project and others like it, volunteers around the world allow their computers to be used for scientific research which shows that some people are willing to share for no direct benefit to themselves (Anderson, 2002; SETI@Home, n.d.). People on the internet can be motivated to contribute their idle resources (Abramson, 2000). The wide variety of resources distributed geographically, are used as a single unified resource which is known as the 'computational grid' (Baker, 2000).

Efforts in Grid Computing, both in academia and industry, continue to grow rapidly worldwide. Various grid projects are being developed for research, scientific and commercial purposes. These include large scale science and engineering projects such as Grid Physics Network (GridPhyn), NASA Information Power Grid (NASA IPG), CERN Data Grid, EU Data Grid, TeraGrid and the Earth System Grid, to name a few. India too has climbed the bandwagon. Leading researchers in the field of Grid Computing have identified the various grid projects worldwide, particularly those of India (Buyya , 2005).

MAIN FOCUS

Building a commanding position in Grid computing is crucial for India. By allowing anyone, anywhere, anytime to easily access supercomputer level processing power and knowledge resources, grids will underpin progress in Indian science, engineering and business. The challenge facing India today is to turn technologies developed for researchers into industrial strength business tools. The major Indian National Grid Computing initiative is Garuda. Other efforts include the BIOGRID and VISHWA.

Major Indian Grid Initiatives

a) GARUDA : India's National Grid Computing Initiative

The Department of Information Technology (DIT), India, has funded the Center for Development of Advanced Computing (C-DAC) to deploy the National Grid Computing Initiative, 'GARUDA'. C-DAC has identified Grid Computing as a major thrust area for future and initiated "Proof Of Concept (PoC)" phase of the nation-wide computational grid, involving high speed communications fabric; aggregation of geographically distributed resources (computing, data, storage, software and scientific instruments); architecture, standards, research and technology development; and end-to-end applications development. The initiative will give a push to Indian science, engineering and business (Garuda, 2007).

GARUDA aims at researching applications characterized by intensive computing and data access requirements like Natural Disaster Management, Bio-informatics applications and applications of national importance that require aggregation of geographically distributed resources. C-DAC, in association with the Space Applications Centre, which conducts space application research and development in satellite communication and remote sensing, will mine data from a network of sensors deployed over vast disaster prone regions and upload it to GARUDA as input to forecast models for disaster management.

GARUDA Architecture

Garuda has the grid system architecture based on Web Services. GARUDA is managed by C-DAC with the Grid monitoring and Management Centre at Bangalore which uses an advanced software named 'Paryavekshanam' for monitoring the utilization of the resources. Access to the GARUDA network and resources is through a grid portal managed by C-DAC wherein, the

users have the option to choose from a fastest response to their task requests by deploying as many available computational nodes to their tasks or simply submitting job.

The fabric component of GARUDA is set-up in partnership with Education and Research Network (ERNET). The current PoC phase of GARUDA is expected to lead to the main national initiative on Grid computing over the next 3-5 years. During this phase of the project, 48 research and academic institutions from 17 cities across the country are being networked which comprise of 11 C-DAC (Centre for Development of Advanced Computing) centers, ERNET (India's Research and Education Network) and 36 academic and research organizations including all the Indian Institutes of Technology (IITs) and The Indian Institute of Science (IISc.), Bangalore. The GARUDA network is a Layer 2/3 MPLS Virtual Private Network (VPN) connecting the 48 institutions all across India at 10/100 Mbps with Stringent Service Level Agreements with the service provider. It is a precursor to the Gigabit

Figure 1. GARUDA Network Connectivity Source: Garuda India Website (http://www.garudaindia. in/network_fabric.asp)

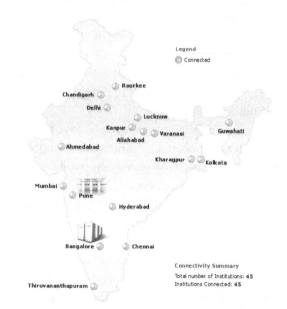

speed nationwide Wide Area Network (WAN). Efforts are also ongoing for using satellite based communication channels (Garuda, 2007).

The de-facto standard for creating computational grids is the Globus Toolkit (Cannataro, 2003). In GARUDA, Globus Toolkit 2.0 is deployed for operational requirements. The researchers at Garuda grid labs are experimenting with Globus Toolkit 4.0. For resource management and scheduling, MOAB scheduler from Cluster Resources and many local schedulers are deployed in a hierarchical architecture. Scheduling, at the cluster level is achieved through Load Leveler for AIX platforms and Torque for Solaris and Linux clusters. Scheduling at the Grid level, is achieved through the MOAB scheduler which interfaces with the various cluster level schedulers. The MOAB scheduler maps user requests onto available resources in the Grid in a transparent manner. MOAB interfaces with Globus for data and user management, job staging and security.

b) BIOGRID

BIOGRID is a high speed and high bandwidth virtual public network (VPN) established by the Department of Biotechnology (DBT), Government of India. BIOGRID will be useful in sharing teaching materials and delivering lectures through video conferencing besides synergizing research in biotechnology and bioinformatics. Commercial software essential to carry out research in bioinformatics will also be made available. The mirror sites of internationally recognized genomic databases such as Genome Data Base(GDB), Protein Databank (PDB), Plant Genome Data Banks, Databases of European Bioinformatics institute (EBI) and Public domain bioinformatics software packages are also available on the BIOGRID. This will provide unhindered mining of high quality data from well established information sources. The BIOGRID allows exchange of database and software, which have been created/acquired by the individual centers/nodes of BTIS (Biotechnology Information System). BIOGRID is also being used for the dissemination of biotechnology information to researchers in the country.

BIOGRID Architecture

The nodes in BIOGRID are interconnected through 2 Mbps dedicated leased circuit line at each location and 4 Mbps Internet bandwidth shared from the central server by all the nodes.

Figure 2. GARUDA Components Source: www.veccal.ernet.in/~iwlsc/IWLSC_Presentations/9FEB/ SessionIII/Mohan 20Ram.ppt

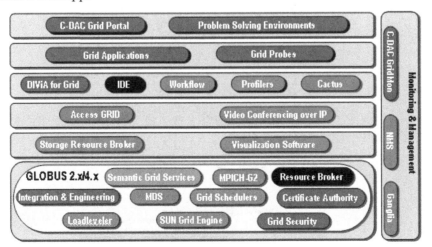

It is envisioned that the BIOGRID will span all the 60+ Bioinformatics centers of the Department of Biotechnology with Gbps bandwidth and 10+ Teraflops of computational power. The network was established through HCL InfiNet and is being coordinated by National Institute of Immunology(NII). Eleven institutions viz. JNU, DBT, Delhi University, South Campus (Rice Genome Project), CBT, NII, NBRC (Gurgaon), MKU Madurai, IISc Bangalore, CDFD, Hyderabad, University of Pune and IMTECH, Chandigarh have been networked under this project in the first phase. In the second and third phase the remaining centers and DBT institutions will be covered.

c) VISHWA: A Reconfigurable Scalable Middleware For Grid Computing

Vishwa is an effort of the Distributed and Object Systems Lab(DOS Lab), Department of Computer Science and Engineering, and Indian Institute of Technology, Chennai, India. The researchers at DOS Lab have identified that the present day grids suffer from various problems like poor scalability across the internet, centralized administration and management and no self organizing behavior. The P2P systems on the contrary have decentralized administration and management, scale well on the Internet and exhibit self organized behavior. Vishwa takes advantages of both P2P and Grid systems. It is a two layered P2P middleware for resource sharing in the Internet. It is a scalable and dynamically reconfigurable middleware. It provides a dependable execution environment for grid applications. The task management layer of the middleware is responsible for initial task deployment on the under-utilized nodes as well as the runtime migration of tasks to handle load dynamics. It is realized as an unstructured P2P layer and allows logical resource clustering based on proximity. The unstructured overlay allows neighbour lists to be constructed based on application specific criteria, whereas in structured overlay, the neighbor lists are based on node identifiers (Venkateswara, 2006).

Figure 3. BIOGRID Network Connectivity Source: http://www.scfbio-iitd.res.in/biogrid/biogrid.htm

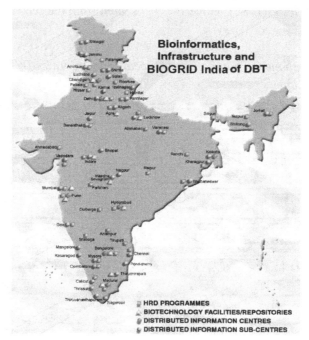

Other Indian Initiatives

To accelerate India's drive to turn its substantial research investment into tangible economic benefits, many leading Indian IT companies have started Grid projects and are actively engaged in the development of Grid technologies or their utilization in driving scientific and business applications. A few other key Indian IT companies have set up separate practices on Grid Computing that offer consulting services for enterprises that want to set up in-house Grids.

a. Infosys, India has set up a Grid Lab and R&D centre to create solutions that address the needs of clients Infosys has developed Grid-based data center management tools. The Grid Computing Center of Excellence (CoE) at Software Engineering and Technology Labs (SETLabs), Infosys has been established with a vision to create an adaptive services Grid through service-oriented architectural constructs and platform (Infosys, 2007).

b. Satyam has established a Grid Computing facility in Chennai. The company has already established an alliance with United Devices Inc., a US-based leader in secured Grid solutions. Satyam recently executed a Grid project for Dr. Reddy's Laboratories (DRL), a leading Indian Pharmacy company engaged in drug discovery. Satyam deployed the molecular docking application on the Grid. It developed interface programs and submitted a large database of 59,000 molecules to run on the Grid of 50 nodes built across two facilities at DRL that yielded phenomenal result (Satyam, 2004).

c. Since sharing is the most important single keyword characterizing a true grid, localization of grid computing interfaces is the key to realize its benefits. Madras Institute of Technologies (MIT) at Anna University, has partnered with C-DAC in developing grid interfaces in Indian languages. One of their effort was the development of Tamil (a language spoken in the south Indian state of Tamil Nadu) interface for their Grid Market Directory (GMD) user-interface. They also developed a Linux shell User Interface in Tamil. This is probably the world's first Grid technology with non-English language interface. The architecture proposed is generic, therefore it can be adapted for other languages such as Chinese and Spanish (Selvi, 2007).

Figure 4. Tamil(Indian Regional Language) Grid Interface Source: http://www.gridbus.org/gmd/tamil/ gmdsnaps.html

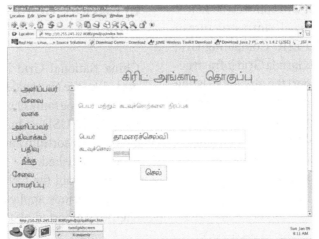

d. Wipro is in the process of setting up an internal grid computing network to connect all its centers of excellence to develop necessary competencies on various platforms .

e. Tata Consultancy Services (TCS) has entered into an alliance with DataSynapse to deliver Grid Computing solutions to TCS' customers worldwide.

f. IIT Kanpur is deploying Grid Computing hardware and software from Sun India, for its computer centre. The installation will make it the largest AMD Opteron HPTC (High Performance Technical Computing) cluster in the education segment in India.

g. HCL Technologies and NEC of Japan are setting up a grid computing joint venture.

INDIA'S INTERNATIONAL GRID PROJECTS

India's major International Grid Project, EU-IndiaGrid, is funded by the European Commission, Research Infrastructure Unit. It links major Indian and European Grid Infrastructures. This international project, comprising five European research, and industrial partners from the UK and Italy, and six Indian research and governmental institutions (Bangalore, Kolkata, Mumbai, New Delhi, and Pune). EU-IndiaGrid will analyze the current Grid network in India and create a strategy for interoperability. It will connect the EGEE (Enabling Grids for E-sciencE) infrastructure of Europe with the regional LHC Computing Grid (LCG) Tier-2 centers and Garuda Grid infrastructures in India. It will support the already existing EU-India collaborative projects. Key application areas include, High Energy Physics, Material Science, Bio-informatics and Earth and Atmospheric Science. This project will bring together over 500 multidisciplinary organizations.

GRID PROJECTS IN THE OTHER BRIC COUNTRIES

The grid computing efforts of Brazil, Russia, India & China, also known as the BRIC countries, are of interest as these countries are foreseen as the four most dominant economies by the year 2050. The major national and international grid projects in India have been discussed in the earlier sections. In this section the major projects of the other three countries are discussed.

a) OURGRID: The Brazilian Grid Computing Project

OurGrid is the major Brazilian computational grid project. It is a joint effort of Hewlett-Packard (HP), Brazil and the Distributed Systems Lab, Universidade Federal de Campina Grande (UFCG), Brazil. A medical research project in Rio de Janeiro used the OurGrid to successfully screen drugs for effectiveness with an HIV variant that is more common in Brazil. The scheduling component is called 'MyGrid'. OurGrid uses a resource allocation mechanism called Network of Favors, which is an autonomous reputation scheme that rewards Peers that contribute more. For security, sandboxing feature, SWAN (Sandboxing Without a Name) is implemented by HP Brazil R&D Labs in Porto Alegre (HP labs, 2005).

b) CNGrid: China National Grid Project

China National Grid Project (CNGrid) is supported by the National High-Tech R&D Program (the 863 program).The China government will invest 12 M USD, to build its infrastructure. The CNGrid consortium and China Grid Forum have been established.

Apart from the CNGrid, China has also developed various applications grids like the ChinaGrid, supported by the ministry of education,

Figure 5. CNGrid Network Connectivity Source: http://i.cs.hku.hk/~clwang/grid/CNGrid.html

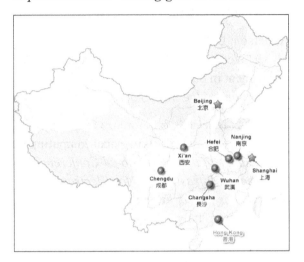

Figure 6. RDIG Network Connectivity Source: http://www.egee-rdig.ru

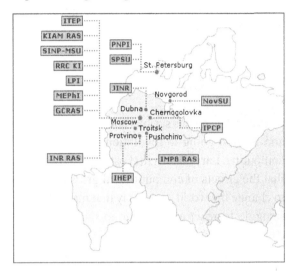

China and the China Science Data Grid (SDG), supported by the Chinese Academy of Science.

c) RDIG: Russian Data Intensive Grid

The Russian Data Intensive Grid (RDIG) is the major grid computing initiative of Russia. It was set up in 2003 to create Grid infrastructure for intensive scientific data operations for the participation of Russian scientists in experiments in high energy physics, chemical physics, biology, earth sciences and other scientific applications. 15 institutes are involved in the RDIG activities: Kurchatov Institute, Moscow; The Institute of High Energy Physics, Protvino; Institute of Mathematical Problems in Biology RAS, Pushchino; Institute of Theoretical and Experimental Physics, Moscow; Joint Institute for Nuclear Research, Dubna,; Keldysh Institute of Applied Mathematics RAS, Moscow; Skobeltsyn Institute of Nuclear Physics at MSU, Moscow; St-Petersburg Institute of Nuclear Physics RAS, Gatchina; Institute for Nuclear Research RAS, Troitsk; Lebedev Physical Institute RAS, Moscow; St-Petersburg State University ; Moscow Engineering Physics Institute; Geophysical Center RAS, Moscow; Novgorod State University, Velikii Novgorod;

and Institute of problems of Chemical Physics RAS, Chernogolovka (EGEE, 2007).

FUTURE TRENDS

While challenges still lie in the path of large-scale adoption of Grid Computing on account of lack of standards, immature solutions, lack of skills and experience at the vendor level, low awareness among users and the cost of initial investment in equipment and software, the technology is expected to proliferate by 2020. Many multi-national companies in India have started active programs in Grid computing. For example, both HP and Oracle have been developing some key Grid technologies needed for taking their current products to the next level. In addition, Oracle, Dell, Intel, EMC have announced their joint project, called MegaGrid. All these developments promise a bright future for Grids.

The importance of international cooperation in grid technologies to benefit collaborative team science is now widely recognized and accepted. Most grids for scientific research are national in nature (e.g., TeraGrid in the U.S., Garuda in India), and are tailored to run on the specific country's infrastructure. To make the infrastructure usable on a routine basis, in future, more work is expected to be done for the interconnection of the national grids.

CONCLUSION

Grid computing has serious social consequences and is soon going to revolutionize the world of computing. Larry Smarr in (Foster, 1999) observes that the effects of computational grids are going to change the world so quickly that mankind will struggle to react and change in the face of the challenges and issues they present. Worldwide a great number of scientific and commercial applications have started harnessing the power of grid computing and India is not far behind. The Govt. of India and many key Indian companies are making efforts to move it beyond scientific applications into mainstream IT infrastructure. The major Indian Initiative is the Government funded GARUDA Project. Several Indian IT Companies too are investing a lot into the research and development of grid computing technology.

The share of the four nations in world growth could double from 20% in 2003 to 40% in 2025. Industrialization in India and China could push the world growth rate to above 4% over the next few years. In a report in March 2005, the adoption of grid computing in India and China was stated to be quite low. But the increasing level of infrastructure standardization in these countries, increases the appeal of implementing Grid Computing. The BRIC countries, especially India, are therefore well positioned to close the gap (Quocirca, 2005).

REFERENCES

Abramson, D., Buyya R., & Giddy, J. (2000). Economy driven resource management architecture for computational power grids. Paper presented at the International Conference on Parallel and Distributed Processing Techniques and Applications (PDPTA'2000), Las Vegas, USA.

Anderson, D. P., Cobb, J., Korpela, E., Lebofsky, M., & Werthimer, D. (2002). Seti@home: An experiment in public-resource computing. *Communications of the ACM, 45*(11).

Baker M., Buyya R. & Laforenza D. (2000). The Grid: International efforts in global computing In *Proceedings of the International Conference on Advances in Infrastructure for Electronic Business, Science, and Education on the Internet.* Aquila, Rome, Italy.

Buyya, R., & Venugopal, S. (2005). A gentle introduction to Grid Computing and technologies, *CSI Communications, 29*(1), 9-19.

Chopra, I., & Kaur, G. (2007). Exploring Grid middleware – A comparative study, *Proceedings of the International Conference on Intelligent Systems and Networks,*(pp. 650-651). Jagadhri, Haryana, India.

Cannataro, M., &Talia, D. (2003). The knowledge Grid. *Communications of the ACM, 46*(1), 89-93.

Chawla, N. (2007). Grid computing. *Developer IQ, 7*(1), 38.

EGEE (2002). Enabling Grids for E-Science. Retrieved October 25, 2007, from http://www.egee-rdig.ru/

Foster, I. & Kesselman, C. (Eds.). (1998). *The Grid: Blueprint for a new computing infrastructure.* San Francisco: Morgan Kaufmann.

Garuda India Portal (2007). Retrieved June 25, 2007, from http://garudaindia.in

Grid Computing Info Centre (n.d.). Retrieved May 5, 2007, from http://www.gridcomputing.com

HP Labs web site (2005). News and Events, 2005 Archives, Stripped-down grid : A lightweight grid for computing's have-nots, February 2005.

Retrieved October 22, 2007, from http://www. hpl.hp.com/news/2005/jan-mar/grid.html

IBM Inc. (n.d.). IBM Grid computing, About Grid computing, What is grid. Retrieved May 5, 2007, from http://www-03.ibm.com/grid/about_grid/what_is.shtml

Infosys (2007). Technology, Centers of Excellence, Grid computing : Center of excellence. Retrieved June 5, 2007, from http://www.infosys.com/technology/grid-computing-coe.asp

Jennifer, M. S. (2003). Grids: The top ten questions. Paper presented at *International Symposium on GridComputing.*

Laforenza, D. (2002). Grid programming: Some indications where we are headed. *ACM Parallel Computing Special Issue: Advanced environments for parallel and distributed computing* (pp. 1733-1752).

Open Grid Forum (n.d.). Retrieved April 5, 2007, from http://www.ogf.org

Quocirca (2005), Retrieved October 2007, from http://www.quocirca.com/report_gridindex2.htm

Satyam Computer Services Limited. (2004). Media Room, Archives: 2004. Retrieved June 10, 2007, from http://www.satyam.com/mediaroom/pr5dec04.html

Selvi, S.T., Buyya, R., Rajagopalan, M. R.,Vijayakumar, K., & Deepak, G.N. (2007). Multilingual interface for Grid market directory services: An experience with supporting Tamil. Retrieved from, http://www.gridbus.org/reports/gmd-tamil.pdf

SETI@Home (n.d.). Retrieved April 5, 2007, from http://setiathome.ssl.berkeley.edu

Venkateswara R. M., Srinivas V., Gopinath T., & Janakiram D. (2006). Vishwa: A reconfigurable P2P middleware for Grid computations. In *Proceedings of International Conference on Parallel Processing (ICPP'06)* (pp. 381-390).

KEY TERMS AND DEFINITIONS

CPU-Scavenging/Cycle-Scavenging: A technique that makes use of instruction cycles on desktop computers that would otherwise be wasted at night,during lunch, or even in the scattered seconds throughout the day when the computer is waiting for user input or slow devices.

Distributed Computing: A computer processing method in which different parts of a program run simultaneously on two or more computers communicating with each other over a network.

Grid Computing: A type of computing which relies on complete computers connected by a conventional network interface, to allow organizations to provision and scale resources as needs arise, thereby preventing the underutilization of resources (computers, networks, data archives, instruments).

High Performance Computing (HPC): HPC refers to the use of supercomputers and computer clusters, that is, computing systems(in or above the teraflop-region) comprised of multiple processors linked together in a single system with commercially available interconnects.

High-Performance Technical Computing (HPTC): It refers to the engineering applications of cluster-based computing (such as computational fluid dynamics and the building and testing of virtual prototypes).

Metacomputing: A particular type of distributed computing which involved linking up supercomputer centers with what was, at the time, high speed networks.

Middleware: It is the software that manages activity on the Grid like enabling the user to access computers distributed over the network and organizing/integrating the disparate computational resources of the Grid into a coherent whole. The middleware is conceptually in between the two types of software (operating systems and applications software).

Virtual Organizations: Virtual Organization is a group of individuals or institutions who share the computing resources of a "grid" for a common goal.

Virtual Private Network (VPN): VPN is a private communications network often used by companies or organizations to communicate confidentially over a public network.

Chapter XXX
Dynamic Maintenance
in ChinaGrid Support Platform

Hai Jin
Huazhong University of Science and Technology, China

Li Qi
Huazhong University of Science and Technology, China

Jie Dai
Huazhong University of Science and Technology, China

Yaqin Luo
Huazhong University of Science and Technology, China

ABSTRACT

A grid system is usually composed of thousands of nodes which are broadly distributed in different virtual organizations. Owing to geographical boundaries among these organizations, the system administrators suffer a great pressure to coordinate when grid system experiences a maintaining period. Furthermore, the runtime dynamicity of service state aggravates the complexity of tasks. Consequently, building an efficient and reliable maintaining model becomes an urgent challenge to ensure the correctness and consistency of grid nodes. In our experiment with ChinaGrid, a dynamic maintenance mechanism has been adopted in the fundamental grid middleware called ChinaGrid Support Platform. By resolving the above problems with system infrastructure, service dependency and service consistency, the availability of the system can be improved even the scope of maintenance extends to wider region.

INTRODUCTION

Dynamic maintenance for large-scale resources in grid environment is a big challenge owing to complexity of grid services and exigent requirement of grid users. Inappropriate processes of maintenance lead to unpredictable failures in wide area. Due to geographical distribution of computing and data resources in different administrative regions, a reliable maintenance mechanism is urgently necessary to coordinate different hosts and ensure the efficiency of maintenance task.

For the administrators of grids, the maintaining task is running through the whole lifecycle of service components. As shown in Figure 1, Jin and Qi (2007) defined that each service component in grid has the lifecycle of: released, deployed, initialed, activated, and destroyed. Responding to these stages, the maintaining tasks include *publish*, *deploy*, *undeploy*, *redeploy*, *configure*, *activate*, and *deactivate*. Especially, these tasks should face the distributed challenges in grid environment.

A number of earlier investigations have addressed providing and standardizing maintenance for distributed resources. The Configuration, Description, Deployment and Lifecycle Management (CDDLM), proposed by Open Grid Forum (2006), is to standardize distributed software deployment and configuration in a validated lifecycle. Another specification of deployment infrastructure, the Installable Unit Deployment Descriptor (IUDD) released by W3C (2004), also provides a solution of supporting dynamic maintenance in run-time execution environment. Web Services Distributed Management (2006), proposed by Organization for the Advancement of Structured Information Standards (OASIS), discusses how management of any resource can be accessed via web services protocols and management of the web services resources via the former. Talwar and Milojicic (2005) discussed the approaches for service deployment, and defined Quality of Manageability to measure the quality and efficiency of maintenance for service components.

Today's domain consumers demand the maintenances without shutting down the system, but the existing specifications and solutions can not efficiently reduce the downtime due to maintenance. Therefore, the performance and availability of grid services during maintenance need further attention when focusing on the maintenance of resources.

As the improvement from infrastructure, researchers believe the feature of dynamic deployment in grid container can achieve higher availability. Weissman (2005) proposed an architecture basing on Apache Tomcat's dynamic deployment functionality which allows service renovating and reconfiguring without taking down the whole

Figure 1. Lifecycle of service component

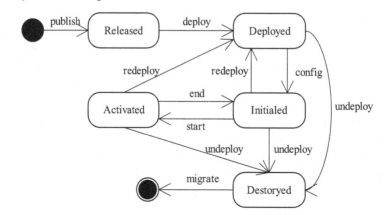

site. Smith and Friese (2005) also introduced a similar solution to support dynamic deployment. Liu and Lewis (2005) designed an intermediate language X# to support the dynamic deployment among heterogeneous implementations of grid container.

Above the infrastructure, the maintaining logics focus on the consistency and complexity of grids. Shankar and Talwar (2006) invented a specification-enhanced ECA model, called Event-Condition-Precondition-Action-Postcondition (ECPAP), for designing adaptation maintaining rules. The policy-based solution can adapt some specific emergencies (e.g. file transferring mistake, maintaining failure, etc.) in grid.

Naturally the efficiency of dynamic maintenance will help achieving high hardware utilization and resource sharing. It demands a suitable mechanism which promises high availability, flexibility, incrementally scalable low cost components, and administrative overhead reducing. Therefore, the capability of dynamic maintenance for service components becomes one of essential attributes for grid middleware.

BACKGROUND AND OVERVIEW

ChinaGrid

ChinaGrid (Jin, 2004), funded by Ministry of Education in China, is an open scientific discovery infrastructure combining 12 top universities in China to create an integrated, persistent computational resource.

Connected by high-performance China Education and Research Network (CERNET), ChinaGrid integrates high-performance computers, data resources and tools, and high-end experimental facilities altogether. Currently, ChinaGrid provides more than 20 teraflops of computing power and over 200 terabytes of online and archival data storage capacity. Researchers can freely access these resources from the member universities.

With this combination of resources, ChinaGrid is the most comprehensive distributed infrastructure for open scientific research in China.

ChinaGrid Support Platform

ChinaGrid Support Platform (CGSP, 2005) is the fundamental platform for ChinaGrid. Without sacrificing local autonomy, CGSP brings people sharing their computational capability, storage capacity and other tools online across corporate virtual organization with geographic boundaries. CGSP includes system services and developing libraries for resource identification, discovery, dynamic management, workflow design, and virtual data management. By using CGSP package, domain developers and experts can easily deploy, share, and run their applications in ChinaGrid.

Based on the common CGSP, ChinaGrid drives five concrete application grids: bioinformatics grid, computational fluid dynamics grid, image processing grid, course online grid, and massive data processing grid. These grids provide powerful utilities and service components for the domain experts of different fields.

Dynamic Maintenance in ChinaGrid Support Platform

To manage thousands of resources and services distributed in ChinaGrid efficiently, the dynamic maintenance becomes an indispensable functional module of CGSP. Despite the specifications and implementations mentioned in section 1 defined the interfaces and maintaining actions formally, they ignored the runtime complexity brought by high distribution, service dependency, and consistency of maintenance tasks. The main objective of CGSP is to promise high availability to consumers during the maintenance, and to ensure the consistency of maintenance tasks. Hence CGSP employs a model-based propagating, dependency-aware, and asynchronous architecture to resolve the challenges from (i) *service dynamicity*, (ii)

Figure 2. Two layers architecture of dynamic maintenance in CGSP

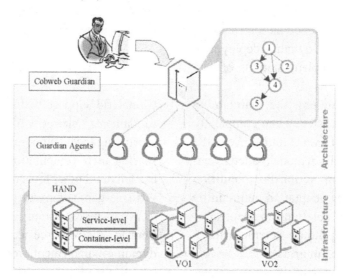

service dependency complexity, and (iii) *maintenance consistency*.

To achieve these objectives, dynamic maintenance is layered into two parts in CGSP as depicted in Figure 2. (i) The infrastructure part is installed on each resource distributed in different virtual organizations, called Highly Available Dynamic Deployment Infrastructure (HAND). It is response for the dynamicity of runtime and promises the availability during the maintenance. (ii) In the higher architecture part, Guardian Agents provide provisioning services and distributed management services. These agents promise the integrity and consistency of maintenance. As a coordinator, Cobweb Guardian is the user interface that is in charge of accepting maintaining requests, analyzing dependencies, and decoupling tasks from administrator or other provisioning modules into atomic maintenances.

MAIN FOCUS

With the evolution of grid system, the demands to dynamic maintenance are increasingly critical. Integration and dynamicity of grid service effectively explore the performance scalability but also pose great stress on service availability problem. Widely addressed by Chu (2005), service availability is the foremost issue to evaluate system performance. One typical way to measure service availability is by calculating system functioning time during a watching period. MTBF (mean time between failures) and MTTR (mean time to recovery) are those metrics which need a long time to observe. Researchers believe that better solution of maintenance requires less time to maintain and greater proportion of system available time. Meanwhile, the correctness of maintenance should not be ignored.

Motivated by need of proving high availability and correctness during the maintenance, a dynamic maintenance mechanism is proposed in CGSP which support dynamic features of service updates in three aspects: service dynamicity, service dependency complexity, and maintenance consistency.

Service Dynamicity

Service upgrade and reconfiguration bring dynamicity to grid system. While a new version of service is preparing for install, or system is migrating to another host environment, the dynamicity will cause the performance degradation. An approach is to implement dynamic maintenance infrastructure which better handle service quality problem caused by dynamicity. Although Weissman (2005) proposed a solution, it provides poor performance since its implementation is totally based on Tomcat's container-level deployment capability.

Dealing with service dynamicity, a smaller scope deployment solution is the primary improvement of HAND infrastructure imported in CGSP. A smaller granularity of deployment denotes that deactivation and reactivation of single service will not affect other services. Consequently, the reloading time can be highly reduced and predictable as a majority of services remain functional during maintenance. Shorter maintenance time is beneficial for enhancement of system availability.

This infrastructure can dynamically reflect the changes of services by reconfiguring at run time. In particular, the reconfiguration, redeployment and undeployment of specific service will not cause the invalidation of other systematic functions. HAND guarantees the efficiency of maintenance and availability of services to grid users simultaneously.

Service-level deployment and container-level deployment are two approaches in HAND:

- Service-level deployment, in which administrators deactivate one or more existing services, install new services, and reactivate those services without reloading the whole container.
- Container-level deployment, in which the installation of new service involves reloading (reinitializing and reconfiguring) the whole container.

A container-level deployment can save time for large scale maintenance. However, service-level deployment will guarantee the efficiency of maintenance, especially when unique grid service maintenance is required. According to the particular demands, HAND can adopt adaptive level to achieve shortest maintaining time.

Service Dependency Complexity

Service dependency is ubiquitous in large-scale grid services. It means that a correct execution of selected service is depending on host environment, the dependent service and deployment of prerequisite component. Accordingly, dependency is classified into three categories: invocation dependency, deployment dependency, and environment dependency. Invocation dependency always happens in composite services which depend on additional service functionality. Deployment dependency denotes that the prerequisite software or service needs to be fixed before installation of dependent component. Environment dependency means that the maintenance of selected service could affect the availability of other service in a same container.

Intricate dependency relations among service components also aggravate the complexity of service maintenance. Incremental service evolvement brings further partition, replication and aggregation of related service components. Several grid services present its functions by combination of dependent services in multiple remote sites' containers. This trend requires highly dynamic deployment mechanism to detect the unavailability of depended service. Therefore, propagating any maintenance of service component is obligatory so that dependent services continue to function correctly. As an attempt of higher availability during service updates, a special mechanism, called Cobweb Guardian system is introduced grounding on special consideration of dependencies. Working over HAND infrastructure, it is considered as a significant part of dynamic deployment mechanism.

Cobweb Guardian system is a two-tier model which is composed of one Cobweb Guardian controller (CG) and multiple Guardian Agents (GA).

To execute the actual maintenance, CG communicates with GAs and delivers them maintenance instructions as depicted in Figure 2. Authorization center, Session Control, Dependency Optimizer, and Policy controller are four main modules of CG. Since illegal users may deploy harmful service which may cause potential danger, the responsibility of Authorization module is to prove the validity of maintenance requests. The progress of the maintenance is controlled by Session Control module. After confirming the critical path from Dependency Optimizer module, it propagates the maintenance tasks to target Guardian Agent. The Policy controller module is designed to execute on-demand maintenance. Dependency Optimizer module is the key component of CG. The input parameter of Dependency Optimizer module is provided by maintenance administrator. Matching it with dynamic building dependency map, a critical deploy path can be automatically generated from established optimal strategies. Building over HAND infrastructure, CG can support both container-level and service-level maintenance.

Comparing with CG, GA also consists of four parts: the Notification module, the Validation module, the Maintenance Interface and the Axis handler. The Notification module reports the maintenance states to all depending services since the latter ones should inform their unavailable states to public before complete execution of maintenance. Meanwhile, system administrators can detect maintenance failure instantly with this module and propagate it to relative GA. The Validation module of GA is responsible of checking maintenance actions of corresponded notifications. The actual execution of service deploying, redeploying and upgrading is supported by Maintenance Interface which accepts the requests from Session Control module. Invocation dependency capturing function is implemented using Axis handler which records different dependencies into service dependency map.

The two-tier and loosely coupled architecture promises the correctness when maintaining the composite services with highly complicated dependencies. Further more, it achieves high availability in runtime by optimizing the maintenance according to dependency type.

Service Consistency

When the resources and services scale grows, the consistency problem becomes further crucial. Currently, the maintenances propagating to heterogeneous resources always need waiting for all the correct ends of replica instructions. The synchronous approach brings unnecessary cost during maintenance. As a simple example, if a maintaining operation (e.g. deploying a replica service for one of storage nodes) is failed due to network congestion, naturally the later operation (e.g. patching the replica service) will be failed. Similarly, if the later maintenance instruction (i.e. patching work) is arrived earlier than the former (i.e. deploying work) in a computational node due to the networking latency, the whole procedure of maintenance will also abort. Meanwhile the maintaining time will be prolonged because of these emergencies.

CGSP introduces an asynchronous model to resolve the consistency challenge. A maintaining stack for each resource is initialized first in the internal of CG. When a maintaining task is delivered to virtual maintainer, CG finds out the possible implicational atomic maintenances due to dependencies. And then, the task is decoupled into multiple atomic maintenances and pushed into the maintaining stack of related resources respectively. However, the real maintenance will not launch immediately. These maintenances should be started asynchronously when the related services are requested. Namely, these atomic maintenances are triggered on-demand.

The on-demand trigger events are delivered by HAND deployed on target resources. Actually, when the ordinary requests arrive, the HAND service will assess the local maintaining states of requested service. After comparing it with the state stored in remote CG, HAND decides whether the maintenance is triggered physically. If necessary, HAND requests a GA to finish the whole maintenance work.

This asynchronous model can promise the maintenances for different resources finishing successfully on demand. Especially, it brings better benefits in the resources with high computing capability and bandwidth (i.e. the maintenance for them will be finished in shorter time.). Furthermore, this approach tolerates a great deal of unpredictable failures (e.g. temporal offline and maintenance failures). Naturally, the availability of global system is enhanced.

FUTURE TRENDS

The dynamic provisioning and maintenance are increasingly being concerned by major grid middleware. In particular, the demands of automatic management and self-healing, self-organization will motivate the dynamic maintenance to wider applicable areas. For instance, the ideas from sensor network and peer to peer computing technique can benefit dynamic maintenance much on real time states collecting and network bandwidth bottleneck. As another point, the multiple agents and neural network techniques from artificial intelligence community help grid to manage its service components and resources smartly and prevent various predictable failures efficiently.

CONCLUSION

Building dynamic maintenance mechanism with ever-increasing demands on service availability is a great challenge. The design and implementation of dynamic maintenance mechanism in CGSP investigates the problem from three principal aspects of dynamicity, complexity and consistency demands of maintenance task. By providing different maintenance granularity, HAND infrastructure in

this mechanism can substantially reduce service upgrading time. In terms of complexity brought by service dependency, Cobweb Guardian guarantees the correctness and efficiency of maintenance task. It supports recognition of dependency type and executes maintenance task abiding by auto-generated optimal solution. Finally, the proposed mechanism adopts an asynchronous maintenance architecture which provides multilevel replication consistency with performance scalability and fault-tolerance support. Comparing with previous proposed mechanism, dynamic maintenance mechanism in CGSP behaves more smoothly to system maintenance failures, and provides an efficient solution for system availability during maintenance.

REFERENCES

ChinaGrid Support Platform Project (2005). http://www.chinagrid.edu.cn/cgsp/

Chu, L., Shen, K., Tang, H. et al (2005). Dependency isolation for thread-based multi-tier Internet services. *Proceedings of InfoCom'05* (pp. 796-806).

Foster, I. (2003). The Grid: A new infrastructure for 21st century science. In F. Berman, G.C. Fox, & A.J.G. Hey (Eds.), *Grid Computing* (pp. 65-100). New York: Wiley.

Jin, H. (2004). ChinaGrid: Making Grid computing a reality. *Digital Libraries: International collaboration and cross-fertilization* (LNCS 3334, pp. 13-24).

Liu, P., & Lewis, M.J. (2005). Mobile code enabled Web services. In *Proceedings of ICWS'05*, (pp. 167-174).

Open Grid Forum (2006). The configuration, description, deployment and lifecycle management version 1.0. Retrieved from, http://www.ogf.org/documents/GFD.85.pdf

Organization for the advancement of structured information standards (2006). Web services distributed management: management of Web services, version 1.1. Retrieved from, http://docs.oasis-open.org/wsdm/wsdm-mows-1.1-spec-os-01.htm

Qi, L., Jin, H., & Foster, I. et al (2007). HAND: Highly Available Dynamic Deployment Infrastructure for Globus Toolkit 4. In *Proceedings of PDP'07* (pp. 155-162).

Shankar, C., Talwar, V., Iyer, S. et al (2006). Specification-enhanced policies for automated management of changes in it systems. In *Proceedings of LISA'06* (pp. 103-118).

Smith, M., Friese, T., & Freisleben, B. (2005). Intra-engine service security for grids based on WSRF. In *Proceedings of CCGrid'05* (pp. 644-653).

Talwar, V., Milojicic, D., Wu, Q. et al (2005). Approaches for service deployment. *IEEE Internet Computing, 9*(2), 70-80.

Weissman, J., Kim, S., & England, D. (2005). A framework for dynamic service adaptation in the grid: Next generation software program progress report. In *Proceedings of IPDPS'05.*

World Wide Web Consortium (2004). Installable Unit Deployment Descriptor Specification Version 1.0. Retrieved from, http://www.w3.org/Submission/InstallableUnit-DD/

Qi, L., Jin, H., Luo, Y. et al (2007). Service dependency model for dynamic and stateful grid services. In *Proceedings of ICA3PP'07* (pp. 278-289).

Wu, Y., Wu, S., Yu, H. et al (2005). CGSP: An extensible and reconfigurable Grid framework. In *Proceedings of APPT'05* (pp. 292-300).

KEY TERMS AND DEFINITIONS

Availability of Maintenance: The proportion of time a system is in a functioning condition in the watching period. More specifically, the availability during the maintenance is the ratio of system's available time to the longest maintaining time (i.e., watching period).

Consistency of Maintenance: Due to the complexity of grid system, the maintenance to particular services always is propagated to many replications. Consistency is a measure to promise the maintenance can be finished in valid period or the correct order.

Dynamic Deployment: It denotes the ability for remote clients to request the upload and deployment of new services into, or the undeployment of existing services from, existing grid containers. It is a special case of dynamic maintenance.

Dynamic Maintenance: Dynamic maintenance includes the operations (e.g., deploy, undeploy, and so forth) to large scale service components in the runtime. The dynamicity of maintenance means that the maintenance will not affect the execution of existing components and promise the downtime as less as possible. Normally the maintaining requests are delivered by the administrators and provisioning modules.

Grid Container: It hosts web or grid services and executes user requests issued by clients that invoke operations defined by those services.

Quality of Manageability: It is a measure of the ability to manage a system component. QoM measures include number of lines of configuration code (LOC) for deployment, number of steps involved in deployment, LOC to express configuration changes, and time to develop, deploy, and make a change.

Service Dependency: The correct execution of a service component is always depending on the hosting environment, the dependent calling services, and the dependent deployment service respectively.

Service-/Container-/Global-level of Maintenance: The maintenance of any new service components involves reloading (reinitializing and reconfiguring) the service (or container or whole grid respectively).

Compilation of References

Abdelkader, K., Broeckhove J., & Vanmechelen, K. (2008). Commodity resource pricing in dynamic computational grids. In *Proceedings of the ACS/IEEE International Conference on Computer Systems and Applications (AICCSA '2008)*, IEEE Computer Society.

Abramson, D., Buyya R., & Giddy, J. (2000). *Economy driven resource management architecture for computational power grids*. Paper presented at the International Conference on Parallel and Distributed Processing Techniques and Applications (PDPTA'2000), Las Vegas, USA.

Abramson, D., Buyya, R., & Giddy, J. (2002). A computational economy for Grid computing and its implementation in the Nimrod-G resource broker. *Future Generation Computer Systems, 18*(8), 1061-1074.

Abramson, D., Lewis, A., Peachey, T., & Fletcher, C. (2001). An automatic design optimization tool and its application to computational fluid dynamics. In *Proceedings of the 2001 ACM/IEEE conference on supercomputing* (pp. 25–25).

Adams, J. R., & Price, C. C. (2004). Boltzmann algorithms to partition and map software for computational grids. In *Proceedings of the 18th International Parallel and Distributed Processing Symposium, High Performance Grid Computing Workshop*.

Adams, S. B. (2006). Stanford and Silicon Valley: Lessons on becoming a high-tech region. *California Management Review, 48*(1), 29-51.

Afgan, E., & Bangalore, P. (2007). Application specification language (ASL) – A language for describing applications in grid computing. *The 4th International Conference on Grid Services Engineering and Management - GSEM 2007*, Leipzig, Germany (LNCS, pp. 24-38).

Afgan, E., & Bangalore, P. (2007). Performance characterization of BLAST for the grid. In *Proceedings of the IEEE 7th International Symposium on Bioinformatics & Bioengineering (IEEE BIBE 2007)* (pp. 1394-1398). Boston, MA: IEEE.

Afgan, E., & Bangalore, P. (2008). Experiences with developing and deploying dynamic BLAST. In *Proceedings of the 15th ACM Mardi Gras conference, Workshop on Grid-Enabling Applications* (pp. 38). Baton Rouge, LA: ACM.

Afgan, E., Sathyanarayana, P., & Bangalore, P. (2006). Dynamic task distribution in the grid for BLAST. *Granular computing 2006* (pp. 554-557). Atlanta, GA: IEEE.

Agostinelli, S. (2003). GEANT4—A simulation toolkit. *Nuclear Instruments and Methods in Physics Research A, 506*, 250-303.

Aiftimiei, C., Andreozzi, S., Cuscela, G., Donvito, G., Dudhalkar, V., Fantinel, S. et al. (2007). Recent evolutions of GridICE: A monitoring tool for Grid systems. In *Proceedings of the 2007 Workshop on Grid Monitoring* (pp. 1-8), Monterey, California, USA.

Ainsworth, J., Newhouse, S., & MacLaren, J. (2006). *Resource usage service (RUS) based on WS-I Basic Profile 1.0* (draft-ggf-wsi-rus-17). Global/Open Grid Forum. Retrieved August 30, 2007, from http://forge.ogf.org/sf/go/doc7965?nav=1

Al-Ali, J., Hafid, A., Rana, F., & Walker, W. (2003). QoS adaptation in service oriented grids. In *Proceedings of the 1st International Workshop on Middleware for Grid Computing (MGC 2003),* Brazil. Retrieved from, http://mgc2003.lncc.br/cam_ready/MGC289_final.pdf

Albrand, S., & Fulachier, J. (2004). ATLAS metadata interfaces (AMI) and ATLAS metadata catalogs. *Computing in high energy and nuclear physics (CHEP 2004),* Interlaken, Switzerland.

Alert, J. & Jiménez J. (2004). Tendencias del tratamiento radiante en los tumores del sistema nervioso central. *Rev Cubana Med,* 43, 2-3.

Alfieri, R., Cecchini, R., Fiaschini, V., Dell'Agnello, L., Frohner, A., Gianoli, A., etl al. (2003). VOMS, an Authorization System for Virtual Organizations. In *Proceedings of the 1st European Across Grids Conference* (pp. 33-40).

Ali, A. (2006). *From Grid middleware to a Grid operating system.* Paper presented at the 5th International Conference on Grid and Cooperative Computing, Oct 21-24, 2006, Changhsa, China.

Aloisio, G., Cafaro, M., Fiore, S., & Mirto, M. (2005). The grid relational catalog project. In L. Grandinetti (Ed.), *Advances in parallel computing, "Grid computing: The new frontiers of high performance computing"* (pp. 129-155). Elsevier.

Altekar, G., Dwarkadas S., Huelsenbeck J.P. & Ronquist F. (2004). Parallel metropolis coupled Markov chain Monte Carlo for Bayesian phylogenetic inference. *Bioinformatics,* 20, 407-415.

Altmann, J., Courcoubetis, C., Darlington, J., & Cohen, J., (2007). GridEcon – The economic-enhanced next-generation Internet. In J. Altmann, & D.J. Veit (Eds.), In *Proceedings of the 4th International Workshop on Grid Economics and Business Models,* Lecture Notes in Computer Science (LNCS 4685, pp. 188-193). Heidelberg: Springer-Verlag.

Altschul, S.F. (1997). Gapped BLAST and PSI-BLAST: a new generation of protein database search programs. *Nucl. Acids Res, 25,* 3389-3402.

Amazon. (2008). *Amazon elastic compute cloud* (Amazon EC2). Retrieved February 18, 2008, from http://www.amazon.com/gp/browse.html?node=201590011

Amigoni, F., Fugini, M.G., & Liberati, D. (2007) Design and execution of distributed experiments. In *Proceedings of the 9th International Conference on Enterprise Information Systems, (ICEIS'07),* Madeira, June.

Anderson, D. P. (2004). BOINC: A system for public-resource computing and storage. *Fifth IEEE/ACM International Workshop on Grid Computing.*

Anderson, D. P., Cobb, J., Korpela, E., Lebofsky, M., & Werthimer, D. (2002). Seti@home: An experiment in public-resource computing. *Communications of the ACM, 45*(11).

Andronico, G., Ardizzone, V., Barbera, R., Catania, R., Carrieri, A., Falzone, A., et al. (2005). In *TRIDENTCOM 2005. GILDA: The Grid INFN Virtual Laboratory for Dissemination Activities.* (pp. 304-305).

Andrzejak, A., Graupner, S., Kotov, V., & Trinks, H. (2002). *Algorithms for self-organization and adaptive service placement in dynamic distributed systems* (Tech. Rep. No. HPL-2002-259). Palo Alto: HP Laboratories.

Anjomshoaa, A., Brisard, F., Drescher, M., Fellows, D., Ly, A., McGough, S., et al. (2005). *Job submission description language (JSDL) specification, Version 1.0* (Tech. Rep. No. GFD-R.056). Global Grid Forum (GGF).

Antonioletti, M., Atkinson, M. P., Baxter, R., Borley, A., Chue Hong, N. P., Collins, B., et al. (2005). The design and implementation of grid database services in OGSA-DAI. *Concurrency and Computation: Practice and Experience, 17*(2-4), 357-376.

Antonioletti, M., Krause, A., Paton, N. W., Eisenberg, A., Laws, S., Malaika, S., et al. (2006). The WS-DAI family of specifications for web service data access and integration. *ACM SIGMOD Record, 35*(1), 48-55.

Aparicio, G. (2006). Blast2GO goes Grid: Developing a Grid-enabled prototype for functional genomics analysis. *Studies in Health Technology and Informatics, 120,* 194-204.

Aparicio, G., Blanquer I., Hernández V. & Segrelles D. (2007). BLAST in Grid (BiG): A Grid-enabled software architecture and implementation of parallel and sequential BLAST. In J. Casado, R. Mayo, & R. Muñoz (Eds.), *Proceedings of the Spanish Conference on e-Science Grid Computing* (pp. 11-22). Madrid: CIEMAT Press.

Apparao, A. (2006). *Characterization of network processing overheads in Xen.* Paper presented at the First International Workshop on Virtualization Technology in Distributed Computing, 17 Nov 2006, Tampa, USA.

Arce, P., & Rato, P. (2006). GAMOS: A user-friendly and flexible framework for medical applications. *GEANT4 Collaboration Workshop and Users Conference,* LIP, Lisbon, Portugal.

Arce, P., & Rato, P. (2007). GAMOS status and plans. *12th GEANT4 Collaboration Workshop and Users Conference*, Hebden Bridge, United Kingdom.

Assunção, M. D. d., Buyya, R., & Venugopal, S. (in press). InterGrid: a case for internetworking islands of Grids. *Concurrency and computation: practice and experience.*

Assuncao, M., & Buyya, R. (2005). A case for the world wide Grid: Interlinking islands of Grids to create an evolvable global cyberinfrastructure. *Technical Report, 43(3).*

Athanasopoulos, G., Tsalgatidou, A., & Pantazoglou, M. (2006). Interoperability among heterogeneous Services. In *Proceedings of the IEEE International Conference on Services Computing* (pp.174-181).

Atkinson, M., Roure, D., Dunlop, A., Fox, G., Henderson, P., Hey, A. J. G., Paton, N. W., Newhouse, S., Parastatidis, S., Trefethen, A. E., Watson, P., & Webber, J. (2005). Web service grids: an evolutionary approach. Concurrency - Practice and Experience, 17(2-4), 377-389.

Attiya, G., & Hamam, Y. (2004). Two phase algorithm for load balancing in heterogeneous distributed systems. *12th Euromicro Conference on Parallel, Distributed and Network-Based Processing* (pp. 434-439).

Aubanel, E., & Wu, X. (2007). Incorporating latency in heterogeneous graph partitioning. In *Proceedings of the 21st Intl. Parallel and Distributed Processing Symposium, Workshop on Parallel and Distributed Scientific and Engineering Computing (PDSEC).*

AuYoung, A., Chun, B.N., Snoeren, A.C., & Vahdat, A. (2004). Resource allocation in federated distributed computing infrastructures. In *Proceedings of the 1st Workshop on Operating System and Architectural Support for the On-demand IT Infrastructure*

Babaoğlu, Ö., Meling, H., & Montresor, A. (2003). Anthill: A framework for the development of agent-based peer-to-peer systems. In *Proceedings of the 22nd International Conference on Distributed Computing Systems* (ICDCS'02), Vienna, Austria.

Babiloni, F., Carducci, F., Cerutti, S., Liberati, D., Rossini, P., Urbano, A., et al. (2000). *Comparison between human and ANN detection of laplacian-derived electroencephalographic activity related to unilateral voluntary movements. Comput Biomed Res, 33,* 59-74.

Baker M., Buyya R. & Laforenza D. (2000). The Grid: International efforts in global computing In *Proceedings of the International Conference on Advances in Infrastructure for Electronic Business, Science, and Education on the Internet.* Aquila, Rome, Italy.

Baker, M., Apon, A., Ferner, C., & Brown, J. (2005). Emerging grid standards. *Computer, 38*(4), 43-50.

Banerjee, S., Basu, S., Garg, S., Garg, S., Lee, S.J., Mullan P., et al. (2005). Scalable Grid service discovery based on UDDI. In P. Henderson (Ed.), *Proceedings of the 3rd Int. Workshop on Middleware for Grid Computing* (pp. 1-6). Grenoble, France: ACM Press.

Baraldi, P., Manginelli, A.A., Maieron, M., Liberati, D., Porro, C.A. (2007). *An ARX model-based approach to trial by trial identification of fMRI-BOLD responsens. NeuroImage, 37,* 189-201.

Barbera, R., Ardizzone, V., & Ciuffo, L. N. (2007). *Grid training and dissemination facilities: The GILDA experience.* Paper presented at IST-Africa Conference, Maputo, Mozambique.

Barbera, R., Falzone A., & Rodolico A. (2003). *The GENIUS Grid Portal.* Paper presented at Conference for

Computing in High Energy and Nuclear Physics (CHEP 2003), La Jolla, California, USA.

Barham, P. (2003). Xen and the art of virtualization. In *Proceedings of the Nineteenth ACM Symposium on Operating Systems Principles*, October 19-22, 2003, Bolton Landing, USA.

Barmouta, A., & Buyya, R. (2003, April). GridBank: A Grid accounting service architecture (GASA) for distributed systems sharing and integration. In *Proceedings of the 17th Annual International Parallel and Distributed Processing Symposium* (pp. 245-252), Nice, France.

Bartholomew, D. (2006, May). QEMU: A multihost, multitarget emulator. *Linux J.*

Baud, J.P, Casey, J., Lemaitre, S., Nicholson, C., Smith, D., Stewart, G. (2005). *LCG Data Management: from EDG to EGEE*. GLAS-PPE/2005-06.

Baud, J.P., & Lemaitre, S. (2005). *The LHC File Catalogue (LFC),* HEPIX 2005, Karlsruhe, Germany.

Baudron, O., & Stern, J. (2001). *Non-interactive private auctions*. Paper presented at the 5th International Financial Cryptography Conference, Grand Cayman, BWI, 19-22.

Bebee, B., & Thompson, B. (2004). Extending rich semantics in an architecture for data sharing and collaboration for counter terrorism. In *IEEE Aerospace Conference Proceedings*. IEEE.

Beckman, P.H. (2005). Building the TeraGrid. *Philosophical transactions of the royal society A*, 363, 1715-1728.

BEgrid (2007). *The Belgian Grid for research*. Deployed through the Belgian federal and state government initiatives. Retrieved from, http://www.begrid.be

Belle (2007). *Belle home page*. Retrieved Feb. 2007, from http://belle.kek.jp/

Bent, J. (2005). *Data-driven batch scheduling*. Ph.D. Dissertation, University of Wisconsin-Madison.

Bent, J., Thain, D., Arpaci-Dusseau, A., & Arpaci-Dusseau, R. (2004, March). Explicit control in a batch-aware distributed file system. In *Proceedings of the First USENIX/ACM Conference on Networked Systems Design and Implementation.*

Berman F., Wolski R., Casanova H., & Cirne W. (2003). Adaptive computing on the grid using AppLeS. *IEEE Transactions on Parallel and Distributed Systems, 14*(4) 369-382.

Berman, F. (1998). High-performance schedulers. In I. Foster & C. Kesselman (Eds.), *The grid: blueprint for a new computing infrastructure* (pp. 279-309). San Francisco, CA: Morgan Kaufmann Publishers, Inc.

Berman, F., Fox, G. & Hey, T. (2003). The grid: past, present, future. In F. Berman, G.C. Fox, & A.J.G. Hey (Eds.), *Grid computing* (pp. 51-63). New York: Wiley.

Berman, F., Hey, A., & Fox, G. (Eds.). (2003). *Grid computing: Making the global infrastructure a reality*. New York: John Wiley & Sons.

Bic, L., & Shaw, A. C. (1974). The organization of computer systems. In *The logical design of operating systems*. Prentice Hall.

Bird, I., Bos, K., Brook, N., Duellmann, D., Eck, C., Fisk, I., et al. (2005). *LHC Computing Grid*. Retrieved June 20, 2005, from http://lcg.web.cern.ch/LCG/tdr/LCG_TDR_v1_04.pdf

Birkin, M. & Clarke, G. (1998). GIS, geodemographics, and spatial modeling in the U.K. Financial Service Industry. *Journal of Housing Research*, 9(1), 87-111.

Booth, D., Haas, H., McCabe, F., Newcomer, E., Champion, M., Ferris, C., & Orchard, D. (2003). *Web services architecture, W3C working draft 8 August 2003*. Retrieved December 4th, 2007, from http://www.w3.org/TR/2003/WD-ws-arch-20030808/.

Borgatti, S., P., & Foster, P., C. (2003). The network paradigm in organizational research. *Journal of Management, 29*(6), 991-1031.

Boris, J. (2002). The threat of chemical and biological terrorism: Roles for HPC in preparing a response. In *Computing in science and engineering-HPC and national security*. IEEE

Bose, A., Wickman, B., & Wood, C. (2004). *MARS: A metascheduler for distributed resources in campus grids* (pp. 110-118).

Bosin, A., Dessì, N., Fugini, M.G., Liberati, D., & Pes, B. (2006a). Applying enterprise models to design cooperative scientific environments (LNCS 3812, pp. 281-292). Springer-Verlag.

Bosin, A., Dessì, N., Fugini, M.G., Liberati, D., & Pes, B. (2007a). *The future of portals in e-science.* In A. Tatnall (Ed.), *Encyclopedia of portal technology and applications* (pp. 413-418). Hershey, PA: IGI Global.

Bosin, A., Dessì, N., Fugini, M.G., Liberati, D., & Pes, B. (2008). Setting the framework of collaboration for E-science. In N. Kock (Ed.), *Encyclopedia of E-Collaboration* (pp. 82-88). Hershey, PA: IGI Global.

Bosin, A., Dessì, N., Fugini, M.G., Liberati, D., & Pes, B. (2008). ALBA cooperative environment for scientific experiments. In M. Freire & M. Pereira (Eds.), *Encyclopedia of Internet technologies and applications* (pp. 52-58). Hershey, PA: IGI Global.

Bosin, A., Dessì, N., Fugini, M.G., Liberati, D., & Pes, B. (2008). Virtual enterprise environments for scientific experiments. In G. Putnik & M. Cunha (Eds.), Encyclopedia *of networked and virtual organizations.* Hershey, PA: IGI Global.

Bosin, A., Dessì, N., Fugini, M.G., Liberati, D., Pes, B. (2007). ALBA architecture as a proposal for OSS collaborative science. In K. St.Amant & B. Still (Eds.), *Handbook of research on open source software* (pp. 68-78). Hershey, PA: IGI Global.

Bosin, A., Dessì, N., Liberati, D., & Pes, B. (2006). Learning Bayesian classifiers from gene-expression MicroArray data. *Lecture Notes in Artificial Intelligence, 3849,* 297-304.

Botadra, H., Cheng, Q., Prasad, S.K., Aubanel, E., & V. Bhavsar, V. (2007). iC2mpi: A platform for parallel execution of graph-structured iterative computations. In *Proceedings of the 21st Intl. Parallel and Distributed Processing Symposium, Workshop on Parallel and Dis-* tributed Scientific and Engineering Computing (PDSEC). March 2007, Long Beach California.

Brandt, F. (2006). How to obtain full privacy in auctions. *International Journal of Information Security, 5*(4), 201-261.

Bredin, J., Maheswaran, R.T., Imer, C., Basar, T., Kotz, D., & Rus, D. (2003). Computational markets to regulate mobile-agent systems. *Autonomous Agents and Multi Agent Systems, 6*(3), 235-263.

Breitbart Y., & Korth, H. F. (1997). Replication and consistency: Being lazy helps sometimes. In *Procedings of the 16th ACM SIGACT-SIGMOD-SIGART Symposium on Principles of Database Systems.*

Breunig, M. (1996). *Integration of spatial information for geo-information systems.* Berlin, New York: Springer.

Brew, C.A.J., Wilson, F.F., Castelli, G., Adye, T., Luppi, E., & Andreotti, D. (2006). BABAR experience of large scale production on the Grid. *E-science,* 151.

Briquet, C., & de Marneffe, P. (2006). Grid resource negotiation: Survey with a machine learning perspective. In T. Fahringer (Ed.), *Proceedings of the 24th IASTED international Conference on Parallel and Distributed Computing and Networks* (pp. 17-22). ACTA Press, Anaheim, CA.

Brobst, R., Chan, W., Ferstl, F., Gardiner, J., Robarts, J. P., Haas, A., et al. (2007). *Distributed resource management application API specification 1.0.* OGF Grid final documents. Retrieved October 29, 2007, from http://www.ogf.org/documents/GFD.22.pdf.

Broeckhove, J., Arickx, F., Hellinckx, P., Vasilevsky, V. S., & Nesterov, A. V. (2007). The ^{5}H resonance structure studied with a three-cluster J-matrix model. *Journal of Physics G: Nuclear and Particle Physics, 34,* 1955-1970

Broeckhove, J., Arickx, F., Vanroose, W., & Vasilevsky V. (2004). The modified J-Matrix method for short-range potentials. *Journal of Physics A: Mathematical and General, 37,* 1-13

Brun, R. & Rademakers, F. (1997). ROOT – An object orientated data analysis framework. *Nucl. Instr. and Methods*, A 389, 81.

Bubendorfer, K., & Thomson, W. (2006). *Resource management using untrusted auctioneers in a Grid economy*. Paper presented at the Second IEEE International Conference on e-Science and Grid Computing.

Bubendorfer, K., Komisarczuk, P., Chard, K., & Desai, A. (2005). *Fine grained resource reservation and management in grid economics*. Paper presented at the International Conference on Grid Computing and Applications.

Bucur, A. I. D., & Epema, D. H. J. (2003). The performance of processor co-allocation in multicluster systems. In *Proceedings of the Third IEEE International Symposium on Cluster Computing and the Grid (CCGrid'03)* (pp. 302).

Burchard, L.O., Linnert, B., Heine, F., Hovestadt, M., Kao, O., & Keller, A. (2005). A quality-of-service architecture for future grid computing applications. In *Proceedings of 19th IEEE International Parallel and Distributed Processing Symposium*, Berlin, Germany.

Burke, S., Campana, S., Delgado Peris, A., Donno, F., Mendez Lorenzo, P., Santinelli, R., et al. (2007). *GLite 3 user guide*. Retrieved January 17, 2007, from https://edms.cern.ch/file/722398/1.1/gLite-3-UserGuide.pdf

Busby, D., Farmer, C. L., & Iske, A. (2007). Hierarchical nonlinear approximation for experimental design and statistical data fitting. *SIAM Journal on Scientific Computing*, 29(1), 49-69.

Buyya, R. (2002). *Economic-based distributed resource management and scheduling for grid computing*. Doctoral dissertation, Monash University, Australia.

Buyya, R., & Venugopal, S. (2005). A gentle introduction to Grid Computing and technologies, *CSI Communications*, 29(1), 9-19.

Buyya, R., Abramson, D., & Giddy, J. (2000). *An economy driven resource management architecture for global computational power grids*. Paper presented at the 2000 International Conference on Parallel and Distributed Processing Techniques and Applications (PDPTA 2000), Las Vegas, NV.

Buyya, R., Abramson, D., & Venugopal, S. (2005). The Grid economy. *Proceedings of the IEEE*, 93(3), 698-714.

Buyya, R., Abramson, D., & Venugopal, S. (2005). The Grid economy. In *Proceedings of the IEEE*, 93(3), 698-714.

Buyya, R., Abramson, D., & Venugopal, S.(2005). The grid economy. *In Proceedings of the IEEE, 93*(3), 698-714.

Buyya, R., Abramson, D., Giddy, J., & Stockinger, H. (2002). Economic models for resource management and scheduling in Grid computing environments. *Concurrency and Computation: Practice and experience, 14*(13-15), 1507-1542.

Buyya, R., Giddy, J., & Abramson, D. (2000). An evaluation of economy-based resource trading and scheduling on computational power grids for parameter sweep applications. In *Proceedings of the Second Workshop on Active Middleware Services (AMS2000), In conjunction with the Ninth IEEE International Symposium on High Performance Distributed Computing (HPDC 2000)*, Pittsburgh, USA.

Buyya, R., Murshed, M., Abramson, D., & Venugopa, S. (2005). Scheduling parameter sweep applications on global Grids: A deadline and budget constrained cost-time optimization algorithm. *Software - Practice & Experience, 35*(5), 491-512.

Bykowsky, M., Cull, R., & Ledyard, J.O. (1995). Mutually destructive bidding: The FCC auction design problem. *Journal of Regulatory Economics, 17*(3), 205-228.

Byrom, R., Cordenonsi, R., Cornwall, L., Craig, M., Djaoui, A., Duncan, A. et al. (2005). *APEL: an implementation of Grid accounting using R-GMA*. Paper presented at the UK e-Science All Hands Conference, Nottingham, UK.

Cachin, C. (1999). *efficient private bidding and auctions with an oblivious third party*. Paper presented at the

ACM Conference on Computer and Communications Security.

Calanducci, A. (2006). *gLibrary: A Multimedia contents management system on the Grid*. EGEE User Forum, CERN, Switzerland.

Calanducci, T., Cherubino, C., Ciuffo, L.N., & Scardaci D. (2006*). gLibrary - Digital asset management system for the Grid*. Retrieved August 22, 2007, from https://glibrary.ct.infn.it/glibrary/

Campbell, A., Aurrecoechea C., & Hauw, L. (1996). A review of QoS architectures. In *Proceedings of 4th International Workshop on Quality of Service (IWQoS)*.

Cannataro, M., &Talia, D. (2003). The knowledge Grid. *Communications of the ACM, 46*(1), 89-93.

Canon, L., & Jeannot, E. (2006). Wrekavoc: A tool for emulating heterogeneity. In *Proceedings of the 20th Intl. Parallel and Distributed Processing Symposium, Heterogeneous Computing Workshop (HCW)*.

Cao, J. (2004). Self-organizing agents for Grid load balancing. In *Proceedings of the Fifth IEEE/ACM international Workshop on Grid Computing* (pp. 388-395). GRID. IEEE Computer Society, Washington, DC.

Cao, J., Jarvis, S. A., Saini, S., Kerbyson, D. J., & Nudd, G. R. (2002). ARMS: An agent-based resource management system for grid computing. *Scientific Programming, 10*(2), 135-148.

Cappuccio, R., Cattaneo, G., Erbacci, G., & Jocher, U. (April 2001). A parallel implementation of a cellular automata based model for coffee percolation. *Parallel Computing, 27*(33), 685-717.

Cardellini, V., Colajanni, M., & Yu, P.S. (2000). Geographic load balancing for scalable distributed Web systems. In *Proceedings of 8th International Symposium on Modeling, Analysis and Simulation of Computer and Telecommunication Systems*, IEEE Computer Society, San Francisco, CA, USA (pp. 20-27).

Cárdenas, M. (2006). Biomedical Applications in EELA. *Studies in Health Technology and Informatics, 120*, 397-400

Casey, J. et al. (2003). Next-generation EU DataGrid data management services. In *Proceedings of the Conference for Computing in High Energy and Nuclear Physics (CHEP 2003)*, La Jolla, California.

CCSP (2003). Strategic plan for the US climate change science program. *CCSP Report*.

CDF (2007). *The collider detector at Fermilab*. Retrieved Feb. 2007, from http://www-cdf.fnal.gov/

Cellary, W., Gelenbe, E., & Morzy, T. (1988). *Concurrency control in distributed database systems*. Amsterdam: North-Holland.

Ceyhan, E. & Kosar, T. (2007). Large scale data management in sensor networking applications. To appear in *Secure Cyberspace Workshop*. Shreveport, LA.

Chalmers, D., & Sloman M. (1999). A survey of quality of service in mobile computing environments. *IEEE Communications Surveys and Tutorials, 2*(2), 2-10.

Chawla, N. (2007). Grid computing. *Developer IQ, 7*(1), 38.

Cheliotis, G., Kenyon, C., & Buyya, R. (2005). 10 Lessons from Finance for Commercial Sharing of IT Resources. In R. Subramanian, & B.D. Goodman (Eds.), *Peer to peer computing: The evolution of a disruptive technology* (pp. 244-264). Hershey, PA: Idea Group Publishing.

Chen, J., & Taylor, V. E. (2002). Mesh partitioning for efficient use of distributed systems. *IEEE Transactions on Parallel and Distributed Systems, 13*(1), 67-79.

Chen, M.L., Geist, A., Bernholdt, D.E., Chanchio, K., & Million, D.L. (2005). The design and prototype of RUDA, a distributed Grid accounting System (LNCS 3482, pp. 29-38).

Chen, X., Lee, B., & Kim, K. (2003). Receipt-free electronic auction schemes using homomorphic encryption. Paper presented at the 6th International Conference on Information Security and Cryptology (pp. 259-273).

Chen, Y., Berry D., & Dantressangle P. (2007). Transaction-based grid database replication. In *Proceedings of the UK e-Science All Hands Meeting*.

Chervenak, A., Deelman, E., Foster, I., Guy, L., Hoschek, W., Iamnitchi, A., et al. (2002). Giggle: A framework for constructing scalable replica location services. In *Proceedings of the Int'l. ACM/IEEE Supercomputing Conference (SC 2002)*. IEEE Computer Society Press.

Chervenak, A., Schuler, R., Kesselman, C., Koranda, S., Moe, B., & Wide (2005). Area data replication for scientific collaboration. In *Proceedings of 6th IEEE/ACM Int'l Workshop on GridComputing (Grid2005)*.

Chien, A. A. (2003). Architecture of a commercial enterprise desktop grid: The entropia system. In F. Berman, G.C. Fox, & A.J.G. Hey, *Grid computing: Making the Global Infrastructure a Reality*. John Wiley & Sons, Ltd.

Chien, C. H., M., & W. (2005). *Market-oriented multiple resource management and scheduling in Grid computing*. Paper presented at the Advanced Information Networking and Applications (AINA'05).

Chignola, R., Schenetti, A., Chiesa, E., Foroni, R., Sartoris, S., Brendolan, A., Tridente, G., Andrighetto, G., & Liberati, D. Forecasting the growth of multicell tumour spheroids: implications for the dynamic growth of solid tumours. *Cell Proliferat, 33*, 219-229.

ChinaGrid Support Platform Project (2005). http://www.chinagrid.edu.cn/cgsp/

Ching, A. L. M., Sacks, L., & McKee, P. (2002). Super resource-management for Grid computing. *In Proceedings of the London Communications Symposium (LCS 2002)*, London.

Chopra, I., & Kaur, G. (2007). Exploring Grid middleware – A comparative study, *Proceedings of the International Conference on Intelligent Systems and Networks,*(pp. 650-651). Jagadhri, Haryana, India.

Choucri, N., Madnick, S. E., Moulton, A., Siegel, M. D., & Zhu, H. (2004). Information integration for counter terrorism activities: Requirements for context mediation. In *Proceedings of the 2004 IEEE Aerospace Conference.*

Chu, L., Shen, K., Tang, H. et al (2005). Dependency isolation for thread-based multi-tier Internet services. *Proceedings of InfoCom'05* (pp. 796-806).

Chun, B. N., Buonadonna, P., AuYoung, A., Chaki, N., Parkes, D.C., Shneidman, J., Snoeren, A.C., & Vahdat, A. (2005). Mirage: A microeconomic resource allocation system for sensornet testbeds. In *Proceedings of the Second IEEE Workshop on Embedded Networked Sensors* (pp. 19-28). Los Alamitos, CA: IEEE Society Press.

Ciaschini, V., Ferraro, A., Ghiselli, A., Rubini, G., Guarise, A., Patania, G. et al., (2006). *An integrated framework for VO-oriented authorization, policy-based management and accounting*. Paper presented at the Conference on Computing in High Energy and Nuclear Physics (CHEP'06), T.I.F.R. Mumbai, India.

Cirne, W., & Berman, F. (2003). When the herd is smart: Aggregate behavior in the selection of job request. *IEEE Transactions on Parallel and Distributed Systems, 14*(2), 181-192.

Cirrone, G.A.P., & Cuttone, G. (2005). Implementation of a new Monte Carlo-GEANT4 Simulation tool for the development of a proton therapy beam line and verification of the related dose distributions. *IEEE Transactions on Nuclear Science, 52*(1), 262-265.

CMS (2007). The Compact Muon Solenoid Project (CMS). Retrieved from, http://cmsinfo.cern.ch/.

Cooke, A.W. et al. (2004). The relational Grid monitoring architecture: Mediating information about the grid. *Journal of Grid Computing, 2*(4), 323-339.

Cowan, R. (2007). *BaBar public Web home page*. Retrieved May 16, 2007, from http://www-public.slac.stanford.edu/babar/

Cramton, P., Shoham, Y., & Steinberg, R. (Eds.). (2006). *Combinatorial auctions*. Cambridge, MA: MIT Press.

Curbera, F., Duftler, M., Khalaf, R., Nagy, W., Mukhi, N., & Weerawarana, S. (2002). Unraveling the Web services: An introduction to SOAP, WSDL, and UDDI. *IEEE Internet Computing, 6*(2), 86-93.

Curbera, F., Duftler, M., Khalaf, R., Nagy, W., Mukhi, N., & Weerawarana, S. (2002). Unraveling the web services: an introduction to SOAP, WSDL, and UDDI. *IEEE Internet Computing, 6*(2), 86-93.

Czajkowski, K., Ferguson, D. F., Foster, I., Frey, J., Graham, S., Sedukhin, I., et al. (2004). The WS-Resource framework. Retrieved March 5, 2004, from http://www.globus.org/wsrf/specs/ws-wsrf.pdf. (last access: June 2007)

Czajkowski, K., Ferguson, DF., Foster, I., Frey, J., Graham, S., Seduknin, I., et al. (2004). *The WS-resource framework* (Version 1.0). Retrieved from http://www-106.ibm.com/developerworks/library/ws-resource/ws-wsrf.pdf

Czajkowski, K., Fitzgerald, S., Foster, I., & Kesselman, C. (2001). Grid information services for distributed resource sharing. *In Proceedings of the 10th IEEE Int. Symposium on High-performance distributed computing (HPDC-10)* (pp. 181-194), San Francisco, CA.

Czajkowski, K., Foster, I., Kesselman, C., Sander, V., & Tuecke, S. (2002). SNAP: A protocol for negotiating service level agreements and coordinating resource management in distributed systems. (LNCS 2537, 153-183).

Dai, Y.S., Xie, M., & Poh, K.L. (2008). Availability modeling and cost optimization for the Grid resource management system. *Systems, Man and Cybernetics, Part A, IEEE Transactions, 38*(1), 170-179.

Dale-Jones, R., & Tjahjadi, T. (1993). A study and modification of the local histogram equalisation algorithm, *Pattern Recognition, 26*, 1373-1381.

Darling, A., Carey, L. & Feng, W. (2003). The design, implementation, and evaluation of mpiBLAST. In Proceedings of the *4th International Conference on Linux Clusters: The HPC Revolution* (In conjunction with the ClusterWorld Conference & Exp San Jose).

Das, S. K., Harvey, D. J., & Biswas, R. (2002). MinEX: A latency-tolerant dynamic partitioner for grid computing applications. *Future Generation Computer Systems, 18*(4), 477-489.

Dash, R.K., Parkes, D.C., & Jennings, N.R. (2003). Computational mechanism design: A call to arms. *IEEE Intelligent Systems, 18*(6), 40-47.

DataCutter (2007). Retrieved October 7, 2007, from http://www.cs.umd.edu/projects/hpsl/ResearchAreas/DataCutter.htm

Datamat. (2001). *Job Description Language how to.* Retrieved December 12, 2001, from http://www.grid.org.tr/servisler/dokumanlar/DataGrid-JDL-HowTo.pdf

Davies, E.R. (1990). *Machine vision: theory, algorithms, practicalities.* Academic Press, London.

Davis, D. M., Baer, G. D., & Gottschalk, T. D. (2004). 21st Century simulation: exploiting high performance computing and data analysis. *Interservice/Industry Training, Simulation and Education Conference (I/ITSEC) 2004, 1517*, 1-14.

De Roure, D., & Hendler, J. (2004). E-Science: The grid and the semantic Web. *IEEE Intelligent Systems, 19*(1).

De Villiers, E.M. (2004). Classification of papillomaviruses. *Virology, 324*, 17-27.

Deelman E., Blythe J., Gil Y., & Kesselman C. (2003). Mapping abstract complex workflows onto grid environments. *Journal of Grid Computing, 1*(1) 25-39.

Deelman, E., Singh, G., Atkinson, M. P., Chervenak, A., Hong, N.P.C., Kesselman, C., et al. (2004). *Grid-based metadata services.* Paper presented at the 16th International Conference on Scientific and Statistical Database Management (SSDBM'04), Santorini Island, Greece.

DeFanti, T. A., Foster, I., Papka, M. E., Stevens, R., & Kuhfuss, T. (1996). Overview of the I-way: Wide-area visual supercomputing. *International Journal of High Performance Computing Applications, 10*(2-3), 123-131.

Deitel, H. M. (1990). I/O Control System. In *An introduction to operating systems,* Addison-Wesley Longman Publishing Co., Inc.

DeMers, M.N. (1997). *Fundamentals of geographic information systems.* New York: John Wiley & Sons.

Deng, Y., & Wang, F. (2007). A heterogeneous storage grid enabled by grid service. *ACM SIGOPS Operating Systems Review, 41*(1), 7-13.

Deng, Y., & Wang, F. (2007). Opportunities and challenges of storage grid enabled by grid service. *ACM SIGOPS Operating Systems Review, 41*(4), 79-82.

Deng, Y., Wang, F., Helian, N., Wu, S., & Liao, C. (2007). Dynamic and scalable storage management architecture for Grid oriented storage device. *Parallel Computing, 34*(1).

DeNicolao, G., Liberati, D., & Sartorio, A. (2000). Stimulated secretion of pituitary hormones in normal humans: a novel direct assessment from blood concentrations. *Ann Biomed Eng, 28*, 1131-1145.

Dennis, A. R., & Carte, T. A. (1998). Using geographical information systems for decision making: Extending cognitive fit theory to map-based presentations. *Information Systems Research, 9*(2), 194-203.

Devine, K. D., Boman, E. G., Heaphy, R. T., Hendrickson, B. A., Teresco, J. D., Faik, J., et al. (2005). New challenges in dynamic load balancing. *Applied Numerical Mathematics, 52*(2-3), 133-152.

Dimitrakos, T., Mac Randal, D., Yuan, F., Gaeta, M., Laria, G., Ritrovato, P., et al. (2003). *An emerging architecture enabling grid based application service provision.* Paper presented at the Seventh IEEE International Conference on Enterprise Distributed Object Computing Conference.

Ding, Q., Chen, G. L., & Gu, J. (2002). A unified resource mapping strategy in computational Grid environments. *J. Softw.,13*(7), 1303-1308.

Distributed parallel storage system project (2007). Retrieved from, http://wwwdidc.lbl.gov/DPSS/

Dobber, M., Koole, G., & van der Mei, R. (2005). Dynamic load balancing experiments in a grid. *International Symposium on Cluster Computing and the Grid (CCGrid)* (pp. 1063-1070), Vol. 2.

DOE (2004, March-May). The data management challenge. *Report from the DOE Office of Science Data-Management Workshops.*

Doherty, T. (2006). *Development of gLite Web Service based security components for the ATLAS metadata interface,* EGEE User Forum, CERN, Switzerland.

Domenici, A., Donno, F., Pucciani, G., Stockinger, H. (2006, May 16-19). Relaxed data consistency with CON-Stanza. *Sixth IEEE International Symposium on Cluster Computing and the Grid (CCGrid06).* Singapore: IEEE Computer Society.

Domenici, A., Donno, F., Pucciani, G., Stockinger, H., Stockinger, K. (2003). Replica consistency in a data grid. In *Proceedings of the IX International Workshop on Advanced Computing and Analysis Techniques in Physics Research*, Tsukuba, Japan.

Dongara, J.J. & Walker, D. (1996). MPI: A standard message passing interface. *Supercomputer, 12*(1), 56-68

Dongarra, J., & Lastovetsky, A. (2006). An overview of heterogeneous high performance and grid computing. In B. Di Martino, J. Dongarra, A. Hoisie, L. Yang & H. Zima (Eds.), *Engineering the grid: Status and perspectives.* American Scientific Publishers.

Dorigo, M. (1992). *Optimization, learning and natural algorithms.* PhD thesis, DEI, Polytecnico di Milano, Milan, Italy. (in Italian).

Dorigo, M., & Stutzle, T. (2004) *Ant colony optimization.* The MIT Press.

Downey, A. (1997). Predicting queue times on space-sharing parallel computers. In *Proceedings of the International Parallel Processing Symposium (IPPS ,97)* (pp. 209-218). Geneva, Switzerland.

Drago, G.P., Setti, E., Licitra, L., & Liberati, D. (2002). Forecasting the performance status of head and neck cancer patient treatment by an interval arithmetic pruned perceptron. *IEEE T Bio-Med Eng, 49*(8), 782-787.

Drtina, R. E. (1994). The outsourcing decision. *Management Accounting, 75*(9), 56-62.

Du, Z.H., Lau, F.C.M., Wang, C.L., Lam, W.K., He C., Wang X.G., Chen Y. & Li S.L. (2004). Design of an OGSA-based MetaService architecture. In *Proceedings of Grid and Cooperative Computing—GCC2004* (LNCS 3251, 167-174).

Düllmann, D., Hoschek, W., Jean-Martinez, J., Samar, A., Stockinger, H., & Stockinger, K. (2002). Models for replica synchronisation and consistency in a data grid. In *Proceedings of 10th IEEE Symposium on High*

Performance and Distributed Computing (HPDC-10). IEEE Computer Society Press.

Dumitrescu, C., Raicu, I., & Foster, I. (2005). DI-GRU-BER: A distributed approach for grid resource brokering. In *Proceedings of the International Conference on High Performance Computing, Networking and Storage*.

Duran-Limon, H.A., Blair, G.S., & Coulson, G. (2004). Adaptive resource management in middleware: A survey. *Distributed Systems Online, 5*(7).

EEGE (2007). *Enabling Grids for E-sciencE*. Retrieved August 21, 2007, from http://www.eu-egee.org/

EELA (2007). *E-Infrastructure shared between Europe and Latin America*. Retrieved August 21, 2007, from http://www.eu-eela.org/

Eerola, P., Konya, B., Smirnova, O., Ekelof, T., Ellert, M., Hansen, J. R., et al. (2003). Building a production grid in Scandanavia. *Internet Computing, IEEE, 7*(4), 27-35.

EGEE (2002). Enabling Grids for E-Science. Retrieved October 25, 2007, from http://www.egee-rdig.ru/

EGEE (n.d.). *Enabling Grids for E-science*. Project funded by the European Commission. Retrieved from, http://www.eu-egee.org.

El-Darieb, M., & Krishnamurthy, D. (2006). A scalable wide-area Grid resource management framework. *International Conference on Networking and Services (ICNS'06)* (pp. 76).

El-Ghazawi T., Gaj, K., & Alexandridis N. (2004). A performance study of job management systems. *Concurrency and Computation: Practice and Experience, 16*(13) 1229-1246.

Engelmore, R., & Morgan, T. (1998). *Blackboard systems*. New York: Addison-Wesley Publishers.

England, D., & Weissman, J. B. (2004). Costs and benefits of load sharing in computational grid. *10th Workshop on Job Scheduling Strategies for Parallel Processing* (LNCS 3277).

Enterprise Management Associates. *A quote from this Information Technology analyst firm.*

Eres, M. H., Pound, G. E., Jiao, Z., Wason, J. L., Xu, F., Keane, A. J., et al. (2005). Implementation and utilization of a grid-enabled problem solving environment in Matlab. *Future Generation Comp. System, 21*(6), 920-929.

Ernemann, C., Hamscher, V., & Yahyapour, R. (2002). Economic Scheduling in Grid Computing. *8th International Workshop on Job Scheduling Strategies for Parallel Processing.* (LNCS 2537, pp. 128-152).

Ernemann, C., Hamscher, V., & Yahyapour, R. (2002). Economic scheduling in Grid computing (LNCS 2537, pp. 128-152).

Ernemann, C., Hamscher, V., & Yahyapour, R. (2004). Benefits of global grid computing for job scheduling. In *Proceedings of the Fifth IEEE/ACM International Workshop on Grid Computing (GRID'04)* (pp. 374-379).

Ernemann, C., Hamscher, V., Schwiegelshohn, U., Streit, A., & Yahyapour, R. (2002). On advantages of grid computing for parallel job scheduling. In *Proceedings of 2nd IEEE International Symposium on Cluster Computing and the Grid (CC-GRID 2002)* (pp. 39-46). Berlin, Germany.

Ernemann, C., Hamscher, V., Streit, A., & Yahyapour, R. (2002). On effects of machine configurations on parallel job scheduling in computational grids. In *Proceedings of International Conference on Architecture of Computing Systems, ARCS 2002* (pp. 169-179).

Ernemann, C., Hamscher, V., Yahyapour, R., & Streit, A. (2002). Enhanced algorithms for multi-site scheduling. In *Proceedings of 3rd International Workshop on Grid Computing, in conjunction with Supercomputing 2002* (pp. 219-231). Baltimore, MD, USA.

Erwin, D., & Snelling, D. (2001). UNICORE: A Grid computing environment. (LNCS 2150, pp. 825-834). Springer.

Estrella, F., Kovacs, Z., LeGoff, J.M., & McClatchey, R. (2001). MetaData objects as the basis for system evolution (LNCS 2118, 390-399).

EUChinaGRID initiative (2007). Retrieved August 21, 2007, from http://www.euchinagrid.org/

EUIndiaGrid (2007). *Joining European and Indian Grids for e-Science network community.* Retrieved August 21, 2007, http://www.euindiagrid.org/

EUMEDGRID (2007). *Empowering eScience across the Mediterranean.* Retrieved August 21, 2007, from http://www.eumedgrid.org/

Eymann, T., Reinicke, M., Streitberger, W., Rana, O., Joita, L., Neumann, D., et al. (2005). Catallaxy-based Grid markets. *Multiagent and Grid Systems, 1*(4), 297-307.

Fagg, G.E., Gabriel, E., Bosilca, G., Angskun, T., Chen, Z., Pjesivac-Grbovic, J., London, K. & Dongara, J. (2004). Extending the MPI specification for process fault-tolerance on high-performance computing systems. In *Proceedings of the International Supercomputer conference (ICS).*

Falkenrath, R. A. (2001). Problem of preparedness: U.S. readiness for a domestic terrorist attack. *International Security, 25*(4), 147-186.

Fang, W., Wong, S. C., Tan, V., Miles, S., & Moreau, L. (2005). Performance analysis of a semantics enabled service registry. In C. Simon (Ed.), *UK e-Science All Hands Meeting*, Nottingham.

Farhang-Mehr, A., & Azarm, S. (2005). Bayesian meta-modeling of engineering design simulations: a sequential approach with adaptation to irregularities in the response behavior. *International Journal for Numerical Methods in Engineering, 62*(15), 2104-2126.

Feitelson, D., Rudolph, L., Schwiegelshohn, U., & Sevcik, K. C. (1997). Theory and practice in parallel job scheduling (LNCS 1291, pp. 1-34).

Feldman, M., Lai, K., & Zhang, L. (2005). A price-anticipating resource allocation mechanism for distributed shared clusters. In *Proceedings of the 6th ACM conference on Electronic commerce* (pp. 127–136). New York: ACM Press.

Fella, A., Andreotti, D., & Luppi E. (2007). *Events simulation production for the BaBar experiment using the grid approach content.* Paper presented at the Third EELA Conference, Catania, Italy.

Feng, W. (2003). High performance transport protocols. *Los Alamos National Laboratory.*

Ferrari, Trecate G., Muselli, M., Liberati, D., Morari, M. (2003). A clustering technique for the identification of piecewise affine systems. *Automatica, 39*, 205-217.

Fidanova, S., & Durchova, M. K. (2006). Ant algorithm for Grid scheduling problem. In *Proceedings of the 5th International Conference on Large-Scale Scientific Computing* (pp. 405-412).

Figueiredo, R., Dinda, P., & Fortes, J.A.B. (2003). A case for Grid computing on virtual machines. In *Proceedings of 23rd International Conference on Distributed Computing Systems* (pp. 550-559).

Fiore S., Cafaro M. & Aloisio G. (2007). *GRelC DAS: A Grid-DB Access Service for gLite Based Production Grids.* Paper presented at the Fourth International Workshop on Emerging Technologies for Next-generation GRID (ETNGRID 2007), Paris, France.

Fiore, S., Cafaro, M., Negro, A., Vadacca, S., Aloisio, G., Barbera, R., et al. (2007). GRelC DAS: A Grid-DB access service for gLite based production Grids. In *IEEE Proceedings of the Fourth International Workshop on Emerging Technologies for Next-generation GRID (ETNGRID 2007).* (pp. 261-266).

Fiore, S., Negro, A., Vadacca, S., Cafaro, M., Mirto, M., & Aloisio G. (2007). Advanced Grid database management with the GRelC data access service. In *Proceedings of the 5th International Symposium on Parallel and Distributed Processing and Applications (ISPA07)* (LNCS 4742, 683-694).

Foster I. & Kesselman C. (2004). The Grid2: Blueprint for a new computing infrastructure. Morgan-Kaufman.

Foster I., (2006). Globus toolkit Version 4: Software for service-oriented systems. *IFIP International Conference on Network and Parallel Computing* (LNCS 3779, 2-13).

Foster I., Roy A., & Sander V. (2000). A quality of service architecture that combines resource reservation and application adaptation. In *Proceedings of the 8th*

International Workshop on Quality of Service (pp. 181-188), Pittsburgh, PA.

Foster I., Voeckler J., Wilde M. & Zhao Y. (2002). *Chimera: A virtual data system for representing, querying, and automating data derivation.* Paper presented at Scientific and Statistical Database Management.

Foster, I. & Kesselman, C. (1997). Globus: A metacomputing infrastructure toolkit. *The International Journal of Supercomputer Applications and High Performance Computing, 11*(2), 115-128.

Foster, I. & Kesselman, C. (2001). A data Grid reference architecture. In *Proceedings of the ACM/IEEE SC2001 Conference.*

Foster, I. & Kesselman, C. (Eds.). (1998). *The Grid: Blueprint for a new computing infrastructure.* San Francisco: Morgan Kaufmann.

Foster, I. (1995). *Designing and building parallel programs.* Addison Wesley.

Foster, I. (2003). The Grid: A new infrastructure for 21st century science. In F. Berman, G.C. Fox, & A.J.G. Hey (Eds.), *Grid Computing* (pp. 65-100). New York: Wiley.

Foster, I. (2005, January 29). *The open Grid services architecture, Version 1.0.* Informational document, global Grid forum (GGF).

Foster, I., & Iamnitchi, A. (2003). On death, taxes, and the convergence of peer-to-peer and Grid computing (LNCS 2735, pp. 118-128).

Foster, I., & Kesselman, C. (1997). Globus: A meta-computing infrastructure toolkit. *Intl J. Supercomputer Applications, 11*(2),115-128.

Foster, I., & Kesselman, C. (1998). *The Grid, blueprint for a new computing infrastructure.* San Francisco: Morgan Kaufmann Publishers Inc.

Foster, I., & Kesselman, C. (1998). *The Grid: blueprint for a new computing infrastructure.* Morgan Kaufmann Publishers, Inc.

Foster, I., & Kesselman, C. (1999). A distributed resource management architecture that supports advance reservation and co-allocation. In *Proceedings Of The International Workshop on Quality of Service* (pp. 27-36).

Foster, I., & Kesselman, C. (1999). *The Grid: Blueprint for a new computing infrastructure.* Morgan Kaufmann Publishers Inc.

Foster, I., & Kesselman, C. (2003). The grid: The first 50 years, lovelace lecture at British computer society (BCS). Lovelace Medal Presentation, London, UK.

Foster, I., & Kesselman, C. (2004). *The Grid 2: Blueprint for a new computing infrastructure.* San Fransisco: Morgan Kaufmann Publishers.

Foster, I., (2002). *The physiology of the Grid: An open Grid services architecture for distributed systems integration - globus project.*

Foster, I., Kesselman C., & Tuecke S. (2001). *The anatomy of the Grid - Enabling scalable virtual organizations.* Retrieved 2001, from http://www.globus.org/alliance/publications/papers/anatomy.pdf

Foster, I., Kesselman, C., & Tuecke, S. (2001). The anatomy of the Grid: Enabling scalable virtual organizations. *International Journal of High Performance Computing Applications, 15*(3), 200-222.

Foster, I., Kesselman, C., Nick, J. M., & Tuecke, S. (2002). Grid services for distributed system integration. *IEEE Computer, 35*(6), 37-46.

Foster, I., Kesselman, C., Nick, J. M., & Tuecke, S. (2002). The physiology of the grid: An open grid services architecture for distributed systems integration. Retrieved June 30, 2007, from http://www.globus.org/alliance/publications/papers/ogsa.pdf

Foster, I., Kesselman, C., Nick, JM., & Tuecke, S.(2002). *The physiology of the Grid: An open Grid services architecture for distributed systems integration.* Retrieved from, http://www.gridforum.org/ogsi-wg/drafts/ogsa_draft2.9_2002-06-22.pdf

Foster, I., Kesselman, K., & Tuecke, S. (2001). The anatomy of the Grid: Enabling scalable virtual organizations.

International Journal of Supercomputer Applications, 2001(3), 200-222.

Fox, G., & Pierce, M. (2007). *Grids challenged by a Web 2.0 and multicore sandwich.* Paper presented at Cluster Computing and the Grid (CCGrid), Rio de Janeiro, Brazil: IEEE.

Franklin, C. (1992). An introduction to geographic information systems: linking maps to databases, *Database 15*(2), 13-21.

Franklin, M., & Reiter, M. (1995). *The design and implementation of a secure auction service.* Paper presented at the Proc. IEEE Symp. on Security and Privacy.

Freund, J. (2006). Health-e-Child: An integrated biomedical platform for Grid-based paediatrics. In *Studies in health technology & informatics* (pp. 259-270). IOS Press.

Fudenberg, D., & Tirole, J. (1991). *Game theory.* Cambridge, MA: MIT Press.

Gannon, D., Fox, G., Pierce, M., Plale, B., Laszewski, G. v., Severance, C., et al. (2003). *Grid Portals: A scientist's access point for grid services.* Global Grid Forum (GGF).

GAO. (2002). Washington DC, USA: GAO; 2002 May 29.

Garatti, S., Bittanti, S., Liberati, D., Maffezzoli, P. (2007). An unsupervised clustering approach for leukemia classification based on DNA micro-arrays data. *Intelligent Data Analysis, 11*(2), 175-188.

Garcia-Molina, H. (1982). Elections in a distributed computing system. *IEEE Transaction on Computers, 32.*

Garrick, B.J., Hall, J.E., Kilger, M., McDonald, J.C., O'Toole, T., Probst, P.S., et al. (2004). Confronting the risks of terrorism: Making the right decisions. *Reliability Engineering and System Safety 86*(2), 129-176 .

Garrison, A. (2007). Terrorism: The nature of its history. *Criminal Justice Studies. 16*(1), 39-52.

Gartner Group (2003, November). *Gartner predicts: Future of IT, symposium/ITxpo.* Cannes.

Garuda India Portal (2007). Retrieved June 25, 2007, from http://garudaindia.in

Geddes, N. I. (1998). *BaBar software release structure.* Retrieved November 18, 1998, from http://www.slac.stanford.edu/BFROOT/www/Computing/Environment/NewUser/htmlbug/node14.html

GENIUS Portal (2007). Retrieved August 21, 2007, from https://genius.ct.infn.it/

Ghazinour, K., Shaw, R.E., Aubanel, E., & Garey, L.E. (2008) A linear solver for benchmarking partitioners. In *Proceedings of the 22nd Intl. Parallel and Distributed Processing Symposium, Workshop on Parallel and Distributed Scientific and Engineering Computing (PDSEC).*

Gibbons, R. (1997). *A historical application profiler for use by parallel schedulers.* (LNCS 1291, 58-77).

Gibson, G., & Meter, R. V. (2000). Network attached storage architecture. *Communications of the ACM, 43*(1), 37-45.

Gibson, G., Stodolsky, D., Chang, F., Courtright II, W., Demetriou, C., Ginting, E., et al. (1995). The Scotch parallel storage system. In *Proceedings of 40th IEEE Computer Society International Conference* (pp. 403-410).

Gibson, R., & McGuire, E. G. (1996). Quality control for global software development. *Journal of Global Information Management, 4*(4), 16-22.

GILDA (2007) *Grid Infn Laboratory for dissemination activities.* Retrieved August 21, 2007, from https://gilda.ct.infn.it/

GILDA Grid Demonstrator (2007) Retrieved August 21, 2007, from https://glite-demo.ct.infn.it/

GILDA Wiki (2007). Retrieved August 21, 2007, from https://grid.ct.infn.it/twiki/bin/view/GILDA/WebHome

Giunta, A., & Eldred, M. (2000). Implementation of a trust region model management strategy in the DAKOTA optimization toolkit. In *Proceedings of the 8th AIAA/USAF/NASA/ISSMO symposium on multidisciplinary analysis and optimization.* Long Beach, CA.

gLite (2007). *Lightweight middleware for Grid computing*. Retrieved August 21, 2007, from http://glite.web.cern.ch/glite/

gLite. *Middleware development initiative as part of the EGEE project*. Retrieved from, http://glite.web.cern.ch/glite/default.asp.

Globus (2008). The Globus Project. Argonne National Laboratory USC Information Sciences Institute, Grid Architecture. Available from: http://www.globus.org

Globus Alliance. (2007). Retrieved August 10, 2007, from http://www.globus.org/

Globus Toolkit (n.d.). Retrieved from, http://www.globus.org/toolkit.

Goldstein, H. (2006). Modelling terrorists: New simulators could help intelligence analysts think like the enemy. *IEEE Spectrum, 43*(9), 18-26.

Gomoluch, J., & Schroeder, M. (2003). Market-based resource allocation for Grid computing: A model and simulation. In *Proceedings of the 1st International Workshop on Middleware for Grid Computing* (pp. 211–218). Rio de Janeiro: PUC-Rio.

Gong L., Sun X.H. & Waston E. F. (2002). Performance modeling and prediction of non-dedicated network computing. *IEEE Trans. on Computers, 51*(9), 1041-1055.

Google (2008). Available from http://maps.google.com

Gorissen, D., Hendrickx, W., Crombecq, K., & Dhaene, T. (2006). Integrating gridcomputing and metamodelling. In *Proceedings of 6th IEEE/ACM international symposium on cluster computing and the grid (CCGrid 2006)* (p. 185-192). Singapore.

Goyal, B., & Lawande, S. (2006). Enterprise grid computing with Oracle. New York: McGraw-Hill.

Grama, A., Karypis, G., Kumar, V., & Gupta, A. (2003). *Introduction to parallel computing* (2nd ed.). Addison-Wesley.

Graupner, S., Kotov, V., Andrzejak, A., & Trinks, H. (2003). Service-centric globally distributed computing. *IEEE Internet Computing, 7*(4), 36-43.

Gray, J., Helland, P., O'Neil, P., & Shasha. D. (1997). The dangers of replication and a solution. In *Proceedings of the 1996 ACM SIGMOD International Conference on Management of Data* (pp. 173-182).

Greene, W. A. (2001). Dynamic load-balancing via a genetic algorithm. In R. Bilof, & L. Palagi (Eds.), *13th IEEE International Conference on Tools with Artificial Intelligence*, (pp. 121-129), Dallas: IEEE Computer Society.

Grid Computing Info Centre (n.d.). Retrieved May 5, 2007, from http://www.gridcomputing.com

Gropp, W. & Lusk, E. (1997). A high-performance MPI implementation on a shared-memory vector supercomputer. *Parallel Computing, 22*(11), 1513-1526

Gropp, W., Lusk, E., & Skjellum, A. (1999). *Using MPI-Portable parallel programming with the message passing interface* (2nd ed.).

Gropp, W., Lusk, E., & Sterling, T. (2003). *Beowulf cluster computing with Linux*. Cambridge, MA: The MIT Press.

Gropp, W., Lusk, E., Doss, N., & Skjellum, A. (1996). A high-performance, portable implementation of the MPI message passing interface standard. *Parallel Computing, 22*(6), 789-828

Gu, L. (2001). A comparison of polynomial based regression models in vehicle safety analysis. Paper DETC/DAC-21063, *Proceedings of DETC'01 ASME 2001 Design Engineering Technical Engineering Conferences and the Computers and Information in Engineering Conference*, Pittsburgh, PA, 9-12 September .

Gupta A., Lin B. & Dinda P. (2004). Measuring and understanding user comfort with resource borrowing. In *Proceedings of the 13th IEEE International Symposium on High Performance Distributed Computing*, Honolulu, Hawaii.

Hafid, A., & Bochmann, G. (1998). Quality of service adaptation in distributed multimedia applications. *ACM Springer-Verlag Multimedia Systems Journal, 6*(5), 299-315.

Halhead, R. (1995). Breaking down the barriers to free information exchange. *Logistics Information Management, 8*(1), 34-37.

Ham, S., & Atkinson, R. D. (2002). Using technology to detect and prevent terrorism. *Technical Policy Report.* Progressive Policy Institute, 102.

Ham, W., Kim, K., & Imai, H. (2003). *Yet another strong sealed-bid auctions.* Paper presented at the Symposium on Cryptography and Information Security (SCIS).

Hamscher, V., Schwiegelshohn, U., Streit, A., & Yahyapour, R. (2000). Evaluation of job-scheduling strategies for grid computing. In *Proceedings of the 7th International Conference on High Performance Computing, HiPC-2000* (pp. 191-202). Bangalore, India.

Hanushevsky, H. (2004). *The Next Generation Root File System.* Paper presented at CHEP04, Interlaken, Switzerland.

Haque, N., Jennings, N. R. and Moreau, L. (2005). Resource allocation in communication networks using market-based agents. *International Journal of Knowledge Based Systems, 18*(4-5), 163-170.

Harchol-Balter, M. (2002). Task assignment with unknown duration. *J. ACM, 49*(2) 260-288.

Harkavy, M., Tygar, J. D., & Kikuchi, H. (1998). *Electronic auctions with private bids.* Paper presented at the 3rd USENIX Workshop on Electronic Commerce.

Harmer, T. J., Donachy, P., Perrott, R.H., Chambers, C., Craig, S., Mallon, B., et al. (2003). In C. Simon (Ed.), *UK e-Science all hands meeting 2003,* Nottingham. Retrieved June 2007, from http://www.nesc.ac.uk/events/ahm2003/AHMCD/

Harrovet, F., Ballet, P., Rodin, V., & Tisseau, J. (1998). ORIS: Multiagent approach for image processing. In *Proc. Parallel and Distributed Methods for Image Processing* (pp. 57-68).

Harsanyi, J. (1967). Games with incomplete information played by Bayesian players, I - III. *Management Science, 14,* 159-182, 320-334, 486-502.

He, L., Jarvis, S.A., Spooner, D.P., Chen, X., & Nudd, G.R. (2004). Dynamic scheduling of parallel jobs with QoS demands in multi-clusters and grids. In *Proceedings of 5th IEEE/ACM International Workshop on Grid Computing,* Coventry, UK (pp. 402-409).

Hellinckx, P., Arickx, F., Broeckhove, J., & Stuer G. (2007). The CoBRA Grid: A highly configurable lightweight Grid system. *International Journal of Web and Grid Services, 3*(3), 267-286

Hendler, J. (2003). Science and the semantic Web. *Science, 299*(5606).

Hendrickson, B. (1998). Graph partitioning and parallel solvers: Has the emperor no clothes? *Workshop on Parallel Algorithms for Irregularly Structured Problems* (LNCS 1457, 218-225).

Hendrickx, W., & Dhaene, T. (2005). Multivariate modelling of complex simulation-based systems. *Proceedings of the IEEE NDS 2005 conference* (pp. 212-216).

Hermida, A. (2001). Computing power on tap. BBC News online. Retrieved June 30, 2007, from http://news.bbc.co.uk/2/hi/science/nature/1470225.stm

Hey, T. & Trefethen, A. (2003). The data deluge: An e-Science perspective. In *Grid computing - Making the global infrastructure a reality* (pp. 809-824). Wiley and Sons.

Hoare, C.A.R. (1985). *Communicating sequential processes.* Prentice Hall, New York.

HP Labs web site (2005). News and Events, 2005 Archives, Stripped-down grid : A lightweight grid for computing's have-nots, February 2005. Retrieved October 22, 2007, from http://www.hpl.hp.com/news/2005/jan-mar/grid.html

Huang, K. C., & Chang, H. Y. (2006). An integrated processor allocation and job scheduling approach to workload management on computing grid. In *Proceedings of the 2006 International Conference on Parallel and Distributed Processing Techniques and Applications (PDPTA'06)* (pp. 703-709). Las Vegas, USA.

Huang, S., Aubanel, E. E., & C., V. (2006). PaGrid: A mesh partitioner for computational grids. *Journal of Grid Computing, 4*(1), 71-88.

Huang, S., Aubanel, E., & Bhavsar, V. C. (2003). Mesh partitioners for computational grids: A comparison. *International Conference on Computational Science and its Applications* (LNCS 2267-2269, 60-68).

Huedo, E, Montero, R.S., & Llorente I.M. (2005). The GridWay framework for adaptive scheduling and execution on Grids. *Nova Science, 6,* 1-8.

Huedo, E., Montero, R. S., & Llorente, I. M. (2004). A framework for adaptive execution on grids. *Journal of Software - Practice and Experience, 34,* 631-651.

Huhns, M. & Stephens, L. (2000). Mutiagent systems and societies of agents. In G. Weiss (Ed.) *Multiagent systems.* Cambridge, MA: The MIT Press.

Iamnitchi, A., & Foster, I. T. (2001). On fully decentralized resource discovery in Grid environments. In C. A. Lee (Ed.), *Proceedings of the Second international Workshop on Grid Computing.* London: Springer-Verlag (LNCS 2242, pp. 51-62).

IBM Grid Computing. (2007). Retrieved August 10, 2007, from http://www-106.ibm.com/developerworks/grid/

IBM Inc. (n.d.). IBM Grid computing, About Grid computing, What is grid. Retrieved May 5, 2007, from http://www-03.ibm.com/grid/about_grid/what_is.shtml

ICEAGE (2007). *The international collaboration to extend and advance Grid education.* Retrieved August 21, 2007, from http://www.iceage-eu.org/

IDC white paper. (2007). The expanding digital universe: A forecast of worldwide information growth through 2010. Retrieved October 7, 2007, from http://www.emc.com/about/destination/digital_universe/

INFNGrid (2002). *The Italian Grid infrastructure.* Retrieved December 2002, from http://grid.infn.it/

Infosys (2007). Technology, Centers of Excellence, Grid computing : Center of excellence. Retrieved June 5, 2007, from http://www.infosys.com/technology/grid-computing-coe.asp

Internet & World Wide Web History (2003). Retrieved June 30, 2007, from www.elsop.com/wrc/h_web.htm

Jacob, B., Ferreira, L., Bieberstein, N., Gilzean, C., Girard, J., Strachowski, S., et al. (2003). Enabling applications for Grid computing with Globus. *IBM RedBooks SG24-6936-00* (pp. 43-69).

Jacq, N. (2006). Demonstration of in silico docking at a large scale on Grid infrastructure. *Studies in Health Technology and Informatics, 120,* 155-157

Jaeger, M. C., Goldmann, G.R., Mühl, G., Liebetruth, C., & Geihs, K. (2005). Ranked matching for service descriptions using OWL-S. In *Proceedings of Communication in Distributed Systems (KiVS),* Kaiserslautern, Germany.

Jamieson, L.H., Delp, E.J., Wang, C., Li, J., & Weil, F.J. (1992). A software environment for parallel computer vision. *Computer, 25,* 73-77.

Jan, S. (2004). GATE: A simulation toolkit for PET and SPECT. *Phys. Med. Biol., 49,* 4543-4561.

Jennifer, M. S. (2003). Grids: The top ten questions. Paper presented at *International Symposium on Grid-Computing.*

Jia, Y., Michael, K., & Rajkumar, B. (2007). Multi-objective planning for workflow execution on grids. *Grid Computing 2007* (pp. 10-17). Austin, TX.

Jin, H. (2004). ChinaGrid: Making Grid computing a reality. *Digital Libraries: International collaboration and cross-fertilization* (LNCS 3334, pp. 13-24).

Johnson, I., Lakhani, A., Matthews, B., Yang, E., & Morin, C. (2007). XtreemOS: towards a Grid operating system with virtual organisation support. *UK eScience All Hands Meeting,* September 2007.

Joita, L., Rana, O., Freitag, F., Chao, I., Chacin, P., Navarro, L., & Ardaiz, O. (2007). A catallactic market for data mining services. *Future Generation Computer Systems, 23*(1), 146-153.

Juels, A., & Szydlo, M. (2003). *A two-server, sealed-bid auction protocol.* Paper presented at the Proc. 6th Financial Cryptography Conference (FC 2002).

Jufeng, W., Hancheng, X., Xiang, L., & Jingping Y. (2004). Multiagent based distributed control system for an intelligent robot. In *Proc. IEEE International Conference on Services Computing*, 633-637.

Karasavvas, K., Antonioletti, M., Atkinson, M. P., Chue Hong, N. P., Sugden, T., Hume, A. C., et al. (2005). Introduction to OGSA-DAI Services (LNCS 3458 1-12).

Karonis, N., Toonen, B. & Foster, I. (2003). MPICH-G2: A grid-enabled implementation of the message passing interface. *Journal of Parallel and Distributed Computing (JPDC), 63*(5), 551-563.

Karypis, G., & Kumar, V. (1998). Multilevel k-way partitioning scheme for irregular graphs. *Journal of Parallel and Distributed Computing, 48*(1), 96-129.

Keahey, K., Chase J. & Foster, I (2006). Virtual playgrounds: managing virtual resources in the grid. In *Proceedings of 20th IEEE International Parallel and Distributed Processing Symposium*, IL, USA.

Keahey, K., Foster I., Freeman T., & Zhang X. (2005). Virtual Workspaces: Achieving quality of service and quality of life in the Grid. *Scientific Programming*. IOS Press.

Keahey, K., Foster I., Freeman T., Zhang X., & Galron D. (2005). Virtual Workspaces in the Grid. (LNCS 3648, 421-431).

Keenan, P. B., Grimshaw, D. J., Pick, J. B., & Ostyn, F. (1999). Panel: IS and GIS: mapping the way forward. In *Proceedings of the Seventh European Conference on Information Systems*. Copenhagen.

Keller, U., Lara, R., Polleres, A., Toma, I., Kifer, M., & Fensel, D. (2004). *WSMO discovery*. Working Draft D5.1v0.1. Retrieved June 2007, from http://www.wsmo.org/2004/d5/d5.1/v0.1/20041112/ (last access: June 2007)

Kennedy, J., & Eberhart, R. C. (1995). Particle swarm optimization. In *Proceedings of IEEE International Conference on Neural Networks* (pp. 1942-1948).

Keung, H.N.L.C., Dyson, J.R.D., Jarvis, S.A., & Nudd, G.R.(2003). Performance evaluation of a Grid resource monitoring and discovery service. *Software, IEEE Proceedings, 150*(4), 243-251.

Khanli, L.M., & Analoui, M. (2006). Grid-JQA a new architecture for QoS-guaranteed Grid computing system. In *Proceedings of the 14th Euromicro International Conference on Parallel, Distributed, and Network-Based Processing (PDP'06)* (pp. 268-271).

Kikuchi, H. (2002). *(M+1)st-price auction protocol*. Paper presented at the 5th International Financial Cryptography Conference.

Kim, D.H. & Kang K.W. (2006). Design and implementation of integrated information system for monitoring resources in Grid computing. In *Proceedings of 10th International Conference on Computer Supported Cooperative Work in Design*, Korea (pp. 1-6).

Kirrily R. (2002). *A brief introduction*. Retrieved March 2002, from http://perldoc.perl.org/perlintro.pdf

Kleijnen, J. P., Sanchez, S. M., Lucas, T. W., & Cioppa, T. M. (2005). State-of-the-art review: A user's guide to the brave new world of designing simulation experiments. *INFORMS Journal on Computing, 17*(3), 263-289.

Koenig, G. A., & Kalé, L. V. (2007). *Optimizing distributed application performance using dynamic grid topology-aware load balancing*. Paper presented at the 21st. International Parallel and Distributed Processing Symposium.

Koh, W. T. H. (2007). Terrorism and its impact on economic growth and technological innovation. *Technology forecasting & social change*, 74129-138. Elsevier.

Kola, G., Kosar, T., & Livny, M. (2005). Run-time adaptation of grid data-placement jobs. *Scalable Computing: Practice and Experience, 6*(3), 33-43

Komisarczuk, P., Bubendorfer, K., & Chard, K. (2004). *Enabling virtual organisations in mobile networks*. Paper presented at the Fifth IEE International Conference on 3G Mobile Communication Technologies.

Kosar, T. (2006, June). A new paradigm in data intensive computing: Stork and the data-aware schedulers. In *Proceedings of Challenges of Large Applications in*

Distributed Environments (CLADE 2006) Workshop. Paris, France.

Kosar, T., & Livny, N. (2004, March). Stork: Making data placement a first class citizen in the Grid. In *Proceedings of 24th IEEE International Conference on Distributed Computing Systems (ICDCS 2004)*, Tokyo, Japan.

Kosar, T., Son, S., Kola, G., & Livny, M. (2005). Data placement in widely distributed environments. In L. Grandinetti (Ed.), *Grid Computing: The New Frontier of High Performance Computing* (pp. 14). Elsevier Press.

Kra, D. (2004, April). Six strategies for grid application enablement: Part 1. *IBM DeveloperWorks series* (pp. 1-8).

Kranzkmuller, D. (2006). White Paper. *e-Infrastructure Reflection Group, version 1.2* (pp. 67), from http://www.e-irg.org

Krauter, K., Buyya, R., & Maheswaran, M. (2002). A taxonomy and survey of Grid resource management systems for distributed computing. *International Journal of Software: Practice and Experience, 32*(2), 135-164.

Kumagai, J. (2006). Nine cautionary tales: If terrorists decide to strike again, are we prepared? Not really, as these scenarios of extremism make clear. *IEEE Spectrum, 43*(9), 28-37.

Kyong, H. K., Buyya, R., & Kim, J.(2006). Imprecise computation Grid application model for flexible market-based resource allocation. *Cluster Computing and the Grid, 2006. CCGRID 06. Sixth IEEE International Symposium on Volume 1, 5.*

Laforenza, D. (2002). Grid programming: Some indications where we are headed. *ACM Parallel Computing Special Issue: Advanced environments for parallel and distributed computing* (pp. 1733-1752).

Lagares, J.I. (2006). Monte Carlo parallelized solution for patients under dynamic radiotherapy treatment. *Science and supercomputing in Europe* (pp. 520-524).

Lagares, J.I., Arce, P., Soler, J.D., Pereira, G., & Embid, M. (2007). The MIRaS (Medical Image Radiotherapy and Simulation) project. *4th International Conference on Imaging Technologies in Biomedical Sciences, ITBS 2007.* Milos Conference Center G. Eliopoulos, Milos Island, Greece.

Lagares, J.I., Soler, J.D., Arce, P., Pereira, G., & Embid, M. (2007). The MIRaS (Medical Image Radiotherapy and Simulation) C++ Radiotherapy Simulation Module. *Xth EFOMP Congress*, Pisa, Italy.

Lai, K., Rasmusson, L., Adar, E., Sorkin, S., Zhang, L., & Huberman, B.A. (2004). *Tycoon: an implementation of a distributed market-based resource allocation system* (Tech. Rep. arXiv:cs.DC/0412038). Palo Alto, CA: HP Labs.

Lambert, H. D., & Leonhardt, C. F. (2004). Federated authentication to support information sharing: Shibboleth in a bio-surveilance information Grid. *International Congress Series*, 1268135-140.

Lamehamedi, H., Szymanksi, B. K., & Conte, B. (2005). *Distributed data management services for dynamic data Grids* (Tech. Rep. No. 05-16). Computer Science, Rensselaer Polytechnic Institute.

Lan, Z., Taylor, V. E., & Li, Y. (2006). DistDLB: Improving cosmology SAMR simulations on distributed computing systems through hierarchical load balancing. *Journal of Parallel and Distributed Computing, 66*(5), 716-731.

Laure. E. (2004). Middleware for the next generation grid infrastructure. In *Proceedings of the Computing in High Energy Physics Conference* (pp. 8-26).

Lawson, M. B. (2001). In praise of slack: Time is of the essence. *The Academy of Management Executive, 15*(3), 125-136.

LCG (n.d.). *Worldwide Large Hadron Collider Computing Grid*. Project of the European Organization for Nuclear Research (CERN).

LCG Middleware (2006). Retrieved August 21, 2007, from ttp://lcg.web.cern.ch/LCG/activities/middleware.html

LCG-3D (2007). *Distributed deployment of databases for LCG*. Retrieved from https://twiki.cern.ch/twiki/bin/view/PSSGroup/LCG3DWiki

Leal, A., Sánchez-Doblado, F., Arráns, R., Roselló, J. V., Carrasco, E., & Lagares, J.I. (2003). Routine IMRT verification by means of an automatic MC simulation system. *Int. J. Rad. Oncol. Biol. Phys*, *56*(1) 58-68.

Lee, H. (1999). Time and information technology: Monochronicity, polychronicity and temporal symmetry. *European Journal of Information Systems*, *8*(1), 16-26.

Lee, T.B., Hendler, J., & Lassila, O. (2001). The semantic Web. *Scientific American, 284*(4), 34-43.

Lehmann, D., Müller, R., & Sandholm, T. (2006). The winner determination problem. In P. Cramton, Y. Shoham, R. Steinberg, R. (Eds.), *Combinatorial auctions* (pp. 297–317). Cambridge, MA: MIT Press.

Lehmann, D., Oallaghan, L. I., & Shoham, Y. (2002). Truth revelation in approximately efficient combinatorial auctions. *Journal of the ACM (JACM), 49*(5), 577-602.

Leitner, T. (1996). Accurate reconstruction of a known HIV-1 transmission history by phylogenetic tree analysis. *Proc. Natl. Acad. Sci. USA, 93* (pp. 10864-10869).

Leitner, T., & Albert, J. (1999). The molecular clock of HIV-1 unveiled through analysis of a known transmission history. *Proc. Natl. Acad. Sci. USA, 96* (pp. 10752–10757).

Leitner, T., Kumar, S., & Albert, J. (1997). Tempo and mode of nucleotide substitutions in gag and env gene fragments in Human Immunodeficiency Virus Type 1: Populations with a known transmission history. *Journal of Virology, 71*, 4761–4770.

Lewis, R., & Torczon, V. (2002). A globally convergent augmented Lagrangian pattern search algorithm for optimization with general constraints and simple bounds. *SIAM Journal on Optimization*, *12*(4), 1075-1089.

Li, L., & Horrocks, I. (2004). A software framework for matchmaking based on semantic Web technology. *Int. J. of Electronic Commerce*, 8(4), 39-60.

Li, M., & Baker, M. (2005). *The Grid: Core technologies*. England: Wiley.

Li, M., Yu, B., & Qi, M. (2006). PGGA: A predictable and grouped genetic algorithm for job scheduling. *Future Generation Computer Systems, 22*(5), 588-599.

Li, M., Yu, B., Huang, C., Song, Y. & Rana, O. (2006). Service Matchmaking with Rough Sets, Proceedings of the 6th IEEE International Symposium on Cluster Computing and the Grid (CCGRID'06) (pp. 123 – 130), Singapore.

Li, Y. W., & Lan, Z. L. (2004). A survey of load balancing in grid computing. *First International Symposium on Computational and Information Science* (LNCS 3314, 280-285).

Li, Y.H., Zhao, D.P., & Li J. (2007). Scheduling algorithm based on integrated utility of multiple QoS attributes on service Grid. In *Proceedings of 6th International Conference on Grid and Cooperative Computing*, Dalian, China (pp. 288-295).

Liberati, D. (2007). Identification through data mining. In J. Janczewski & A.M. Colarik (Eds.), *Cyber warfare and cyber terrorism* (pp. 374-380). Hershey, PA: IGI Global.

Liberati, D. (2008). Attention facilitation via multimedia stimulation. In I.K. Ibrahim (Ed.), *Handbook of research on mobile multimedia*. Hershey, PA: IGI Global.

Liberati, D. (2008). Multi-target classifiers for mining in bioinformatics. In M. Song & & Y.-F. Wu (Eds.), *Handbook of research on text and web mining technologies*. Hershey, PA: IGI Global.

Liberati, D. (2008). System theory: From classical state space to variable selection and model identification. In L. Tomei (Ed), *Encyclopedia of information technology curriculum integration*. Hershey, PA: IGI Global.

Liberati, D. (2008). Information technology in brain intensive therapy. In N. Wickramasinghe & E. Geisler (Eds.), *Encyclopedia of healthcare and information systems*. Hershey, PA: IGI Global.

Lin, Y.-C., Fregly, B., Haftka, R., & Queipo, N. (2005). Surrogate-based contact modeling for efficient dynamic simulation with deformable anatomic joints. In *Proceed-*

ings of the tenth international symposium on computer simulation in biomechanics (p. 23-24).

Linesch, M. (2007). *Grid - Distributed computing at scale, An overview of Grid and the Open Grid Forum.* OGF Grid final documents. Retrieved October 29, 2007, from http://www.ogf.org/documents/GFD.112.pdf

Lipmaa, H., Asokan, N., & Niemi, V. (2002). *Secure Vickrey auctions without threshold trust.* Paper presented at the 6th International Financial Cryptography Conference.

Liu, P., & Lewis, M.J. (2005). Mobile code enabled Web services. In *Proceedings of ICWS'05*, (pp. 167-174).

Liu, X., & Chien, A. A. (2006). Realistic large-scale online network simulation. *International Journal of High Performance Computing Applications, 20*(3), 383-399.

Lueckenhaus, M., & Eckstein, W. (1997). Multiagent based system for parallel image processing. *Proc. Parallel and Distributed Methods for Image Processing* (pp. 21-30).

Mach, R., Lepro-Metz, R., Jackson, S., & McGinnis, L. (2006) *Usage Record -- Format Recommendation* (Version 1, GDF.98). Open Grid forum. Retrieved August 30, 2007, from http://www.ogf.org/documents/GFD.98.pdf

Machado, M. (2004, June). Enable existing applications for Grid. *IBM developerWorks series* (pp. 1-11).

MacKie-Mason, J. K., & Varian, H. R. (1994). *Generalized Vickery auctions* (Working Paper). University of Michigan.

Madnick, S. E., & Donovan J. J. (1973). Application and analysis of the virtual machine approach to information system security and isolation. In *Proceedings of ACM SIGARCH-SYSOPS Workshop on Virtual Computer Systems*, Boston, MA. (pp. 210-224).

Madnick, S. E., & Donovan, J. J. (1974). I/O Scheduler. In *Operating Systems.* McGraw-Hill, Inc.

Maheswaran, M., Ali, S., Siegel, H. J., Hensgen, D., & Freund, R. F. (1999). Dynamic mapping of a class of independent tasks onto heterogeneous computing sys-

tems. *Journal of Parallel and Distributed Computing, 59*(2), 107-131.

Majithia, S., Ali, A.S., Rana, O., & Walker, D. (2004). Reputation-based semantic service discovery. In *Proc. of Int. Workshops on Enabling Technologies: Infrastructures for Collaborative Enterprises (WETICE)* (pp. 297-302). Modena, Italy: IEEE Computer Society.

Malone, M., S. (2001). Internet II: Rebooting America, Forbes online. Retrieved June 30, 2007, from http://members.forbes.com/asap/2001/0910/044.html

Malone, T. W., Fikes, R. E., Grant, K. R., & Howard, M. T. (1988). Enterprise: A market-like task scheduler for distributed computing environments. In *The Ecology of Computation* (pp. 177-205). North-Holland: Elsevier Science Publishers.

Mani, A., & Nagarajan, A. (2002). Understanding quality of service for Web services. Retrieved October 7, 2007, from http://www-106.ibm.com/developerworks/library/ws-quality.html

Martin, D. L., et al. (2004). Bringing semantics to Web services: The OWL-S approach. In J. Cardoso & A.P. Sheth (Eds.), *Proceedings of the 1st Int. Workshop on Semantic Web Services and Web Process Composition (SWSWPC)* (pp. 26-42). San Diego: IEEE Computer Society.

Mastroianni, C., Talia, D., & Verta, O. (2005). A super-peer model for building resource discovery services in Grids: Design and simulation analysis. *European Grid Conference 2005.* (LNCS 3470, pp. 132-143).

Mattmann, C. A. (2006). A reference framework for requirements and architecture in biomedical Grid systems. *IEEE International Conference on Information Reuse and Integration, 2007* (pp. 418-422). Las Vegas, NV.

McGuinness, D. L., & Harmelen, F. (2004). *OWL Web ontology language overview.* W3C Recommendation. Retrieved June 2007, from http://www.w3.org/TR/owl-features (last access: June 2007)

Meeks, W.L., & Dasgupta, S. (2004). Geospatial information utility: An estimation of the relevance of geospatial information to users. *Decision Support Systems, 38*(1), 47-63.

Milanovic, N., & Malek, M. (2004). Current solutions for web service composition. *IEEE Internet Computing, 8*(6), 51-59.

Miles, S., Papay, J., Dialani, V., Luck, M., Decker, K., Payne, T., & Moreau, L. (2003). Personalised Grid service discovery. *IEEE Proceedings Software: Special Issue on Performance Engineering, 150*(4), 252-256.

Min, W. H., Wilson, W. Y., Ngi, Y. H., Wang, D., Li, Z., Hong, L. K., et al. (2005). Dynamic storage resource management framework for the Grid. In *Proceedings of the 22nd IEEE / 13th NASA Goddard Conf. on Mass Storage Systems and Technologies*, (pp. 286-293).

Min, Y., Shao-yin, H., Zhi, W., Zunping, C., dilin, M., & Chuanshan, G. (2005). *PICC: a secure mobile agent framework based on garbled circuit*. Paper presented at the 19th International Conference on Advanced Information Networking and Applications.

Mineter, M.J., Dowers, S., & Gittings, B.M. (2000). Towards a HPC Framework for integrated processing of geographical data: encapsulating the complexity of parallel algorithms. *Transactions in GIS, 4*(3), 245-261.

Ming, A, & Ma, H. (2007). Proposal of an architecture for a biometric Grid. *LNCS, 44*(39),195-208.

Minyard, T., & Kallinderis, Y. (2000). Parallel load balancing for dynamic execution environments. *Computer Methods in Applied Mechanics and Engineering, 189*(4), 1295-1309.

Montagnat, J. (2006). Bridging clinical information systems and Grid middleware: A Medical Data Manager. In *Proc. HealthGrid 2006*, Valencia, Spain.

Montresor, A., Meling, H., & Babaoğlu, Ö. (2002). Messor: Load-balancing through a swarm of autonomous agents. In *Proceedings of the 1st International Workshop on Agents and Peer-to-Peer Computing* (pp. 125-137). Springer Berlin / Heidelberg.

Morariu, C., Waldburger, M., & Stille, B. (2006). *An accounting and charging architecture for mobile Grids*

(Tech. Rep. No. 2006.06). Zurich, Switzerland: University of Zurich, Department of Informatics (IFI).

Moretti, C., Faltemier, T. C., Thain, D., & Flynn, P. J. (2006). Challenges in executing data intensive biometric worloads on a desktop Grid. Tech Report (pp. 13).

Morin, C., et al. (2004). Kerrighed: A single system image cluster operating system for high performance computing. *International Conference on Parallel and Distributed Computing, Parallel Processing, 2790/2004* (pp. 1291-1294).

Morris, R.J.T., & Truskowski, B. J.(2003).The evolution of storage systems. *IBM System Journal, 42*(2), 205-217.

Moscicki, J.T., Lee, H.C., Guatelli, S., Lin, S.C., & Pia, M.G. (2004). Biomedical Applications on the GRID: Efficient management of parallel jobs. In *NSS IEEE 2003, Rome*. Retrieved from,http://it-proj-diane.web.cern.ch/it-proj-diane/papers/DIANE-NSS2004.pdf

Moulitsas, I., & Karypis, G. (2006). *Architecture aware partitioning algorithms*. (Tech Rep. No. 06-001). University of Minnesota.

Müller-Pfefferkorn, R., Neumann, R., Borovac, S., Hammad, A., Harenberg, T., Husken, M., et al. (2006). Monitoring of jobs and their execution for the LHC computing Grid. In *Proceedings of the Cracow Grid Workshop (CGW 06)*, Cracow, Poland.

Murch, R., & Johnson, J. (1998). *Intelligent software agents*. New York: Prentice Hall.

Muselli, M., & Liberati, D. (2000). Training digital circuits with hamming clustering. *IEEE T Circuits I, 47*, 513-527.

Muselli, M., & Liberati, D. (2002). Binary rule generation via hamming clustering. *IEEE T Knowl Data En, 14*(6), 1258-1268.

Naor, M., Pinkas, B., & Sumner, R. (1999). *Privacy preserving auctions and mechanism design*. Paper presented at the 1st ACM Conference on Electronic Commerce.

Navarro, D. (2004). Epidemiología de las enfermedades del tiroides en Cuba. *Rev Cubana Endocrinol, 15*.

Negroponte, N. (2000, Jun 19). Will everything be digital? *Time, 155*, 86-87.

NeST (2007). *Network Storage Technology*. http://www.cs.wisc.edu/condor/nest

Neumann, D., Stoesser, J., Anandasivam, A., & Borissov, N., (2007). SORMA – Building an open Grid market for Grid resource allocation. In J. Altmann, D.J. Veit (Eds.), *Proceedings of the 4th International Workshop on Grid Economics and Business Models* (LNCS 4685, pp. 194-200). Heidelberg: Springer-Verlag.

Ng, H.-K., Ong, Y.-S., Hung, T., & Lee, B.-S. (2005). Grid enabled optimization. In *Advances in Grid Computing - EGC 2005* (LNCS, 296-304).

Nicolescu, C., & Jonker, P. (2000). Parallel low-level image processing on a distributed memory system. In *Proc. 15th Workshop on Parallel and Distributed Processing* (pp. 226-233).

Nisan, N., & Ronen, A. (2000). *Computationally feasible VCG mechanisms*. Paper presented at the 2nd ACM conference on Electronic commerce.

No, J., & Park, H. (2005). GEDAS: A data management system for data Grid environments. *Computational Science – ICCS 2005* (pp. 485-492).

Nolle, L., Wong, K.C.P., & Hopgood, A.A. (2001). DARBS: A distributed blackboard system. *Research and Development in Intelligent Systems XVIII*, 161-170.

Novak, M. (2005).A discovery service for very large, dynamic Grids. *Sixth IEEE/ACM International Workshop on Grid Computing*.

Novotny, J. (2003). The Grid portal development kit. In F. Berman, G.C. Fox, & A.J.G. Hey (Eds.), *Grid computing: Making the global infrastructure a reality* (pp. 657-673). England: John Wiley & Sons Ltd.

NSF (2005). Research challenges in distributed computer systems. *NSF Workshop Report*.

NSF (2006, January). NSF's Cyberinfrastructure Vision for 21st Century Discovery. *NSF Cyberinfrastructure Council Report*.

Nurmi D., Brevik J., & Wolski R. (2003). *Modeling machine availability in enterprise and wide-area distributed computing environments* (UCSB Computer Science Tech. Rep.CS2003-28), 2003.

Nzouonta, J. (2003). *An algorithm for clearing combinatorial markets* (Technical Report No. CS-2003-23). Florida Institute of Technology.

Octopus (2007). *Enhydra octopus, JDBC data transformation*. Retrieved from http://www.enhydra.org/tech/octopus/

Oetiker, T. (2005). *Write your own monitoring software with RRDtool*. Retrieved August 3, 2005, from http://oss.oetiker.ch/rrdtool/pub/oscon2005-slides.pdf

Open Grid Forum (2006). The configuration, description, deployment and lifecycle management version 1.0. Retrieved from, http://www.ogf.org/documents/GFD.85.pdf

Open Grid Forum (n.d.). Retrieved April 5, 2007, from http://www.ogf.org

Open Grid Forum. (2007). Retrieved August 10, 2007, from http://www.ogf.org

Organization for the advancement of structured information standards (2006). Web services distributed management: management of Web services, version 1.1. Retrieved from, http://docs.oasis-open.org/wsdm/wsdm-mows-1.1-spec-os-01.htm

Otero, B., Cela, J. M., Badia, R. M., & Labarta, J. (2005). Data distribution strategies for domain decomposition applications in grid environments. *6th International Conference on Algorithms and Architectures for Parallel Processing, ICA3PP*. (LNCS 3719, 214-224).

Otsu, N. (1979). A threshold selection method for gray level histograms. *IEEE Transactions on Systems, Man and Cybernetics, 9*, 62-66.

Özsu, M.T., & Valduriez, P. (1999). *Principles of distributed database systems*. Prentice Hall.

Padala, P. & Shin, K. (2006). GVU: A view-oriented

framework for data management in Grid environments. *High Performance Computing - HiPC 2006* (pp. 629-640).

Palmer, B., Bubendorfer, K., & Welch, I. (2007). *Combinatorial auctions using Garbled circuits* (No. CS-TR-07-2). School of Mathematics, Statistics and Computer Science at Victoria University of Wellington.

Palmer, B., Welch, I., & Bubendorfer, K. (2007). *Adding verification to a privacy preserving combinatorial auction* (No. CS-TR-07-3). School of Mathematics, Statistics and Computer Science at Victoria University of Wellington.

Paoli, G., Muselli, M., Bellazzi, R., Corvò, R., Liberati, D., & Foppiano, F. (2000). Hamming Clustering techniques for the identification of prognostic indices in patients with advanced head and neck cancer treated with radiation therapy. *Med Biol Eng Comput, 38,* 483-486.

Paolucci, M., Kawamura, T., Payne, T., & Sycara, K. (2002). Semantic matching of Web service capabilities. In I. Horrocks & J. Hendler (Eds.), *Proceedings of the 1st International Semantic Web Conference (ISWC)* (pp. 333-347). Berlin: Springer-Verlag.

Papazoglou, M.P., Traverso, P., Dustdar, S., Leymann, F., & Krämer, B.J. (2005). Service-oriented computing: a research roadmap. In F. Curbera, B. J. Krämer, M. P. Papazoglou (Eds.), *Service Oriented Computing (SOC)*. Germany: Schloss Dagstuhl.

Parallel Workloads Archive. (2007). Retrieved August 10, 2007, from http://www.cs.huji.ac.il/labs/parallel/workload/

Paraskevas, A., & Arendell, B. (2007). A strategic framework for terrorism prevention and mitigation in tourism destination. *Tourism management.* Elsevier.

Parkes, D. C. (2001). *An iterative generalized Vickery auction: Strategy-proofness without complete relevation.* Paper presented at the AAAI Spring Symposium on Game Theoretic and Decision Theoretic Agents.

Parkes, D. C., Rabin, M. O., Shieber, S. M., & Thorpe, C. A. (2006). *Practical secrecy-preserving, verifiably cor-*
rect and trustworthy auctions. Paper presented at the 8th International Conference on Electronic Commerce.

Paton, N. W., Atkinson, M. P., Dialani, V., Pearson, D., Storey, T., & Watson, P. (2002). *Database access and integration service on the Grid.* Global Grid Forum OGSA-DAIS WG.

Patterson, D. A. (2002, January). Availability and maintainability >> Performance: New Focus for a new century. *Key Note Lecture at FAST '02.*

Pattnaik, P., Ekanadham, K., & Jann, J. (2003). Autonomic computing and Grid. In F. Berman, G.C. Fox, & A.J.G. Hey (Eds.), *Grid computing: Making the global infrastructure a reality* (pp. 351-361). England: John Wiley & Sons Ltd.

Pavani, G. S., & Waldman, H. (2006). Grid resource management by means of ant colony optimization. In *Proceeding of the third International Workshop on Networks for Grid Applications* (GridNets 2006), San Jose, CA, USA.

Pawlak, Z. (1982). Rough sets. *Int. J. of Computer and Information Science, 11*(5), 341-356.

Pellegrini, F., & Roman, J. (1996). SCOTCH: A software package for static mapping by dual recursive bipartitioning of process and architecture graphs. In *Proceedings of the International Conference and Exhibition on High-Performance Computing and Networking: HPCN Europe 1996* (pp. 493-498).

Peng, K., Boyd, C., & Dawson, E. (2005). *A multiplicative homomorphic sealed-bid auction based on goldwasser-micali encryption.* Paper presented at the 8th International Conference on Information Security.

Peng, K., Boyd, C., Dawson, E., & Viswanathan, K. (2002). *Robust, privacy protecting and publicly verifiable sealed-bid auction.* Paper presented at the 2nd International Conference on Information, Communications and Signal Processing.

Peng, K., Boyd, C., Dawson, E., & Viswanathan, K. (2003). *Five Sealed-bid auction models.* Paper presented at the Australasian Information Security Workshop Conference on ACSW Frontiers.

Peng, L., Ng, L. K., & See, S. (2005). YellowRiver: A flexible high performance cluster computing service for Grid. In *Proceedings of the 8th International Conference on High Performance Computing in Asia-Pacific Region (HPCASIA'05)* (pp. 553-558).

Peris, A.D., Lorenzo, P.M, Donno, F., Sciabà, A., Campana, S., & Santinelli, R. (2004). *LCG-2 User Guide, v2.1.*

Perrow, C. (2006). Shrink the targets: We can't defend everything, so we should take steps that protect against both terrorism and natural disasters. *IEEE Spectrum, 43*(9), 38-41.

PetaShare (2007). Retrieved from, http://www.petashare.org

Petcu, D., Vizman, D., & Paprzycki, M. (2006). Heuristic load balancing for CFD Codes executed in heterogeneous computing environments. *Scalable Computing: Practice and Experience* (SCPe), *7*(2), 15-24.

Pick, J. B., Hettrick, W. J., Viswanathan, N., & Ellsworth, E. (2000). Intra-censal geographical information systems: Application to binational border cities. *Proceedings of the Eighth European Conference on Information Systems.* Vienna.

Piro, R.M., Guarise, A., & Werbrouck, A. (2003). An economy-based accounting infrastructure for the DataGrid. In *Proceedings of the 4th International Workshop on Grid Computing* (pp. 202-204), Phoenix, AZ.

Piro, R.M., Guarise, A., & Werbrouck, A. (2004). Simulation of price-sensitive resource brokering and the hybrid pricing model with DGAS-Sim. In *Proceedings of the 13th International Workshops on Enabling Technologies: Infrastructures for Collaborative Enterprises (WETICE 2004)*, Modena, Italy.

Piro, R.M., Guarise, A., & Werbrouck, A. (2006). Price-sensitive resource brokering with the hybrid pricing model and widely overlapping price domains. *Concurrency and Computation: Practice and Experience, 18*(8), 837-850.

Piro, R.M., Pace, M., Ghiselli, A., Guarise, A., Luppi, E., Patania, G., et al. (2007). Tracing resource usage over heterogeneous Grid platforms: A Prototype RUS interface for DGAS. In *Proceedings of the 3rd IEEE International Conference on e-Science and Grid Computing 2007 (eScience2007)*, Bangalore, India.

Platform. (2007). Retrieved August 10, 2007, from http://www.platform.com/

Pollock, A., and Benjamin, L. (2002). Why Web Services and Grid Computing will Turn the Travel Industry on Its Head – and Why that's a Good Thing!. White Paper, DestiCorp.

Popp, R., Armour, T., Senator, T., & Numrych, K. (2004). Countering terrorism through information technology. *Communications of the ACM, 47*(3), 36-43.

Porter, M. E., & Millar, V. E. (1985). How information gives you competitive advantage. *Harvard Business Review, 64*(4), 149-160.

Powles, A., & Krishnaswamy, S. (2005). Extending UDDI with recommendations: an association analysis approach. In S. Bevinakoppa, L.F. Pires, & S. Hammoudi (Eds.), *Proceedings of Web Services and Model-Driven Enterprise Information Services (WSMDEIS)* (pp. 45-54). Miami: INSTICC Press.

Pucciani, G. (2008). *The replica consistency problem in data grids*. Ph.D. Thesis, Information Engineering, University of Pisa, Italy.

Qi, L., Jin, H., & Foster, I. et al (2007). HAND: Highly Available Dynamic Deployment Infrastructure for Globus Toolkit 4. In *Proceedings of PDP'07* (pp. 155-162).

Qi, L., Jin, H., Luo, Y. et al (2007). Service dependency model for dynamic and stateful grid services. In *Proceedings of ICA3PP'07* (pp. 278-289).

Qian, Z., Seepersad, C. C., Joseph, V. R., Allen, J. K., & Wu, C. F. J. (2006). Building surrogate models based on detailed and approximate simulations. *Journal of Mechanical Design, 128*(4), 668-677.

Quocirca (2005), Retrieved October 2007, from http://www.quocirca.com/report_gridindex2.htm

Rajasekaran, S., Ammar, R., Demurjian, S., & Greenshields, I. (2004). Strategies to process voluminous data in support of counter-terrorism. *IEEEAC, 1253*(8).

Raman, R., Livny, M., & Solomon, M. (1998, July). Matchmaking: Distributed resource management for high throughput computing. In *Proceedings of the Seventh IEEE International Symposium on High Performance Distributed Computing (HPDC7)*. Chicago, Illinois.

Raman, V., Narang, I., Crone, C., Haas, L., Malaika, S., Mukai, T., et al. (2002). *Data access and management services on Grid*. Global Grid Forum 5.

Ranganathan, K., & Foster, I. (2001). Identifying dynamic replication strategies for a high performance data grid. In *Proceedings of the International Grid Computing Workshop*, Denver, CO.

Rao, A.R.M. (2006). Explicit nonlinear dynamic finite element analysis on homogeneous/heterogeneous parallel computing environment. *Advances in Engineering Software, 37*(11), 701-720.

Regev, O., & Nisan, N. (1998). The POPCORN market – an online market for computational resources. In *Proceedings of the 1st International Conference on Information and Computation Economies* (pp. 148-157). New York: ACM Press.

Resnick, M. (1997). *Turtles, termites, and traffic jams - explorations in massively parallel microworlds*. Cambridge, MA: MIT Press.

Reynolds, C. W. (1987). Flocks, herds, and schools: A Distributed behavioral model. *Computer Graphics, 21*(4), 25-34.

Rilling, L. (2006, August). Vigne: Towards a self-healing Grid operating system. *International Conference on Parallel and Distributed Computing, Dresden, Germany.*

Ritchie, G., & Levine, J. (2004). A hybrid ant algorithm for scheduling independent jobs in heterogeneous computing environments. In *Proceedings of the 23rd Workshop of the UK Planning and Scheduling Special Interest Group.*

RLS (2007). Data management: Key concepts of RLS. Retrieved from http://www.globus.org/toolkit/docs/4.0/data/key/rls.html

Roman, D., Keller, U., Lausen, H., Bruijn, J., Lara, R., Stollberg, M., et al. (2005). Web service modeling ontology. *Applied Ontology, 1*(1), 77-106.

Ronquist, F., & Huelsenbeck, J.P. (2003). MrBayes 3: Bayesian phylogenetic inference under mixed models. *Bioinformatics, 19*, 1572-1574.

Rosenblum, M., & Garfinkel, T. (2005). Virtual machine monitors: current technology and future trends. *Computer 38*(5), 39-47.

Ross-Flanigan, N. (2003). MGRID to lead to third wave of computing, The University record online, University of Michigan. Retrieved June 30, 2007, from http://www.umich.edu/~urecord/0203/May05_03/08.shtml

Rotaru, T., & Nägeli, H. (2004). Dynamic load balancing by diffusion in heterogeneous systems. *Journal of Parallel and Distributed Computing, 64*(4), 481-497.

Rothkopf, M. H., Pekec, A., & Harstad, R. M. (1995). *Computationally manageable combinatorial auctions*. New Jersey, USA: DIMACS, Center for Discrete Mathematics and Theoretical Computer Science, Rutgers.

Roure, D., Jennings, N. R., & Shadbolt, N. R. (2003). The semantic Grid: A future e-Science infrastructure. F. Berman, G.C. Fox, & A.J.G. Hey (Eds.), *Grid computing: Making the global infrastructure a reality* (pp. 437-470). England: John Wiley & Sons Ltd.

Rowstron A., & Druschel, P. (2001). Pastry: Scalable, distributed object location and routing for large-scale peer-to-peer systems. In R. Guerraoui (Ed.), *Proceedings of Middleware 2001* (pp. 329-350). Heidelberg: Springer-Verlag.

Ruby, C. L. (2002). The definition of terrorism. *Analyses of Social Issues and Public Policy, 2*(1), 9-14.

Rudolph, L. (2001). *Project oxygen: Pervasive, human-centric computing - An initial experience*. Paper presented at the 13th International Conference on Advanced Information Systems Engineering.

Sacco, E., Farina, M., Greco, C., Busti, S., DeGioia, L., Fantinato, S., et al. (2007). Molecular and computational analysis of regulation of hSos1, the major activator of the proto-oncoprotein Ras. *Proc SysBioHealth.*

Saito, Y., & Shapiro, M. (2005). *Optimistic replication.* ACM Computing Surveys.

Samaras, G., Karenos, K., & Christodoulou, E. (2004). A Grid service framework for metadata management in self-e-learning networks. *Grid Computing 2004* (pp. 260-269).

Sander, V., Adamson W., Foster I., & Roy A. (2001). *End-to-end provision of policy information for network QoS.* In *Proceedings of the Tenth IEEE Symposium on High Performance Distributed Computing (HPDC-10).* IEEE Press.

Sandholm, T. W. (1996). *Limitations of the Vickery auction in computational multiagent systems.* Paper presented at the Second International Conference on Multi-Agent Systems.

Sandholm, T., Gardfjäll, P., Elmroth, E., Johnsson, L., & Mulmo, O. (2004). An OGSA-based accounting system for allocation enforcement across HPC centers. In *Proceedings of the 2nd International Conference on Service Oriented Computing,* New York, USA.

Santos, N. & Koblitz, B. (2006). *Distributed metadata with the AMGA metadata catalog.* Paper presented at Workshop on Next-Generation Distributed Data Management. HPDC-15, Paris, France.

Santos, N., & Koblitz, B. (2005). Metadata services on the Grid. In *Proc. of Advanced Computing and Analysis Techniques (ACAT'05),* Zeuthen, Berlin.

Santos, R., Brasileiro, F., Andrade, A., Andrade N., & Cirne, W. (2005). Accurate autonomous accounting in peer-to-peer Grids. In *ACM International Conference Proceeding Series,* 117, 1-6. *3rd International Workshop on Middleware for Grid Computing (MGC'05),* Grenoble, France.

Sartorio, A., De Nicolao, G., & Liberati, D. (2002). An improved computational method to assess pituitary re-sponsiveness to secretagogue stimuli. *Eur J Endocrinol, 147*(3), 323-332.

Sartorio, A., Pizzoccaro, A., Veldhuis, J., Liberati, D., DeNicolao, G., & Faglia (2000). Abnormal LH pulsatility in women with hyperprolactinaemic amnorrhoea normalizes after bromocriptine treatment: Deconvolution-based assessment. *Clin Endocrinol 52*(6), 703-712.

Satyam Computer Services Limited. (2004). Media Room, Archives: 2004. Retrieved June 10, 2007, from http://www.satyam.com/mediaroom/pr5dec04.html

Schloegel, K., Karypis, G., & Kumar, V. (2003). Graph partitioning for high-performance scientific simulations. In J. Dongarra, et al. (Eds.), *The sourcebook of parallel computing.* Morgan Kaufmann.

Schnellmann, P., & Redard, A. (2006). *Accounting for the authentication and authorization infrastructure (AAI) - Pilot Study* (Technical Report, version 1.0). Zurich, Switzerland: SWITCH - The Swiss Education & Research Network.

Schnizler, B. (2007). *Resource allocation in the Grid: A market engineering approach.* Doctoral dissertation, Universitätsverlag Karlsruhe, Karlsruhe.

Schopf, J. M., Pearlman, L., Miller, N., Kesselman, C., Foster, I., D'Arcy, M., et al. (2006). Monitoring the Grid with the Globus Toolkit MDS4. *Journal of Physics: Conference Series, 46,* 521–525.

Sciolla, C. (2007). *Implementazione e valutazione di un sistema di trasferimento file basato su SOAP in ambiente GRID.* Master's Thesis at the University of Pisa.

Segal, I. (2006). The communication requirements of combinatorial allocation problems. In P. Cramton, Y. Shoham, & R. Steinberg, R. (Eds.), *Combinatorial Auctions* (pp. 265–294). Cambridge, MA: MIT Press.

Seinstra, F.J., Koelma, D., Geusebroek, J.M. (2002). A software architecture for user transparent parallel image processing. *Parallel Computing, 28,* 967-993.

Selvi, S.T., Buyya, R., Rajagopalan, M. R.,Vijayakumar, K., & Deepak, G.N. (2007). Multilingual interface for Grid market directory services: An experience with supporting Tamil. Retrieved from, http://www.gridbus. org/reports/gmd-tamil.pdf

SETI@Home (n.d.). Retrieved April 5, 2007, from http:// setiathome.ssl.berkeley.edu

ShaikhAli, A., Rana, O., Al-Ali, R., & Walker, D. (2003). UDDIe: An extended registry for Web service. *Proceedings of 2003 Symposium on Applications and the Internet Workshops (SAINT)* (pp. 85-89). Orlando: IEEE Computer Society.

Shankar, C., Talwar, V., Iyer, S. et al (2006). Specification-enhanced policies for automated management of changes in it systems. In *Proceedings of LISA'06* (pp. 103-118).

Shapiro, C., & Varian, H. R. (1999). *Information rules: a strategic guide to the network economy.* Boston: Harvard Business School Press.

Shen, Z., Dongping, M., & Qinghui, S. (2004). Architecture design of Grid GIS and its applications on image processing based on LAN. *Information Sciences, 166*(1-4), 1-17.

Shneidman, J., Ng, C., Parkes, D.C., AuYoung, A., Snoeren, A.C., Vahdat, A., & Chun, B. (2005). Why markets could (but don't currently) solve resource allocation problems in systems. In *Proceedings of the 10th conference on Hot Topics in Operating Systems.* Berkeley: USENIX Association

Shoshani, A. (2003). Storage resource managers: Essential components for the grid. In J. Nabrzyski, J.M. Schopf, & J. Weglarz (Eds.), *Grid resource management: State of the art and future trends.* Kluwer Academic Publishers.

Siegrist, D. (2000). Advanced information technology to counter biological terrorism. *ACM SIGBIO, 20*(2), 2-7.

Simpson, T. W., Booker, A. J., Ghosh, D., Giunta, A. A., Koch, P. N., & Yang, R.-J. (2004). Approximation methods in multidisciplinary analysis and optimization: A panel discussion. *Structural and Multidisciplinary Optimization, 27*(5), 302-313.

Sinclair, B., Goscinski, A., & Dew, R. (2005). Enhancing UDDI for Grid service discovery by using dynamic parameters. In O. Gervasi, et al. (Eds.), *Proceedings of the Int. Conference on Computational Science and its Applications (ICCSA)* (pp.49-59). Singapore: Springer.

Sinha, S., & Parashar, M. (2002). Adaptive system sensitive partitioning of AMR applications on heterogeneous clusters. *Cluster Computing, 5*(4), 343-352.

Skowron, A., & Rauszer, C. (1992). The discernibility matrices and functions in information systems. In R. Slowinski (Ed.), *Decision support by experience - Application of the rough sets theory* (pp. 331-362). Kluwer Academic Publishers.

Smale, S. (1976). A convergent process of price adjustment and global Newton methods. *Journal of Mathematical Economics, 3*(2), 107-120.

Smith, D. (2001). *ProdTools man pages.* Retrieved December 10, 2001, from http://www.slac.stanford. edu/BFROOT/www/Computing/Offline/Production/ prodtools.pdf

Smith, D. A., Blanc, F., Bozzi, C., Andreotti, D., & Khan, A. (2006). Babar Simulation Production – A millennium of work in under a year. *Nuclear Science, IEEE Transactions on 53*(3), 1299–1303.

Smith, M., Friese, T., & Freisleben, B. (2004). Towards a service-oriented Ad Hoc grid. In *Proceedings of the 3rd International Symposium on Parallel and Distributed Computing/Third International Workshop on Algorithms, Models and Tools for Parallel Computing on Heterogeneous Networks (ISPDC/HeteroPar'04)* (pp. 201-208).

Smith, M., Friese, T., & Freisleben, B. (2005). Intra-engine service security for grids based on WSRF. In *Proceedings of CCGrid'05* (pp. 644-653).

Smith, W., Foster, I., & Taylor, V. (1998). Predicting application run times using historical information. In *Proceedings of the Workshop on Job Scheduling Strategies for Parallel Processing* (pp. 122-142). Springer-Verlag.

Snedecor, G., Cochran, W.G. (1967). *Statistical methods* (pp. 62-64). Ames, IA: The Iowa State University Press.

Sotomayor, B., & Childers, L. (2005). *Globus toolkit 4: Programming java services.* Morgan Kaufmann.

SRB (2007). The SDSC storage resource broker. Retrieved from, http://www.sdsc.edu/srb/index.php/Main_Page

Srinivasan, N., Paolucci, M., & Sycara, K.P. (2004). An efficient algorithm for OWL-S based semantic search in UDDI. In J. Cardoso & A.P. Sheth (Eds.), *Proceedings of the 1ˢᵗ Int. Workshop on Semantic Web Services and Web Process Composition (SWSWPC)* (pp. 96-110). San Diego: IEEE Computer Society.

Srivastava, B., & Koehler, J. (2003). Web service composition—Current solutions and open problems. IN *Proceedings of the ICAPS 2003 Workshop on Planning for Web Services* (pp. 28-35).

Stanoevska-Slabena, K., Talamanca, C.F., Thanos, G.A., & Zsigri, C. (2007). Development of a generic value chain for the grid industry. In J. Altmann, & D.J. Veit (Eds.), *Proceedings of the 4th International Workshop on Grid Economics and Business Models* (LNCS 4685, pp. 44-57). Heidelberg: Springer-Verlag.

Stockinger H. (2007). Defining the Grid: A Snapshot on the Current View, *Journal of Supercomputing*, Springer Verlag. Retrieved June 30, 2007, from http://www.springerlink.com/content/906476116167673m/

Stockinger, H. (2001). *Database replication in worldwide distributed data grids.* Ph.D. Thesis, Institute of Computer Science and Business Informatics, University of Vienna, Austria.

Stockinger, H. (2007). Defining the grid: A snapshot on the current view. *The Journal of Supercomputing, 42*(1), 3-17.

Stoica, I., Morris, R., Liben-Nowell, D., Karger, D., Kaashoek, M., Dabek, F., & Balakrishnan, H. (2003). Chord: A scalable peer-to-peer lookup protocol for Internet applications. *IEEE/ACM Transactions on Networks, 11*(1), 17-32.

Stonebraker, M., Aoki, P.M., Litwin, W., Pfeffer, A., Sah, A., & Sidell, J. (1996). Mariposa: A wide-area distributed database system. *The International Journal on Very Large Databases, 5*(1), 48-63.

Storage resource broker (2007). Retrieved October 7, 2007, from http://www.sdsc.edu/srb/index.php/Main_Page

Stuer, G., Vanmechelen, K., & Broeckhove, J. (2007). A commodity market algorithm for pricing substitutable Grid resources. *Future Generation Computer Systems, 23*(5), 688-701.

Sun Grid Engine. (2007). Retrieved August 10, 2007, from http://wwws.sun.com/software/gridware/sge.html

Sun X.-H., & Wu M. (2003). Grid harvest service: A system for long-term, application-level task scheduling. In *Proceedings of 2003 IEEE International Parallel and Distributed Processing Symposium,* Nice, France.

Sun X.-H., & Wu M. (2007). Quality of service of grid computing: Resource sharing. In *Proceedings of the 6th International Conference on Grid and Cooperative Computing* (pp. 395-402).

Sun. (2008). *Sun Grid.* Retrieved February 18th, 2008, from http://www.sun.com/service/sungrid

Sundararaj, A., & Dinda, P. (2004). Towards virtual networks for virtual machine grid computing. In *Proceedings of 3rd USENIX Conference on Virtual Machine Technology.*

Suomi, R. (1990). Lowering transaction costs with information technology. *Nordisk Försäkringstidskrift, 70*(4), 264-285.

Susarla, S., & Carter, J. (2005). Flexible consistency for wide area peer replication. In *Proceedings of the 25th International Conference on Distributed Computing Systems.*

Sutherland, I.E. (1968). A futures market in computer time. *Communications of the ACM, 11*(6), 449-451.

Suzuki, K., & Yokoo, M. (2002). *Secure combinatorial auctions by dynamic programming with polynomial secret sharing.* Paper presented at the 6th International Financial Cryptography Conference.

Sweet, W., & Cass, S. (2007). How to fight crime in real time: New York City's rapid data retrieval accelerates investigations. *IEEE Spectrum, 44*(6), 46-49.

Tait, R.J., Schaefer, G., & Hopgood, A.A. (2006). iDARBS – A distributed blackboard system for image processing. In *Proc. 13th International Conference on Systems, Signals and Image Processing*, 431-434.

Talwar, V., Milojicic, D., Wu, Q. et al (2005). Approaches for service deployment. *IEEE Internet Computing, 9*(2), 70-80.

Taniar D., G. S. (2007). Concurrency control issues in grid databases. *Future Generation Computer Systems 23*(1).

Taniguchi, R., Makiyama, Y., Tsuruta, N., Yonemoto, S., & Arita, D. (1997). Software platform for parallel image processing and computer vision. In *Proceedings of Parallel and Distributed Methods for Image Processing* (pp. 2-10).

Taylor, J. (2002). Plenary keynote, GGF 5. Retrieved June 30, 2007, from www.gridforum.org/Meetings/ggf5/ plenary/Mon/

Taylor, V., Wu, X., Geisler, J., Li, X., Lan, Z., Stevens, R., et al. (2000). Prophesy: An infrastructure for analyzing and modeling the performance of parallel and distributed applications. *High Performance Distributed Computing (HPDC) 2000* (pp. 302-303). Pittsburgh, PA.

Teresco, J., Devine, K., & Flaherty, J. (2005). Partitioning and dynamic load balancing for the numerical solution of partial differential equations. In *Numerical solution of partial differential equations on parallel computers*. Springer Verlag.

The Globus Toolkit (n.d.). Retrieved from, http://www.globus.org/toolkit/

The Washington Post (2006). 325,000 on terrorism list.

Thigpen, W., Hacker, T.J., McGinnis, L.F., & Athey, B.D. (2002). Distributed accounting on the Grid. In *Proceedings of the 6th Joint Conference on Information Sciences* (pp. 1147-1150), Durham, North Carolina, USA.

Tian, M., Voigt, T., Naumowicz, T., Ritter, H., & Schiller, J. (2004). Performance considerations for mobile web services. *Computer Communications, 27*(11), 1097-1105.

Torterolo, L., Corradi, L., Canesi, B., Fato, M., Barbera, R., Scifo, S., et al. (2007). A new paradigm to design, implement and deploy Grid oriented application: A biomedical use case. *Proceedings of the Symposium Open Grid*, Palermo, Italy.

Trombetti, G.A., Merelli, I., Orro, A., & Milanesi, L. (2007). BGBlast: A BLAST Grid implementation with database self-updating and adaptive replication. *Stud Health Technol Inform, 126*, 23-30.

Tsouloupas, G., & Dikaiakos, M. (2003). GridBench: A tool for benchmarking grids. In *Proceedings of 4th International Workshop on Grid Computing (Grid2003)* (pp. 60-67). Phoenix, AZ: IEEE.

Tuecke S. (2001). Grid security infrastructure (GSI) roadmap. Retrieved from, http://www.gridforum.org/security/ggf1_-200103/drafts/draft-ggf-gsi-roadmap-02.pdf

Tuecke, S., Czajkowski, K., Foster, I., Frey, J., Graham, S., Kesselman, C., et al. (2003). Open grid services infrastructure (OGSI) Version 1.0. Retrieved from, http://forge.gridforum.org/projects/ggf-editor/document/draft-ogsi-service-1/en/1

Tummala, S. & Kosar, T. (2007). Data management challenges in coastal applications. To appear in *Journal of Coastal Research*.

Umbaugh, S. (1998) *Computer vision and image processing*. New York: Prentice Hall.

Vanmechelen, K., & Broeckhove, J., (2007). A comparative analysis of single-unit Vickrey auctions and commodity markets for realizing Grid economies with dynamic pricing. In J. Altmann, D.J. Veit (Eds.), *Proceedings of the 4th International Workshop on Grid Economics and Business Models* (LNCS 4685, pp. 98-111). Heidelberg: Springer-Verlag.

Vanmechelen, K., Depoorter, W., & Broeckhove, J., (2008). Economic Grid resource management for CPU bound applications with hard deadlines. In *Proceedings of the 8th IEEE International Symposium on Cluster Computing and the Grid (CCGrid 2008)*. Lyon (France), IEEE Computer Society.

Vanmechelen, K., Stuer, G., & Broeckhove, J. (2006). Pricing substitutable Grid resources using commodity market models. In H.Y. Lee, & S. Miller (Eds.), *Proceedings of the 3rd International Workshop on Grid Economics and Business Models* (pp. 103-112). Singapore: World Scientific.

Vapnik, V. (1998). *Statistical learning theory.* New York: Wiley.

Varian, H. R. (1995). *Economic mechanism design for computerized agents.* Paper presented at the Usenix Workshop on Electronic Commerce.

Vasilevsky, V. S., Nesterov, A. V., Arickx, F., & Broeckhove, J. (2001). The algebraic model for scattering in three-s-cluster systems: Theoretical background. *Physical Review, C63 034606* (pp. 1-16).

Venkateswara R. M., Srinivas V., Gopinath T., & Janakiram D. (2006). Vishwa: A reconfigurable P2P middleware for Grid computations. In *Proceedings of International Conference on Parallel Processing (ICPP'06)* (pp. 381-390).

Vercesi, A., Sirtori, C., Vavassori, A., Setti, E., & Liberati, D. (2000). Estimating germinability of Plasmopara Viticola oospores by means of neural networks. *Med Biol Eng Comput, 38,* 109-112.

Vickrey, W. (1961). Counterspeculation, auctions and competitive sealed tenders. *The Journal of Finance, 16*(1), 8-37.

Vickrey, W. (1961). Counterspeculation, auctions, and competitive sealed tenders. *Journal of Finance, 16*(1), 8-37.

Voss, K., Djemame, K., Gourlay, I., & Padgett, J., (2007). AssessGrid, economic issues underlying risk awareness in Grids. In J. Altmann, D.J. Veit (Eds.), *Proceedings of the 4th International Workshop on Grid Economics and Business Models* (LNCS 4685, pp. 170-175). Heidelberg: Springer-Verlag.

Waldspurger, C.A., Hogg, T., Huberman, B.A., Kephart, J.O., & Stornetta, W.S. (1992). Spawn: A distributed computational economy. *IEEE Transactions on Software Engineering, 18*(2), 103-117.

Walker, R. (ed.) (1993). *AGI Standards Committee GIS Dictionary.* Association for Geographic Information.

Walshaw, C., & Cross, M. (2001). Multilevel mesh partitioning for heterogeneous communication networks. *Future Generation Computer Systems, 17*(5), 601-623.

Wang, G. G., & Shan, S. (2007). Review of metamodeling techniques in support of engineering design optimization. *Journal of Mechanical Design, 129*(4), 370-380.

Wang, M., Du, Z.H., Cheng, Z.L., & Zhu, S.H. (2007). A pipeline virtual service pre-scheduling pattern and its application in astronomy data processing. *Simulation, 83*(1), 123-132.

Wang, S. & Armstrong, M.P. 2003. A quadtree approach to domain decomposition for spatial interpolation in Grid computing environments. *Parallel Computing, 29*(10), 1481-1504.

Wanschoor, R., & Aubanel, E. (2004). Partitioning and mapping of mesh-based applications onto computational grids. *Fifth IEEE/ACM International Workshop on Grid Computing* (pp. 156-162).

Watkinson, J. (1990). *The art of digital video.* Focal Press.

Watson, P. (2003). Databases and the Grid. In F. Berman, G.C. Fox, & A.J.G. Hey (Eds.), *Grid computing* (pp. 363-384). New York: Wiley.

Wei, J., Cai, W., Wang, L., & Procter, R. (2007). A secure information service for monitoring large scale grids. *Parallel Computing, 33*(7-8), 572-591.

Weiss, A. (2007). Computing in the clouds. *Networker, 11*(4), 16-25.

Weiss, L., Amon, C., Finger, S., Miller, E., Romero, D. & Verdinelli, I. (2005). Bayesian computer-aided experimental design of heterogeneous scaffolds for tissue engineering. *Computer Aided Design, 37,* 1127-1139.

Weissman, J., Kim, S., & England, D. (2005). A framework for dynamic service adaptation in the grid: Next generation software program progress report. In *Proceedings of IPDPS'05.*

Weitzel, T., Wendt, O., & v. Westarp, F. (2000). Reconsidering network effect theory. *Proceedings of the Eighth European Conference on Information Systems.* Vienna.

Wikipedia – Service Level Agreement. Retrieved from, http://en.wikipedia.org/wiki/Service_Level_Agreement

Williamson, O. E. (1985). *The economic institutions of capitalism. Firms, markets, relational constructing.* New York: The Free Press.

WLCG (2007). *Worldwide LHC computing grid.* Retrieved from http://lcg.web.cern.ch/LCG/

Wolskĩ, R., Brevik, J., Plank, J., & Bryan, T. (2003). Grid resource allocation and control using computational economies. In F. Berman, A. Hey, & G. Fox (Eds.), *Grid computing - Making the global infrastructure a reality* (pp. 747-771). New York: J. Wiley.

Wolski, R., Plank, J.S., Brevik, J., & Bryan, T. (2001). Analyzing market-based resource allocation strategies for the computational Grid. *International Journal of High Performance Computing Applications, 15*(3), 258-281.

Wolski, R., Spring N. T., & Hayes J. (1999). The network weather service: A distributed resource performance forecasting service for metacomputing. *Journal of Future Generation Computing Systems, 15*(5-6) 757-768.

Wong, A. K. Y., Ray, P., Parameswaran, N., & Strassner, J. (2005). Ontology mapping for the interoperability problem in network management. *IEEE Journal on Selected Areas in Communications, 23*(10), 2058-2068.

World Wide Web Consortium (2004). Installable Unit Deployment Descriptor Specification Version 1.0. Retrieved from, http://www.w3.org/Submission/InstallableUnit-DD/

Woslki, R., Brevik, J., Plank, J.S., & Bryan, T. (2003). Grid resource allocation and control using computational economies. In F. Berman, G. Fox, & A. Hey (Eds.), *Grid computing: making the global infrastructure a reality* (pp. 747-772). John Wiley & Sons.

Wu M., & Sun X.-H. (2006). Grid harvest service: A performance system of grid computing. *Journal of Parallel and Distributed Computing, 66*(10), 1322-1337.

Wu M., Sun X.-H., & Chen Y. (2006). QoS oriented resource reservation in shared environments. In *Proceedings of the 6th IEEE International Symposium on Cluster Computing and the Grid* (pp. 601-608).

Wu, J., Cheng, D., & Zhao, W. (2004). Detecting Grid-abuse attacks by source-based monitoring. In *Proceedings of the 1st International Workshop on Security.*

Wu, M. (2006). *System support of quality of service in shared network environments.* Dissertation, Department of Computer Science, Illinois Institute of Technology.

Wu, Y., Wu, S., Yu, H. et al (2005). Cgsp: An extensible and reconfigurable Grid framework. In *Proceedings of APPT'05* (pp. 292-300).

Xia, H., Dail, H., Casanova, H., & Chien, A. A. (2004). The MicroGrid: Using online simulation to predict application performance in diverse grid network environments. In *Proceedings of the Second International Workshop on Challenges of Large Applications in Distributed Environments (CLADE)* (pp. 52- 61). Honolulu, HI.

Yokoo, M., & Suzuki, K. (2002). *Secure multi-agent dynamic programming based on homomorphic encryption and its application to combinatorial auctions.* Paper presented at the First International Joint Conference on Autonomous Agents and Multiagent Systems.

Yu, B., Guo, W., Li, M., Song, Y., Hobson, P. & Qi, M. (2006). *Proceedings of Semantics, Knowledge and Grid, 2006 (SKG '06)* (pp. 80). Gulin, China: IEEE Computer Society.

Yu, H., Vahdat, A. (2002). Design and evaluation of a Conit-based continuous consistency model for replicated services. *ACM Transactions on Computer Systems (TOCS).*

Yu, J., & Buyya, R. (2005). Taxonomy of Workflow management systems for grid computing. *Journal of Grid Computing, 3*(3-4), 171-200.

Yu, J., Kirley, M., & Buyya, R. (2007). Multi-objective planning for workflow execution on Grids. *Grid 2007* (pp. 10-17). Austin, TX: IEEE/ACM.

Yuan, E., & Wenzel, G. (2002). Enabling total information awareness with Grid services. *IEEEAC, 6-2980*(1209).

Zhang, W., Cheng, A. M. K., Hu, M. (2006, April). Multisite co-allocation algorithms for computational grid. In *Proceedings of the 20th International Parallel and Distributed Processing Symposium* (pp. 8).

Zhu, C. (2007). *Construction of a Webportal and user management framework for Grid*. Paper presented at the 21st International Symposium on High Performance Computing Systems and Applications (HPCS'07), Saskatoon, Saskatchewan, Canada.

Zhu, Y., Han, J., Liu, Y., Ni, L. M., Hu, C., & Hua, J. (2005). TruGrid: A self-sustaining trustworthy grid. *Proceedings of the First International Workshop on Mobility in Peer-to-Peer Systems (MPPS) (ICDCSW'05)* (pp. 815-821).

Zomaya, A.Y., & Teh, Y.H. (2001). Observations on using genetic algorithms for dynamic load-balancing. *IEEE Transactions on Parallel and Distributed Systems, 12*(9), 899-911.

About the Contributors

Emmanuel Udoh is an assistant professor of computer science at the Indiana–Purdue University, Fort Wayne. He is currently serving as the editor-in-chief of the *International Journal of Grid and High Performance Computing* and also of the *Encyclopedia of Grid Computing Technologies and Applications*. In addition to being interested in grid computing, Dr. Udoh has been active in database research. Dr. Udoh has published a book and over 25 articles in journals and conference proceedings. He served as the organizing and session chairs of the IASTED International Conference on Software Engineering/Applications and International Conference on Information Technology. Dr. Udoh has been listed in American Marquis Who's Who in the World 1993-1994.

Frank Zhigang Wang is the director of Centre for Grid Computing, Cambridge-Cranfield High Performance Computing Facility (CCHPCF), Cranfield University. He is chair in e-Science and Grid Computing. Prof. Wang is on the editorial board of IEEE Distributed Systems Online, *International Journal of Grid and Utility Computing, International Journal of High Performance Computing and Networking*, and *International Journal on Multiagent and Grid Systems*. He is on the High End Computing Panel for the Science Foundation Ireland (SFI). Prof. Wang is the chair (UK & Republic of Ireland Chapter) of the IEEE Computer Society.

* * *

Khalid Abdelkader is a PhD-student in the Department of Mathematics and Computer Science at the University of Antwerp (UA), Belgium. His research interests are distributed systems and grid computing. Currently, his main research focus is the study of grid economies in dynamic, large-scale settings.

Enis Afgan is currently a PhD candidate in the Department of Computer and Information Sciences at the University of Alabama at Birmingham, under the supervision of Dr. Purushotham Bangalore. His research interests focus around grid computing with the emphasis on user-level scheduling in heterogeneous environments with economic aspects. His other interests include distributed computing, optimization methods, and performance modeling. He received his BS degree in computer science from the University of Alabama at Birmingham in 2003. More information about his research activities can be found at: http://www.cis.uab.edu/afgane/.

Giovanni Aloisio is full professor of Information Processing Systems at the Engineering Faculty of the University of Salento, Lecce, Italy. His research interests are in the area of high performance computing, distributed and grid computing and are carried out at the Department of Innovation Engineering of the University of Salento. He is also director of the CACT (Center for Advanced Computational Technologies) of the National Nanotechnology Laboratory\ (NNL/CNR-INFM).

Daniele Andreotti was born in Ferrara (Italy) in 1975. Since 2001 has collaborated and worked on the BaBar experiment as developer of tools for managing data generated by the simulation production workflow. At the end of 2002 he also joined the INFN-Grid project, created by the National Institute for Nuclear Physics. Actually he is involved in the management of the local grid farm services at the University of Ferrara and in the development of tools for interfacing the traditional Monte Carlo simulation production of BaBar with the grid facilities provided by the INFN-Grid framework.

Ashiq Anjum works in the CCCS research centre at University of the West of England, Bristol UK and carries out research in collaboration with CERN Geneva. His areas of interest are grid and high performance computing, grid resource management and operating systems, distributed data mining and sensor networks. He has more than 30 peer reviewed publications to his credit. He holds a BS in electrical engineering, and an MS and PhD in computer science and has seven years of industry experience before entering academic research in 2001.

Gabriel Aparicio is a researcher in the Institute for the Applications of Advanced Information and Communication Technologies (ITACA) since 2005. He has been involved in parallel and grid computation and genomic analysis processing since this date participating in six national and European research project, being the author and co-author of more than 10 papers and posters in national and international conference proceedings.

Valeria Ardizzone graduated in computer science at the University of Catania (Italy). Since 2004, she is involved in the Enabling Grid for E-Science Project (EGEE and EGEE-II - http://www.eu-egee. org, as a member of NA3 (User Training and Induction) and NA4 (Application Identification and Support) activities. She is an accredited trainer on grid computing technology attending many induction and dissemination event on Grid and LCG/gLite middleware held all over the world.

Frans Arickx is a full professor in the Department of Mathematics and Computer Science at the University of Antwerp (UA), Belgium, and member of its computational Modeling and Programming research group. He received his PhD in physics, in 1976 at the Free University of Brussels (VUB), Belgium. His current research interests include computational science and distributed computing, applied to theoretical quantum problems.

Eric Aubanel is associate professor in the Faculty of Computer Science at the University of New Brunswick, Fredericton. He received his PhD in theoretical chemistry from Queen's University, Canada. He leads the grid computing research group at UNB. His research interests include high performance parallel computing, scientific and grid computing.

Purushotham Bangalore is an assistant professor in the Department of Computer and Information Sciences at the University of Alabama at Birmingham (UAB) and also serves as the director of Collaborative Computing Laboratory. He has a PhD in computational engineering from Mississippi State

University where he also worked as a research associate at the Engineering Research Center. His area of interest includes programming environments for parallel and grid computing, scientific computing, and bioinformatics. More information about his research activities can be found at: http://www.cis.uab. edu/puri/.

Roberto Barbera was born in Catania (Italy) in October 1963. He graduated in physics at the University of Catania where he currently holds an associated professorship. His main research activity has been done in the areas of nuclear and particle physics. Since 1999 he's interested in grid computing. He is the director of two grid projects in Italy (TriGrid VL and PI2S2) while, at international level, he is the technical coordinator of the EELA-2 Project and has several responsibilities in other projects such as EGEE-III and EU-IndiaGrid. Since 2002 he's the responsible of the GENIUS grid portal and, in 2004, he created the international GILDA e-infrastructure for training and dissemination.

Fernando Blanco graduated in physics from Universidad Complutense de Madrid (1983). From 1985 has been working at CIEMAT where his main interest was focused on systems administration and architecture, scientific informatics, clusters and grid computing. He previously was a fellow in the National Institute of Geology working on data acquisition. He has been involved in several national and international projects and he is currently head of the ICT Division of CIEMAT.

Ignacio Blanquer is an assistant professor at the Computer System Department of the Technical University of Valencia since 1999 and member of the GRyCAP since 1993. He has been involved in parallel computation and medical image processing since 12 years ago participating in 17 national and European research projects, being the author and co-author of more than 60 papers in national and international journals and conference proceedings. He is also a research fellow of the ITACA and CRIB and member of the board of directors of HealthGRID association.

Cesar Bonavides is an electronic engineer and received his masters degree in 1999, on information technology management. In the same year he started his scientific and academic career in the Program of Computational Genomics at the Center for Genomic Sciences, of the National University of Mexico, CCG-UNAM (formerly known as the Nitrogen Fixation Research Center); he is an academic technician at the UNAM assisting research in bioinformatics; his activities have broadened from software design and development for bioinformatics, to database design and administration of computer networks. He is co-author of RegulonDB and collaborator of EcoCyc, both are databases which perform literature-based curation of the entire genome of Escherichia coli.

Jan Broeckhove is a professor in the Department of Mathematics and Computer Science at the University of Antwerp (UA), Belgium, and member of its Computational Modeling and Programming research group. He received his PhD in physics in 1982 at the Free University of Brussels (VUB), Belgium. His current research interests include computational science and distributed computing, in particular cluster and grid computing.

Kris Bubendorfer is a senior lecturer at Victoria University of Wellington. His primary research topics are: market oriented grid computing, secure and verifiable auctions and reputation. Other projects that Kris has been involved (and is still interested) in, include: SLAs and migration in service containers, SLAs and QoS scheduling and Content Distribution Networks. He has been on the academic staff at Victoria University since 2002, teaching operating systems, data communications and topics in distributed systems including mobile agents and grid computing.

Massimo Cafaro is an assistant professor at the Department of Innovation Engineering of the University of Lecce and a member of the Center for Advanced Computational Technologies. His research covers high performance, distributed and grid computing. He is also interested in computer security. Since the beginning of 1998 he is involved in grid projects. He received a degree in Computer Science from the University of Salerno and a PhD in computer science from the University of Bari. He is a member of IEEE and IEEE Computer Society, ACM and holds a visitor position at CACR Caltech.

Juan L. Chaves got the MS degree in computational engineering (Universidad de Los Andes-Venezuela) in 2005. His research area is focused on clusters and grid computing. Nowadays, he is working at the Information Centre of the Technological Park of Merida, Venezuela.

Zhili Cheng received his bachelor's degree in department of computer science and technology, Tsinghua University, Beijing, China, in 2006. He is now studying for the master's degree in department of computer science and technology, Tsinghua University, Beijing, China. His current research interests include grid computing, QoS, data replica, and virtualizations.

Dominic Cherry received the MS from School of Engineering and Design at Brunel University in 2005. He is currently a software engineer at the ITV Transmission Office in London.

Lin Chuang received the PhD degree in department of computer science from Tsinghua University, Beijing, China, in 1994. He is a professor and has been the head of the Department of Computer Science and Technology, Tsinghua University. His current research interests include computer networks, performance evaluation, logic reasoning, and Petri net theory and its applications. He has co-authored more than 150 papers in research journals and IEEE conference proceedings and has published three books.

Yeh-Ching Chung received a BS degree in information engineering from Chung Yuan Christian University in 1983, and the MS and PhD degrees in computer and information science from Syracuse University in 1988 and 1992, respectively. He joined the Department of Information Engineering at Feng Chia University as an associate professor in 1992 and became a full professor in 1999. From 1998 to 2001, he was the chairman of the department. His research interests include parallel and distributed processing, cluster systems, grid computing, multi-core tool chain design, and multi-core embedded systems. He is a member of the IEEE computer society and ACM.

Leandro Neumann Ciuffo was born in Brazil in 1978 and holds a BS in computer science from the Universidade Federal de Juiz de Fora (UFJF) and an MS in computing from the Universidade Federal Fluminense (UFF), both Brazilian universities. Since September 2006 he collaborates with EELA project (http://www.eu-eela.org) at the Italian National Institute of Nuclear Physics (INFN – Catania), works as WP4 Manager for dissemination and training activities. Before joining INFN he acted as an assistant professor in some Brazilian universities.

Jie Dai is a PhD candidate in computer architecture at the Huazhong University of Science and Techonology, Wuhan, China. He obtained his BS and MS from the Huazhong University of Science and Technology, Wuhan, China.

Piet Demeester received his degree in electrical engineering (1984) and his PhD degree (1988) at Ghent University, where he became professor in 1993. He is heading a research group on broadband communication networks and distributed software, IBCN. The IBCN-group is also part of IBBT (the Interdisciplinary institute for BroadBand Technology). His current research interests include: multilayer networks, Quality of Service (QoS) in IP-networks, mobile and sensor networks, access networks, grid computing, energy efficient ICT, distributed software, network and service management and applications. He is co-author of over 600 publications in international journals or conference proceedings. He has been involved in over 40 European funded research projects.

Yuhui Deng received his PhD degree in computer architecture from Huazhong University of Science and Technology in 2004. He joined Cranfield University in February 2005 as a research officer. Dr. Deng has served as committee members for several professional conferences in the field. He has authored and co-authored more than ten international journal papers and several leading conference papers. He is on the editorial board of *International Journal of Grid and High Performance Computing*. His research interests cover data storage and computer architecture, Grid computing, parallel and distributed computing, performance evaluation etc.

Wim Depoorter is a PhD-student and member of the Computational Modeling and Programming (CoMP) group of the Department of Mathematics and Computer Science at the University of Antwerp (UA), Belgium. His research interests include grid economics, grid computing and aspect-oriented programming.

David Dewolfs is a PhD student at the Department of Mathematics and Computer Science at the University of Antwerp (UA), Belgium, and a member of its Computational Modeling and Programming research group. He currently works as a developer at Siemens. His research interests include MPI-based cluster computing, fault tolerant MPI and high performance distributed computing in general.

Tom Dhaene received the PhD degree in electrical engineering from Ghent University, Belgium, in 1993. In 1993, he joined the EDA company Alphabit (now part of Agilent). He was one of the key developers of the planar EM simulator ADS Momentum, ADS Model Composer, and ADS Broadband SPICE. Since 2007, he has been a full professor in the IBCN research group of the Department of Information Technology, Ghent University. He has authored or coauthored more than 120 peer-reviewed papers and abstracts in international conference proceedings, journals, and books. He is a holder of 3 U.S. patents.

Andrea Domenici obtained his PhD in information engineering in 1992 with a thesis on the implementation of the G\" model logic programming. He has been an assistant professor at the Sant'Anna School of University Studies and Doctoral Research, Pisa, and he is currently at the Department of Information Engineering of the University of Pisa, where he teaches Software Engineering and does research in the fields of Object-oriented design and Grid architectures. In this latter field, he took part in the European Datagrid Project and is now in the EGEE project, in cooperation with the Italian National Institute of Nuclear Physics (INFN).

Flavia Donno holds a PhD in information engineering from the University of Pisa, Italy. She has been involved in grid computing since the early years working in the areas of storage and data management and access, and grid infrastructures. Flavia has participated in various projects: European Data Grid (EDG), DataTag, and Worldwide LHC Computing Grid (WLCG). Flavia has also taught several Grid tutorials all over the world. She currently works at CERN in Geneva where she is in charge of the coordination of Grid Storage Services in WLCG.

Zhihui Du received his bachelor's degree in Tianjing University, Tianjing ,China, and his master's degree and PhD in Peking University, Beijing, China. Now he is an associate professor at Tsinghua University, Department of Computer Science and Technology, Beijing, China. His research interests include cluster computing/grid computing/P2P computing, parallel algorithm based on cluster architecture, high performance communication/user level network communication, computational science and engineering research and application.

Miguel Embid graduate in chemistry but a doctorate degree in physics from Universidad Autónoma de Madrid (1999). He has been associate professor at Universidad Nacional de Educación a Distancia and works at CIEMAT since 1998. He was fellow at CERN and Unión Fenosa in the Nuclear Energy department. He has been involved in 10 international and national projects and has more than 90 contributions in journals, reviews, technical reports and books.

Armando Fella has MS in computer science and worked as a system engineer. He joined INFN-CNAF in 2006 and participated in CNAF/Tier1 computing centre and BaBar experiment. He is actually involved in the GRID middleware and service support for the experiment environment. He is responsible for Monte Carlo simulation production in the INFN-GRID approach. He is working in management and deployment of data handling systems xRootD and GPFS at CNAF too, the physics data are imported from SLAC centre in San Francisco, USA and are analyzed at CNAF by the BaBar collaboration.

Sandro Fiore was born in Galatina (LE) in 1976. He received a summa cum laude Laurea degree in computer engineering from the University of Lecce (Italy) in 2001, as well as a PhD degree in informatic engineering on innovative materials and technologies from the ISUFI-University of Lecce in 2004. Research activities focus on parallel and distributed computing, specifically on advanced grid data management. Since 2001 he has been the project principal investigator of the GRelC project. Since June 2006, he leads the Data Grid group of the Euro-Mediterranean Centre for Climate Change (CMCC) in Lecce (Italy).

Emidio Giorgio obtained his MSc degree in computer science in 2003; soon after has begun its collaboration with INFN on computational grids, joining the EGEE project in the NA3/NA4 areas, i.e., training and applications support; as trainer, he has delivered more than 30 grid tutorials in 4 years. In the context of the ICEAGE project, he has been manager for WP 4, concerning the operations for its shared training Infrastructure. He is interested also in programming and system administration, and he has developed several tools and configured services for both the grid and IT infrastructures in Catania.

Dirk Gorissen received his masters degree in computer science from Antwerp University, Belgium in 2004. In addition, he obtained a master in artificial intelligence from the Katholieke Universiteit Leuven in 2007. Currently, he is a PhD student at the INTEC Broadband Communication Networks (IBCN) research group at Ghent University, Belgium. The IBCN-group is also part of IBBT (the Interdisciplinary Institute for BroadBand Technology). His current research interests include: adaptive global surrogate modeling and its application to real world problems, distributed computing and artificial intelligence.

Gokop Goteng is a PhD student of grid computing applications at Cranfield University and is a professional member of the British Computer Society (BCS) and student member of IEEE Computer Society. Gokop's research interests are in grid computing, multidisciplinary optimization and collaborative IT solutions. He is the winner of the UK Grid Computing Now! Competition in 2006.

Irfan Habib is a post graduate research student at the Centre for Complex Co-operative Systems at the University of the West of England, Bristol. His areas of interest include grid and high performance distributed computing, operating systems, virtualization, cloud computing, machine learning. He holds a BEng in software engineering.

Jin Hai is currently the director of Services Computing Technology and System Lab, Cluster and Grid Computing Lab and the dean of School of Computer Science and Technology, Huazhong University of Science and Technology, China. He obtained his BS, MS and PhD from the Huazhong University of Science and Technology, Wuhan, China.

Na Helian received her PhD degree in computer science in 1992. She has various working experience in Japan, Singapore, and the United Kingdom. She is now a senior lecturer and the director of the MSc Data Mining Program in the Department of Computing, Communication & Mathematics, London Metropolitan University, United Kingdom. She is the co-investigator of the United Kingdom Government EPSRC/DTI grant "Grid-Oriented Storage (GOS)."

Peter Hellinckx is a PhD-student at the Department of Mathematics and Computer Science at the University of Antwerp (UA), Belgium, and a member of its Computational Modeling and Programming research group. His research interests include desktop grids, grid scheduling, Runtime predictions, resource availability predictions, resource management in general and computer graphics.

Álvaro Hernández is a research scientist of CECALCULA. He graduated in biology at the University of Los Andes. After his graduation, he worked in bioinformaitcs and as network, system and security administrator, he administered UNIX systems.

Vicente Hernández is a full professor in computer science and artificial intelligence. He is the leader of the GRyCAP (Grid and High Performance Computing Research Group). He has large experience in parallel and distributed computing, numerical methods and computer applications, applied matrix analysis, control systems and signal processing. He has managed and participated in more than 25 European projects, from the III to the VI Framework Programme, and national projects. He is also a research fellow of the ITACA and CRIB and member of the board of directors of HealthGRID association. He was a vice-chancellor of Research, Development and Innovation of the Technical University of Valencia.

Kuo-Chan Huang received his BS and PhD degrees in computer science and information engineering from National Chiao-Tung University, Taiwan, in 1993 and 1998, respectively. He is currently an assistant professor in Computer and Information Science Department at National Taichung University, Taiwan. He is a member of ACM and IEEE Computer Society. His research areas include parallel processing, cluster and grid computing, workflow computing.

Raul Isea is currently an associate researcher at the Fundación Instituto de Estudios Avanzados IDEA in Baruta-Venezuela from Aug. 2007. He got the PhD in chemistry (Universidad Complutense de Madrid–Spain) in 1996 and the BS in physics (Universidad Central de Venezuela, Caracas-Venezuela) in 1993. He was a postdoctoral research fellow at the Instituto Venezolano de Investigaciones Científicas in Caracas from 1997 until 1999. In 2000, he got a postdoctoral position at the Rice University in Texas, USA. His research interest is focused on computational biology.

Vineet Khare received his BTech degree from India Institute of Technology (IIT) Kanpur, India, in 2001. His PhD degree in computer science was awarded by The University of Birmingham in December 2006. Currently he is working as a research officer at the Centre for Grid Computing. His research interests include swarm intelligence, co-evolution, multiple neural network systems and multi-objective evolutionary algorithms.

Tevfik Kosar is an assistant professor of Computer Science at Louisiana State University. He received his MS in computer science from Rensselaer Polytechnic Institute in 1999 and his PhD in computer science from University of Wicsonsin-Madison in 2005. Tevfik Kosar has profound experience in building blocks for solving the distributed data handling problem. He has introduced the concept that the data placement efforts should be regarded as first class entities and these tasks should be automated and standardized just like the systems that support and administer computational jobs. Kosar has designed and implemented the first prototype batch scheduler specialized in data placement – Stork.

Juan I. Lagares has PhD in physics. His main interest is medical and computational physics. He has been working in radiotherapy in several hospitals from Seville and Madrid with several techniques. He currently works in a project to extend the supercomputation and grid paradigms to the public hospitals in order to improve the radiation doses to be prescribed.

Maozhen Li received the PhD in 1997 from Institute of Software, Chinese Academy of Sciences, Beijing. He is a lecturer in the School of Engineering and Design at Brunel University. His research interests are in the areas of grid computing, distributed problem-solving environments for large-scale simulations, intelligent systems, service-oriented computing, semantic web. He has over 50 publications in these areas. He co-authored *The Grid: Core Technologies*, a research-level textbook on grid computing published by Wiley in 2005. He has been serving as a TPC member for various conferences in the area of grid computing, e.g., IEEE CCGrid'05. He is a member of IEEE.

Diego Liberati has a PhD in electronic and biomedical engineering, Milano Institute of Technology and is the director of Research, Italian National Research Council. He has authored 50 papers on ISI journals, edited books and chapters. He is the secretary of the Biomedical Engineering Society of the Italian Electronic Engineering Association (and Milano prize laureate in 1987), and has chaired

Scientific Committees for Conferences and Grants. Visiting scientist at Rockefeller University, New York University, University of California and International Computer Science Institute, he has directed joint projects granted by both private and public institutions and mentored dozens of pupils toward and beyond their doctorate.

Daniel López is head of CUBAENERGIA. He graduated in nuclear engineering at the University of Havana in 1985. He obtained his master degree in reactor techniques in 1988 at the Technical University of Budapest. He has worked in transport simulations and nuclear data processing for fission, fusion and well logging applications. He is an IAEA expert in the field of nuclear data bases and nuclear data dissemination through web applications.

Yaqin Luo is a PhD candidate in computer architecture at the Huazhong University of Science and Techonology, Wuhan, China. She obtained her BS and MS from the Huazhong University of Science and Technology, Wuhan, China.

Eleonora Luppi was born in Ferrara (Italy) in 1958. Since 1983 she is member of the High Energy Physics group of the Physics Department of Ferrara University and currently an associate professor in Experimental Physics. She participated in several elementary particle physics experiments, at Cern, Fermilab, Frascati INFN National Laboratory and SLAC, with responsibilities in simulations, event reconstruction and analysis, and in detector development and construction. She is involved in computing for high energy physics projects and currently is the international coordinator of the BaBarGrid project.

Rafael Mayo has a doctorate degree in physics from the Universidad Complutense de Madrid (2004). From 2006 he is also adjunt faculty at the same University in the Physics of Materials Department. Since his graduation his main research activity has been done in experimental atomic and molecular physics developing also software for the spectral analysis and data Networks. He works at CIEMAT since 2005 and has been involved in several European and National Projects in the information and communication technologies. He has more than 40 papers.

Richard McClatchey is director of the Centre for Complex Co-operative Systems at the University of the West of England, Bristol. He is a fellow of the Institute of Electrical Engineers (FIEE) and of the British Computer Society (FBCS) as well as a chartered information technology practitioner and a chartered engineer. His specialty is in the management of distributed data and processes, grid computing and the design of data models for the capture of workflow information. He has published over 150 articles in journals or in international conferences and has been on program committees of numerous conference series during his 16 years at UWE. McClatchey holds a PhD in high energy physics (from University of Sheffield in 1982) and was awarded a DPhil acknowledging his contribution to the field of Computer Science in 1999.

Esther Montes graduated in mathematical science from the Universidad Complutense de Madrid (1999), obtained an MS in mathematical engineering in 2003, and, at present time, she is preparing her master thesis in grid computing research. She is, since 2005, system architect of the ICT unit of CIEMAT in Madrid, Spain, where she is involved in several grid projects like EELA, ALICE, etc. She has published 5 papers. Before joining CIEMAT, she worked for 3 years at Telefónica R&D division as application developer.

Henry R. Mora is an associate researcher to CUBAENERGIA. He graduated in nuclear engineering at the Higher Institute of Nuclear Science and Technology in 1998. He obtained his master degree in Environmental impact and protection. He has worked in mass transfer phenomena modelling, energy planning modelling and database design.

Alessandro Negro was born in S. Pietro Vernotico (BR) in 1981. He received a summa cum laude bachelor degree in Computer Engineering from the University of Lecce, Italy in February 2004 and a summa cum laude master degree in computer engineering from the same University in April 2006. His research interests include GUI development, data management, distributed, grid computing and Web services. He is also interested in web and pattern-oriented design. Since 2003 he is a team member of the GRelC Project. Since September 2006 he holds a contract position in the LIBI project for the University of Lecce.

Ben Palmer is currently completing a masters degree in computer science at Victoria University in Wellington, New Zealand. His thesis is on the verification of privacy preserving combinatorial auction protocols. This research has concentrated on using zero knowledge proofs of knowledge to construct practical protocols to provide confidence in auction results in environments with no pre-existing trust. One of the research goals is to allow anyone to run an auction, removing the need to use trusted servers. Verification plays an important part in this process by providing arguments that the auction result was conducted correctly.

Rosario M. Piro studied physics at the University of Heidelberg/Germany and the University of Torino/Italy, where he obtained his Laurea Specialistica degree in 2004, and a master's degree in bioinformatics in 2006. He has worked on grid accounting and economic scheduling within the EDG, EGEE and OMII-Europe projects. Currently, he is continuing his research for INFN Torino within the EGEE-II project and as a co-chair of the Resource Usage Service working group (RUS-WG) of the Open Grid Forum, while pursuing a PhD in molecular medicine, with focus on bioinformatics, at the Molecular Biotechnology Center of the University of Torino.

Gianni Pucciani has been working at CERN since 2006. He obtained his PhD in information engineering at the University of Pisa in 2008 with a thesis on the replica consistency problem in data grids. From 2003 to 2006 he worked at the Italian National Institute of Nuclear Physics (INFN) where he was involved in R&D within the INFN Grid project. He collaborated with Webster University in Geneva where he taught a course on Database Applications. His research interests are in grid computing, data management, cross-technology database replication and testing and performance evaluation of grid services.

Li Qi is a PhD candidate in computer architecture at the Huazhong University of Science and Techonology, Wuhan, China. He obtained his BS and MS from the Huazhong University of Science and Technology, Wuhan, China. He is a research assistant and has managed VMGrid, WAGA and CGSP systems.

Man Qi is a lecturer in Dept. of Computing at Canterbury Christ Church University, UK. She was a research fellow in Dept. of Computer Science at University of Bath, UK from Jan. 2001 to Oct. 2003. Her research interests are in the areas of computer graphics, computer animation, multimedia and grid computing applications.

Rajkumar Roy has been leading the competitive design research at Cranfield for the last ten years. Professor Roy is known for his qualitative cost modeling, requirements management and design optimization research and has published over 20 Journals and 100 conference papers. He is currently the principal investigator of three Product-Service System projects in the areas of whole life cost and service knowledge capture. He is currently leading the new initiative on competitive creative design at Cranfield and collaboration with University of the Arts London. Professor Roy has a PhD in design optimization using soft computing techniques.

Gerald Schaefer obtained his PhD in computer vision from the University of East Anglia. He worked at the Colour & Imaging Institute, University of Derby as a research associate (1997-1999), as senior research fellow at the School of Information Systems, University of East Anglia (2000-2001), and as senior lecturer in Computing at the School of Computing and Informatics at Nottingham Trent University (2001-2006). In September 2006 he joined the School of Engineering and Applied Science at Aston University. His research interests include colour image analysis, physics-based vision, image retrieval, and medical imaging. He has published more than 150 papers in these areas.

Salvatore Scifo graduated in computer science at the University of Catania in 2001. He is currently employed with the Cometa Consortium where he works in the Grid R&D and Application Support areas. He worked as a scientific researcher at the INFN (Istituto Nazionale Fisica Nucleare) of Catania) in the Grid R&D and Application Support areas. He worked with comunicando società per azioni of Catania (CT) Italy as senior software engineer on activities concerning the design and development of live services for the Vodafone Italy mobile operator. He worked with the garanet s.r.l. - Catania (CT) Italia.

Jyotsana Sharma is a research scholar at Thapar University, India. Under guidance of Dr. Maninder Singh, she has focused her research on deep packet inspection for forensics analysis using grid infrastructure. She has presented her work at several international and Indian meetings. In 1996 she received the Suman Sharma Award for academic distinction in the computer engineering discipline. Currently she is a senior lecturer at Maharaja Agrasen Institute of Management & Technology, Jagadhri (India)

Po-Chi Shih received the BS and MS degrees in computer science and Information Engineering from Tunghai University in 2003 and 2005, respectively. He is now pursuing his PhD degree in computer science at the National Tsing Hua University.

Patrik Skogster is currently working as a senior lecturer at the Rovaniemi University of Applied Sciences in Finland. Previously he has operated for several years in the retailing industry in various positions concerning location planning process and in various academic positions. He has master's and Licentiate's (lower doctoral) degrees from the Helsinki University of Technology. He is finalizing his doctoral thesis about location planning in the shopping centre context to the same institution. His recent research work has been concentrated on geographic information systems applied to the retailing and real estate industries.

Heinz Stockinger has been working in grid projects in Europe (CERN, etc.) and in the USA (Stanford Linear Accelerator Center) in various technical and management functions. Heinz is affiliated with the Swiss Institute of Bioinformatics where he works on diverse Grid subjects. He has been appointed "Privatdozent" at the University of Vienna - leading the Research Lab for Computational Technologies and Applications in 2005. Currently, he is also a lecturer at the Swiss Federal Institute of Technology in Lausanne (EPFL). Heinz holds a PhD degree in computer science and Business Administration from the University of Vienna, Austria.

Xian-He Sun received his BS in 1982 from Beijing Normal University, P.R. China, and completed his MS and PhD in 1987 and 1990, respectively, from Michigan State University. He was a post-doctoral researcher at the Ames National Laboratory, a staff scientist at ICASE, NASA Langley Research Center, an ASEE fellow at the US Navy Research Laboratories, and was a professor at Louisiana State University before joining Illinois Institute of Technology (IIT) in 1999. Currently, he is a professor of computer science at IIT. Dr. Sun's research interests include high performance computing, performance evaluation, and distributed systems. More information about Prof. Sun can be found at www.cs.iit.edu/~sun/.

Roger Tait obtained his PhD in computer science from Nottingham Trent University. During his PhD he carried out research into image processing and artificial intelligence for use in non-destructive evaluation and in medical imaging. He is currently working as a research fellow in the School of Science and Technology at Nottingham Trent University.

Ashutosh Tiwari is a senior lecturer in Design Optimization and course director of the IT for Product Engineering MS. He is leading the research in design optimization within the Manufacturing Department. In 1998, he joined Cranfield University from where he successfully obtained his MS in manufacturing and PhD degree. He obtained the award for Best MS Student in Manufacturing. He was awarded the Academic Excellence Award for his achievements in the course. Dr Tiwari is a fellow of the Higher Education Academy, member of the Institution of Electrical and Electronics Engineers (IEEE), World Federation on Soft Computing (WFSC).

Salvatore Vadacca was born in Galatina (LE) in 1982. He received summa cum laude bachelor and master degrees in computer engineering from the University of Lecce, Italy in 2003 and 2006, respectively. His research interests include data management; distributed, peer-to-peer and grid computing; as well as web design and development. Since 2003, he has been a team member of the GRelC Project. In 2006 he joined the Euro-Mediterranean Centre for Climate Change (CMCC) in Lecce, Italy, where he works in the Data Grid group.

Kurt Vanmechelen is a PhD student and member of the Computational Modeling and Programming (CoMP) group of the Department of Mathematics and Computer Science at the University of Antwerp (UA), Belgium. His current research interests include grid economics in particular and grid resource management in general. He is a member of the steering board of the national Belgian Research Grid Initiative BEgrid.

Man Wang received his bachelor's degree in department of computer science and technology, Fudan University, Shanghai, China, in 2005. Now, she is studying for the master's degree in department of computer science and technology, Tsinghua University, Beijing, China. Her current research interests include grid computing and scheduling.

Xiaoying Wang is a PhD candidate in the Department of Computer Science and Technology at Tsinghua University, China. She received her bachelor degree in 2003 and then joined the High Performance Computing Institute at Tsinghua University. Her research interests include parallel and distributed computing, grid computing systems, and autonomic computing.

Ian Welch is a senior lecturer at Victoria University of Wellington. His research interests related to security include developing more efficient ways to identify malicious activity on the Internet, improving the intrusion tolerance of online auctions and developing tools for managing large scale deployments of security and network measurement instruments. His teaching interests include the foundations of engineering, concurrency, distributed systems, professional ethics for software engineers and operating systems. He has served as a reviewer for conferences and journals including the Dependability and Performance Symposium (part of the Distributed Systems and Network conference) and the *Journal of Concurrency: Practice and Experience.*

Ming Wu received his BE degree from Xidian University, China, in 1994, the MS degree from the University of Science and Technology of China, in 1997, and PhD degree in computer science from Illinois Institute of Technology, in 2006. His research interests include Quality of Service support in network computing, performance evaluation and task scheduling systems in distributed computing, failure analysis and modeling in high performance computing.

Bin Yu received the PhD from School of Engineering and Design at Brunel University in April 2007. He is currently a system analyst at Level E Limited in Edinburgh. His research interests are in the areas of service oriented computing, grid computing and applications, service discovery and composition optimization.

Index